Race and Inequality in American Politics

Authored by three of the USA's most well-known scholars on American politics, this undergraduate textbook argues that racial considerations are today—and have always been since the nation's founding—central to understanding America's political system writ large. Drawing on decades of teaching experience and compelling original research, Hajnal, Hutchings, and Lee present an up-to-date and comprehensive survey of race's role in American democracy, spanning topics as wide-ranging as public opinion, voting behavior, media representation, criminal justice, social policy, and protest movements. The reader will examine the perspectives of multiple racial groups, learn how to bring empirical analysis to bear on deeply divided viewpoints, and debate solutions to the many problems of governance in an America that is polarized by party, riven by race, and divided by inequality. Chapters open with a vignette to introduce the core issues and conclude with discussion questions and annotated suggested readings. Full color photos, figures, and boxed features elaborate on and reinforce important themes. Instructor resources are available online.

Zoltan L. Hajnal is the author of several award-winning books, has published in the top political science journals, and has been featured in the *New York Times*, *Washington Post*, and a range of other media outlets. He is actively involved in voting rights litigation and local election law reform.

Vincent L. Hutchings was elected as a Fellow to the American Academy of Arts and Sciences (AAAS) in 2012 and was elected to the National Academy of Sciences (NAS) in 2022.

Taeku Lee is Bae Family Professor of Government and President-Elect of the American Political Science Association. Prior to Harvard, Lee was Professor of Political Science and Law at UC Berkeley for two decades.

"Like all countries, the United States is an imperfect union. But each union is imperfect in its own way; the U.S. shows a distinctive structure of liberal democratic aspirations overlaid on racial, ethnic, and class inequality. Coming from these authors, this book is our best guide to understanding how that conundrum plays out in politics, daily life, and policies. Students will gain invaluable insight by engaging with *Race and Inequality in American Politics*—and will learn ways to make our union less imperfect.**"

Jennifer Hochschild, *Harvard University*

"Written by several of *the* leading political science scholars who have long studied the fundamental importance of race in American politics, *Race and Inequality in American Politics: An Imperfect Union* is a strikingly comprehensive, rigorous, and intellectually thoughtful work, particularly notable in its rich combination and blending of breadth and depth."

Rodney E. Hero, *Arizona State University*

"This is a terrific book, perfect for the classroom. The authors are exceptional at providing a great range of topics and research within a larger narrative of the foundational nature of race and discrimination in American history and today. Moreover, authored by three of the foremost scholars in racial and ethnic politics today, the book provides a synthesis of the leading cutting-edge work of the moment that will benefit scholars at all levels of the academy."

Paul Frymer, *Princeton University*

"Leveraging extensive original research and an exhaustive review of the existing literature on race and American politics, Hajnal, Hutchings, and Lee provide an incisive and compelling overview of how, when, and under what circumstances race has played and continues to play a central role in American politics. This cogent and accessible text provides students with a more substantive orientation to U.S. political history than traditional textbooks, with a focus not only on the inputs but also on the outcomes of elections and policy making. With elegance and depth, the authors craft a narrative that offers students a robust and meaningful understanding of U.S. political institutions, including how they evolved into their current forms and why their actions matter to real people. This is the robust empirical foundation undergraduate students need in order to be able to meaningfully and effectively engage in our democracy."

Lisa García Bedolla, *University of California, Berkeley*

Race and Inequality in American Politics

An Imperfect Union

Zoltan L. Hajnal
University of California, San Diego

Vincent L. Hutchings
University of Michigan, Ann Arbor

Taeku Lee
Harvard University, Massachusetts

CAMBRIDGE
UNIVERSITY PRESS

Shaftesbury Road, Cambridge CB2 8EA, United Kingdom

One Liberty Plaza, 20th Floor, New York, NY 10006, USA

477 Williamstown Road, Port Melbourne, VIC 3207, Australia

314–321, 3rd Floor, Plot 3, Splendor Forum, Jasola District Centre, New Delhi – 110025, India

103 Penang Road, #05–06/07, Visioncrest Commercial, Singapore 238467

Cambridge University Press is part of Cambridge University Press & Assessment,
a department of the University of Cambridge.

We share the University's mission to contribute to society through the pursuit of
education, learning and research at the highest international levels of excellence.

www.cambridge.org
Information on this title: www.cambridge.org/highereducation/isbn/9781108484114

DOI: 10.1017/9781108633352

First published 2025

A catalogue record for this publication is available from the British Library

A Cataloging-in-Publication data record for this book is available from the Library of Congress

ISBN 978-1-108-48411-4 Hardback
ISBN 978-1-108-73555-1 Paperback

Additional resources for this publication at www.cambridge.org/riap1e.

Contents

Note from the Authors

As this book heads into print, America remains deeply polarized. A 2022 Pew Research Center study found that supermajorities of Republicans see Democrats as dishonest, immoral, and close-minded and similar supermajorities of Democrats see Republicans in the same, negative way.[1] In such a climate, a growing number of Americans are fed up with both parties and with politics writ large. In a 2023 Pew study, 65 percent of us say we feel "exhausted" when we think about politics and 55 percent feel "angry." Only 10 percent feel "hopeful" and only 4 percent are "excited."[2]

This is the shaky political landscape of the United States today. Even the common ground of shared facts, standards of evidence, and critical thinking that a healthy democracy requires is wobbly. Growing numbers of Americans not only mistrust their fellow Americans across partisan lines, but they also mistrust those individuals and institutions with expertise and experience whose traditional role has been to referee contested facts, evidence, and truths. Individuals like the three of us and institutions like the universities where we work.

As educators, as researchers, and as citizens, we are deeply troubled by these cracks in the bedrock of our democracy. We wrote this book as part of our efforts to step up to the moment we are in. Yet we understand that some students will read this text with skepticism, based on their political beliefs or based on their assumptions about our political beliefs. Other students may read this text far too uncritically, based on their political beliefs or based on their assumptions about our political beliefs.

Our goal throughout this book is to ask whether and how race is a factor in our democratic politics and then follow the evidence in pursuit of answers. That evidence points to the persistence of racial inequalities and a central role of race. Of course, we may not have gotten all of it right all of the time. Given our polarized, shaky political landscape, we urge you to read this text with an open mind and a critical eye. The contents of this book should spark debate, not stonewall it. As much as you, as students, will learn from *Race and Inequality in American Politics,* we hope that we, as authors and teachers, will learn from your experience with this text.

---

[1] Pew Research Center, August 2022. "As Partisan Hostility Grows, Signs of Frustration With the Two Party-System." https://www.pewresearch.org/wp-content/uploads/sites/20/2022/08/PP_2022.09.08_partisan-hostility_REPORT.pdf

[2] Pew Research Center, September 2023. "Americans' Dismal Views of the Nation's Politics." https://www.pewresearch.org/wp-content/uploads/sites/20/2023/09/PP_2023.09.19_views-of-politics_REPORT.pdf

Preface

The last two decades have produced two pivotal, perhaps even epochal, elections in the nation's 228-year history of electoral democracy. Barack Obama's victory at the ballots as the nation's 44th president in 2008 represented a radical departure from an uninterrupted, invariant chronology of forty-three successive presidents who were White men. For many, this shift in the descriptive character of our president signaled a collective abnegation of race as a basis for organizing our politics and ushered in a hopeful new era of color-blind politics.

Yet just eight years later, at the end of Obama's two terms in the White House—a period roiled by partisan and racial polarization—any remnants of optimism in hopes for racial harmony were in tatters. Among other factors, Donald J. Trump won the presidency by appealing to nativist and nationalist sentiments, and in so doing exacerbated an already unparalleled partisan racial divide by increasing Republican support among America's White working class. While the centrality of race to Trump's success remains contested, the campaign unquestionably began with Trump's now infamous reference to Mexicans crossing America's southern border as "criminals" and "rapists," a kindling of anti-immigrant sentiments that was regularly stoked throughout the campaign and spread across to religious tests of belonging, staunch support for the safety and rights of law enforcement over that of civilians, and nationalist sloganeering such as "Make America Great Again" and "America First."

Against these snapshots in recent electoral history are the grinding wheels of two of the most significant social transformations over the last half century: America's growing economic inequality and its increasing racial diversity. Growth in income inequality has been prolonged, massive, and perhaps unprecedented in American history. Since 1970, the share of income going to the top 1 percent has more than doubled. Disparities in wealth are even greater. The wealthiest 1 percent possesses 40 percent of the nation's wealth, while the bottom 80 percent only own 7 percent. Economic disparities are also stark in the context of race. For example, data drawn from the 2019 Survey of Consumer Finances indicates that the typical White family has $188,200 in wealth compared with only $24,100 for the typical African American family. In other words, for every dollar of wealth held by the average White family the average Black family has about 12 cents.

Likewise, growth in racial diversity has been inexorable, and unparalleled. As late as 1950, non-Hispanic Whites represented 88 percent of the US population, and "minority" politics was by far the domain of Black politics. Today, half of all babies born in this country are non-White and the country is rapidly moving toward being a "majority-minority" nation within the next two to three decades. Moreover, the meaning of racial diversity is undergoing transformation: today, Latinos outnumber Blacks, Asian Americans are the fastest growing racial group, and multiracial Americans are now officially recognized by the federal government and growing exponentially.

Race and Inequality in American Politics offers a timely and in-depth exploration and analysis of the relationship between perceptions of plural identities, attributions of group differences, and the allocation of power and resources in American politics, broadly defined. In framing our text, we view politics as the art and noise of collective governance under conditions of scarce resources, conflicting interests, diverse beliefs, uncertain outcomes, and unequal power. We also see in politics the enduring struggle to organize human affairs in harmony with our loftiest normative aspirations for freedom, equality, justice, accountability, legitimacy, diversity, citizenship, and community. The empirical and normative realms come to a head on a single, perhaps defining question about American politics: are our politics designed to reinforce and perpetuate existing inequalities and injustices, or to resist and purge them?

In other words, are our current politics an essential manifestation of, or an exception from, the tradition of liberal democracy in the United States? Is ethnoracial hierarchy woven into the fabric of our history, politics, and policies, or is it an eradicable stain in an otherwise just and democratic nation? Alongside the default assumption of pluralism—that democracy flourishes when comprising a diversity of organized interests that compete freely to win the day—are competing narratives on the mobilization of bias. Is political representation in America largely the province of well-heeled elites who look after their own interests? Is it largely the province of older White men motivated to reinforce and perpetuate their exclusionary privilege?

In wrestling with these questions, students will learn about the institutions, ideologies, processes, and contexts that constitute politics in the United States. This learning starts with the basic architecture of our government: the Constitution, federalism, civil rights and liberties, and the core institutions of Congress, the presidency, the judiciary, and the bureaucracy. To this framework readers will also learn how the democratic inputs into this architecture—public opinion, electoral and non-electoral participation, and the (de)mobilizing influence of institutions like political parties, interest groups, and the mass media—are translated into law and policy ranging from voting rights and immigration policy to healthcare, affirmative action, and criminal justice. Throughout, we underscore both the importance of understanding today's racial politics within the historic context of Black–White relations in the United States and the importance of going beyond this "Black–White paradigm" given the multichrome diversity of contemporary American society.

Our Approach

This text differs from others in several key respects. First, we aim to do more than compose in our own words a dry litany of "textbook" facts. We have in mind an argument, specifically, on the question of the centrality of race in American politics. Our main thesis is that understanding racial–ethnic politics is indispensable to understanding American politics writ large. This thesis is not without controversy or critics. Yet our firm belief is that precisely because the subject matter of racial–ethnic politics and American politics is rife with contested viewpoints, students stand to gain most from being challenged to examine their own views against a sustained argument, defended with reasoning and facts that we will subject to critical analysis throughout the text. Few, if any, of the existing texts offer this kind of overarching narrative.

Second, in addition to this overarching argument, the text brings to bear a substantial amount of original research conducted by the authors. In this respect, we anticipate that students will not only learn about the fundamentals of racial and ethnic politics in the United States, but also that they will, along the way, learn how to use empirical analysis to understand deeply divided viewpoints. Further, where we are unable to offer original research, we incorporate the best available social science research, carefully walking the reader through the studies and their findings. None of the existing texts presents as much original research or takes such care in familiarizing students with empirical analysis and reasoning.

Third, whenever possible, our text offers explicit comparisons between race and ethnicity as dimensions of identity and difference alongside other salient dimensions of identity and difference like class, gender, age (generation), religion, and sexual orientation. Comparison here is critical to evaluating whether race is central to American politics. It also introduces students to the reality that the social identities that are salient to politics are multiple, intersectional, and interconnected. Existing texts, for the most part, focus exclusively on race and ethnicity. Moreover, while older texts primarily focus on race in a Black–White dimension, we consider four major groups (Whites, Blacks, Latinos, and Asian Americans) wherever the data allow and also examine subgroup differences (e.g., comparing Mexican Americans to Cuban Americans, Asian Indians to Vietnamese Americans).

Fourth, we examine the scope of politics more comprehensively than most existing texts. These texts generally emphasize the inputs of democracy—opinions, votes, and individual participation—to the neglect of how those inputs are linked to the outputs of democracy. We include chapters on responsiveness that assess how the actions or inactions of governmental actors align with the interests of racial and ethnic minorities and how those outputs impact their well-being across time and context. We also take seriously the idea that democracy is about more than elections and laws, and include a concluding chapter on protest movements and more radical forms of political participation.

Fifth, and finally, we do more than existing texts to outline, assess, and recommend potential reforms. We believe the most effective undergraduate texts not only require that students deepen their knowledge base and hone their analytic skills, but also challenge them to debate solutions to the many problems of governance. Where our own research or other studies identify effective and feasible solutions to problems related to race and minority representation, we highlight them. Where chapters touch on clashes over policy and regulation (e.g., affirmative action, racial profiling, religious tests, voter identification), we note that and cover the competing sides on the issue.

Instructional Tools

Race and Inequality in American Politics is designed for undergraduate courses in racial and ethnic politics. It would also serve well in American Government courses—either as a supplement to a standard introductory American Government text or as the primary text with other supplements. As such, the book is written with accessibility and student engagement in mind.

Each chapter of the text includes five key elements to increase student interest and aid learning. Chapters begin with a *narrative* or *case* that introduces and highlights the chapter's core issues and gives students something to relate to that is tangible and real. Boldfaced *key terms* are defined where introduced to give students a strong command of the most important concepts and are listed at the end of each chapter. *Boxed material* elaborates on and reinforces themes introduced in the text. These themes alternatively explain the core logic of an event or outcome ("How It Happened"), illustrate in more graphic ways the experience of race in the past or present ("Digging Deeper" and "What it Looks Like Today"), or demonstrate how social science answers contentious questions on race ("Testing the Theory"). Each chapter concludes with a set of *discussion questions* that are designed to help students think more deeply about the core questions and concepts raised in the chapter. Finally, to encourage students to expand their studies of racial politics beyond the pages of this volume, we offer and annotate *suggested readings* that provide pathways for deeper analysis of specific topics.

Online Resources

Lecture slides and a test bank are available for verified instructors on the Cambridge University Press Higher Education platform. Simply go to www.cambridge.org/riaple.

Organization of the Book

Our primary goal in this textbook is to investigate the role of race in American democracy in a comprehensive and systematic way. To help with that endeavor, the chapters follow a logical pathway that begins with a focus on the basic underpinnings of democracy and our Constitution.

Part I, "Diversity and American Democracy" includes three chapters:

Chapter 1 Setting the Stage: Diversity and Democracy

This framing chapter focuses on the nation's founding and the salience of inequality and race that is baked into our founding documents. It also discusses the concept of democracy that prevailed at the time of the founding and why it represented a radical departure from the past influences of Anglo and French political thought. It introduces the concept of multiple political traditions within American democracy.

Chapter 2 *E Pluribus Unum*: Citizenship, Demographic Change, and Diversity

This chapter explains different definitions of citizenship, including citizenship as status, as rights, as participation, and as identity. It highlights key immigration laws and periods of immigrant inclusion and exclusion. The chapter also presents basic data on demographic change through American political history.

Chapter 3 Democracy, Inequality, and Polarization

Chapter 3 provides a review of democratic theory, moving from the "minimal conception" of democratic politics to democracy in its representative, constitutional, participatory, deliberative, and epistemic forms. The chapter offers a comparison of where America stands today among the world's democracies and introduces the question of whether democracy carries the assumption of equality; it also reviews data on inequality throughout American history and on the more recent increase in inequality. We propose the idea that inequality is not extraneous to our democratic politics, but a direct result of it.

In Part II, we proceed to try to understand how race is lived in America, with two chapters that focus on the role of discrimination in our individual lives as well as in our institutions:

Chapter 4 How Do Individuals Experience Discrimination in the United States?

How has discrimination changed over time? What does discrimination look like today? This chapter begins by highlighting severe and systematic acts of discrimination throughout American history. It then assesses contemporary discrimination through a range of audit studies and other methods and then delves into individual perceptions of discrimination.

Chapter 5 How Do Institutions Contribute to Racism in the United States?

How can institutions be "racist"? What additional challenges are posed when bias is produced and reproduced by everyday institutional practices? This chapter traces the historical evolution of institutional discrimination from Reconstruction to the present, highlighting explicit legal and implicit policy-level discrimination in the Jim Crow era, the New Deal, and historical immigration policy. It also provides more in-depth analysis of the role of race in the present-day housing market, in the criminal justice system, and in election administration.

Our next task is to delve more deeply into inputs into our system of government from public opinion to the media, parties, and elections. All of this, we hope, will inform us about the openness of our democracy and about the desires and actions of the public. Part III discusses these inputs in four chapters:

Chapter 6 Public Opinion: Divided by Race?

Chapter 6 begins by looking at how Americans of different racial and ethnic stripes think about politics and how these views have changed over time. This chapter looks not only at racial divisions in policy preferences but also at racial differences in public trust and confidence in institutions. Excerpts examine the echo chamber and skepticism over polling and the measurement of public opinion as well as the role of social media in shaping public opinion.

Chapter 7 Political Participation

Here we first highlight the central role played by the vote and political participation in the democratic process. We then look at who votes and who participates in politics. The chapter underscores severe racial imbalances across most types of participation—both conventional and less conventional. It then seeks to explain these imbalances through a rigorous examination of factors such as socioeconomic status, group identity and consciousness, institutions, and mobilization. We also look at the impact of uneven participation on outcomes in American democracy and introduce potential solutions for existing inequities.

Chapter 8 Media, Campaigns, and the Politics of Race

This chapter covers the media, race, and politics. It begins by introducing the key concepts of priming, framing, and agenda-setting. It then offers a history of the use of race in electoral campaigns, highlighting the difference between racially explicit and racially implicit frames on crime, welfare, and other policy areas. That history includes the progression from a Republican "Southern Strategy" focused primarily on race and African Americans to one increasingly focused on immigration and religion in recent years. The chapter then turns to different assessments of the impact of these campaigns. Excerpts cover media conglomeration and the debate over whether the media has a liberal bias and/or an anti-minority bias.

Chapter 9 Race and Elections

To what extent does race predict vote choice in the array of American elections? How does the impact of race compare with class, gender, age, and other demographic factors? And how has racially polarized voting changed in the face of the growing diversity of the American electorate? After demonstrating an increasingly close connection between race and the vote, this chapter seeks to explain the link between race and vote choice. Although we note that a series of nonracial factors account for some of the racial divide in the vote, research also clearly shows that racial considerations and increasing concerns about immigration greatly shape both sides of the vote. We also focus on the rise of nonpartisanship among the minority population and on the role that parties have played in the past and could play in the future in incorporating immigrants.

We believe that these inputs into our system represent only the beginning of the democratic process. Thus, in the second half of the textbook we shift the focus to the *outputs* of the democratic process. In Part IV "Outcomes in American Democracy," Chapters 10–15 ask: who wins office? What policies do they pursue? Whose voices are heard and whose are ignored? And ultimately how are these patterns of inclusion and exclusion reflected in core policy areas like criminal justice, voting rights, and social rights?

Chapter 10 Do Elected Officials Look Like Their Constituents?

The chapter begins with a brief introduction to different conceptions of representation. It proceeds to focus on descriptive representation and the degree to which elected leaders in this nation have demographically mirrored the public over time. Despite enormous gains, it is clear that the halls of power remain overwhelmingly White. The text assesses the implications of the dearth of minorities in office for both policy and minority well-being. Next, we seek to understand the causes of the underrepresentation of minorities. We assess the role that institutions, financial resources, candidates, and, perhaps most importantly, White voters play in limiting minority representation.

Chapter 11 Does Government Carry Out the Will of the People?

The outcomes that we should perhaps care most about are substantive representation and responsiveness, and in particular the extent to which policy matches the interests and preferences of different segments of the public. Here we systematically assess the link between individual preferences and aggregate policy outcomes and conclude that race, more than any other factor, determines who wins and who loses on policy. We also look at variation in responsiveness by time and across context to try to identify factors that lead to more equitable representation.

Chapter 12 Race and Criminal Justice

This chapter delves into mass criminalization and mass incarceration. It examines the role that race plays at each level of the criminal justice system from the initial decision of law enforcement officials to engage with members of the public through to the trial and sentencing phases. Throughout, we seek to understand and illustrate the impact of individual bias and structural discrimination. We then end by highlighting the enormous racial disparities that the system fosters and by considering several alternative avenues for reform.

Chapter 13 Voting Rights

Chapter 13 surveys and assesses the different ways in which election laws and practices impact racial equality in the political process and the distribution of resources and power that stems from those elections. Topics include voter ID laws, felon disenfranchisement, and racial redistricting, as well as immigrant political incorporation and language access. Themed boxes include recent court cases on voter ID, specific voting rights cases, and non-citizen voting.

Chapter 14 Race and the Shaping of American Social Policies

In Chapter 14, we examine policy debates and policy outcomes across a range of areas that tend to be viewed as core to a minority agenda or that could alternatively be framed as the social rights of citizenship. These include affirmative action, Obamacare, education, and welfare reform. We will provide historical context on the race-targeted versus universalism debate. Insets will examine the link between legal status and access to social services.

Chapter 15 Diversity and Democracy from the Bottom up: The Past, the Present, and the Future

Our concluding chapter examines race, civil society, and social movements. What do political actors do when the chain of democratic accountability and responsiveness is broken? How do we understand the origins of protest movements and more radical forms of political participation? How do ordinary citizens in a diverse democracy contest and claim power for the people and effect change?

Part I

Diversity and American Democracy

1   Setting the Stage: Diversity and Democracy

The United States is the longest standing constitutional democracy in the world. For nearly 250 years since a group of propertied gentlemen began meeting in Philadelphia to draft a formal proclamation of independence from England and then design the framework for a new nation, the bedrock of our politics has been regular elections and a peaceful transition of power almost without exception. Yet today, there are alarming signs that our democracy is in serious trouble.

Three Episodes That Illustrate the Central Themes of This Text

We introduce some of the central themes and aims of this text by highlighting three of the most important events and movements of our recent past—episodes and undertakings that starkly capture the fragile state of our democratic tradition. These events, ripped from today's headlines, also reveal how the fragility of our democratic politics is connected to race as a marker of identity and an axis of inequality. In short, they exemplify why we cannot think about democracy without also considering diversity. We have kept these discussions short because we have all witnessed them and/or have been directly involved and affected by them.

A Global Pandemic

This episode in our recent history starts in December 2019 with whispers of a novel coronavirus named SARS-CoV-2, originating in Wuhan, China, that appeared both unnervingly contagious and unusually life-threatening. Into the early months of 2020, the initial concern quickly turned into the reality of a global pandemic with devastating consequences. As of May 19, 2022, there were more than 80 million confirmed cases and over 1 million confirmed deaths from COVID-19 in the United States alone (Hassan 2022).

    COVID-19 is ostensibly neither about politics nor about race. Yet the United States' experience with COVID-19 provides an instructive illustration of the state of our democracy. There is a basic expectation that governments—especially ones premised on an ideal of popular sovereignty—ought to be responsive to the needs and demands of the governed and ought to be held accountable when they are not. Furthermore, political science research tells us that when those needs and demands are urgent and come from an external threat like a global pandemic, democratic societies generally "rally around the flag" with unified support to fight that external threat. Heads of state like the president enjoy a big boost in popularity, allowing them to act swiftly and decisively to thwart that external threat.[1] Yet in the United States, Donald Trump, who presided over the onset of the pandemic, never received a boost in his historically low approval ratings during the pandemic. What is more, rather than unifying the nation against the public health crisis, Trump regularly downplayed the seriousness of the pandemic, cast doubts on his own scientific agencies trying to fight it, fueled misinformation and conspiratorial views on the virus, and ultimately further deepened the already sharp social and political divisions in the nation. Even with a transition to the Biden administration, which promised and delivered a more scientific and full-bore approach to combat the pandemic, the nation remained sharply divided on vaccines and masks, and Joe Biden has not enjoyed a crisis-charged boost in popular approval.

COVID-19 also provides an instructive lens on the role of diversity in democracy because of the pandemic's disproportionate effects on communities of color. The health menace and economic consequences of the pandemic fell especially hard on Blacks, Latinos, and Native Americans. In the initial waves of the pandemic, these groups were significantly more likely to become infected with the virus, to die from the virus, be exposed to the virus as "essential workers," or to struggle financially from the strain on the economy beset by COVID-19. Asian Americans, for their part, faced an outbreak of hate, violence, and scapegoating related to the origins of the pandemic. In addition, as America's response to the pandemic became mired in political polarization and misinformation and mistrust of science, the later waves of the pandemic saw a shift in the geography of COVID-19's death toll. Whereas the early phases of the pandemic hit densely populated, Democratic-leaning, and more racially diverse areas the hardest, the delta and omicron variants hit less densely populated, Republican-leaning, and Whiter areas the hardest (Jones 2022). As an unprecedented external threat to the nation, the microbe SARS-CoV-2 is color-blind. Yet the destructive consequences of the pandemic show all too plainly how polarized and unequal the United States is today, politically, racially, socially, and geographically.

An Attempted Insurrection

With COVID-19 wreaking havoc in the background, the nation also faced an attempted insurrection on January 6, 2021. The run-up to this insurgency and insurrection at the United States Capitol was the bitterly contested 2020 presidential election. Faced with a decisive loss to Joe Biden, the incumbent President Donald

---

[1] See, for example, Mueller (1973); Brody (1991).

Photo 1.1 On January 6, 2021, supporters of outgoing U.S. President Donald Trump breached security and entered the Capitol as Congress debated the 2020 presidential election Electoral Vote Certification.
Source: Photo Consistency Saul Loeb © Saul Loeb/Contributor/AFP/Getty Images.

Trump generated and intensified a hue and cry about stolen elections, and he plotted to overturn the election results on many fronts. Inflaming his supporters after the election with lies about fraudulent voting and ballot counting (none of which were able to be proven in court), the popular furor came to a head on January 6. Several thousands of Trump supporters flocked to a planned rally to "Save America" on the Ellipse of the National Mall and then marched toward the U.S. Capitol to "Stop the Steal." With the frenzy of a mob, hundreds breached police perimeters, vandalized and looted offices in the Capitol, and inveighed against an outgoing vice president who was at the Capitol for the ceremonial task of certifying the election with chants of "Hang Mike Pence." As facts of that day continue to be discovered by the U.S. House Select Committee on the January 6 Attack, it is clear how alarmingly close the insurrectionists came to disrupting the peaceful transition of power in America.

The events of January 6 shed light on some of the vulnerabilities of our democracy. An insurrection aimed at the legislative branch of government, stoked by the incendiary rhetoric of a defeated incumbent politician threatens the very premise of free and fair elections that ensure a peaceful transfer of power. A baseline standard for countries that have successfully transitioned out of authoritarianism to democracy is, as Adam Przeworski puts it, when democratic elections are "the only game in town, when no one can imagine acting outside of the democratic institutions, when all the losers want to do is to try again within the same institutions under which they have just lost" (1991: 26). The 2020 election is now several years in our past, yet Donald Trump remains a vanquished ex-president bent on rewriting history.

January 6 is also instructive because of the racial undertones of that day and the events that have occurred in the wake of the 2020 presidential election. We do not need a full recapitulation of the racial dog-whistling that contributed to Trump's ascendancy to the White House and his one term in office. Suffice it to say that central to the context preceding January 6 was Trump's penchant for sowing the seeds of racial division that fed and fueled his White nationalist base. Thus, the racial antecedents to January 6 include Trump's reference to undocumented immigrants from Mexico as "criminals, drug dealers, rapists"; to places like Haiti and African nations as "shithole countries"; to refugees from Syria as a "200,000-man army" who "could be ISIS"; to presidential candidate Elizabeth Warren as "Pocahontas"; to calling the SARS-CoV-2 virus the "Chinese virus" and "kung flu."

Dividing America's electorate for political gain is one kind of challenge diversity poses to democracy. An entirely different challenge is to exploit racial markers to try to engineer electoral outcomes in one party's favor. The wake of Trump's electoral loss has been characterized not just by the frontal assault on the U.S. Capitol on January 6, but also by the longer-term behind-the-scenes assault on the fundamental right to vote occurring in state capitols throughout the nation. As of October 2021, Republican-majority state legislatures in nineteen states had passed new election laws that were likely to make it harder for citizens in their states to exercise their right to vote. Many more states have similar laws on the docket. The restrictions include imposing harsher voter identification requirements, purging voter registration rolls and absentee voting lists, making it generally harder to vote by mail or vote absentee, limiting early voting, limiting language access and assistance to citizens with limited English proficiency, reducing the availability of polling places, even banning the provision of water and snacks to election day voters who often have to wait hours on end to cast their vote. Many of these laws are, by design, expected to have an especially restrictive effect on the ability of voters of color to exercise their franchise. The implication here, at least to Democrats and voters of color, appears to be that the long-term strategy of one of America's two major political parties is: if you cannot win outright by winning more votes, resort to winning by selectively limiting who can vote.

A Movement of Racial Reckoning

The Black Lives Matter movement began in 2013 in response to the acquittal of George Zimmerman for the killing of teenager Trayvon Martin. Since 2013, Americans have witnessed a seemingly endless and enraging outbreak of violent

Photo 1.2 Thousands gathered in New York's Times Square on June 7, 2020, for a demonstration organized by Black Lives Matter Greater New York in support of police reform policies.
Source: Photo Michael Nigro © Pacific Press/Contributor/LightRocket/Getty Images.

deaths of young African Americans—Eric Garner, Michael Brown, Tamir Rice, Alton Sterling, Philando Castile, Stephon Clark, Breonna Taylor, to name just a few—many at the hands of police officers. When Minneapolis police brutally killed George Floyd on May 25, 2020, anger and despair boiled over into mass protests on an unprecedented national scale. In the subsequent month, between 15 and 26 million Americans took to the streets to demonstrate against racially targeted police violence (Buchanan, Bui, and Patel 2020). By many accounts, Black Lives Matter is the single largest protest movement in American history.

Unlike COVID-19 and January 6, which many might think of as at least superficially non-racial events, Black Lives Matter is by definition about racial justice. For our purposes, it is also an instructive illustration of the state of diversity and democracy in the United States. We noted in the discussion of COVID-19 that representative democracies like the United States are premised on the expectation that our politicians will be responsive to the needs and demands of *all* its citizens. When they are not, we expect that those citizens will hold politicians accountable and vote them out of office come election time. What is true for a global pandemic is also true for racial violence. Yet as we will see in this book, this expectation has long been unmet on those issues—criminal justice, racial violence, structural racism—that set the context for the Black Lives

Matter movement. Too often, our elected officials appear conspicuously invisible or unresponsive on these issues and with little electoral accountability. This dynamic persists for institutional and structural reasons that we will closely examine in later chapters of this text.

The Black Lives Matter movement invites us to explore the questions at the heart of this book. Are issues that disproportionately fall hard on communities of color less likely to get policy attention and response by our democratic politics? Do some of those issues fall disproportionately hard on communities of color *because* of the ways that policy gets made by our democratic politics, or in spite of them? Are the fires that erupt in collective protest when our politics fails to address these issues a sign of democracy in distress or democracy at work?

Rule or Exception? Our Argument

Each of the three events described above poses unprecedented challenges to democratic governance in the United States. Each one alone would be an exceptionally rare moment in our political history, one that would define a generation and a lifetime. Each of these deserves more thorough discussion, analysis, and fuller examination than we can give in one text. That all three have unfolded in the last few years is astonishing, even to three world-weary political scientists like us.

Rare and unique as these events are, they share some common elements, and these are the elements that form the central argument of this book. Democracy in the United States is rooted in the principle of equal standing among every member of a political society. Yet that principle coexists all too often in practice with a reality of unequal standing for many. The SARS-CoV-2 virus infected millions upon millions of Americans, but not everyone was equally at risk of contracting that virus or dying from it, losing their job or home, or being blamed for the pandemic itself. A defeated political candidate foments an insurrection to a battle cry of election fraud, but not everyone is equally riled up, equally accused of fraudulently voting, or equally likely to be affected by the succession of restrictions to voting rights that the claims of stolen elections has brought about. An historic number of Americans of all backgrounds march in the streets because our criminal justice system seemingly serves and protects some Americans more than it does others, and because the deaths of Black Americans seem all too often ignored.

The through line connecting these events and the chapters of this book is that in America today, equality as an ideal coexists in tension with the lived realities of diversity and difference. This tension is not ubiquitous, but it is neither an aberration nor an accident. Rather, the deep roots of inequality and identity can be found encoded in our constitutional framework, inscribed into our institutions, and etched deeply into the hearts and minds of our body politic. This view may strike some readers as self-evident. To quote James Baldwin in the language of his time, "To be a Negro [sic] in this country and to be relatively conscious is to be in a rage almost all the time … It isn't only what is happening to you. But it's what's happening all around you and all of the time in the face of the most extraordinary and criminal indifference" (Baldwin et al. 1961: 205).

At the same time, this view may strike others as heretical, even unpatriotic. In our current hyper-polarized political environment, some might label our argument on the centrality of race as "critical race theory." Let us take a moment to flesh out why. **Critical race theory** is a relatively esoteric, marginalized legal theory that for decades has been kindling reserved for academic debates among law professors. Today it is on the verge of being an inferno, igniting anger and mobilizing voters who resent any insinuation that institutional, structural bias infects our body politic. President Trump helped to fuel this uproar by issuing an Executive Order in 2020 that banned the federal government (as well as federal contractors, subcontractors, and any federal grantees) from diversity and sensitivity training programs on race or gender bias in the workplace. These training programs were, in fact, not based on critical race theory per se, but the order nonetheless declared that such training constituted a "malign ideology from the fringes of American society and threatens to infect core institutions of our country" and is "rooted in the pernicious and false belief that America is an irredeemably racist and sexist country." In a preceding memo from the White House Office of Management and Budget, OMB Director Russell Vought specifically targeted critical race theory, describing it as the belief "either (1) that the United States is an inherently racist or evil country or (2) that any race or ethnicity is inherently racist or evil" (Vought 2020).

Following suit, more than two dozen Republican-led state legislatures have passed or proposed laws with a similar goal. A Texas law (H.B. 3979, 2021), for example, goes so far as to exclude from school curricula "the concept that … slavery and racism are anything other than deviations from, betrayals of, or failures to live up to, the authentic founding principles of the United States, which include liberty and equality."

As is often the case with hot-button issues and catch-all phrases, "critical race theory" as people talk about it today is widely misunderstood. For instance, in an election poll on the 2021 gubernatorial race in Virginia, 73 percent of registered voters reported that "the debate over teaching critical race theory in schools" was "an important factor" in their vote; 25 percent reported that it was "the single most important factor" (Fox News Voter Analysis 2021). What made this sudden rise in the salience of critical race theory among Virginia voters even more remarkable is the lack of any evidence that it was being taught in Virginia's public schools. The current debate over critical race theory may simmer down, or it may continue to boil over and inflame voters as it did in the 2022 midterm elections and threatens to do in the 2024 elections. But because it bears a family resemblance to the central theme of this book—that racial inequality is and has long been deeply rooted in our politics—we want to be clear about what we are saying and what we are not saying (see box, "Digging Deeper: Critical Race Theory—What it Is and What it Isn't" for a discussion of the underpinnings of this theory).

DIGGING DEEPER: CRITICAL RACE THEORY—WHAT IT IS AND WHAT IT ISN'T

Critical race theory is an intellectual movement whose origins date back to the 1970s and 1980s and the writings of a handful of law professors of color who were dissatisfied with existing legal approaches to race and inequality. The scholars within the legal academy who are usually identified as the pioneers of this movement include Derrick Bell, Kimberlé Williams Crenshaw, Richard Delgado, Neil Gotanda, Mari Matsuda, and Patricia Williams. These law faculty saw an intimate connection between who was writing about civil rights and anti-discrimination law and what they wrote. Specifically, the almost exclusively liberal White men who wrote in this field at that time described in their writings a triumph of law over injustice, seeing the sweeping court decisions and legislation of the Civil Rights era as sufficient to eradicate segregation and end racial discrimination. Yet by the 1970s and 1980s, it was clear that despite landmark Supreme Court rulings like *Brown v. Board of Education* (1954) and sweeping new laws like the 1964 Civil Rights Act and the 1965 Voting Rights Act, segregation, discrimination, and racial inequality remained persistent features of American life.

To understand why de facto (actual) inequality persisted in spite of *de jure* (legally recognized) equality, these scholars proposed a new theoretical framework for understanding law and its relation to equality and justice. This new framework builds on another movement within the legal academy, *critical legal studies*, which argues that laws are not neutral or applied formally and universally across all contexts. Rather, critical legal studies sees laws as political instruments that generally serve to uphold the status quo. For critical race theory, importantly, laws are not color-blind. Critical race theorists thus see race and racism as constructed, both in law and in society, for the benefit of dominant groups in power in a society. As Kimberlé Crenshaw describes it, critical race theory "is a practice—a way of seeing how the fiction of race has been transformed into concrete racial inequalities" (Lang 2020).

In addition, critical race theorists reject the default view among legal scholars that the basic societal units of law are anonymous individuals in particular situations. Rather, the inequalities that law produces and reproduces are institutional and structural. As Mari Matsuda puts it, "The problem is not bad people. The problem is a system that reproduces bad outcomes" (Fortin 2021). Systemic racism and discrimination (defined and described in more detail in Chapter 5) are thus manifest as everyday phenomena that affect groups and not just individuals, and that operate through institutions. Racism and discrimination are seen as pervasive in American society and not a time-bound anomaly easily rectified by legislating equality and inclusion.[2]

---

[2] While critical race theory foregrounds race, it has also been at the forefront of recognizing that the identities that shape one's life are **intersectional** and that individuals are situated in complex social positions that all have some impact on an individual's life.

While critical race theory is not actually taught in public schools, the firestorm over whether critical race theory can be taught in schools has become a battle over whether schools will continue to tell the story of America's founding and our shared creed that older generations of Americans learned as their civic education, or whether they will update and complicate that story. We include, under "Discussion Questions" at the end of the chapter, some puzzles to think about regarding critical race theory.

Our Starting Point: Two American Realities

In this book, we do not take as our starting point the view that "America is an irredeemably racist and sexist country," if this phrase is meant to convey that achieving racial justice is impossible. Nor do we take as our starting point the view that slavery, racism, and other structures of inequality and injustice are mere "deviations" from our cherished founding principles. Our views on racial inequality and democratic politics—whether and how they are related—are not based on doctrinal assertions or theoretical assumptions. Rather, as social scientists, *we follow the evidence*. This book examines politics and government in the United States broadly, covering topics that range from public opinion and political participation to elections and representation to areas of law and policy like criminal justice, voting rights, education, and healthcare. For each topic, we curate the evidence from the existing literature from other social scientists and, where needed, contribute evidence from our own research. And the evidence, we find, points to the continuing significance of race and to persistent and substantial racial inequality across multiple facets of American society.

You will, of course, come to your own judgment about whether you agree or disagree with our conclusions on where the evidence points us. Agree or disagree, we expect you to do so not because they confirm and validate the views you held before opening this book but based on how you critically evaluate the evidence we present and the arguments we draw from them. Our stance vis-à-vis critical race theory is best explained by invoking a slogan of sorts that many social scientists repeatedly summon. That slogan is the statement, "It's an empirical question." What do we mean by that? In the social world and perhaps even more so in the political world, much of what we believe to be true are, in reality, only suppositions or received wisdoms. Many of you may believe that our mainstream media has a liberal bias. Many of you may believe that government-run services are inefficient, while those same services run by the private sector are efficient. Many of you may believe that your interests are better served when the politicians look like you or share your background than when they don't. These and many other beliefs about politics are widespread, but each of them can and should be held up against evidence. Then, based on a critical analysis of that evidence, you should either confirm, correct, or contextualize your beliefs.

Putting our prior beliefs up against available evidence and then reasoning through whether those beliefs hold up or require revision is really the crux of critical thinking and learning. It is also very much the core motivation behind this textbook. Throughout the text we will attempt to do this not just for grand theories and overarching beliefs like whether racial inequality is systemic or a mere anomaly, but also for more specific standpoints on media bias, the efficiency of the private sector, descriptive representation, and a host of other topics linked to politics and representation.

To launch this critical thinking process and to help our readers better work through the complex realities that will follow in this textbook, we want to begin by highlighting two central facts about America. The two facts are certainly important in and of themselves—they tell us much about where America is today and perhaps even where it is headed tomorrow. But we place them so early in the text primarily because we believe they are critical for each of us to absorb if we hope to eventually develop an understanding of how and why race matters in this nation and in our democracy.

Growing Racial Diversity

Perhaps the most significant social transformation that America has contended with over the last half century is the increasing racial diversity of our national population. A half century ago, as Figure 1.1 illustrates, America was almost entirely White. As late as 1960, non-Hispanic Whites represented almost 90 percent of the US population. Whites visibly dominated almost every sphere of the national consciousness. But in the interim years we have been inexorably transformed from a world of White numerical dominance to one in which that numerical majority is under siege. Today, half of all babies born in this country are non-White.

Racial diversity in the present moment is very different and more complex than in the past. A couple of generations ago, racial boundaries were, for the most part, characterized along a Black–White dichotomy. Blacks were by far and away the largest racial and ethnic minority group and discussions of race relations and racial discrimination were centrally focused on African Americans. Today, Latinos outnumber Blacks, Asian Americans are the fastest growing racial or pan-ethnic group, Americans are identifying as Native Americans in numbers that far exceed birth and death rates, and multiracial Americans have emerged as a vocal entity. Decades of massive and almost unparalleled immigration have contributed heavily to this altered landscape. Immigrants and their children now represent one in four Americans. That titanic demographic change is impossible for Americans of all stripes to ignore.

And it is not just the change that has already occurred. Equally significant may be the changes that we are likely to see in the future. The Census Bureau projects that the country will move toward being a "majority-minority" nation within the next two to three decades. As of 2022 (noted by the dotted yellow vertical line in Figure 1.1), non-Hispanic Whites still make up 58 percent of the

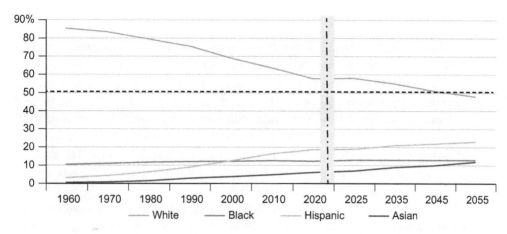

Figure 1.1 America's Growing Racial Diversity: Population Share by Race Over Time.
In 1960, America was predominantly White, but the steady rise in Hispanics and Asians along
with a declining share of non-Hispanic Whites has fueled growing racial–ethnic diversity, with
Whites poised to fall below the 50 percent threshold some time around the middle of the twenty-
first century.
Source: U.S. Census Bureau.

population. But as the declining blue line in the figure indicates, Whites' share of
the population is expected to slowly decline to the point where some time
around the middle part of the twenty-first century Whites' share of the population could dip below the 50 percent mark. Exactly when the nation will be
minority White is not entirely clear. Racial change in the future will depend
heavily on how individual Americans choose to identify themselves racially, on
immigration and birth patterns, on exactly who does and who does not get
included in the White category, as well as a host of other factors. But there is no
doubt that we are in the midst of a massive racial transformation the likes of
which this nation has rarely experienced.

What do radical shifts in the racial diversity of the nation mean for our nation
and our politics? Growing diversity could certainly bring us closer together.
Increasing diversity is sure to bring about greater interracial contact as well as
more interracial marriages, and with these changes blurred and fluid racial and
ethnic lines. Ultimately, these changes could result in greater interracial cooperation and less conflict. But increasing diversity could also push us further apart.
Growing diversity could represent a threat to White Americans, some of whom
may feel that their numerical dominance and access to power is under siege.
That perceived threat could generate resentment and a backlash among some
Whites. Indeed, how White Americans respond to their declining numerical
dominance and the impending loss of their majority status are defining questions
that have fundamentally shaped and will likely continue to profoundly shape
race relations and democratic outcomes in this country in the years and decades
ahead.

Persistent Racial Hierarchy

The fact that America is more diverse today than it was a generation or two ago is undeniable. It is also beyond dispute that across most measures of social, economic, and political well-being America remains a nation with a clear racial hierarchy and profoundly uneven outcomes. On almost every core metric, there are sharp differences in average well-being by race with Whites and Asian Americans often falling near the top of the racial spectrum and Blacks, Latinos, Native Americans, and others often residing near the bottom of that hierarchy with lower incomes, less wealth, higher rates of poverty and unemployment, more limited educational attainment, and worse health outcomes.

Critically, those racial differences are not only very real but also often very large. As we will see, Latinos are only half as likely as Whites to graduate from college, more than twice as likely as Whites to be poor, and almost twice as likely as Whites to be unemployed. Black households likewise have about one-eighth of the net wealth of White households, earn on average only 60 percent of what White households earn and less than half (47 percent) of the wages of the average Asian American household. In America, race and well-being are closely related.

Throughout the text we will provide more detailed assessments of the well-being of each of America's major racial and ethnic groups across a number of political, social, and economic metrics. In this chapter, we highlight a few key indicators that illustrate how racial boundaries define the life opportunities and material conditions of Americans today.

Educational Attainment by Race

We begin with education. Of all of the possible measures of well-being, educational achievement is perhaps the most important—or at least one of the most telling. For most Americans, educational achievements are not only critical in shaping current earnings but are also central in shaping future life opportunities.

Figure 1.2 reveals some stark racial disparities in educational attainment from 1964 to 2015. Whites are far more likely than Blacks or Hispanics to hold a bachelor's degree. In fact, Whites are more than twice as likely as Hispanics to have attained a bachelor's degree or higher and they are almost twice as likely as African Americans to have done so. Asian Americans land even higher up on this scale of educational attainment. In 2015, more than half of Asian American adults (53 percent) had a degree, compared with only a third of Whites (36 percent), a quarter of Blacks (23 percent), and 15 percent of Latinos. Although not included in the figure, educational attainment for Native Americans falls near the bottom of the hierarchy. The American Council of Education reports that in 2017 roughly 20 percent of American Indian and Alaska Natives aged 25 and older had obtained a bachelor's degree or higher. Glaring differences by race on this fundamental indicator are a strong sign that outcomes in American society are profoundly shaped by race.

% of U.S. adults ages 25 and older who have at least a bachelor's degree

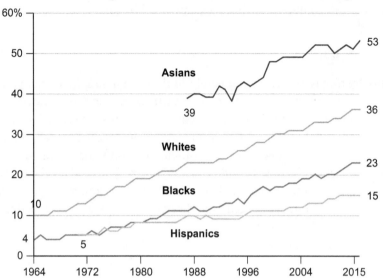

Figure 1.2 Educational Attainment by Race, 1964–2015
The upward trending lines indicate significant improvement in college graduation rates over
time for all groups, but stark disparities among the groups.
Source: Pew Research Center and the Current Population Survey (2016).

There is certainly good news here as well. As the figure illustrates, over the last
half century, college graduation rates have grown significantly for Americans
generally and for all racial and ethnic groups in particular. Blacks, for example,
improved from a college graduation rate of only 4 percent in 1964 to a more
impressive 23 percent in 2015. Gains for Asian Americans, Whites, and
Hispanics—as each of their upwardly trending lines indicates—have also
been substantial.

Those gains, however, have done little to diminish racial and ethnic gaps in
educational attainment. If anything, those racial gaps have actually grown over
time. In 1964, the gap between white graduation rates (10 percent) and Black
graduation rates (4 percent) was only six percentage points—very real but not
insurmountable. Unfortunately, over time that racial gap has increased steadily to
the point where the White graduation rate now exceeds the Black graduation by 13
points. Likewise, the Hispanic–White gap has grown from 12 points in 1972 to a
whopping 21 points in 2015. The only racial gap that has held relatively steady is the
Asian American advantage over Whites which has hovered around 15 points over
the entire time period. Importantly, aggregated statistics like those shown in
Figure 1.2 can also obscure significant gaps in attainment and well-being within a
group. Thus, while 53 percent of Asian Americans have a bachelor's degree or
higher, for a group like Laotian Americans, that figure is only 17 percent, far below

the national average. In sum, at least on this one measure, America's growing racial diversity has unfortunately not been accompanied by greater racial equality.

Economic Well-being by Race

Inequality by race is also readily apparent in the economic sphere. In a pattern that we will see time and time again, there are sharp racial disparities in earnings and a clear racial hierarchy with Whites and Asian Americans generally located toward the upper end and Latinos and African Americans tending to fall closer to the bottom. As Figure 1.3 shows, median household income for Asian Americans far surpasses the median income for other racial groups. The median Asian American household in the country earns roughly $95,000 per year, a number that exceeds the $75,000 figure for White households and dwarfs the $55,000 and $46,000 figures for Hispanics and Blacks, respectively.

Just as alarming is the fact that racial gaps in earnings have not declined in the last few decades. In 1972, the first year for which we have data on White, Black, and Latino earnings, the median Black household earned just under 60 percent of the median White household. Almost fifty years later, the ratio between Black and White median household incomes is almost exactly the same. Likewise, Hispanic households only earn about 70 percent of White households today, a figure that almost perfectly matches the 70 percent ratio of Hispanic to White median household incomes in 1972. The one group at the top of the economic ladder, Asian Americans, has, if anything, gained further ground relative to other groups over

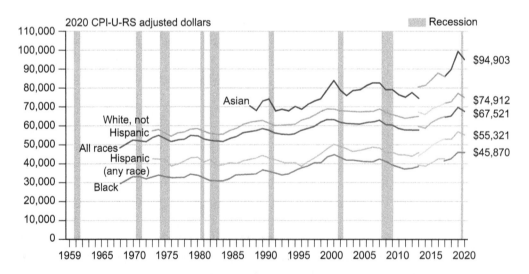

Figure 1.3 Household Incomes Over Time, 1968–2019
Median incomes for Whites and Asian Americans dwarf household incomes for Black and Hispanic Americans. While income levels for all groups have risen over time, the gaps between groups have not narrowed. Due to a change in measurement, there is a gap in the lines around 2013.
Source: U.S. Census Bureau, Current Population Survey, 1968–2019, Annual Social and Economic Supplements

time. Household incomes are growing appreciably for all groups over time, but that has not translated into declining racial disparities.

As with education, aggregated numbers here can obscure enormous variation within each group. Taking Asian Americans again as a case in point, the median household income for Burmese Americans, the least well-off national origin group in the larger Asian pan-ethnic population, was only $45,903 in 2019.[3] For Latinos, outcomes also vary significantly by national origin group and in many cases by immigration status and nativity. Indeed, the relatively flat trends in Latino well-being that are evident in this figure—and in others below—can in part be explained by an influx of immigrants who often arrive with less education and limited skills. This broad range of outcomes within each group underscores an emerging reality: inequality within these large and diverse groups is massive and frequently growing (Kochhar and Cilluffo 2018).

Income is the most widely used measure of economic well-being, but it is certainly not the only one. Patterns in wealth, poverty, homeownership, and labor force participation tell a similar story—great inequality that has unfortunately not diminished much over time.

The degree of difference in wealth is, perhaps, the most startling. In 2019, the median White household had a total net worth of roughly $188,000—a figure that is five times higher than the net worth of Hispanic households ($38,000) and almost eight times higher than the net worth of the median Black household ($24,000). The total net worth of "other" racial groups (combining Asian Americans, Native Americans, and Pacific Islanders together) was $74,000 (Boshara, Emmons and Noeth 2015). Moreover, that wealth gap has hardly declined in the last few decades. The ratio of median Black to White wealth is largely unchanged over the past thirty years and the Hispanic to White wealth ratio has slightly improved over the same period but clearly remains large (Kent and Ricketts 2021).

Homeownership rates also vary widely by race. Roughly three-quarters of all White households (73 percent) owned a home in 2019 compared with less than half of Black (42 percent) and Latino households (48 percent). On this measure, Asian Americans landed closer to the middle with a 58 percent homeownership rate. Native Americans had a slightly higher homeownership rate (50 percent) than either Blacks or Latinos. Latino and Asian American households have caught up slightly with White households in the homeownership rates over time (USA Facts 2023).

White Americans and Asian Americans are also much less likely than racial and ethnic minorities to experience poverty (see Figure 1.4). In fact, in 2019, the Black poverty rate (18.8 percent) and the Hispanic poverty rate (15.7 percent) both more than doubled the White (7.3 percent) and Asian American (7.3 percent) poverty rates. Those racial gaps have hardly changed over the last fifty years. On this measure, Native Americans came out worse than all others with a 23 percent

---

[3] See at: https://usafacts.org/articles/the-diverse-demographics-of-asian-americans.

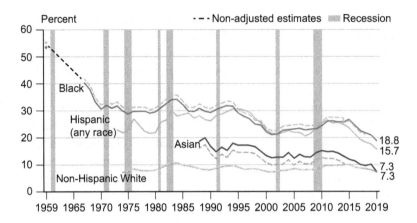

Figure 1.4 Poverty Rates Over Time for Each Racial and Ethnic Group, 1959–2019
Whites and Asian Americans are much less likely than Blacks and Hispanics to
experience poverty.
Source: U.S. Census Bureau, Current Population Survey, 1968–2019, Annual Social and
Economic Supplements.

poverty rate in 2019 (Pathak 2021). Those who are in need and are struggling come
disproportionately from the racial and ethnic minority population.

Wages, wealth, and poverty are, of course, highly dependent on employment—yet
another metric that is closely tied to race and ethnicity. Statistics on unemployment
rates by race are collected quarterly by the U.S. Bureau of Labor Statistics (BLS).
Those statistics tell a now familiar story. In the third quarter of 2021, among
Americans 16 years of age or older, Whites (4.6 percent) and Asian Americans (4.7
percent) had the lowest unemployment rates, whereas Hispanics (6.2 percent) and
African Americans (8.4 percent) had the highest rates.[4] The BLS does not provide this
information for American Indians or Alaskan Natives, but the Native American
Labor Market Dashboard estimates that the rolling three-month average unemployment rate for American Indians/Alaskan Natives as of September 2021 was 8.7
percent for non-metro areas and 7.2 percent for metro areas—rates that highlight a
widespread problem and numbers that place Native Americans close to both Blacks
and Hispanics in terms of labor force participation.[5] Given that these figures capture
only those Americans who are still actively seeking employment, the problem of
nonemployment is undoubtedly worse for all groups than these numbers suggest.

Health and Life Expectancy by Race

Racial and ethnic minority group members also fare worse than their non-
Hispanic White counterparts on a broad range of health outcomes ranging from

[4] See at: www.bls.gov/web/empsit/cpsee_e16.htm.
[5] See at: www.minneapolisfed.org/indiancountry/resources/native-american-labor-market-dashboard.

Number of health status measures for which group fared better, the same, or worse compared to White counterparts:

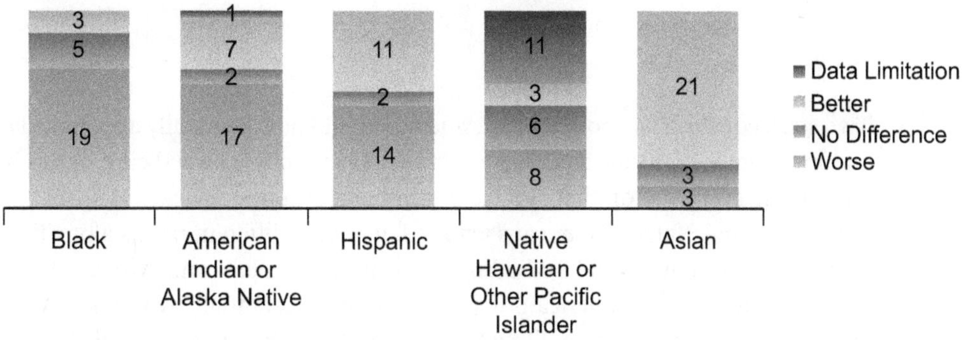

					■ Data Limitation
					▨ Better
					▥ No Difference
					▧ Worse

Black: 3, 5, 19
American Indian or Alaska Native: 1, 7, 2, 17
Hispanic: 11, 2, 14
Native Hawaiian or Other Pacific Islander: 11, 3, 6, 8
Asian: 21, 3, 3

Figure 1.5 Health Outcomes by Race in America, 2018
Most racial minorities fare worse than Whites across a broad range of health outcomes.
Source: Kaiser Family Foundation, www.kff.org/racial-equity-and-health-policy/report/key-data-on-health-and-health-care-by-race-and-ethnicity.

heart disease, strokes, various forms of cancer, infant mortality, pregnancy-related deaths, and HIV or AIDS diagnosis, to name just a few. The Kaiser Family Foundation (KFF), a nonprofit and nonpartisan organization devoted to collecting and disseminating data on national health issues, have developed a helpful summary figure of their findings across twenty-seven different health status measures—including infant mortality, mental health status, pregnancy-related deaths, and various chronic conditions such as heart disease and strokes (see Figure 1.5). As shown in the figure, Blacks have worse outcomes than Whites on nineteen of the twenty-seven measures. They are followed by American Indian and Alaskan Natives who fare worse than Whites on seventeen of twenty-seven health measures.

The results are somewhat less extreme for Hispanics and Native Hawaiians or Pacific Islanders, but in each case the group fares worse than Whites on health outcomes more often than it ends up better than Whites. Only in the case of Asian Americans do we find a group that frequently does better than Whites on a majority (twenty-one) of these twenty-seven measures, although this result may mask significant differences among subgroups within this population.

One inevitable consequence of these broad and pervasive health disparities is that some minorities, such as Blacks and American Indians and Alaskan Natives, have shorter lifespans than non-Hispanic White Americans and Asian Americans. The National Center for Health Statistics estimates that a non-Hispanic White female born in 2020 can expect to live to the age of 80.2. Similarly, the projected life expectancy for an Asian American female born in 2020 was 82.7 years. By contrast, the figure for non-Hispanic Blacks is only 75.7 years. Perhaps surprisingly, Hispanics have traditionally had higher life expectancy rates than Whites—even though Hispanics generally have lower incomes and lower levels of education, which are factors negatively associated with life expectancy. In 2020, Hispanic female infants had a life expectancy of 82.4 years.

Stark Conclusions

Two stark conclusions about race in America should now be readily apparent. The first and most obvious is that there is a clear racial hierarchy to well-being in this nation. On almost every factor that we have examined, Whites, Blacks, Hispanics, Asian Americans, and Native Americans tend to fall at very different points along the socio-economic spectrum. Racial and ethnic minorities in general and African Americans, Hispanics, and Native Americans in particular fare substantially worse than Whites on almost every major outcome. On education, in the economy, and on health, their life chances and their outcomes are generally lower than those of the White population.

This is true not only for the social and economic indicators we have already examined. It is also true for many of the political outcomes that will be the focus of the remainder of this textbook. We will see that despite the increasing racial diversity of the population, the halls of power are still dominated by White faces. We will see that despite some major advances in voting rights, racial and ethnic minorities tend to vote less and participate in politics less than Whites do. And we will see that when Americans express their views and advocate for policies that they think will make the nation better, politicians tend to hear and heed White voices more than minority voices. The political sphere is far from even. There is, in short, stark racial inequality on almost everything that matters in America.

The other thing we have learned from this introductory examination is that things are generally not getting better over time. While there has been some narrowing of racial and ethnic disparities in well-being in some areas—areas that we will delve into in more detail later in the textbook—racial gaps on most basic measures of economic and social well-being have persisted for decades and in some cases have even widened. Put simply, racial and ethnic minorities are not catching up to their White counterparts. Persistent and pervasive racial inequality is certainly troubling. It means that some of us are doing much worse than others. It means that some of us are suffering much more than others.

All of this alerts us to the fact that race is central to outcomes in American society. Of course, simply knowing that these racial disparities exist does not tell us why they exist or how we can alleviate them. Racial disparities could be a function of direct discrimination; of indirect disadvantages like family poverty and educational status, underresourced local institutions, environmental risk factors; of failed government policies, or of any number of other factors. Thus, to better understand why America is where it is and how we can move forward, we will have to dig much deeper. We will have to learn more about the processes driving and underlying racial differences, we will have to learn more about the attitudes and actions of members of each racial and ethnic group, and we will have to learn more about the structures and rules that help to shape these outcomes from within the political sphere. With that in mind, each subsequent chapter will go into much greater depth about different aspects of the political process with the ultimate goal of providing a better understanding of how race works in America and how it impacts or does not impact most of the decisions we make in American democracy.

American Creeds

In this section, we reintroduce the book's perspective by taking on the question of whether there is a defining American "creed," "ethos," or national identity. To animate the difference in viewpoints about our nation's origins, consider the contrast between the following two more modern-day accounts. Samuel Huntington, one of the most influential political scientists of the twentieth century, penned a controversial essay in *Foreign Policy* in 2004 in which he argued that immigration from Mexico posed an existential threat to America's national identity. Huntington begins the essay with the declaration, "America was created by 17th and 18th century settlers who were overwhelmingly white, British, and Protestant. Their values, institutions, and culture provided the foundation for and shaped the development of the United States in the following centuries" (2004: 31). Huntington goes on to describe our national creed as "the product of the distinct Anglo-Protestant culture of the founding settlers. Key elements of that culture include the English language; Christianity; religious commitment; English concepts of the rule of law ... and Protestant values of individualism, the work ethic, and the belief that humans have the ability and the duty to try to create a heaven on earth" (2004: 31–32).

By contrast, consider the *1619 Project*, a Pulitzer Prize winning piece in the *New York Times* that reframed United States history around the existence of slavery from its earliest days and the consequences of slavery and contributions of Blacks to the national narrative. In her introduction to the project, Nikole Hannah-Jones writes, "our democracy's founding ideals were false when they were written." Hannah-Jones goes on to add, "The United States is a nation founded on both an ideal and a lie. Our Declaration of Independence ... proclaims that 'all men are created equal' and 'endowed by their Creator with certain unalienable rights.' But the white men who drafted those words did not believe them to be true for the hundreds of thousands of black people in their midst" (Hannah-Jones 2019). Or consider this succinct statement from Ta-Nehisi Coates in his celebrated essay in *The Atlantic*, "The Case for Reparations": "America begins in black plunder and white democracy, two features that are not contradictory but complementary" (Coates 2014).

The origin story that Huntington retells is the narrative about who we are as a nation that older generations of Americans grew up learning as their truth. It is also the narrative that political projects like the Trump administration's executive order banning diversity training and state laws forbidding the teaching of critical race theory zealously seek to safeguard. The origin story that Hannah-Jones, Coates, and others want to lift up is the "minority report" to that narrative. It is not new, but the historical and present-day experiences that form its basis have often been hidden from the limelight and, when surfaced, have always been vigorously contested.

There is a parallel between these opposing accounts and debates among political scientists about the American political tradition. We find this parallel instructive and one that informs our approach. For much of the history of the discipline, political scientists investigated the topic of a national creed, ethos, and identity by asking what made the United States *different*. Different, peculiarly, from European nations from where most of the settlers who immigrated to the United States came until the mid-twentieth century. This thesis of American exceptionalism has a long tradition tracing back to prominent Europeans visiting the New World and publishing their thoughts on the distinct character of the United States. The authors and works here include Hector St. John de Crevecoeur's *Letters from an American Farmer* (1782), Alexis de Tocqueville's *Democracy in America* (1835 and 1840), James Bryce's *American Commonwealth* (1888), and Gunnar Myrdal's *An American Dilemma* (1944).

The central claim of scholars writing about exceptionalism is that Americans are defined, and define themselves, not by common heritage or bounded geography, but by shared beliefs and values. Until recently, to be German meant to have a German bloodline. And to be French meant being born on French soil.[6] To be Americans, so this account of exceptionalism goes, meant first and foremost adhering to a common, shared American creed and ethos. The creed, according to renowned political scientists of the twentieth century like Louis Hartz, is a defining and distinct American liberalism. Hartz saw liberalism as a distinct view that was enabled by the absence of a feudal, entrenched class system in the United States. With philosophical roots in the writings of John Locke, American liberalism is defined by fierce commitments to political freedom, economic freedom, and limited government. For Hartz and others, American liberalism so infused the American way of life and became such a consensus that it effectively buffered the United States from the revolutionary socialist impulse that Karl Marx viewed as an historical inevitability.[7]

The key point for us is that there is a long tradition of political scientists who see a common thread through the nation's history—a unifying, single, pervasive set of liberal beliefs, centered around the rights and freedoms of individuals. In contrast to this view of a single, consensus American political tradition, an alternative narrative has surfaced in the last generation. This revisionist account is often identified with Rogers Smith's *Civic Ideals* (1999) and stresses multiple traditions of political thinking in American history. The multiple traditions include liberalism, but also

---

[6] See, for example, Brubaker (1998) on the difference between French and German ideas and laws on citizenship.

[7] What beliefs constitute the American creed vary a bit, depending on who is writing about them. McCloskey and Zaller (1984), for instance, stress that the core beliefs shared by Americans are support for liberty, equality, and economic individualism. In another example, for Seymour Martin Lipset the American creed is the shared belief in liberty, egalitarianism, individualism, populism, and a laissez-faire view toward private commerce.

traditions quite distinct from liberalism. None are anomalies and all have been present throughout our history, even as they often coexist in tension with one another. The multiple traditions view is, in effect, what Ta-Nehisi Coates meant by describing "black plunder and white democracy" as "not contradictory but complementary" elements of America's origin story.

For Smith, in addition to the long-standing tradition of liberalism, Americans have also held fiercely to a civic republican tradition and an inegalitarian ascriptive tradition. For the liberalist, to be American is to hold Lockean commitments to individual rights like religious freedom, freedom of thought, movement, and expression, and to espouse a separation of private from public spheres of life. To the *civic republican*, to be American is to believe in a common good and collective purpose (*res publica*), and to manifest civic virtues like participation, deliberation, and a communitarian spirit. Finally, to the believer in *ascriptive hierarchy*, to be American is to attach oneself to assigned or inherited traits like one's race, gender, class, religion. Recall that for Samuel Huntington, to be American is to come from, or at least adhere to, the Anglo-American Protestant tradition on which the nation was supposed to have been founded. Advocates of ascriptive Americanism go as far back as the founding moment of the nation. Benjamin Franklin, for instance, railed against the perceived threat of German immigrants to his sense of common creed: "Why should Pennsylvania, founded by the English, become a colony of Aliens, who will shortly be so numerous as to Germanize us instead of our Anglifying them, and will never adopt our Language or Customs, any more than they can acquire our Complexion?" (1751).

In this respect, the United States is not particularly exceptional. The consensus among political scientists is that all nations, and the sense of national identity that accompany them, are socially constructed and historically contingent. Which is to say, there is no imminent sense of American national identity that is singular, pre-ordained, and fixed in time. While nationalist movements aim to mobilize people around the idea of a single national creed, nation-building more often than not entails the contestation between beliefs about that creed. Some forms of nationalism are more inclusive civic, or liberal, nationalisms; others are more exclusionary ethnic nationalisms.

The United States, from its founding, has had both inclusionary and exclusionary elements. We are currently in a moment of racial reckoning. Yet the demographic changes that we will review in the next chapter, the back-to-back electoral earthquakes of Obama in 2008 and Trump in 2016, and the Black Lives Matter movement are just the latest episodes of an ongoing, seemingly perpetual struggle over who we are as a nation. We share Rogers Smith's view that the American political tradition over the course of our nation's history is composed of multiple creeds. We are sometimes egalitarian, sometimes inegalitarian; sometimes inclusionary, sometimes exclusionary. Our celebrated founding beliefs and the constitutional framework they set were not pre-ordained, self-evident truths carried down from the mountaintop on tablets by our Founding Fathers. They were the product of political contestation and compromise.

The Terms of Construction

One of the first challenges in writing a text on race, ethnicity, and American politics is the language we use to write about it. Terms of description in one era can be terms of disrespect in another. Terms sometimes function as conventions, the way societies decide whether to drive on the right side or left side of a road, so we are all agreed on language to avoid confusion and misunderstanding. Terms also sometimes function as characterizations, to convey color, complexity, and content beyond the mere word that is used, often also to convey a value judgment. Because the terms we use can disrespect and can judge, even when unintended, language contains power—both the power to put and keep someone down and the power to rise up and resist being put down.

We thus try to be as careful and intentional as possible in our choice of terms. In this section, we present and define some of the essential terms and labels we use throughout this book. Where terms are contested or controversial, we try to highlight the reasons behind disagreements and explain where we come down and why. In addition, the terms we use are used every day in casual conversation. But in many cases, these everyday terms also represent underlying social science concepts that, too, can be contested or controversial. Thus, we also try to explain our terms as social science concepts wherever they apply.

Race as a Social Construction

Let us start with the terms *race* and *ethnicity*. Often used interchangeably and rarely defined explicitly, race and ethnicity are often confused for one another but have distinct origins as concepts to describe differences between groups. The origins of race as a concept in the United States is often dated to the seventeenth century, when White European colonists used the concept to differentiate themselves as a group from Native Americans, whose territory they were expropriating, and from Africans who were forcibly kidnapped and trafficked to the New World as slave labor. Ethnicity as a concept is more recent. By one account, the first uses of "ethnic group" is traced to Jewish American activists in the early decades of the twentieth century who sought to maintain their distinctiveness as a group without being considered a "race."[8] Moreover, as we shall see later in this chapter, ethnicity was not recognized as a way to categorize the American population by the federal government until the 1970 decennial census, and then only to differentiate "Hispanic" ethnicity from all other "races."

To understand why groups might want to maintain their distinctiveness without being classified as a separate race, we have to understand the origins of racial classification. This is a vast topic, so our key point in this discussion is that "race" is an idea with a past. As an idea with a past, *race* is a "social construction." By this

---

[8] See Victoria Hattam (2007).

we mean that race is a concept that does not exist in an independent, predetermined form outside the meaning and value human societies have given it and continue to give to it. The social construction of race serves the reductionist purpose of sorting and classifying the diversity and complexity of observable differences between humans into crudely simplified and bounded populations. Furthermore, this sorting and classifying is often accompanied by evaluative judgments that often justify and perpetuate the differential treatment of the categorized groups. It is precisely when these constructed racial differences sanction unequal treatment that the social construct of race bleeds into the ideology of racism.

The origins of racial classification as we know it today lie in a belief system that historians refer to as "scientific racism" and that dates back to the Enlightenment Era of the eighteenth and early nineteenth centuries. Among the most eminent scientists in Europe and America of that time pursued what they called "race science," premised on taxonomy as a branch of science, where plants, animals, and minerals could be classified into classes, orders, genera, and species. As applied to humans and racial classification, these scientists described differences in phenotype that were assumed to not only reflect differences in underlying genotype, but also to reflect differences in attributes and abilities. Unsurprisingly, these "race scientists"—all White European men—generally imbued positive abilities and attributes to their own race while imbuing negative abilities and attributes to other races. For instance, Carolus Linnaeus, considered the inventor of taxonomy, discerned four distinct races and differentiated these races according to their allegedly observable physical differences and their allegedly observable behavioral differences:

- *Europeanus*, which Linnaeus described "physically" as "white, sanguine, muscular" and "behaviorally" as "light, wise, inventive."
- *Africanus*, described by Linnaeus "physically" as "black, phlegmatic, lazy" and "behaviorally" as "sly, sluggish, neglectful."
- *Americanus*, described "physically" as "red, choleric and straight" and "behaviorally" as "unyielding, cheerful, free."
- *Asiaticus*, described "physically" as "sallow, melancholic, stiff" and "behaviorally" as "stern, haughty, greedy."[9]

Today, we would call Linnaeus' four "distinct races" Whites, Blacks, American Indians, and Asians. His characterization of what defines and differentiates these groups are to our eyes and ears shocking and offensive. Yet such characterizations were widely respected and regarded as objective and real since they were advanced by some of the leading scientists of the day like Robert Boyle before Linnaeus (of Boyle's Law in chemistry) and, after Linnaeus, Johann Friedrich Blumenbach (among the founders of zoology and anthropology) and Benjamin Rush (a Founding Father of the United States and among the founders of American psychiatry).

---

[9] See at: www.linnean.org/learning/who-was-linnaeus/linnaeus-and-race.

The current scientific consensus, of course, is that race has no biological basis in fact. Yet the origins of race as a concept in science continues to influence how many everyday Americans think about race. Namely, that race is about bloodline. Consider the fact that almost every newborn in the United States has a "Certificate of Live Birth" (i.e., birth certificate) form that collects data on the race of the parents to determine the race of the newborn. The idea of a biological basis to race even continues to hold sway in some corners of scientific inquiry like DNA ancestry testing, pharmaceuticals marketed to Black Americans, and reproductive technologies.[10]

The resilience of this view underscores a common definition of *race* and *ethnicity* as concepts. Namely, that race is a social construct based on alleged biologically based differences between groups, and ethnicity is a social construct based on alleged culturally based differences between groups. What sets race apart from ethnicity is the claim that some differences are inborn and immutable, as opposed to others that are acquired and adaptable. Thus, alleged racial differences are often described in terms of coloration (skin, hair, eyes) and other physical observable attributes. Alleged ethnic differences, by contrast, are often described in terms of traits like language, religion, and cultural practices like in-group social norms, observed rituals, even cuisine and clothing.

This definition comes with caveats. First, in both instances, the differences between groups are *alleged*, meaning that the definitions describe differences in how race and ethnicity are *constructed*. We do not mean to imply that in the case of racial categories, biologically based differences *are real* or that in the case of ethnic categories, culturally based differences *are real*. The second clarification is that we use the term "social construct" as shorthand for the many ways that people and societies come to a view about ideas and concepts. Specifically, by *social* we do not mean to imply that race is only constructed through social processes, and we especially do not mean to imply that race is exclusively defined by everyday social encounters between acquaintances and strangers devoid of the institutional contexts in which people interact and create meanings. Race and ethnicity as concepts are made and remade in specific economic, legal, political, and social institutional contexts—both historically and in the present day. We illustrate this below in our discussion of the current U.S. federal government's ethno-racial classification system as well as in the next chapter on the legal construction of race through citizenship test cases.

Finally, while populations may sometimes be described in terms of the alleged biologically based or culturally based differences between groups, there are no clear, clean-cut criteria for designating one group as *racial* and another as *ethnic*. The boundaries between what is allegedly biologically based and what is allegedly culturally based are subjective and contingent. So too are the economic, political, and social incentives to organize as an ethnic group rather than as a racial group. To see how this is so, consider how "race" and "ethnicity" have been constructed and reconstructed over time by the U.S. federal government in its decennial census.

---

[10] To read more about the resilience of scientific racism in modern science, see Dorothy Roberts' *Fatal Invention* (2011) and Angela Saini's *Superior* (2019).

Racial Categories and Terms Used in the Census

The United States Constitution requires that the nation's population be fully counted every ten years. Tucked just beneath "We the People" in the preamble sits Article 1, section 2, paragraph 3, which states:

Representatives and direct Taxes shall be apportioned among the several States which may be included within this Union, according to their respective Numbers, which shall be determined by adding to the whole Number of free Persons, including those bound to Service for a Term of Years, and excluding Indians not taxed, three fifths of all other Persons. The actual Enumeration shall be made within three Years after the first Meeting of the Congress of the United States, and within every subsequent Term of ten Years.

The purposes of the enumeration are thus clear: representation of political offices like the House of Representatives were designated to be population based and the distribution of taxed resources too were stipulated to be population based. In short, these counts determine the distribution of power and resources between states.

Racial categories are not explicitly mentioned, but the Constitution does explicitly differentiate the U.S. population by "free persons," "Indians not taxed," and "all other persons." When this constitutional mandate was implemented in 1790 in the first decennial census, the meaning of these seemingly nonracial categories is made clear, as that census counted the population of the United States by "free white males over 16," "free white males under 16," "free white females," "all other free persons," and "slaves." Thus, Native Americans and free Blacks were counted as "all other free persons" and "all other persons," counted in three-fifths, were the enslaved population of Americans of African descent. Still, the only racial category mentioned in this enumeration for the purposes of determining political representation and redistribution is the category of "White."

Since this first census in 1790, the categories the federal government uses to count the U.S. population have both changed and proliferated.[11] For instance, in 1820, the census began to differentiate "free colored males and females" from "slaves." In 1850, it added categories of "mulatto" and "mulatto slaves." In 1870, following the Civil War, the Census Bureau removed the category of "slave." Then, in 1890, reflecting White Americans' post-Emancipation anxieties about Black freedom and the predominant "one-drop" rule of racial assignment of the time, the Census Bureau added "quadroon" and "octaroon" to "mulatto" to measure even fractions of Black lineage. Ethno-racial classification by the U.S. federal government continues to evolve in more recent times. Perhaps the most consequential recent changes have been: the shift in 1960 from having a census worker come to your home and fill in your racial category for you to what we are familiar with today, self-identifying by race and ethnicity; the introduction in 1970 of a separate "ethnicity" question created exclusively to capture Americans

---

[11] For a visualization of changes in racial classification over the nation's history, see: www.census.gov/data-tools/demo/race/MREAD_1790_2010.html.

of "Hispanic" origin; the change in 2000 to allow Americans to "mark one or more" among the given categories to the race question, acknowledging mixed race identities in the census.

The fact that racial categories have changed so regularly and often so dramatically over time illustrates just how subjective and contingent concepts like race and ethnicity are, and what is meant by describing race and ethnicity as social constructs. Imagine, for instance, an American of Mexican origin traveling through time and how they might be counted by the census. That person, in 1910 would have been counted racially as "White"; in 1930, counted as "Mexican"; in 1940 counted again as "White"; in 1970 counted ethnically as "Hispanic" and, more than likely, racially as "other." Or, to take another example, consider the explosive growth in the nation's Native American population. In 1960, the census counted 508,700 American Indians. In the most recent 2020 census, it counted 3.7 million Americans who only identified as American Indian or Alaska Native and 9.7 million who identified as American Indian/Alaska Native and identified with another racial category. These enormous population increases simply cannot be explained in terms of birth and death rates. Americans who had previously not identified as American Indian are, in greater and greater numbers with each census, now choosing to do so.

We describe demographic changes in the nation's racial and ethnic composition that correspond to these changes in classification in further detail in the next chapter. For now, we will name and discuss the racial–ethnic categories that we use in this book. For the most part, the categories we use in our analysis correspond to the current U.S. federal ethno-racial classification guidelines set by the Office of Management and Budget's 1997 "Revised Directive 15." Those OMB standards identify six groups for the purposes of federal data collection:

- "American Indian or Alaska Native," described as "a person having origins in any of the original peoples of North and South America (including Central America), and who maintains tribal affiliation or community attachment."
- "Asian," described as "a person having origins in any of the original peoples of the Far East, Southeast Asia, or the Indian subcontinent, including, for example, Cambodia, China, India, Japan, Korea, Malaysia, Pakistan, the Philippine Islands, Thailand, and Vietnam."
- "Black or African American," described as "a person having origins in any of the black racial groups of Africa. Terms such as 'Haitian' or 'Negro' can be used in addition to 'Black or African American.'"
- "Hispanic or Latino," described as "a person of Cuban, Mexican, Puerto Rican, South or Central American, or other Spanish culture or origin, regardless of race. The term, 'Spanish origin,' can be used in addition to 'Hispanic or Latino.'"
- "Native Hawaiian or other Pacific Islander," described as "a person having origins in any of the original peoples of Hawaii, Guam, Samoa, or other Pacific Islands."
- "White," described as "a person having origins in any of the original peoples of Europe, the Middle East, or North Africa."

Each of these terms is not without controversy. Most have evolved over time and continue to evolve. Moreover, while we mostly follow the OMB categorizations, we do not always use the same terms. To start, we use Native American and American Indian interchangeably. There has been and continues to be debate over which is proper between the use of the terms "Native American," "American Indian," "Indigenous," "Native," and others. American Indian is the term that the Census Bureau continues to use and has legal footing in its use by Federal Indian Law. Native American is a term whose popularity emerged with the political movements of the 1960s and 1970s. Objections have been raised to both terms, and a common view is that most people prefer to be identified by their specific tribal affiliation. At the same time both terms are widely used, so we use both throughout this book. Our use of Native American and American Indian is not, in most instances, inclusive of Alaska Natives for the simple reason that the research we describe and discuss does not include Alaska Natives.

Next, we use the term Asian American and, at times, Asian Americans and Pacific Islanders (or AAPIs). Like the term Native American, "Asian American" also emerged out of political movements of the 1960s, as an alternative to the derogatory "Oriental" that had previously been used to refer to Americans of Asian descent. Asian American is often used together with Pacific Islander—in previous years with the terms "Asian Pacific Islander" and "Asian Pacific Islander American"—in part as a legacy of previous federal classification guidelines that combined Americans of Asian and Pacific Islander descent and in part as an expression of solidarity, common interest, and community-building. Wherever the research that we describe and discuss does not include Pacific Islanders (which is quite often), we use the term Asian American. We follow the convention from the OMB guidelines in using "Asian" to be inclusive of Asian Americans from East, Southeast, and South Asia, but exclusive of Americans of Middle Eastern descent.

We also use Black and African American interchangeably throughout this book. Both terms are widely used and have, at different moments been championed in political movements, "Black" in the 1960s as part of the Civil Rights and Black Power movements and "African American" in the late 1980s in a campaign led by the Reverend Jesse Jackson. These terms have now clearly replaced older ones like "Afro-American" and "Negro" (which the Census Bureau used as recently as 2000). There is, of course, some debate over whether Black or African American best describes this group—for instance, whether identity should be defined by pigment or geography of origin—and we expect debate to continue as the proportion of Black Americans who are Black and Latino, Black and multiracial, Black and immigrant continues to grow. At the present time, we find no prevailing argument to favor one over the other exclusively and use both terms.

Perhaps the most vigorously contested of the racial and ethnic terms used to describe American diversity today is between Hispanic, Latino, and a relatively new alternative, Latinx. Both Hispanic and Latino are widely used today to describe or identify Americans with origins in any of the Spanish-speaking nations of Latin America. Where one term privileges common language origin the other privileges common geographic origin. As scholars have documented, "Hispanic" as a term is relatively new, invented in the post-Civil Rights Movement era as a compromise between government bureaucrats, community activists, and media executives.[12] While widely used, especially by demographers and federal agencies, the term has its detractors for evoking a shared history of colonialism under Spanish rule among the countries of origin, and "Latino" became popular in the 1990s and by 2000 was included alongside "Spanish/Hispanic origin" in the decennial census. Most recently, the label "Latinx" has been proposed as a gender-neutral and LGBTQ+-inclusive alternative to Latino. While widely used (especially in progressive circles, like universities and the entertainment industry), a recent survey by the Pew Research Center found that only 3 percent of Latino adults used the term and 76 percent reported that they had never heard of the term. In this book, we generally use the term Latino but also occasionally use Hispanic.

Finally, we use the term White as a more inclusive and current label than alternatives like "Caucasian," "European American," "Anglo-American," and others. "White" is the one and only racial label that has remained unchanged throughout the 230-year history of the United States Census. It is tempting to infer from this constancy that racial categories, like many laws, serve to uphold the status quo and maintain the privileges of the dominant group in power. Yet it is important to remember that the category of White is a capacious umbrella term that contains within it an enormous diversity of subgroups, each with their own history, often a history of struggle and unequal treatment. As we quoted earlier, Benjamin Franklin vilified German immigrants and saw them as a threat; a century later, immigrants from Ireland, Southern Europe, and Eastern Europe were similarly vilified and seen as a threat; just a few years ago, White nationalists converged on Charlottesville, Virginia, to participate in a torchlight march to chants of "Jews will not replace us." Thus, while the category "White" has a 230-year history, the question of who is included and who is excluded under that term has long been contested.

The category of Whites also underscores a few final points about racial labels and the diversity of background and experiences in the American body politic. First, each one of our primary categories—American Indian, Asian American, Black, Latino, and White—is a "pan-ethnic" umbrella that contains within it an enormous diversity of subgroups. Second, the boundaries between these categories were never impermeable and are increasingly fluid and hybrid. As we shall see in Chapter 2, one of the most dynamic changes to the nation's ethnic and racial composition is the growth of the multiracial population in America. Third, some racialized minorities in America continue to be miscategorized and thus rendered invisible under the current OMB guidelines. The most conspicuous such group is the Arab American community who face significant barriers to full inclusion, especially since the 9/11 attacks on American soil, but who are currently expected to self-identify as White according to the OMB guidelines.

---

[12] See especially Mora (2014).

KEY TERMS

Alaska Native
American exceptionalism
American liberalism
Asian American
Asian American and Pacific Islander (AAPI)
Black, African American
Critical race theory
Ethnicity
Hispanic, Latino, Latinx
Native American, American Indian
Native Hawaiian or Other Pacific Islander
Race
Racism
White

DISCUSSION QUESTIONS

1. Are racism and discrimination fundamental to American society or an aberration? Explain why you think that way.
2. What is Critical Race Theory and why has it received so much attention?
3. Were Supreme Court rulings like *Brown* v. *Board of Education* and new laws like the 1964 Civil Rights Act and the 1965 Voting Rights Act ineffective in eradicating racial inequality because they were the wrong laws and rulings? Or because laws alone cannot fix the problem?
4. Is increasing racial diversity bringing Americans together or pushing us further apart? Why do you think that is the case?
5. How have America's racial and ethnic minorities fared relative to Whites on economic and social outcomes?
6. Why do you think there are such large racial disparities in economic and social outcomes?
7. How has America's racial hierarchy changed over the last few decades?
8. What factors have led to the persistence of racial and ethnic inequality over time?
9. Is race socially constructed? Why or why not?

ANNOTATED SUGGESTED READINGS

See Philip Klinkner and Rogers Smith. 1999. *The Unsteady March: The Rise and Decline of Racial Equality in America*. Chicago: University of Chicago Press, for an excellent account of how racial inequality has shifted over the course of American history.

See Samuel Huntington. 2004. "The Hispanic Challenge," *Foreign Policy* 141: 30–45, which offers an account of why racial diversity in general and Hispanic immigration in particular are a threat to American society.

See Rogers M. Smith. 1993. "Beyond Tocqueville, Myrdal, and Hartz: The Multiple Traditions in America," *American Political Science Review* 87: 549–566, for a powerful counter-narrative that explains how beliefs in racial inequality have shaped and reshaped American political traditions.

See Michael Omi, and Howard Winant. 1994. *Racial Formation in the United States*. New York: Routledge, on the social construction of race and the centrality of race for American politics and society

This readable report by the Pew Research Center uncovers profound differences between Black and White Americans in their views on race and racial discrimination and also demonstrates and describe sharp racial differences in economic and social well-being: Pew Research Center. 2016. "On Views of Race and Inequality, Blacks and Whites Are Worlds Apart." www.pewresearch.org/social-trends/2016/06/27/1-demographic-trends-and-economic-well-being.

CHAPTER REFERENCES

Baldwin, James et al. 1961. "The Negro in American Culture." *CrossCurrents* 11(3): 205–225.

Boshara, Ray, William Emmons, and Bryan Noeth. 2015. "The Demographics of Wealth. Essay No. 1: Race, Ethnicity, and Wealth." Saint Louis, MO: Federal Reserve Bank of Saint Louis.

Brody, Richard A. 1991. *Assessing the President: The Media, Elite Opinion, and Public Support*. Stanford: Stanford University Press.

Brubaker, Rogers. 1998. *Citizenship and Nationhood in France and Germany*. Cambridge, MA: Harvard University Press.

Buchanan, Larry, Quoctrung Bui, and Jugal K. Patel. 2020. "Black Lives Matter May Be the Largest Movement in U.S. History." July 3. www.nytimes.com/interactive/2020/07/03/us/george-floyd-protests-crowd-size.html.

Coates, Ta-Nehisi. 2014. "The Case for Reparations." *The Atlantic.* June. www.theatlantic.com/magazine/archive/2014/06/the-case-for-reparations/361631.

Fortin, Jacey. 2021. "Critical Race Theory: A Brief History." *New York Times.* November 8. www.nytimes.com/article/what-is-critical-race-theory.html.

Fox News Voter Analysis. 2021. "2021 Virginia Gubernatorial Election." November 2. https://static.foxnews.com/foxnews.com/content/uploads/2021/11/FNVA-Virginia_as-of-8pm-results.pdf.

Hannah-Jones, Nikole. 2019. "The 1619 Project." *New York Times.* August 14. www.nytimes.com/interactive/2019/08/14/magazine/black-history-american-democracy.html.

Hassan, Adeel. 2022. "The U.S. Surpasses 1 Million Covid Deaths, the World's Highest Known Total." *New York Times.* May 19. www.nytimes.com/2022/05/19/us/us-covid-deaths.html.

Hattam, Victoria. 2007. *In the Shadow of Race: Jews, Latinos, and Immigrant Politics in the United States.* Chicago: University of Chicago Press.

House Bill 3979. 2020. https://capitol.texas.gov/tlodocs/87R/billtext/pdf/HB03979F.pdf.

Jones, Bradley. 2022. "The Changing Political Geography of COVID-19 Over the Last Two Years." Pew Research Center. March 3. www.pewresearch.org/politics/2022/03/03/the-changing-political-geography-of-covid-19-over-the-last-two-years.

Kent, Ana Hernández and Lowell Ricketts. 2021. "Wealth Gaps between White, Black, and Hispanic Families in 2019," On the Economy Blog, Federal Reserve Bank of St. Louis, January 5.

Kochhar, Rakesh and Anthony Cilluffo. 2018. "Income Inequality in the U.S. is Rising Most Rapidly Among Asians," Pew Research Center, July 12. www.pewresearch.org/social-trends/wp-content/uploads/sites/3/2018/07/Pew_Research_Center_Inequality-Report_FINAL.pdf.

Lang, Cady. 2020. "President Trump Has Attacked Critical Race Theory. Here's What to Know About the Intellectual Movement." *Time*, September 29. https://time.com/5891138/critical-race-theory-explained.

McCloskey, Herbert and John Zaller. 1984. *The American Ethos: Public Attitudes toward Capitalism and Democracy.* Cambridge, MA: Harvard University Press.

Mora, Cristina. 2014. *Making Hispanics: How Activists, Bureaucrats, and Media Constructed a New American.* Chicago: University of Chicago Press.

Mueller, John E. 1973. *War, Presidents, and Public Opinion.* New York: Wiley.

Pathak, Arohi. 2021. "How the Government Can End Poverty for Native American Women," Center for American Progress. www.americanprogress.org/article/government-can-end-poverty-native-american-women.

Przeworski, Adam. 1991. *Democracy and the Market.* Cambridge: Cambridge University Press.

Roberts, Dorothy. 2011. *Fatal Invention: How Science, Politics, and Big Business Re-create Race in the Twenty-First Century.* New York: New Press.

Saini, Angela. 2019. *Superior: The Return of Race Science.* Boston, MA: Beacon Press.

Smith, Rogers. 1999. *Civic Ideals: Conflicting Visions of Citizenship in U.S. History.* New Haven, CT: Yale University Press.

USA Facts. 2023. "Homeownership Rates Show That Black Americans Are Currently the Least Likely Group to Own Homes." https://usafacts.org/articles/homeownership-rates-by-race.

Vought, Russell. 2020. Memorandum for the Heads of Executive Departments and Agencies. M-20-34. September 4. www.whitehouse.gov/wp-content/uploads/2020/09/M-20-34.pdf

2 *E Pluribus Unum*: Citizenship, Demographic Change, and Diversity

The political scientist Benedict Anderson famously defined nations as "imagined political communities" (1983). Nations as political communities are, of course, comprised of people—real people. Yet even in the smallest republics—even European "micro-states" like Lichtenstein, Monaco, and San Marino—not every person will know every other person. Residents inhabiting Lichtenstein, Monaco, and San Marino who are strangers to one another will nonetheless imagine themselves bound by community and common membership as Lichtensteiners, Monagasques, and Sammarinese. That bond is forged not just by external markers like living within the boundaries of a nation, or holding legal citizenship in that nation, but also by internalized beliefs and claims of shared tradition, common culture, and so on.

What is true of even the smallest republics is true too for a population as big and diverse as the United States of America. While we face seemingly insurmountable social, economic, and political divisions today, echoes of unity and solidarity have been fixed in our collective consciousness from the very founding of the republic. Thus starts the unforgettable preamble to our 1789 Constitution: "We the People of the United States, in Order to form a more perfect Union." The Great Seal of the United States is emblazoned with the motto, *E Pluribus Unum*, Latin for "out of many, one." And in the concluding sentence of the Declaration of Independence are found these powerful words, "And for the support of this Declaration … we mutually pledge to each other our Lives, our Fortunes, and our sacred Honor."

Words like these reveal how people imagine a nation. Such stirring words are meant to inspire solidarity and invoke inclusion. But they can, and often do, coexist with a reality of disunity, hostility, and exclusion. Understanding this tension is at the heart of this book, and so in this chapter we examine what makes the United States a people, an imagined political community.

In Chapter 1 we looked at two perspectives on the American founding: one, illustrated in Samuel Huntington's 2004 essay arguing that the American national creed is guided by the distinct Anglo-Protestant culture of the country's early founders; and the other, represented in Nikole Hannah-Jones' 2019 essay acknowledging the ideals of the founding while pointing out the apparent hypocrisy of those ideals—in particular, that "all men are created equal"—when compared with the reality for non-Whites at the time of the founding and beyond. In this chapter we dig a little deeper

Photo 2.1 Americans celebrating.
Source: © MediaNews Group/Orange County Register via Getty Images/Contributor/
MediaNews Group/Getty Images.

into the origin stories about the United States as a political community. We contrast the idealized "textbook" account of "we the people" to two alternative origin stories about our political community: a story of settler colonialism and a story of chattel slavery. As a nation founded on settler colonialism, the making of the United States as a people entailed territorial conquest and the forced displacement of an already existing indigenous population of Native Americans. As a nation also founded on chattel slavery, the making of the United States as a people also involved the trafficking of humans abducted from their homelands, exchanged as property and exploited as labor, with enduring, destructive consequences for racial inequality even today.

Next, to these origin stories, we add a third account of the making of America as a nation of immigrants. We will describe the expansion and diversification of the U.S. population through four waves of migration from precolonial times to the mid-1960s. The growing diversity of the U.S. population has been especially dramatic since the mid-1960s, and we will explore those demographic changes. Demographic change, especially when the change brings racial and ethnic diversity, is not always easily achieved or warmly welcomed. Thus, the chapter also describes how, with this growing diversity over time, a set of laws governing immigration emerged. These laws are notable for singling out certain migrants for exclusion from entry and labeling certain Americans as "illegal" and thus unqualified for membership.

At the heart of these laws and the politics around them are questions of whether immigrants of different backgrounds can "become American," and if they have to assimilate into "whiteness" to do so. The chapter reviews competing social science theories about whether and how immigrants adapt to a new homeland and become incorporated into a new body politic. Racial boundaries and anxieties over racial diversity play a central role in immigrant incorporation and our governing laws on immigration, as they have been for debates over American citizenship throughout our history. The chapter closes with a discussion of what it means to be a citizen, how political identity and racial identity have intersected in defining citizenship, and how debates over immigration and citizenship today continue to be shaped by competing and contested visions of who "we the people" are and what imagined political communities accompany those visions.

America's Origin Stories

Every nation has a story that gets told and retold about its founding, passed down like folklore through the ages. These origin stories typically have a ring of truth to them and are based on verifiable facts about a nation's history. They are also often adorned with embellishments that stretch the truth and obscure other truths about a nation's history. Origin stories are thus contested narratives.

The Idealized Origin Story

The textbook version of America's origin story—the one that has been taught in schools for many generations—focuses on the discovery of America by European explorers. The protagonists in that account include Leif Ericson in Newfoundland in the tenth century, Christopher Columbus in San Salvador in 1492, and English colonists in Virginia and Massachusetts in the early seventeenth century. The narrative typically acclaims the heroism of these explorers and the positive, cultivating influence of Europe on an undiscovered and undeveloped "New World." This textbook account typically culminates by hailing the crowning achievements of our "Founding Fathers," who crafted the Declaration of Independence in 1776 and the Constitution in 1787 and composed tracts like *The Federalist Papers* which have served as a blueprint for America's soaring success as a beacon for democracy and its preeminence as a global superpower. It is an origin story that fits tidily into the political traditions of liberalism and civic republicanism which we introduced in Chapter 1.

That textbook version, of course, has been vigorously challenged and amended. The current firestorm over "Critical Race Theory" discussed in Chapter 1 is only the most recent iteration of the debate. Just as "ascriptive Americanism" (attaching certain racial, religious, or other traits to one's vision of being American) surfaces a part of our political tradition that adherents to liberalism and civic republicanism would rather ignore, so too do the alternate origin stories we present in this section. While mottos like "we the people" and "*e pluribus unum*" are stirring, they were never meant to include just anybody and certainly not meant to include *everybody*.

Equality, in the American tradition, has always come with qualifications. Thus, "we the people" is followed in the U.S. Constitution by further words that tell us which "people" mattered to the architects of our founding document. Article 1 of the Constitution defines "people" as "free Persons . . . excluding Indians not taxed, three fifths of all other Persons." And in practice, the boundaries of belonging were even more restrictive and exclusionary. In the first federal election held in 1788—the one that elected George Washington as our inaugural president—only a small fraction of the thirteen colonies' total population had voting rights. Each state set its own voting requirements and nearly without exception, the states set those requirements based on age, gender, race, and class. Excluded were women and, among men, those who had not "attained their majority" (i.e., who were not yet adults), Native Americans, most African Americans, and those who did not hold property or pay requisite taxes.[1]

Settler Colonialism

The first alternative origin story is that of the United States as an archetype of settler colonialism. The European discoverers of our fabled past like Ericson, Columbus, and the Pilgrims did not simply come upon virgin, uninhabited lands. The Americas they found were already thriving, cultivated lands with established, sovereign communities. The history of "we the people" thus begins with territorial occupation, conquest, and expansion. The colonies of Jamestown and Plymouth would not have been established without the displacement and uprooting of the Powhatan and the Wampanoag. Settler colonialism is that form of colonialism in which the rule and governance of a preexisting, original population within a territory is replaced by the rule and governance of a new society of settlers. Settler colonialism then involves more than the founding of a new society of settlers from foreign lands. It also entails the exercise of power and dominion over a territory and the subjugation of the original population within that territory. Through a combination of violent conflicts and the introduction of infectious diseases from Europe like chicken pox, measles, and smallpox, European settlement had devastating, genocidal consequences. By some estimates, the total population of the Western Hemisphere at the end of the fifteenth century approximated 50 million indigenous peoples, with almost 4 million in the parts of North America that eventually became the United States and Canada. By 1890, the Native American population in the U.S. had declined to a low mark of about 228,000.[2]

As an origin story, the account of settler colonialism in the United States starts with the Spanish empire's conquest of the Americas in the late fifteenth and sixteenth centuries. This was then followed by Great Britain and France colonizing parts of North America in the sixteenth century, and then Sweden and the Netherlands settling into small colonies on the eastern shores of what is now the

---

[1] Vermont was the exception to the property requirements for voting rights in 1788.
[2] See Thornton (1987); Reddy (1995).

United States in the seventeenth century. The relationship of one people's rule over another prior, original people's sovereignty continued even as colonial rule was supplanted by a newly formed republic. The exclusionary language "free Persons . . . excluding Indians not taxed, three fifths of all other Persons" is infamous not just for the dehumanization of enslaved Africans into fractional counts, but also for the exclusion of "Indians not taxed," a clause that is nowhere defined in the Constitution.[3] In practice, unless Native Americans were willing to disavow their tribal affiliations and able to leave them, they would not only be excluded from enumeration but also excluded from citizenship. This exclusion carries over into section 2 of the Fourteenth Amendment in 1868, which revised Article 1 of the Constitution to provide that, "Representatives shall be apportioned among the several states according to their respective numbers, counting the *whole* number of persons in each state, *excluding Indians not taxed*" [emphasis added]. In fact, it was not until 1924, with the passage of the Indian Citizenship Act, that full birthright citizenship was extended to all Native Americans.

Chattel Slavery

The second, related origin story is the central role of the institution of chattel slavery, a form of bondage of one human to another where the agency of the enslaved is legally possessed by the slaveholder, who by law can own other humans as personal property to be bought, sold, exploited, and abused. In the founding of the American republic, alongside the qualification that "we the people" excluded "Indians not taxed" is the qualification that the decennial census will count "three fifths of all other Persons." These words are striking because "all other Persons" referred specifically and exclusively to one population: those who were forcibly abducted from their homelands and brought to America to be traded as property and exploited for their labor. The Constitution further stipulates that African slaves were to count in fractional terms, as less than full persons. The general historical account of this "three fifths" stipulation is that it was a necessary political compromise between Southern states and Northern states to achieve agreement on the Constitution. Southern states wanted to fully count their slave population for the purpose of maximizing their political representation in Congress vis-à-vis Northern states, all while maintaining chattel slavery. Northern states, by and large, argued against counting African slaves and included many who were also opposed to chattel slavery on moral grounds.

Whether there were champions of manumission among our Founding Fathers or not, chattel slavery would remain in place as a social, economic, legal institution in America for nearly a century until the nation waged a civil war and passed the Thirteenth, Fourteenth, and Fifteenth Amendments in 1865, 1868, and 1870, respectively. This institution of owning and selling the freedom and labor of fellow

---

[3] Scholars generally seem to agree that "Indians not taxed" referred to Native Americans who retained their tribal affiliations.

humans was the key to transforming the fledgling new nation from a colonial and mostly agricultural economy to the second most formidable economic power in the industrial world by the end of the nineteenth century (behind Great Britain). Slave labor was the economic engine of the South in plantation farms that cultivated cash crops like sugar cane, tobacco, rice, and the "King" of them all, cotton. In the pre-Civil War era, cotton was America's dominant export and the United States produced more than half of the world's cotton. The capital and profits from cotton from the agricultural South, moreover, was essential to the rise and success of industrialization in the North. "King Cotton," historians argued, was instrumental to the rise of modern capitalism itself.[4] Putting the origin story of settler colonialism together with the origin story of chattel slavery, then, the United States achieved its remarkable rise to global economic power in its first century as a nation by dint of exploiting coerced labor to till the soil of lands that were forcibly expropriated from America's indigenous peoples.

A Nation of Immigrants?

There is a third alternative origin story. This one builds on the textbook "we the people" account in many ways, but also in important ways subverts that account by explicitly recognizing the dominant role of a plural, multiethnic population to America's growth as a nation. The historian Oscar Handlin began his classic work, *The Uprooted*, with the lines, "Once I thought to write a history of immigrants in America. Then I discovered that immigrants were American history" (1951). This quote is often repeated to make the point that the United States is a "nation of immigrants." America as a nation of immigrants is an idea that is deeply woven into our political consciousness, evoking the creedal belief that the American liberal tradition includes a history of welcoming immigrants with open arms and giving refugees safe haven. Even today, American civic education includes learning the famous words from Emma Lazarus' "The New Colossus" inscribed into the pedestal of the Statue of Liberty: "Give me your tired, your poor, your huddled masses yearning to breathe free ... Send these, the homeless, tempest-tost to me."

The First Wave of Immigrants

The "nation of immigrants" mythos is rooted in a history of multiple waves of tired, poor, huddled masses yearning for freedom and opportunity. In the colonial era, the first wave of immigrants were initially Pilgrims and Puritans from the British Isles seeking refuge from religious persecution in the seventeenth and eighteenth

---

[4] For examples of historical research on the centrality of chattel slavery and cotton farming to nation-building in the United States and the rise of global capitalism, see Sven Beckert, *Empire of Cotton* (2015), Edward Baptist, *The Half Has Never Been Told* (2016), and Walter Johnson, *River of Dark Dreams* (2017).

centuries, but eventually included such diverse roots as the Dutch establishing colonies in New York, the Quakers and Germans in Pennsylvania, the Spanish in Florida, and the French along the Saint Lawrence Seaway, the Mississippi, and the Gulf Coast. Notwithstanding that diversity, the enumerated population of colonial America was decidedly Anglo in origins.

The results of the first enumeration of the U.S. population by race appear in Figure 2.1. The first U.S. Census in 1790 counted over 3.9 million people.[5] The census did not ask about national origin explicitly, but for 2.8 of that 3.9 million, national origin can be ascribed based on the ethnic names of the heads of each household. From this assignment, census estimates are that of this 2.8 million, 83 percent were categorized as of English origin, 7 percent of Scottish origin, 6 percent of German origin, 2 percent of French origin and another 2 percent of Irish origin (U.S. Census Bureau 1793). While this enumerated count is overwhelmingly from the British Isles, we have to keep in mind too, that this first census also counted more than 750,000 Blacks, more than 690,000 of whom were slaves and about 60,000 who were free. The first census did not count the Native American population.

Importantly, while the population inhabiting American soil at the end of the eighteenth century was clearly multiracial, the population of citizens of the United States was uniformly monoracial. Citizenship was not explicitly addressed in the Constitution itself. Rather, citizenship was implied until it became clear that with new immigrants arriving, policies regarding citizenship were needed. In this earliest period of the nation, there were no federal policies governing our borders and entry into the United States; that power was largely left to the states. Congress did, however, hold the constitutional authority to establish laws governing citizenship and so enacted the Naturalization Act of 1790, which stipulated that "... any alien, being a free white person, may be admitted to become a citizen of the United States."[6] The law further required two years of residence and applicants could petition "any common law court of record" and be granted citizenship upon demonstrating their "good moral character."

Subsequent Waves of Immigrants

The first group of immigrants was followed by a second wave, the large majority of which came to the United States between the 1830s and the 1850s, mostly from Britain, Ireland, and Germany. While some of these migrants still sought freedom from religious persecution, most sought economic opportunity and freedom from famine and political upheaval. By one estimate, the influx of new immigrants to the United States increased from about 152,000 arrivals between 1820 and 1830 to

---

[5] The first U.S. Census in 1790 counted the population by "Free white males of 16 years and upwards, including heads of families," "Free white males under 16 years," "Free white females, including heads of families," "All other free persons," and "Slaves."

[6] Congress also exercised the authority to ban the slave trade, passing the Act Prohibiting Importation of Slaves in 1807 at the behest of then President Thomas Jefferson. Abolishing the slave trade into the United States, however, had no effect on the domestic slave trade in Southern states.

The Return for SOUTH CAROLINA having been made since the foregoing Schedule was originally printed, the whole Enumeration is here given complete, except for the N. Weſtern Territory, of which no Return has yet been publiſhed.

DISTICTS	Free white Males of 16 years and upwards, including heads of families.	Free white Males under ſixteen years.	Free white Females, including heads of families.	All other free perſons.	Slaves.	Total.
Vermont	22435	22328	40505	255	16	85539
N. Hampſhire	36086	34851	70160	630	158	141885
Maine	24384	24748	46870	538	NONE	96540
Maſſachuſetts	95453	87289	190582	5463	NONE	378787
Rhode Iſland	16019	15799	32652	3407	948	68825
Connecticut	60523	54403	117448	2808	2764	237946
New York	83700	78122	152320	4654	21324	340120
New Jerſey	45251	41416	83287	2762	11423	184139
Pennſylvania	110788	106948	206363	6537	3737	434373
Delaware	11783	12143	22384	3899	8887	59094
Maryland	55915	51339	101395	8043	103036	319728
Virginia	110936	116135	215046	12866	292627	747610
Kentucky	15154	17057	28922	114	12430	73677
N. Carolina	69988	77506	140710	4975	100572	393751
S. Carolina	35576	37722	66880	1801	107094	249073
Georgia	13103	14044	25739	398	29264	82548
	807094	791850	1541263	59150	694280	3893635

Total number of Inhabitants of the United States excluſive of S. Weſtern and N. Territory.	Free white Males of 21 years and upwards.	Free Males under 21 years of age.	Free white Females.	All other perſons.	Slaves.	Total
S.W. territory	6271	10277	15365	361	3417	35691
N. Ditto	—	—	—	—	—	—

Figure 2.1 Enumeration in the 1790 Census
Results for the first U.S. Census from South Carolina. Guidance for the first U.S. Census was set in an Act of Congress approved March 1, 1790. The census began on Monday, August 2, 1790 and was finished in about nine months.
Source: U.S. Census Bureau, 1790.

nearly quadruple that number, 599,000, between 1830 and 1840, and then nearly triple that number, 1.7 million, between 1840 and 1850 (Willcox 1931). The total U.S. population had also grown dramatically from 3.9 million in 1790 to more than 23 million by 1850. Growth in the slave population continued over this period as well, rising from nearly 700,000 in 1790 to roughly 3.2 million by 1850 (U.S. Census Bureau 1850).

This second wave of migration to the United States is perhaps best known for the massive influx of Irish immigrants escaping the Great Famine. In the 1840s, newcomers from Ireland made up roughly half of all the migration into the United States. In this period, America also provided safe harbor to political refugees who were seeking to escape failed revolutions in the 1848 "Springtime of Nations" throughout continental Europe. For the first time in its history, there were also significant numbers of new Americans by the 1840s who were not migrating from Europe. The Treaty of Guadalupe Hidalgo in 1848 officially ended the Mexican War and incorporated all or part of ten states between Oklahoma and Texas in the south to California in the west. With that territorial expansion, citizenship was extended to thousands of Mexicans inhabiting the American southwest and California. Finally, the 1849 California Gold Rush brought thousands of prospectors and others seeking to profit from the economic boom brought about by the Gold Rush, including some 25,000 immigrants from China by the 1850s.

The "nation of immigrants" self-image of the United States—a land of opportunity and safe haven for refugees—is built on this history. At the same time, even in this second wave of migration, newcomers from faraway lands fanned the flames of xenophobia (prejudice against and perceived threat from foreigners) and **nativism** (prejudice in favor of native-born over foreign-born people). The basis for the fear and persecution of these newcomers was religious as much as it was ethnic. The influx of large numbers of Catholics from Ireland and Germany fueled the rise of conspiracy theories, secret societies, and by the 1850s led to the formation of a nativist and populist political party known informally as the "Know Nothings" and formally as the "American Party." Know Nothing candidates successfully won political control in states like Massachusetts and Rhode Island, and the mayoralty in cities like Philadelphia and Washington, D.C. In a dynamic eerily similar to today, many Know Nothing supporters were mobilized by conspiracy theories of widespread illegal voting by non-citizen Catholics, leading to flare-ups of electoral violence in the 1850s. The resentments that fueled Know Nothings were not always aimed at Catholics; in California, for instance, Know Nothing chapters were organized around opposition to Chinese immigrants.

The momentum behind this nativist political movement ultimately fizzled out almost as quickly as it gathered force. America became increasingly divided on the issue of slavery in the 1850s, and this issue also split Know Nothing supporters into pro-slavery and anti-slavery factions. Migration in the United States also slowed considerably in the Civil War years and its aftermath. By the 1880s, however, a convergence of forces propelled an unprecedented third wave of immigration. In addition to the lure of a land of opportunity and freedom, expanded train routes in Europe made access to ports of call easier, steamships dramatically increased capacity and reduced travel time across the Atlantic, and rapid industrialization and urbanization in the United States created a post-Civil War boom of employment opportunities. Between 1880 and 1920, more than 20 million new immigrants arrived in the

United States. In this era, roughly one in every seven Americans was an immigrant, a peak that was unmatched for more than 100 years (Campbell and Jung 2006).

The majority of arrivals in this third wave were from Eastern, Central, and Southern Europe. At its height, 1.3 million immigrants entered the United States via Ellis Island in a single year, 1907. Many Southern European immigrants (e.g., Italians and Greeks) crossed the Atlantic for better economic opportunities, while many Eastern Europeans (primarily Jewish) fled religious persecution in their homelands. This wave of immigration slowed by the 1910s as the United States and Europe became ensnared in the First World War. At home, xenophobia and perceived economic competition from immigrants grew into demands for stronger curbs on migration into America. By 1917, Congress established a literacy test to gain admission into the United States, and the Immigration Act of 1924 (the Johnson–Reed Act) effectively slammed the door shut by drastically cutting the total number of immigrants allowed into the country and setting quotas for in-migration by ethnicity and nationality.

The 1924 law marked the end of the third wave of immigration, and U.S. immigration policy was defined by a quota system for the next four decades. Two percent of the total number of each national origin group in the United States as of the 1890 census would be allowed in and migration from Asia would be completely excluded, defining what came to be known as the "Asiatic Barred Zone." Senator David Reed, co-sponsor of the bill, proclaimed that "The racial composition of America at the present time thus is made permanent" and the *New York Times* ran the headline, "America of the Melting Pot Comes to End." The dramatic effect of more restrictive immigration policies like the Johnson–Reed Act is obvious in Figure 2.2: as a share of the total U.S. population, immigrants declined from a peak of 14.7 percent in 1920 to a low of 4.7 percent by 1970.

The Immigration Act of 1924 also marked a key turning point in how Americans saw immigrants. The law required, for its implementation, the prescreening of immigrants, establishing a visa system and the U.S. Border Patrol, and enforcement power to deport undocumented arrivals. In effect, the law and its aftermath created what had not existed before: a category of Americans labelled as "illegal." While the issue of "illegal immigrants" and whether they merit a pathway to citizenship is fiercely debated today, it is important to remember that the category of "illegal immigrant" did not exist as a federal matter for roughly the first hundred years of U.S. history. That is, for something to be labeled "illegal," there has to be a law to break or abide by, and there were no federal laws governing who could and who could not enter the United States until the late nineteenth century. States like California did pass local immigration laws, but these were generally either select-ively implemented at best or did not survive legal challenges in courts.

The Role of Race in the Emergence of Immigration Laws

Xenophobia and nativism against immigrants of many different ethnic backgrounds have been present since the founding of the Republic, and settler colonialism and

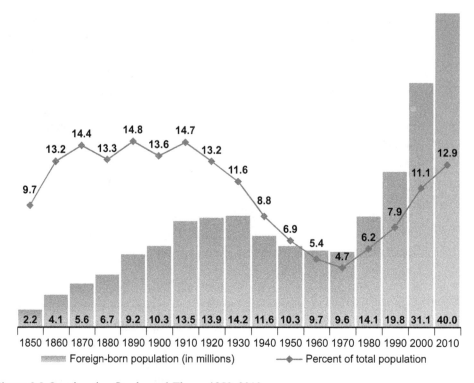

Figure 2.2 Immigration Stocks and Flows, 1850–2010
The foreign-born population in the United States is shown here by decade, from 1850 to 2010, with the total number of foreign-born illustrated by the bars and the percentage of the total U.S. population that was foreign-born shown by the red line.
Source: U.S. Census Bureau, Census of Population, 1850–2000, and the American Community Survey, 2010.

chattel slavery were early integral elements of structural racism in the United States (see Chapter 5 for more details). Race also played a key role in the emergence of federal laws governing immigration in America. When the first federal laws restricting migration into the United States were passed, however, they targeted a very specific racialized minority: Chinese Americans. Probably the first restrictive law on the books was the Immigration Act of 1875 (or the Page Act), which was introduced to "end the danger of cheap Chinese labor and immoral Chinese women" and prohibited the recruitment of laborers from "China, Japan, or any Oriental country" for "lewd and immoral purposes." The Page Act effectively blocked all but a few Chinese women from migrating to the United States. It was then followed by the even more restrictive Chinese Exclusion Act of 1882. From the 1850s on, thousands of Chinese workers had been coming to the United States to work as miners, farm laborers, and factory workers, and to work construction jobs building railroads that connected the West Coast to the rest of the nation. While Chinese immigrants in places like California and Washington made up a miniscule fraction of the total population in these states, they found themselves increasingly scapegoated for wage competition and targeted for racial violence. Thus, even before the 1882 federal law, local jurisdictions enacted policies targeting Chinese Americans. California, for instance, passed a "foreign miner's tax" and required special licenses for Chinese-owned businesses. San Francisco banned laundries in wooden buildings without a permit, with wide discretion given to the city over the permits, which effectively shuttered all but one Chinese-owned laundromat. The anti-Chinese bias in the law's application served as the basis for *Yick Wo* v. *Hopkins* (1886), the first Supreme Court case that established a *disparate impact* basis for a discrimination claim (see Chapter 4 for further discussion of disparate impact).

The Chinese Exclusion Act of 1882 set a ten-year moratorium on Chinese workers coming to the United States, barred Chinese Americans who were already in the United States from naturalizing as citizens, and required every American of Chinese descent traveling in and out of the United States to carry an identification card. The 1882 law not only marked the first federal law in American history to set restrictions on immigration, but it set those restrictions by targeting immigrants of a specific race and from a specific nation. This selective exclusion continued in the following decades. The ten-year exclusion of Chinese immigrants was extended for another ten years with the Geary Act of 1892 and then made permanent in 1902. By 1917, the selective exclusion expanded to define an "Asiatic Barred Zone" that stretched from Turkey to Japan.

Legislative and Demographic Change from the Mid-1960s to the Present

The fourth and most recent wave of immigrants to the United States is commonly identified with the Immigration and Naturalization Act of 1965, or the Hart–Celler Act. While the 1924 Johnson–Reed Act marked a watershed in the nation's immigration history, many Americans opposed the closing of the country's borders to strangers from distant shores. Efforts to undo such sweeping restrictions on immigration gathered momentum as the United States took on a leading role in the arena of global affairs during the Second World War and the Cold War. In particular, American efforts to stem the tide of authoritarianism and communism were hampered by the seeming double standard of abiding Jim Crow laws and closed borders at home. Thus, the Chinese Exclusion Act was eventually repealed by 1943 with the Magnuson Act and the Immigration and Nationality Act (the Walter–McCarran Act) in 1952 formally ended the Asiatic Barred Zone and the targeted exclusion of Asians from immigrating to the United States.[7]

Efforts to fully annul the 1924 Johnson–Reed Act, however, were not successful until 1965, when Lyndon Johnson sought to devote his presidency to pushing through John F. Kennedy's legislative agenda, after Kennedy was assassinated. The Hart–Celler Act was passed into law in 1965 alongside the twin pillars of legislation, the Civil Rights Act of 1964 and the Voting Rights Act of 1965. The

---

[7] To read more on the period between 1924 and 1965, see Yang (2020).

Hart–Celler Act abolished the prior system of national quotas and replaced it with a multipronged approach that prioritized family reunification and labor skills. While it was widely celebrated as a landmark piece of legislation, few politicians at the time expected it to dramatically change American society. Lyndon Johnson, at a signing ceremony beneath the Statue of Liberty on October 3, 1965 declared, "The bill that we will sign today is not a revolutionary bill. It does not affect the lives of millions. It will not reshape the structure of our daily lives ... Yet it is one of the most important acts of this Congress and of this administration. For it does repair a very deep and painful flaw in the fabric of American justice. It corrects a cruel and enduring wrong in the conduct of the American nation."

The Hart–Celler Act stands as one of the most prominent examples of the unintended consequences of enacted laws. Then Attorney General Robert F. Kennedy, testifying before a House subcommittee on immigration noted, "I would say for the Asia-Pacific Triangle it [immigration] would be approximately 5,000 ... after which immigration from that source would virtually disappear." As it turned out, the demand to come to the United States was not equal throughout the world and the family reunification proviso opened the door for the transformation of the United States into a much more multiethnic, multiracial society. As shown in Figure 2.2, the foreign-born population in the United States grew from 9.6 million in 1970 to 40 million by 2010.

In addition to a major increase in the number of immigrants coming into the United States, the Hart–Celler Act also precipitated a dramatic shift in the geography of immigration and with it, its racial composition. Note in Figure 2.3 the regions from which in-migration begins, divided very roughly into "Western"

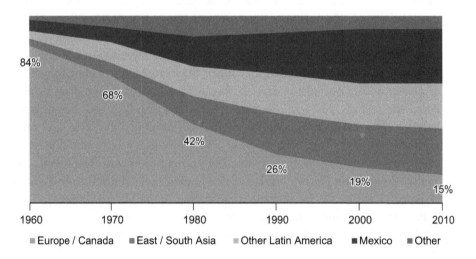

Figure 2.3 The Geography of Immigration, 1960–2010
This figure shows the dramatic decline of immigrants coming from home countries in Europe beginning in the 1960s and the growth of immigrants coming from Mexico, Latin America, and Asia over the same years.
Source: Authors' representation of data taken from Census Bureau.

(Europe and Canada), "Eastern" (East and South Asia), and "Southern" (separately shown for Mexico and the rest of Latin America). In the 1960 Census, just prior to the law's passage, fully 84 percent of the foreign-born population in the United States came from Europe or Canada, with 6 percent from Mexico, 4 percent from other Latin American nations, and 4 percent from Asia. By 2010, those proportions had flipped, with European nations and Canada contributing to just 15 percent of the United States' foreign-born population, and Mexico, other Latin American countries, and Asia contributing 29 percent, 24 percent, and 25 percent. respectively.

The Hart–Celler Act, quite contrary to expectations in 1965, has generated nothing short of a transformation of the racial and ethnic landscape of the United States. Whereas previous waves of immigration contributed to growing numbers of White ethnics to the U.S. population, the post-1965 boom in the U.S. population via immigration resulted in multiplying the number and diversity of racial and ethnic minorities in America, with the emergence of large and growing Hispanic and Asian American communities. Consider the radical demographic changes between 1790, 1960, and today. As noted before, the first decennial census in 1790 counted a population of 3.9 million Americans, with a biracial categorization: 81 percent White and 19 percent Black (of whom 8 percent were categorized as free Blacks). By the 1960 Census, the U.S. population had grown to 179 million, still with a mostly biracial classification of that population into "Whites," "Negros" [sic], and "Other Races." The 1960 Census continued to show a White-dominant nation, with 88.6 percent Whites, 10.5 percent Blacks, and 0.9 percent all other racial groups. That all changed over the next several decades. The most recent 2020 census counted a population of 329 million Americans and sorted that population by ethnicity (as Hispanicity) and separately by race, with five primary racial categories excluding Hispanicity. That classification yielded a population count that was 60 percent (non-Hispanic) Whites, 18 percent Hispanics, 13 percent African Americans, 6 percent Asian Americans, 2.7 percent mixed race Americans, 1.3 percent Native American.

The outsized impact of rising Asian American and Latino population growth on the U.S. racial composition can also be seen in recent decade-to-decade changes. In the first decade of the twenty-first century, both Asian American and Latino populations in America grew far faster than other racial groups—at an astonishing 43 percent, while total population growth in the United States was only 10 percent. Population demographers who track these changes over time expect that at some point in the decade of the 2040s, the United States will become a "majority-minority" nation, meaning that no one racial group will form a majority. The most recent such projections predict that in 2045, 49.7 percent of the population will be White, with 25 percent Latino, 13 percent Black, 8 percent Asian American, 4 percent multiracial (Frey 2018).

Changes to the nation's demographic diversity have been even more striking in the most recent decennial census. Between 2010 and 2002, the size of the Asian American and Latino populations continued to grow considerably, at 36 percent and 23 percent growth, respectively. But the headline findings on change in the 2020 census were the unexpectedly high increase in the nation's multiracial population, at 127 percent, and the equally unexpected negative growth of the nation's White population, which decreased by almost 3 percent. This 3 percent figure, furthermore, includes as Whites those who identify as White and with another racial group. When the "White alone" category (those who only identify as Whites and with no other racial group) is examined, the decrease from 2010 to 2020 is 8.6 percent. These declines in the nation's number of White Americans is the first ever recorded since 1790. Moreover, the 2020 Census already finds, among Americans aged 18 and younger, a majority-minority youth: 47 percent are White, 26 percent Latino, 13 percent Black, 5 percent Asian, and 7 percent multiracial (Frey 2018; Vespa, Medina, and Armstrong 2018).

These demographic changes have measurable consequences for our racial and ethnic politics. In fact, the perception of demographic change alone can be consequential. For example, consider the following experiments conducted by psychologists Maureen Craig and Jennifer Richeson of the attitudes of White Americans. Craig and Richeson randomly selected White participants in their study to be informed of census projections that Whites will no longer be a majority by the 2040s. Those White participants were significantly more hostile toward Latinos, Blacks, and Asian Americans and exhibited a significantly more pro-White bias than their White counterparts who did not receive this piece of information (Craig and Richeson 2014a). In a second study, Craig and Richeson found that White participants who were randomly selected to being informed that California is already a "majority-minority" state became significantly more conservative in their political views and more Republican in their partisanship than White participants who did not get this information. They further found that this effect was driven by Whites' fears that their status in American society is threatened by this demographic diversity. When Whites who were told about the impending "majority-minority" nation were also told that "despite the shift in the demographic make-up, the relative social status of different racial groups is likely to remain steady," Craig and Richeson found no shift in conservatism or partisanship (Craig and Richeson 2014b).

Other Changes Affecting the Nation's Racial Diversity

While projections of a demographic future where Whites are no longer a majority seems to foreshadow far-reaching changes in race relations and racial politics, it is important to remember that demographics are not destiny. Change is a constant, and so even as the remarkable growth in the Asian and Latino populations in America continues to drive such projections of demographic change, there are other dynamic changes to the nation's racial diversity to note. We describe a few other dynamic changes, but this list of dynamic changes is far from exhaustive. One change is the stunning increase in the Native American population. As recently as the 1970 Census, only 827,000 Americans identified as American Indian. By 2020,

Photo 2.2 Montaukett Indian Nation descendants gather to look at a heritage designation marker displaying the Montaukett seal in North Amityville, New York, on December 4, 2021. The town of Babylon unveiled these markers on six streets to acknowledge where the Montaukett natives once lived in the 1600s.
Source: Photo Newsday LLC © Newsday LLC/Contributor/Newsday/Getty Images.

that figure had grown to 3.7 million who identified only as American Indian, with an additional 5.9 million who identified as Native American and as another race ("alone or in combination"), for a total estimated Native American population approaching 10 million. This explosion in the number of Native Americans cannot be explained by immigration or additions by high birth rates (net of death rates). Rather, this rise appears to be due primarily to subjective shifts in how Americans with partial or distant Indian ancestry have chosen to identify racially.[8]

Another change is that the nation's Black population is increasingly also immigrant. Figure 2.4 shows that in 1980, immigrants made up only 3.1 percent of the African American population, or some 816,000 in number. By 2010, those figures jumped up to 8.7 percent and nearly 3.8 million, respectively. This diversity within the African American community has the potential to reshape how we think about issues like reparations, intergroup conflict (e.g., the common view that Blacks and immigrants are in conflict with one another), and structural racism.

A third major change to the nation's racial and ethnic diversity is the emergence of multiracial identity—Americans with mixed racial ancestries. While mixed ancestries have been present since the Blacks, Whites, and Native Americans first came into contact with one another, their histories have been largely hidden and their present-day realities have been largely invisible until recent decades. A combination

---

[8] See Nagel (1995); Sandefur et al. (1996).

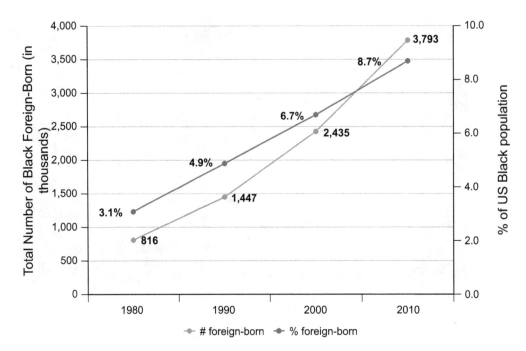

Figure 2.4 The New Black Migration
Immigrants are a growing share of the Black population in the United States, a trend that is
expected to continue into the foreseeable future.
Source: Data from Christine Tamir, "Key Findings about Black Immigrants in the U.S.," Pew
Research Center, January 27, 2022.

of grassroots activism (led mostly by the White parents of interracial children who
sought a broader range of identification options for their children) and political
entrepreneurialism from conservatives like House Speaker Newt Gingrich and
affirmative action opponent Ward Connerly created a window of opportunity for
a radical change in how federal agencies saw and counted the nation's population in
racial terms (DaCosta 2007; Williams 2006).

While Americans of multiple racial backgrounds before the revision to the
1997 OMB Directive on ethno-racial classification had to choose between identifying with the race of one parent's lineage or the other, they could not specifically
identify in a way that best described their unique background. The 2000 Census saw
only 2.4 percent of all Americans who identified with more than one racial category.
However, an increasingly greater share of Americans with mixed backgrounds or
forgotten family histories or seeking more information about their ancestry are
choosing to identify as multiracial. The separation between an ethnicity question
for Americans of Hispanic origin and a race question for all other origins does,
however, represent an ongoing limitation to the freedom to describe oneself in a
multiplicity of backgrounds. The multiracial identification excluded those who were
"Hispanic and" another race. We discuss some of the implications of mixed-race
identity in the box below.

WHAT IT LOOKS LIKE TODAY: MIXED RACE IDENTITY AND THE 2020 CENSUS

While many multiracial Americans celebrated the inclusion of a "mark one or more" category with the 2000 Census, not everyone welcomed the change. Prominent civil rights organizations like the NAACP and the National Council of La Raza opposed a separate "multiracial" category for fear that a new category would dilute the population counts of minority groups, given the use of population counts for the allocation of federal funds and apportionment of political seats. In addition, the initial estimates of the nation's mixed race population for the 2000 Census fell well below estimates from demographers, suggesting an "undercount" of the multiracial population. For the 2020 Census, the Census Bureau implemented seemingly minor changes to the race question (see Figure 2.5): among them were six examples for the White, Black, and American Indian racial categories; areas to write-in one's specific background under each racial category such as German if White and Jamaican if Black (Marks 2021). These changes led to a dramatic increase in the nation's multiracial population count, from 9 million in 2010 to 33.8 million in 2020. Think about and discuss how seemingly minor alterations to the Census race question could yield such a dramatic change in population counts.

The introduction of a multiracial identifier in the 2000 Census also produced a controversial and complex way of counting groups by race. Since 2000, population counts by race are given in two ways: "alone," counting only those Americans who identify with a given racial category; "alone or in combination," taking into account individuals who identify with multiple racial categories. For instance, the Census Bureau reported 3.7 million "American Indian or Alaska Native" people in the 2020 Census in their "alone" count, meaning 3.7 million Americans marked only that category. But they also reported an additional 5.9 million people who identified as "American Indian or Alaska Native" and identified with another race category. Thus, the official "alone or in combination" count approached 10 million. Another example is the estimate of the White American population. The headline from the 2020 Census was the first-ever decline in the population of Whites. Here, if Whites are counted as "alone or in combination," the population decrease is 3 percent compared with 2010 figures. If Whites are counted as "alone," the decrease is a far more dramatic 8.6 percent from 2010 to 2020 (Jones et al. 2021).

Comparing groups using "alone or in combination" counts opens up an interesting window into how racial boundaries are being remade today. For example, 92 percent of the 33.8 million Americans who identified as multiracial in the 2020 Census identified as "White" and another racial category. Yet because Whites are so numerous, multiracial Whites only make up 13 percent of all White Americans. For other, smaller sized populations, the total number of multiracial identifiers is much smaller, but they make up a much larger proportion of that racial group. For instance, a large majority (61 percent) of the 9.7 million who identify with the "American Indian and Alaska Native" category identify multiracially, that is, they also identify with another racial category (Jones et al. 2021).

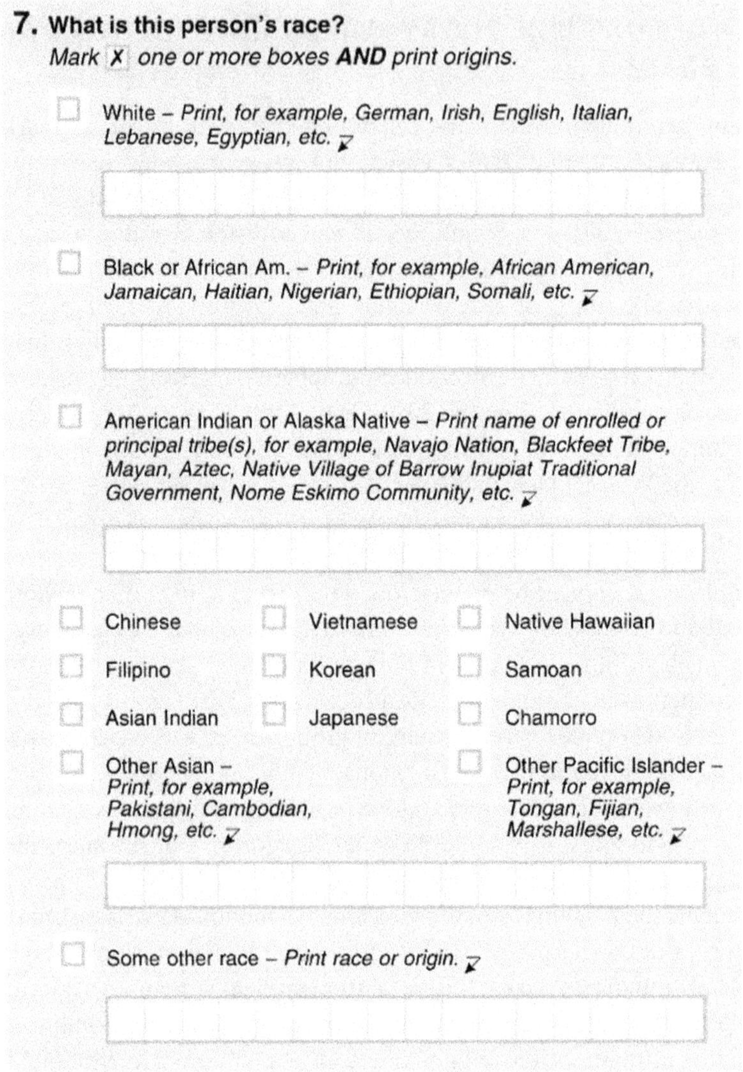

7. **What is this person's race?**
Mark X *one or more boxes AND print origins.*

☐ White – *Print, for example, German, Irish, English, Italian, Lebanese, Egyptian, etc.* ↗

[ ]

☐ Black or African Am. – *Print, for example, African American, Jamaican, Haitian, Nigerian, Ethiopian, Somali, etc.* ↗

[ ]

☐ American Indian or Alaska Native – *Print name of enrolled or principal tribe(s), for example, Navajo Nation, Blackfeet Tribe, Mayan, Aztec, Native Village of Barrow Inupiat Traditional Government, Nome Eskimo Community, etc.* ↗

[ ]

☐ Chinese   ☐ Vietnamese   ☐ Native Hawaiian

☐ Filipino   ☐ Korean   ☐ Samoan

☐ Asian Indian   ☐ Japanese   ☐ Chamorro

☐ Other Asian – *Print, for example, Pakistani, Cambodian, Hmong, etc.* ↗   ☐ Other Pacific Islander – *Print, for example, Tongan, Fijian, Marshallese, etc.* ↗

[ ]

☐ Some other race – *Print race or origin.* ↗

[ ]

Figure 2.5 2020 Census Race Question
The 2020 Census race question added more examples for various race categories, fill-in spaces for Whites, Blacks, and American Indian/Alaska Natives to specify their group origins, and eliminated some "legacy" terms like "Negro" for the Black or African American category.
Source: U.S. Census Bureau paper questionnaire.

What implications does the rise of multiracial identities have for our politics? Early research suggests that members of this new category tend to hold culturally and politically progressive views and on some issues—such as abortion and gender/ marriage equality—even express more liberal views than their peers of monoracial parentage (Davenport 2018). At a minimum the growth of this population in the Census raises questions that we encourage you to think about. Is mixed race identity or being multiracial a distinct identity? Or is it a hybrid of multiple distinct identities, say, as Afro-Latino, biracial Asian, or in Tiger Woods' version,

"Cablinasian"? If the multiracial population of the United States continues to grow at the pace it did in the last decade, will the significance of racial boundaries matter more or less?[9] If the Hispanic ethnicity question is combined together with the race question in the 2030 Census, what implications do you think that would have for the size of the multiracial population in America?

Race, Immigration, and Citizenship

This chapter has examined the idea of America as a people. As a people, the United States today is a remarkably diverse, plural society. While we celebrate our multiracial, multicultural heritage, that diversity did not happen overnight and was not achieved by design. America's demographic diversity has been achieved through several transformative changes over its history. The changes have been driven by territorial conquest, by the trafficking of humans in the transatlantic slave trade, and by multiple waves of immigrants coming to flee religious and political persecution or find peace and prosperity. In short, race, ethnicity, and national origin have been at the center of clashes over the boundaries of belonging and over our national identity from our founding moment to the present day.

In this last section of the chapter, we examine these clashes in two key contexts: the legal challenges related to race and immigration in the late nineteenth and early twentieth centuries and the contemporary debate over "illegal immigration." We have already discussed some of the contested history of citizenship and the role of race in it. Native Americans were not even counted in the census until 1860 and were not conferred citizenship until 1924. African Americans in slave states were counted in fractions and denied formal citizenship until the Fourteenth Amendment in 1868 and then continued to have their political and civil rights nullified by Jim Crow laws and de facto segregation for another century. From this history, it is clear that being "American" has not always implied status as "citizen" if being American accompanies membership in a racial or ethnic minority. The two cases we discuss below show how that dynamic has been true for newer entrants to the racial landscape of America. The landmark legal challenges of the late nineteenth and early twentieth centuries largely involved plaintiffs of Asian heritage and were instrumental in defining the racial boundaries of American citizenship at that time. Today, fierce fights over whether Americans without documents or authorization belong or whether they should be deported and our borders closed is a politicized struggle focused on Mexican Americans.

Citizenship and Race

There is arguably no more fundamental a marker of belonging in a country and a society than citizenship. As former Chief Justice Earl Warren put it, citizenship is

---

[9] Given that a significant source of the increase in multiracial identification is the change of racial categories in the 2020 census, it is difficult to know what future trends in multiracial identification will look like.

"the right to have rights" (*Perez* v. *Brownell* 1958). These rights include civil rights, which in our founding documents were specified as those positive liberties necessary for each individual's freedom, like their personal liberty, freedom of speech, freedom of thought, and right to own property. Today, we also understand civil rights to include "negative liberties," such as *freedom from* slavery, *freedom from* the arbitrary exercise of government's coercive powers, and *freedom from* torture, violence, and inhumane treatment. Citizenship rights also include political rights, which are our protected rights to expression, participation, and power in the political sphere. Most important among these are the right to vote and the right to run for elected office. Finally, in most societies, citizenship also entails certain social rights, or economic rights. These are the rights to have basic needs met and uncertain risks mitigated. Debates over universal health insurance, guaranteed minimum wage, unemployment benefits, social security pensions, and so on are debates over the social rights of citizenship. Fundamental to many social welfare states is the ideal that freedom also entails freedom from fear and freedom from want.[10]

At its core, then, citizenship is a political identity that carries with it the legal standing of membership in a nation and, with that legal standing, the fundamental right to have rights as well as the civic duty to participate in collective decision-making. Because citizenship is by definition linked to countries and because it confers a status that comes with rights and privileges, citizenship is inherently exclusive. Countries set laws and policies qualifying some of its inhabitants for citizenship and disqualifying others. We take it as a given, for instance, that a foreign tourist traveling through the United States on summer vacation should be ineligible for citizenship. So, too, we assume that a lifelong resident of the United States born to parents who are U.S. citizens should qualify for citizenship. These are easy cases, but what about seasonal agricultural workers needed to feed the nation? Or an undocumented immigrant who is willing to enlist in the U.S. military to fight for the nation? Each country sets its own rules for membership as well as its own limits on the rights of membership. In the United States today, for example, the right to vote is limited by age and, in many states still, nullified by a criminal record.

Some of the most impassioned political debates today center on setting limits on citizenship and citizenship rights. Democratic partisans, for instance, see the right to vote as being under siege in states governed by Republican-controlled legislatures and question whether proposals to reform election laws at the state level are motivated by a genuine concern about the integrity of democratic elections or by a naked interest in winning political office by suppressing the votes of racial and ethnic minorities. They see in these legislative initiatives echoes of the past when the right to vote was subject to constraints and qualifications like poll taxes and literacy tests designed to restrict the value and power of citizenship for African Americans. Citizenship is thus constantly changing and constantly contested, and racial conflict is often at the heart of those changes and contests.

---

[10] The elaboration of citizenship rights into civil, political, and social rights is attributed to Marshall (1950).

Consider the period of American history that we discussed earlier as the "third wave" of immigration from (roughly) 1880 to the 1920s. The United States had just emerged from a bloody civil war fought in large part over slavery and resulting in a watershed expansion of liberty, equality, and citizenship in the United States with the Thirteenth, Fourteenth, and Fifteenth Amendments to the Constitution. In particular, the Fourteenth Amendment, passed in 1866 and ratified in 1868, was written to secure equal treatment for African Americans and to guarantee citizenship as a birthright for all persons born on American soil. With this guarantee, moreover, came the right to expect equal protection and due process under the law. The Fourteenth Amendment was followed in short order by the Naturalization Act of 1870, which expressly deemed "aliens of African nativity and to persons of African descent" as eligible for citizenship.

The first major test of this expansion of citizenship and naturalization laws came a decade after the Fourteenth Amendment's ratification, with the Supreme Court case *In re Ah Yup* (1878). Ah Yup was a Chinese immigrant who petitioned for naturalization as a U.S. citizen, but the Court determined that "Chinese" was neither White nor Black and therefore denied his petition. *In re Ah Yup* is the first of some fifty-two legal cases between 1878 and 1944 that challenged immigration and naturalization laws. The legal scholar Ian Haney Lopez calls them "racial prerequisite laws" because the laws of the day established racial prerequisites for eligibility for citizenship—you had to be deemed "White" or "aliens of African nativity and to persons of African descent."[11] Together, these cases represent a series of test cases that open a window into how the courts attempted to navigate legal precedent, "science," and where needed "common knowledge" to render legal definitions of race and uphold the boundaries of Whiteness. Interestingly, there is only one instance out of the fifty-two cases in which the plaintiff petitions for citizenship and the grounds that they should be recognized as "of African descent"; in the remaining fifty-one cases, plaintiffs ask the court to recognize their background as "White."[12]

The racial prerequisite cases are also notable because in a majority of the cases, the plaintiffs were of Asian descent. Twenty-eight of the fifty-two cases were brought by Asian Americans (twelve by Asian Indians), another twelve by Arab Americans, two by Armenian Americans, with lone cases brought by a Native Hawaiian, a Mexican American, and a Native American and eight cases brought by plaintiffs of mixed racial backgrounds. While most cases were unsuccessful, in twelve cases the plaintiffs were able to win their petition for citizenship. Perhaps the two most well known of these racial prerequisite cases go all the way to the Supreme

---

[11] See Lopez (1996).

[12] That case is *In Re Cruz* in the Eastern District of New York court in the U.S. District Courts in 1938. The court determined that the plaintiff, who presented as "one-quarter" African descent and "three-quarter" Indian descent, was ineligible because "his African descent must be shown to be at least an affirmative quantity, and not a neutral thing as in the case of the half blood, or a negative one as in the case of the one-quarter blood."

Court, *Ozawa* v. *United States* (1922) and *United States* v. *Thind* (1923). These two cases are usually compared alongside one another to illustrate the pretzel-like logic the Court used to exclude non-Whites from passing as White.

In *Ozawa* v. *United States*, Takao Ozawa petitioned for citizenship on the grounds that both socially and racially, he was "White." Socially, Ozawa argued that he had assimilated into Whiteness and that he manifested the "good moral character" deemed to be required of citizens in the Naturalization Act of 1790. Ozawa, who had lived in the United States at the time for twenty years, spoke fluent English, had graduated from the University of California, Berkeley, converted to Christianity, and wrote in his petition, "In name, General Benedict Arnold was an American, but at heart he was a traitor. In name, I am not an American, but at heart I am a true American." Racially, Ozawa argued that he was "whiter" than other Americans who had been classified as White for the purposes of naturaliza-tion, writing that Japanese Americans were "whiter than the average Italian, Spaniard, or Portuguese." The Court rejected Ozawa's petition. In doing so, it relied partly on legal precedent, citing *In re Ah Yup*. But the Court also leaned heavily on what they considered the science of the day, which was the belief that only persons of Caucasian origin could be defined as "White."

In *United States* v. *Thind*, brought to the Supreme Court just one year later, the Court did a complete about-face. Bhagat Singh Thind's petition for citizenship capitalized up on the Court's reasoning in *Ozawa*. Thind thus argued that as "a high caste Hindu of full Indian blood, born at Amrit Sar, Punjab" he was Caucasian and Aryan in origin and therefore White. The Court, however, also rejected Thind's petition. Now, the Court wrote in its opinion that the Founding Fathers intended for citizenship to apply only "upon that class of persons whom the fathers knew as white, and to deny it to all who could not be so classified," adding further, "[i]t may be that the blond Scandinavian and the brown Hindu have a common ancestor in the dim reaches of antiquity, but the average man knows perfectly well that there are unmistakable and profound differences between them today." The contrast here is striking. In Ozawa, "science" deems the plaintiff not "White." In Thind, "the average man" deems the plaintiff not "White."

Does "Mexican" = "Illegal"?

The *Ozawa* and *Thind* cases show how closely Whiteness has been associated with Americanness, even in the eyes of Supreme Court justices. That association of race and belonging remains prominent even today. We are reminded again of Chapter 1's discussion of Samuel Huntington's controversial essay, "The Hispanic Challenge," in which a preeminent Harvard professor worries aloud that immigration from Mexico poses an existential threat to American national identity. That threat comes from two premises. The first premise is that the Anglo-Protestant background of colonial settlers is at the heart of American national identity. The second is that Mexican American immigrants are not "assimilable," a premise that is baked into the proposition that our national identity is Anglo-Protestant.

Assimilation, a concept that we return to in the next section, is the idea that some immigrants are capable of being absorbed into the body politic while others are not.

Huntington wrote his essay in 2004, but his is a view that continues to fuel xenophobia and nativism in America today. During the Trump presidency, rallying cries to "Make America Great Again" were tethered to harsh policies like the mass deportation of Mexican Americans from their homes and communities in the United States and the separation of children from their parents at the U.S.– Mexico border. They were also stoked by political rhetoric about "drug dealers, criminals, rapists" and building "a great wall" that Mexico would pay for. Not surprisingly, by the summer of 2019, 23 percent of Americans in a Gallup poll named "immigration" as the "most important problem facing the country," second only to "government" (at 26 percent). That 23 percent figure marked the highest level ever measured for immigration by Gallup since it tracked their most important problem question in 1993 (Jones 2019).

Alongside the dangerous stereotype that "American" implies "White" is the equally dangerous view that "Mexican" implies "immigrant" or worse, that "Mexican" implies "illegal immigrant." A key historical context for this elision is the Bracero Program. In the aftermath of the Second World War the United States faced an unprecedented labor shortage that led to diplomatic accords between the United States and Mexico to address the country's need for short-term agricultural and transportation labor. Signed in 1942, the Bracero Program was the largest contract labor program in American history, resulting in 4.6 million contracts signed between 1942 and 1964, when the program was officially shuttered. The millions of Mexicans who came to the United States under this program, primarily in Texas and California, suffered through extremely harsh working conditions, wage exploitation, racial discrimination, and violence.

The Bracero Program is often identified as a key turning point in the rise of an undocumented, unauthorized population of Americans in the nation's history. Illegal migration across the nation's southern border certainly existed before the program, but the demand for cheap, exploitable labor from Mexico created the conditions for an unparalleled population flow between the United States and Mexico. While most laborers returned home, often penniless, after their short-term contracts were over, many chose to overstay their contracts and tried to make a life in America in the shadows. The labor demand also resulted in millions of Mexican nationals who were unable to obtain work permits through the Bracero Program deciding to enter the United States without papers. By some estimates, the number of migrants entering the United States illegally during the period of the Bracero Program equaled or surpassed the number of braceros. Many American farmers used bracero labor and undocumented immigrant labor as a bargaining chip against agricultural workers in the United States, creating even greater resentment and discrimination against Mexican Americans.

That program, decades of substantial northbound migration, and perhaps most importantly, an immigration threat narrative, regularly perpetuated by both the media and strategic politicians, which scapegoats immigrants for much of what ails

America, has resulted in widespread anxiety about immigration. It has also led to a close association between "Mexican" and "undocumented" in the minds of many Americans who, in fact, believe that the immigrant population is largely undocumented and largely Latino (Citrin and Sides 2008). The unfortunate result is that anxiety dominates economic concerns in explaining immigration policy views and that attitudes toward Latinos in particular account for nearly all of the effect (Valentino, Brader, and Jardina 2013).

The data, however, very clearly show that each of the three common misperceptions about Mexican Americans and immigration is faulty. First, not all immigrants are illegal. Of the nearly 46 million foreign-born in the United States, 77 percent are here legally: 45 percent as naturalized citizens, 27 percent as "green card"-holding permanent residents, and 5 percent as "temporary lawful residents" here to stay for a defined period of time, such as for business, education, or other reasons. Only 23 percent (or 10.5 million) are in America without documents or authorization (see Budiman 2020; Lopez, Passel, and Cohn 2021).

Second, not all immigrants are of Mexican origin. Of the 44.8 million people in America in 2018 who were born outside the United States, only one in four (or 11.2 million) were Mexican American (Budiman 2020). In fact, Mexican Americans have been a declining share of the U.S. foreign-born population over time. In 2007, there were 38.1 million Americans who were first-generation immigrants. Of that number, 11.7 million or roughly 31 percent were Mexican Americans (Grieco 2010).[13]

Third, not all illegal immigrants are of Mexican origin. While it is true that in 2007 Mexican unauthorized immigrants were a majority of the total undocumented population in America, making up 6.9 million (57 percent) of the estimated 12.2 million in that year, the reality is that the number of undocumented immigrants has—despite the heated political rhetoric—been declining in recent years. Note that even at the peak level of the estimated undocumented population in America (roughly 12.2 million in 2007), more than 40 percent were *not* Mexican Americans. Since 2007, the proportion of undocumented immigrations of Mexican descent has actually been declining. Pew estimates are that in 2017, of the 10.5 million estimated undocumented immigrants, a little over 4.9 million (or 47 percent) were of Mexican background (Lopez, Passel, and Cohn 2021). An additional 1.9 million (18 percent) were from Central America, and 1.5 million (14 percent) were from Asia.

The facts thus clearly show that immigration should not be assumed to be "illegal," that immigration should not be assumed to be Mexican in origin, and that undocumented immigration too should not be assumed to be Mexican in origin. That such beliefs remain widespread, in spite of the facts, reveals more about how politicians create and then exploit misperceptions about immigration than it does about immigration itself or about actual threats to American national identity.

---

[13] See at: www2.census.gov/library/publications/2010/acs/acs-11.pdf.

DIGGING DEEPER: DACA AND LIVING WHILE UNDOCUMENTED IN AMERICA

For millions who do live in the country without documentation, life can be a struggle. Legally, undocumented residents cannot hold a job. In many cases, public services are out of reach. Even access to education can be difficult. Fear of deportation is a near constant. Americans, as a whole, recognize those problems and want to help. That is likely why most favor some sort of pathway to legal status. Indeed, three-quarters of all Americans believe that the undocumented should be able to remain in this country legally (Krogstad 2020).

Yet despite the problems the undocumented face and despite the fact that so many Americans want to do something about it, efforts to enact comprehensive immigration reform over the last few decades have been contentious and have all eventually failed. In the early 2000s, John McCain and Ted Kennedy worked to create landmark bipartisan legislation that would include legalization, guest worker programs, and border enforcement. But in the end, their Secure America and Orderly Immigration Act was not even voted on. A similar attempt at comprehensive reform led by Senator Arlen Specter in 2005 also failed. And in 2013, a major piece of amnesty legislation sponsored by the infamous "Gang of Eight" senators would have provided 11 million undocumented residents with a path to citizenship. Like the previous efforts, it faced significant grassroots resistance and ultimately died in Congress.

With little hope for significant bipartisan reform on the horizon, President Barack Obama enacted an executive order entitled Deferred Action for Childhood Arrivals (DACA) in August 2012. DACA provided for temporary protection from deportation as well as legal work permits and identity documents for undocumented immigrants who had arrived in the United States as children. That was followed in 2014 by the Deferred Action for Parents of Americans (DAPA) that granted renewable work permits and exemption from deportation to undocumented adults with children who are U.S. citizens—a program that was eventually blocked by lawsuits.

Since its inception the DACA has enabled over 800,000 young adults to work lawfully, to attend school, and to plan their lives without the imminent threat of deportation. The gains for young adults as well as for the American economy have been meaningful. Surveys indicate that recipients' average hourly wages increased by 86 percent after receiving DACA (Wong, Flores, and Kmec 2019). Forty percent of recipients are in school, and of those 83 percent are working toward a bachelor's degree or higher. For recipients like Julia Verzbickis who moved to the United States with her family when she was 9, the program has had a huge impact on their lives. Within days of hearing she had been approved for DACA, Julia had applied for dozens of jobs, a social security card, and a driver's license. She joined Teach for America and has since started teaching in middle school. In the end, for Julia, "DACA gave me my independence back. It's the single reason I am able to teach, and live on my own, and pay for my car, and feel like I belong in the country I have lived in for 15 years" (*New York Times* 2017)

Photo 2.3 Immigration rights activists take part in a rally in front of the U.S. Supreme Court in Washington, D.C. on November 12, 2019, in advance of Supreme Court arguments on the fate of the "Dreamers," an estimated 700,000 people brought to the country illegally as children but allowed to stay and work under the DACA program created by former President Barack Obama.
Source: Photo Mandel Ngan © Mandel Ngan/Contributor/AFP/Getty Images AFP/Getty Images.

Nevertheless, DACA, which only provides temporary status and requires recipients to reapply every two years has been under attack. President Trump's administration attempted to terminate the program. After those efforts were overturned by the Supreme Court, Trump's Acting Secretary of Homeland Security Chad Wolf placed limits on DACA that eventually blocked the federal government from approving any new, first-time DACA applications. While President Biden has reaffirmed the federal government's commitment to DACA, the future of the program remains unclear. Moreover, DACA is limited. Current recipients only gain temporary relief and have no long-term path to citizenship. DACA also does not cover the millions of other undocumented Americans who are not eligible for the program.

All of this raises deep questions about what we can and should do moving forward. For noncitizens, is temporary protection like DACA sufficient or should we pursue longer-term solutions? More broadly, should citizenship be a rightful claim for anyone who has set up roots in the United States and contributed to American society? Or is it a special privilege reserved for those born on U.S. soil, born to U.S. citizens, and those who have immigrated with legal authorization?

Theories of Immigrant Incorporation

Immigrants everywhere share a common experience of wondering how they will adapt to their new environs, whether they will feel welcomed or be asked to "go back to where you came from." At the heart of the fabled view of America as a "nation of immigrants" is the chronicle of citizenship. The chronicle evokes a long-standing question that the philosopher Michael Walzer provocatively posed by asking, "What Does It Mean to Be an 'American'?" (2004).

America has, of course, provided different answers for different groups across different contexts and time periods. On one extreme stand Presidents Woodrow Wilson and Theodore Roosevelt who viewed hyphenated Americans—those who chose to identify themselves both by their adopted nation and by their country of origin (e.g., Irish-American) with a deep sense of mistrust. In his final speech in support of the League of Nations, Wilson famously asserted that "Any man who carries a hyphen about with him carries a dagger that he is ready to plunge into the vitals of this Republic whenever he gets ready." Roosevelt likewise declared that "There is no room in this country for hyphenated Americanism ... There is no such thing as a hyphenated American who is a good American. The only man who is a good American is the man who is an American and nothing else" (*New York Times* 1915). The assumption underlying this perspective is that in order to truly be American, immigrants need to renounce all foreign allegiances and fully devote themselves to assimilating into (or conforming to) American society and culture.

On the other extreme stand scholars like Michael Walzer and many others who assert that it is both unnecessary and often unconstructive to require this unitary allegiance and near-complete assimilation into American mores and ways. Rather, as a nation of immigrants, American can and should be tolerant of ethnic pluralism and racial diversity. This sentiment is powerfully expressed by President Barack Obama: "I am the son of a black man from Kenya and a white woman from Kansas ... I am married to a black American who carries within her the blood of slaves and slaveowners—an inheritance we pass on to our two precious daughters. I have brothers, sisters, nieces, nephews, uncles and cousins, of every race and every hue, scattered across three continents, and for as long as I live, I will never forget that in no other country on Earth is my story even possible."[14]

These debates over what it means to be American are yoked to competing views of immigrant political incorporation, or the process by which foreigners and their descendants come to think of themselves as members with sufficient standing in a new society to have a voice in the inputs to democratic decision-making and to make claims on the outputs of democratic decision-making. Immigrant incorporation is an idea and a question that has long been debated, and the polar extremes with which we began this section are reflected in contrasting scholarly perspectives

---

[14] Speech at the National Convention Center, Philadelphia, March 18, 2008, see at: https://constitutioncenter.org/amoreperfectunion.

over how immigrants adapt to a new host society and whether that host society successfully incorporates newcomers. We review several such theories of immigrant incorporation below.

Cultural Monotheism

At one end of the spectrum is the account of cultural monotheism, or the view that there is a foundational identity to any society and that each new group successfully adapts to the extent that they adopt that foundational identity. Diverse elements are made and remade into one larger, homogeneous and monocultural society. That model is perhaps best illustrated as a simple formula: A + B + C = A. Out of many, comes one and only one. When new immigrant groups (B and C above) arrive to a nation with a majority group (A), cultural monotheism suggests that B and C meld in with and ultimately mirror and reinforce the culture of the majority group A. In the American context, immigrant incorporation means relatively strict conformity with Anglo-Protestant traditions or "Anglo-conformity." As Samuel Huntington sees it:

The creed [is] the product of the distinct Anglo-Protestant culture of the founding settlers. Key elements of that culture include the English language; Christianity; religious commitment; English concepts of the rule of law; and dissenting Protestant values of individualism, the work ethic, and the belief that humans have the ability and the duty to try to create a heaven on earth, a "city on a hill." Historically, millions of immigrants were attracted to the United States because of this culture and the economic opportunities and political liberties it made possible. Contributions from immigrant cultures modified and enriched the Anglo-Protestant culture of the founding settlers. The essentials of that founding culture remained the bedrock of U.S. identity, however, at least until the last decades of the 20th century.

The notion of America as a place that can transform people of all stripes and backgrounds into "Americans" has structured our treatment of waves of immigrants for centuries and still holds great sway in our politics and in our national imagination.

Cultural Relativism

The "monotheistic" view of immigrant incorporation has drawn many critics who object to it on both empirical and normative grounds. Many scholars of American history and culture have questioned whether we were ever a monocultural nation whose entire basis derived from Anglo-Protestantism. Others point out that, whether or not America once was Anglo-Protestant in its cultural roots, the United States today is decidedly not simply Anglo-Protestant. Certainly, many aspects of the creed Huntington describes remain prevalent today, such as pledging our allegiance to "one nation, under God, indivisible," extolling the virtues of individualism and hard work, and the ubiquity of English as our common language. Yet describing the United States solely in these terms would present a highly skewed portrait. Finally, critics of a monocultural view question the very value of conformity to one culture and the social norm of assimilation to that culture, either for a nation and for its immigrants themselves. Should we require or even expect assimilation of this form? Or is it possible that a different model that allows for more individual expression and more cultural diversity could be beneficial to both immigrant and nation?

A second perspective on immigration, then, is the idea that out of many can come something different and better. This is essentially the commonly held view of America as a "melting pot." The idea of the melting pot is that America has survived and thrived for so long because in bringing together different cultures and insights from around the world it has managed to create something new— something better. The melting pot model is perhaps best illustrated by the formula: $A + B + C = D$. That is, when new immigrant groups (B and C above) arrive to a nation with a majority group (A), a new society and culture, D, emerges. It conjures the words of Israel Zangwill:

There she lies, the great Melting Pot—listen! Can't you hear the roaring and the bubbling? There gapes her mouth—the harbour where a thousand mammoth feeders come from the ends of the world to pour in their human freight. Ah, what a stirring and a seething! Celt and Latin, Slav and Teuton, Greek and Syrian, black and yellow, Jew and Gentile, Yes, and East and West and North and South … how the Great Alchemist fuses them with his purging flame! Here they shall all unite to build the Republic of Man and the Kingdom of God (Zangwill 1926).

Photo 2.4 Muslim leaders and allies held a rally and march against Islamophobia, White supremacy, and anti-immigrant bigotry in Times Square on March 24, 2019.
Source: Photo Erik McGregor © Erik McGregor/Contributor/LightRocket/Getty Images.

Cultural Pluralism

To these two perspectives, scholars of immigration and assimilation would add a third account, cultural pluralism, a version in which smaller groups are able to maintain their unique identities, values, and practices that are, in turn, accepted by the larger or more dominant culture. Proponents of this latter theory of immigration incorporation see America more as a "salad bowl" in which a medley of groups come together and coexist in harmony while retaining their essential character as distinct groups. In other words, A + B + C = A + B + C. That view of cultural pluralism is well articulated by theorist Michael Walzer (2004): "It is not the case that Irish-Americans, say, are culturally Irish and politically American, as the pluralists claim. Rather, they are culturally Irish-American and politically Irish-American ... America has no singular national destiny—and to be an 'American' is, finally, to know that and to be more or less content with it." This kind of pluralism considers the unique traits of incoming groups as potentially valuable and places much greater emphasis on integration, with reduced expectations for assimilation to society's norms or for the acquisition of the previously dominant culture. Cultural pluralism is seen by advocates not only as a more factually accurate representation of the reality of immigration in America, but also as an aspirational goal in a welcoming and inclusive society.

Race and Assimilation

These theories of immigrant incorporation are complicated by the experience of race as a powerful social structure in American social, economic, and political life. In the American context, the traditional version of a racial assimilation model is one of "straight-line assimilation" in which new racial and ethnic minority groups slowly allow their unique cultural traits to fade and, in their place, assimilate and transform into the cultural mores of mainstream society. Sociologist Richard Alba, for example, describes the process by which White Catholic ethnic immigrants (e.g., by and large, Irish, Italian, Polish, many Germans) were maligned and marginalized in their first generation and remained faithful to their cultural heritage, but eventually saw a decline into a "twilight of ethnicity" (Alba 1985). In essence, even ethnic minorities who are initially excluded are expected to lose their ethnic distinctiveness and "pass" into Whiteness.

This straight-line model is often juxtaposed with the ethnic disadvantage (or, by some accounts, "ethnic resilience") model in which racial and ethnic minorities either choose to or are forced to maintain their distinct position as different, lesser, or outsider. Sociologist Alejandro Portes and his colleagues argued that what is patently true for descendants of enslaved Africans who were forcibly brought to the United States under the institution of chattel slavery is also true for newer racialized minorities like Latinos and Asian Americans (Portes and Bach 1985). Through discrimination, language barriers, and a host of other exclusionary rules and structures, newly immigrated minorities remain disadvantaged and are unable and unwelcome to "pass" into Whiteness.

The ethnic disadvantage model ultimately evolved into a third, more nuanced account of the ways in which ethnic migrants successfully adapt to their new environs while continuing to face systemic, structural barriers to advancement. Reflecting the views of a growing segment of sociologists studying immigrant incorporation, segmented assimilation is a more complex model in that it maintains that there is no one pathway to incorporation that fits every immigrant group (Portes and Zhou 1993). Immigrants instead come with different class, racial, or religious backgrounds as well as different kinds of ethnic and immigrant cultural resources and social capital. As Portes, Fernandez-Kelly, and Haller argue, "[c]-hildren of Asian, black, mulatto, and mestizo immigrants cannot escape their ethnicity and race, as defined by the mainstream. Their enduring physical differences from whites and the equally persistent strong effects of discrimination based on those differences … throw a barrier in the path of occupational mobility and social acceptance. Immigrant children's identities, their aspirations, and their academic performance are affected accordingly" (Portes, Fernandez-Kelly, and Haller 2005). Complicating matters further, it should be clear that the contexts of "reception" differ and include local labor markets, spatial segregation, and political regimes, among others. Compare an Afro-Caribbean immigrant in Iowa versus an Afro-Caribbean immigrant in Jamaica Plains, New York. In Iowa that immigrant may have to attempt to navigate the local labor market without the support of an extensive social network of fellow immigrants and against the barriers imposed by a less sympathetic local political regime. By contrast, the Afro-Caribbean immigrant in Jamaica Plains is likely to be aided in their search for employment by a deep network of immigrants and a more welcoming political environment.

Conclusion

We have covered a lot of ground in this chapter, offering some different perspectives that draw attention to the widely divergent understandings of the immigrant experience in the United States as well as to the often contradictory ways the nation has responded to immigrants and to demographic change. To begin with, America's origin stories vary greatly, and the place of immigration in those stories is also seen from many different points of view. Some see an historical legacy and national mythology that insists on strict assimilation to a singular Anglo-Protestant monocultural identity, while others emphasize moments of greater openness to difference and more inclusive processes of incorporation where at least some of the unique features of an immigrant's cultural background endure and reshape America as a result. Still others contend that the process of assimilation and incorporation is heterogeneous and will vary greatly depending on time and context.

These different perspectives also raise deep normative questions about what assimilation should be. Should we require newcomers to erase their origins and instead mold themselves to an American way of life, if we could even agree on such a thing? Or should we value those origins and allow for or even encourage an assimilation process that is less one-way and more multifaceted? In other words, is it better to try to create uniformity or to celebrate difference? Americans have passionately debated these questions through history, they continue to do so today, and they will likely continue to do so long into the future.

What all of this should tell us is that immigration and citizenship in America are best characterized by a complicated and troubled reality. Citizenship may be an inclusionary and egalitarian concept by definition—something that many Americans herald and aspire to. But the deeper truth is that citizenship has been marked by an exclusionary and inegalitarian history in the United States. What was once true, largely remains true today. The current political milieu continues to be one of sharp lines and sharp elbows drawn between members and those excluded from membership, as we will see in the chapters that follow.

KEY TERMS

Bracero Program
Chattel slavery
Chinese Exclusion Act 1882
Civil rights
Cultural monotheism
Cultural pluralism
Cultural relativism
Ethnic disadvantage
Hart–Celler Act (Immigration and Naturalization Act) 1965
Immigrant political incorporation
Johnson–Reed Act 1924
Multiracial identity
"Nation of immigrants"
Political rights
Segmented assimilation
Settler colonialism
Social rights
Straight-line assimilation
Xenophobia

DISCUSSION QUESTIONS

1. How important are a nation's founding myths to you? Can the benefits to national unity and patriotism be achieved while recognizing our history of settler colonialism and chattel slavery?
2. Is it inevitable that demographic change and increasing racial diversity will lead to greater interracial conflict? Can you think of examples where that is not the case?

3. Is there a "right" or "wrong" way to count groups by race? How should we compare population numbers from Census data before 2000, when the option to identify with multiple races was introduced, to population numbers since 2000?

ANNOTATED SUGGESTED READINGS

See Ned Blackhawk. 2023. *The Rediscovery of America: Native Peoples and the Unmaking of U.S. History*. New Haven, CT: Yale University Press, which retells five centuries of history and the role of Native peoples in shaping America's constitutional democracy.

See Gloria Anzaldua. 1987. *Borderland: La Frontera, the New Mestiza*. San Francisco, CA: Aunt Lute Books, a ground-breaking, semi-autobiographical book, which offers a deeply personal account of the idea of a border and the history of Chicano/Latino history.

See Erika Lee. 2019. *America for Americans: A History of Xenophobia in the United States*. New York: Basic Books, for an insightful, comprehensive, and authoritative account of anti-immigrant sentiment in America.

See Beth Lew Williams. 2018. *The Chinese Must Go: Violence, Exclusion, and the Making of the Alien in America*. Cambridge, MA: Harvard University Press, which begins in the 1850s and highlights the role of anti-Chinese violence and vigilantism in advancing immigration controls.

See Alejandro Portes and Ruben Rumbaut. 1996. *Immigrant America: A Portrait*. Berkeley: University of California Press, an acclaimed classic text about immigrant life in America has been updated several times to provide readers with a comprehensive and current overview of immigration to the United States.

See Kenneth Prewitt. 2013. *What Is "Your" Race? The Census and Our Flawed Efforts to Classify Americans*. Princeton: Princeton University Press, for an historical overview of the census race question—and a proposal for eliminating it.

See Lynn Jia Yang. 2020. *One Mighty and Irresistible Tide: The Epic Struggle over American Immigration*. New York: W. W. Norton, for a powerful account of the twentieth-century battle for immigration reform beginning with the harsh system of ethnic quotas instituted by Congress in 1924.

CHAPTER REFERENCES

Alba, Richard. 1985. *Italian-Americans: Into the Twilight of Ethnicity*. Upper Saddle River, NJ: Prentice Hall.

Anderson, Benedict. 1983. *Imagined Communities: Reflections on the Origin and Spread of Nationalism*. London: Verso.

Baptist, Edward. 2016. *The Half Has Never Been Told: Slavery and the Making of American Capitalism*. New York: Basic Books.

Beckert, Sven. 2015. *Empire of Cotton: A Global History*. New York: Vintage.

Budiman, Abby. 2020. "Key Findings about U.S. Immigrants," Pew Research Center, August 20. www.pewresearch.org/fact-tank/2020/08/20/key-findings-about-u-s-immigrants.

Campbell, Gibson and Kay Jung. 2006. "Historical Census Statistics on the Foreign-Born Population of the United States, 1850 to 2000," Working Paper No. 81. U.S. Census Bureau.

Citrin, Jack and John Sides. 2008. "Immigration and the Imagined Community in Europe and the United States," *Political Studies* 56(1): 33–56.

Craig, Maureen and Jennifer Richeson. 2014a. "More Diverse, Yet Less Tolerant? How the Increasingly Diverse Racial Landscape Affects White Americans' Racial Attitudes," *Personality and Social Psychology Bulletin* 40(6): 750–761.

Craig, Maureen and Jennifer Richeson. 2014b. "On the Precipice of a 'Majority-Minority' America: Perceived Status Threat from a Racial Demographic Shift Affects White Americans' Political Ideology," *Psychological Science* 25(6): 1189–1197.

DaCosta, Kimberly McClain. 2007. *Making Multiracials: State, Family, and Market in the Redrawing of the Color Line.* Stanford: Stanford University Press.

Davenport, Lauren. 2018. *Politics Beyond Black and White: Biracial Identity and Attitudes in America.* Cambridge: Cambridge University Press.

Frey, William. 2018. "The US Will Become 'Minority White' in 2045, Census Projects," www.brookings.edu/blog/the-avenue/2018/03/14/the-us-will-become-minority-white-in-2045-census-projects.

Grieco, Elizabeth. 2010. "Race and Hispanic Origin of the Foreign-Born Population of the United States: 2007," U.S. Census Bureau American Community Survey Reports. www2.census.gov/library/publications/2010/acs/acs-11.pdf.

Handlin, Oscar. 1951. *The Uprooted: The Epic Story of the Great Migrations That Made the American People.* Philadelphia: Pennsylvania University Press.

In re Ah Yup 5 Sawy. 155 (1878).

Johnson, Walter. 2017. *River of Dark Dreams: Slavery and Empire in the Cotton Kingdom.* Cambridge, MA: Harvard University Press.

Jones, Jeffrey. 2019. "New High in U.S. Say Immigration Is Most Important Problem," June 21. https://news.gallup.com/poll/259103/new-high-say-immigration-important-problem.aspx

Jones, Nicholas, Rachel Marks, Roberto Ramirez, and Merarys Ríos-Vargas. 2021. "2020 Census Illuminates Racial and Ethnic Composition of the Country," August 12, 2021. www.census.gov/library/stories/2021/08/improved-race-ethnicity-measures-reveal-united-states-population-much-more-multiracial.html.

Krogstad, Jens Manuel. 2020. "Americans Broadly Support Legal Status for Immigrants Brought to the U.S. Illegally as Children," Pew Research Center, June 17. www.pewresearch.org/short-reads/2020/06/17/americans-broadly-support-legal-status-for-immigrants-brought-to-the-u-s-illegally-as-children.

Lopez, Ian Haney. 1996. *White by Law.* New York: New York University Press.

Lopez, Mark Hugo, Jeffrey R. Passel, and D'Vera Cohn. 2021. "Key Facts about the Changing U.S. Unauthorized Immigrant Population," Pew Research Center, April 13. www.pewresearch.org/fact-tank/2021/04/13/key-facts-about-the-changing-u-s-unauthorized-immigrant-population.

Marks, Rachel. 2021. *"Improvements to the 2020 Census Race and Hispanic Origin Question Designs, Data Processing, and Coding Procedures,"* August 31, 2021. www.census.gov/newsroom/blogs/random-samplings/2021/08/improvements-to-2020-census-race-hispanic-origin-question-designs.html.

Marshall, T. H. 1950. *Citizenship and Social Class.* Cambridge: Cambridge University Press.

Nagel, Joanne. 1995, "Politics and the Resurgence of American Indian Ethnic Identity," *American Sociological Review* 60: 953.

New York Times. 1915. "Roosevelt Bars the Hyphenated,"*New York Times*, October 13, 1, 5. https://timesmachine.nytimes.com/timesmachine/1915/10/13/105042745.pdf.

Ozawa v. *United States* 260 U.S. 178 (1922).

Perez v. *Brownell* 356 U.S. 44 (1958).

Portes, Alejandro and Zhou Min. 1993. "The New Second Generation: Segmented Assimilation and Its Variants," *Annals of the American Academy of Political and Social Sciences* 530: 74–96.

Portes, Alejandro and Ruben Rumbaut. 1985. *Latin Journeys: Cuban and Mexican Immigrants in the United States.* Berkeley: University of California Press.

Portes Alejandro, Fernandez-Kelly Patricia, and Haller William. 2005. "Segmented Assimilation on the Ground: The New Second Generation in Early Adulthood," *Ethnic and Racial Studies* 28(6): 1000–1040.

Reddy, Marlita. 1995. *Statistical Record of Native North Americans*, 2nd ed. Detroit, MI: Gale Research.

Sandefur, Gary, Ronald R. Rindfuss, and Barney Cohen (eds.). 1996. *Changing Numbers, Changing Needs: American Indian Demography and Public Health.* Washington, D.C.: National Academies Press.

Tamir, Christine. 2022. "Key Findings about Black Immigrants in the U.S.," Pew Research Center, January 27. www.pewresearch.org/fact-tank/2022/01/27/key-findings-about-black-immigrants-in-the-u-s.

Thornton, Russell. 1987. *American Indian Holocaust and Survival: A Population History since 1492.* Norman: University of Oklahoma Press.

United States v. *Bhagat Singh Thind* 261 U.S. 204 (1923).

United States Census Bureau. 1793. *Return of the Whole Number of Persons within the Several Districts of the United States.* Philadelphia. www.census.gov/library/publications/1793/dec/number-of-persons.html.

United States Census Bureau. 1850. *1850 Census: Compendium of the Seventh Census.* www.census.gov/library/publications/1854/dec/1850c.html.

Valentino, Nicholas, Ted Brader, and Ashley Jardina. 2013. "Immigrant Opposition among U.S. Whites," *Political Psychology* 34(2): 149–166.

Vespa, Jonathan, Lauren Medina, and David M. Armstrong. 2018. "Demographic Turning Points for the United States: Population Projections for 2020 to 2060." *Current Population Reports, P25-1144.* Washington, D.C.: U.S. Census Bureau.

Walzer, Michael. 2004. "What Does It Mean to Be an 'American'?" Social Research 71(3): 633–654.

Willcox, Walter F. (ed.). 1931. *International Migrations, Vol. II: Interpretations.* National Bureau of Economic Research. www.nber.org/system/files/chapters/c5104/c5104.pdf.

Williams, Kim. 2006. *Mark One or More: Civil Rights in Multiracial America.* Ann Arbor: University of Michigan Press.

Wong, Tom, Claudia Flores, and Ignacia Rodriguez Kmec. 2019. "2021 Survey of DACA Recipients Underscores the Importance of a Pathway to Citizenship," Center for American Progress. www.americanprogress.org/article/2021-survey-of-daca-recipients-underscores-the-importance-of-a-pathway-to-citizenship.

Yang, Jia Lynn. 2020. *One Mighty and Irresistible Tide.* New York: W. W. Norton.

Yick Wo v. *Hopkins* 117 U.S. 356 (1886).

Zangwill, Israel. 1926. *The Melting Pot.* New York: Macmillan.

3   Democracy, Inequality, and Polarization

In the United States, democracy is the closest thing we have to a common political creed. It is well known to everyone everywhere that the United States is a democratic system of government. Democracy's premise is etched indelibly into the very first words of the Constitution, "We the People of the United States ..." In the political history of the twentieth century, one of the most dramatic story lines is the clash over how nation-states would govern themselves and whether political systems would spread to other nation-states, even if against their will. On the global stage and in at least three acts—the First World War, the Second World War, and the Cold War—democracy has effectively won out over monarchy, dictatorship, and communism. The United States is the lead actor in this triumphant tale of twentieth-century democracy, aggressively investing in a foreign policy goal of "democracy promotion," and realized with a forceful combination of economic carrots and military sticks.

Despite this, there have always been critics of democracy as a system of government, with such criticism founded in skepticism about the capacity of ordinary people to govern themselves. Thomas Jefferson, even as he championed a democratic republic to replace the British monarchy, wrote of "a natural aristocracy among men [sic]. The grounds of this are virtue and talents" (Letter to John Adams, October 28, 1813).[1] The early twentieth-century essayist and social critic, H. L. Mencken, wrote the memorable barb that "democracy is the art and science of running the circus from the monkey cage" (Mencken 1982). Even the former British Prime Minister Sir Winston Churchill—best known to history for his steely-eyed defense of liberal democracy against the scourge of rising fascism during the Second World War—is well known for commenting that "democracy is the worst form of government except for all those other forms that have been tried from time to time."[2]

Views like these make quick, clever points at the expense of the average voter. But how does democracy hold up under deeper scrutiny? Does democracy, as conceived by our "Founding Fathers," work best in a select subgroup of "average voters" only (defined by race, gender, class, and territorial conquest) who held the franchise to

---

[1] Jefferson, notably, made this point to argue against Adams' partiality for what Jefferson describes as "an artificial aristocracy founded on wealth and birth." Jefferson thus saw the role of democratic citizens as discerning and voting for "the aristoi from the pseudo-aristoi ... [to] elect the real good and wise."

[2] Speech to the House of Commons, 1947.

Photo 3.1 One of the strongest defenders of liberal democracy, Winston Churchill famously said, "Many forms of Government have been tried, and will be tried in this world of sin and woe. No one pretends that democracy is perfect or all-wise. Indeed it has been said that democracy is the worst form of Government except for all those other forms that have been tried from time to time ..."
Source: © *Evening Standard*/Stringer/Hulton Archive/Getty Images.

elect the natural aristocracy of which Jefferson wrote? Can a nation that was founded at least in part on the basis of exclusion by race, gender, class, and territorial conquest evolve and adapt into a more inclusive and diverse democracy? How well does democracy endure as a political system when the average voter is more diverse and inclusive? These questions animate this textbook. To answer them, we need to first dig a little deeper into the concept of democracy.

In this chapter we explore the meaning of democracy and how it compares with "all those other forms of government" to which Churchill refers. While many systems of government and many approaches to popular rule go by the name "democracy," they are not all alike, or cut from the same cloth. We thus describe the variety of ways that a society can be democratic and discuss how this variety can either support or stifle an evolving, diversified polity. Once we have a good handle on democracy as an ideal and the institutional forms that ideal can take, we introduce several trends and themes that illustrate contemporary challenges confronting the state of democracy in the United States, trends and themes that we will return to in many of the chapters in this text.

Defining Democracy

Democracy is a term that carries different meanings to different people in different contexts. There is no uncertainty about its origins, however, as it comes from the Greek root words, *demos*, generally translated as "the people," and *kratos*, translated as "power." Democracy in practice is often traced back to Ancient Greece and their polis, or city-state. The idea that democracy is "people power" lends itself to the idea that democracy is popular sovereignty, a simple enough concept to understand.

At the same time, however, the application of this root meaning of the term democracy in practice has long been the source of vigorous disagreement. If democracy refers to the power of people, then one must ask "who are the people?" Even in the city-states of Ancient Greece, leading minds like Plato and Aristotle split sharply over who should rule. Plato was a skeptic who argued for the rule of "philosopher-kings" (someone like himself, we assume) who could best judge what was in the best interests of his fellow Athenians. Aristotle, who insisted that it was in every person's nature to be a "political animal," held firmly to the view that his fellow Athenians could and *should* govern themselves. Importantly, however, *both* Plato and Aristotle did not think of the *demos* as "the many." In fact, Athenian democracy explicitly excluded voting rights to women and children, excluded citizenship to slaves (a common practice throughout Ancient Greece), and recognized the institution of ostracism (where, by popular vote, unpopular or threatening citizens could be expelled from the city-state for a period of ten years).

Today, there is a general presumption that the "people" in a democracy is "the many." At least, that is the aspiration, if not the reality. Thus, our Declaration of Independence insists, as "self-evident" that "all Men are created equal, that they are endowed ... with certain unalienable rights" and that "governments are instituted among Men deriving their just powers from the consent of the governed." This proclamation will likely strike today's readers as ironic, even as it may continue to inspire us. The Founders after all were, literally, all men writing as though claims to equality applied only to men. Yet a central theme throughout the history of the nation has been that of defining "we the people" in ever expansive and inclusive terms. Thus, while the "people" in 1776 and 1789 explicitly limited the scope of democracy to White men who held property rights (not unlike the Greeks), the "people" today includes persons of all genders, all races, all socioeconomic backgrounds—nearly the entire adult population. In the coming chapters, we examine how this change has been achieved only through great strife, struggle, and sacrifice. And as we shall see, the work of fully democratizing our "more perfect nation" is not yet done, as even today claims to equal citizenship are limited by age, legal status, disability, the mark of a prison record, and so on.

For now, the idea of *demos* as "the many" helps to differentiate democracy from other forms of government. Compared with the rule of many, for instance, there is autocracy, which quite literally means rule by one. In autocracies, the ruler wields absolute power over their subjects, without restraint from laws, constitutions, or countervailing popular will. Monarchy includes a variety of modes of autocratic rule, whether by a king, queen, emperor, empress, or some other titled ruler. In rule by royals, governing rights are often justified in terms of divine will, rights that stay within the family (except for "Game of Thrones"-type intrigues) and passed on from generation to generation. When the control over governing institutions is seized and maintained by force, we typically apply the terms despotism and dictatorship.

Along with autocracy, or rule by one, there are also forms of rule by a select few. The most general of these is oligarchy, which by definition is rule by the few. In theory, oligarchy as a term is neutral with respect to how the few come to be selected into power; however, most recognized oligarchies are distinguished on the basis of nobility, wealth, or control over business, religious, or military power. When those few are selected because they represent a recognized elite, the system is called an aristocracy, the "rule of the best." The list of alternatives to democracy continues to multiply even today. In recent years, for instance, we see the growing use of the term netocracy—a combination of *networked* and *aristocracy*—to denote the rule by those in control of information and communication technologies. And even more recently, in a broadside against the rise of "fake news" and the alleged incompetence of ordinary voters, a political philosopher has argued the merits of epistocracy, or rule by those with knowledge.

Varieties of Democracy

We review so many alternatives to democracy in part to highlight a defining tension between the *theory* that the people in a society should have an equal and final say in how they are governed, and the *practice* of giving everyone an equal and final say. The practice is perpetually mired in the suspicion, as we quoted Mencken earlier, that governing by popular sovereignty is much like "running the circus from the monkey cage." In fact, societies that are solely governed as a direct democracy—that form in which all people in a polity participate and collectively decide how to govern themselves—are practically political unicorns.

WHAT IT LOOKS LIKE TODAY: DIRECT DEMOCRACY IN ACTION

The ideal of direct democracy is considered to be so rare in practice that textbooks often cite as examples the agora of ancient Athens or faraway cantons of Switzerland like Appenzell Innerrhoden. Yet the ideal of direct self-governance is embodied every time a jury convenes in an American courthouse and is vested with the power to discern the guilt or innocence of a fellow citizen. It also animates town hall meetings; and countries and localities throughout the world are, more and more often, turning to varieties of "citizen assemblies" as a means of institutionalizing more direct inputs into collective decision-making. Since 2009, voters in Oregon

Photo 3.2 Chris Rodgers of Eugene, Oregon, speaks to reporters about the new Citizens' Initiative Review process outside the state Capitol in Salem. The panel of twenty-four citizens recommended by a 19-5 vote that Oregon voters support Measure 85, which would eliminate corporate tax rebates known as the "kicker."
Source: © Jonathan C. Cooper/Associated Press/ Alamy Stock Photo.

have blended together two elements of direct democracy. In addition to the initiative and referendum process in which citizens can propose new statutes or decide whether to uphold or repeal existing laws, Oregonians can also participate in and are informed by a Citizens' Initiative Review (CIR) board. The CIR convenes a representative cross-section of between twenty and twenty-four participants who spend four or five days deliberating over each proposed ballot measure. These participants then submit a "Citizens' Statement" with key facts, a tally of whether they support or oppose the proposed measure, and their reasons to vote for and against it. That Citizens' Statement is then sent out by Oregon's Secretary of State to all voters before Election Day.

Why are experiments in direct democracies so rare? How well would experiments like the Oregon Citizens' Initiative Review work for the United States as a whole? Or in the community where you live?

We will see in the coming chapters that a central focus of decades of political science research is the question of whether citizens are capable of what democracy requires of them. You might ask at this point: what exactly does democracy require of its citizens? After all, there are many ways the people can actively contribute to democratic politics. Here, we briefly introduce five key descriptions of democratic participation that political scientists often discuss: electoral, representative, participatory, deliberative, and constitutional. For each, the American story of contested, yet continuing diversity and inclusion poses particular challenges and opportunities. These will be themes that recur throughout this text.

Electoral Democracy

We will start with the minimalist conception of electoral democracy. Most often attributed to the Austrian political economist Joseph Schumpeter, **electoral democracy** requires that "democracy is just a system in which rulers are selected by competitive elections" (Przeworski 1999: 23). For a political system to be considered democratic, we need ask only whether regular elections are held and whether they are competitive (typically that means the existence of more than one party). After all, countries like China, North Korea, Russia, and Venezuela hold elections regularly, but no one would seriously claim that these are democracies because the elections are not competitive. Note that in theory, minimal democracies can be neutral about a lot of things, such as political freedoms, civil and social rights, or the equal participation of all members of a polity in an election. Thus, by simply equating regular elections with democracy, countries like the Philippines, Hungary, and Turkey might count as democracies. Yet Rodrigo Duterte's wanton practice of extrajudicial killings via death squads in the Philippines, or Viktor Orbán's chokehold on a free press, an independent judiciary, and a multiparty system in Hungary, or Recep Erdogan's media censorship and sweeping arrests of journalists, social critics, and intellectuals in Turkey would strike most observers as falling far short of a common-sense understanding of democracy.

Furthermore, defining democracies simply according to whether elections are regular and competitive also implies neutrality about who is eligible to vote, who turns out to vote, and whether those who are elected actually represent who the voters are and what they want. These aspects of elections and their consequences will strike most people as fundamental to democracy. That brings us to the intuition that democracies should be representative and participatory.

Representative Democracy

Why do "strong man" rulers like Duterte, Orbán, and Erdogan run afoul of our intuitions about what is appealing about democracy? For one thing, elections are not supposed to be an end in themselves, but a means to obtaining political outcomes that benefit the many, and not the few in power. A fuller account of democracy requires certain expectations of those in power. Representative democracy is the idea that the people in a democracy exercise their popular sovereignty by voting for those political candidates and those party platforms that optimize their set of preferences over politics and policy. There is a separate class of elected officials and political elites who, on a daily basis, do the politics on behalf of the people. Representative democracy is often described in terms of principal–agent theory in economics, where citizens are principals and politicians are their agents. Importantly, representative democracies aim to achieve responsiveness and accountability. When voters express their needs and demands to their politicians, representative democracies expect them to be *responsive* to those needs and demands. If they are not responsive, representative democracies expect citizens to hold their politicians *accountable* and vote them out of office.

In terms of diversity and democracy, there are many kinds of questions we would ask of representative democracy that will be addressed in this text. For instance, do the elected and appointed officials chosen to represent citizens in a polity need to mirror what the polity looks like on dimensions such as race, gender, class, sexual orientation? In short, should Latino politicians represent Latino voters and women represent women? Is this kind of *descriptive representation* more important than *substantive representation*—that is, representation on the basis of common policy goals, collective political interests, and shared partisanship? Is an African American Democrat better represented by a White Democrat or a Black Republican?

Representative democracies expand upon the minimalist view of electoral democracy by stipulating what politicians voted into office are expected to do. So, what about voters? Strictly speaking, electoral and representative conceptions of democracy should not care about something most of us assume is a good of democratic politics—namely, whether people voted or not. Strictly speaking, under either electoral and representative democracies, we should be neutral between an election in which only 20 percent of all eligible voters turned out to vote and an election in which 80 percent voted. As it turns out, electoral participation is low in the United States, as Figure 3.1 shows. When voter turnout is measured as a percentage of each country's voting age population, the United States is the bottom half of this list of the world's advanced industrialized democracies. When turnout is measured as a percentage of registered voters in that country, however, the United States leapfrogs to near the top third of that list. What does this contrast tell us about democracy in America?

Participatory Democracy

Participatory democracy is the view that the cornerstone of democracy is action and engagement among the people itself. Often contrasted to representative democracy, the spirit of participatory democracy is captured by the philosopher Jean-Jacques Rousseau who argued that "the moment a people allows itself to be represented, it is no longer free; it no longer exists." Participation includes, but is not limited to, the act of voting. A *demos* that is more fully engaged in politics in both amount and avenues—protesting, contributing money, contacting elected officials, signing petitions, writing editorials for local papers, attending town hall meetings, even talking about politics with one's Uber driver—is more truly democratic than one in which its citizens are disengaged, alienated, distrustful, and generally inactive in politics.

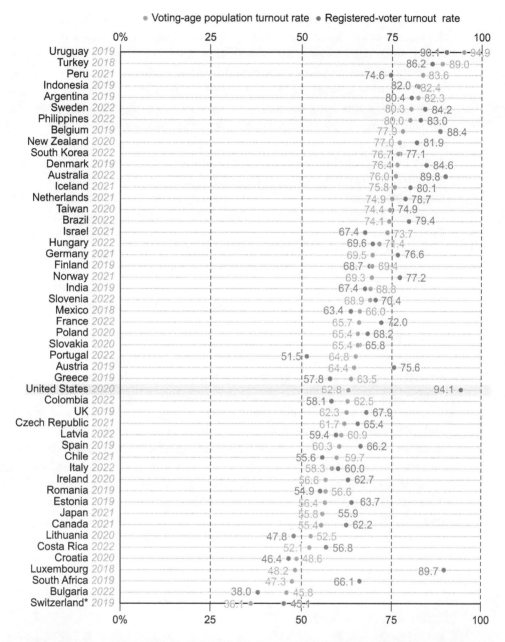

Figure 3.1 Voter Turnout in the United States Compared with Other Developed Countries. Turnout in the United States has increased in recent elections, but it still trails that of many other countries.

Source: Pew Research Center calculations based on data from International Institute for Democracy and Electoral Assistance, European Election Database, United States Election Project, Office of the Clerk of the U.S. House of Representatives, and various national election authorities.

Direct democracy, which we noted earlier as extremely rare as the principal form of democracy in any society, is a subtype of participatory democracy in which citizen engagement determines what government does, and not just who is voted to represent us. Citizens actually govern themselves, whether by taking turns serving in government, as with the Ancient Athenian practice of choosing politicians by lottery, or by bypassing politicians entirely and directly voting on policy matters through referenda, popular mandates, and other citizen-initiated ballots.

As an end in itself, our views about participatory democracy are likely to vary depending on whether engagement in politics advances the democratic values of equality and liberty. From the standpoint of equality, do all citizens in a participatory democracy share equal rights and access to participation? And are their expressed political views heard with equal influence by elite decision-makers? Campaign contributions, for instance, require disposable income as a precondition to participation, and presumptively influence politicians in a different way than votes, emails from their constituents, or protest marches in the streets. And from the standpoint of liberty, are citizens freely choosing to participate, or are they coaxed or coerced to do something they would not otherwise have done? Freedom, after all, includes the liberty to opt out of politics altogether. The British comedian Russell Brand, for instance, states a commonplace view that, "Obviously I don't vote as I believe democracy is a pointless spectacle where we choose between two indistinguishable political parties, neither of whom represent the people but instead the interest of powerful business elites that run the world."[3]

Later chapters will address whether the various venues for political engagement and civic activism are inclusive and equally open to all. Societies like the United States in 1789 in which the right to vote was exclusive to propertied White men may be democratic in some sense (i.e., they hold elections and are founded on a constitution that embodies democratic principles), but they are not terribly participatory. Societies like the United States today in which the right to vote is formally recognized for all citizens may not be terribly participatory either. Depending on what state you live in, that formal equality may coexist with political districts that are drawn so that the impact of voters of color is diluted or with voter identification laws designed to target voters of color for disenfranchisement.

Deliberative Democracy

In going from electoral to participatory ideals of democracy, the demands on citizens are ratcheted up. These demands are even higher for deliberative democracy, which is the view that democracy is realized when citizens roll up their sleeves and engage in a specific, intensive, public form of participation—namely, when they deliberate together about politics. What distinguishes deliberative democracy from other forms is the premise that, for a collective decision to be legitimate, it must be

---

[3] From the 2012 MTV Movie Awards ceremony, at: www.politico.com/blogs/click/2012/06/russell-brand-democracy-is-pointless-125168.

preceded by free, reasoned, and respectful exchange of information, ideas, and arguments. Rather than take our preferences over politics as given, deliberative democrats would argue that citizens are more likely to reach *better* decisions about politics after competing viewpoints have been argued and differences in those viewpoints settled through information and persuasion. Oregon's Citizens' Initiative Review described in this chapter's "What It Looks Like Today" box is an example of an initiative aimed at putting more deliberation into democratic decision-making at the state level.

In terms of diversity and deliberative democracy, the key questions again concern how fully inclusive and equal deliberation renders our politics. Are the public spaces in which we converse and contemplate politics equally open to all? Are all persons in a collective discussion equally engaged and authorized to contribute to the exchange? Does deliberation improve the unequal rates of participation (by race, gender, age, class, and so on), or does it make them worse? Who gets to set the agenda for what is discussed and what kind of information make for a free, reasoned, and respectful exchange?

A growing source of skepticism about the possibility of deliberative democracy in the United States is recent research suggesting that "public spheres" are not free, open, vibrant spaces for informed exchange of ideas and arguments. Rather, in reality, they are "echo chambers" where birds of an ideological feather stick together. In the United States today, the phenomenon of *"homophily"* (in which likes attract likes) is increasingly the norm, and people who can afford the choice choose to live with their political tribe. Liberals prefer living with liberal neighbors, conservatives prefer living with conservative neighbors. As Walter Lippmann, journalist and philosopher from the early twentieth century, wrote, "where all think alike, no one thinks very much." When citizens self-select by ideological beliefs, race, class, gender, and other badges of affinity and familiarity, the places where people talk politics (such as social media platforms) may serve as the breeding grounds for hate, intolerance, and greater social division rather than thriving public spheres of deliberation.

TESTING THE THEORY: BIRDS OF A FEATHER TWEET TOGETHER?

There is something close to a consensus today that too many Americans live in "echo chambers" and "filter bubbles" of confirmation bias in which people tend to only pay attention to and believe in information that validates their preexisting social and political worldviews. But what happens when such people are exposed to more diverse viewpoints? To find out, a team of sociologists surveyed both self-identified Republicans and Democrats and then randomly selected respondents from both groups with a financial incentive to share their Twitter ID (Bail et al. 2018). Those respondents then received retweeted messages with views from the opposing political perspective—twenty-four retweeted messages a day for a period of a month. Both respondents in the initial survey who received these retweets and those who did not were then reinterviewed after the one-month period. The study finds that conservatives who were exposed to retweeted liberal messages—counter-arguments and evidence that might challenge their views—actually became significantly more conservative. Liberals who were exposed to retweeted conservative messages, also became more liberal on average, but the effect was not statistically significant. How believable is this finding? Are we doomed to remain polarized and talk past one another, or does the problem reside in the medium of social media platforms like Twitter itself?

Constitutional Democracy

Finally, most recognized democracies are constitutional democracies. This variety exists in political societies built from a blueprint that both explicitly empowers and constrains the ideals of popular sovereignty. Constitutions are an agreed-upon and inscribed set of rules for governing. In the United States—the longest standing constitutional democracy in the world—we are all familiar with rules like articulated powers of different branches of government, rules that establish the scope of federal government versus state governments, rules for how laws are to be made, interpreted, amended, and so on. What makes such blueprints democratic is their emphasis on the balance of powers between the people and the state.

Constitutional democracies like the United States take seriously the idea that people in a society are born free and that they cede these natural liberties to a government and its constitution. Thus, as a blueprint, constitutions are the actualization of a social contract between governments and the people, much like the one that America's Founding Fathers made with one another on behalf of their fellow Americans and their progeny. As a social contract, constitutions are generally negotiated agreements between competing interests and contested visions for a political society. The U.S. Constitution, for instance, required the ratification of nine of the thirteen state legislatures after being drafted in 1787. That ratification was by no means assured and sparked off a spirited war of words between the Federalists, who defended the Constitution, and the Anti-Federalists, who feared a central government so powerful that it would threaten individual liberties and weaken the sovereignty of states. Ultimately, organized opposition from the Anti-Federalists and the threat that ratification might fail resulted in the inclusion of a Bill of Rights to the Constitution, which we today consider a bedrock of our constitutional democracy.

In terms of diversity and inclusion, constitutional democracies recognize basic principles like individual liberty, political equality, and human dignity, principles that are meant to apply to everyone equally, regardless of race, gender, class, religion, sexual orientation, political beliefs, or any other indelible or valued aspect of diversity and difference. In the United States, these principles are inscribed in the preamble to the U.S. Constitution and the Bill of Rights. And the triumphal story of America's struggle for freedom and equality is the story of successive additions to that initial realization, such as the articulation of due process and equal protection clauses in the

Fourteenth and Fifteenth Amendments; the passage of specific constitutional amendments that have expanded the scope of our democratic politics like the Thirteenth (abolishing slavery), Seventeenth (establishing direct elections of senators by popular vote), Nineteenth (prohibiting the denial of voting rights based on sex), Twenty-Fourth (prohibiting the denial of voting rights due to nonpayment of poll taxes or any other taxes), and the Twenty-Sixth (setting eighteen as the age of voter eligibility) amendments. Major legislative acts like the Civil Rights Act of 1964, the Voting Rights Act of 1965, and the Americans with Disabilities Act of 1990 have also extended the basic principles upon which our Constitution was founded.

Democracy in Crisis?

Democracy in America—whether appraised by its electoral, representative, participatory, deliberative, or constitutional ideals—remains a constantly changing work in progress. At the same time, democracy in America has been remarkably durable. The United States has withstood myriad tests over time from changes to its party system, presidential impeachments, multiple wars, large-scale protest movements, and even a full-scale civil war. To admirers, the durability of America's democracy is achieved by design, a system of checks and balances and off-setting institutional arrangements between levels of government, bodies of legislature, and branches of government. Ironically, the intuition behind designing a democracy this way is a deep distrust of certain forms of popular rule. James Madison famously articulated this wariness of democracy itself in *Federalist No. 10*, noting that "[a] pure democracy, by which I mean a society consisting of a small number of citizens, who assemble and administer the government in person, can admit of no cure for the mischiefs of faction." Factions for Madison were groups "united and actuated by some common impulse of passion, or of interest, adverse to the rights of other citizens, or to the permanent and aggregate interests of the community."

The mischiefs of faction that Madison, Hamilton, and other Federalists were keen to avoid in conceiving a constitution were popular uprisings like Shay's Rebellion in western Massachusetts in 1786 and 1787. Shay's Rebellion was borne out of the inequality and economic precarity that faced soldiers-turned-farmers in the aftermath of the American Revolutionary War. Veterans who turned to farming for their subsistence faced a deep recession, broken promises to be compensated for their military service, and unpayable debts that led to foreclosures and even prison. The result was a deepening schism between rural Americans and the merchant and manufacturing class based in cities, a divide that ultimately fueled civil disobedience, mass insurrection, and violent conflict.

Growing Factions

The fact that the oft-praised durability of American democracy has been achieved (at least in part) within a constitutional framework designed to limit the scope of "common impulses of passion or of interest" is a powerful reminder that the past is once again prologue to the present. As we write this text, America is rife with factions that seem to strain the idea of national unity and common political ends to breaking point. There are Americans from the left who see Tea Party activists and "Make America Great Again" Trump supporters as extremist factions that prelude a descent into authoritarianism and ethnonationalism, adverse to "the permanent and aggregate interests" of the nation. Similarly, there are Americans from the right who see organized groups like Occupy Wall Street, Black Lives Matter, Dreamers, and #MeToo, as engaged in a kind of radicalized "identity politics" or "cancel culture," also adverse to "the permanent and aggregate interests" of the nation. In short, the factionalization of American politics, together with dramatic changes in technology, wealth and inequality, globalization and mass migration, and declining public trust and social capital, are currently tinder to the view that democracy is in crisis in the United States.

Increasing Polarization

Many Americans believe that democracy is not just backsliding, but also on the verge of a precipitous descent into violence and chronic civil strife. In a recent book titled *How Democracies Die* (2018), Harvard political scientists Steve Levitsky and Daniel Ziblatt identify two diagnostic criteria for democracies at mortal risk. First, democracies are at mortal risk when competing political parties lose the norm of "mutual toleration," where mutual toleration is defined by a recognition that electoral competition is the only game in town, and the losers of one election turn their attention to trying again and winning the next election, rather than resorting to acting outside democratic institutions. Consider here that polling in the summer of 2021 continued to show that one out of every three Americans still believe that Joe Biden did not legitimately win the 2020 election and that Republican-led legislatures in states like Arizona were conducting sham audits of the 2020 vote count in heavily Democratic counties despite zero evidence of any election irregularities.

Second, Levitsky and Ziblatt argue that democracies are at mortal risk when competing political parties lose the norm of "forbearance," where forbearance is defined by an institutional commitment to playing the long game and opposing parties are willing to respect both the letter of the law and the spirit of the law. Consider here the lack of forbearance in the Republican-led Senate's unwillingness to consider Barack Obama's nomination of Merrick Garland to the U.S. Supreme Court in the last year of his presidency and their mad rush to approve Donald Trump's nomination of Amy Coney Barrett in the last months of his presidency. Or consider the active debate to suspend Senate filibuster rules on the Democratic side of the aisle in order to pass voting rights legislation.

Levitsky and Ziblatt further describe a four-part test for distinguishing when a leader is authoritarian and not democratic: when they actively question the legitimacy of their political opposition; when they rebuff and undermine democratic institutions; when they incite political violence; when they advocate limits to our civil liberties (Levitsky and Ziblatt 2018). In *How Democracies Die*, no major party candidate for president in the 100 years leading up to 2016 met even one of these four criteria except for Richard Nixon, who resigned his presidency in 1974 under a cloud of criminal suspicion from the Watergate scandal. By Levitsky and Ziblatt's scorecard, Donald Trump, our 45th President of the United States, met all four conditions of authoritarian rule. *How Democracies Die*, moreover, is only one among a long and growing list of books to publicly question the stability of democratic politics, including Jason Brennan, *Against Democracy* (2016); Nancy MacLean, *Democracy in Chains* (2017); David van Reybrouck, *Against Elections* (2016); Yascha Mounk, *The People versus Democracy* (2018); and Chris Hedges, *America: The Farewell Tour* (2018). The titles of these books alone speak volumes.

While the existential matter of whether America's centuries-old tradition of democratic politics will hold remains an open question, it is clear that one root cause of this loss of mutual toleration, the lack of institutional forbearance, and the descent into authoritarian rule is the political, social, cultural, and racial polarization of the United States. Ziblatt and Levitsky write that, "If one thing is clear from studying breakdowns throughout history, it's that extreme polarization can kill democracies (2018: 9)." We will examine the extent and sources of polarization—and the role race plays in it—in Chapter 7, "Political Participation." For now, just looking at Figure 3.2 makes it clear how far apart Democrats and Republicans in the U.S. House of Representatives and the U.S. Senate have grown since the 1970s.

Along the horizontal axis, members of Congress in the Senate and House of Representatives are placed along an ideological continuum from most liberal to most conservative using the DW-NOMINATE scoring system devised originally by political scientists Keith Poole and Howard Rosenthal. The figure compares the distribution of Democratic and Republican members of Congress across three slices of time: the 93rd Congress (1973–1974); the 103rd Congress (1993–1994); and the 112th Congress (2011–2012). The takeaway from the figure is arresting, especially considering that it does not even address the polarization of the last ten years. A half century ago, while Democrats were more liberal than Republicans, in both the Senate and the House, there was a significant degree of overlap across party lines with liberal Republicans and conservative Democrats. By the mid-1990s, much of that overlap had disappeared and in the most recent congresses, members of Congress who cross party lines ideologically (i.e., liberal Republicans or conservative Democrats) are effectively political unicorns. The middle ground for bipartisanship has nearly vanished into thin air.

This basic pattern is mirrored not just in the halls of Congress. Ordinary voters are also growing increasingly polarized as well, with self-identified Democrats becoming more liberal over time and self-identified Republicans becoming more conservative. What is perhaps most shocking, however, is that the Democrats have also become increasingly intolerant of Republicans, and Republicans intolerant of Democrats. In fact, in America today, partisans see fellow countrymen from the other parties as national threats. According to a Pew Research Center survey in 2016, 91 percent of Republicans hold an unfavorable view of Democrats, 58 percent

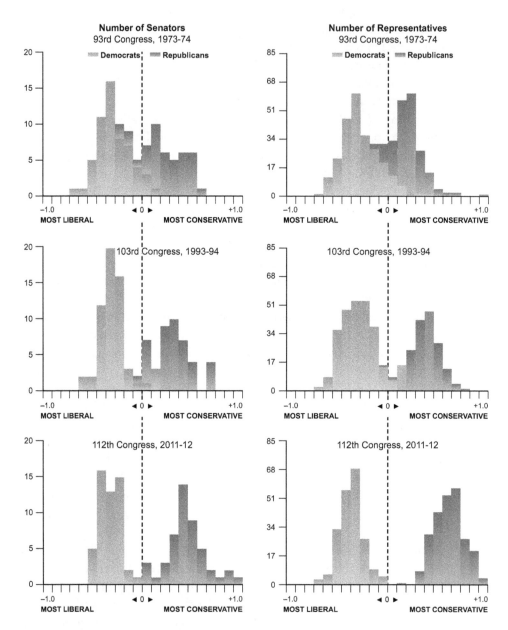

Figure 3.2 The Evolution of Political Polarization in Congress
The graphs here demonstrate how far the two parties have moved away from each other in
terms of their liberal and conservative views.
Source: Royce Carroll, Jeff Lewis, Jamels Lo, Nolan McCarty, Keith Poole and Howard
Rosenthal, Voteview.com as reported at Pew Research Center, www.pewresearch.org/fact-tank/
2014/06/12/polarized-politics-in-congress-began-in-the-1970s-and-has-been-getting-worse-ever-
since.

of them, "very unfavorable." Similarly, 86 percent of Democrats hold an unfavorable view of Republicans, 55 percent of them, "very unfavorable." Even worse, 45 percent of Republicans see the Democratic Party's policies as a threat to the nation's well-being; 41 percent of Democrats take the same dim view of the Republican Party's policies (Pew Research Center 2016).

Declining Public Trust in Government

Beyond the dangers of increasing polarization, there are other signs of trouble and crisis seemingly everywhere and seemingly all the time. American democracy is threatened by a disquieting decline in the public's trust in government. As we noted earlier, representative democracies like the United States rely on a healthy relationship between citizens (the principals) and their politicians (their agents), one in which elected and appointed officials can be entrusted to pass laws, regulations, and generally govern on behalf of citizens. Yet public trust in government has sunk to dismally low levels in the United States. Figure 3.3 combines the responses of those who trust the U.S. federal government "most of the time" and those who trust it "all of the time." That combined number has declined from a high of nearly 80 percent in the early 1960s to regularly around 20 percent in recent years.

Similarly, wherever democracies rely on institutions of governance, we should expect citizens to have high confidence in those institutions. Parents should have high confidence that their child will be in a safe, respectful learning environment when they send them off to school. Grocery shoppers should have high confidence that the food they buy is not spoiled or contaminated. So, too, should citizens have high confidence that their democratic institutions are governing well. Yet in the United States, confidence in the "people's branch of government," the United States

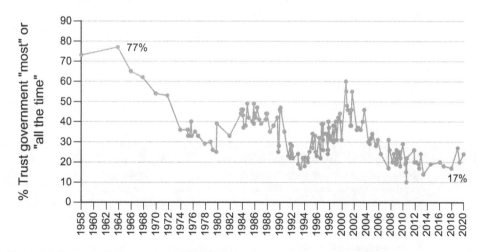

Figure 3.3 Trust in Government, 1960–2020
Source: This figure combines data from multiple polls over time: Pew Research Center, National Election Studies, Gallup, ABC/*Washington Post*, CBS/*New York Times*, and CNN Polls, www.pewresearch.org/politics/2021/05/17/public-trust-in-government-1958-2021.

Figure 3.4 Confidence in Congress, 1973–2021
From 1973 (when the question was first asked), to 2021, confidence in Congress has fallen
precipitously, with a lows of 7 percent in 2014 and 2021.
Source: "Confidence and Institutions," Gallup, https://news.gallup.com/poll/1597/confidence-
institutions.aspx.

Congress, has dropped precipitously. In 1973, the first year that the Gallup poll
asked its respondents the question, 42 percent of Americans either had "a great
deal" or "quite a lot" of confidence in Congress. By 2014, the bottom had fallen
from these numbers, with just 7 percent of Americans today with "a great deal" or
"quite a lot" of confidence in Congress. Only 4 percent had "a great deal" of
confidence, a figure that is essentially statistically indistinguishable from zero, given
the likely **margin of error** for the poll in which the data are collected (see
Figure 3.4).[4] Though confidence bounced back up to 13 percent in 2021, it was
back down to 7 percent again in 2022.

These trends and statistics paint a portrait of Americans who are increasingly
intolerant of each other across party lines and increasingly distrustful of their
government. It is little surprise then that support for democracy itself is surprisingly

---

[4] Margin of error is a number that tells you how close your sample estimate is to a true underlying statistic
in the population from which you are drawing a sample. Say, for example, you want to know what
percentage of Americans support a constitutional amendment lowering the voting age to 16 years old, and
we drew a random sample of 1,500 adults to survey their views on this question. A poll of this sample size
would have a 3 percent margin of error at the 95 percent confidence level. That means that if we field this
survey over and over 100 times, drawing one random sample of 1,500 respondents after another, we
should expect our estimate to be within 3 percentage points of the level of support for this constitutional
amendment in the U.S. adult population as a whole 95 times out of that 100 times that we fielded the poll.
Here's another way to think about the margin of error statistic: if our poll showed that 52 percent of the
1,500 Americans we surveyed favored lowering the voting age to 16, that means that we can be confident,
at the 95 percent level, that the true percentage of adult Americans favoring a lowered voting age is
somewhere between 49 percent and 55 percent.

low? In an Axios/Survey Monkey 2016 poll, 40 percent of Americans stated that they had "lost faith" in U.S. democracy and another 6 percent volunteered that they never had faith to lose (Persily and Cohen 2016).

Another indicator of support for democracy is the extent to which voters accept the results of an election as legitimate. Legitimacy is the key to a consolidated democracy, when democracy is "the only game in town, when no one can imagine acting outside of the democratic institutions, when all the losers want to do is to try again within the same institutions under which they have just lost" (Przeworski 1991: 26). Here, a Politico/Morning Consult poll fielded just after the November 2020 election found that 74 percent of Republicans did not view the election as "free and fair" and only 34 percent trusted the U.S. election system.[5] Another poll, conducted by Associated Press and the National Opinion Research Center in early 2021, after Biden was sworn in as president, found that 65 percent of Republicans did not think that Joe Biden was legitimately elected president in November 2020.[6]

Unequal Democracy?

The discussion above, along with the figures and statistics tell a sobering story about what Americans think about each other, about their government, and about democracy. Beyond a breakdown in civility and democratic sentiments, however, is the United States also in crisis in terms of what politics can or cannot deliver *substantively* for Americans? Does a political system premised on popular sovereignty generate the policies, laws, and services that the people want? One troubling sign is that democracies regularly result in extreme and worsening inequalities, and the U.S. case is especially bad. Figure 3.5 shows the astonishing rise in inequality over a generation. The share of the nation's total income garnered by its top 1 percent of earners increased from just below 11 percent of all the income earned in the United States in 1980 to more than a 20 percent share in 2018. Over the same period, the share of income earned by the bottom 50 percent of wage earners nationally—half the country's population—has moved drastically in the other direction from over 20 percent of the national income in 1980 to around 13 percent today.

Economists like Thomas Piketty (2018) have pointed out that this dynamic is visible in almost all advanced industrialized democracies. Figure 3.6 shows the picture for Western Europe. There, too, the share of total income reaped by the top 1 percent of earners has been rising since the 1980s, but the increase is far more modest. Just as importantly, the share of Western Europe's total wealth enjoyed by the bottom 50 percent has remained effectively unchanged since the 1990s. This prompts two questions. First, why is a political system that stipulates equality

---

[5] These numbers combine those who said the election was "probably" or "definitely" "free and fair" and those who said they trusted the election system "a lot" or "some," at: https://morningconsult.com/form/tracking-voter-trust-in-elections, last accessed August 30, 2021.

[6] AP/NORC, https://apnorc.org/projects/trumps-legacy-as-president, last accessed August 30, 2021.

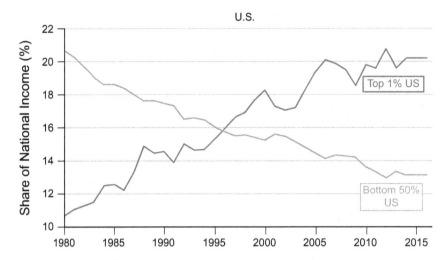

Figure 3.5 Wealth Inequality in the United States, 1980–2016
It is clear from this data that inequality in the United States has grown dramatically since the late 1990s, when the share of income earned by the top 1 percent of earners exceeded all of the earnings from the bottom 50 percent of earners.
Source: Figure E3 (top) from World Inequality Report 2018, wir2018-summary-english.pdf (wid.world).

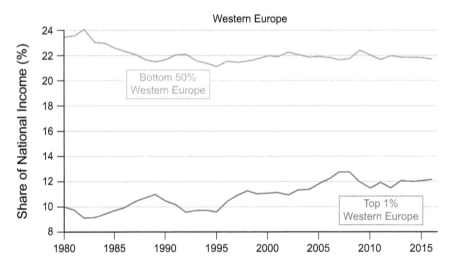

Figure 3.6 Wealth Inequality in Western Europe, 1980–2016
In Western Europe, during the same period of time as shown for the United States, the share of total income earned by the top 1 percent of earners shows a far more modest increase, and the share of earnings enjoyed by the bottom 50 percent has remained effectively unchanged since the 1990s.
Source: Figure E3 (bottom) from World Inequality Report 2018, wir2018-summary-english.pdf (wid.world).

among all citizens so good and consistent at achieving outcomes that benefit the very, very few at the expense of the many? Second, why is the U.S. case so much worse than it is for other advanced industrialized democracies?

As we will see in the coming chapters, it is not just that inequality is growing at such alarming rates in America. Certain groups like African Americans are vastly overrepresented among the least well-off and vastly underrepresented among the most well-off, a racial wealth gap that has only increased since the 1980s. In addition, as a growing body of research shows, the U.S. case is not just a story about corporate greed or the unanticipated spillover effects of a laissez-faire approach to the economy. Rather, economic inequality is both political and partisan.

Princeton economists Alan Blinder and Mark Watson find that, by nearly any measure of economic success (growth in the gross domestic product (GDP), employment and unemployment rates, wage levels, stock market returns, and so on), the U.S. economy consistently fares better under a Democratic president than it does under a Republican president (Blinder and Watson 2016). Larry Bartels' *Unequal Democracy* (2016) delves deeper into the partisan nature of inequality in America. Figure 3.7 shows that income grows at a higher rate under Democratic presidents than Republican

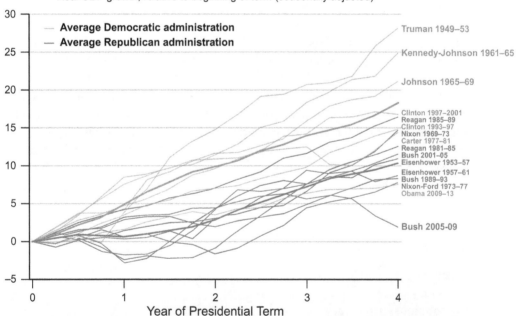

Figure 3.7 Post-Tax Income Growth under Democratic and Republican Presidents, 1949–2013 Growth in annual real income is greater under Democratic presidents than Republican presidents. The income growth under Democratic presidents also increases across the income distribution, whereas under Republican presidents, income increases the most for high income earners and the least for low income earners.

Source: Tim Hyde, "Why Does the Economy Do Better when Democrats are in the White House?" American Economic Association, June 20, 2016, www.aeaweb.org/research/why-does-the-economy-do-better-democrats-white-house Data is taken from U.S. Federal Reserve FRED database.

presidents, on average. Second, income growth is unequal under Republican presidents; Americans at the upper echelons of the income brackets can expect higher real income while those at the lowest ranks will actually see averaged losses in real income. Why are Republican presidents able to get away with this, you might ask? Bartels' answer is both political and cynical: Republican presidents time their highest rates of economic growth to coincide with presidential election years, while Democratic presidents do not.[7]

Conclusion: Democracy, if We Can Keep It?

A story is commonly told about the moments immediately after the Constitutional Convention in 1787. Elizabeth Willing Powel, a woman well known in Philadelphia's high society, asks Benjamin Franklin what sort of government the Founders had agreed to. Franklin replies wryly, "A republic, if you can keep it."[8] This quote from Franklin has been invoked repeatedly in recent years, especially to sound an alarm on the Trump presidency—during both impeachment proceedings and after a legion of Donald Trump supporters stormed the U.S. Capitol on January 6, 2021, to protest at what they saw as an illegitimate presidential election.

A key takeaway of this chapter—beyond the multiple definitions and types that democracy can take—is that democracy is complex and contested, both as an ideal and in its realization on American soil. We reviewed many figures and statistics on distrust, polarization, and inequality that are sobering and that paint a portrait of a democracy on the ropes. They make the powerful point that a bedrock of the American republic, the idea of democracy, has proven to be far more fragile and friable than we have grown accustomed to expect. What remains to be seen, and what the chapters in this text will explore in great detail, is the extent to which our tenuous democracy coexists with the remarkable and growing diversity that we reviewed in Chapter 2. The animating question once again is whether that diversity is a source of the nation's strength and stability or increasingly a root of seemingly constant threats of discord and dissensus to the nation.

KEY TERMS

Aristocracy
Autocracy
Constitutional democracy
Deliberative democracy

---

[7] Bartels is cautious about the extent to which this is achieved by design. There is, after all, a lag between proposing and enacting legislation and a further lag between enacted policies and their consequences on the economy.

[8] From Gillian Brockell, "'A Republic, If You Can Keep It': Did Ben Franklin Really Say Impeachment Day's Favorite Quote?" *Washington Post*, December 18, 2019, www.washingtonpost.com/history/2019/12/18/republic-if-you-can-keep-it-did-ben-franklin-really-say-impeachment-days-favorite-quote.

Despotism/dictatorship
Direct democracy
Epistocracy
Monarchy
Netocracy
Oligarchy
Participatory democracy
Polis
Popular sovereignty
Principal–agent theory
Representative democracy

DISCUSSION QUESTIONS

1. How democratic is politics in the United States today? By which of the many conceptions of democracy is the United States a successful democracy? By which does it fall short?
2. Is diversity a source of strength or a threat to the stability of democratic societies? What evidence supports either point of view?
3. Think about polarization in your own daily lives. Do you find that friends, family, classmates sort into "us" versus "them" according to their partisan identities? If so, how would you change this dynamic?

ANNOTATED SUGGESTED READINGS

See Danielle Allen. 2023. *Justice by Means of Democracy*. Chicago: University of Chicago Press, for a fresh philosophical argument that liberal democracies focus too much on redistribution at the expense of political equality and power sharing.
See Steve Levitsky and Daniel Ziblatt. 2018. *How Democracies Die*. New York: Penguin, two leading scholars of politics in Latin America and Europe offering a sober warning that the breakdown of "mutual toleration" could lead to the demise of democracy in the United States.
See Liliana Mason. 2018. *Uncivil Agreement: How Politics Became Our Identity*. Chicago: University of Chicago Press, describing how partisanship has become a mega-identity dividing America and absorbing what used to be cross-cutting differences by race, religion, class, gender, and region.
See Barbara Walter. 2022. *How Civil Wars Start: And How to Stop Them*. New York: Penguin, for a tough-minded analysis about the prospects for civil war in the United States, based on lessons learned from over twenty countries.

CHAPTER REFERENCES

Bail, Christopher A., Lisa P. Argyle, Taylor W. Brown, and Alexander Volfovsky. 2018. "Exposure to Opposing Views on Social Media Can Increase Political Polarization," *Proceedings of the National Academy of Science* 115(37): 9216–9221.

Bartels, L. 2016. *Unequal Democracy*. Princeton: Princeton University Press.

Blinder, A. and M. Watson. 2016. "U.S. Presidents and the US Economy," *American Economic Review* 106(4): 1015–1045.

Brennan, Jason. 2016. *Against Democracy*. Princeton: Princeton University Press

Hedges, C. 2018. *America: The Farewell Tour*. New York: Simon & Schuster.

Levitsky, S. and D. Ziblatt. 2018. *How Democracies Die*. New York: Penguin.

MacLean, Nancy. 2017. *Democracy in Chains*. New York: Random House.

Mencken, Henry Louis. [1916] 1982. *A Mencken Chrestomathy*. New York: Vintage.

Mounk, Y. 2018. *The People vs. Democracy: Why Our Freedom is in Danger and How to Save It*. Cambridge: MA: Harvard University Press.

Persily, N. and J. Cohen. 2016. "Americans are Losing Faith in Democracy—and in Each Other," *The Washington Post*, October 14. www.washingtonpost.com/opinions/americans-are-losing-faith-in-democracy–and-in-each-other/2016/10/14/b35234ea-90c6-11e6-9c52-0b10449e33c4_story.html.

Pew Research Center. 2016. "Partisanship and Political Animosity in 2016," June 22. www.pewresearch.org/politics/wp-content/uploads/sites/4/2016/06/06-22-16-Partisanship-and-animosity-release.pdf.

Piketty, T. 2018. *Capital in the Twenty-First Century*. Cambridge, MA: Harvard University Press.

Poole, K. and H. Rosenthal. 1985. "A Spatial Model for Legislative Roll-Call Analysis," *American Journal of Political Science* 29: 3547–3524.

Przeworski, A. 1991. *Democracy and the Market*. Cambridge: Cambridge University Press.

Przeworski, A. 1999. "Minimalist Conception of Democracy: A Defense," In I. Shapiro and C. Hacker-Cordon, eds., *Democracy's Value*. Cambridge: Cambridge University Press, 23–55.

Reybrouck, D. V. 2016. *Against Elections: The Case for Democracy*. London: Bodley Head.

Schumpeter, J. A. 1942. *Capitalism, Socialism, and Democracy*. New York: Harper & Bros.

Part II

The Experience of Race in the United States

4   How Do Individuals Experience Discrimination in the United States?

On July 27, 2004, Illinois State Senator—and Democratic nominee for the U.S. Senate seat from Illinois—Barack Obama delivered the keynote address at the Democratic National Convention (DNC). His rousing performance at the DNC helped to launch his national reputation within the party and was followed by a comfortable victory in the Senate race that fall. As we know, Senator Obama would go on to capture the Democratic nomination for president four years later, and was ultimately elected the 44th president of the United States with 52.9 percent of the popular vote. On January 20, 2009, Barack Obama became the first president of African descent in the 220-year history of the American presidency. Many political observers celebrated Obama's 2008 victory and understandably interpreted it as an indicator of the progress this country has made in race relations (Nagourney 2008). Somewhat surprisingly, one of the first politicians offering congratulations to the newly elected president was none other than his Republican opponent, Senator John McCain (Arizona). In his concession speech on the night of November 4, 2008, McCain went beyond the obligatory compliments that the losing candidate offers to the victorious candidate. The Arizona senator made the following comments minutes after the election had been called for President-elect Obama:

This is an historic election, and I recognize the special significance it has for African Americans and for the special pride that must be theirs tonight. I've always believed that America offers opportunities to all that have the industry and will to seize it. Senator Obama believes that, too. But we both recognize that, though we have come a long way from the old injustices that once stained our nation's reputation and denied some Americans the full blessing of American citizenship, the memory of them still have the power to wound. A century ago, Theodore Roosevelt's invitation of Booker T. Washington to visit—to dine at the White House—was taken as an outrage in many quarters. America today is a world away from the cruel and prideful bigotry of that time. There is no better evidence of this than the election of an African-American to the presidency of the United States. Let there be no reason now for any American to fail to cherish their citizenship in this, the greatest nation on Earth. (McCain 2008)

Obama's victory notwithstanding, the popular narrative about the implications of the 2008 campaign often overlook the role that racial discrimination played in the presidential contest and in contemporary American society more broadly. For example, Hutchings (2009) found that as a consequence of anti-Black prejudice,

Photo 4.1 On Tuesday, November 4, 2008, Senator Barack Obama of Illinois was elected the 44th president of the United States by a wide margin, opening a new chapter in the country's history as the first African American president-elect.
Source: Photo Andrew Harrer © Emmanuel Dunand/Contributor/AFP/Getty Images.

candidate Obama performed about three percentage points lower among Whites than he would have in the absence of racial intolerance (see also Kinder and Dale-Riddle 2012; Piston 2010). Lewis-Beck and his colleagues provide a more extensive analysis of the 2008 election cycle (Lewis-Beck, Tien, and Nadeau 2010). They report that, although decisive, Obama's 2008 victory falls short of a "landslide," which they define as 75 percent of the 538 Electoral College votes or 55 percent of the popular vote. One way in which Lewis-Beck and his co-authors highlight Obama's underperformance is by noting that in elections for the House of Representatives, Democrats received a higher percentage of the popular vote in 2008 than any political party had received since 1982. Finally, relying on a forecasting model that utilizes macroeconomic indicators to predict presidential vote share as well as national survey data, Lewis-Beck and his collaborators conclude that Obama lost about 5 percent of the popular vote due to anti-Black prejudice.

One of the racially tinged challenges candidate Obama faced in the 2008 presidential campaign, and to some degree in his reelection bid in 2012, were the

Photo 4.2 Senator John McCain of Arizona, Republican presidential nominee, delivers his speech conceding to Barack Obama, during an election night gathering outside the Biltmore Hotel in Phoenix, Arizona.
Source: © Bloomberg/Contributor/Getty Images.

persistent rumors about his religion and citizenship status. In short, some of his political opponents—including his eventual successor in the White House, Donald J. Trump—argued that Obama was not born in the United States and was therefore ineligible to hold the office of the president. Barack Obama's birth certificate confirms that he was in fact born in the United States, in the state of Hawaii.[1] Similar misperceptions arose about Obama's religion. Some suggested that he was secretly a Muslim, even though Obama frequently professed his Christian faith. In spite of the mainstream media's efforts to debunk both rumors, a significant fraction of Americans continued to subscribe to them both before and after the 2008 election. For example, an April 2011 survey from USA Today/Gallup found that 9 percent of Americans believed that President Obama was "definitely" not born in the United States (Newport 2011). About 15 percent indicated that he was "probably" born outside the United States. Not surprisingly, these figures varied considerably across party lines. This same USA Today/Gallup survey found that 43 percent (combining "definitely" and "probably") of

---

[1] Ironically, Obama's 2008 opponent, John McCain, was not born in the United States but on a Naval Air base in the Panama Canal Zone. Both of McCain's parents were U.S. citizens, however, so, in spite of the minor controversy this matter caused during the presidential campaign, there is little doubt that McCain was eligible to serve as president.

Republican Party identifiers indicated some skepticism regarding whether the president was born in the United States.

The anti-Black prejudice encountered by Barack Obama during the 2008 presidential campaign and the widespread belief in the negative, and erroneous, rumor about his citizenship are contemporary examples of discrimination. For a significant number of American voters, candidate Obama was considered unacceptable for the office of the presidency simply because of his racial background. This chapter will provide a working definition and brief history of discrimination in America—paying particular attention to the period following the Civil War when passage of the Thirteenth, Fourteenth, and Fifteenth Amendments to the Constitution (collectively known as the Civil War Amendments) extended formal citizenship rights to all Americans (although Native Americans would have to wait until 1924 before Congress granted them full citizenship). Our aim will be to highlight some of the more prominent, and neglected, examples of discrimination throughout American history and across a broad range of socially salient groups with a particular focus on race, ethnicity, and color. After reviewing this issue from a historical perspective, we will devote most of the remainder of the chapter to exploring the contemporary manifestations of race-based discrimination and other forms of discrimination. This discussion will summarize some of the ways that discrimination is measured as well as how it is perceived by various groups in society. As Senator John McCain indicated in his concession speech following the 2008 presidential election, there is in fact much to celebrate about the country's progress over time regarding race-based discrimination. Nevertheless, the weight of the evidence will demonstrate that the senator was unduly optimistic when he indicated that "America today is a world away from the cruel and prideful bigotry" of previous eras.

Defining Discrimination

Social psychologist Gordon W. Allport offered a succinct definition of discrimination in his classic 1954 book, *The Nature of Prejudice*. He wrote that, "Discrimination only comes about when we deny to individuals or groups of people equality of treatment which they may wish" (Allport 1954: 51). Allport recognized that this definition was overly broad however as, for example, excluding someone on the basis of their *individual quality* of unruliness, criminality, or disagreeableness seems quite reasonable to most people. The form of discrimination that we are most concerned with in this chapter involves differential treatment based on racial or ethnic categorization (Allport 1954). In short, discrimination of this sort involves singling out an individual or group of individuals for mistreatment on the basis of their membership in a particular racial or ethnic group. The United Nations provides a useful definition of racial discrimination in the International Convention on the Elimination of All Forms of Racial Discrimination:

[Racial discrimination in international law is] any distinction, exclusion, restriction or preference based on race, colour, descent or national or ethnic origin which has the purpose or effect of nullifying or impairing the recognition, enjoyment or exercise, on an equal footing, of human rights and fundamental freedoms in the political, economic, social, cultural or any other field of public life. (United Nations Human Rights: Office of the High Commissioner 1965)

Another useful definition of discrimination comes from the National Research Council (NRC), who convened a panel of the nation's leading social scientists to set common standards on how best to define and measure discrimination. The NRC panel offers the important distinction that racial discrimination can come from direct and indirect origins: directly, as "differential treatment on the basis of race that disadvantages a racial group" and indirectly as "treatment on the basis of inadequately justified factors other than race that disadvantages a racial group (differential effect)" (National Research Council 2004: 39). The differential treatment and differential effect bases are similar to the two current legal standards for discrimination in U.S. case law: disparate treatment discrimination and disparate impact discrimination. As the NRC report defines it, disparate treatment racial discrimination occurs when "an individual is treated less favorably—for example, is not hired for a job—because of his or her race," while disparate impact racial discrimination occurs "if a behavior or practice that does not involve race directly has an adverse impact on members of a disadvantaged racial group without a sufficiently compelling reason" (2004: 40–41). Using a check-box to ask if job applicants have a criminal record is an example of an employment hiring practice that typically has a disparate racial impact. As this example illustrates, such practices may or may not be illegal. In the next two chapters, we consider two other key ways in which discrimination, whether based on race, color, ethnicity, religion, or any other arbitrary classification, can manifest itself: individual discrimination and institutional discrimination (Ture and Hamilton [1967] 1992). This framework, first introduced by social activist Kwame Ture[2] and political scientist Charles Hamilton, defines individual level discrimination as discrimination that is typically unplanned or unsanctioned by the state (e.g., politicians, the local police, etc.). Institutional discrimination, on the other hand, is discrimination associated with state action, or the seemingly race-neutral codified rules and procedures of governmental and non-governmental institutions such as the mass media, private businesses, and higher education. Ture and Hamilton (1992) provide an example of each type of discrimination in their landmark book, *Black Power: The Politics of Liberation*:

When white terrorists bomb a black church and kill five black children, that is an act of individual racism, widely deplored by most segments of the society. But when in that same city—Birmingham, Alabama—five hundred black babies die each year because of the lack of proper food, shelter and medical facilities, and thousands more are destroyed and maimed physically, emotionally and intellectually because of conditions of poverty and discrimination in the black community, that is a function of institutional racism. When a black family

---

[2] Kwame Ture was formerly known as Stokely Carmichael, a prominent leader of the Student Non-Violent Coordinating Committee, in the 1960s.

moves into a home in a white neighborhood and is stoned, burned or routed out, they are victims of an overt act of individual racism which many people will condemn—at least in words. But it is institutional racism that keeps black people locked in dilapidated slum tenements, subject to the daily prey of exploitative slumlords, merchants, loan sharks and discriminatory real estate agents.

In this chapter we will focus on individual rather than institutional manifestations of racial or ethnic discrimination, although we will at times discuss the actions of individual actors within powerful institutions who may be engaged in unofficial acts of discrimination. For example, during the era of Reconstruction, the period after the Civil War when the federal government took control of the South to help rebuild the region, White mobs or paramilitary groups frequently sought to discourage African American political participation. As discussed below, these actions were sometimes aided and abetted by local law enforcement officials (Foner 2014). However, because the law did not sanction this violence, it falls more under the category of individual discrimination as opposed to institutional discrimination. We will delve more deeply into institutional discrimination in Chapter 5.

Discrimination before and after Reconstruction

Individual acts of discrimination—race-based or otherwise—have obviously unfolded in this country since the founding of the Republic. These acts were encouraged by a contemporary political climate that regarded most African-descended people as chattel slaves and most Native Americans as bloodthirsty savages. For Blacks at least, this situation would begin to shift with the conclusion of the Civil War in 1865. As a consequence of the defeat of the Confederacy, events were set in motion that would culminate with the formal abolition of slavery (Thirteenth Amendment to the Constitution); the incorporation of the Bill of Rights such that its freedoms applied to both federal and state governments (Fourteenth Amendment); the establishment of birthright citizenship (Fourteenth Amendment); and the extension of voting rights to all adult males over the age of 21, "regardless of race, color, or previous condition of servitude" (Fifteenth Amendment). These events are important because they ultimately gave rise to countervailing efforts to restrict these newly acquired freedoms. The people who opposed these efforts adopted a variety of different tactics that can be broadly characterized as discrimination. Swedish economist Gunnar Myrdal noted in his classic work *An American Dilemma* that these tactics included, "... legal trickery, unfair administration, intimidation and forthright violence" (Myrdal 1944: 446).

At the conclusion of the Civil War, federal troops were stationed throughout many parts of the South. In order to ensure the region's orderly reintegration into the Union, the majority Republican Congress passed what came to be known as the Reconstruction Acts of 1867 and 1868. Essentially, these four statutes divided the rebellious Southern states into five military districts that would be administered by military governors until the state constitutions could be rewritten to the satisfaction of Congress. These Acts also extended voting rights to all freedmen—formerly enslaved African American adult males—andb facilitatead their participation in the state Constitutional Conventions that were charged with rewriting the various state constitutions (the Fifteenth Amendment would not be ratified until 1870).

One important point to bear in mind about the era of Reconstruction is that African Americans represented a much larger fraction of the South's population than is the case today. For example, of the eleven states that made up the Confederacy, seven had populations that were at least 40 percent Black according to the 1870 U.S. Census.[3] Today, there are no states where Blacks make up 40 percent or more of the population. At the end of the Civil War, African Americans represented the majority of the population in three states: Louisiana, Mississippi, and South Carolina. Consequently, if elections were conducted fairly in each state, voters interested in the reestablishment of White supremacy in the South would have a difficult time mobilizing a winning electoral coalition. This is one of the primary reasons why White paramilitary groups (i.e., quasi-military forces unauthorized by state or local government) with the express purpose of undermining democracy in the region sprang up during this period. At the same time, many laws were passed in local and state governments in the South to marginalize Blacks and effectively deny them the rights granted during Reconstruction. These laws, which established different rules for Blacks and Whites, came to be known as Jim Crow laws and led to the Jim Crow era of legalized racial segregation. In the next chapter we will discuss this period in greater detail.

Sociologist Guy B. Johnson is quoted at length on the rampant anti-Black violence during Reconstruction in Myrdal's *An American Dilemma*:

The Ku Klux Klan and a dozen similar organizations which sprang up over the South were as inevitable as a chemical reaction. Their purpose was punitive and regulatory, the restoration of absolute white supremacy. They flogged, intimidated, maimed, hanged, murdered, not only for actual attacks and crimes against whites, but for all sorts of trivial and imagined offenses ... Every Negro militia drill, every meeting or convention for the political or social advancement of the Negro took on the aspect of a "conspiracy" or an "insurrection." The number of Negroes killed during Reconstruction will never be known. Five thousand would probably be a conservative estimate. (Myrdal 1944: 449–450)

The Colfax Massacre

Perhaps the deadliest example of anti-Black violence during the Reconstruction era occurred in 1873 in Louisiana and has variously been described as "The Colfax Riot," or the "The Colfax Massacre" (Foner 1988). This incident arose from the disputed gubernatorial election of 1872. Forces aligned with the Democratic candidate, John McEnery, declared victory in the contest, as did allies of Republican candidate, William Pitt Kellogg. The state courts adjudicated in favor of the Democrat but a federal court judge in New Orleans overruled the decision in favor of the Republican. Armed skirmishes between Democrats and Republicans erupted

[3] The eleven Confederate states were Alabama, Arkansas, Florida, Georgia, Louisiana, Mississippi, North Carolina, South Carolina, Tennessee, Texas, and Virginia.

Photo 4.3 This engraving depicting Blacks gathering the dead and wounded after the Colfax Massacre on May 10, 1873, was published in *Harper's Weekly*.
Source: Photo MPI © MPI/Stringer/Archive Photos/Getty Images.

throughout Louisiana in the aftermath of the disputed election. However, because the freedmen were overwhelmingly aligned with the Republicans, the violence often broke down along racial lines. In the spring of 1873, Black Republicans occupied the Colfax courthouse in Grant Parish, in part because of fears that the Democrats might take control of the building. White paramilitary groups, inflamed by media reports of atrocities committed by local Black residents, engaged in an hours-long battle with the Republicans on Easter Sunday, April 13. Eventually, the inhabitants of the courthouse were overwhelmed and many of the fleeing Republicans were shot dead. Estimates of the death toll are imprecise, as many of the bodies were subsequently dumped into the river. However, historian Eric Foner cites one source as estimating that 280 Blacks were killed in the Colfax massacre. Whatever the exact number of deaths, Foner describes the event as "the bloodiest single instance of racial carnage in the Reconstruction era ..." (Foner 1988: 437).

Lynchings and Riots

In the next chapter, we will discuss in greater detail how Reconstruction was succeeded by the Jim Crow era of legalized racial segregation, but here we concern ourselves with one of the chief forms of unauthorized violence visited upon African

Americans in the Reconstruction and Jim Crow eras: lynching. Although the practice of lynching is often associated with hanging, victims might be killed in a variety of different ways, including being shot or burned alive. Castration and other forms of dismemberment were not uncommon. Lynching was widespread throughout the Reconstruction and Jim Crow periods and, although typically carried out by nongovernmental actors, was nevertheless tolerated or condoned by local, state, and federal officials. In *An American Dilemma*, Myrdal cites figures from the Tuskegee Institute that identifies 3,833 lynchings between 1889 and 1940 (Myrdal 1944: 561). About 80 percent of the victims were African American, according to this study. Roughly 90 percent of the lynchings documented by the Tuskegee Institute occurred in the South. Of the remaining 10 percent, most occurred in states that border the South.[4] Myrdal reports that lynching mostly occurred in rural and high poverty locales. He also notes that, although the slightest infraction or perceived infraction (e.g., testifying in court against a White man, seeking employment "out of place," offensive language, boastful remarks, etc.) could lead to lynching, the unmistakable goal was, ". . . not merely a punishment against an individual but a disciplinary device against the Negro group" (Myrdal 1944: 561).[5]

HOW IT HAPPENED: IDA B. WELLS-BARNETT AND THE CRUSADE AGAINST LYNCHING

One of the most renowned and effective activists against the practice of lynching was journalist and social activist Ida B. Wells-Barnett. Wells was born into slavery in Mississippi in 1862 and freed by the Emancipation Proclamation in 1865; she was orphaned at age 16. To support her four younger siblings, Wells became a teacher. Later, she moved to Memphis, Tennessee, where she became increasingly outspoken about the unfair treatment of Blacks and women. One incident propelled Wells in her activism. She had purchased a first-class railroad ticket in Memphis, Tennessee, but was ordered to leave the ladies' car because the emerging Jim Crow laws forbade Blacks from riding in first class. Wells refused to leave and was subsequently removed after a brief struggle (she initially bit the conductor who tried to remove her). She sued on the grounds that the railroad company had accepted her payment for first-class accommodation but refused to provide them on account of her race. Although Wells' suit was successful at the lower court level, she ultimately lost in the Tennessee State Supreme Court. However, the publicity surrounding her case led her to write a series of letters describing her suit in various Black newspapers. The popularity of these essays helped to launch her new career as a pioneering journalist.

---

[4] Border states where lynching was relatively prominent include Maryland, West Virginia, Ohio, Indiana, Illinois, and Kansas.

[5] The conventional wisdom holds that lynchings were often employed against Black men accused of sexually assaulting White women. However, Myrdal cites a report that found that in only 23 percent of lynchings was the victim accused of raping or attempting to rape a White woman.

Photo 4.4 American journalist and civil rights activist, Ida B. Wells in 1920.
Source: Photo Chicago History Museum © Chicago History Museum/ Contributor/Archive Photos/Repetition Getty Images.

In keeping with her defiant personality, Wells began writing a series of columns condemning lynching and praising Black efforts to resist racial violence. Her controversial efforts intensified in 1892 when three Black men with whom she was acquainted were lynched because a rival White businessman felt threatened by the men's economic success (Dray 2002). This lynching was a turning point for Wells. She began documenting the reasons Black men were lynched and noted that— contrary to popular opinion at the time—the allegation that a Black man had raped a White woman was only raised in about two-thirds of these crimes. Moreover, according to her reporting, the allegation of "rape" when it was levied, was simply a face-saving effort to conceal a consensual interracial romance. Wells' courageous reporting frequently placed her in great danger, and in 1892 the Memphis office of her newspaper was ransacked, and threats were issued in the local White press that Wells herself would be lynched if she ever returned to the city. She relocated to New York City but continued her activism against lynching. And in 1909, she helped to co-found the National Association for the Advancement of Colored People (NAACP).

More recently, the Equal Justice Initiative (EJI), led by attorney and civil rights activist Bryan Stevenson, has investigated the frequency of lynching in the South and provides a figure slightly higher than that derived from the Tuskegee

Photo 4.5 Bryan Stevenson speaks at the opening of the Equal Justice Initiative Memorial for Peace and Justice in Montgomery, Alabama, on April 26, 2018. The memorial is in memory of those who were lynched in each county in the South.
Source: © Associated Press/Alamy Stock Photo.

Institute: 4,075.[6] In April 2018, the EJI opened the National Memorial for Peace and Justice, which they describe as "... the nation's first memorial dedicated to the legacy of enslaved black people, people terrorized by lynching, African Americans humiliated by racial segregation and Jim Crow, and people of color burdened with contemporary presumptions of guilt and police violence."[7]

Violence against Mexicans and Other Minorities

African Americans were not the only minority group targeted for lynching. Other marginalized groups in the United States, including Jewish Americans, Native Americans, and Chinese immigrants were also victimized by this illegal practice. Historians William D. Carrigan and Clive Webb summarize some of the more egregious examples in their 2013 book, *Forgotten Dead: Mob Violence against*

---

[6] The Equal Justice Institute report focuses on lynchings directed specifically at African Americans in the states of Alabama, Arkansas, Florida, Georgia, Kentucky, Louisiana, Mississippi, North Carolina, South Carolina, Tennessee, Texas, and Virginia between 1877 and 1950, https://eji.org/racial-justice/legacy-lynching.

[7] See at: https://museumandmemorial.eji.org/memorial.

Mexicans in the United States, 1848–1928, and in their subsequent *New York Times* editorial (Carrigan and Webb 2013; 2015). These authors argue that during the period of their study, vigilantes may have murdered thousands of Mexicans, although they can only document 547 specific episodes. In one incident they uncovered, a 20-year-old Mexican laborer named Antonio Rodriguez was arrested and charged with killing a local rancher's wife in Rock Springs, Texas, in November of 1910. Some time later, a mob abducted Rodriguez from the jail, tied him to a tree and burned him alive. As with many lynchings of Blacks in the Jim Crow South, the local newspapers reported that thousands attended Rodriguez's lynching, as if it were some kind of sporting event. According to Carrigan and Webb, no one was ever charged with Rodriguez's torture and subsequent murder.

One important difference between the experiences of African Americans and Mexican Americans during this period involves the country of Mexico. The United States had a very contentious relationship with its southern neighbor in the years covered by the Carrigan and Webb study. In 1846, the United States and Mexico were involved in a war that ended in Mexico's defeat two years later. The agreement that officially ended hostilities between the two countries, the Treaty of Guadalupe Hildalgo, stipulated that roughly half of Mexican territory (including the present-day states of Arizona, California, Nevada, Utah, most of New Mexico and Colorado, and portions of several other states) would now become part of the United States. The former Mexican citizens who remained in these territories would become American citizens, but they and their descendants would nevertheless face discrimination in their new country. Moreover, when Mexico experienced political turmoil—as was the case in the early 1900s—this also had implications for the treatment of Mexican Americans. For example, the violence associated with the Mexican Revolution (1910–1920) would occasionally spill over into parts of the United States that bordered Mexico. Carrigan and Webb recounted one incident that occurred in 1917–1918. Sometime during this period, Mexican rebels had attacked a ranch in Presidio County, Texas. When a band of Texas Rangers and local ranchers arrived on the scene, they assumed that Mexican American locals had assisted the Mexican rebels. Roughly fifteen Mexican American men were rounded up, directed to a rock bluff near the village of Porvenir, and executed on the spot. This event has come to be known as the "Porvenir Massacre."

The 1919 Race Riots

Riots represent yet another form of extrajudicial violence directed at racial minorities. Unlike lynching, race riots have historically been as likely to occur in the North as in the South (Myrdal 1944). Although the urban unrest of the 1960s is well known, some may be less familiar with the country's most deadly racial disturbances, which occurred following the end of the First World War. These events, which unfolded in the summer and fall of 1919 in twenty-six cities, are collectively referred to as the Red Summer. The scholar-activist, W. E. B. Du Bois described the factors contributing to the Red Summer in his book, *Dusk of Dawn* (Du Bois 1940).

He notes that the year 1919 was a particularly difficult one for African Americans. He reports that seventy-seven Blacks were lynched that year, including one Black woman and eleven First World War veterans. Eleven of these individuals were burned alive. Du Bois, who was the editor of the NAACP journal, *The Crisis*, identified two major causes of the outbreak in racial violence in 1919. The first was the economic competition that emigrating Black workers represented to Whites in other parts of the country. As Blacks began migrating out of the South following the war, they inevitably began competing with Whites for factory jobs throughout the Northeast and Midwest, which stirred up resentment among Whites about their job security.

The second explanation for the racial violence was the bitterness that many White servicemen, particularly those in the South, felt toward African American veterans of the war. In short, Black servicemen received both gratitude and a measure of freedom while in France during the war, and these experiences made the returning soldiers less inclined to tolerate the unyielding racial hierarchy of the segregated South.

HOW IT HAPPENED: THE GREAT MIGRATION, 1915–1970

Between 1915 and 1970 approximately 6 million Black southerners left the Jim Crow South for the comparatively greater economic and political freedoms in the Northeast, Midwest, and West. Historians and political observers refer to this period as "The Great Migration." The First World War was perhaps the greatest factor leading to the Great Migration. Many factories in the North faced severe manpower shortages because of the war due to the draft and declining immigration levels. Employers addressed this problem by recruiting Blacks from the South—where, prior to the First World War, about 90 percent of the African American population resided. This movement did not simply change the fortunes of these fleeing families, but also transformed the demographics of major American cities and fundamentally altered national politics (Wilkerson 2010). During the early decades of the twentieth century, for example, Harlem went from being a majority-White neighborhood to majority-Black. And free from "grandfather clauses," poll taxes, literacy tests, and other efforts to disenfranchise them, Blacks in the North were able to exercise their voting rights for the first time since the end of Reconstruction. This was most evident in the 1948 presidential election where the Black vote (outside the Jim Crow South) was widely regarded as being instrumental to President Truman's narrow electoral victory (Anderson 2003).

Of all the outbreaks of race-based violence in 1919, the riot—or more accurately, the massacre—that occurred near Elaine, Arkansas, was by far the deadliest. The journalist Robert Whitaker, describes the tragic events in his book, *On the Laps of Gods* (2009). On the night of September 30 in the small town of Hoop Spur in rural

Photo 4.6 U.S. soldiers of 57th Infantry from Camp Pike in Little Rock were dispatched during the race/riot/massacre that occurred in Elaine, Arkansas, in 1919.
Source: Photo Circa Images © Universal History Archive/Contributor/Universal Images Group/Getty Images.

Phillips County, a group of 100 or so African American sharecroppers had come together to discuss unionizing in order to obtain better pay and working conditions from plantation owners. The White landowners were opposed to plans to form a union and had previously sought to disrupt such meetings. On the night in question, Black armed guards were stationed at the meeting location, a local church, in order to prevent any disruptions. There was a confrontation at the church involving the armed guards as well as a White deputy sheriff and a White security officer, employed by the Missouri-Pacific Railroad. Both White men were shot, with the security guard suffering fatal injuries.

Over the next few days, a White mob drawn from the local area, including parts of nearby Mississippi, acting in concert with federal troops responding to the request of the governor, descended on the Black community in Elaine. In the ensuing massacre, some reports suggest that as many as 200 African American men, women, and children were killed. No Whites were ever prosecuted for this mayhem. Instead, 122 Blacks were charged with various offenses, with over seventy being charged with murder. Twelve were quickly tried and convicted for murder and given the death penalty. The remaining defendants charged with murder pleaded to lesser charges, such as second-degree murder, receiving sentences as high as twenty-one years. The murder convictions for the twelve men initially convicted were appealed, with one group eventually freed by the Arkansas Supreme Court, and another group eventually freed after a successful appeal to the U.S. Supreme Court. As part of the negotiation for their release, this second group had to plead guilty to second-degree murder and serve five-year sentences beginning with the time when they were initially incarcerated.[8]

Assessing Contemporary Discrimination

The discrimination underlying the race-based violence in Elaine, Arkansas, seems clear-cut and unmistakable, and there are many more instances of racial violence in twentieth-century America that could be mentioned here. In 1943 alone, the country was racked by the "Zoot Suit" riots in Los Angeles; the Beaumont, Texas, race riot; the Harlem, NY, race riot in August; and the 1943 Detroit race riot, at Belle Isle Park. Fortunately, we do not witness such widespread acts of racial violence today, but one only needs to pay attention to the daily news to know that individual acts of racial violence are still committed against Blacks and other minorities. And, of course, nonviolent forms of discrimination also are prevalent. It is important to know how to assess incidents of violence and other forms of discrimination in order to determine how to end them.

Incidence of Hate Crimes

One way to quantify discrimination is with the official accounting of hate crimes. The Federal Bureau of Investigation (FBI) has collected information on hate crimes committed throughout the country since 1992. Hate crimes are defined by the FBI as a "criminal offense committed against a person or property motivated in whole or in part by an offender's bias against a race, religion, disability, sexual orientation, ethnicity, gender, or gender identity" (Federal Bureau of Investigation: Hate Crimes, n.d.). The most recent hate crime statistics at the time of this writing are from 2019. In that year, the FBI reported that there were 8,812 victims of hate crimes. Hate crimes based on race or ethnicity are by far the most common type of offense. According to the FBI report, over half or about 56 percent of hate crime victims were targeted because of their racial or ethnic background. The second highest category (19 percent) involves religion. Of the 4,930 victims of racially motivated hate crimes, the FBI reports that almost half (48 percent) were singled out because of the offender's anti-Black bias. Interestingly, about 16 percent of hate crime victims in 2019 were targeted because of anti-White bias. They report that 14 percent were victimized because of anti-Hispanic or anti-Latino bias, about 3 percent were the victims of anti-Native American bias, and 4 percent were victims of anti-Asian American bias.

Audit Studies

Of course, as we have discussed, violence is not the only form of discrimination people face. Determining whether one has been discriminated against is not always

---

[8] See at: https://encyclopediaofarkansas.net/entries/elaine-massacre-of-1919-1102.

easy. An individual may genuinely believe that he or she has faced discrimination but that conclusion could nevertheless be mistaken. Similarly, an individual may have no suspicion that they have been discriminated against when, in fact, they have been victimized by racial or ethnic bias. For example, the typical job applicant will usually not be awarded the job for which he or she has applied—if only because the demand for the position often outstrips the supply of available jobs. Since the applicant is not privy to the decision-making process of their prospective employer, they will have no way of knowing why they did not get the job and likely assume a more qualified applicant was chosen. In short, they will have no direct knowledge of whether they were unlawfully discriminated against based on their race or ethnicity.

In order to assess more directly whether an individual has encountered discrimination, researchers and community activists in the 1950s devised what are known as audit studies. Audit studies can be conducted either in person or through correspondence. With in-person audit studies, individuals of different racial or ethnic background are chosen to apply for rental housing units, to contact a realtor regarding a home purchase, or to apply for advertised job openings. The individuals involved in the audit are typically selected so as to be essentially similar on all relevant characteristics other than race. So, for example, the testers are selected to be comparable on age, educational background, income, personality, attractiveness, etc. If, therefore, it is found that the minority tester is less likely to rent a room, or receive a call-back for a job interview, then we can conclude that the discrepancy is likely due to racial bias. In the case of correspondence audits, researchers contact landlords or employers via mail or online to inquire about an opening. If inquiries associated with minority applicants (often conveyed through ethnic-sounding names) are less likely to result in a favorable response, relative to a White applicant, then this would also be interpreted as evidence of racial bias.

Researchers have conducted numerous audit studies in both the housing and employment markets. Oh and Yinger (2015) provide an excellent summary of the literature on housing audits in their article titled, "What Have We Learned From Paired Testing in Housing Markets?" These authors review the results of housing audits sponsored by the U.S. Department of Housing and Urban Development (HUD) conducted in 1977, 1989, 2000, and 2012. Each study involved at least 3,000 testers operating in at least twenty-three metropolitan areas. In the most recent Housing Discrimination Study (2012), Oh and Yinger found that White renters were favored over Black renters about 9 percent of the time. (Specific features of the four studies differed over time, so direct comparisons are not possible.) Whites were favored over Latino renters about 10 percent of the time. In the case of home buying, the authors report that Whites were given more favorable treatment than equally qualified African Americans approximately 10 percent of time. There was no indication in 2012 that Whites were favored over Latinos when it came to buying a home. The authors also report that some forms of housing discrimination have diminished over time, such as whether minorities would be shown rental units. However, other forms of discrimination have increased over time, such as steering minority home-seekers away from predominantly White neighborhoods and toward majority-minority neighborhoods (Oh and Yinger 2015).

Quillian et al. (2017) provide a summary of the literature on audit studies in U.S. labor markets. These authors examined every study, published or unpublished, on employment audits since 1972. They included both in-person audit studies and correspondence audit studies. Quillian and his colleagues find on average that Whites receive 36 percent more "call-backs" or follow-up interviews after an initial job application than African Americans, and 24 percent more call-backs than Latinos. The bulk of the studies examined by Quillian and his co-authors occurred in 1989 or later. When focusing on this group of studies they find no evidence that anti-Black discrimination has declined in the 1989 to 2015 period. In the case of Latinos, there is some evidence of a decline in discrimination over time, but because of the relatively small number of audit studies involving Latino participants, there was some uncertainty regarding this result.

In a follow-up study, Quillian, Lee, and Oliver (2020) examine whether discrimination also unfolds *after* the call-back stage of the job search process. The authors note that most audit studies seeking to document racial discrimination in the labor market focus only on the stage at which the applicant is called back for an interview. However, even if one gets past this stage, racial and ethnic minorities may encounter discrimination as to whether a job offer is ultimately extended to them. Fortunately, the authors found that some audit studies do cover the stage involving job offers and in a systemic evaluation of a dozen such studies—half in the United States and half in Europe—they found "considerable additional discrimination in hiring after call-back" (Quillian et al. 2020: 732). Specifically, across twelve studies from 1991 to 2010, involving 13,000 applications, they found that "minority candidates experience on average more than twice as much discrimination overall in the job offer outcome as in the call back outcome" (748). This suggests that, on average, White applicants receive about 48 percent more job offers than equally qualified Latino applicants, and about 72 percent more offers than equally qualified Black applicants (Quillian et al. 2020).

Attitudes about Discrimination over Time

Survey researchers have measured American attitudes about race and discrimination since at least the 1940s. Scholars in the National Opinion Research Center (NORC) at the University of Chicago initially carried out the pioneering work in this area. Relying on earlier work by Herbert H. Hyman and Paul B. Sheatsley (1956), Greeley and Sheatsley summarized the results from a series of national surveys conducted as early as 1942, and as late as 1970 in an article in *Scientific American* titled, "Attitudes toward Racial Integration" (Greeley and Sheatsley 1971). These surveys focused on White attitudes about African Americans only, but they provide an invaluable record of some of the ways that attitudes regarding racial discrimination have changed over time. For example, Greeley and Sheatsley

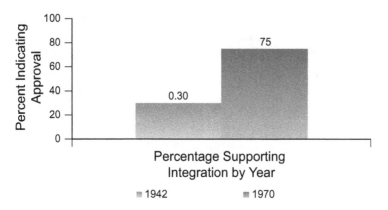

Figure 4.1 White Attitudes about Discrimination Over Time
When asked "Do you think White students and Negro students should go to the same schools or separate schools?" only 30 percent of Whites indicated approval in 1940, while this number jumped to 75 percent by 1970.
Source: Data from Greeley and. Sheatsley (1971).

report that in 1942 only 30 percent of Whites in their national sample approved of school integration (see Figure 4.1). By 1970, that number had risen to 75 percent. Not surprisingly, Greeley and Sheatsley found considerable regional differences across both time periods, with Whites in the North far more supportive of school integration in principle (40 percent in 1942 and 82 percent in 1970) than were their Southern counterparts (2 percent in 1942 and 42 percent in 1970). The most noteworthy aspect of these results, as well as comparable analyses carried out by the authors on similar questions, is that in both the North and the South, support for integration was steadily increasing.

WHAT IT LOOKS LIKE TODAY: INTERPRETING PUBLIC OPINION SURVEYS

Public opinion surveys are designed to provide reliable estimates of a specific population (e.g., a particular state or the entire nation). But, one might reasonably ask, how can a survey consisting of hundreds or even thousands of participants (also known as respondents) accurately reflect the views of a country like the United States, with over 300 million citizens? The short answer is that most surveys rely on probability sampling, or random sampling, to select the participants in their study. In theory, with this method every eligible citizen (e.g., adults over the age of 18) has an equal probability of being selected to participate in the survey. As a result, by interviewing 1,000 or 1,500 randomly selected respondents in the United States a researcher can estimate the views of all 330 million Americans with a relatively high degree of accuracy. Metaphorically, it is similar to tasting a spoonful of soup to determine what the soup tastes like. The problem with this straightforward description of modern survey techniques is that even the most diligent surveys have some sampling bias. That is, for a variety of reasons everyone does not have an equal probability of participating in surveys.

For example, survey researchers have known for decades that Americans with less formal education and those with less interest in politics are also less likely than others to agree to participate in political surveys. More recently, pollsters have found that Trump supporters were also systematically undercounted in many pre-election surveys in both 2016 and 2020. Although potentially consequential given the relative closeness of both presidential contests, one analysis found that the discrepancies between the official outcome in 2020 and the average bias in preelection polls was not dramatic. "At the state level, presidential polls understated Trump's support by 3.3 percentage points on average, while overstating Joe Biden's support by about 1 point" (Edwards-Levy 2021).

Even in the absence of sample bias, surveys represent only an imprecise representation of a target population. In practice, this means that all surveys have a certain amount of sampling error or margin of error. Usually, surveys are designed with confidence intervals of 95 percent. This means that, for example, with a sample size of 1,000 respondents the survey estimates have a confidence level of plus or minus 2.5 percent. Thus, if the survey were repeated twenty times on the same target population we would expect similar results (plus or minus 2.5 percentage points) in nineteen out of twenty cases. So, if a survey estimate is 45 percent support for some policy then in this hypothetical example the "true" value is probably somewhere between 42 percent and 48 percent.

The important take-away message from this brief discussion about the mechanics and limitations of sample surveys is that they are a valuable, but imperfect, indicator of public opinion. And, given the impracticalities of interviewing all adult residents in the country, surveys are one of the most cost-effective and efficient ways to assess the national mood on politically relevant topics.

In 2012, Bobo, Charles, Krysan, and Simmons summarized survey data from the General Social Survey (GSS) in order to update the earlier time series analysis by Greeley, Sheatsley, and their colleagues. In their article, titled "The *Real* Record on Racial Attitudes," Bobo and his co-authors examined survey data from 1972 through 2008. In keeping with the theme of the earlier studies, they found that White support for the principles of Jim Crow segregation—including a belief in the innate inferiority of African Americans and opposition to interracial marriage—had almost entirely evaporated in modern times. However, they also found that there is more nuance and complexity in contemporary White attitudes on race if one scratches beneath the surface. For example, although explicit support for racial inequality exists only at the margins of White society today, a substantial proportion of Whites still express tepid or no support for interacting with minorities in social settings. One study cited by the authors found that approximately 25 percent of Whites in a national sample indicated a preference for neighborhoods with no African American residents (Charles 2003). Opposition to Latino and Asian American neighbors was even higher at 32 percent and 33 percent, respectively.

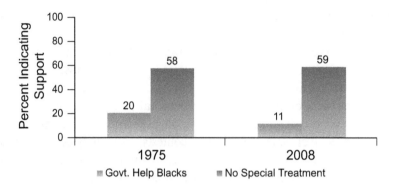

Figure 4.2 White Attitudes Regarding Assistance to Blacks to Improve Their Living Standards in 1975 and 2008
Survey respondents were asked: "Some people think that (Negroes/Blacks/African Americans) have been discriminated against for so long that the government has a special obligation to improve their living standards. Others believe that the government should not be giving special treatment to (Negroes/Blacks/African Americans). Where would you place yourself on this scale, or haven't you made up your mind on this?" Respondents were instructed to place themselves on a five-point scale with values 1–2 indicating that government should help Blacks, 4–5 indicating that Blacks should receive no special treatment, and 3 indicating agreement with both perspectives. *Source*: Greeley and Sheatsley (1971).

Bobo and his colleagues also noted a distinction in White public opinion between support for the principles of racial equality and support for government efforts to enforce or promote equality. That is, support for the principles of Jim Crow segregation is extremely low in contemporary public opinion (Bobo et al. 2012). For example, support among Whites for segregated schools dropped below 10 percent in the mid-1980s, and opposition to interracial marriage had plummeted to just above 10 percent by the start of the twenty-first century. However, governmental action to implement racial equality has not risen over the last few decades, with most Whites expressing opposition to such efforts. For example, in 1975 only about 20 percent of Whites thought that the government should provide assistance to African Americans in order to improve their living standards (Bobo et al. 2012). By 2008, support for this view had declined to about 11 percent (see Figure 4.2).

Throughout this thirty-plus year period, most Whites (between 50 and 60 percent) indicated that the government should provide no "special treatment" to Blacks. Scholars have not yet reached a consensus regarding what accounts for this "principle–policy gap," or the disconnect between the embrace of racially egalitarian principles and opposition to policies to implement these principles. In Chapter 6, "Public Opinion: Divided by Race," we explore this question in more detail, but we note here that the possible explanations range from the emergence of a new, more subtle form of racial bias, to principled ideological objections to big government, to a desire on the part of many Whites to preserve their racial privileges (Hutchings and Valentino 2004).

More recent survey data from the 2020 American National Election Study (ANES) also suggests that racial intolerance is not just an issue on the margins of contemporary society. The ANES is a nationally representative survey of the United States, typically involving both face-to-face interviews and self-administered online interviews. However, because of the COVID-19 pandemic, all surveys for the 2020 American National Election Study were conducted online. In 2020, ANES survey respondents were asked to place different ethnic and racial groups on a seven-point scale assessing how well different traits applied to the group. One such trait involved the tendency to be hardworking or not hardworking.[9] Researchers can determine how groups are perceived in relation to one another by comparing responses across groups. For example, if a White respondent places Latinos at "4" on this scale, suggesting that on average the group is neither hardworking nor lazy, but places their own racial group at "2," suggesting that on average their group possesses a strong work ethic, then this would provide some evidence of racial bias. If, on the other hand, both groups are placed at "3," then this would suggest that the respondent sees no difference in the industriousness of the two groups. How did Whites view the work ethic of Asian Americans, Latinos, and African Americans—relative to their own racial group—in the 2020 ANES? Most Whites either indicated that there are no differences between their group and racial minorities, or they viewed minorities as harder workers. Still, a significant and troubling percentage of Whites indicated more favorable views of their group on this dimension. For example with Asian Americans, about 12 percent of Whites in the survey indicated that this group is less hardworking than their own group. And about 14 percent of Whites indicated that Latinos are less hardworking. When it comes to their view of African Americans, over one-third (36 percent) of Whites indicated that Blacks are less hardworking than their racial group.

Similar results unfold for the stereotype about violence. As with the "hardworking" question, this question asks if people in each group tend to be peaceful or violent. Only 8 percent of Whites in the 2020 ANES reported that Asian Americans tend to be more violent than their own racial group. Twenty percent of Whites reported that Hispanic Americans were more violent than Whites, and 37 percent of Whites reported that they felt African Americans were more violent than Whites.

Contemporary Perceptions of Discrimination

In this section, we discuss how both Whites and ethnic and racial minorities experience discrimination with the most recent and comprehensive survey data available. We look at several surveys that ask respondents about their perceptions of discrimination.

---

[9] "Now I have some questions about different groups in our society. I'm going to show you a seven-point scale on which the characteristics of the people in a group can be rated. In the first statement a score of 1 means that you think almost all of the people in that group tend to be 'hardworking.' A score of 7 means that almost all of the people in the group are 'lazy.' A score of 4 means that you think that most people in the group are not closer to one end or the other, and of course you may choose any number in between. Where would you rate [Whites, Blacks, Latinos, etc.] on this scale?"

The American National Election Study Survey

We turn first to the American National Election Study (ANES), which asked their respondents about discrimination in their 2016 and 2020 surveys. The face-to-face and online surveys in 2016 and the online samples in 2020 provide sufficient numbers of White, Latino, and Black respondents to provide reliable results for each of these populations. Unfortunately, the 2016 survey did not contain large enough samples of Asian Americans or Native Americans to evaluate the views of these two groups. However, later in this chapter we will discuss additional survey data that examines these groups and some others.

The 2016 and 2020 ANES surveys asked three questions about respondent perceptions of discrimination. The first question focused on personal experiences with racial or ethnic discrimination.[10] The results for the 2016 survey are presented in Figure 4.3. In this survey, respondents across racial groups were much more likely to indicate that they encountered little or no discrimination rather than a lot or a great deal. Not surprisingly, however, the results varied considerably across the three groups. Among Whites, over 80 percent reported little or no experience with racial discrimination. Only 4 percent indicated that they encountered a lot or a great deal of racial discrimination. Hispanics and Blacks were much less likely to report infrequent experiences with discrimination. About half of Hispanics indicated that they had none or only a little exposure to discrimination. Slightly less than one-third of African Americans reported little or no experience with racial discrimination. Relative to Whites, however, a significant fraction of both Latinos (16 percent) and Blacks (44 percent) reported that they frequently encountered racial discrimination. These figures are roughly consistent with the audit studies and hate crimes reports discussed earlier. In short, these data indicate that even in the twenty-first century, Latinos and Blacks are far more likely than Whites to encounter racial discrimination in their daily lives.

The results from 2020, as shown in Figure 4.4, present a similar story. Indeed, the results are mostly unchanged across all groups. Again, the vast majority of Whites (86 percent) rarely experience racial discrimination. Almost 2 out of 5 (18 percent) of Latinos, on the other hand, experience a lot or a great deal of discrimination. Again, African Americans report the most frequent experiences with discrimination in 2020. According to this most recent survey, over one-third of Blacks (37 percent) indicate that they routinely confront racial discrimination. Less than one-third characterized their experiences with discrimination as infrequent.

Researchers have found that an individual's personal experiences with discrimination and their perceptions of the level of discrimination encountered by their racial group are not necessarily the same thing. For this reason, the ANES asked an additional question about the level of discrimination that the respondent believed

---

[10] Respondents were asked the following question about discrimination: "How much discrimination have you personally faced because of your ethnicity or race? A great deal, a lot, a moderate amount, a little, or none at all?"

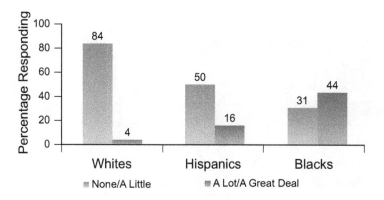

Figure 4.3 Personal Experiences with Racial Discrimination, 2016
In the 2016 American National Election Survey, Whites, Hispanics, and Blacks were asked
about their personal experiences with racial discrimination; the results varied considerably
across the three groups.
Source: Data from American National Election Studies, University of Michigan, and Stanford
University, 2017.

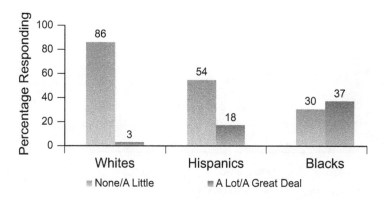

Figure 4.4 Personal Experiences with Racial Discrimination, 2020
In the 2020 American National Election Survey, Whites, Hispanics, and Blacks were asked the
same question about their personal experiences with racial discrimination; the results were very
similar to those for 2016.
Source: Data from American National Election Studies, University of Michigan, and Stanford
University, 2021.

was experienced by their racial group.[11] Figure 4.5 documents the results from the
2016 ANES. In each case, groups are more likely to report that their group experiences race-based discrimination than they are to say that they have personally

---

[11] Respondents were asked about their own racial or ethnic group, as well as other groups. Specifically, they
were asked the following question: "How much discrimination is there in the United States today against
each of the following groups. How about (Whites/Latinos/Blacks, etc.)? Would you say that there is a
great deal, a lot, a moderate amount, a little, or none at all?"

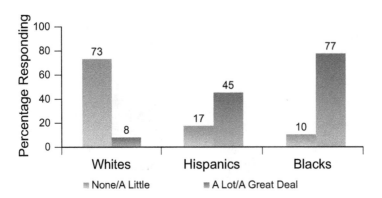

Figure 4.5 Perceptions of Discrimination against Own Racial Group, 2016
When asked in 2016 about their perception of how much their own racial group is discriminated against, groups are more likely to report that their group experiences race-based discrimination than they are to say that they have personally experienced bias.
Source: Data from American National Election Studies, University of Michigan, and Stanford University, 2017.

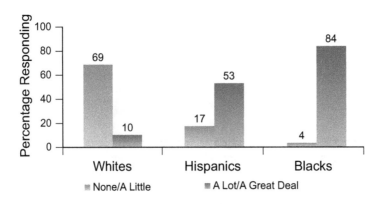

Figure 4.6 Perceptions of Discrimination against Own Racial Group, 2020
When asked in 2020 about their perception of how much their own racial group is discriminated against, all three groups showed an increase in their perception of discrimination against their own group over what was reported in 2016.
Source: Data from American National Election Studies, University of Michigan, and Stanford University, 2021.

experienced bias. Nevertheless, a familiar pattern emerges. The overwhelming majority of Whites reported that their group experiences little or no racial discrimination. Fewer than 10 percent of Whites indicated that racial bias is a major problem for their group in 2016. In contrast, a near-majority of Latinos (44 percent) and a super-majority of Blacks (77 percent) indicated that their groups experienced significant amounts of ethnic or racial discrimination. The results for 2020 (see Figure 4.6) suggest similar patterns and, not surprisingly, given that these surveys were conducted at the height of the nationwide demonstrations for racial justice in the summer and fall of that year—if anything—heightened perceptions of racial bias. A majority of Latinos (53 percent) and well over three-quarters of Blacks (84 percent) reported that their group encounters "a lot" or "a great deal" of discrimination in this country. Relatively few Whites (10 percent), on the other hand, reported in 2020 that their racial group experienced substantial racial barriers.

Clearly, discrimination based on race or ethnicity remains an important problem in contemporary society, at least for ethnic and racial minorities. However, discussions of race and ethnicity can leave the impression that all members of marginalized groups experience bias in the same way. Legal scholars and social scientists have argued for many years that women, the poor, LGBTQ+ individuals, and other marginalized groups within minority communities often experience heightened levels of discrimination (Cohen 1999; Crenshaw 1995; Harris-Perry 2011; Strolovitch 2007). While we foreground racial and ethnic discrimination throughout this book, it is important to keep in mind that discrimination is intersectional, by which we mean that there are multiple, interlocked systems at work that co-produce inequality and injustice and that focusing on race, gender, class, sexuality, nation, ability, age, and so on in isolation from one another can obscure the specificity of discrimination or render it invisible altogether. For illustrative purposes, consider how race and class intersect focusing just on the categories "Black" and "White" and "Middle Class" and "Working Class." A key insight from an intersectional analysis is that the experience of the Black Middle Class is distinct from that of the Black Working Class, as is the experience of the White Middle Class and the White Working Class and so too for White and Black Working Class and White and Black Middle Class.

Recently, scholars have also begun to focus on another marker of disadvantage within minority communities: skin tone. In short, darker skinned members of minority groups have poorer health outcomes and encounter more discrimination in the criminal justice system, the voting booth, the labor market, and a variety of other domains (Eberhardt et al. 2006; Frank, Akresh, and Lu 2010; Monk 2015; Weaver 2012). In order to assess whether these experiences are reflected in perceptions of color, as opposed to race-based, discrimination, the ANES fielded a new question on discrimination in 2016.

In this portion of the survey, respondents were first asked to rate their skin tone on a ten-point scale ranging from light to dark.[12] Then, in a variant of the question on personal experiences with racial discrimination, respondents were asked how much discrimination they had personally encountered because of their skin tone. These results are presented in Figure 4.7. Virtually no Whites and few Latinos reported significant levels of color-based discrimination. However, among African Americans, fully one in three indicated that they faced "a lot" or "a great deal" of

---

[12] The 2016 ANES used the Massey and Martin scale, which is composed of a picture of ten hands corresponding to the numbers 1–10. The hands start out at lower values as extremely light and become progressively darker until, at 10, the hand is a very dark brown/black shade.

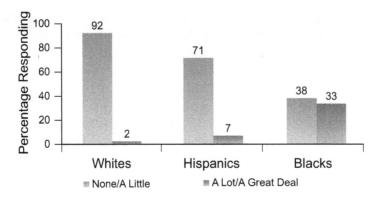

Figure 4.7 Personal Experiences with Color-based Discrimination by Racial Group, 2016
ANES respondents were asked to rate their skin tone on a ten-point scale ranging from light to dark and then were asked about the amount of discrimination they faced on the basis of their skin tone. Virtually no Whites and few Latinos reported significant levels of color-based discrimination, but one in three Blacks indicated that they faced a lot or a great deal of discrimination based on the color of their skin.
Source: Data from American National Election Studies, University of Michigan, and Stanford University, 2017.

discrimination based on the color of their skin (as distinct from their racial group membership). To place this percentage in context, Blacks are about twice as likely to report substantial levels of color-based discrimination as Latinos are to report race-based discrimination in 2016 or 2020 (see Figures 4.3 and 4.4). Similarly, Blacks are eight to ten times more likely to report color-based discrimination as Whites are to report personal experiences with race-based discrimination in both 2016 and 2020.

The results in Figure 4.7 demonstrate that color-based discrimination is a serious problem among Blacks, but it remains unclear as to which group of African Americans faces the most difficult challenges with this form of bias. That is, we know that Blacks report more color-based discrimination than other groups but we do not know the characteristics of those African Americans who most frequently experience this type of discrimination. In order to further explore this issue, we need to assign Blacks to different groups based on the darkness or lightness of their skin. As indicated earlier, each respondent characterized his or her skin color with a number ranging from 1 to 10. To simplify our analyses, we grouped African American respondents into three color-based groups: light-skinned, medium skinned, and dark-skinned.[13] The experiences of each of these groups with color discrimination are shown in Figure 4.8. Interestingly, Blacks in the middle of the color spectrum reported the least amount of color-based discrimination—although

[13] Blacks who identified their skin color as ranging from 1 to 4 were categorized as "light-skinned," those selecting 5 or 6 were categorized as "medium-skinned," and those selecting from 7 to 10 were coded as "dark-skinned."

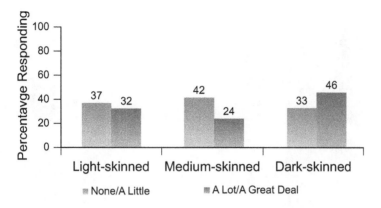

Figure 4.8 Personal Experiences with Color-based Discrimination among Blacks, 2016
Based on their self-identification of skin tone, Blacks were divided into three groups. Roughly one-third of lighter skinned Blacks indicated that they faced a lot or a great deal of color-based discrimination, while Blacks in the middle of the color spectrum reported the least amount of color-based discrimination; darker skinned Blacks reported the highest levels of color-based discrimination, with almost half indicating that they face a lot or a great deal.
Source: Data from American National Election Studies, University of Michigan, and Stanford University, 2017.

still considerably more than either Whites or Latinos. Roughly one-third of lighter skinned Blacks indicated that they faced a lot or a great deal of color-based discrimination. And, consistent with expectations, darker skinned Blacks reported the highest levels of color-based discrimination, with almost half indicating that they face a lot or a great deal. To provide some context to this latter figure, in 2020, 37 percent of Blacks in the ANES survey reported significant personal experiences with race-based discrimination. In that same year, darker-skinned Blacks reported slightly higher levels of experience with color-based discrimination.[14]

The NPR Telephone Survey

The ANES survey provides an important overview of experiences with, and perceptions of, race and color-based discrimination. However, the insights we can draw from this analysis are limited because the survey has an insufficient number of respondents who do not identify as White, Latino, or Black. A telephone survey jointly fielded in 2017 by National Public Radio (NPR), the Robert Wood Johnson Foundation, and the School of Public Health at Harvard University includes a

---

[14] It is also worth noting that darker skinned African Americans also report higher levels of personal experience with *racial* discrimination. Among lighter skinned Blacks, about 44 percent indicate that they encounter race-based discrimination a lot or a great deal of the time, and medium skinned Blacks report such experiences about 36 percent of the time. The comparable figure for darker skinned Blacks is 59 percent.

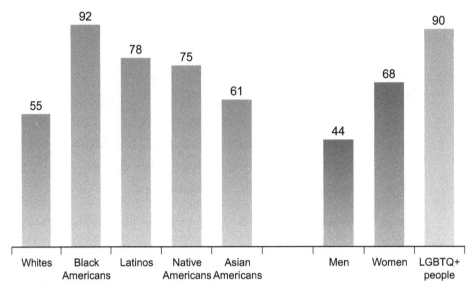

Note: Total N = 3,453 U.S. adults.

Figure 4.9 Belief that Discrimination against Own Group Exists Today
The bars represent the percentage of each group that believes, generally speaking, that
discrimination against their own group exists in America today.
Source: Data from NPR Robert Wood Johnson Foundation/Harvard T.H. Chan School of
Public Health, Discrimination in America, January 26–April 9, 2017, fig. 1.

much broader range of groups (Robert Wood Johnson Foundation: Discrimination
in America 2017). The NPR survey, as we shall refer to it here, relied on a nationally
representative sample of Whites, Latinos, African Americans, Asian Americans,
and Native Americans. The survey also included a large sample of, and corresponding questions focusing on, Lesbian, Gay, Bisexual, Transgender, and Queer
(LGBTQ+) individuals. Respondents in this survey were asked a range of questions
focusing on their racial, ethnic, gender, and sexuality-based experiences with discrimination in variety of domains. For example, respondents were asked about their
experiences with discrimination in the criminal justice system, in interactions with
the police, in the labor market, housing, etc.

As with the ANES survey, the NPR survey also asked respondents their perceptions about the discrimination faced by their group. These results are summarized in
Figure 4.9. One important difference between the NPR survey and the ANES
survey is that the ANES asked respondents how much discrimination their group
encountered. The NPR survey, on the other hand, simply asked respondents if they
believed discrimination against their group exists. Still, in spite of the difference in
question wording, the pattern of results is similar to what we found in Figures 4.5
and 4.6. In general, racial and ethnic minorities are more likely to believe their
group experiences discrimination than is the case with White Americans. Latino
Americans, Native Americans, and especially African Americans are much more

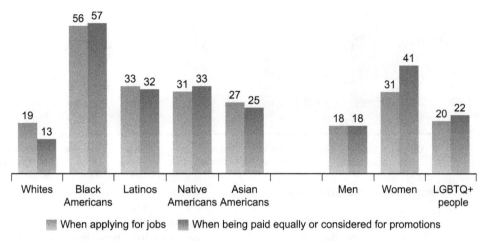

Note: Total N = 3,453 U.S. adults.

Figure 4.10 Perceptions about Discrimination Faced by One's Group
The bars represent the percent of each group saying they have been personally discriminated against in each situation because of their race or ethnicity (for racial and ethnic groups); because of their gender (for men and women); or because of their LBGTQ+ (Lesbian, Gay, Bi-sexual, Transgender, and Queer) identity for (LGBTQ+ people).
Source: Data from NPR Robert Wood Johnson Foundation/Harvard T.H. Chan School of Public Health, Discrimination in America, January 26–April 9, 2017, fig. 2.

likely to report that their group faces discrimination compared with Whites. Interestingly, the perceptions of Whites (55 percent) and Asian Americans (61 percent) are not dramatically different. Also, women in general and LGBTQ+ people report beliefs about discrimination that are roughly comparable with that of racial and ethnic minorities. Indeed, aside from African Americans, the LGBTQ+ community is more likely than any other group to agree that they encounter discrimination.

Figure 4.10 summarizes results on workplace discrimination. This experience— whether in the application process or with respect to pay and promotion—is something most African Americans have faced. Other groups report lower, although still substantial levels of employment discrimination. Women in general seem particularly attuned to pay discrimination, with a greater percentage (41 percent) reporting that they have been discriminated against in this way than any other group, aside from Blacks. White Americans are the group least likely (13 percent) to report discrimination with respect to payment or promotion.

Perceptions of discrimination in interactions with the police have been a high-profile issue in the news since the deadly encounter between Michael Brown and Officer Darren Wilson in Ferguson, Missouri, in 2014. The NPR survey asked about respondents' personal experiences with discrimination by the police, as shown in Figure 4.11. The differences across groups are striking, although by now familiar. Blacks and Whites represent two ends of the spectrum in terms of experiences with police discrimination. Half of African Americans report such experiences compared with only 10 percent of Whites. The remaining groups, defined by race/ethnicity,

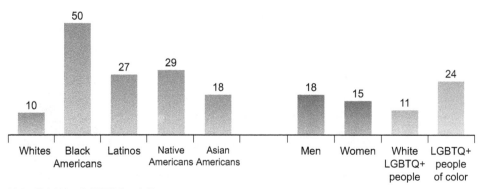

Note: Total N = 3,453 U.S. adults.

Figure 4.11 Personal Experiences with Discrimination by the Police
The bars represent the percent of each group saying they have been personally discriminated against when interacting with the policy because of their race or ethnicity, gender, or LGBTQ+ identity.
Source: Data from NPR Robert Wood Johnson Foundation/Harvard T.H. Chan School of Public Health, Discrimination in America, January 26–April 9, 2017, fig. 3.

gender, or sexuality, fall somewhere between Blacks and Whites, with Native Americans reporting slightly more negative encounters with the police than any other non-Black group. Interestingly, the effects of race are even present within the LGBTQ+ community. Non-White sexual minorities are more than twice as likely (24 percent) as their White counterparts (11 percent) to report discrimination at the hands of the police.

In the case of housing discrimination, as shown in Figure 4.12, the NPR study again found that a significant percentage of their respondents indicate that they have had this experience. Among Whites, and among men in general (based on perceived gender discrimination), relatively few have been affected by housing discrimination. The experience is much more common among minority groups and, to a lesser extent, women in general. Almost half of Blacks (45 percent) and approximately one-third (31 percent) of Latinos indicate that they have been victimized by discrimination in the housing market. The percentages reporting this form of discrimination are also high, relative to Whites, among Asian Americans and LGBTQ+ people.

The NPR survey also asked about experiences with discrimination in applying to or attending college and in trying to vote or participate in politics. Whites were, on average, the least likely to report discrimination in higher education (11 percent) and political participation (4 percent). Blacks were most likely to report being discriminated against in education (36 percent) and politics (19 percent).

Lastly, the NPR study focused on respondent experiences with discrimination in the healthcare industry. Again, in 2017 this experience was uncommon among Whites and men in general, as shown in Figure 4.13. The situation among minority groups and women is quite different. When seeking medical treatment,

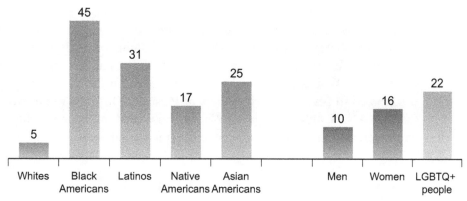

Note: Total N = 3,453 U.S. adults.

Figure 4.12 Personal Experiences of Discrimination When Seeking Housing
The bars represent the percent of each group saying they have been personally discriminated against when seeking housing because of their race or ethnicity, gender, or LGBTQ+ identity.
Source: Data from NPR Robert Wood Johnson Foundation/Harvard T.H. Chan School of Public Health, Discrimination in America, January 26–April 9, 2017, fig. 6.

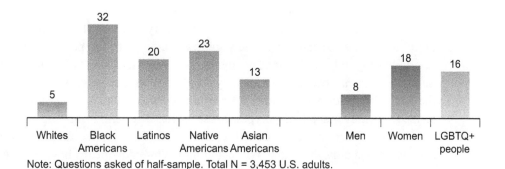

Note: Questions asked of half-sample. Total N = 3,453 U.S. adults.

Figure 4.13 Personal Experiences of Discrimination When Seeking Medical Care
The bars represent the percent of each group saying they have been personally discriminated against when going to a doctor or health clinic because of their race or ethnicity, gender, or LGBTQ+ identity.
Source: Data from NPR Robert Wood Johnson Foundation/Harvard T.H. Chan School of Public Health, Discrimination in America, January 26–April 9, 2017, fig. 8.

approximately one in five Latinos (20 percent), Native Americans (23 percent), and women (18 percent) reported experiences with discrimination. Among African Americans, the prevalence was one in three (32 percent).

The unmistakable conclusion from the ANES and NPR surveys is that discrimination in the twenty-first century is a common occurrence for racial and ethnic minorities (and, in many instances, for women and LGBTQ+ people as well). The findings for African Americans were particularly high across both surveys.

In contrast, there was scant evidence that Whites encounter significant race-based discrimination in contemporary society. Rarely did more than a single-digit percentage of Whites indicate that they were discriminated against because of their racial group. Indeed, personal experiences with discrimination are uncommon even among those Whites who, based on media reports on their views, might be most predisposed to perceive it—supporters of President Donald Trump. According to the 2020 ANES, only 4 percent of Whites who voted for Trump indicated that they had experienced a lot or a great deal of discrimination on account of their race.

Conclusion

The evidence in this chapter indicates that the late Senator John McCain's optimistic characterization of racial inequity in contemporary American society was, at best, misleading. While in some respects it is true that "... we have come a long way from the old injustices that once stained our nation's reputation and denied some Americans the full blessing of American citizenship," it is also true that many profound racial disparities remain in the twenty-first century. The country has experienced an enormous amount of racial violence and discrimination since its founding, and while instances of bias (and especially the acceptance of it) have diminished, it is clearly still a problem in the country today. FBI hate crime statistics are dominated by racial bias. Audit studies demonstrate the persistence of racial discrimination in both the housing and employment markets. And although White public opinion has become increasingly tolerant on matters of race since the end of the Second World War, substantial portions of this population continue to subscribe to negative racial stereotypes. Most Whites also tend to oppose government efforts to enforce anti-discrimination legislation. Finally, recent public opinion surveys consistently show that White and non-White Americans have dramatically different experiences with racial discrimination in a variety of settings. In short, individual expressions of racial discrimination are not just the subject of history books. For many ethnic and racial minorities, they remain a routine aspect of life in contemporary American society.

KEY TERMS

Audit studies
Civil War Amendments
Correspondence audits
Discrimination
Disparate impact
Disparate treatment
Individual level discrimination
In-person audit studies
Institutional discrimination

Intersectionality
Jim Crow era
Reconstruction
Reconstruction Acts 1867 and 1868
Red Summer

DISCUSSION QUESTIONS

1. In what ways was Senator McCain right when he said that "America today is a world away from the cruel and prideful bigotry [of previous eras]"? In what ways was he wrong?
2. Why do you think that housing and employment discrimination remain so common over fifty years after such practices were declared illegal at the end of the Civil Rights Movement?
3. Why do you think that most Whites have become more supportive of racial equality in principle but continue to oppose concrete efforts to bring about this equality?
4. Americans are much more likely to perceive discrimination against their racial or ethnic group than they are to report that they have personally experienced discrimination. What factors do you think might be responsible for these different attitudes?

ANNOTATED SUGGESTED READINGS

See Vincent L. Hutchings and Nicholas A. Valentino. 2004. "The Centrality of Race in American Politics," *Annual Review of Political Science* 7: 383–408, for a comprehensive overview of the social science literature on race and political attitudes.
See Lawrence D. Bobo and Mia Tuan. 2006. *Prejudice in Politics: Group Position, Public Opinion, and the Wisconsin Treaty Rights Dispute.* Cambridge, MA: Harvard University Press, for an extensive discussion on the different theoretical explanations for racial discrimination.
See Mara Cecilia Ostfeld and Nicole Yadon. 2022. *Skin Color, Power, and Politics in America.* New York: Russell Sage Foundation, for an excellent examination of the ways in which color-based, as opposed to race-based, identities can shape political perspectives.
See Philip Dray. 2002. *At The Hands of Persons Unknown: The Lynching of Black America.* New York: Modern Library, for more information on lynchings in America.
See Devah Pager. 2009. *Marked: Race, Crime, and Finding Work in an Era of Mass Incarceration.* Chicago: University of Chicago Press, for a closer look at audit studies on employment discrimination.

CHAPTER REFERENCES

Allport, Gordon W. [1954] 1979. *The Nature of Prejudice: 25th Anniversary Edition.* New York: Basic Books.

Anderson, Carol. 2003. *Eyes Off the Prize: The United Nations and the African American Struggle for Human Rights, 1944–1955*. New York: Cambridge University Press.

Bobo, Lawrence D, Camille Z. Charles, Maria Krysan, and Alicia D. Simmons. 2012. "The *Real* Record on Racial Attitudes," In *Social Trends in American Life: Findings from the General Social Survey since 1972* (ed.) Peter V. Marsden. Princeton: Princeton University Press, 39–83.

Carrigan, William D. and Clive Webb. 2013. *Forgotten Dead: Mob Violence against Mexicans in the United States, 1848–1928*. Oxford: Oxford University Press.

Carrigan, William D. and Clive Webb. 2015. "When Americans Lynched Mexicans," *New York Times.* February 20, www.nytimes.com/2015/02/20/opinion/when-americans-lynched-mexicans.html.

Charles, Camille Z. 2003. "The Dynamics of Racial Segregation," *Annual Review of Sociology* 29: 167–207.

Cohen, Cathy J. 1999. *The Boundaries of Blackness: AIDS and the Breakdown of Black Politics.* Chicago: University of Chicago Press.

Crenshaw, Kimberlé. 1995. "Mapping the Margins: Intersectionality, Identity Politics, and Violence against Women of Color," In *Critical Race Theory: The Key Writings That Formed the Movement* (eds.) Kimberlé Crenshaw, Neil Gotanda, Gary Peller, and Kendall Thomas. New York: New Press, 357–383.

Dray, Philip. 2002. *At the Hands of Persons Unknown: The Lynching of Black America*. New York: Modern Library.

Du Bois, W. E. B. 1940. *Dusk of Dawn: An Essay toward an Autobiography of a Race Concept*. New York: Harcourt Brace.

Eberhardt, Jennifer L., Paul G. Davies, Valerie J. Purdie-Vaughns, and Sheri Lynn Johnson. 2006. "Looking Deathworthy: Perceived Stereotypicality of Black Defendants Predicts Capital Sentencing Outcomes," *Psychological Science* 17(5): 383–386.

Edwards-Levy, Ariel. 2021. "Here's What Pollsters Think Happened with 2020 Election Surveys," CNN.com., May 13. www.cnn.com/2021/05/13/politics/2020-polling-error-research/index.html.

Federal Bureau of Investigation: Hate Crimes. n.d. www.fbi.gov/investigate/civil-rights/hate-crimes.

Foner, Eric. 1988. *Reconstruction: America's Unfinished Revolution 1863–1877.* New York: Harper and Row.

Frank, Reanne, Ilana Redstone Akresh, and Bo Lu. 2010. "Latino Immigrants and the U.S. Racial Order: How and Where Do They Fit in," *American Sociological Review* 75(3): 378–401.

Greeley, Andrew M. and Paul B. Sheatsley. 1971. "Attitudes toward Racial Integration," *Scientific American* 225(6): 13–19.

Harris-Perry, Melissa V. 2011. *Sister Citizen: Shame, Stereotypes, and Black Women in America.* New Haven, CT: Yale University Press.

Hyman, Herbert H. and Paul B. Sheatsley. 1956. "Attitudes towards Desegregation," *Scientific American* 195(6): 35–39.

Hutchings, Vincent L. 2009. "Change or More of the Same? Evaluating Racial Attitudes in the Obama Era," *Public Opinion Quarterly* 73(5): 917–942.

Hutchings, Vincent L. and Nicholas A. Valentino. 2004. "The Centrality of Race in American Politics," *Annual Review of Political Science* 7: 383–408.

Kinder, Donald R., and Allison Dale-Riddle. 2012. *The End of Race? Obama, 2008, and Racial Politics in America.* New Haven, CT: Yale University Press.

Lewis-Beck, Michael S., Charles Tien, and Richard Nadeau. 2010. "Obama's Missed Landslide: A Racial Cost?" *Political Science & Politics* 43(1): 69–76.

McCain, John. 2008. "Transcript of John McCain's Concession Speech," *Npr.com*, November 5. www.npr.org/templates/story/story.php?storyId=96631784.

Monk, Ellis P. 2015. "The Cost of Color: Skin Color, Discrimination, and Health among African Americans," *American Journal of Sociology* 121(2): 396–444.

Myrdal, Gunnar. [1944] 1996. *An American Dilemma: The Negro Problem and Modern Democracy*. New Brunswick: Transaction (original ed., Harper & Row).

Nagourney, Adam. 2008. "Obama Elected President as Racial Barrier Falls," *New York Times*, November 4. www.nytimes.com/2008/11/05/us/politics/05elect.html.

Newport, Frank. 2011. "Americans' Belief about Obama's Birth," *News.gallup.com*, April 27. https://news.gallup.com/opinion/polling-matters/169724/americans-beliefs-obama-birth.aspx.

National Research Council. 2004. *Measuring Discrimination*. Washington, D.C.: National Academies Press.

Oh, Sun Jung and John Yinger. 2015. "What Have We Learned from Paired Testing in Housing Markets?" *Cityscape: A Journal of Policy Development and Research* 17(3): 15–60.

Piston, Spencer. 2010. "How Explicit Racial Prejudice Hurt Obama in the 2008 Election," *Political Behavior* 32: 431–451.

Quillian, Lincoln, John J. Lee, and Mariana Oliver. 2020. "Evidence from Field Experiments in Hiring Shows Substantial Additional Racial Discrimination after the Callback," *Social Forces* 99(2): 732–759.

Quillian, Lincoln, Devah Pager, Ole Hexel, and Arnfinn H. Midtbøen. 2017. "Meta-Analysis of Field Experiments Shows No Change in Racial Discrimination in Hiring over Time," *Proceedings of the National Academy of Sciences of the United States of America* 114(41): 10870–10875.

Robert Wood Johnson Foundation: Discrimination in America. 2017. www.rwjf.org/en/library/research/2017/10/discrimination-in-america–experiences-and-views.html.

Strolovitch, Dara Z. 2007. *Affirmative Advocacy: Race, Class, and Gender in Interest Group Politics*. Chicago: University of Chicago Press.

Ture, Kwame and Charles Hamilton. [1967] 1992. *Black Power: The Politics of Liberation*. New York: Vintage.

United Nations Human Rights: Office of the High Commissioner. 1965. International Convention on the Elimination of All Forms of Racial Discrimination. www.ohchr.org/en/instruments-mechanisms/instruments/international-convention-elimination-all-forms-racial.

Weaver, Vesla. 2012. "The Electoral Consequences of Skin Color: The 'Hidden' Side of Race in Politics," *Political Behavior* 34(1): 159–192.

Whitaker, Robert. 2009. *On the Laps of Gods: The Red Summer of 1919 and the Struggle for Justice That Remade a Nation*. New York: Crown.

Wilkerson, Isabel. 2010. *The Warmth of Other Suns: The Epic Story of America's Great Migration*. New York: Vintage.

5 How Do Institutions Contribute to Racism in the United States?

Rachelle Faroul, a gainfully employed 33-year-old African American woman with savings and a good credit score, was making approximately $60,000 a year when she was turned down for a home loan by Philadelphia Mortgage Advisors. The Northwestern University graduate was surprised but tried again, a year later, this time at Santander Bank, a Spanish firm with U.S. headquarters in Boston. Here, "the process dragged on for months." Only after Faroul's partner, Hanako Franz—a half-White and half-Japanese woman—agreed to co-sign her loan application did the mortgage get approved. At the time, Franz was making $144.65 every two weeks, or $3,760 a year. When contacted about the loan denials by the Center for Investigative Reporting, the mortgage companies denied that discrimination was involved in their decisions. Nonetheless, having been denied multiple times and after asking for more and more information to support her application, Faroul was left feeling bitter and humiliated: "The things that happen behind the scenes is what's disturbing," she said (Glantz and Martinez 2018).

Racial discrimination in the provision of mortgage loans has been illegal since the passage of the Community Reinvestment Act of 1977. That bill was aimed at encouraging banks to lend and invest more in low- and moderate-income areas in an effort to correct the damage done in the preceding decades. The Act charges the Office of the Comptroller of the Currency—located in the United States Department of the Treasury—with regulating banks and curtailing **redlining**, the term used to describe denial of loans to communities based on race rather than creditworthiness (see Figure 5.1 for an example from 1938, in Brooklyn, New York). However, this office has done almost nothing to remedy the damage of previous policies (Glantz and Martinez 2018). The office has rated virtually all banks (99 percent) as satisfactory or outstanding in recent years. Such lax standards have existed under both Republican and Democratic administrations. This is in part a function of the way the 1977 Community Reinvestment Act was written and in part because of changes in the mortgage business over the last few decades (Henderson and Marchiel 2021). First, to avoid excessive regulation of banks, the law allows oversight only with respect to discouraging redlining when banks seek to merge or expand. At all other times, the law is not applicable. Second, the law applies only to banks, savings and loan institutions. However, since the 1990s, non-depository mortgage companies—not subject to the regulations in this law—have

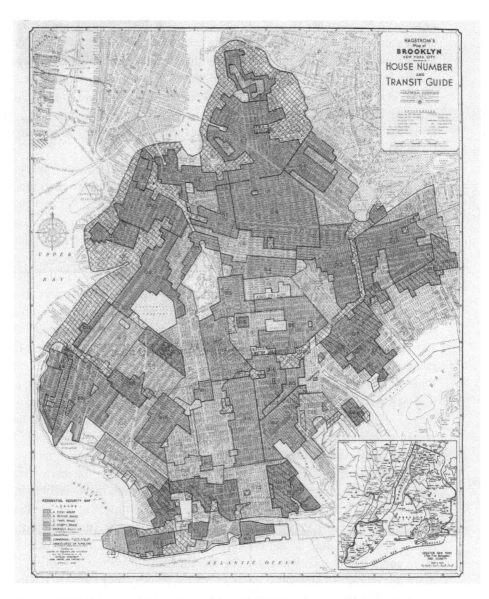

Figure 5.1 Homeowner's Loan Corporation, map of Brooklyn, New York, 1938
Maps like these were used by mortgage lenders to divide an area's housing stock by graded levels of lending "security." The practice was labeled "redlining" because the riskiest areas were outlined in red. These were often areas with large non-White populations.
Source: National Archives and Records Administration, Mapping Inequality. See at: www .nytimes.com/2017/08/24/upshot/how-redlinings-racist-effects-lasted-for-decades.html.

surpassed traditional lending institutions (i.e., savings and loans, and banks) as the dominant mortgage lenders in the housing market.

It is not easy to determine whether decisions made by lending agencies are influenced by the race of the applicant. This is in part because the 1975 Home Mortgage

Disclosure Act does not require lending agencies to disclose information on customer credit scores, so banks can argue that any existing racial disparities in loan provisions are due to differences in creditworthiness rather than race. Since credit score information is not public, no one can evaluate the validity of this argument. Even if credit scores were publicly available, they are not race-neutral (Rice and Swesnik 2013). For example, credit scores do not reflect on-time rent payments. This omission disproportionately, and negatively, affects people of color rather than Whites because they are far more likely to be renters and not homeowners.

The persistence of racial disparities in the provision of mortgage loans illustrates some of the key distinctions between individual and institutional discrimination. In the case of individual discrimination, we are usually referring to overt prejudicial acts that are unsanctioned by major institutions in society such as the government (local, state, and federal), as well as religious organizations, the mass media, banks, and corporations. With institutional discrimination, we are typically referring to codified rules and procedures associated with major governmental and nongovernmental institutions that—whether intentionally or otherwise—result in unequal outcomes across racial groups (Ture and Hamilton 1992). In the example above, it is possible that Rachelle Faroul experienced racial discrimination in her efforts to secure a mortgage loan because of the particular way that conventional loans are provided (i.e., the traditional criteria used to determine eligibility) by banks in the Philadelphia area, and throughout the country.

If Ms. Faroul were merely the victim of a racially biased loan officer, or if race played no role at all in their decision to deny her a loan, then we would have little reason to expect a broader pattern of discrimination in the Philadelphia banking industry. However, the 2016 revealnews.org study of conventional home purchase loans in Philadelphia (based on an analysis of 11,367 cases in the metro area) found that African American borrowers were almost three times more likely than Whites to be denied a loan (Glantz and Martinez 2018). The rate was approximately 1.6 times more likely for Latino borrowers. In both cases, the study found that these results held even after taking into account income, neighborhood racial composition, and a host of other factors. The Reveal study also examined over 30 million mortgage records in 409 metro areas across the country and found that Blacks were more likely to be denied a conventional mortgage loan, or a loan with lower interest rates, than comparable Whites in forty-eight metropolitan areas. Reveal found that Latinos were less likely to receive conventional mortgage loans in twenty-five metro areas. Racial disparities were also uncovered for Asian Americans in nine metro areas, and in three areas for Native Americans (Glantz and Martinez 2018). More recent data indicate that these results are not unusual. The Urban Institute finds, based on their analysis of the 2020 Home Mortgage Disclosure Act data, that national mortgage denial rates differ significantly by race (Choi and Mattingly 2022). As illustrated in Figure 5.2, all communities of color—unfortunately, Native Americans were not included in their analyses—were denied home mortgage loans at higher rates than non-Hispanic Whites. The disparities were particularly high for Hispanics and African Americans. In short, Ms. Faroul's experience

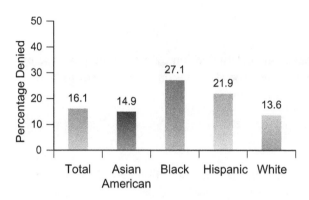

Figure 5.2 Home Mortgage Denial Rates by Race and Ethnicity, 2020
National mortgage denial rates differ significantly by race, with Blacks being denied nearly twice as often as Whites.
Source: Data adapted from the Urban Institute and Choi and Mattingly (2022), www.urban.org/urban-wire/what-different-denial-rates-can-tell-us-about-racial-disparities-mortgage-market.

appears to be more of a feature, rather than a bug within the banking system. People of color are systematically denied home loans at a greater rate than Whites, even when they have comparable economic profiles.

While individual acts of discrimination are disturbing (and, in the current era, often illegal), it is institutional discrimination that represents the primary source of contemporary racial group inequality. Because institutional racism flows from established rules and procedures, often although not always couched in race-neutral language, it often cannot be attributed to the racially biased motives of a single actor. Even when a specific alleged perpetrator can be identified, it can be difficult to determine whether the motive was racial animus. These points are important because, in the absence of an identifiable perpetrator, a specific individual victim, and most importantly an undeniable racially biased motive, *discrimination is not illegal*. In fact, as noted by legal scholar Daria Roithmayr (2018), racially unequal outcomes, promoted by government as well as private individuals, have been so common throughout American history that racially discriminatory intent may no longer be necessary to maintain White advantage. In other words, institutional discrimination can be baked into the laws and routine bureaucratic procedures that are seldom questioned by ordinary citizens. Moreover, the damage inflicted by these laws and procedures has a lingering negative impact on the ability of communities of color to prosper and accumulate wealth as well as to pass on that wealth to subsequent generations—even if the original discriminatory intent that may have motivated these practices no longer exists. The aim of this chapter is to identify these often-overlooked rules and regulations, and analyze their long-term impact.

In the sections that follow, we provide some historical context by focusing on institutional discrimination in the aftermath of the Civil War through the Great Depression in the 1930s and 1940s. We also discuss the role of institutional discrimination in shaping immigration policy from the late nineteenth century up until the middle of the twentieth century and then focus on governmental policies to displace or eradicate Native American nations in the nineteenth and twentieth centuries. We spend the remainder of the chapter discussing examples of institutional discrimination in various domains (e.g., housing and criminal justice) in the latter part of the twentieth and into the twenty-first centuries.

History of Institutional Discrimination in the United States

We begin our discussion of institutional discrimination by examining how discrimination has been woven into the political, social, and economic fabric of the United States at different points in the country's history.

Institutional Discrimination during Reconstruction

We start at the end of the Civil War, with the Reconstruction period, because prior to this time, African Americans and other people of color were not regarded as citizens of the United States. This was made crystal clear in the wording of the Dred Scott decision of 1857, in which the Supreme Court (by a vote of 7 to 2), held that the Constitution did not apply to Blacks, who were "regarded as beings of an inferior order [with] no rights which the white man was bound to respect." Even after the adoption of the Thirteenth, Fourteenth, and Fifteenth Amendments to the Constitution, government policies and processes were applied in different ways for Blacks and Whites. This is evident in the type of federal programs enacted by Congress at the end of the Civil War. Much of the Southern economy had been devastated by the war and roughly 4 million emancipated formerly enslaved people, along with hundreds of thousands of Union veterans, required assistance to be reintegrated into society. The manner in which Congress responded to the needs of these two constituencies—the formerly enslaved and Civil War veterans—demonstrates the way in which racial bias can unfold in the design and implementation of governmental policy—even if policies appear to be racially neutral (Williams 2003).

The Freedmen's Bureau and the Civil War Veterans Pension Program

At the conclusion of the Union victory in the Civil War, the federal government developed two national programs to address the economic hardships that were so widespread at that time. These were the Bureau of Refugees, Freedmen, and Abandoned Lands (known informally as the Freedmen's Bureau), which operated from 1865 to 1872, and the Civil War Veterans Pension Program, established in 1862. The Freedmen's Bureau was designed to help both African Americans and Whites by providing food, clothing, and fuel to the formerly enslaved and White war refugees. It was also charged with establishing schools, supplying medical services, overseeing contracts between the freedmen and their employers, managing confiscated or abandoned land, and securing equal justice before the law for Blacks (Williams 2003).

According to political scientist Linda Faye Williams, in spite of some impressive success stories, the goals of the Freedmen's Bureau were undermined by antagonistic elements in the federal government almost from the beginning. This opposition made it difficult for the bureau to succeed. First, the Bureau was initially designed to operate for just one year, and Congress appropriated no funds to carry out its duties, so the Bureau operated on donations. Eventually, after much struggle, congressional funding was provided and the life of the Bureau was extended to six years, but even this was inadequate considering the length of time for which slavery had existed in the country (almost 250 years, dating from 1619 to 1865).

Bureau efforts to redistribute confiscated Confederate land to the freedmen faced strong political opposition (most notably from President Andrew Johnson), and therefore were ultimately abandoned. Eventually, after President Johnson gained control over the Bureau, the organization encouraged the newly freed slaves to "lay aside their bitter feelings, and become reconciled to their old masters" (Williams 2003: 44). In other words, instead of becoming landowners, Blacks were encouraged to become sharecroppers and tenant farmers—essentially one step removed from chattel slavery. The Bureau was unpopular throughout its seven years of existence. For example, when President Johnson vetoed the Freedmen's Bureau Bill in February 1866, he argued that Congress had never passed legislation to provide economic relief to "our own people—the thousands, not to say millions of the white race, who are honestly toiling from day to day for their subsistence" (Williams 2003: 50). According to Johnson and other critics, the Bureau was too expensive and fostered dependency among the freedmen. Congress eventually passed a compromised version of the legislation in spite of yet another veto from President Johnson. Still, the Bureau was constantly struggling for funding and restrictions were imposed on who was eligible for aid. In October 1866, support was limited to orphans, the disabled, the elderly, or members of Union soldiers' families. In early January 1867, additional restrictions were imposed so that assistance was provided only to orphans and Blacks in "regularly organized hospitals" (Williams 2003: 49). Eventually, the Bureau was disbanded and folded into the War Department in 1872.

The stinginess and controversy of the Freedman's Bureau stood out because federal social policy during this period of American history was *not* inherently controversial and stingy. Take, for example, the Civil War Veterans Pension Program, whose beneficiaries were primarily White (Blacks made up about 10 percent of Union forces). The Veterans Pension Program differs from the Freedmen's Bureau on a number of dimensions. First, the Veterans program provided generous cash assistance rather than mostly goods and services as offered by the Freedmen's Bureau. Moreover, unlike the Freedmen's Bureau, beneficiaries of the Veterans program were viewed as "deserving," and "dependency" concerns were never an issue. Also, unlike the Bureau, the Veterans program became more expansive over time. Although initially authorized in 1862, it remained in place over several decades, and by 1890, the Veterans program was extended to cover veterans who had become disabled *after* their service in the Civil War. Lastly, the Veterans program was not means-tested, or conditional on destitution.

Williams derives several lessons from her comparison of the Freedmen's Bureau and the Civil War Veterans Pension Program. First, federal efforts to address racial inequality were typically short-lived, under-funded, and half-hearted. Second, federal relief efforts distinguished between the "deserving" and "undeserving." And, third, ideological opposition to federal efforts to address racial inequality was most effective when adopting racially neutral criticisms such as an overreliance on "big government," charges of "unfairness," references to "special interests," and—perhaps most importantly—leveling charges of "dependency." Although in theory, all of these criticisms could have been leveled at the Civil War Veterans Pension Program, in the end, they were not. In short, federal efforts to reduce racial inequality were often stigmatized whereas federal efforts directed at White constituencies were generally popular and well funded. As we indicate later in this chapter and throughout this textbook, this practice would continue well into the twentieth and twenty-first century.

How did the Veterans program deal with Black Civil War veterans? Although the administration of the Veterans program was *not* overtly discriminatory (i.e., Black veterans were not officially denied access to benefits), institutional racism (specifically how Black soldiers were used during the war compared with White soldiers) still contributed to a racial bias in the provision of the benefits Blacks received. For example, Black soldiers were often forced to serve under dangerous or unsanitary conditions, which contributed to greater casualties among Black soldiers. About 21 percent of Black soldiers died during the war compared with 16 percent of White Union soldiers. When the Veterans program was expanded in 1890, far fewer Black soldiers (28 percent) than White soldiers, Union (51 percent) or Confederate (49 percent), had survived to take advantage of it (Williams 2003).

Because the Veteran's Pension Program was a national program, those Black veterans who resided in the North benefited about as much as White veterans. However, only about a quarter (27 percent) of Black Union veterans lived in the North at the time when benefits were greatly expanded (1890). In the South, a variety of strategies were adopted to prevent Blacks from taking full advantage of benefits they had fairly earned. Thus, by 1890, only about 51 percent of Black veterans' families had received their Civil War pensions, compared with 80 percent of Whites.

Confederate Veterans Pension Programs

Confederate soldiers were not eligible for the federally administered Veteran's Pension Program, but they did eventually receive pensions from each of the former Confederate states (as well as Kentucky, Missouri, and Oklahoma). For obvious reasons, Blacks did not serve in large numbers as combatants in the Confederate army, but according to the Mississippi Historical Society they did "serve," typically in the capacity of nonvoluntary enslaved people, providing support by working on specific military projects or in "war-related foundries, munitions factories, and mines" (Hollandsworth 2008). Enslaved people were also compelled to assist the Confederate war effort by serving as servants and company cooks. In spite of this service, Blacks were not initially eligible for Confederate pensions in any state except for Mississippi. Several additional states opened up their pensions to African Americans who had worked on behalf of the Confederacy but only after 1921, when the vast majority of Black veterans had long since passed away.

Economists Shari Eli and Laura Salisbury argue that Confederate Veterans' pensions intentionally excluded African Americans—and in fact, they argue that this was the point of establishing the program (Eli and Salisbury 2016). In the 1880s and 1890s the Democratic Party in the South—at that time, almost exclusively White—was still locked in an electoral battle with the Republican Party, to which almost all African Americans belonged. In order to attract White support, Democratic leaders across the South advanced the Confederate Veterans program as a form of patronage, especially courting the vote of the White rural poor—but without making such overtures to Southern Blacks (Republicans).

Confederate Veterans pensions were paid for by drawing on taxes collected by the state. Thus, African American taxpayers were partially responsible for subsidizing these pensions. During this period, three states (Mississippi, Louisiana, and South Carolina) had majority African American populations and several others (e.g., Alabama, Florida, and Georgia) had at least 40 percent Black populations. So, during this period, the taxes paid by Black Southerners helped to fund pensions for veterans who fought to keep them enslaved, and from which they were systematically excluded.

The Push for (and Rejection of) Reparations

What about pensions—or reparations—for the formerly enslaved? A number of efforts were proposed within the federal government to address the widespread economic uncertainty facing the newly emancipated African Americans. However, each of these efforts was successfully challenged and squashed. The first effort to compensate African Americans for their centuries of involuntary servitude came when Union General William Tecumseh Sherman issued Special Field Order No. 15 in January 1865, near the end of the Civil War. This order, approved by President Lincoln, promised 40 acres of abandoned and/or confiscated land in Florida, Georgia, and South Carolina to the former slaves. General Sherman also planned to provide mules, for rent, to those who settled on these lands. Additionally, section 4 of the Freedmen's Bureau Act of March 1865 had authorized the Bureau to rent up to "40 acres of confiscated or abandoned land to freed people and loyal white refugees for a term of three years. At the end of the term, or at any point during the term, the male occupants renting the land had the option to purchase it and would then receive a title to the land" (Perry 2010). The assassination of President Lincoln in April 1865 brought an abrupt end to this plan. Lincoln's successor, former Vice President Andrew Johnson, was a Southerner and far more sympathetic to the former slave owners. President Johnson provided pardons to many of the Confederate officers and ordered the restoration of their land with Circular No. 15. This policy, issued under the auspices of the Freedmen's Bureau under the direct orders of the new president, had the effect of ending any land redistribution plans overseen by the federal government.

Some additional efforts in Congress were made to provide compensation for the former slaves, including a plan introduced in March 1867 by House Speaker

Thaddeus Stevens (R-Pennsylvania). This specific passage from H.R. 29 lays out the stated intention of the legislation:

Out of the lands thus seized and confiscated, the slaves who have been liberated by the operations of the war and the amendment of the Constitution or otherwise, who resided in said "confederate States" on the 4th day of March, A.D. 1861 or since, shall have distributed to them as follows namely: to each male person who is the head of a family, forty acres; to each adult male, whether the head of a family or not, forty acres; to each widow who is the head of a family, forty acres; to be held by them in fee simple, but to be inalienable for the next ten years after they become seized thereof . . . At the end of ten years the absolute title to said homesteads shall be conveyed to said owners or to their heirs of such as are then dead. (Perry 2010)

In the end neither this plan, nor others introduced during this period, were enacted due to opposition in Congress and from President Lincoln's successor, Andrew Johnson.

The Movement for (and Opposition to) a Pension Plan for Former Slaves

As the federal government was seeking to expand the Civil War Veterans Pension plan, and the Southern states were instituting the Confederate Veterans pension plan, a movement emerged among African Americans to fight for a pension plan for the formerly enslaved population. A number of organizations, inspired in part by the Veterans pension plan, arose to support this movement. The most prominent was the National Ex-Slave Mutual Relief, Bounty and Pension Association of the United States of America (MRB&PA), established in 1894 with headquarters in Nashville, Tennessee (Berry 1972). The MRB&PA claimed that its national membership numbered in the hundreds of thousands. The two leaders most closely associated with this organization were Isaiah H. Dickerson, a minister and educator, and Callie D. House, a formerly enslaved widow and laundress. Aside from lobbying Congress on behalf of a pension plan for emancipated African Americans, the group also received financial support from its membership to fund their lobbying activities, support work-related travel for the leadership of the organization, and for "mutual aid purposes (to aid the sick, the disabled, and for burial expenses)" (Perry 2010).

As the MRB&PA grew in numbers and influence it attracted opposition from the Federal Bureau of Pensions (the agency that preceded the Veterans Administration), the U.S. Post Office Department, and the U.S. Department of Justice. Each of these agencies adopted a variety of strategies to undermine the pension plan movement for ex-slaves. For example, the Bureau of Pensions investigated movement leaders and kept them under surveillance to determine if they were engaged in fraud—even though the group had a First Amendment right to peacefully assemble and lobby Congress on behalf of its perceived interests. As with the Bureau of Pensions, the Post Office concluded, without any evidence, that movement leaders were engaged in fraud. Consequently, acting assistant attorney general for the Post Office Department, Harrison Barrett, issued a fraud order against the

MRB&PA, which had the effect of preventing the organization from sending or receiving mail, the primary means by which it communicated with its members and received financial support. The organization was also investigated by the Department of Justice. House, Dickerson, and other movement leaders denied all wrongdoing and hired a lawyer to combat what they regarded as government harassment. The Post Office Department continued to investigate House, eventually having her arrested and indicted for mail fraud (the charge, which she denied, was that she made false claims in information sent through the mail guaranteeing pensions to association members). She was tried by an all-White jury and found guilty in September 1917. She was sentenced to a year in jail at the Missouri State Prison. As a result of House's conviction, the organization was effectively destroyed. In a pattern that would repeat itself over the next 100-plus years, local, state, and federal government entities would continue to target and disrupt activists working on behalf of African Americans, including Marcus Garvey, W. E. B. DuBois, Rosa Parks, Dr. Martin Luther King Jr., Fannie Lou Hamer, Malcolm X, Black Panther Party leader Fred Hampton, Black Lives Matter Movement activists, and many more (Breitman, Porter, and Smith 1976; Gage 2014; Mitchell 2019; Stafford 2021).

Institutional Discrimination under Jim Crow

Although African Americans did not receive compensation for their involuntary servitude, the end of the Civil War brought on greater social and political freedom than the group had ever known in the United States. This included—at least for Black men over the age of 21—the right to vote and hold elective office. The Reconstruction Act of 1867 authorized military commanders of the ten Southern districts to establish procedures wherein the freedmen, as well as Whites, would be registered to vote for any proposed Constitutional Convention in the various states. The state constitutions had to be rewritten to reflect the reality that Blacks were now citizens and that all adult males were eligible to vote. The passage of the Fifteenth Amendment in 1870 solidified this point. As a result of these changes, Blacks were elected to a variety of offices in the post-Civil War South. One such official was Hiram Revels, who in 1870 became the first African American to serve in the U.S. Congress when he was elected by the Mississippi state legislature to represent the state in the U.S. Senate (senators were not elected by popular vote until the ratification of the Seventeenth Amendment in 1913). Several other Black men served in the U.S. House of Representatives during this time. These political successes were soon curtailed, however, with the Compromise of 1877 and the rise of Jim Crow.

The Compromise of 1877 and the End of Reconstruction

Whites affiliated with the Democratic Party used a variety of illegal tactics, including fraud, intimidation, and outright violence, to reacquire political control throughout the South. Union troops were stationed in many parts of the South to prevent politically motivated violence, but over time Republican politicians in the North became less committed to protecting the civil rights of Blacks in the region. As a result, White Southern Democrats began to regain political control culminating in yet another instance of institutional discrimination: the Compromise of 1877. In the closely contested presidential contest of 1876, Democratic candidate Samuel J. Tilden won the popular vote against his Republican opponent, Rutherford B. Hayes. However, in a controversial decision, Hayes was awarded the tie-breaking electoral vote, granting him a 185 to 184 victory. Historians argue that in order to resolve this impasse, Republican and Democratic leaders cut a deal that would result in Hayes being declared the winner of the election in exchange for the removal of—or, more accurately, the refusal to actively deploy—the last federal troops stationed in the South. The last remaining troops were stationed in Louisiana, South Carolina, and parts of Florida in order to keep the peace and provide support to the newly enfranchised African Americans. With the deal resulting in the Compromise of 1877, Reconstruction was effectively ended, thus ushering in nearly a century of state-sponsored efforts to undermine the civil and human rights of Black Americans, the period that is generally referred to as the Jim Crow era.

The Role of Federal Court Decisions

A series of Supreme Court decisions facilitated the implementation of Jim Crow laws. One of the more consequential decisions during this period involved the overturning of the Civil Rights Act of 1875. The Civil Rights Act of 1875 was initially drafted by Republican Senator Charles Sumner and African American abolitionist John Mercer Langston, and sought to ensure that Blacks received equal treatment in public accommodations, public transportation, and in their service on juries. Denial of such rights, in the view of the authors of this legislation, represented an unconstitutional badge of slavery and violated the Equal Protection Clause. In short, the law drew its authority from the Thirteenth and Fourteenth Amendments to the Constitution, which abolished slavery, established birthright citizenship, and declared that no state shall deprive citizens of equal protection of the laws. In both cases, the Congress was given the explicit power to "enforce by appropriate legislation," the provisions outlined in the amendments. Nevertheless, the Supreme Court declared the 1875 Civil Rights Act to be unconstitutional in 1883 in an 8 to 1 decision. Essentially, the Court found that the Fourteenth Amendment protections regarding equal treatment under the law applied only to state actions but not to the actions of private citizens. This meant that while Congress could regulate the actions of state actors, they could not prevent private citizens from discriminating based on race. Justice Joseph P. Bradley authored the majority decision, writing:

When a man has emerged from slavery, and, by the aid of beneficent legislation, has shaken off the inseparable concomitants of that state, there must be some stage in the progress of his elevation when he takes the rank of a mere citizen and ceases to be the special favorite of the laws, and when his rights as a citizen or a man are to be protected in the ordinary models by which other men's rights are protected.[1]

In other words, the Court is saying that eighteen years (the Thirteenth Amendment abolishing slavery was ratified in 1865) is a sufficient amount of time to overcome the lingering influences of approximately 250 years of chattel slavery. On its face this decision has the veneer of being race-neutral, but in practice it had the effect of removing institutional support from a politically vulnerable population surrounded by powerful and hostile adversaries.

Following this ruling, it did not take long for Southern and Border states to establish laws requiring separate accommodations for Black and White citizens in virtually all aspects of public life, including schools, cemeteries, churches, public transportation, etc. African Americans challenged these laws in the courts, reasoning that when they involved official actions taken by the state they represented violations of the equal protection clause of the Fourteenth Amendment. The most famous case challenging segregationist laws was *Plessy* v. *Ferguson*, decided in 1896.

In *Plessy* v. *Ferguson*, the plaintiff (Plessy) objected to an 1890 Louisiana law that required separate railway cars for White and "colored" customers. Plessy, who described himself as "seven-eighths Caucasian and one-eighth African blood," sought to challenge the constitutionality of the law by sitting in the "White" section.[2] He was subsequently arrested for violating the law. In the Supreme Court's 8 to 1 decision, the scope of the Fourteenth Amendment was reduced even more than with their judgment on the 1875 Civil Rights Act. The doctrine of "separate-but-equal" in public accommodations was declared constitutional. This decision would remain the law of the land for over fifty years before being reversed by a unanimous Supreme Court in the celebrated 1954 *Brown* v. *Board of Education* decision. In the interim period, however, segregated facilities sanctioned by the local, state, and federal government became commonplace throughout the South and in many Border states.

Other Mechanisms for Undermining Political Power of Blacks in the South

A number of institutional mechanisms were employed throughout the Jim Crow era to undermine Black political power in the South—where the vast majority of African Americans still lived. As Gunnar Myrdal wrote in *An American Dilemma* "... the most efficient device in use today to keep Negroes from voting where the vote would count most in the South is the 'white primary.' The Democratic Party prohibited Negroes from participating in its primary by means of state-wide rule ... in nine Southern states: Mississippi, Alabama, Georgia, Florida, South Carolina,

---

[1] You can read the full text at: www.law.cornell.edu/supremecourt/text/109/3.
[2] See at: www.law.cornell.edu/supremecourt/text/163/537.

Louisiana, Arkansas, Virginia, and Texas" (Myrdal 1996: 480). And, in case there was any confusion, Myrdal points out that the exclusion was entirely about race and not partisanship: "In many areas white *Republicans* are permitted to vote in the Democratic primaries, but Negro *Democrats* are not" (481). Most of the Southern states adopted White primaries between 1896 and 1908. One of the reasons that excluding African Americans, as well as Mexican Americans and other people of color, from participating in Democratic primary activities was so effective was that, during the Jim Crow era, the Democratic Party was effectively the only political party in the South (Key 1949; Mickey 2015). This meant that in the general election the Democratic candidate typically ran unopposed. The only contested elections were in the Democratic primaries. The federal courts went back and forth on the constitutionality of White primaries from the late 1920s through the 1940s, before finally declaring the practice unconstitutional in the 1944 *Smith* v. *Allwright* decision.

Daria Roithmayr (2018) argues that the widespread use of White primaries were not simply motivated by irrational prejudice, but were more similar to a business cartel or in this case, a racial cartel. A cartel is an association of businesses that have organized to artificially reduce competition so as to inflate the price of their goods or services. Traditionally, cartels use such strategies as boycotts, intimidation, and violence to shut out their competition. Roithmayr argues that Southern Whites adopted these same strategies in order to artificially inflate the political influence of their racial group. As discussed previously, many Southern states had substantial Black populations, with Black majorities in Mississippi, South Carolina, and Louisiana well into the 1920s. Thus, Roithmayr maintains that the Democratic Party in the South utilized the White primary—with the tacit approval or acquiescence of the federal government up until the 1940s—in order to gain a political advantage vis-à-vis African Americans. One of the hallmarks of institutional racism is that the specific perpetrators are often difficult to identify, and it is unclear whether the motives are necessarily driven by racial animus.

Institutional Discrimination and the New Deal

Some scholars have argued that institutional discrimination was a central component of American politics at the federal level even during one of the most politically progressive eras in our history: the presidential administrations of Franklin D. Roosevelt and Harry S. Truman (Katznelson 2005). In fact, the New Deal policies of Franklin D. Roosevelt and the Fair Deal policies of his successor Harry Truman are arguably responsible for exacerbating racial inequalities, even as they led to the creation of the White middle class (Katznelson 2005). This was a result of the manner in which these policies were designed and implemented in the 1930s and 1940s. The disproportionate political strength of the segregationist South and the acquiescence of Northern (White) Democrats allowed New Deal legislation to be designed and implemented in a discriminatory manner that privileged Whites and disadvantaged African Americans and other people of color.

With the stock market crash of 1929, the United States and eventually most of the industrialized world would be plunged into the Great Depression. President Herbert Hoover's administration was caught off-guard by the widespread economic misfortune and many viewed his response as inadequate. This set the stage for Hoover's challenger in the 1932 presidential contest, the Democratic Governor of New York, Franklin D. Roosevelt. Roosevelt won the presidency in a landslide and quickly moved to institute his "New Deal" policies, involving public work projects designed to address the skyrocketing unemployment rate, as well as various regulations and financial reforms. Some of the most prominent programs that came out of the New Deal were the Civilian Conservation Corps, the Farm Security Administration, the National Industrial Recovery Act, the Civil Works Administration, the Works Progress Administration, and the Social Security Administration. Roosevelt transformed the federal government into a much more proactive institution. The programs created by his administration provided support for the unemployed, farmers, the poor, and the elderly.

The New Deal provided much-needed relief to Americans struggling during the Great Depression—and laid the groundwork for the expansion of the middle class in the 1950s. But what is often overlooked is the way that institutional racism determined who benefited from New Deal programs.

President Roosevelt experienced unprecedented political success throughout the 1930s and the early 1940s. He remains the only individual in American history to have been elected to the presidency four times, relying heavily on the unified support of the "solid South" (the Twenty-Second Amendment, passed in 1951, limited the presidency to two four-year terms). Since the end of Reconstruction, the South had voted consistently for the Democratic presidential candidate. Since the "solid South" during this period was also the Jim Crow South, this meant that Blacks were effectively disenfranchised throughout the region and members of Congress from the South typically faced no significant opposition in the general election. As a result, Southern members of Congress had no electoral incentive to be responsive to their Black "constituents." And, due to the lack of competition, Southern members had an advantage, relative to other parts of the country with competitive elections, in gaining seniority on influential congressional committees. Because segregationist Democrats chaired many of the influential committees in the House of Representatives—which they acquired through seniority—they were able to exercise outsized influence on the New Deal legislation proposed by the Roosevelt administration. This influence was used in a variety of ways to discriminate against African Americans and other people of color.

Katznelson (2005) identifies three strategies undertaken by Southern Democratic lawmakers to ensure that Whites would be advantaged relative to Blacks within any proposed New Deal legislation. First, laws such as the 1935 Social Security Act (SSA) intended to assist the poor and workers in general were designed so as to systematically exclude African Americans. This was not done overtly, by inscribing racial restrictions into the new laws, but covertly, by excluding occupations that were disproportionately Black. For example, in the 1930s roughly 60 percent of

Photo 5.1 View of a passenger under a sign that reads "Colored Waiting Room" at a bus station in Durham, NC, 1940.
Source: Photo Jack Delano © Library of Congress/Interim Archives/Contributor/Archive Photos/Getty Images.

Blacks throughout the country worked as either farmworkers or maids. In the South, this figure was closer to 75 percent. The job categories of maid or farmworker were specifically excluded from the anti-poverty language of the SSA thereby preventing these workers from receiving minimum wage and regulated work hour protections. These jobs were also excluded from the law creating the modern unions and, at least until the 1950s, from protections associated with Social Security.

A second strategy used by Southern Democrats involved designing how the New Deal legislation would be implemented. Southern lawmakers insisted that the new agencies developed by the Roosevelt administration be administered at the local level. In the case of the South, this meant that local officials—typically ones sympathetic to segregation—would be charged with administering programs designed to assist the poor, the unemployed, senior citizens, and veterans. As a result, local administrators could deny African Americans access to benefits, such as Aid to Families with Dependent Children (AFDC), without fear of federal oversight.

The third strategy involved an act of omission rather than commission. When the New Deal legislation was being designed, segregationists in Congress insisted that the laws would not contain any anti-discrimination provisions. As a result, it was legally permissible to allocate goods and services on a racially discriminatory basis, even as the nation was seeking to recover from the worst economic calamity in history. As Katznelson (2005) argues, this amounted to an aggressive affirmative action policy for Whites only.

The ways in which racial considerations shaped New Deal legislation illustrate yet again the hallmarks of institutional discrimination. As with the demise of the Freedmen's Bureau and the abrupt ending of Reconstruction by federal inaction and unfavorable court decisions, it is difficult to attribute the discriminatory foundation built into Roosevelt's New Deal to a specific perpetrator. Additionally, attributing the discriminatory act to racial prejudice is also difficult since the legislation was written in such a way so as to obscure any racial motivation. All of this makes it more difficult to combat the unseen forces responsible for rules and bureaucratic procedures that promote racial inequality. And, as discussed later in this chapter, one contemporary manifestation of these historical patterns is the modern-day racial wealth gap. In short, Whites have over several generations been able to amass wealth and pass it down to their children whereas ethnic and racial minorities have been denied this opportunity.

Institutional Discrimination and U.S. Immigration Policy

Another area where institutional discrimination has exerted considerable influence is in U.S. immigration policy. As was the case during the periods of Reconstruction and the Great Depression, the design of immigration legislation, the ways in which the federal courts interpreted these laws, and the way they have been implemented have often been biased against immigrants who do not come from Europe.

Race and Citizenship

The United States government has imposed a racial litmus test on citizenship since the founding of the republic. The earliest legislation designed to specify who was eligible to become a citizen was the Naturalization Act of 1790. This law limited naturalization, or the process by which immigrants can petition to become American citizens, to "free white person[s] … [of] good moral character" (Masuoka and Junn 2013: 44). As a practical matter, this legislation excluded Native Americans and individuals of African and Asian descent. Following the Civil War, this law was overridden by new legislation that extended citizenship and the possibility of naturalization to individuals of African ancestry. Restrictions remained, however, for Asian immigrants and Indigenous populations.

Mexican immigrants during this period fell into a gray area in terms of their eligibility to become naturalized citizens. On the one hand, the 1848 Treaty of Hidalgo Guadalupe—negotiated after the United States defeated Mexico in the 1846 Mexican–American war—stipulated that those former Mexican citizens who wished to remain in the territories acquired by the United States (i.e., California,

Nevada, Utah, most of Arizona, Colorado, and New Mexico, and parts of Kansas, Oklahoma, Texas, and Wyoming) at the conclusion of the war would have full citizenship rights (Garcia Bedolla 2009). This presumably meant that Mexicans immigrating to the United States after the treaty had been ratified would also be eligible to become American citizens. On the other hand, the Naturalization Act of 1870, which amended the Naturalization Act of 1790, indicated that only Whites and people of African descent could become U.S. citizens. Did Mexicans, who often had both European (Spanish) and Indigenous ancestry, qualify as White? A federal judge (*In re Rodríguez* 1897) concluded that in the eyes of the law Mexicans were "White," but Bureau of Immigration and Naturalization regional officers remained unconvinced (Molina 2010). This ambiguity took on more urgency in the 1910s as more Mexicans immigrated to the United States due to the instability of the Mexican Revolution (1910–1920) and the increased demand for Mexican labor during the First World War.

Whatever the uncertainty of the racial status of Mexicans, a series of legislative and administrative acts would prove effective in discouraging Mexican immigration (Molina 2010). First, the Immigration Act of 1917, although primarily designed to deter Asian immigration, also imposed restrictions such as literacy tests for the first time on Mexicans seeking to immigrate to the United States. Second, border stations began adopting humiliating medical inspections for immigrants at the southern border as an additional deterrent. Third, in 1924 the United States–Mexican Border Patrol was created, thereby providing additional practical (e.g., checkpoint harassment) and symbolic barriers to immigration from Mexico. Finally, in 1928, the U.S. State Department significantly reduced Mexican immigration by "instructing its consular offices in Mexico to curtail the number of visas issued" (Molina 2010: 188–189). As a result, authorized immigration from Mexico declined sharply.

Efforts to restrict Asian immigration were often less subtle. For example, in 1882 Congress passed the Chinese Exclusion Act. As its name suggests, this law imposed a ten-year ban, or moratorium, on Chinese immigration into the United States. Ten years later the ban was extended for another ten-year period before being made permanent in 1902.

Legislators added even more exclusionary policies to immigration laws in the twentieth century. For example, the 1917 Immigration Act mentioned earlier imposed literacy tests on immigrants and provided immigration officials with greater discretion in deciding who would be excluded. More importantly, the legislation established an "Asiatic Barred Zone," which essentially barred all Asian immigrants from entry into the United States. The 1924 Immigration Act pushed this effort even further by establishing national origin quotas. The law was designed so that immigration visas could only be issued to "two percent of the total number of people of each nationality in the United States as of the 1890 national census."[3] This provision sought to obscure its nativist motivations by adopting an

---

[3] See at: https://history.state.gov/milestones/1921-1936/immigration-act.

indirect way of sharply limiting the number of immigrants from eastern or southern Europe—and thus limiting the number of Jewish, Italian, Greek, Slavic, or Polish immigrants. At the time, these groups were not regarded as authentically "White" in the same way as their Anglo-Saxon counterparts. A provision in the 1924 legislation stipulated that those immigrants who could not become naturalized citizens were barred from immigrating to the United States. Since the Naturalization Act of 1790 (and its successor in 1870) excluded Asians from naturalization, this provision effectively banned all immigration from Asia. The quota system introduced with this Act would remain official U.S. policy until the passage of the Immigration and Nationality Act of 1965.

Government efforts to prevent immigration from Asia and Mexico, as well as from southern Europe in the first half of the twentieth century are in sharp contrast to the more welcoming posture to immigrants adopted in earlier periods of American history. Indeed, even in the early twentieth century, unlawful or "illegal" immigrants from Europe were rarely criminalized and deported at the rates common in the twenty-first century. For example, immigrants unlawfully entering the country prior to 1940—a disproportionately European population—were "protected from deportation by statutes of limitations, and in the 1930s and 1940s, tens of thousands of unauthorized immigrants ... were given amnesty" (Kamasaki 2021). Undocumented immigrants in the late twentieth and early twenty-first centuries, however, have faced a far more punitive environment. The fact that these immigrants are overwhelmingly from Asia and Latin America, rather than Europe, highlights the racially biased ways in which immigration laws have been enacted and enforced.

The Incarceration of Japanese Americans

On December 7, 1941 the Japanese bombed Pearl Harbor, the U.S. naval base in Hawaii. The following day, the United States declared war on Japan, thereby entering the Second World War and also setting the stage for the federal government to relocate and incarcerate over 100,000 Japanese Americans in concentration camps. The official reason for the internment was the concern that Japanese Americans, virtually all of whom were located on the West coast, might pose a security risk during the war. The concern was that at least some might have a greater allegiance to Japan than to the United States, and that they therefore might be motivated to engage in espionage. Since most individuals of Japanese descent in America (over 60 percent) were natural-born citizens, this prospect seems unlikely (Backman and Gonchar 2017). The remaining percentage—those born outside the United States—may have also wanted to become citizens, but unlike European immigrants during this time period, Asian immigrants were legally barred from becoming naturalized citizens.

The relocation and internment process, unfolding between 1942 and 1945, resulted in tremendous financial, psychological, and physical loss for Japanese Americans. They were ordered to leave their homes with only the property they could carry. Many lost their homes or businesses as a result of their incarceration. Also, the stress and depression associated with captivity was common throughout the internment camps. There were also life and death consequences of the federally sanctioned incarceration. Several camp residents were shot and killed by armed guards, some while attempting to escape.[4]

Was Japanese internment a case of institutional discrimination? It is hard to see it in any other way. First, the federal government undeniably sanctioned the action. President Roosevelt authorized the internment with Executive Order 9066. The War Department implemented the incarceration process with the full assistance of the state of California, where most Japanese Americans resided. Fred Korematsu, a Japanese American who had been born in California, challenged the legality of the internment in the courts. The Supreme Court eventually heard his case, *Korematsu* v. *United States*, in 1944. In a landmark 6-3 decision the Court held that the internment was constitutional. Thus, the state of California, along with the executive and judicial branches of the federal government, all endorsed the relocation and internment of Japanese Americans.

Consider as well the groups that were disproportionately affected. Given the anti-Japanese climate in the country following the attacks on Pearl Harbor, it is perhaps not surprising that Japanese Americans were rounded up and relocated to concentration camps located away from the West coast. However, the United States also declared war on Germany and Italy just days after declaring war on Japan. Some German and Italian immigrants, as well as German American and Italian American citizens were also imprisoned during the war because of security concerns. For example, over 11,000 people of German ancestry were interned during the Second World War, as were more than 400 individuals of Italian ancestry. Neither of these numbers is trivial nor should we discount the disruption that internment had on these populations. Nevertheless, the number of Japanese Americans interned is many times larger than the number of German or Italian Americans. It is fair to conclude that concerns about treasonous activity were focused primarily on the racially distinctive Japanese American population rather than those with ancestral ties to the European countries of Germany or Italy.

Perhaps the clearest evidence that the internment of Japanese Americans should be classified as institutional discrimination is that the United States government admitted as much many decades after the end of the war. In 1976, President Gerald R. Ford acknowledged that the internment was "a national mistake." In 1982, a unanimous congressional commission concluded that the internment was not motivated by legitimate wartime considerations and that there were no substantiated instances of Japanese Americans engaging in sabotage or espionage. Moreover, the report indicated that the internment was driven by "race prejudice, war hysteria and a failure of political leadership."[5] In 1988, Congress passed the Civil Liberties Act which granted each Japanese American internee—provided that they were American citizens or legal residents—$20,000 in compensation.

---

[4] See at: https://encyclopedia.densho.org/Homicide_in_camp.

[5] See at: https://encyclopedia.densho.org/Commission_on_Wartime_Relocation_and_Internment_of_ Civilians/#Specific_Findings_and_Recommendations.

Photo 5.2 A sign installed by Tatsuro Matsuda on the Wanto Co. grocery store in Oakland, CA, on December 8, 1941, reads, "I AM AN AMERICAN." The store was closed after the attack on Pearl Harbor and the Matsuda family, who owned it, were relocated and incarcerated under the U.S. government's policy of internment of Japanese Americans. Matsuda was a University of California graduate.
Source: Photo Dorothea Lange © Historical/Contributor/Corbis Historical/Getty Images.

Institutional Discrimination and Native Americans

Institutional discrimination has not simply targeted enslaved Africans and their descendants, or non-European immigrants. The power of government and other significant institutions has also been used to expand the boundaries of the United States through the acquisition of Native American lands, and the use of a variety of methods ranging from deceit, to forced removal, to genocide.[6] The nineteenth-century

---

[6] The United Nations Office on Genocide Prevention and the Responsibility to Protect defines genocide as "killing members of the group; causing serious bodily or mental harm; deliberately inflicting on the group conditions of life calculated to bring about its physical destruction in whole or in part; imposing measures intended to prevent births within the group; and forcibly transferring children of the group to another group" (Dunbar-Ortiz 2014).

philosophy that justified these actions was known as "Manifest Destiny," which held that it was preordained by God that the United States would inevitably conquer, and bring under its control, the North American continent. The fact that hundreds of Native American nations already resided on this territory and had done so for centuries was regarded as, at best, inconvenient. It is beyond the scope of this chapter to provide a comprehensive review of the extensive litany of broken treaties with Native American nations, and the numerous bloody military engagements that constitute what is euphemistically referred to as the "settling of the American West." In this section, however, we will summarize some of the more consequential steps taken by the government to undermine, remove, and eradicate the populations that inhabited this continent before the arrival of Europeans.

The Trail of Tears and Its Aftermath

Relations between the newly formed American government and the Native American societies located east of the Mississippi River took many forms in the late eighteenth and early nineteenth centuries. At times these encounters could be described as bureaucratic and even cooperative, while at other times they were more brutal and one-sided. Invariably, the goal was to acquire Indigenous lands and open them up to American settlers. For example, in 1805 the United States gained possession of most of the land of the Choctaws and Chickasaws—nations located primarily in the southeast—by purchasing them for $50,000 and $20,000, respectively (Dunbar-Ortiz 2014). The Muskogee (Creek) Nation, located throughout parts of what are now the states of Alabama, Florida, Georgia, and Tennessee, was less receptive to this strategy. Elements within the Muskogee Nation, known as the Red Sticks, resisted settler expansion into their ancestral territory and came into armed conflict with the Tennessee militia, led by future president Andrew Jackson. In the decisive battle between the two forces in March 1814, Jackson's militia killed 800 Muskogee and allied fighters. Jackson lost only forty-nine men. In addition to the lopsided casualties, the Red Sticks ultimately surrendered because Jackson had captured and held hostage 300 of the Muskogee wives, and children. The treaty that the defeated Muskogee were forced to sign required them to relinquish most of their lands and move out west (Dumbar-Ortiz 2014).

A series of conflicts between the United States and Indigenous nations followed the battle with the Red Sticks. Despite this, the so-called "Five Civilized Tribes" (Cherokee, Chocktaw, Chickasaw, Muscogee, and Seminole) had sought to remain in their ancestral homes east of the Mississippi River, with many of these societies hoping to coexist with the Americans by adopting western traditions, including Christianity, English literacy, and even slavery. However, in 1830, Congress—at the urging of President Andrew Jackson—enacted the Indian Removal Act, effectively ending the policy of coexistence. As the name suggests, this policy called for the federal government to transfer Native populations from their homes in the southeast to federal territory in Oklahoma (see Figure 5.3).

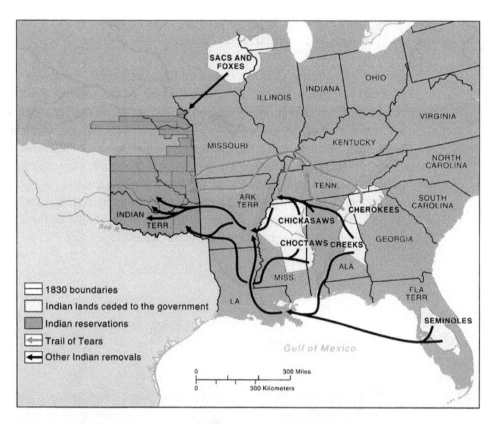

Figure 5.3 Native American Removal from the southeast
Congress passed the Indian Removal Act on May 28, 1830, which began the forced relocation of thousands of Native Americans from their lands in the southeast to federal territory in Oklahoma.
Source: Own work by Nikater, submitted to the public domain. Background map courtesy of Demis, www.demis.nl and Wilcomb E. Washburn (Ed.), *Handbook of North American Indians. Vol. 4: History of Indian–White Relations*. Smithsonian Institution Press, Washington, D.C., 1988.

The eventual impact of the Indian Removal Act was far-reaching and devastating. A series of involuntary migrations of Native Americans occurred after the passage of this legislation. For example, "the 1838 forced march of the Cherokee Nation, now known as the Trail of Tears, was an arduous journey from the remaining Cherokee homelands in Georgia and Alabama to what would later become northeastern Oklahoma" (Dunbar-Ortiz 2014). The forced march unfolded on foot, in the dead of winter. Approximately half of the 16,000 Cherokee men, women, and children who endured the involuntary migration died along the way. One Georgia volunteer who helped to oversee the migration and later became a colonel in the Confederate army, made the following observation about the deadly journey: "I fought through the civil war and have seen men shot to pieces and slaughtered by the thousands, but the Cherokee removal was the cruelest work

I ever knew" (Dunbar-Ortiz 2014). Other Indigenous groups, such as the Seminoles and the Muskogee, experienced similar casualty rates in their forced removal to "Indian country."

Armed battles between U.S. forces and Indigenous nations continued after the Trail of Tears, especially among the Plains Indians of the southwest such as the Apache and the Sioux. However, by the end of the nineteenth century—particularly after the 1890 Wounded Knee Massacre in South Dakota, in which roughly 300 Sioux men, women, and children were killed by the 7th U.S. Cavalry Regiment—such conflicts became increasingly rare. By the early twentieth century, the "Indian Wars" were effectively over. From the perspective of the federal government, one Indian problem had been solved (thereby fulfilling the promise of Manifest Destiny) but another problem remained. What should be done with the Indigenous populations living within the United States?

Photo 5.3 After the Battle of Wounded Knee in 1890 in which as many as 300 Lakota Sioux men, women, and children, including Minneconjou-Teton Sioux Chief Big Foot, were killed by the 7th U.S. Cavalry Regiment, only a small portion of the chief's people remained alive. Here, a group of children, an elderly man and some women pose for a moment outside their tepees in 1891.

Source: Photo John C. H. Grabill © Library of Congress/Contributor/Corbis Historical/Getty Images.

The Push for Assimilation

One recurring theme of U.S. Indian policy in the twentieth century was assimilation. This theme was embedded in the 1924 Indian Citizenship Act, which provided, at least in some cases, unsolicited citizenship to Native Americans, although this Act did not require them to relinquish their tribal citizenship. Assimilation was more forcefully pursued with the 1953 Termination Act. This legislation was designed to eventually eliminate the sovereignty claims of Native nations and to end their special relationship with the federal government, including treaty rights and guaranteed subsidies. Similarly, the 1956 Indian Relocation Act sought to encourage Native Americans to leave the mostly rural reservations where many had been assigned and to relocate into designated urban settings. Both policies were eventually abandoned in the face of Indigenous resistance, especially from the activists associated with the American Indian Movement of the late 1960s and 1970s.

In summary, there were multiple instances throughout history when Indigenous populations were subject to what can only be described as acts of discrimination that went beyond random individual acts of bias but were instead fully authorized acts of American institutions (e.g., the military, Congress, etc.). Indeed, the government persecution of newly emancipated African Americans in the latter part of the nineteenth century, the barely disguised nativism enshrined in U.S. immigration policy since 1790, the internment of Japanese Americans during the Second World War, and the systematic effort to eradicate Indigenous nations, either through bureaucratic or military means, all have something in common. In each case, the full power of the federal government was brought to bear on vulnerable and marginalized populations for supposedly lofty goals: equality under the law, restricting the "socially inadequate" from immigrating to the United States, national security, or assimilation. In spite of how these actions may have been justified, however, running throughout each of these efforts was the common thread of utilizing the power of government to preserve White supremacy.

Institutional Discrimination in the Housing Market

Our opening vignette discussed discrimination in the home mortgage lending market, but that is just one aspect of housing where we find discrimination. The history of institutional discrimination in the housing market is particularly insidious because of the widespread nature of such actions and because of its contribution to the enormous racial gap in the acquisition of family wealth.

Efforts to Preserve All-White Neighborhoods

Throughout the twentieth and twenty-first centuries, the local, state, and federal government have incorporated discriminatory practices within their official housing policy (Rothstein 2017). These include a wide variety of institutional procedures, both blatant and subtle, adopted at different times to prevent Blacks and other ethnic and racial minorities from moving into predominantly White residential areas.

In the 1930s and into the 1950s, such practices were unambiguous. For instance, the federal government routinely constructed public housing in both the North and the South on a segregated basis, with some units explicitly designated for Whites and other, often less desirable, units reserved for Blacks.

Another particularly effective segregation strategy was to rely on local zoning laws, or laws that stipulated who was allowed to purchase homes in a particular area or what kind of homes could be constructed. In the early years of the twentieth century cities like Baltimore prevented Blacks from moving into White areas simply by adopting racially restrictive local ordinances (Rothstein 2017). Specifically, these laws prohibited African Americans from buying homes on blocks where Whites were already in the majority. The Supreme Court declared such zoning practices unconstitutional with the 1917 case, *Buchanan* v. *Warley*. However, many cities either ignored this ruling or found clever ways to get around it (Rothstein 2017).

One common strategy for keeping potential Black homeowners out of White residential areas was to pass zoning laws which required that only single-family homes could be built within the jurisdiction. This meant that apartment buildings, which catered to more low-income families, could not be built in the city. In other words, if zoning laws excluding African Americans were unconstitutional, then cities would adopt zoning laws to prevent low-income families from moving into the neighborhood. This had the intended effect of also excluding most African Americans, since most of this population would be working class. This practice of using class as a proxy for race is similar to the strategy that Southern Democrats used to exclude Blacks from the New Deal policy reforms advanced during the Roosevelt administration. Zoning laws were also used to direct the establishment of undesirable businesses (e.g., polluting industries, liquor stores, night clubs, etc.) into Black neighborhoods and to prevent them from being established in White neighborhoods.

Another strategy for preserving all-White neighborhoods was through the use of restrictive covenants. Restrictive covenants are obligations that purchasers of a new home are legally required to meet. Restrictive covenants based on race involved the obligation that the owner would not resell the home to a Black family. This way, the neighborhood would remain entirely White. Rothstein notes that racially restrictive covenants (which sometimes also barred the resale of homes to Jews, Irish, Mexican, and other minorities, as well as African Americans), were common throughout much of the twentieth century. The U.S. Commission on Civil Rights reported in 1973 that the practice was so common, that by 1940, 80% of property in Los Angeles and Chicago carried restrictive covenants barring the sale of homes to non-White families (see Figure 5.4).

As objectionable as this practice may have been, it is only relevant for our purposes if important institutions such as the local, state, or federal government also reinforced restrictive covenants. According to Rothstein (2017), this was in fact said Tracts to a corporation or association formed by residents or owners of property in Innis Arden No. 2, or to a corporation or association formed by residents or owners of Innis Arden, for community purposes, in the activities of which corporation or association residents of Innis Arden No. 2 shall have the right to participate, subject to reasonable restrictions and requirements imposed by such corporation or association.

14. *RACIAL RESTRICTIONS*. No property in said addition shall at any time be sold, conveyed, rented or leased in whole or in part to any person or persons not of the White or Caucausian race. No person other than one of the White or Caucausian race shall be permitted to occupy any property in said addition or portion thereof or building thereon except a domestic servant actually employed by a person of the White or Caucausian race where the latter is an occupant of such property.

15. *ANIMALS*. No hogs, cattle, horses, sheep, goats, or or similar livestock shall be permitted or maintained on said property at any time. Chicken hens, pigeons, rabbits and other similar small livestock, not exceeding a total of twenty-five in number, shall be permitted but must be kept on the premises of the owner. Not more than one dog and cat may be kept for each building site. No pen, yard, run, hutch, coop or other structure or area for the housing and keeping of the above described poultry or animals shall be built or maintaied closer

Figure 5.4 Example of a Restrictive Covenant Based on Race
This comes from a restrictive covenant on a Seattle property.
Source: The Seattle Civil Rights & Labor History Project, University of Washington, https://depts.washington.edu/civilr/covenants.html.

the case. For much of the twentieth century various levels of government actively enforced restrictive covenants—thus, facilitating residential segregation. For example, state courts ordered the eviction of Black families that had purchased homes in violation of restrictive covenants in states across the country, including in Alabama, California, Colorado, Kansas, Kentucky, Louisiana, Maryland, Michigan, Missouri, New York, North Carolina, West Virginia, and Wisconsin (Rothstein 2017). In all of these hundreds of cases, the state courts held that restrictive covenants did *not* violate the Constitution because they were merely "private agreements." Of course, if the agreements were merely private, then this would not explain why the government was enforcing them (Rothstein 2017).

Although state and local government authorities helped to enforce restrictive covenants, the most powerful endorsement of this discriminatory practice came from the federal government. For example, in the 1926 Supreme Court case—*Corrigan* v. *Buckley*—the Court held that racially restrictive covenants were in fact constitutional because they were voluntary private contracts (Rothstein 2017). This perspective was not just endorsed by the federal courts. The executive branch also endorsed it. The Federal Housing Administration (FHA) explicitly recommended restrictive covenants in their 1936 official manual. It is worth emphasizing here that one of the primary duties of the FHA was to appraise mortgage loan applications, and if they rated an application as high—in effect, the FHA agreed to insure the loan application—then the prospective home buyer was more likely to receive a low-interest loan from the bank. For many working- and middle-class families, this was the only practical way they could hope to acquire the necessary down-payment to purchase a home. By recommending restrictive covenants, the FHA was essentially excluding Blacks from acquiring low-interest loans. One study found that between 1945 and 1959, only 2 percent of FHA-backed loans went to African Americans (Rothstein 2017).

In the 1948 case, *Shelly* v. *Kraemer*, the Supreme Court finally declared restrictive covenants to be unconstitutional. In spite of this ruling, it took the FHA another year and a half before they agreed *in principle* to no longer insure mortgages with restrictive covenants—and only for new mortgages executed after February 1950. In practice, however, the FHA continued to insure housing developments that excluded African Americans throughout the 1950s. Only in 1962, when President Kennedy issued an executive order, did the FHA stop financing new housing subdivisions with racially restrictive covenants. The practice of *officially* reserving neighborhoods for Whites only ended when Congress passed the 1968 Fair Housing Act.

Finally, Rothstein notes that some of these discriminatory practices continue into the twenty-first century. One such practice is known as "reverse redlining," where banks—with the tacit acceptance of federal regulators—target Black and Hispanic communities for subprime mortgages. Subprime mortgages are nontraditional loans that have higher interest rates and less favorable terms—making it more likely that recipients would ultimately default on the loan and lose their property. Blacks and Hispanics are disproportionately targeted for these subprime loans. According to Rothstein, in 2006, 61 percent of borrowers of all races who received subprime loans would have qualified for conventional loans with lower rates. However, during this same time period Blacks received subprime loans at *three times* the rate of Whites. Among higher-income Blacks, the rate was *four times* that of comparable Whites. One recent study found that even after controlling for credit scores and other risk factors, "Hispanics are 78 percent more likely [than whites] to be given a high-cost mortgage, and black Americans are 105 percent more likely" (White 2016).

The many decades spent preventing Blacks and other minorities from purchasing homes, and therefore accruing equity that they could later pass on to their children, has significant implications for rates of homeownership and levels of financial security across racial groups in the twenty-first century. First, according to the U.S. Census Bureau, White families are currently much more likely to own their own home than are the families of racial or ethnic minority groups. Based on data from the third quarter of 2021, 74 percent of non-Hispanic White families owned their own home compared with just 60 percent of Asian families, 48 percent of

Latino families, and 44 percent of African American families.[7] The 30-point gap in homeownership between Black and White families is greater today than in 1968, when housing discrimination was still legal. And this gap cannot be easily attributed to contemporary racial differences in socioeconomic status. To illustrate this point, White high-school dropouts are more likely to own a home (60 percent) than are Black college graduates (56 percent) (Young 2019).

Another legacy of discrimination in social policy and the housing market is the racial wealth gap. There are a number of different ways to define wealth, but one of the most common ways defines wealth as household debt subtracted from household assets (e.g., home mortgage, car, savings account, stocks, bonds, etc.). Using this formula, the typical (median) Latino household in 2019 had about $36,100 in wealth and the typical Black household had about $24,100. The average level of wealth for White Americans in 2019 was about $188,200. In other words, for every dollar in wealth possessed by the typical White family, the typical Latino family had about 19 cents and the typical Black family had about 12 cents (Bhutta et al. 2020). As with homeownership, these staggering racial discrepancies cannot be dismissed as simply reflections of modern-day differences in socioeconomic status across racial groups. The median White household where the head failed to graduate from high school has essentially the same wealth ($71,652) as an African American head of household who graduated from college ($72,515) (Hutchings et al. 2021).

The Role of Local Governments in Maintaining Segregated Neighborhoods

Local governments have played a large role in promoting housing segregation according to Jessica Trounstine (2018), who documents how local business interests and White homeowners used zoning laws and other land use regulations to make it difficult for minorities and poor Whites to purchase homes in middle-class White neighborhoods. The motivation here, according to Trounstine, was not irrational racial hatred but a desire on the part of White middle-class homeowners to maintain their property values and deny minorities and the poor access to neighborhood amenities (e.g., local schools, parks, etc.) (Trounstine 2018). In other words, Whites' efforts to promote segregation are largely motivated by the desire to gain an advantage for their racial (and class) group at the expense of other groups (Trounstine 2018; Roithmayr 2018). According to Trounstine, individual level racial prejudice is insufficient to account for the high levels of residential segregation that still exists in this country; the specific tools of local government are necessary in order to successfully promote segregation. For instance, zoning laws can be used to require that the lot sizes on which houses are built are so large as to price lower-income—and thus most minority—families out of the market (Trounstine 2018: 24). Another way in which local governments can shape the class and racial

---

[7] See at: www.census.gov/housing/hvs/files/currenthvspress.pdf. In these analyses, Asian families are combined with Native Hawaiian and Pacific Islander families.

characteristics of their community is through the presence or absence of bus lines, the location of public housing (e.g., in majority-Black areas), the placement of highways, and the location of local businesses.

What Is the Effect of Segregated Neighborhoods?

What are the real-world consequences of maintaining segregated neighborhoods? Scholars have long argued that it is easier to discriminate against a population when it is segregated. For example, Gunnar Myrdal wrote that: "Housing segregation necessarily involves discrimination ... It further permits any prejudice on the part of public officials to be freely vented on Negroes without hurting whites" (Myrdal 1996: 618). Trounstine (2018) notes that by segregating Whites from non-Whites, and the affluent from the poor, local leaders could, "... collect taxes from poor and minority residents, but underprovide services to them—thereby holding down the total tax bill" (p. 59). In other words, city government was able to keep local taxes relatively low because the poor and non-Whites were essentially subsidizing the amenities of the affluent Whites.

Differentiated Levels of Public Spending

Trounstine theorized that city governments would have smaller budgets and thus lower per capita expenditures in more racially segregated communities. In order to test this proposition, she relied on city government expenditure data on over 3,000 cities from the early 1980s until 2012 (Trounstine 2018: 150). In keeping with her expectations, she found that more segregated cities allocated lower levels of spending on public goods compared with cities with lower levels of segregation. Specifically, she found that moving from the 25th percentile to the 75th percentile on her index of segregation resulted in slightly more than a $100 decline, per resident, in direct general expenditures. And these effects hold even after taking into account alternative influences on government expenditures, such as ethnic and racial diversity, median household income, population size, the percentage of the city population with a college degree, and the percentage of city residents who were renters as opposed to homeowners: higher segregation levels translated into lower spending on road maintenance, police services, parks, and sanitation, presumably because city officials could deny segregated populations access to these amenities.

Differentiated Social Networks

Residential segregation is so foundational to the maintenance of modern-day racial inequality precisely because it affects so many other things. That is, in addition to affecting the kind of neighborhood amenities to which one has access, segregation also influences the composition of one's neighbors, friends, classmates, and co-workers. These social networks have implications for racial inequality because they can in turn influence access to information about employment opportunities.

Indeed, some scholars report that many, if not most, Americans get their jobs through informal social networks rather than through advertised job openings (Waldinger 1996). DiTomaso explored this idea in some detail when she interviewed 246 non-Hispanic White adults in New Jersey, Ohio, and Tennessee (DiTomaso 2013). She found that, at some point in their lives, all but two of her interviewees had received help from family and friends to obtain jobs. This was especially true for "good" jobs that provided higher salaries and benefits (DiTomaso 2013: 53). However, because racial and ethnic minorities remain largely segregated from Whites, people of color tend to have very different social networks. As a result, they are far less likely to have access to informal channels indicating the availability of "good jobs." In this way, racial inequality replicates itself even in the absence of overt racial prejudice (Roithmayr 2018).

Residential Segregation in the Twenty-First Century

Residential segregation along racial and ethnic lines are the inevitable consequence of the different types of housing discrimination discussed in the previous chapter, as well as the government sanctioned practices discussed in this chapter. However, by many accounts, levels of residential segregation have been declining since the latter decades of the twentieth century (Logan and Stultz 2011; Rugh and Massey 2013). For example, one popular measure of racial segregation is known as the index of dissimilarity. Essentially, this measure—ranging from 0 to 100—provides a score that captures the percentage of minorities who would need to move in order to achieve an even distribution of their group in a particular geographic area (e.g., a city like New York or San Francisco). The higher the index score, the greater the segregation in a given area, with 100 representing complete segregation. When examining the fifty largest metropolitan areas in the country, Logan and Stults (2011) found that the index of dissimilarity score for Black–White neighborhood segregation was 67 in 1970, but 59 in 2010. Thus, although segregation levels remain quite high, they have been declining over time—although only for Blacks and not other racial minority groups. It is also worth noting that, even in 2010, Black–White levels of neighborhood segregation are noticeably larger than the comparable figures for Asian–White (41) and Hispanic–White (48) segregation.

Some scholars have raised a note of caution regarding the over-time declines in residential segregation (Lichter, Parisi, and Taquino 2015; Trounstine 2018). It is possible that segregation is simply evolving rather than declining. Trounstine points out that typically researchers have measured segregation *within* cities and suburbs, but segregation can also arise *across* cities and suburbs. She argues that segregation across geographic areas has been on the rise since the 1970s. Lichter, Parisi, and Taquino (2015) provide an excellent example of this phenomenon by referencing the city of Detroit: "Detroit today is over 80 percent black—up from 62 percent in 1980. Over the same period, black–white neighborhood segregation nevertheless declined from 67.5 to 61.2 (Logan and Stults 2011). In this case, declining Black–White

Figure 5.5 Stylized Illustration of Low and High Macro Segregation Metropolitan Area
Figure shows stylized examples of how racial segregation can manifest as a high concentration of Blacks within the central city and surrounding suburbs of a metro area (high macro segregation) or with Blacks concentrated in the central city and more dispersed across suburban communities within a metro area (low macro segregation). In the latter case, segregation still occurs in the central city and surrounding communities, but also *within* the smaller jurisdictions of outlying suburban communities.
Source: Lichter, Parisi, and Taquino (2015).

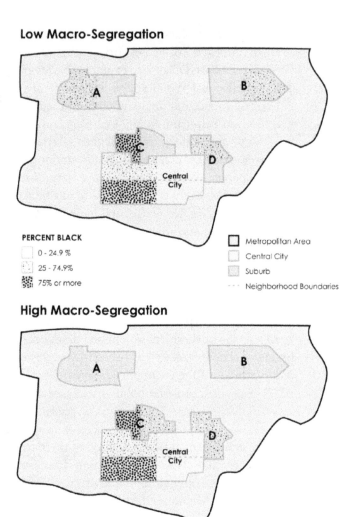

segregation occurred in tandem with massive white depopulation" (Lichter et al. 2015: 844). Labeling this more recent version of segregation "macro segregation" (see Figure 5.5) the authors examine U.S. Census data from 1990 through 2010 and demonstrate that although segregation levels within metropolitan areas have declined over time, macro segregation has increased over the same time period. In effect, Americans of different racial groups are becoming increasingly separated across city boundaries. This trend is important because cities and suburbs, unlike neighborhoods, have the institutional tools—land use regulations and zoning to promote and reinforce segregation more effectively.

As Trounstine writes, "Segregation is *not* simply the result of individual choices about where to live. Neither racial antipathy nor economic inequality between groups is sufficient to create and perpetuate segregation. The maintenance of property values and the quality of public goods are collective endeavors. And like all collective endeavors, they require collective action for production and stability. Local governments provide this collective action" (Trountsine 2018: 3).

Institutional Discrimination and Criminal Justice Policies

A broad range of social science studies has documented the pervasive presence of institutional discrimination throughout the criminal justice system (see Balko 2019 or Kurlychek and Johnson 2019 for an overview of this literature). Thus, Blacks and Latinos are more likely to be stopped by the police, arrested, charged with a crime, prosecuted, convicted at trial, and given lengthier sentences than Whites in comparable situations. Even when researchers account for class differences, the severity of the alleged crime, and the fact that racial and ethnic minorities commit a disproportionate share of some crimes, these racial differences often remain.

In Chapter 12 we explore racial disparities in the criminal justice system in much greater detail, but in this section we will discuss only briefly how these outcomes are influenced by institutional discrimination. One area where institutional discrimination affects criminal justice policies is with mass incarceration. The racial disparities associated with mass incarceration are often staggering. According to the Sentencing Project, Blacks, Hispanics, and other people of color make up about 37 percent of the U.S. population but they make up 67 percent of the prison population.[8] Although African Americans and Hispanics are also more likely to commit certain types of crimes than are Whites—largely because poor Americans in general are more likely to commit property crimes and violent crimes, and racial minorities are more likely to be mired in poverty—this explains only part of the racial disparity in incarcerations. Legal scholar, Michelle Alexander, places some of the blame on racially discriminatory policing of drug crimes (Alexander 2010).

According to Alexander (2010) and others, racially discriminatory policing occurs because federal court decisions have given law enforcement officers wide discretion in how they exercise their authority. This discretion, coupled with levels of racial bias among police officers that is comparable with that found within the general public, can lead to racially disparate rates of arrest, traffic stops, and misconduct (Baumgartner, Epp, and Shoub 2018; Goff et al. 2014; LeCount 2017).

WHAT IT LOOKS LIKE TODAY: THE ROOTS OF RACIAL UNREST IN FERGUSON, MISSOURI

On March 4, 2015, the U.S. Department of Justice released a 102-page report on the origins of the racial unrest in Ferguson, Missouri. After interviewing numerous governmental officials in Ferguson, including the mayor, chief of police, and roughly half of the Ferguson Police Department, the report provided the

---

[8] See at: www.sentencingproject.org/criminal-justice-facts.

following conclusion: "This investigation has revealed a pattern or practice of unlawful conduct within the Ferguson Police Department that violates the First, Fourth, and Fourteenth Amendments to the United States Constitution, and federal statutory law" (p. 1). Specifically, the DOJ report found that Blacks in Ferguson were targeted for minor traffic violations—which frequently resulted in a fine—in order to generate revenue for the city. The racial disparities in Ferguson were dramatic (also see Baumgartner, Epp, and Shoub 2018). According to the report: "Data collected by the Ferguson Police Department from 2012 to 2014 shows that African Americans account for 85% of vehicle stops, 90% of citations, and 93% of arrests made by FPD officers, despite comprising only 67% of Ferguson's population. African Americans are more than twice as likely as white drivers to be searched during vehicle stops even after controlling for non-race based variables such as the reasons the vehicle stop was initiated, but are found in possession of contraband [illegal substances] 26% less often than white drivers, suggesting officers are impermissibly considering race as a factor when determining whether to search" (4). Racial disparities were also uncovered in the use of force by the Ferguson Police Department. The report found that in almost 90 percent of documented cases of use of force by officers the civilian was an African American.

Photo 5.4 Protesters march down South Florissant Road prior to a demonstration at the Ferguson, Missouri Police Department on May 31, 2020. Major cities nationwide saw demonstrations over the death of George Floyd.
Source: Photo Michael B. Thomas © Michael B. Thomas/Stringer/Getty Images News/Getty Images.

In August 2019, the *New York Times* ran a story on the status of racial equality in Ferguson and the state of Missouri five years after the shooting of Michael Brown.[9] During the ensuing years, *New York Times* journalist John Eligon reported that there had been several positive changes such as the once majority-White police department becoming about half African American. As of June 2019, the police chief is also an African American. Additionally, lawmakers in the state of Missouri passed legislation in 2015 capping the percentage of revenue that cities were allowed to obtain from fees associated with traffic fines and court appearances at 20 percent. As a result, there has been a 45 percent decline in the collection of municipal court fines throughout the state. Still, Eligon reports that Black drivers are still stopped by police at greater rates than White drivers. "Statewide, black motorists were nearly twice as likely as other motorists to be stopped, based on their share of the driving-age population, according to the Missouri attorney general's annual report on traffic stops. White drivers were stopped 6 percent less than would be expected. In Ferguson, the disparity in traffic stops of black drivers has increased by five percentage points since 2013, while it has dropped by 11 percentage points for white drivers."

Conclusion

The aim of this chapter was to define institutional racism and to outline its far-reaching implications for both historical and contemporary American society. Unlike individual level discrimination, institutional discrimination cannot usually be linked to the actions of a single individual. And, even when the discriminatory act can be associated with a specific individual or group of individuals, the racial motivations driving the actions are in some cases obscured or may in fact be completely absent. In short, racially biased outcomes may unfold from racially neutral legislation, court decisions, and established rules and procedures in both the public and private sector. Because racial inequality has been so thoroughly embedded in the structures and institutions of American society from its founding until the late 1960s, institutional discrimination today has become almost routine.

We highlighted two frequent characteristics of contemporary institutional discrimination—uncertain origins and indeterminate motivations—in this chapter. Of course, in earlier eras of American history there was often little subtlety in biased governmental actions, such as with the 1830 Indian Removal Act, the 1857 Dred Scott decision, or the 1882 Chinese Exclusion Act. Because these unambiguous Acts were not merely transgressions of unauthorized individuals but backed by the considerable power of the federal government, they nevertheless constitute acts of institutional discrimination. In the contemporary era, we have seen more

---

[9] See at: www.nytimes.com/2019/08/06/us/black-drivers-traffic-stops.html.

understated expressions of institutional discrimination in the home mortgage lending industry, where racial and ethnic minorities are less likely than Whites to receive a loan to purchase a home even when they have comparable economic profiles. This chapter also discussed how Blacks and Hispanics are disproportionately targeted for subprime loans, which tend to be associated with higher interest rates and much higher default rates. Another example of both historic and contemporary discrimination in the housing and banking industries is that minorities have much lower rates of homeownership compared with Whites. These racial differences persist even when socioeconomic class factors are taken into account.

Housing discrimination has been illegal since 1968, but segregated communities remain common in the twenty-first century. As outlined in this chapter, powerful institutions have been used to promote and maintain segregated enclaves, primarily by using local zoning laws to discourage both class and racial integration. These actions are perfectly legal and have the added benefit of maintaining segregated schools and making it more difficult for minorities and the working class to compete for jobs located near affluent suburbs.

Institutional discrimination is also present in the criminal justice system. For example, racial and ethnic minorities are more likely to be arrested for drug offenses, even though they are no more likely to use or sell drugs than are Whites (Alexander 2010). Also, scholars have consistently shown that Black offenders convicted of killing Whites (especially women) are disproportionately targeted for the death penalty—even though cross-racial murders are far less common than murders committed within racial groups (Baumgartner, Grigg, and Mastro 2015). Lastly, numerous studies have shown that the police disproportionately target minorities for traffic stops, often in order to generate revenue for local municipalities. Because these actions may lack an easily discernible racial motive and often cannot be attributed to a specific individual, federal court decisions have made it difficult to challenge their legality.

KEY TERMS

Border Patrol
Cartel
Chinese Exclusion Act 1882
Civil Liberties Act 1988
Compromise of 1877
Immigration Act 1917
Index of dissimilarity
Indian Citizenship Act 1924
Indian Relocation Act 1956
Indian Removal Act 1830
Manifest Destiny
Naturalization Act 1790
Restrictive covenants

Social Security Act 1935
Subprime mortgages
Termination Act 1953
Trail of Tears
Wounded Knee Massacre

DISCUSSION QUESTIONS

1. How is institutional discrimination different from individual discrimination?
2. Why do you think that Japanese Americans imprisoned during the Second World War were given financial compensation by the U.S. government but the formerly enslaved were unable to receive reparations for slavery?
3. Why did American settlers believe it was necessary to forcibly remove Native Americans from their homes in the southeast to such places as Oklahoma?
4. How has racial segregation in the housing market evolved over time?
5. What are some of the ways that institutional discrimination affects immigration policy today?

ANNOTATED SUGGESTED READINGS

See Richard Rothstein. 2017. *The Color of Law: A Forgotten History of How Our Government Segregated America.* New York: Liveright Publishing, for one of the best references on the history of housing discrimination by local, state, and federal authorities.

See Roxanne Dunbar-Ortiz. 2014. *An Indigenous Peoples' History of the United States.* Boston, MA: Beacon Press, for an excellent overview of various ways in which Native Americans have been discriminated against by the American government throughout history.

See Nikole Hannah-Jones, Caitlin Roper, Ilena Silverman, and Jake Silverstein (eds.) 2021. *The 1619 Project: A New Origin Story.* New York: One World, for an alternative interpretation of American history, including the origins of institutional discrimination.

CHAPTER REFERENCES

Alexander, Michelle. 2010. *The New Jim Crow: Mass Incarceration in the Age of Colorblindness.* New York: New Press.

Backman, Marjorie and Michael Gonchar. 2017. "Teaching Japanese-American Internment Using Primary Sources," *New York Times*, December 7. www.nytimes.com/2017/12/07/learning/lesson-plans/teaching-japanese-american-internment-using-primary-resources.html.

Balko, Radley. 2019. "Opinion: 21 More Studies Showing Racial Disparities in the Criminal Justice System," *Washington Post*, April 9. www.washingtonpost.com/opinions/2019/04/09/more-studies-showing-racial-disparities-criminal-justice-system.

Baumgartner, Frank R., Derek A. Epp, and Kelsey Shoub. 2018. *Suspect Citizens: What 20 Million Traffic Stops Tells Us about Policing and Race.* Cambridge: Cambridge University Press, ch. 8, 165–186.

Baumgartner, Frank R., Amanda J. Grigg, and Alisa Mastro. 2015. "#BlackLivesDon'tMatter: Race-of-Victim Effects in U.S. Executions, 1976–2013," *Politics, Groups, and Identities* 3(2): 209–221.

Berry, Mary F. 1972. "Reparations for Freedmen, 1890–1916: Fraudulent Practices or Justice Deferred?" *Journal of Negro History* 57(3): 219–230.

Bhutta, Neil, Andrew C. Chang, Lisa J. Dettling, Joanne W. Hsu, and Julia Hewitt. 2020. *FEDS Notes*, September 28. www.federalreserve.gov/econres/notes/feds-notes/disparities-in-wealth-by-race-and-ethnicity-in-the-2019-survey-of-consumer-finances-20200928.htm.

Breitman, George, Herman Porter, and Baxter Smith. 1976. *The Assassination of Malcolm X.* New York: Pathfinder Press.

Choi, Jung Hyun and Peter J. Mattingly. 2022. "What Different Denial Rates Can Tell Us about Racial Disparities in the Mortgage Market," *Urban Institute*, January 13. www.urban.org/urban-wire/what-different-denial-rates-can-tell-us-about-racial-disparities-mortgage-market.

Diamond, Anna. 2020. "The 1924 Law That Slammed the Door on Immigrants and the Politicians Who Pushed It Back Open," *Smithsonian Magazine*, May 19. www.smithsonianmag.com/history/1924-law-slammed-door-immigrants-and-politicians-who-pushed-it-back-open-180974910.

DiTomaso, Nancy. 2013. *The American Non-Dilemma: Racial Inequality without Racism.* New York: Russell Sage Foundation.

Dunbar-Ortiz, Roxanne. 2014. *An Indigenous People's History of the United States.* Boston, MA: Beacon Press.

Eli, Shari and Laura Salisbury. 2016. "Patronage Politics and the Development of the Welfare State: Confederate Pensions in the American South," *Journal of Economic History* 76(4): 1078–1112.

Eligon, John. 2019. "Stopped, Ticketed, Fined: The Pitfalls of Driving While Black in Ferguson," *New York Times*, August 6. www.nytimes.com/2019/08/06/us/black-drivers-traffic-stops.html.

Gage, Beverly. 2014. "What an Uncensored Letter to M.L.K Reveals," *New York Times Magazine*, November 11. www.nytimes.com/2014/11/16/magazine/what-an-uncensored-letter-to-mlk-reveals.html.

Garcia Bedolla, Lisa. 2009. *Latino Politics*. Malden, MA: Polity Press.

Glantz, Aaron and Emmanuel Martinez. 2018. "For People of Color, Banks Are Shutting the Door to Homeownership," *Revealnews.org*, February 15. www.revealnews.org/article/for-people-of-color-banks-are-shutting-the-door-to-homeownership.

Goff, Phillip Atiba, Matthew Christian Jackson, Brooke Allison Lewis Di Leone, Carmen Marie Culotta, and Natalie Ann DiTomasso. 2014. "The Essence of Innocence: Consequences of Dehumanizing Black Children," *Journal of Personality and Social Psychology* 106(4): 526–545.

Henderson, Robert and Rebecca Marchiel. 2021. "The Keys to Ensuring a New Anti-Redlining Initiative Succeeds: History Offers Some Pointers for Government Regulators," *Washington Post*, November 15. www.washingtonpost.com/outlook/2021/11/15/keys-ensuring-new-anti-redlining-initiative-succeeds.

Hollandsworth Jr., James G. 2008. "Black Confederate Pensioners after the Civil War," *Mississippi History Now*, May. www.mshistorynow.mdah.ms.gov/articles/289/black-confederate-pensioners-after-the-civil-war.

Hutchings, Vincent L., Sydney Carr, Kamri Hudgins, and Zoe Walker. 2021. "'If They Only Knew': Informing Blacks and Whites about the Racial Wealth Gap," unpublished manuscript, presented at the American Political Science Association Meeting, Seattle, Washington, October 3.

Kamasaki, Charles. 2021."U.S. Immigration Policy: A Classic Unappreciated Example of Structural Racism," *Brookings Institute*, March 26. www.brookings.edu/blog/how-we-rise/2021/03/26/us-immigration-policy-a-classic-unappreciated-example-of-structural-racism.

Katznelson, Ira. 2005. *When Affirmative Action Was White: An Untold History of Racial Inequality in Twentieth-Century America*. New York: W. W. Norton.

Key Jr., V. O. 1949. *Southern Politics in State and Nation*. New York: A. A. Knopf.

Kurlychek, Megan C. and Brian D. Johnson. 2019. "Cumulative Disadvantage in the American Criminal Justice System," *Annual Review of Criminology* 2: 291–319.

LeCount, Ryan Jerome. 2017. "More Black than Blue? Comparing the Racial Attitudes of Police to Citizens," *Sociological Forum* 32(S1): 1051–1072.

Lichter, Daniel T., Domenico Parisi, and Michael C. Taquino. 2015. "Toward a New Macro-Segregation? Decomposing Segregation within and between Metropolitan Cities and Suburbs," *American Sociological Review* 80(4): 843–873.

Logan, John R. and Brian J. Stults. 2011. *The Persistence of Segregation in the Metropolis: New Findings from the 2010 Census*. New York: Russell Sage Foundation/Brown University.

Masuoka, Natalie and Jane Junn. 2013. *The Politics of Belonging: Race, Public Opinion, and Immigration*. Chicago: University of Chicago Press.

Mickey, Robert. 2015. *Paths out of Dixie: The Democratization of Authoritarian Enclaves in America's Deep South, 1944–1972*. Princeton: Princeton University Press.

Mitchell, Robert. 2019. "The Police Raid That Killed Two Black Panthers, Shook Chicago and Changed the Nation," *Washington Post*, December 4. www.washingtonpost.com/history/2019/12/04/police-raid-that-left-two-black-panthers-dead-shook-chicago-changed-nation.

Molina, Natalia. 2010. "'In a Race All Their Own': The Quest to Make Mexicans Ineligible for U.S. Citizenship," *Pacific Historical Review* 79(2): 167–201.

Myrdal, Gunnar. [1944] 1996. *An American Dilemma: The Negro Problem and Modern Democracy*. New Brunswick: Transaction (original ed., Harper & Row).

Perry, Miranda Booker. 2010. "No Pensions for Ex-Slaves: How the Federal Government Suppressed Movement to Aid Freedpeople," *Prologue Magazine* 42(2). www.archives.gov/publications/prologue/2010/summer/slave-pension.html#page-header.

Rice, Lisa and Deidre Swesnik. 2013. "Discriminatory Effects of Credit Scoring on Communities of Color," *Suffolk University Law Review* 46: 936–966.

Roithmayr, Daria. 2018. *Reproducing Racism: How Everyday Choices Lock in White Advantage*. New York: New York University Press.

Rothstein, Richard. 2017. *The Color of Law: A Forgotten History of How Our Government Segregated America*. New York: Liveright Publishing.

Rugh, Jacob S. and Douglas S. Massy. 2013. "Segregation in Post-Civil Rights America: Stalled Integration of End of the Segregated Century?" *Du Bois Review: Social Science Research on Race* 10(2): 1–28.

Stafford, Kat. 2021. "Movement for Black Lives: Feds Targeted BLM Protestors," *Associated Press News*, August 18. https://apnews.com/article/joe-biden-death-of-george-floyd-health-race-and-ethnicity-racial-injustice-07a91fd5c210f8b809d019292c3ec0c0.

Trounstine, Jessica. 2018. *Segregation by Design: Local Politics and Inequality in American Cities*. Cambridge: Cambridge University Press.

Ture, Kwame and Charles Hamilton. [1967] 1992. *Black Power: The Politics of Liberation.*
New York: Vintage.

Waldinger, Roger. 1996. *Still the Promised City? African-Americans and New Immigrants in Postindustrial New York.* Cambridge, MA: Harvard University Press.

White, Gillian B. 2016. "Why Blacks and Hispanics Have Such Expensive Mortgages: High-Cost Lenders Are Targeting These Communities, Preventing Them from Building Wealth to Pass on to Their Children," *The Atlantic.* www.theatlantic.com/business/archive/2016/02/blacks-hispanics-mortgages/471024.

Williams, Linda Faye. 2003. *The Constraint of Race: Legacies of White Skin Privilege in America.* University Park: Pennsylvania State University Press.

Young, Caitlin. 2019. "These Five Facts Reveal the Current Crisis in Black Homeownership," *Urban Institute*, July 31. www.urban.org/urban-wire/these-five-facts-reveal-current-crisis-black-homeownership.

Part III

The Inputs of Democratic Decision-Making in a Racially Divided America

6   Public Opinion: Divided by Race?

As Yuanyuan Zhu walked to her gym in San Francisco, she wondered if it would be her last workout. It was March 2020, in the early days of the coronavirus pandemic, so fear was rampant, and no one knew what would happen. Yuanyuan, however, had one extra burden. On her way to the gym, a man shouted at her, yelling hateful insults about China. When a bus passed by, he screamed "Run them over." She attempted to get away, but the man spit in her face. In shock, Ms. Zhu found a quiet corner and cried. Most troubling to her, as she later said, was that "That person didn't look strange or anything . . . He just looked like a normal person" (Tavernise and Oppel 2020). In the early days of the pandemic, her experience was unfortunately far from unique.

The coronavirus—discovered in China's Wuhan province—soon became all too well known to almost every human on the planet. It killed millions and challenged almost every basic element of human interaction. At least at first glance, there is nothing racialized about the virus. It can infect anyone. But Yuanyuan's encounter that day and our broader experience with COVID-19 underscore several themes about race and public opinion that will be the subject of this chapter.

The fact that a White man screamed racial epithets at an Asian woman only days into a healthcare crisis that affected all Americans regardless of race underlines how much race can, and often does, shape people's views and actions. The man's actions that day reveal a deep-seated prejudice that was easily triggered by fear. It also highlights how ostensibly nonracial issues can, and often do, become infused with race, and how this connection can be fostered intentionally for strategic or political reasons. In this case, then-President Donald Trump frequently referred to the virus as the "Chinese virus," and he broadcast the theory that the virus had spread because of a Chinese cover-up, all of which racialized the issue.

But an association between race and a seemingly nonracial event like the coronavirus pandemic can also emerge without anyone's conscious effort to promote it. For example, as we noted earlier, the virus may not discriminate, but its effects have been anything but racially neutral. Due to differences in access to healthcare, the ability to stay at home and isolate rather than work, preexisting health conditions, and other factors, the virus has had extremely racially disparate effects. Blacks and Latinos have been three times as likely as Whites to become infected and twice as likely to die from the disease (Oppel et al. 2020). Race, in short, has been and will

Photo 6.1 The large "Stop Asian Hate" rally and march held to protest against anti-Asian hate crimes, Foley Square, New York, Sunday April 4, 2021.
Source: Photo Wang Ying © Xinhua Alamy Stock Photo.

continue to be infused in many different policy areas. Also, the swiftly changing events surrounding the coronavirus pandemic teach us that public opinion about different racial groups and how much the public fears or supports them can change quickly. In this case, to return to the story of Yuanyuan Zhu on the way to her gym in San Francisco, Asian Americans, a group that is often put on a pedestal as a "model minority," very quickly became a scapegoat for the virus. Asian Americans are, of course, not the only group to emerge as a target and a scapegoat in response to real crises or perceived threats. Muslim Americans garnered relatively little attention prior to the 9/11 terrorist attacks. But since then, animosity and discrimination toward the group has been widespread. Depending on events, issues, and moments in our political history, Latinos, African Americans, and White ethnic minorities have also at times elicited more or less attention and more or less ire from the American public.

This chapter focuses on the views held by the public-at-large. Public opinion, or what we sometimes describe as the will of the people, is the life force of a democracy. Politicians who ignore it do so at their peril. James Bryce, the noted nineteenth-century British jurist and author of *The American Commonwealth*, perhaps the first systematic analysis of the role of the public's views on politics in the United States, wrote that "towering over Presidents and State governors, over Congress and State legislatures, over conventions and the vast machinery of party, public opinion stands out, in the United States, as the great source of power, the master of servants who tremble before it" (1888: 225). However, as we will see in this chapter, the public typically does not hold a single view on most matters of public policy. Americans largely agree on America's founding principles of individualism and equality of opportunity; we also all tend to profess support for the principle of racial equality. But that is often where any common rendering of the public will ends. As we detail in this chapter, there are important racial divisions in support for various policies. That division begins with how we think of each other and ourselves. Across the public, there is widespread racial stereotyping of minority and ethnic groups. Large swathes of the public view Blacks as lazy, violent, and unintelligent. Assessments of the Latino population are not much better: assumptions about a lack of intelligence and illegality are common. Stereotypes of Asian Americans are more complex, with many believing in a model minority myth that sees Asian Americans as intelligent and hardworking; many of the same Americans also believe that Asian Americans are particularly foreign or unassimilable.

Racial divisions filter into how we think about policy. There are massive differences of opinion between White Americans and racial and ethnic minorities on policies such as affirmative action that are explicitly designed to help minorities level the playing field. That White–non-White divide lessens somewhat on a host of policies like welfare, healthcare, education, and crime that are implicitly connected to race, but across a broad swathe of policy, race remains a primary driver of opinions. With almost all of these issues, Whites appear reluctant to see government action as necessary, while minorities place a greater emphasis on redistribution and other policies that they believe will foster greater equality. Only on foreign affairs and issues of morality do racial differences largely subside.

In addition to identifying the contours of the racial divide on opinion, this chapter explores the sources of that division. The sharp difference of opinion between Whites on one side and racial and ethnic minorities on the other is partly driven by White America's more conservative core values and its stronger attachment to individualism and limited government. But the racial divide is also very much a function of Whites' racial views. Resentment over minority gains and concerns over losing their place in the power and status hierarchy play deeply into White policy views.

Overall, public opinion divisions between Blacks, Hispanics, and Asian Americans are smaller than those between Whites and minorities. However, across many of the issues we examine, Blacks are clearly the most liberal group, with Hispanics often following not too far behind and Asian Americans landing somewhere in the middle of the liberal-to-conservative spectrum. But we also find plenty of divisions within each racial and ethnic minority population. Blacks, Hispanics, and Asian Americans are never totally of one mind on policy, and factors like country of origin, religion, and class can and often do create divisions within each group. Overall, the key point is that one cannot truly understand public opinion in America without recognizing its racial contours.

Understanding and Measuring Public Opinion

V. O. Key, a famed observer of politics, noted long ago that public opinion consists of "those opinions held by private persons which governments find it prudent to heed" (Key 1967). That statement provides insight into both the substance and the importance of public opinion. In terms of substance, public opinion is simply the views of the masses—what each of us individually and what all of us collectively feel about the issues of the day. In terms of importance, we study public opinion because it matters—or at least should matter. The will of the public—often as expressed through public opinion—should be one of the primary driving forces of our democracy. As such, it is imperative that we try to measure and understand just what it is that the public wants from government.

Of course, politicians do not always actually respond to what the public wants. Many believe that money and special interests dominate over the public. In Chapter 11, we will return to the question of how much policy decisions are shaped by the public will. That chapter will also assess whose opinions most influence policy. Moreover, we explore the question of whether politicians *should* respond to a public that is often divided, ill-informed, and subject to biases and prejudices. All of these are valid concerns, but, for now, we are content to recognize the potential importance of public opinion and to outline and understand the voices of the public.

How Is Public Opinion Expressed?

Before we can understand public opinion, we need to measure it. Political scientists, journalists, and political strategists often rely on surveys and polling to assess public opinion. We shall return to these measures soon, but first, it is important to remember that the public can express its will through a range of actions that extend far beyond participating in a traditional opinion survey. Researchers can assess what the public wants by studying anything from the letters they write to politicians to the sentiments they express through bumper stickers, or to whom they donate money. The public also expresses its will through more contentious political acts like protests and boycotts.

These kind of actions often provide distinct insights into the public's views. They can, for example, help us to learn about the intensity of the views. It is easy to answer a survey, but it takes more time and energy and is sometimes more dangerous to take part in a protest. Thus, by engaging in a protest, members of the public are showing us how much they care about an issue. Also, when citizens take actions that go beyond responding to surveys, they can express their thoughts with more specificity. In a survey, for example, you may be asked whether you want to spend more or less money on policing. In a blog post, however, you can express exactly what it is about policing that you do or don't like and exactly how you think the government should fix it. Finally, by monitoring the public's actions beyond polls, we can learn about emerging issues. Surveys only ask citizens about the issues that pollsters think are important. But rallies and boycotts can rapidly shift the focus to new problems of public concern.

Of course, the main problem with these other forms of public opinion is that they often do not represent the entire public's views. For example, by tracking political donations, we may learn the preferences of the wealthy, but we learn little about the wants of the disadvantaged, who have little or no money to donate.

The Science of Public Opinion Polling

While all these alternative means of measuring public opinion have advantages and offer complementary insights, for now we turn to public opinion polling. The key advantage of public opinion surveys—and the main reason we tend to rely on them so heavily to gauge the public will—is that they are specifically designed to be representative. The underlying goal of most surveys is to select a random sample of the population so that the views expressed represent the views of the broad public. Statistically speaking, with a random sample of 1,000 people, pollsters can get a reasonably accurate picture of the entire population. Nineteen times out of twenty (95 percent of the time) the estimate from the survey should match up within 3 percentage points of the public's views.

Of course, acquiring a truly representative sample in a survey is not easy. Pollsters have to overcome a range of obstacles to get there. To begin with, they have no complete list of residents from which to randomly sample. A bigger problem is that much of the public is difficult to reach. Some do not have phones at all, and many do not have landlines—negating a traditional method that pollsters used to contact the public in the past. Even worse, much of the public does not want to answer surveys. Those who opt-in to phone surveys are unlikely to be representative of the public. Opt-in internet surveys may be even more problematic. Survey firms have developed techniques to adjust for these issues that typically involve weighting the responses of underrepresented demographic categories more heavily. But none of these techniques is foolproof. In addition, there is the complex problem of predicting who will actually turn out to cast a vote and who will stay home.

An equally significant problem lies in the survey questions themselves. A poor fit between the words and concepts in the question and how the public thinks about the issue may result in an inaccurate assessment of underlying attitudes. We know all too well that the same question asked with slightly different wording can lead to radically different responses. But perhaps the biggest problem lies with the public itself. Few Americans have devoted sufficient time and energy to fully understand the complex issues on which they are regularly polled. Indeed, since polling began in the 1930s, researchers have repeatedly found that the public is woefully ignorant of basic facts relevant to key policy decisions. Plus, many Americans—perhaps more so over time—lie to pollsters.

Given all these problems, it is not surprising that public opinion polls have been much maligned over the years. For many, the failure to accurately predict the election of Donald Trump in 2016 (and subsequently to understate his support in 2020) sealed the view that public opinion surveys are deeply flawed. But the reality is that polls—at least in terms of predicting election outcomes— are reasonably accurate and indeed have become more accurate over time. Figure 6.1 shows the difference between

Orange line represents average absolute error
Bars represent average signed error (red bars indicate overestimation of Republican
vote margin; blue bars indicate overestimation of Democratic vote margin)

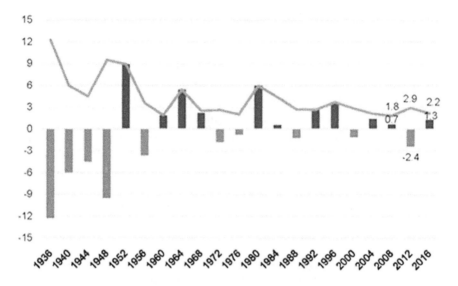

Figure 6.1 Election Eve Polls and Election Outcomes for Presidential Elections,
1936–2016
The red bars in this graph indicate the degree to which the Republican vote was
overestimated and the blue bars show how much the Democratic vote was
overestimated in any given election. The orange line shows the trend in the average
error over time, which was quite large in the 1930s—around ten percentage points—
but then showed a steady decline over time. In recent elections, for example,
preelection polls have only missed the election results by one or two points.
Source: Kennedy et al. (2018), www.archive.aapor.org/education-resources/reports/
an-evaluation-of-2016-election-polls-in-the-u-s.aspx.

election eve polls and actual election outcomes for presidential elections from 1936 to
2016. The red bars indicate the degree to which the Republican vote was overestimated and the blue bars show how much the Democratic vote was overestimated in
any given election. The orange line shows the trend in the average error over time,
which were quite large in the 1930s—around ten percentage points—but then showed
a steady decline over time. In recent elections, for example, preelection polls have
only missed the election results by one or two points. So what happened in 2016?
Polls accurately predicted that Hilary Clinton would go on to win the popular vote.
But Clinton's margin was overestimated by 1.3 percentage points—not a lot but
enough to make the margin small enough for Trump to lose the popular vote but
win the Electoral College and the presidency. The polls in 2016 more or less got it
right, but in an extremely tight election it is incredibly difficult to predict the winner.
The polls in 2020 were, in fact, less accurate (about three points off), but since they
were lucky enough to predict the winner, criticism was more muted.

WHAT IT LOOKS LIKE TODAY: ERRORS IN ASSESSING MINORITY OPINIONS

Although public opinion surveys can provide a reasonably accurate portrayal of the national mood, their assessments of the views of subsets of the public should be read with some caution. Because national surveys are not designed to gauge the attitudes of subsets of the public, their samples of smaller groups are often neither random nor large, and this applies to estimates of the views and votes of the racial and ethnic minority population. For example, a typical national survey of voters might include only 50 Asian American and 100 Latino respondents. Making matters worse, most national surveys only interview in English, effectively eliminating a substantial share of the Latino and Asian American population and almost certainly skewing results. Other polls sample minorities only in geographic areas where that particular group is concentrated, a method that can introduce more error. Furthermore, whether a sample of Latinos happens to include more Cuban Americans from Florida or more Mexican Americans from California can radically alter estimates of Latino positions, as these two groups often differ in their partisan proclivities and issue preferences. These flaws explain why scholars who focus on minority politics often remain skeptical of the national exit poll's estimates of the Latino and Asian American vote.

Photo 6.2 People hold placards after U.S. Vice President Mike Pence addressed supporters at a Latinos for Trump campaign rally at Central Christian University, October 10, 2020, in Orlando, FL. With twenty-four days until the 2020 presidential election, both Donald Trump and Democrat Joe Biden were courting the Latino vote.

Source: Photo Paul Hennessy © NurPhoto/Contributor/Getty Images.

More specifically, national exit polls in 2016 reported that Donald Trump won 29 percent of the Asian American vote and an identical 29 percent of the Latino vote. If true, those numbers represented a substantial uptick in Republican voting in both groups and a sign of a potential reversal in party fortunes going forward. The only problem is that both numbers were probably wrong. Polls that interviewed in multiple languages and that targeted Asian Americans and Latinos across the country all reached different conclusions about the minority vote in 2016. Three major surveys of the Latino population estimated that only 17–19 percent of the Latino vote went for Trump in 2016. And the one major election eve survey of Asian Americans found that only 19 percent of that group favored Trump. Both figures suggest declining rather than increasing minority support for Republican candidates. Interestingly, the national exit polls once again reported an uptick in Latino support for Trump in 2020. And once again, the media ran countless stories highlighting the shift. But just how big the shift really was and whether it signals an ongoing shift in the vote will have to await better numbers.

American Core Values

America—so the founding story goes—is exceptional. We were founded, so the story continues, on values that set us apart from all other nations and that continue to drive our nation. As we noted in Chapter 1, for many, the American ethos is defined by core values: most notably, commitments to individualism and equality. By individualism we mean a focus on individual liberty, prioritized above other possible values, and an inherent suspicion of government. According to this view, Americans believe that hard work should pay off and the government should be peripheral and only active when absolutely necessary. Equality, on the other hand, is about the belief that everyone deserves an equal chance at success. For Americans, perhaps unlike citizens in other nations, equality is not a desire for all to end up at the same level, with the same wealth or identical outcomes, but rather a strongly felt desire to create a system that is fair and that provides all with an equality of opportunity.[1]

Belief in Individualism and Equality of Opportunity

The notion that America is different from and perhaps even better than all other nations is well-trodden ground, but is it actually true? Is there a distinct American

---

[1] Another difference between Americans and those in other nations may be the degree to which U.S. residents believe that there is, in fact, equality of opportunity and the chance of raising one's rank in the future. Fully 63 percent of Americans are satisfied with the opportunities for people to get ahead (Newport 2018).

creed? And how does it square with the racial inequities and divides that we have so far highlighted in this textbook?

Some truth certainly underlies this national mythology. At its founding, America was in some ways more equal economically and more democratic than almost any other nation—although as we have discussed in some depth in Chapter 2 and elsewhere, that equality extended to only a select segment of the population. Since that time, hard work, ingenuity, and invention have continued to serve as core values, producing remarkable achievements and fostering wide-ranging socioeconomic mobility—although that mobility has waned in recent decades. As well, our commitment to individualism seems to have endured. Today, we devote less to social spending than other developed nations. Unlike our European counterparts, we do not have a universal healthcare system nor family allowance. Compared with those European nations, we have less labor protection, more limited parental leave, and a lower minimum wage.

Clearly, large segments of the American public continue to hold these values dear. Survey data reveal a deep-rooted skepticism about the government. In the American National Election Study—the survey that we introduced in Chapter 4 and rely on for most of the data in this chapter—fully 72 percent of Americans believe that the government wastes "a lot" of tax money. Americans also almost universally believe in equality of opportunity. Almost 80 percent agree that "Our society should do whatever is necessary to make sure that everyone has an equal opportunity to succeed." Moreover, this basic commitment to both individualism and equality extends to all racial and ethnic groups. We are indeed an individualistic and egalitarian nation.

The United States also stands somewhat apart from most nations in our views on individualism and limited government. The World Values Survey, which is a global project to interview the opinions of ordinary individuals in nearly 100 countries, reveals that on average only 38 percent of residents of other countries believe that "government has too much power." In the United States, by contrast, fully 65 percent agree with that statement. Also, 73 percent of Americans believe that hard work is important to getting ahead, while only 50 percent concur elsewhere.

At the same time, no one can or should claim that all Americans hold these views. The public is divided on these values, and at least some of that division is across racial and ethnic lines. As Figure 6.2 reveals, the commitment to individualism is appreciably more pronounced among White Americans than it is in the racial and ethnic minority population. A clear majority (60 percent) of White Americans contend that "government is involved in things people should do for themselves," while most racial and ethnic minorities disagree. Only 35 percent of Blacks, 48 percent of Hispanics, and 48 percent of Asian Americans concur. Likewise, the majority of Whites (55 percent) believe that "the less government, the better." But racial and ethnic minorities largely disagree. Only 24 percent of Blacks, 34 percent of Hispanics, and 31 percent of Asian Americans believe that less government is generally better. Whites and minorities also do not see eye to eye on the question of whether government should "see to jobs and a standard of living" for all

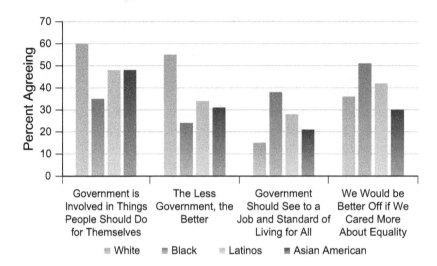

Figure 6.2 Commitment to Individualism and Equality by Race
The survey data summarized here indicate, among other things, that White Americans are more committed to beliefs around individualism than are Black, Hispanic, and Asian Americans, while Black and Hispanic Americans show more commitment to equality than Whites.
Source: 2016 American National Election Survey.

Americans or "let each person get ahead on their own." Only 15 percent of White Americans think it is the government's role to provide jobs and a standard of living. Blacks and Latinos are much more likely to view government as having a valid role in that regard (38 and 28 percent, respectively), and Asian Americans are slightly more likely to hold that view (21 percent). Racial differences—albeit smaller ones— also emerge on the topic of equality. Only 36 percent of Whites agree that we would be better off "if we cared more about equality." That figure increases to 51 percent for Blacks, 42 for Hispanics, and 30 percent for Asian Americans. Individualism and a belief in equality of opportunity are very American but far from universally American values.

Belief in Ascriptive Difference

Some contend that individualism and equality are not the only two values that define the American creed. Critics throughout American history have argued that a darker side permeates our beliefs. These critics maintain that a deeply held belief in ascriptive difference—that some people are more deserving or more able than others—is just as central to the American ethos. Thus, although we may aspire to be a free and equal society, we often define the borders of our society to include some and exclude others. This inegalitarian ideology, which was famously outlined by Gunner Myrdal in *An American Dilemma* and then detailed more clearly in scholarly work by Rogers Smith, has allowed us to create a hierarchical system in which the political and legal status of racial and ethnic minorities, women, immigrants, and others have been curtailed or limited in fundamental ways (Myrdal 1944; Smith 1993).

From this perspective, American society is best understood as the often conflictual and contradictory product of multiple political traditions, some of which push us toward a free and equal society and some of which seek to solidify inequalities by race, gender, and the like. The ebb and flow of those two forces can then explain the uneven arc of American history—one that surges back and forth between periods of expanding rights and periods of regression and retrenchment (Klinkner and Smith 1999). It can also explain the ambivalence that many individual Americans feel about groups that differ from their own, and what the rights of those other groups should be.

If a belief in ascriptive difference is central to American thought, then its presence represents an important corrective to the rather rosy American exceptionalism story. But is a belief in ascriptive difference really central? At least in terms of our laws and actions, there is a lot that fits. Although our Constitution aspired to an ideal of equality for all, for most of our history the majority of the domestic population has been ineligible for full citizenship rights, including the right to vote. Likewise, although our laws have typically moved over time toward greater formal equality (e.g., the expansion of the vote to women and minorities), we have often followed those expansions with laws that have re-enshrined racism (e.g., Jim Crow laws that mandated separate drinking fountains, accommodation, transportation, and schools for Blacks and Whites), and we have sometimes adopted laws that explicitly exclude racial groups from our society (e.g., the Chinese Exclusion Act).

Deep down, what do Americans really believe about racial and ethnic minorities? Do many or most of us believe that some Americans are more deserving than others? Is prejudice really core to who we are? This is an extraordinarily difficult question to answer, since few Americans are willing to openly express racist views. In the next sections, we attempt to assess views on race and the extent to which Americans of different races and ethnicities hold negative views of each other.

Increasing Support for the Principle of Racial Equality

At least at first glance, Americans today firmly believe in the principle of racial equality. But as Figure 6.3 illustrates, Americans were once quite willing to support different laws for different races. In the middle of the twentieth century, the overwhelming majority of Americans (96 percent) did not approve of interracial marriage. More than half admitted that they would not vote for a "qualified Black candidate" nominated by their own party, and more than half said Blacks and Whites should not go to the same schools.[2] But over time, support for interracial marriage, integrated schools, and Blacks in politics has dramatically increased to the point where almost

---

[2] The trend showing growing support for interracial schools is slightly exaggerated because data for 1956 and 1962 are only available for Whites.

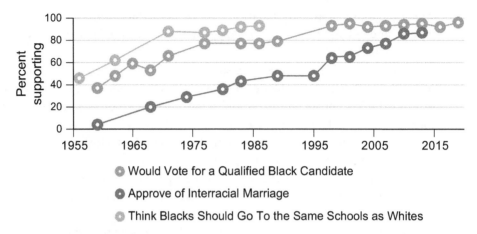

Figure 6.3 Americans' Increasing Support for Racial Equality in Principle, 1955–2015
Over time, an increasing percent of Americans have shown support for racial equality, but in
1955, a large percentage of Americans did not support such ideals.
Source: GSS Cumulative File and Gallup Trends.

everyone agrees on equality—at least in principle. Indeed, most of these questions
have been dropped from surveys because they have reached maximum or near-
maximum support levels, and this improvement is largely due to changes in White
attitudes. African American support for the principle of racial equality has been
nearly unanimous since these questions were first asked on surveys. All of this
suggests that the public now broadly or even universally accepts racial equality.

Measuring Our Views on Race

Ascertaining what Americans really think about race is difficult. Individual
Americans may not want to admit to holding views that others might see as
undesirable. This notion that we might hide our true views on a survey to look
better in front of others is what researchers call social desirability bias. The existence
and potential prevalence of social desirability bias has made understanding views on
race extremely difficult and has forced researchers to come up with subtle and
imaginative ways of measuring our views on race.

Widespread Racial Stereotyping

One way to try to get at our true attitudes on race is to ask people specific questions
about a particular racial group and then combine those separate questions to get a
relative evaluation of racial minorities. More concretely, we can ask individual
Americans to rate a racial group—say Blacks—on some trait. For example, we
might ask someone to rate how "hardworking" Blacks tend to be, using a scale

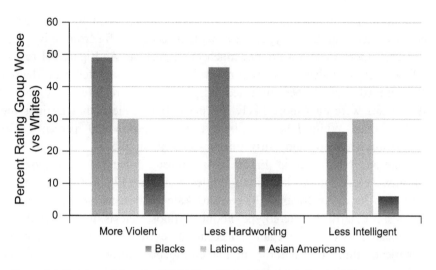

Figure 6.4 Percent of Americans Viewing Minorities as Inferior to Whites
According to survey data, Americans as a whole carry negative stereotypes of racial and
ethnic minorities.
Source: Data from General Social Survey 2016 and National Longitudinal Survey of
Freshmen 1999.

from 1 to 7, with 1 meaning that almost all members of that group are "lazy" and
7 meaning that almost all members of that group are "hardworking." We can then
ask the same individual to rate Whites on the same scale. Combining the two
responses, we can determine how many Americans rate Whites as superior or in
this case as more hardworking than Blacks (also see Chapter 4 for a discussion of
similar survey measures). This method—or any method that we will introduce in
this chapter—is not perfect. People could still be lying. But we suspect they are less
likely to do so in this format. Indeed, when questions are posed this way, many
answers conform to common stereotypes about minorities.

In fact, as you can see in Figure 6.4, stereotypes of racial and ethnic minorities are
widespread—particularly so for African Americans. About half of all Americans
rate African Americans as more violent than Whites. Almost half view African
Americans as less hardworking than Whites. And about 30 percent of people believe
that Blacks tend to be less intelligent than Whites. The 30 percent figure is especially
troubling not only because it is focused on a largely innate quality like intelligence,
but because it is based on responses from college freshmen. We might have hoped
that a younger generation of college students would be more racially progressive,
but instead we find that almost a third appear to believe that one racial group is on
average less intelligent than another. Critically, very few Americans end up rating
Blacks as superior to Whites on any of these scales. Only 12 percent rate Blacks as
less violent, only 12 percent rate Blacks as more hardworking, and only 8 percent
rate them as more intelligent. At the same time, large shares of the public do place
Blacks and Whites at the same point of each scale. Very roughly, about half of

Americans rate Blacks and Whites as equally violent, equally hardworking, and equally intelligent. Stereotypes are broadly held but are far from universal.

Stereotypes of Latinos are not much more positive. As Figure 6.4 reveals, fully 30 percent of college freshmen rated Latinos as less intelligent than Whites. By contrast, only 7 percent rated Hispanics as more intelligent than Whites. Americans were also more likely (30 percent) to believe that Latinos are more violent than Whites than to believe the opposite (20 percent). However, Americans seem to hold fairly mixed views about the work rate of the Latino population. Note that in Figure 6.4, almost 20 percent of respondents rate Latinos as less hardworking than Whites; but what Figure 6.4 does not show is that even more Americans—30 percent—rate Latinos as *more hardworking* than Whites. Perhaps the stereotype about Latinos that is most prevalent in the American public is of illegality. Recent survey data show that the majority of Americans think the majority of the Latino population is undocumented (Pew 2018). The reality is that less than a quarter of the Latino population is, in fact, undocumented.

At least at first glance, stereotypes of Asian Americans appear to be positive. As Figure 6.4 hints, Asian Americans tend to be viewed as less violent, harder working, and more intelligent than Whites or other groups. Americans are more than seven times more likely to view Asian Americans as more intelligent than Whites (45 percent) than they are to see Asian Americans as less intelligent than Whites (6 percent). Asian Americans are also much more likely to be viewed as more hardworking than Whites (43 percent) than they are to be viewed as less hardworking (13 percent). Very few Americans (13 percent) judge Asian Americans to be more violent than Whites, but almost half (48 percent) feel that Asian Americans are on average less violent than Whites. Such positive stereotypes fuel the prevailing perception that Asian Americans are a "model minority." In a nutshell, the model minority stereotype is the belief that Asian Americans are an exemplar among racial minority groups by virtue of cultural traits like valuing education and hard work and knowing to keep out of trouble, and by virtue of the assumed benefits that come with those traits like high socioeconomic attainment.

The model minority stereotype is, however, not entirely positive. For one thing, it is often deployed to draw a sharp contrast between Asian Americans and other minorities—most notably, Blacks and Latinos. The contrast leans heavily on false stereotypes, such as the belief that Asian Americans succeed socioeconomically because of traits like valuing education and hard work while Blacks and Latinos fail to achieve high socioeconomic attainment because they lack those traits. Implied in this view of America is the belief that inequality is the result of individual traits and not institutional barriers. That is, the thinking goes, if Asian Americans can succeed, Blacks and Hispanics should be able to do the same without any special favors. As we have already demonstrated in Chapter 5, institutional racism and structural barriers to opportunity and advancement are rife in America, even today. It is important to remember, furthermore, that stereotypes are beliefs about a group that overgeneralize or mischaracterize that group. Thus, even though the stereotypes that fuel widespread perceptions of a model minority may be positive beliefs about a group, they can have adverse effects. For instance, the model minority stereotype clearly overlooks the sizeable share of the Asian American population that is socioeconomically disadvantaged or that do not manifest cultural traits like valuing education and hard work. And generalizations about a minority group's alleged successes can breed contempt of others. For example, when asked which groups hold "too much economic power," Whites, Blacks, and Hispanics are all more likely to point to Asian Americans than to any other racial group (Lee 2000).

The picture is further complicated by a broad sense among the American public that Asian Americans are unassimilable or less likely than other groups to assimilate to the American way of life. Survey data are limited and somewhat dated, but one study found that roughly half of the population thinks that Asian Americans "are particularly puzzling and mysterious," and a third indicated that Asian Americans "have more in common with Asians in Asia than with other Americans" (Lee 2000). Almost all Asian Americans, regardless of how long they and their families have lived in the United States, are familiar with the question, "Where are you really from?"—a question that assumes foreign origins and attachments. At worst, the implied foreignness of Asian Americans can lead to a sense of fear—a view of this population that is often referred to as the Yellow Peril. The internment of tens of thousands of Japanese Americans (and fewer German Americans) during the Second World War in concentration camps around the United States is one glaring historical case of the negative consequences of this stereotype. Recent slurs against Chinese Americans in light of COVID-19, as presented in the opening story of this chapter, and trade wars with China represent others.

What is interesting and perhaps frightening is that these stereotypes tend to be held not only by Whites but also by racial and ethnic minorities themselves. When we break down the survey data by race, we find that each minority tends to have a slightly more positive view of members of its own group. Blacks, for example, are half as likely as Whites, Hispanics, and Asian Americans to rate Blacks as more violent than Whites. Hispanics are, likewise, considerably less likely than other racial groups to see Hispanics as more violent than Whites. But the sad truth is that racial and ethnic minorities tend to hold negative views of other racial and ethnic minority groups. Asian Americans are, for example, as likely or more likely than Whites to believe that Blacks are violent, lazy, and unintelligent. The same is true for Latino views of African Americans, while the views of Blacks and Latinos regarding Asian Americans often align with White views of Asian Americans. We view the prevalence of these racial stereotypes among all groups as one of the most damning findings about race in America that we will present in this textbook. Given how widespread these stereotypes are, it would be startling if racial and ethnic minorities received the same treatment and privileges as Whites do in American society. Real progress on race is likely to require changes in our deeply held stereotypical views of each other.

Photo 6.3 Exclusion order posted at First and Front Streets in San Francisco directing the removal and imprisonment of persons of Japanese ancestry from the first section of the city to be affected by evacuation, stating that "Evacuees will be housed in War Relocation Authority centers for the duration."
Source: NAID: 196319.

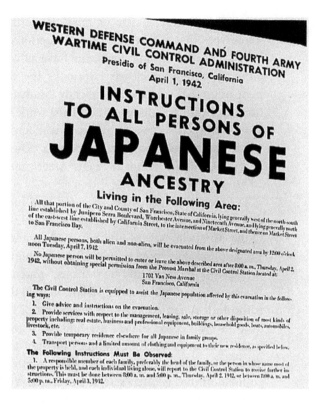

America's Racial "Hierarchy"

Summing together these racial stereotypes, we can get a picture of America's racial hierarchy. One approximation of that hierarchy is illustrated in Figure 6.5. The figure shows the placement of Blacks, Latinos, Asian Americans, and Whites on two dimensions. The vertical dimension shows the degree to which a group is viewed as superior or inferior. Because Blacks are stereotyped as less intelligent, lazy, and violent, they are found at the bottom, or so-called inferior, part of that scale. By contrast, as a group often viewed as a Model Minority, Asian Americans are placed toward the superior end of that scale. The horizontal dimension places each group on the foreigner–insider dimension. As a group that is viewed as particularly foreign, Asian Americans are placed on the foreigner end of the scale. Latinos, for whom a primary stereotype is illegality, might also be placed near the foreign end of the scale. Of course, each of these placements is somewhat subjective. You and your classmates could have an interesting debate about where each group truly fits in the minds of individual Americans.

One group that is not placed in the figure is Muslim Americans. We do not have much systematic data on stereotypes of Muslim Americans, so it is hard to know where to place them. Most Americans probably don't know it, but in terms of socioeconomic status, Muslim Americans closely mirror the American public with near average levels of education and income. Moreover, we also know that three-quarters of Muslim Americans are immigrants or the children of immigrants. But what do Americans actually think when they see Muslims on the street?

Photo 6.4 Muslims from the U.S. and abroad, organized by Hassen Abdellah, a criminal lawyer who is president of the Dar-ul-Islam mosque in Elizabeth, NJ, pray on the West Front of the U.S. Capitol.
Source: Photo Scott J. Ferrell © Scott J. Ferrell/Contributor/CQ-Roll Call, Inc./Getty Images.

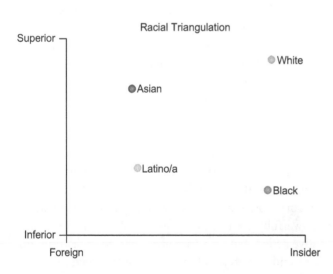

Figure 6.5 America's Racial Hierarchy In this figure, Blacks, Latinos, Asian Americans, and Whites are placed on two dimensions. The vertical dimension shows the degree to which a group is viewed as superior or inferior. The horizontal dimension places each group on the foreigner–insider dimension.
Source: Adapted from Kim (1999).

Given that much of the media coverage of (and much of the political rhetoric about) Muslims and Muslim Americans centers on the potential for violence and terrorism, we suspect that violence is a central feature of Muslim American stereotypes. Thus, we might need to add a third dimension (from violent to peaceful) to accurately place Muslim Americans in America's racial hierarchy. What we do know is that discrimination against Muslim Americans is widespread. Experiments by political scientist Nazita Lajevardi show that politicians are less responsive to an email from a citizen with a Muslim-sounding name than a non-Muslim-sounding name (Lajevardi 2020). Her experiments also reveal that Americans are less apt to support a Muslim candidate than an otherwise identical candidate who is not Muslim.

Other Measures of Racial Views

Another widely used measure of racial views is called the racial resentment scale. The scholars who created this scale are Donald Kinder and Lynn Sanders, who based their measure on an earlier "symbolic racism" or "modern racism" scale by Kinder and David Sears (Kinder and Sanders 1996; Kinder and Sears 1981). These authors argue that White American views on race have shifted over time, especially since the Civil Rights Movement. In their account, we have progressed from a nation where most White Americans believed in the innate inferiority of racial minorities prior to the Civil Rights Movement to a nation where most Americans will publicly endorse the principle of racial equality, but privately harbor resentment and animus toward racial minorities (in particular, African Americans) for demanding too much in "special favors and accommodations." Racially resentful Whites believe that formal racial barriers were removed following the Civil Rights Movement and that by asking for government support and protection, Blacks are not adhering to traditional American values associated with the Protestant work ethic. This new type of racial prejudice is thus a subtle combination of anger at Blacks for not taking advantage of opportunities and support for individualism. To gauge racial resentment (or symbolic racism as it is sometimes called) scholars ask individual Americans how they feel about statements like these: "Irish, Italians, Jewish and many other minorities overcame prejudice and worked their way up. Blacks should do the same without any special favors." Or, "It's really a matter of some people not trying hard enough; if blacks would only try harder, they could be just as well-off as whites." Those who agree are labeled as racially resentful.

In the 2020 American National Election Study, we find that about 40 percent of Americans (and almost 50 percent of White Americans) could be categorized as racially resentful, or as scoring above the midpoint of the scale. These figures suggest that this more subtle form of prejudice is widely held. Moreover, in study after study, racial resentment powerfully predicts positions on policies that explicitly deal with race, such as affirmative action, but also on policies related to distribution of resources, such as healthcare and welfare, and even on policies such as social security and foreign aid—policies that are only weakly tied to race (Kinder and Sanders 1996; Winter 2006). Racial resentment is also one of the most powerful predictors of the vote. In 2020, 93 percent of Whites who scored highest on the racial resentment scale voted for Trump, whereas 90 percent of the least racially resentful Whites voted for Biden. While racial resentment is undoubtedly powerful, it is difficult to interpret its meaning. Given that measures of racial resentment

Photo 6.5 Members of the National Socialist Movement (NSM) rally near City Hall on April 17, 2010, in Los Angeles, CA.
Source: © David McNew/Stringer/Getty Images News/Getty images.

incorporate both feelings on race and views on individualism and government intervention, it is hard to know whether the primary driver is attitudes about race or conservatism.

More recently, several racial resentment scales have been created to assess attitudes toward Latinos, Asian Americans, and Muslims. Here research shows that resentment tends to drive opposition to policies designed to aid each group (Lajevardi 2020; Ramirez and Peterson 2020).

An even subtler method used to get at underlying racial attitudes is the implicit attitude test (IAT). The idea behind the IAT is that implicit, unconscious associations play an important role in our perceptions and actions about social groups. Psychologists like Daniel Kahneman (2011), for instance, distinguish between "System 1" and "System 2" thinking, both of which are ubiquitous in human cognition. System 1 thinking is our brain's automatic, unconscious responses to new situations and stimuli; everyday activities like talking, walking, and driving rely heavily on System 1 processes. System 2 thinking, by contrast, is slower, more effortful, and requires reasoning and deliberation. The goal of the IAT is to identify people's "System 1" automatic or uncontrolled thoughts on race (Banaji and Greenwald 2013). The IAT does this by assessing how quickly test subjects pair two concepts that stereotypically go together (e.g., the concepts "Black" and "lazy") compared with concepts that stereotypically do not go together (e.g., the concepts

"White" and "lazy"). Because the test detects millisecond differences in response times, it can identify hesitancy or difficulty with incongruous pairings. Since these racial associations are deeply held by many Americans and are thus part of automatic processes in our brains, even those who prefer not to reveal their racial views cannot but do so. Results of the test show that upwards of 50 percent of White Americans associate racial minorities with negative stereotypes and thus at least implicitly view Whites more positively than racial minorities (Pew 2015). Only a tiny fraction of Whites favor racial minorities over Whites. By contrast, racial minorities are roughly evenly split between favoring their own group and favoring Whites. Interestingly, racial biases revealed by the IAT are not highly correlated with standard measures of racial resentment, suggesting that the two measures reveal different aspects of our racial views.

TESTING THE THEORY: DO YOUR OWN IMPLICIT ATTITUDE TEST

We would like each of you to take an Implicit Attitude Test. The test is free and only takes a few minutes, available at the following link: https://implicit.harvard.edu/implicit/takeatest.html. A variety of IATs are available. We encourage you to start with one on race, but you are welcome to do more. In fact, it can be informative to take the same test multiple times as the same person taking the same test can get widely different results. After you complete the test or tests, reflect on the results. What do the test results say about you?

You should know that intense debate surrounds the question of what the IAT actually measures. Is it simply measuring cultural knowledge of racial stereotypes? Is it measuring automatic processes that we can control and overcome? Or is it providing an accurate window into our views? It is worth noting that scores on the race IAT can predict racially biased actions, although the evidence is mixed as to whether it can also influence our political choices. For example, some research has found that those who implicitly favored Whites over Blacks when taking the Affect Misattribution Procedure or AMP, an alternative to the IAT, were less likely to support Barack Obama in the 2008 presidential election, even after taking into account racial resentment and other factors that could drive the vote (Payne et al. 2010). Subsequent work, however, has found that implicit prejudice has essentially no effect on presidential vote choice once more traditional survey measures of racial attitudes are taken into account (Kalmoe and Piston 2013; Kinder and Ryan 2015).

Scholars have come up with one other rather ingenious way of measuring prejudice. Recall that earlier in this chapter, we noted that survey data are sometimes susceptible to social desirability bias when respondents give the answers that they think the researchers or pollsters want to hear, rather than what they actually think. To the extent that there are strong social norms against being (or at least appearing) racially prejudiced, questions about race on surveys can be subject to this bias. To avoid this possibility, researchers sometimes use a technique known as a *list experiment*. In list experiments, subjects are presented with several statements and then asked only to indicate *how many* of those statements they agree with, not which ones. Subjects are randomly assigned to get either a list of all neutral statements (i.e., none of which pertain to potential prejudice toward a minority group) or an list that is nearly identical but for the addition of one more, nonneutral, sensitive statement (e.g., the statement "Muslim immigrants should be banned from entering the United States"). Because subjects only have to say how many items they agree with and do not have to identify which ones, they may worry less about social norms and feel freer to express their true views. Since subjects are randomly assigned to one of two groups, and the lists are identical between the groups except for the one sensitive item, researchers infer that any difference in the mean number of statements agreed to in the two groups reflects agreement with the nonneutral, sensitive item. Using this technique, scholars have shown that many more Americans object to, for example, a Black family moving in next door, than they would admit if they were asked directly (Kuklinski et al. 1997).

Finally, one of the most recent additions to the toolbox is conjoint analysis. Conjoint analysis is actually a method of marketing research that has been around for about a half century, where the goal is to determine how consumers make decisions based on the many different attributes of any product. Decisions on where to dine out for a meal, for example, can be based on taste, cost, ambience, location, cuisine, and so on. In social science research, they are used, for instance, in experiments on immigration, in which respondents evaluate a pair of immigrants, each of whom has been randomly assigned a wide range of characteristics that include their age, education, gender, work history, country of origin, religion, and other factors. These experiments have offered significant insights. The large number of factors that are asked about can lower how inhibited respondents feel about expressing their true views about immigrants who are Muslim or who belong to a racial minority. Because the immigrant characteristics that are asked about are randomly assigned, conjoint analysis experiments allow researchers to measure how Americans value different characteristics in a group. For example, two important studies have revealed that a sizeable share of Americans favor Christian over Muslim immigrants (Adida, Lo, and Platas 2019; Hainmeuller and Hopkins 2014).

Policy Opinions

We should be concerned by the extent to which individual Americans hold negative views of other racial and ethnic minority groups. But it is not yet clear how much those negative racial views and racial stereotypes translate into an individual's views regarding government policies. We may have different views of each other, but we might still want the same things. In the next sections, we look more concretely at one of the most respected public opinion surveys—the American National Election

Study—to see what members of each racial and ethnic group want from government. Are the policy preferences of various groups largely aligned or largely in conflict? The reality, as we will soon see, is somewhere in the middle and depends at least in part on the kinds of policy we focus on.

Race-Conscious Issues

We begin by looking at an area where racial differences are likely to be the most pronounced—on matters of policy that explicitly or directly deal with racial and ethnic minorities and immigrants. One of the most controversial areas in these racial-explicit policy debates is what, if anything, government should do to improve the well-being of African Americans. In light of centuries of individual and institutional discrimination (see Chapters 4 and 5), how much is intervention justified or not justified? In Figure 6.6 we look at the share of Whites, Blacks, Latinos, and Asian Americans who favor three governmental actions to address racial inequities.

The first pattern you will notice in this figure is that African Americans want action. Half of the Black population believes that the federal government should "make every effort to improve the social and economic position of Blacks." Two-thirds favor preferential hiring for Blacks. And almost three-quarters agree that reparations for the slavery of African Americans are warranted. Indeed, the finding that a majority of African Americans want government action to improve the status of Blacks and to reduce the racial gap in well-being is one of the most consistent and clear results in survey research.

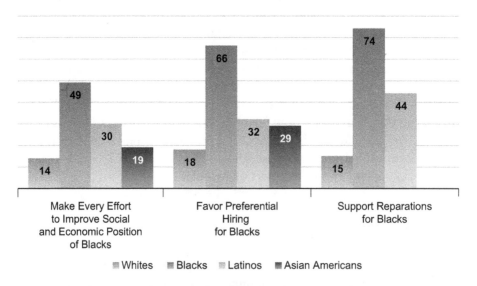

Figure 6.6 Americans' Approval of Policies Affecting Blacks
The bars here indicate the share of Whites, Blacks, Latinos, and Asian Americans who favor three governmental actions to address racial inequities.
Source: 2016 American National Election Study and 2019 NORC Center for Public Affairs Research Poll.

The second major pattern revealed by Figure 6.6 is that a substantial gap exists between Black views and the views of all other groups. Only small percentages of Whites, Latinos, and Asian Americans think that government should "make every effort." Moreover, relatively small percentages of these groups favor affirmative action for Blacks and reparations to Blacks for slavery. The gap between what Blacks want on racial policy and what other racial and ethnic groups want on racial policy has likely been the primary barrier to moving forward with policies that would lessen racial inequality.

We also see that Whites, as a group, are the most resistant to investing resources to help Blacks and reduce racial inequities. Only 14 percent think government should "make every effort" to improve the position of Blacks. Only 18 percent of Whites favor preferential hiring for Blacks. And only 15 percent support reparations for slavery. The overwhelming majority of Whites do not want the policies that the overwhelming majority of Blacks want. This massive Black–White gap in opinion on racial policy is also one of the most enduring and emphatic patterns in public opinion research.

Note also the differences between the groups featured in the figure. Hispanics are slightly more favorably inclined to policies designed to help Blacks than are Asian Americans, but both groups are substantially more favorably inclined than Whites. Moreover, and now moving beyond Figure 6.6, differences between minority groups decline further when the policy in question asks not only about support for African Americans but instead about support for minorities as a whole. Thus, for example, when minorities are asked about affirmative action policies that would benefit all racial and ethnic minorities, Latinx and Asian American support grows appreciably—although these two groups have not thus far favored such policies to the same level as Blacks do. Overall, however, the more a racial policy focuses explicitly on one racial minority and therefore excludes other racial minorities, the more differences emerge between communities of color.

Immigration Policy

With Donald Trump's presidency and more generally the Republican Party devoting considerable attention to immigration and the potential threats that it poses, immigration has taken on an outsize role in the political arena. Across the nation, Americans hold an extremely diverse range of opinions on the topic. For example, on the broad topic of how the nation should deal with undocumented immigrants, 17 percent of Americans say that the United States should make them "all felons and send them back to their home country," 14 percent favor a guest worker program that would limit the amount of time undocumented immigrants could remain in the United States, 59 percent indicate that the United States should allow them to stay and apply for citizenship as long as they meet certain strict conditions, and 10 percent say that all should be allowed to stay and eventually become citizens. Likewise, on the question of whether anyone born in the United States should automatically become a citizen, 31 percent are in favor, 28 percent are not sure,

Photo 6.6 A group of about thirty Brazilian migrants who had just crossed the border, sit on the ground near U.S. Border Patrol agents on March 20, 2019. U.S. President Donald Trump branded such migrants a threat to national security, demanding billions of dollars from Congress to build a wall on the southern U.S. border.
Source: Photo Paul Ratje © Paul Ratje/Contributor/AFP/Getty Images.

and 40 percent are opposed—even though the Fourteenth Amendment to the Constitution already ensures birthright citizenship.

Attitudes on immigration also vary widely depending on the type of immigrant. Americans reserve their most negative views for undocumented immigrants and tend to look more favorably on legal immigrants. But studies also suggest that these attitudes are highly racialized. In particular, Americans are more negative about Latino and Muslim immigrants than they are about European or Asian immigrants. Research also indicates that many Americans are ambivalent about immigration—holding positive views about those they perceive as hardworking immigrants, while simultaneously worrying about crime, lost jobs, and a lack of assimilation.

Amidst all of this, we see once again that there are sizeable racial and ethnic divides in opinion. Once again, Whites are generally the most resistant or conservative on the topic. As Figure 6.7 illustrates, of all the racial and ethnic groups, compared with Blacks, Hispanic, and Asian Americans, Whites are by far the most likely to say that legal immigration levels should be decreased (49 percent) and by far the most likely to favor building a wall along the border with Mexico (39 percent). Along with Blacks, Whites are also the least likely to believe that immigrants are generally good for the economy (49 percent). It should, however, be noted that in each case, White opinions are divided. For example, on the question of

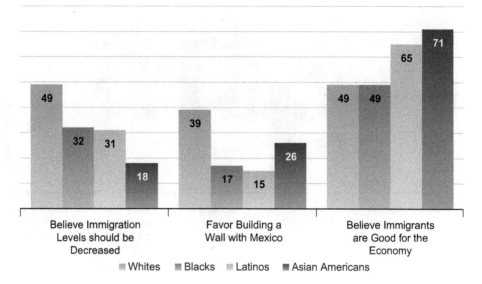

Figure 6.7 Americans' Views on Immigration Policy
Whites are generally the most resistant or conservative on immigration policy compared with Blacks, Latinos, and Asian Americans.
Source: 2016 American National Election Study and 2019 NORC Center for Public Affairs Research Poll.

whether we should increase or decrease current immigration levels, 15 percent of Whites want immigration levels increased, and the rest—36 percent—favor keeping immigration at its current level. Likewise, although 39 percent favor building a wall, another 40 percent oppose the border wall.

At the other end of the racial divide regarding immigration issues stand Latinos and Asian Americans. This is not surprising given that much of the Hispanic and Asian American population has such close ties to the immigrant experience. Only about one in five Asian Americans (18 percent) wants immigration levels decreased. For Latinos, the figure is only one in three, or 31 percent. Only small percentages of Latino and Asian Americans favor a border wall (15 and 26 percent, respectively). Overwhelming majorities of both groups think that immigrants are good for the economy.

In general, African Americans tend to fall somewhere in the middle—perhaps reflecting both their status as a racial minority group that understands the disadvantages minorities can face and their status as a largely native-born group that sometimes competes with immigrants for working-class jobs and other resources.

Public Services

The category of public services includes a wide range of policies from welfare and health to education and policing—all of which address basic services the

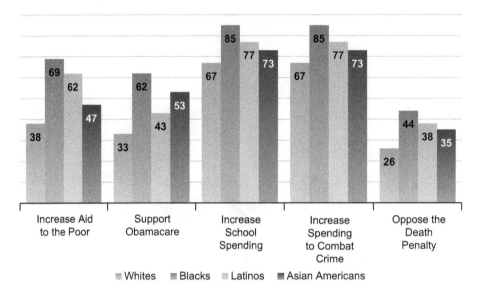

Figure 6.8 Americans' Views on Public Services
There is a clear racial divide on the topic of public services, with Whites typically the least likely to support these services.
Source: 2016 American National Election Study and 2019 NORC Center for Public Affairs Research Poll.

government provides to members of the public. Some of these policies (welfare, health, education) can also often be thought of as redistributive, in that they tend to redirect resources toward less advantaged segments of society. As a result, these policies are often framed around issues of class and questions about who needs or deserves help.

Although none of these policies has an explicit connection to race, because of America's racial hierarchy in well-being, most policies that seek to aid the disadvantaged affect racial minorities more than Whites. As such, how we think about these policies is likely to at least in part reflect how we think of racial and ethnic minorities. We explore that possibility in more depth later in this chapter.

In a pattern that is now likely to be familiar, we find major racial divides on questions related to public services, with Whites typically the least likely to support these services, Blacks typically the most likely to support them, and Latinos and Asian Americans in the middle but often closer to Blacks. That pattern is illustrated in Figure 6.8, which highlights the share of each racial and ethnic group supporting four major policies on welfare, health, education, and criminal justice.

The racial gaps are probably the most pronounced on supporting economically disadvantaged Americans where only 38 percent of Whites favor an increase in "aid to the poor." By contrast, racial and ethnic minorities tend to strongly support most anti-poverty programs. In terms of aid to the poor, large majorities of Blacks (69 percent) and Latinos (62 percent) want to increase aid. Almost half of Asian Americans (47 percent) agree. This pattern, in which Whites largely oppose efforts to reduce poverty and minorities generally support such efforts is another long-standing finding in public opinion surveys. In our survey, we also find that Whites have much less positive views of the poor than do Blacks and Latinos, a pattern that helps to explain both White resistance to expanded aid as well as the racial gap.

Questions about healthcare spending—at least recently—tend to generate similarly racialized patterns. For a long time—and especially since President Obama introduced the Affordable Care Act (Obamacare) in 2010, opinions on healthcare have divided Americans by race, with Whites generally much more opposed to government involvement in healthcare than racial minorities. In Figure 6.8 we see that only a third of Whites supported Obamacare in 2016, while majorities of Blacks and Asian Americans and almost half of Latinos did so.

Patterns on education are hard to characterize and vary substantially across different aspects of education policy. Policies that are more redistributive—for example, free school lunch, Head Start, or loan forgiveness for university students—tend to be associated with sharper racial divisions than do programs that are less redistributive, like general school funding, Charter Schools, or research grants for professors. Support for charter schools, for example, tends to divide Americans within each racial group but hardly at all across racial groups. And as Figure 6.8 shows, most Americans support increased spending on schools, although Whites are somewhat less likely than Blacks, Hispanics, and Asian Americans to do so.

Racial divides on crime are equally pronounced but also vary across aspects of criminal justice policy. As Figure 6.8 illustrates, racial divides on spending to combat crime have until recently been generally small. All four groups tended to favor expanding the federal crime budget, though Blacks and Asian Americans were the most supportive. The killing of George Floyd by a Minneapolis police officer that was caught on camera in May 2020 and the ensuing Black Lives Matter protests led to a shift in thinking about the role of local police departments and calls for the reduction of budgets. Some cities have reduced their police budgets in response, but the changes have been modest—and have met with some backlash. As might be expected, racial groups are more divided over support for the death penalty, a punishment that disproportionately affects Black Americans and also one that tends to discriminate against Black Americans (Baldus and Woodworth 2003). In the 2016 study, many Americans opposed the death penalty, but Whites (26 percent) were much less likely than African Americans (48 percent) and Hispanics (38 percent) to do so. As is often the case, Asian Americans fall in the middle on this question.

The Environment

Between 80 and 85 percent of the members of each racial and ethnic group agree that global warming is a problem. But when the public is asked about solutions, moderate racial divisions emerge. Contrary to a lot of the media reports, Whites are once again the least likely to favor investing time and resources to protect the environment. Only about half of Whites (47 percent) favor increased spending to

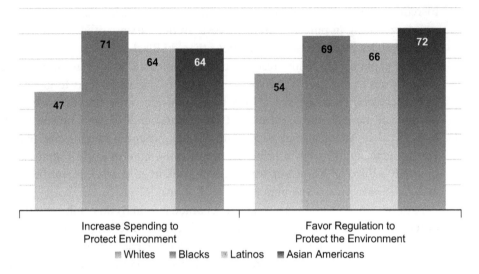

Figure 6.9 Americans' Views on Environmental Policy
While most Americans recognize the danger of global warming, moderate racial divisions
emerge when it comes to doing something about it. Among the groups polled, Whites are the
least likely to favor investing time and resources to protect the environment compared with
Blacks, Latinos, and Asian Americans.
Source: 2016 American National Election Study and 2019 NORC Center for Public Affairs
Research Poll.

protect the environment, whereas roughly two-thirds of the racial and ethnic
minority population wants to spend more money on the environment (see
Figure 6.9). Similarly, when it comes to regulations to protect the environment,
Whites are substantially less likely (54 percent) to favor regulations than are Blacks
(69 percent), Latinos (66 percent), or Asian Americans (72 percent). The greater
willingness of all three racial and ethnic minority groups to invest in reducing
humankind's impact on the environment may relate to the fact that racial and
ethnic minorities tend to be the most exposed to environmental degradation and
the most vulnerable to environmental disasters.

Gender and Social Morality

Figure 6.10 provides a glimpse into Americans' views by race on a number of
important policies related to gender equality and social morality. This is the first
time we see small to nonexistent racial differences. Despite some claims in the media
and elsewhere, Blacks and Latinos are not substantially more conservative when it
comes to these gender-equity issues or to many questions related to social morality.

More specifically, all four racial and ethnic groups agree in principle on gender
equality. As the figure illustrates, 85 percent or more of each group believes that
women should get equal pay. Almost two-thirds of each group also support women's

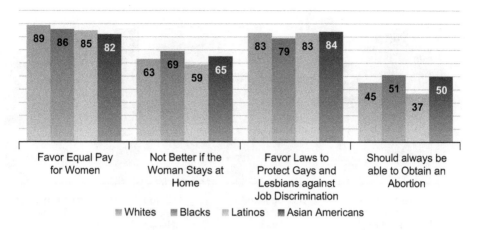

Figure 6.10 Americans' Views on Gender and Morality
There is not a lot of difference of opinion among the different groups on the subject of gender-equity and social morality issues.
Source: 2016 American National Election Study and 2019 NORC Center for Public Affairs Research Poll.

right to work outside the home. Although not reflected in the figure, Americans are more divided over what to think of feminists as well as the degree to which they think women face barriers in the workforce, but even here racial divisions are minor.

LGBTQ+ rights also do not divide Americans by race. Over time, members of all racial and ethnic groups have grown more accepting of Lesbians, Gays, and Bisexual Americans. Roughly 80 percent of all Whites, Blacks, Latinos, and Asian Americans now favor laws barring discrimination against the lesbian and gay communities in the workplace. However, many Americans of all racial and ethnic stripes remain opposed to extending full rights to the LGBTQ+ community. Slightly more than half of the members of each racial and ethnic group agree that gay marriage should be legal (Pew 2019). Members of all four groups also have lukewarm feelings toward transgender Americans, and support for laws that protect transgender Americans is relatively weak among all racial and ethnic groups.

Similarly, there are few major racial divisions on abortion. About half of the Black, Hispanic, and White population support full access to abortion, while very roughly, only 15 percent of each group contends that abortion should never be legal. This is, however, one area where Asian Americans stand out. On abortion Asian Americans are the most conservative of the four groups in this study. An important point about attitudes toward abortion is that they have not changed much over time. Americans of all racial and ethnic stripes remain divided over how we should regulate abortion.

Foreign Affairs

Foreign affairs is another area where we see few large or consistent differences in attitudes between racial groups. On most questions of foreign policy, the opinions of

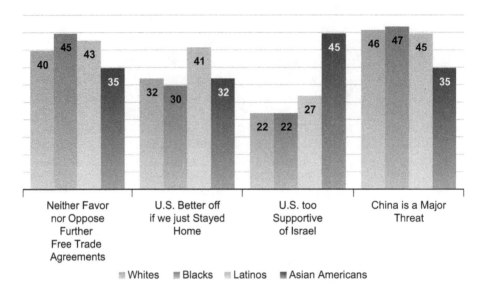

Figure 6.11 Americans' Views on Foreign Affairs
There are few large or consistent differences in attitudes between racial groups on the subject of foreign affairs.
Source: 2016 American National Election Study and 2019 NORC Center for Public Affairs Research Poll.

each racial and ethnic group largely match up with each other. All four groups are largely ambivalent about signing more free trade agreements, and all four groups are equally unsure of whether it would be better if the United States stayed at home rather than becoming entangled in the problems of other countries (see Figure 6.11). Indeed, when we asked for opinions across a wide range of foreign interventions, from combatting terrorism to providing foreign aid, we found no clear racial patterns, and no one racial and ethnic group was consistently more interested in engaging with the rest of the world. Not surprisingly, Asian Americans tended to see China as less of a threat than did other racial and ethnic groups. For all the groups and for most of the questions, the most common survey response was to give moderate or middle of the road views—perhaps reflecting a lack of knowledge or disinterest in foreign affairs. Regardless of the reason, America's racial and ethnic groups largely agree on the aspects of foreign policy addressed in the survey.

What Accounts for the Racial Divide in Public Views?

Remarkably, in most of the areas of public policy that we have examined, racial and ethnic groups divide sharply over which policies this country should pursue. More often than not, that division is most pronounced between Whites, on one hand, and racial and ethnic minorities, on the other. And not too infrequently, what the majority of Whites want is the opposite of what the majority of minorities want. Critically, all of this is most severe on areas of racial policy. Here Whites and minorities seem often to live in separate, opposing worlds. In this next section, we try to understand the source of those divisions. Why is it that Whites and minorities disagree so often over policy? To answer that question, we focus on one group at time. We begin with Whites because as both the majority and the group that seems most resistant to policies explicitly designed to aid minorities, their support is critical to moving policy forward.

Understanding White Views

Perhaps the most remarkable aspect of White views is the contrast between support for racial equality in principle and opposition to government policies that might lead to equality in practice. We highlight this gap in Figures 6.12 and 6.13, which show trends over time for the *principle* of equality as well as White support for the *implementation of policies* designed to generate racial equality. Over a period of thirty years (the mid-1950s to 1985), Whites came to overwhelmingly support the principle of racial equality (see Figure 6.12). That is, by 1985, almost all Whites agreed that Blacks and Whites "should go to the same schools." When asked, almost all Whites also agreed that "Blacks should have as good a chance as Whites to get jobs." Both questions got such unanimous support that they are no longer asked in surveys.

But when we shift to policies that would require effort and resources to attain equality, Whites are much less supportive. Scholars call this the principle–implementation gap. Moreover, on this implementation of policies, White views have not changed much over time. As Figure 6.13 reveals, very roughly, only about a third of Whites believe that the "government in Washington" should see to it that Black

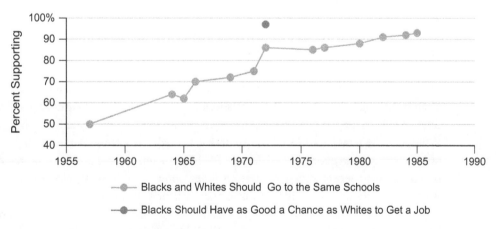

Figure 6.12 White Support for the Principles of Racial Equality, 1957–1985
Over a period of thirty years (1957–1985), White support for the principle of racial equality grew dramatically.
Source: American National Election Study, 1957–1985.

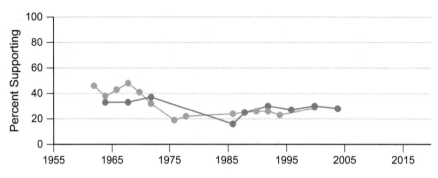

Figure 6.13 White Support for Implementing Racial Equality, 1960–2004
From 1955 to 2004, White support for policies implementing racial equality remained fairly stagnant, in fact, slightly decreasing rather than increasing.
Source: American National Election Study, 1962–2004.

people get "fair treatment in jobs," and that level of support has slightly decreased over time. And a similar percentage of Whites are opposed to government intervening to assure that Blacks and Whites go to the same schools. That low level of support for school integration has remained stagnant over time.

Note that this principle–implementation gap is unique to White views. African Americans, the group that could most benefit from these policies, overwhelmingly favor *both* the principle of racial equality and the implementation of policies that might get them there.

Scholars have offered two explanations for this principle–implementation gap. One centers around race and racial prejudice and the other around principled conservatism. The race story has several versions, but the crux of the argument is that while White America may genuinely believe in racial equality under the law, many Whites continue to hold negative views of Blacks and other minorities and therefore remain reluctant to expend resources to bring about change. Perhaps driven by the stereotypes we discussed earlier, they may think that Blacks are already getting too much in terms of special favors, or they may simply fear losing their own privileged status—again either consciously or not-fully-consciously. Whatever the exact nature of the reluctance, we have strong evidence that racial attitudes help to explain the resistance of Whites to supporting policies that have the potential to generate racial change. Studies show that how Whites think about Blacks strongly predicts which policies they will or will not support.

Take welfare, for example. Surveys have shown that most Americans (wrongly) believe that most welfare recipients are Black. As we discussed earlier in the chapter, surveys also reveal that many Americans view Blacks as lazy. If the two are put together, they can create powerful sentiments against welfare. In fact, landmark work by Martin Gilens has demonstrated that one of the best predictors of attitudes

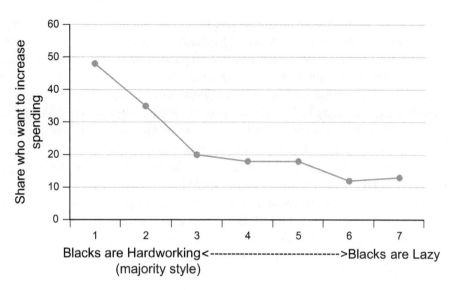

Figure 6.14 The Link Between Racial Attitudes and Welfare Views
The data plotted here show that as individual Americans' views of Blacks improve, their willingness to increase welfare spending grows.
Source: Adapted from Gilens (2001).

on welfare is a person's views on how lazy or hardworking African Americans are. His research, which we have partially reproduced in Figure 6.14, shows that as individual Americans' views of Blacks improve, their willingness to increase welfare spending grows. In other words, how we think about Blacks is intricately related to how we think about welfare. Respondents' willingness to increase welfare spending is higher when attitudes about Blacks are more positive—and vice versa.

Similar tests have shown that our preferences on healthcare, gun control, education, and even Social Security are closely linked to how we think about racial and ethnic minorities (Filindra and Kaplan 2016; Tesler 2012; Winter 2008). Going further, how we think about Latinos shapes a number of policies related to immigration, education, and taxation (Abrajano and Hajnal 2015; Ramirez and Peterson 2020). More broadly, the degree to which White Americans are racially resentful predicts their policy preferences even after scholars take into account many factors, including where they fall on the liberal-to-conservative spectrum and their views on individualism and small government. Indeed, when racial resentment is thrown together with other factors, it usually comes out as one of the most powerful predictors of White policy views.

The principle–implementation gap can, however, also be explained by pointing to values associated with political conservatism—what some may call *principled conservatism*. The argument is that Whites oppose most of these policies, not because of racial animus but because of a commitment to values like individualism, hard work, and equality of opportunity. In other words, Whites might want to help Blacks but at the same time believe that government intervention is not the right avenue for those efforts. Likewise, Whites might oppose affirmative action, not because it helps

Blacks, but because these programs give Blacks special advantages and do not treat everyone equally. Empirically, an individual's support for small government and self-reliance correlates with the principle–implementation gap among Whites. One well-known experiment supports the idea that the race of the recipient is not the key factor in determining whether Whites favor government social programs. More specifically, the study indicated that overall, Whites were no more or less willing to provide job assistance or welfare support to an African American than to a "White immigrant from Europe" (Sniderman and Carmines 1997).

The main problem in trying to determine the driving force behind White policy views is that it is difficult to disentangle racial views from principled conservatism. The reality is that how we feel about race, how we feel about government and equality, and how we feel about policy have all become so intricately intertwined that empirically separating one from the other well enough to test them is extremely difficult. One recent experiment demonstrated just how enmeshed the concepts are. That study by Christopher DeSante (2013) asked individual Americans to decide how much money to give to two individual welfare applicants. The applicants were randomly assigned different races as well as different past work histories. Overall, Americans were just as willing to provide monetary assistance to a Black applicant as an otherwise identical White applicant. But respondents rewarded White applicants a lot more (by giving them higher monthly welfare benefits) than Black applicants for having a strong work history, and Blacks applicants were punished much more, with lower monthly benefits, than otherwise identical White applicants for being described as "lazy" in the past. In a twist, respondents in the experiment could also set aside some of the money to reduce the deficit. The author found that when respondents were presented with two theoretical welfare applicants who were Black, the amount of money they wanted to reserve for the deficit increased, and when both welfare applicants were White (but again otherwise identical), it declined. Also, all these patterns were more pronounced for respondents who scored high on a racial resentment scale.

One final way to try to explain the principle–implementation gap—and also understand why Whites and Blacks so strongly disagree over policy—is to point to the fact that Black and White Americans see American society and the role of race in that society very differently. When White Americans look at the nation, they tend to see very little racial discrimination. By contrast, when racial and ethnic minorities assess the country, they tend to see widespread discrimination—a pattern we highlighted in Chapter 5. That contrast in views is central because the things that one thinks should be done or not done related to race depend critically on whether one thinks discrimination is widespread. Those who feel that racial discrimination is limited or nonexistent will likely see no need to take special steps to help African Americans or other minorities. By contrast, those who perceive widespread discrimination are likely to think that major policy initiatives are required to address the problem and to bring us closer to racial equality. That difference of opinion is evident in Figure 6.15, which shows the percentage of each racial and ethnic group that believes there is a lot of discrimination against Blacks, against Latinos, and against Asian Americans. The most striking aspect of the figure is that the

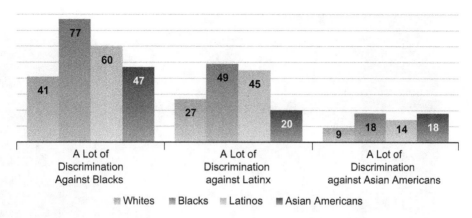

Figure 6.15 Americans' Views on Discrimination in America
Whites are less likely than Blacks, Latinos, and Asian Americans to believe there is a lot of discrimination against racial and ethnic minorities.
Source: 2016 American National Election Study.

overwhelming majority of African Americans (77 percent) think there is a lot of discrimination against Blacks, while fewer than half of Whites (41 percent) hold that view. If White and Black Americans cannot agree on whether there is a problem, they likely will not agree on a solution.

This particular Black–White divide may, however, be changing. The gruesome murder of George Floyd in 2020 and the seemingly endless flow of videos demonstrating police brutality against minorities appear to be raising White awareness of discrimination and perhaps shifting White views on a range of race-related questions. Only time will tell if this ultimately leads to a closing of the racial gaps shown in Figure 6.15.

Notably, it is not just Whites and Blacks who disagree about discrimination. As Figure 6.15 shows, Whites and Latinos also differ. A little under half of all Latinos think there is a lot of discrimination against Hispanics in America, while only about a quarter of Whites agree. That gap is also likely to make it difficult to agree on how much policy support Latinos need in this country.

The only case where there is widespread agreement related to discrimination relates to views regarding Asian Americans. All four racial and ethnic groups largely agree that there is not a lot of systematic discrimination against Asian Americans. But even here the story is more complicated than it appears. When Asian Americans are asked if they have ever personally experienced racial discrimination, about half typically say yes. Unfortunately, the problem appears to be getting worse. As you read in the opening story to this chapter, President Trump's efforts to blame China for the coronavirus have filtered into widespread acts of discrimination. The vast majority of Asian Americans (81 percent) report that violence against their group has increased since the coronavirus outbreak (Ruiz et al. 2021). Fully a third have feared that someone could threaten or physically attack them (Ruiz et al. 2021).

Photo 6.7 Demonstrators wearing face masks and holding signs take part in a rally "Love Our Communities: Build Collective Power" to raise awareness of anti-Asian violence, at the Japanese American National Museum, Little Tokyo, Los Angeles, CA, March 13, 2021. Reports of attacks, primarily against Asian American elders, had spiked in recent months at that time.
Source: Photo Ringo Chiu © Ringo Chiu/Contributor/AFP/Getty Images.

The United States' citizens increasingly disagree about the extent of discrimination against Whites. Very few Americans of any race contend that there is "a great deal" of discrimination against Whites, but Whites are much more likely than racial and ethnic minorities to perceive at least some discrimination against Whites. Roughly half of the Black, Hispanic, and Asian American populations believe there is no discrimination against Whites. But only 28 percent of White Americans believe that their racial group does not face any discrimination. Moreover, the percentage of Whites who believe that their group faces at least a little discrimination has been increasing in recent years. Studies show that White Americans, particularly those who strongly identify with their racial group, are more and more likely to feel that their group is significantly disadvantaged in American society (Jardina 2018). In other words, a new fissure is opening up in the race debate.

Understanding Racial and Ethnic Minority Views

Racial and ethnic minorities, as we have seen, tend to support more liberal policy-making than do Whites. But as we have also seen, there is considerable variation *within* the minority community. Blacks tend to be more liberal than Hispanics, who in turn are often more liberal than Asian Americans. And within each group, there is often a mix of views. In this section, we offer some explanations for both the similarities and differences within groups.

Group Consciousness

One factor that might drive unity within racial and ethnic minority communities is *group consciousness*. One of the most basic questions about Hispanics, Asian Americans, and to a lesser extent African Americans, is whether, in fact, the members of each group actually identify with and feel attached to their racial or pan-ethnic group. The question is especially relevant for Asian Americans and Hispanics because members of these groups are not only extremely diverse in terms of economic well-being but also because members hail from so many different countries, speak different languages, and belong to different religions. The fact that the terms Asian American and Latino largely did not even exist until a few decades ago further raises questions as to whether the terms are meaningful in describing groups that are cohesive in any way.

While the answer to that question was murky several decades ago, it has become much less so today. Figure 6.16 shows the degree to which Latinos, Asian Americans, African Americans, and Whites identify with their racial group. Here, we show two different ways of measuring how strongly someone might identify with

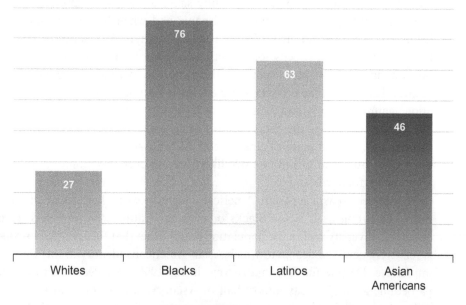

Figure 6.16 Americans Who Say Racial Identity is "Extremely" or "Very Important"
According to the ANES data, African Americans profess the strongest sense of attachment to their racial identity, but some share of every group polled professed a strong racial identity.
Source: 2016 American National Election Study.

their racial group. The first is to simply ask how important belonging to a group is to one's identity. A second way in which political scientists measure the strength of group identity draws on the work of Michael Dawson (1994) and others on a "linked fate" orientation. The idea behind linked fate is the belief that your fate is tied to the fate of your group as a whole. A linked fate orientation thus serves as a heuristic, or cognitive short-cut, for members of a racial group when faced with important policy proposals or political choices.

In line with past findings, African Americans exhibit the strongest sense of attachment to their race. Three-quarters of the Black population indicate being Black is "extremely important" or "very important" to their identity. That strong sense of identity is also manifest as a strong sense of linked fate. In the American National Election study, fully 76 percent of Black Americans agree that what happens to Black people generally in this country will affect their own lives. That robust belief in linked fate means that when faced with a new policy proposal or political option, African Americans generally evaluate alternatives based on how they are likely to impact the collective well-being of the group—what Dawson calls the "Black Utility Heuristic." That logic helps to explain why African Americans are the most unified racial group in the political arena and in particular why their support for the Democratic Party and a liberal pro-Black agenda is so extensive.

But as Figure 6.16 shows, African Americans are not the only group with a strong sense of identity. Fully 63 percent of Latinos also say that their racial identity is extremely or very important. That is a far cry from the numbers we would have seen a couple of decades ago when only a tiny share of the Latino population actually identified with the terms Latino or Hispanic and when the vast majority instead identified with their country of origin or with a hybrid American identity (e.g., Mexican American). A sense of pan-ethnic identity is growing for lots of reasons, but among the most important are likely the use of anti-immigrant rhetoric by political leaders and the growing sense among the Latino population that discrimination against them is widespread. Latinos have also begun to feel a stronger sense of linked fate with other members of the Latino community. Already 61 percent of Latinos express this sense of linked fate. As with African Americans, a stronger sense of identity and linked fate will likely lead to even more unity in the political arena going forward.

The degree to which Asian Americans identify with their racial group is not nearly as strong as it is for Blacks or even for Latinos. Nevertheless, given the enormous diversity within the population and the fact that the term Asian American is relatively new, the degree to which Asian Americans identify in this way today is impressive. Despite the fact that surveys in the 1990s revealed little to no sense of pan-ethnic identity, today almost half of Asian Americans (46 percent) state their Asian American identity is very important to them. Even more remarkable, 70 percent of Asian Americans express a sense of linked fate with their racial group. Again, many factors are likely to be driving this trend, but discrimination and political scapegoating are likely to be primary.

The other relatively recent development is an increased sense of White identity—almost 30 percent, as shown in Figure 6.16. Whites in America generally identified more strongly as American than as White. But as America has become more racially diverse and as racial and ethnic minorities have accumulated more power and resources, White identity has become more fully activated. Other research supports this same conclusion, estimating that for roughly 30–40 percent of White America, racial identity has become politically meaningful (Jardina 2018). And, increasingly, how strongly Whites identify with their own racial group impacts their views on social security, Medicare, and other policy areas.

There is, of course, nothing wrong with having a sense of one's own racial identity, but in-group affinity can often mean out-group antipathy. As our racial identities grow and as we become increasingly racially divided politically, we increasingly face the risk of interracial conflict and violence.

Other Divisions within Minority Groups

Given all the differences that exist within each racial and ethnic minority group—socioeconomic class, gender, age, religion, and national origin—we should not be surprised to find political divisions and differences in policy choices among Blacks, Latinos, and Asian Americans.

Of all these factors that divide and unite, national origin may be the most significant. Among Hispanics, Cuban Americans stand out from every other national origin group in their political views. In particular, on questions related to immigration, such as whether to build the border wall; on healthcare questions, such as whether the government should provide universal healthcare; and on foreign affairs, such as whether to impose sanctions on North Korea or tariffs on Chinese goods, Cuban Americans are 10–15 percent more likely to take what we think of as the more conservative view than are other groups within the Hispanic community. Within the Asian American population, no country of origin stands out as sharply or as consistently, but Filipinos are substantially more likely than other Asian Americans to label themselves as conservative and are particularly likely to express conservative views on abortion and other moral and religious issues. Other national origin groups—for example, Chinese Americans—tend to stand out on issues of particular relevance to their home country.

WHAT IT LOOKS LIKE TODAY: A PROFILE OF YOUNGER AMERICANS

America's youth often think of themselves as more enlightened than their elders on the issues of the day. Our surveys show that younger Americans do, in fact, differ from their elders when it comes to policy preferences. Across almost every arena, from immigration and race to welfare and especially to the environment and LGBTQ+ issues, younger Americans are more liberal and more supportive of government action to rectify inequalities and problems. That is true within every

Photo 6.8 Activist group Earth Strike NYC announced a radical frontline coalition gathering in Sunset Park to support a campaign for local community-led climate justice at the Communities Strike for Climate Over Colonialism rally and march.
Source: Photo Erik McGregor © Erik McGregor/Contributor/LightRocket/Getty Images.

racial and ethnic group, but it is especially true within the White population. White Americans under age 21 are 15–25 percent more likely than White Americans over age 70 to support liberal immigration policies, favor gay marriage and other pro-LGBTQ+ policies, advocate for more active environmental regulation, and back economic redistribution for the poor. If the youth of America have their say, and if they maintain these attitudes as they grow older, the nation may move in a more progressive and inclusive direction in the future.

Other significant factors predicting policy views among minority populations are as follows:

- Religion: with Evangelicals and Catholics often expressing more conservative views, especially on moral and religious policy questions.
- Socioeconomic class: some evidence indicates that among minorities, class gains are less likely to lead to more conservative views than they are among Whites.
- Gender: Black women, for example, are especially liberal on a variety of policy issues. Overall, however, gender differences within the minority population tend to mirror gender differences within the U.S. population as a whole with women slightly more supportive of social welfare programs, slightly more liberal on many economic issues, slightly more concerned about the environment, slightly less

supportive of military force, and slightly more liberal on domestic issues like the death penalty and gun control.
- Age (see "What It Looks Like Today" box).
- Nativity and level of assimilation.
- Region and state.

Indeed, as we have emphasized throughout this chapter, any effort to speak of a fully unified Black, Hispanic, or Asian American community or to claim that one policy or another is *the* policy of a racial group will always ignore significant differences of opinion within the population.

Conclusion

As this chapter has argued, individuals' views on policy often intricately intertwine with their race and ethnicity. Moreover, racial and ethnic biases shape perceptions and behavior, with differential impacts. The COVID-19 pandemic has only served to highlight all of this. Although the virus threatened everyone, regardless of race or ancestry, it was nevertheless sometimes called the "Kung flu,"—a name that fostered resentment toward, and in some cases, violence against Asian Americans. The targeting of Asian Americans was at least in part fueled by political entrepreneurs looking for a scapegoat and was helped by individual Americans with preexisting racial stereotypes.

Similarly deep and complex connections exist between race, ethnicity, and public opinion more generally. Americans may agree on some core principles, but sharp racial divides exist in most areas of policy from welfare and crime to the role of government. Generally speaking, White Americans tend to be more conservative on the array of policy problems facing the public, while minorities and especially African Americans tend to favor more liberal, redistributive solutions. Even sharper racial divides—even in some cases a racial chasm—exist when it comes to policy on race itself. Here the majority of White America favors little government intervention in policies designed explicitly to aid minority groups, perhaps to protect their privileged status. On the other side, the majority of racial minorities support a range of such policies, perhaps to rectify widespread historical and systemic racial discrimination. Underlying all of this are deep-seated stereotypes about the abilities and inabilities of the Black, Latino, and Asian American communities. Of course, within each racial and ethnic group, people are divided by country of origin, religion, age, class, gender, and other factors, but the overarching lesson of this chapter is that racial division is pronounced and exists almost everywhere in the policy world.

Where all of this will go is impossible to tell. We have not looked at trends over time all that much in this chapter, but it is likely that racial divides over policy have been growing, and it is certainly possible that they could continue to expand in the future. It is less clear whether racial stereotyping is declining or not.

Can we do anything to increase understanding and reduce these racial divides? Fortunately, there may be some steps we can take. Several recent experiments in persuasion have highlighted promising ways of increasing understanding and reducing antipathy toward minorities. One study showed that short interactive sessions that encourage individual Americans to think about issues from the perspective of immigrants leads to increased sympathy for refugees. Another set of experiments demonstrated that engaging in short conversations in which participants exchanged nonjudgmental personal narratives facilitated durable declines in stereotypes of transgender Americans and increased not only compassion for unauthorized immigrants but also favorable views toward policy interventions to improve their lives (Adida et al. 2019; Kalla and Broockman 2020). If these efforts can be expanded, so too may be cross-racial consensus and unity.

KEY TERMS

Ascriptive difference
Equality
Implicit attitude test (IAT)
Individualism
Model minority
Principle–implementation gap
Public opinion
Racial resentment
Racial resentment scale
Social desirability bias
Unassimilable

DISCUSSION QUESTIONS

1. How would you define America's core values, and how does race fit or not fit into them?
2. How would you characterize stereotypes for each racial group?
3. What techniques or tools would you use to gauge someone's racial views?
4. What factors contribute to the divisions in this country related to race, ethnicity, and related policy preferences?
5. Do you think the policy views of many White Americans are shaped by a preference to maintain the racial status quo? Why or why not?
6. Why do you think the U.S. citizenry is divided by race on policies that are not explicitly about race?
7. What is group consciousness and what role does it play in shaping public opinion?

ANNOTATED SUGGESTED READINGS

See Rogers Smith. 1993. "Beyond Tocqueville, Myrdal, and Hartz: The Multiple Traditions in America," *American Political Science Review* 87(3): 549–566, for a deeper understanding of how belief in racial difference is central to America's core values.

See Donald R. Kinder and Lynn Sanders. 1996. *Divided by Color: Racial Politics and Democratic Ideals*. Chicago: University of Chicago Press, for a detailed description of racial resentment and its consequences.

See Paul M. Sniderman and Edward G. Carmines. 1997. *Reaching beyond Race*. Cambridge, MA: Harvard University Press, representing the best argument for the role of conservatism in shaping attitudes on racial policy.

See Martin Gilens. 2001. *Why Americans Hate Welfare: Race, Media, and the Politics of Antipoverty Policy*. Chicago: University of Chicago Press, for a better understanding of the link between race, racial attitudes, and redistributive policy.

See Michael C. Dawson. 1994. *Behind the Mule: Race and Class in African-American Politics*. Princeton: Princeton University Press, for more on the role of group consciousness and linked fate.

See Nazita Lajevardi. 2020. *Outsiders at Home: The Politics of American Islamaphobia*. New York: Cambridge University Press, highlighting the increasingly central role that Muslim Americans play in the racial politics of this nation.

See Ashley Jardina. 2018. *White Identity Politics*. New York: Cambridge University Press, for a compelling account of the growth and impact of White racial identity.

See Lauren Davenport. 2018. *Politics beyond black and White: Biracial Identity and Attitudes in America*. New York: Cambridge University Press, for an explanation of the complex views of Americans who identify with more than one race.

See J. L. Kalla and D. E. Broockman. 2020. "Reducing Exclusionary Attitudes through Interpersonal Conversation: Evidence from Three Field Experiments," *American Political Science Review* 114(2): 410–425, to learn more about how exchanging personal narratives can reduce prejudice against disadvantaged groups.

CHAPTER REFERENCES

Abrajano, Marisa and Zoltan Hajnal. 2015. *White Backlash: Immigration, Race, and American Politics*. Princeton: Princeton University Press.

Adida, Claire L., Adeline Lo, and Melina R. Platas. 2019. "Americans Preferred Syrian Refugees Who Are Female, English-Speaking, and Christian on the Eve of Donald Trump's Election," *PLoS One* 14(10): e0222504. https://doi.org/10.1371/journal.pone .0222504.

Baldus, D. C. and Woodworth, G. 2003. "Race Discrimination and the Death Penalty: An Empirical and Legal Overview," In *America's Experiment with Capital Punishment: Reflections on the Past, Present, and Future of the Ultimate Penal Sanction* (eds.) J. R. Acker, R. M. Bohm, and C. S. Lanier. Durham, NC: Carolina Academic Press.

Banaji, Mahzarin and Anthony Greenwald. 2013. *Blindspot: Hidden Biases of Good People*. New York: Delacorte Press.

Bryce, James. 1888. *The American Commonwealth*, vol. 2. Indianapolis, IN: Liberty Fund.

Dawson, Michael C. 1994. *Behind the Mule: Race and Class in African-American Politics*. Princeton: Princeton University Press.

DeSante, Christopher D. 2013. "Working Twice as Hard to Get Half as Far: Race, Work Ethic, and America's Deserving Poor," *American Journal of Political Science* 57: 342–356.

Filindra, Alexandra and Noah J. Kaplan. 2016. "Racial Resentment and Whites' Gun Policy Preferences in Contemporary America," *Political Behavior* 38: 255–275.

Gilens, Martin. 2001. *Why Americans Hate Welfare: Race, Media, and the Politics of Antipoverty Policy*. Chicago: University of Chicago Press.

Hainmueller, Jens and Daniel Hopkins. 2014. "Public Attitudes toward Immigration," *Annual Review of Political Science* 17: 1–25.

Jardina, Ashley. 2018. *White Identity Politics*. New York: Cambridge University Press.

Kahneman, Daniel. 2011. *Thinking, Fast and Slow*. New York: Farrar, Straus & Giroux.

Kalla, J. L. and D. E. Broockman (2020). "Reducing Exclusionary Attitudes through Interpersonal Conversation: Evidence from Three Field Experiments," *American Political Science Review* 114(2): 410–425.

Kalmoe, Nathan P. and Spencer Piston. 2013. "Is Implicit Prejudice against Blacks Politically Consequential? Evidence from the AMP," *Public Opinion Quarterly* 77: 305–322.

Kennedy, Courtney et al. 2018. "An Evaluation of the 2016 Election Polls in the United States," *Public Opinion Quarterly* 82(1): 1–33.

Key, V. O. 1966. *The Responsible Electorate: Rationality in Presidential Voting 1936–1960*. Cambridge, MA: Harvard University Press.

Kim, Claire Jean. 1999. "The Racial Triangulation of Asian Americans," *Politics and Society* 27: 10–138.

Kinder, Donald R. and Timothy J. Ryan. 2015. "Prejudice and Politics Re-Examined: The Political Significance of Implicit Racial Bias," *Political Science Research and Methods* 5: 241–259.

Kinder, Donald R. and Lynn Sanders. 1996. *Divided by Color: Racial Politics and Democratic Ideals*. Chicago: University of Chicago Press.

Kinder, Donald R. and David O. Sears. 1981. "Prejudice and Politics: Symbolic Racism versus Racial Threats to the Good Life," *Journal of Personality and Social Psychology* 40: 414–431.

Klinkner, Philip A. and Rogers M. Smith. 1999. *The Unsteady March: The Rise and Decline of Racial Equality in America*. Chicago: University of Chicago Press.

Kuklinski, James H., Paul M. Sniderman, Kathleen Knight, Thomas Piazza, Philip E. Tetlock, Gordon R. Lawrence, and Barbara Mellers. 1997. "Racial Prejudice and Attitudes toward Affirmative Action," *American Journal of Political Science* 41: 402–419.

Lajevardi, Nazita. 2020. *Outsiders at Home: The Politics of American Islamaphobia*. New York: Cambridge University Press.

Lee, Taeku. 2000. "Racial Attitudes and the Color Line(s) at the Close of the Twentieth Century," In *The State of Asian Pacific Americans: Race Relations* (ed.) Paul Ong. Los Angeles: LEAP.

Myrdal, Gunnar. [1944] 1996. *An American Dilemma: The Negro Problem and Modern Democracy*. New Brunswick: Transaction (original ed., Harper & Row).

Nazaryan, Alexander. 2017. "75 Years Later, Internment of Japanese Remains Stain on American History," *Newsweek*, February 15.

Newport, Frank. "Majority in U.S. Satisfied with Opportunity to Get Ahead," Gallup. https://news.gallup.com/poll/228914/majority-satisfied-opportunity-ahead.aspx

Oppel, Richard A. Jr., Robert Gebeloff, K. K. Rebecca Lai, Will Wright, and Mitch Smith. 2020. "The Fullest Look Yet at the Racial Inequity of Coronavirus," *New York Times*, July 5.

Payne, B. Keith, Jon A. Krosnick, Josh Pasek, Yphtach Lelkes, Omair Akhtar, and Trevor Tompson. 2010. "Implicit and Explicit Prejudice in the 2008 American Presidential Election," *Journal of Experimental Social Psychology* 46: 367–374.

Pew Research Center. 2015. "Exploring Racial Bias among Single Race and Bi-racial Adults: The IAT." www.pewsocialtrends.org/wp-content/uploads/sites/3/2015/08/2015-08-17_IAT.pdf.

Pew Research Center. 2018. "Shifting Public Views on Legal Immigration into the U.S." www.pewresearch.org/politics/2018/06/28/shifting-public-views-on-legal-immigration-into-the-u-s/#many-overestimate-the-share-of-the-immigrant-population-that-is-in-the-u-s-illegally.

Pew Research Center. 2019. "Attitudes on Same-Sex Marriage." www.pewforum.org/fact-sheet/changing-attitudes-on-gay-marriage.

Ramirez, Mark D. and David A. M. Peterson. 2020. *Ignored Racism: White Animus toward Latinos*. Cambridge: Cambridge University Press.

Ruiz, Neil G., Khadijah Edwards, and Mark Hugo Lopez. 2021. "One-Third of Asian Americans Fear Threats, Physical Attacks and Most Say Violence against Them Is Rising," Pew Research Center, April 21. www.pewresearch.org/fact-tank/2021/04/21/one-third-of-asian-americans-fear-threats-physical-attacks-and-most-say-violence-against-them-is-rising.

Smith, Rogers M. 1993. "Beyond Tocqueville, Myrdal, and Hartz: The Multiple Traditions in America," *American Political Science Review* 87: 549–566.

Sniderman, Paul M. and Edward G. Carmines. 1997. *Reaching beyond Race*. Cambridge, MA: Harvard University Press.

Tavernise, Sabrina and Richard A. Oppel Jr. 2020. "Spit on, Yelled at, Attacked: Chinese-Americans Fear for Their Safety," *New York Times*, March 23.

Tesler, Michael. 2012. "The Spillover of Racialization into Health Care: How President Obama Polarized Public Opinion by Race and Racial Attitudes," *American Journal of Political Science* 56: 690–704.

Winter, Nicholas J. G. 2006. "Beyond Welfare: Framing and the Racialization of White Opinion on Social Security," *American Journal of Political Science* 50(2): 400–420.

Winter, Nicholas J. G. 2008. *Dangerous Frames: How Ideas about Race and Gender Shape Public Opinion*. Chicago: University of Chicago Press.

7   Political Participation

The polling site opened bright and early Tuesday morning in Racine County, Wisconsin. Everything was all set for throngs of voters to descend. Signs pointing to the church as a polling location were in place, volunteer workers were on hand, the voting machinery had been tested, and the ballot boxes were secure. The only problem? No one—or almost no one—showed up. How slow was it? According to Mary Bieniek, a poll worker at St. Louis Catholic Church, it was so slow that she was able to finish a 1,000-piece jigsaw puzzle. In fact, in the first 90 minutes only one person voted. And it was Mary's own son. Poll workers spent most of the day staring at empty voting booths in an eerily quiet church. All told, only 5.2 percent of eligible voters took part. As Bieniek lamented, "This is pathetic" (Rogan 2019).

On another Tuesday in Phoenix, Arizona, in what seems like a different world, Cynthia Perez stopped by her polling place on her way to work hoping to vote early. A line so long that she could not see the end of it forced her to change plans. She came back in the mid-afternoon to endure a 3-hour long wait to cast her ballot. By the time she had voted, the lines were even longer. Perez was not alone. All around the county, "lines meandered along church courtyards, zigzagged along school parking lots, and snaked around shadeless blocks as tens of thousands of voters waited to cast their ballots (Santos 2016). For many the wait felt interminable. Anger and frustration ensued. All of this for a primary election.

These two polling places—one empty and another inundated—highlight two powerful patterns in our democracy. The first is that participation is often quite low. Despite the importance of voting for the democratic process, this chapter will show that large shares—often the majority—of Americans choose not to get involved. The second is that participation is uneven. As this chapter will also show, those who do participate tend not to look like those who do not participate. In particular, there is a sharp racial skew to democratic involvement. Whites are much more likely than most racial and ethnic minority groups—with the occasional exception of African Americans—to vote and to engage in most other forms of participation.

These patterns are alarming. Voting is, after all, the foundation of our democracy. Through the vote citizens convey information about their needs and preferences, they make important decisions about whom to elect, and they hold leaders accountable for their actions. Democracy is unworkable and unthinkable without

Photo 7.1 People wait in line for early voting for the 2022 midterm elections at Ponce De Leon Library, Atlanta, GA. Long lines were seen at several polling locations in Atlanta where Georgians were voting for the hotly contested state governor and senator races.
Source: Photo Michael M. Santiago © Michael M. Santiago/Staff/Getty Images News/Getty Images.

broad participation. Yet the reality is that most of us do not participate when given the choice.

Uneven participation patterns raise further concerns. The skewed nature of the vote means that the subset of Americans who participate may be well represented, while other Americans who do not participate may be ignored. As one famous political scientist put it, "The old saw remains profoundly true: if you don't vote, you don't count" (Burnham 1987: 99). If these fears are true, elections will be unrepresentative, outcomes will be skewed, and in the end American democracy will represent the interests of the privileged few more than the concerns of the masses. And all of this could have severe racial consequences.

But are these fears truly warranted? In this chapter, we will also look closely at how much voting and nonvoting matters. Put simply, we will ask if electoral outcomes would be different if everyone voted. The answer is not quite as clear as it would at first seem. Although the media and the public generally believe that broader participation would benefit the Democratic Party, political scientists have traditionally found that higher turnout wouldn't make much of a difference. However, as America is becoming more and more racially diverse and America's politics are becoming more racially divided, the impact of turnout appears to be growing. Recent studies reveal that the implications of not voting are now profound. Today, fuller, more even participation would translate into more Democrats in office and would often mean that a different political party controls the nation's levers of power.

The two precincts—one vacant and one overwhelmed—also lead us to wonder why. Why is it that some people choose to participate and others choose not to exercise their right? This chapter will raise deeper questions about why people participate in the first place. Much of our effort will be directed at trying to explain the racial gap in participation. We will show that a big part of the answer relates to resources. Whites generally participate more than racial and ethnic minorities in no small part because they generally have more economic and educational resources to bring to bear in the political arena. Another part of the story is related to immigration. Attitudes about democracy also factor in. Finally, the degree to which political parties and other actors mobilize us also go a long way to explain who participates and in particular the racial differences in rates of participation. The structure of our electoral institutions greatly shapes who votes. The harder we make it to vote, the fewer people who actually participate—and often, the larger the racial skew in turnout. Sometimes those electoral institutions are even designed to exclude minorities. Voter suppression efforts—everything from poll taxes and literacy tests in centuries past to voter identification laws, voter purges, and reductions in poll locations and hours today—can exacerbate already alarming racial gaps in turnout.

Answers to the question of why some of us get involved while others stay on the sidelines can also help us to answer the final and perhaps the most important question of this chapter. Can we do anything about the low and racially uneven nature of political participation? That analysis will point clearly to a set of reforms and actions that could encourage political involvement and ultimately reduce substantial disparities in participation.

Who Participates?

Despite the centrality of the vote for democracy, we know that large numbers of U.S. citizens stay away from the polls. Our presidential elections draw the most voters, but even here the numbers are far from impressive. In 2020, two-thirds of eligible Americans turned out to vote, the highest voter turnout in the twenty-first century. While five points higher than the turnout in 2016, 2020's turnout was still not that far off the norm. For almost a century, turnout for presidential elections has hovered at around 60 percent of those eligible to vote. As we saw in Figure 3.1, that puts America near the bottom of the international barrel. A recent international study found that America ranked twenty-six of thirty-two in terms of voter turnout among nations surveyed who are members of the Organization for Economic Cooperation and Development (Desilver 2020).

And presidential elections are our best case. Most of those who can vote fail to show up at the polls for midterm elections, where many House and Senate seats are contested as well as many gubernatorial races. Turnout in the 2018 midterm election was 50 percent of eligible votes, higher than any midterm election since 1920. Over the last century, midterm turnout has generally been closer to 40 percent of those eligible to vote. The numbers are even worse for statewide primaries, where turnout often hovers around one-third of eligible voters; the numbers continue to fall as you move down the ballot to county and local elections, where posts such as mayors, judges, and county supervisors are decided and where voter turnout often falls below one-quarter of the voting age population. Contests for hyperlocal elections such as school boards regularly bring in less than 10 percent of the population.

Why does poor turnout matter? It means that generally speaking, a minority—sometimes a slim minority—of the population decides who to elect and determines what our government should do or not do. This raises serious questions about the representativeness and responsiveness of American democracy.

Historical Turnout by Race

Where does race fit into the turnout equation? To answer this question, it helps to begin at the birth of our democracy. Although the nation was founded on the principle of equality and the U.S. Constitution proclaims that "all men are created equal," that very phrase indicates that the reality of our early democracy was far from equal. The ability to vote—often called the franchise—was severely restricted from the very beginning. In 1776, voting was generally confined to White males over age 21 who owned property—a category that represented only about 6 percent of the population. That left out all women. It excluded all racial and ethnic minorities and most non-European immigrants. And it effectively denied the vote to economically disadvantaged people who did not have title to property. Indeed, for most of our history, much of the population has been ineligible to participate in our democracy.

America has slowly opened up the franchise to larger and larger segments of the population, but only very slowly and usually only after those who were disenfranchised fought long and hard for change. The first major national changes came about with the end of the Civil War and the freeing of enslaved Blacks. In 1868, three years after the end of the Civil War, the Fourteenth Amendment was ratified, providing voting rights for all men 21 years of age or older—but effectively Black men were still largely denied the vote. And then in 1870, the nation adopted the Fifteenth Amendment, which proclaimed that "the right of citizens of the United States to vote shall not be denied or abridged by the United States or by any State on account of race, color, or previous condition of servitude." With the passage of the Nineteenth Amendment in 1920, women were granted the right to vote. And in 1924, the Indian Citizenship Act gave Native Americans the right to vote.

However, the passage of these amendments did not mean that all barriers to participation were gone. In fact, with each major opening up of the right to vote came swift, sometimes violent, and often extremely effective countermeasures. Shortly after African Americans were given the legal right to vote, Whites in the South—where most Blacks lived—mobilized to restrict access to that vote in a

Photo 7.2 Martin Luther King, Jr.
and his wife, Coretta, lead a five-day
march to the Alabama State Capitol
in Montgomery in 1965.
Source: © Bettmann/Contributor/
Getty Images.

variety of ways. They imposed poll taxes (a fee for the right to vote, which many
Blacks were unable to afford), or required literacy tests (which many Blacks were
unable to pass, because they had little access to education at that point).
Intimidation and outright violence were also used to prevent most of the African
American population from actually utilizing the franchise. After these measures
were enacted, Black turnout for voting dropped from 45 percent to 1 percent in
Mississippi, from 84 percent to 14 percent in Florida, and from 70 percent to
30 percent in Tennessee (Foner 1984).

The civil rights movement of the 1950s and 1960s was in no small part a response
to this electoral exclusion. Despite grave threats to their well-being, Blacks mobilized in the millions to demand equal treatment under the law. After a prolonged
struggle, the passage of the 1965 Voting Rights Act outlawed many of the tactics
Whites in the South had used to limit voting among racial and ethnic minorities. But
minority empowerment once again met with White resistance. Shortly after the
passage of the Voting Rights Act, legislatures throughout the South enacted a range
of inventive measures designed to reduce the influence of the minority vote. For

example, in one single session and in a marvel of legislative efficiency, the Mississippi legislature was able to pass electoral laws that effectively stripped Blacks of any power with their votes. Among the measures that were passed:

- Electoral offices in areas that had Black majorities were added to at-large elections in larger areas where Blacks were the minority and had little chance of electing representatives of their choice
- Requirements to register to vote and/or to run for office were made more onerous in ways that disproportionately impacted Blacks
- Outlying areas that had higher Black populations were annexed to cities with White majorities, diluting the power of Black vote; this shifting of boundaries to favor the White vote is known as gerrymandering.
- Poll hours were shortened and polling locations were shifted in key sites, making it difficult for Black voters to get to the polls

Progressive activists have worked to eliminate these barriers, and the courts have ruled at least some of these measures as unconstitutional in some circumstances, but the reality is that voter suppression continues today with states in all regions of the country limiting early voting, implementing voter identification laws, disenfranchising millions of felons, and enacting a range of other measures that discourage participation. As we will see in Chapter 13, those electoral laws and many others are still being contested and litigated today.

Turnout by Race Today

Given that barriers to the participation of Blacks, Hispanics, Asian Americans, Native Americans and others persist today, how does the turnout of these groups compare to that of White Americans? The numbers make it clear that the barriers are successful in tamping down the voting power of minorities across the United States. There is still a major racial imbalance at ballot box. In the 2016 presidential election, as Figure 7.1 shows, 61.6 percent of White citizens turned out to vote. That far surpasses the 55.5 percent figure for African Americans and it dwarfs the 47.3 percent figure for Latinos and the 41.1 percent figure for Asian Americans. This difference between White participation on one side and racial and ethnic minority voting on the other is what is known as the racial gap in turnout.

And the 2016 election is by no means an anomaly. The 2020 presidential election had more voters participate, but saw large racial gaps in turnout. In fact, the racial skew in turnout in presidential elections has not changed that much over the last few decades. Black turnout did grow appreciably when Barack Obama ran for president in 2008 and 2012 (briefly outpacing White turnout by some estimates) and then dropped substantially in 2016, but since the 1980s African American turnout has typically been about 5–10 points lower than White turnout. Over the same time period, Asian Americans and Hispanics generally turned out in numbers of about

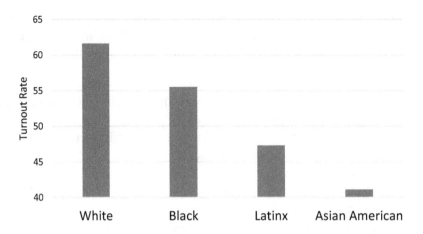

Figure 7.1 Presidential Turnout by Race 2016
In the 2016 presidential election, White turnout far surpassed Black, Latino, and Asian American turnout.
Source: 2016 CCES. Figures are for turnout of adult citizens.

15–20 percentage points less than Whites. When it comes to the vote, Whites have a disproportionate say in American democracy.

That same racial hierarchy in turnout, with Whites the most active, followed by African Americans, and then Latinos and Asian Americans trailing further behind, persists at most levels of voting.[1] In fact, as we move down the ballot to lower-level offices and turnout declines across the board, the racial skew in turnout often increases. Lower turnout and a similar or perhaps even a slightly elevated racial skew is apparent in midterm elections for Congress. In 2018, for example, White citizens turned out at a rate of 59 percent. African Americans lagged much further behind, with 45 percent, followed by Latinos at 43 percent, and Asian Americans at 41 percent. Primary elections, in which the candidates of both major parties (and some third parties as well) are selected to run for office, are tilted even more heavily toward the voices of White Americans. Over the last seven primary contests for the candidates chosen to run for president, White turnout averaged 29 percent, a figure almost double the racial and ethnic minority turnout in those same contests. Across those primaries, turnout for Blacks, Latinx, and Asian Americans was 18 percent, 16 percent, and 14 percent, respectively.

The situation is even more skewed at the local level. Data from a recent study of municipal elections in California show that Whites are greatly overrepresented in urban politics (Hajnal, Kogan, and Markarian 2021). California is now a **majority-minority state**, meaning that non-Hispanic Whites represent less than half the

---

[1] Figures for midterm and primary turnout are from the CCES Cumulative File, 2006–2018.

population in the state; as of 2019, 42 percent of all adults in the state were White. However, Whites account for fully 68 percent of all voters in local elections. The flip side is minority underrepresentation at the local level: Hispanic residents account for 35 percent of the adult population in California but make up only 20 percent of the voters in cities across the state. Likewise, Asian Americans represent 15 percent of the population but only 6 percent of the voters. Blacks represent 6 percent of the adults in California but only 3 percent of the voters.

The one constant in all of this is rate of participation by race. At every level, Whites have an oversize say in democracy, while the voices of racial and ethnic minorities and in particular those of Hispanics and Asian Americans are muted.

Other Ways to Participate

Voting is, of course, not the only way through which citizens can participate in the democratic process. Individual Americans can have their say and can try to influence government actions and public policies through an array of activities from wearing a campaign button to donating money to protesting in the streets. Scholars often break down political activity into electoral participation and non electoral participation. Electoral participation includes actions that we can take within the context of political campaigns to help influence the outcome of those contests, such as calling registered voters for a particular party to urge them to go to the polls on election day. Nonelectoral participation includes individual political acts that typically occur outside the confines of a campaign and that tend to be more focused on shifts in policy or the administration of those policies for one's own private gain (e.g., attending a rally to protest high taxes in order to keep your taxes down) or for public benefit (e.g., protesting against restrictions on immigration).

Figures 7.2 and 7.3 break down by race these two different types of participation. The types of participation vary in terms of the effort involved, the skills required, whether they are solitary or group-based, and whether the goals sought are private or collective, but remarkably they hardly vary from one racial pattern: In almost every case, Whites participate more than any other racial and ethnic group. And in most cases, that racial imbalance is severe:

- Whites are almost three time more likely than Asian Americans to have displayed a lawn sign or a bumper sticker in the last twelve months.
- Whites are almost twice as likely as Asian Americans and Latinx to have worked on a campaign.
- Whites are about 40 percent more likely than other racial groups to have donated money to a campaign, candidate, or political organization.
- White Americans are almost three times as likely as African Americans to have written a letter to a politician.
- Very few Americans have ever run for office (less than 4 percent) but Whites once again are much more likely than Blacks, Hispanics, or Asian Americans to have sought elective office.

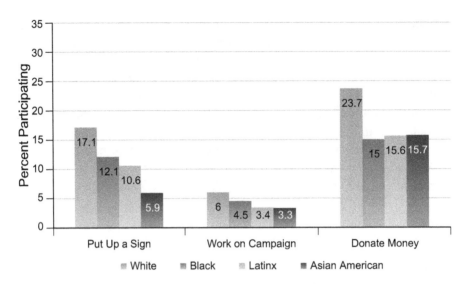

Figure 7.2 Electoral Participation by Race in American Democracy, 2015–2018
White Americans participate more than other racial and ethnic groups on almost every form of electoral participation.
Source: 2018 and 2016 CCES.

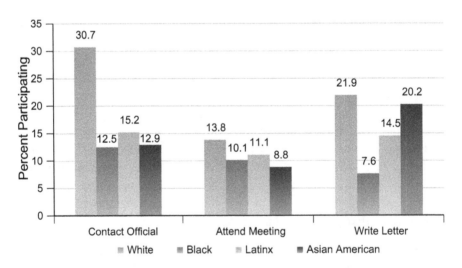

Figure 7.3 Nonelectoral Participation by Race in American Democracy, 2015–2018
White Americans are more active than other racial and ethnic groups across a wide array of political activities.
Source: 2018 and 2016 CCES.

Unfortunately, these figures may actually be understating how steep the imbalance is. When you look not just at who is donating money but also at how much they are donating, an even more troubling picture emerges. Tallying up all of the major donors for House elections between 1980 and 2012, we find that White donors accounted for 91 percent of all of dollars contributed. Latinos were the least well represented in the donor pool—accounting for only 2.2 percent of the total contributions even though they represent almost 18 percent of the population. Blacks and Asian Americans were also severely underrepresented in the donor pool—accounting for 4.9 percent and 1.9 percent of dollars, respectively.[2] If money is the main driving force behind American democracy, as many believe, then that force is overwhelmingly dominated by White Americans.

Moreover, there is little sign that the uneven nature of political participation is likely to change measurably in the future. New data on social media posts such as on Twitter or Facebook reveal a similar pattern, with Whites much more likely to report posting about politics (34.9 percent), than Blacks, Hispanics, or Asian Americans (roughly 25 percent each).[3] Regardless of the political arena, the voice of the nation is skewed toward White America and is likely to stay that way. Later in this chapter, we will attempt to explain why.

The relative positioning of these three racial and ethnic minority groups does, however, vary depending on the type of participation, the year when the survey was conducted, and even which firm or group conducts the survey. In some cases—as in wearing buttons and putting up signs or working on a political campaign—African Americans are substantially more active than are Hispanics and Asian Americans. But in others, there is relatively little difference in the propensity of African Americans, Latinos, and Asian Americans to participate. The three groups roughly equally underperform relative to Whites in terms of political donations, contacting an elected official, attending a local meeting, or engaging in a protest.

The last thing to note about participation rates in U.S. politics is how few Americans of any race actually engage in most of these activities. Voting—a relatively easy and costless act that requires limited skills—brings together large swaths of the public. Other more involved forms of political participation typically draw in a tiny segment of the population—often 10 percent or less of all adults are involved. Our political system is being driven by a small and racially unrepresentative segment of the American public.

Does Uneven Participation Matter?

The data on electoral participation should raise alarm bells. What does a country look like if government responds to those who participate and ignores those who do not? A prominent political scientist noted in 1949, "The blunt truth is that politicians and officials are under no compulsion to pay much heed to classes and groups of citizens that do not vote" (Key [1949] 1984: 99). The skewed nature

---

[2] Contribution figures are for all donations over $200 and are from Grumbach and Sahn (2020).

[3] Data on social media posts are from the 2016 American National Election Study.

of participation raises serious concerns about some groups of Americans being ignored by our democracy.

For a long time political scientists thought that these fears were not warranted. When they looked at the political views of nonvoters, they found that they looked strikingly similar to the views of voters. One famous early study concluded that "voters are virtually a carbon copy of the citizen population" (Wolfinger and Rosenstone 1980:109). And when scholars looked to see how electoral outcomes shifted when turnout rose or fell, they could find few clear patterns. Sometimes higher turnout benefited Democrats, but at other times higher turnout benefited Republicans. Almost all of the time, the effects of higher or lower turnout were negligible in terms of election outcomes. The conclusion—at least through the late twentieth century—was that very few elections would actually shift from one winner to another if everyone voted (Citrin, Schickler, and Sides 2003).

But all of that may be changing, for three reasons. First, as we have already seen, the racial and ethnic minority population is growing. In the past, when Blacks, Latinos, Asian Americans, and others represented a relatively small share of the electorate, their participation (or nonparticipation) did not matter as much to outcomes. As we approach becoming a majority-minority nation, their participation matters a lot. Second, the gap between White and minority turnout has also been increasing. This trend requires a little explanation. It is not that the turnout of any one racial group is changing all that much. Turnout among each racial and ethnic group as we noted earlier in this chapter has been relatively flat over the last few decades. But the racial mix of the minority population has changed radically over time. The Hispanic and Asian American populations have been growing rapidly. Over time these two pan-ethnic groups have made up a larger and larger share of the minority population. Because these two groups vote at much lower rates than Blacks, the gap between White and non-White turnout has been growing. Third, as we have also already noted, the racial divide in American politics is also growing. On one side, White Americans are increasingly identifying with the Republican party and on the other side, racial and ethnic minorities now overwhelmingly identify with the Democratic party. All three trends should make uneven participation more consequential.

Do Voters Have the Same Political Views as Nonvoters?

When we look at the data today, we find that turnout is, in fact, very consequential. Table 7.1 compares the views of voters and nonvoters across a range of key policy areas. Although there is some variation in the magnitude of the difference from policy to policy, it is readily apparent that conservative views are overrepresented among voters, while liberal views are underrepresented. Often the gap is substantial. For example, on the broad question of how much government should be responsible for providing jobs and a guaranteed standard of living, those who strongly favor

Table 7.1 **Comparing the Policy Views of Nonvoters and Voters in 2016 (% of voters agreeing with each statement)**

	Nonvoters	Voters	Difference
Employment			
Government should guarantee employment	24.8	15.9	8.9
Favor the status quo	21.6	20.9	0.7
Up to each person to find job	23	31.5	8.5
Welfare Programs			
Should increase	22.3	17.1	5.2
Favor status quo	36.8	33.8	3
Should decrease	40.9	49.1	8.2
Environment			
Favor more regulation	43.4	42	1.4
Favor status quo	23	17.4	5.6
Favor less regulation	10.5	14.3	3.8
Defense			
Should spend less	12.8	10.8	2
Favor the status quo	27.9	26.7	1.2
Should spend more	25.7	30.6	4.9
Assistance for Blacks			
Support more assistance	20.9	19.5	1.4
Favor the status quo	23.8	22.2	1.6
Oppose assistance	33.15	35.4	2.25
Education			
Should spend more	72.6	68.5	4.1
Favor the status quo	22	23.5	1.5
Spend less	5.4	8.1	2.7
Gay Marriage			
Should be legal	63.1	56.7	6.4
Favor the status quo	17.9	25.5	7.6
Should not be legal	19.1	17.8	1.3

Note: Responses do not add up to 100 percent because some survey respondents provided no opinion.
Source: 2016 American National Election Study.

government involvement make up 24.8 percent of nonvoters but only 15.9 percent of voters. If government only responds to voters, then the more liberal wishes of nonvoters are being ignored. The 8.9-point gap on the government's role in guaranteeing individual well-being is the largest gap in the table but on every policy area shown, nonvoters are more liberal than voters. Nonvoters are significantly more likely than voters to favor increases in welfare spending, greater regulation to protect the environment, less defense spending, more assistance for Blacks, more education spending, and legalizing gay marriage—all of which are traditionally liberal positions. Importantly, the gap between the views of voters and the

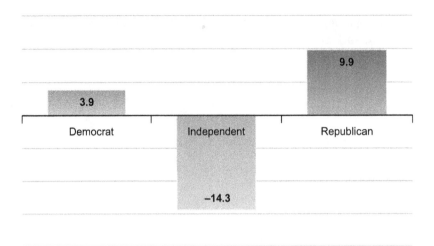

Figure 7.4 The Over- or Underrepresentation of Partisan Identities among Voters
Voters are more Republican and less Independent than the public as a whole.
Source: 2016 American National Election Study.

preferences of nonvoters exists for issues well beyond those illustrated in Table 7.1. When we looked across a wider array of survey questions, a similar pattern emerged, although the difference between voters and nonvoters was not always substantial.

The other important finding that emerges from Table 7.1 is that more moderate views also tend to be underrepresented in the voting population. Especially so on the environment and gay marriage, but also on most other issues that we looked at, those that hold "middle-of-the-road" views are not as well represented among voters as they are among the entire population. The fact that moderate views are not well represented among voters means that more extreme views, on the left and the right, tend to draw more attention. Is this driving polarization of views across the United States?

The differences between voters and nonvoters on individual policy positions are important. But given that American politics is effectively a battle between two major parties, we also want to know whether uneven turnout leads to distortions in the partisan makeup of the electorate. The answer, as we see in Figure 7.4, is "yes." Republicans are highly overrepresented among the voting population. Only 22.4 percent of nonvoters identify as Republican but among voters that figure rises to 32.3—meaning that voters are 9.9 points more Republican than nonvoters. Those who identify as Democratic are also overrepresented among voters, but not by nearly as much—only 3.9 points. The group most excluded by the vote is independents, or those people who do not identify with a party. These nonpartisans account for fully 23 percent of nonvoters but only 8.7 percent of voters—leading to a 14.3-point representational gap. All of this means that the vote will not reflect the partisan proclivities of the entire public and will instead be skewed away from more

Table 7.2 **What Would Happen If Everyone Voted? Democratic Gains from Simulated Full Turnout, 2006–2016**

	President	U.S. House	U.S. Senate
	Democratic Gains in Electoral College Votes (270 votes to win)	Democratic Gains in Seats (435 total seats)	Democratic Gains in Seats (100 total seats)
2006		2	−2
2008	25	1	−3
2010		4	0
2012	113	42	4
2014		−1	6
2016	122	19	5

Source: Adapted from Fraga (2018). Survey data are from the CCES, 2006–2016.

moderate nonpartisans and in favor of Republicans. That is true whether we look at the American National Election Study data as we do in Figure 7.4 or whether we focus on other major surveys of the American public.

Would Outcomes Be Different if Everyone Voted?

The critical question at the end of the day is whether all of this impacts electoral results. Would outcomes actually be different if everyone voted? To answer this question, political scientist Bernard Fraga used nationally representative surveys of the public to compare the electoral preferences of voters and nonvoters in federal elections between 2006 and 2016. The key to the surveys is that they asked adult Americans which candidate they preferred *even if they did not turn out to vote* in the election. To determine the outcome with full turnout, Fraga summed up the candidate preferences for everyone in the survey (voters and nonvoters alike) within each state (or U.S. House district) and then combined all the state (or district) totals to determine the counterfactual full turnout across the nation. Table 7.2 shows the number of Electoral College votes Democratic presidential candidates would gain, the percentage of House districts that would shift to the Democratic Party, and the share of U.S. Senate seats that would become Democratic by shifting to full turnout.

The table shows that outcomes would, in fact, change if everyone voted.[4] Although there is some variation from election year to election year and from office to office, Fraga's analysis indicates that if all members of every racial and

---

[4] Other studies have reached similar conclusions about the growing impact of turnout on elections (Hansford and Gomez 2010; Leighley and Nagler 2013). One such study found that increased turnout also leads to less incumbent support and more volatility in the vote (Hansford and Gomez 2010).

ethnic group voted, electoral outcomes would generally shift toward the Democratic Party—sometimes in ways that would determine which party controls the nation.

Looking first at the 2016 presidential election in Table 7.2, turnout clearly matters a lot. In the actual election, Republican Donald Trump won a clear Electoral College victory amassing 304 votes to Democratic candidate Hillary Clinton's 232 votes. But in a counterfactual simulation in which all eligible voters participated, and based on polling of the preferences of all nonvoters, Clinton would have won an additional 122 Electoral College votes, giving her the majority of Electoral College votes and the presidency. More specifically, if we include the preferences of the entire adult population, Clinton would have had additional wins in the two Midwestern states of Wisconsin and Michigan and she would have had added victories in the Sunbelt states of Florida, Georgia, North Carolina, and Texas, which have large minority populations. In the actual election, Donald Trump won in these mostly swing or traditionally Democratic states. Indeed, with full turnout, Clinton would have won in a landslide, garnering 354 Electoral College votes. Barack Obama, the Democrat, won the 2008 and 2012 presidential contests but he likely would have won by much larger margins if everyone had voted. Indeed, the simulated outcome suggests he would have won with landslides not earned by a Democrat since Lyndon Johnson in 1964.

For House elections, according to Fraga's study, the consequences of full turnout are generally smaller. This is in large part because most House elections are not competitive. Unprecedented levels of partisan gerrymandering (redistricting to ensure a win of one party) and the fact that more and more often these days Democrats and Republicans live in different communities, mean that House elections are rarely close. Fewer than 7 percent of House seats were decided by a margin of victory less than 10 percent in 2016. Nevertheless, full turnout would have helped Democrats make gains in the House in every election except one (2014). Critically, the data suggests that Democrats would have won an additional forty-two seats (or 9.7 percent of all seats) in 2012. That would have been enough for them to keep their majority and control of Congress.

With only about a third of seats up for election in any given year, the effects of full turnout in Senate races are also diminished. Senate outcomes under full turnout are also more mixed. Early on in the time period of Fraga's study, Republicans would have actually gained under full turnout—two seats in 2006 and three seats in 2008. That two-seat gain in 2006 would have cost the Democrats their majority in the Senate. However, over time, full turnout has led to increasingly large gains for the Democratic Party in the Senate. As Table 7.2 shows, Democrats would have won extra states in 2012, 2014, and 2016. Critically, with full turnout, Democrats would have retained the majority of Senate seats in both 2014 and 2016. Finally, although we are not able to systematically calculate results for 2020, many believe that the main reason why Georgia flipped Democratic at both the Senate and

Photo 7.3 Hillary Clinton supporters react to her speech during a rally with Vice President Joe Biden at Riverfront Sports athletic facility on August 15, 2016, in Scranton, PA.
Source: Photo Mark Makela © Mark Makela/Stringer/Getty Images News/Getty Images.

presidential levels and thus one of the main reasons why, since 2021, the Democrats have controlled the presidency and both chambers of Congress is that African Americans in the state turned out in exceptionally high numbers.

All told, the results are revealing. In the real world, between 2006 and 2016 the Democratic Party went from control of the presidency and the Congress to minority status in both institutions. That occurred despite a growing racial and ethnic minority population that increasingly favored the Democratic Party. That expanding demographic advantage clearly did not translate into electoral victory for Democrats (at least until 2020). But in the counterfactual world of even turnout across the races, the Democratic Party would have controlled the Presidency and Senate from 2008 through to 2016 and would have been extremely close to a majority in the House in 2016. In short, even turnout could radically change who governs.

It is not only at the federal level where turnout matters. Shifting toward full turnout also has consequences at the local level. One of the co-authors of this book simulated even turnout by race and ethnicity in big city mayoral elections. He found that the winner would have changed in 30 percent of the contests (Hajnal 2010). Often, the new winner was a Latino candidate backed by a majority of Latino voters. When they don't vote, racial and ethnic minorities lose out at every level of government.

Why Do People Participate—or Not?

If turnout matters so much, why do so few Americans participate? And in particular, why are racial and ethnic minorities—groups that are disproportionately disadvantaged economically and could often use greater government support—disproportionately less likely to vote?

Voting as a Rational Choice

To help understand why some people participate and others do not, political scientists often begin with a rational actor approach, which assumes that people act when the benefits of that action outweigh the costs. In the case of voting, that leads to the following equation describing the costs and benefits of going to the ballot box:

$$V = pB - C$$

These are the four factors in the equation:

V = the probability that the voter will turn out
p = the probability that an individual's vote will determine the outcome of the election
B = the benefit of having your candidate win
C = the costs of voting, which include time and effort

If the benefit outweighs the costs—or more precisely, if the value of $pB - C$ is greater than zero—then we would expect an individual to vote. If, on the other hand, the costs outweigh the benefits, then that individual is unlikely to vote.

When we think through the equation, we can see that voting usually does not make sense. The main reason is that p—the probability that your one vote will determine the outcome of the election—is almost always incredibly small. In a presidential election, for example, there is only an infinitesimal chance that your single vote will determine the winner. To do that, your vote would have to be the tiebreaker in a state that itself was the tiebreaker state determining who wins the Electoral College. How often has something like that happened? Never. But voters in Florida in 2004 came close when George W. Bush won the state by only a few votes in a highly contested election that determined who won the presidency. Since p is so small, pB (the probability that your vote will determine the election multiplied by the benefit of having your candidate win) is small as well—even if you think there is big difference between the candidates. And given that C is very real—that is, it takes significant time and effort to learn about the candidates, make your decision, and go to the polls—the costs of voting generally outweigh the benefits. If everyone is rational, then everyone should stay home, and no one should vote.

The incentive to engage in other forms of political participation, where the costs are often much higher and the benefits still unclear, can be even lower. Consider whether it makes sense to protest for immigrants' rights. The costs of participating are relatively high. You need to travel to the event and devote considerable time and

Photo 7.4 Judge Charles Burton, chairman of the Palm Beach County canvassing board, holds up a ballot as he continues the manual recount of 800–1,000 disputed presidential ballots November 26, 2000, in West Palm Beach, FL, despite the fact that the Florida Supreme Court deadline of 5 pm had already expired.
Source: Photo Robert King/Newsmakers © Robert King/Staff/Hulton Archive/Getty Images.

energy to the effort. In some cases, protestors are arrested. And, once again, the probability that your participation will change the outcome and ultimately impact immigrants' rights is minuscule. Or think about the costs and benefits of writing a letter to a member of Congress to ask for a change in policy. Writing a letter also takes time and effort, yet the probability that your one letter would convince your representative to change their vote is tiny. And the probability that your representative's vote would in turn become the pivotal vote in Congress is microscopic.

All these examples relate to what political scientists call the logic of collective action. The crux of this logic is two-fold. First, your one contribution (or participatory act) is not enough to make a difference. The outcome will almost assuredly be the same whether or not you are involved. Second, because the benefits are public goods, you can typically enjoy the benefits without contributing—referred to as free-riding. If, for example, immigrants' rights protests lead to significant reform and new protections for undocumented workers in the future, anyone who is undocumented will benefit, whether or not they actively joined the protests. In the same vein, even if you don't vote, you can still enjoy the benefits of a functioning democracy. As such, it often makes sense *not* to contribute to the collective good. The problem is that if everyone adopted this view and decided not to vote or participate, democracy would collapse.

The reality, of course, is that everyone doesn't stay home. Many of us vote and participate in the political arena even though it generally doesn't make rational sense to do so. Thus, from this rational actor perspective, the real question is not why so few of us vote but rather why so many of us do.

DIGGING DEEPER: WHY YOU SHOULD VOTE

We have just explained the rational actor model of voting, which argues that voting is *not* rational. More precisely, the model claims that because the odds of your one vote affecting the outcome of the election are infinitesimal, the costs of voting generally outweigh the benefits. But as political scientists we are loath to discourage political participation. Indeed, the three of us strongly believe that voting is critical to democracy, and we would all like to see broader participation in America. So, with that in mind, let us now tell you why you *should* vote.

Although it is true that your one individual vote is unlikely to determine the outcome of an election, your vote may still matter. One way your vote can matter is by increasing the influence you have over the policy decisions of your elected leaders. Politicians generally want to be reelected. To be reelected, they need votes. As such, it behooves them to pay attention to the needs, wants, and desires of voters. The same logic does not necessarily apply to nonvoters, who can largely be ignored as part of the electoral equation. Indeed, political scientists John Griffin and David Newman found that over a thirty-year period, the votes of U.S. Senators were more closely aligned with the policy preferences of voters in their states than they were with the preferences of nonvoters in their state (Griffin and Newman 2005). In fact, in their studies Senators appeared to ignore the views of nonvoters and only paid attention to their voting constituents.

The importance of voting for influencing policy has been underlined in a number of studies.[5] One study shows that areas within congressional districts that vote at higher rates received more federal spending than areas with lower turnout (Martin 2003). Another study found that in states where lower-income Americans turned out to vote at higher rates—relative to higher-income Americans—welfare benefits were appreciably higher. In other words, the poor get more of what they want when they vote more regularly. Higher turnout by lower-class Americans can even lead to smaller gaps in overall income in a state.

We do not want to overstate the power of the vote, so we have to offer an important caveat. The caveat is that all voters in American democracy may not count equally. Voters who are more important to a politician's reelection strategy are likely to count more. In a follow-up study, John Griffin and David Newman demonstrated that senators relied on the policy views of voters from their own party twice as much as

[5] There are, however, other studies that question whether officials really weigh voters' views more heavily (Ellis, Ura, and Robinson 2006; Flavin 2012).

they relied on the views of voters who identified with the other major party (Griffin and Newman 2013). They also found that swing voters—those that sometimes voted Democratic and sometimes voted Republican—had the most influence. The latter finding was particularly disturbing for African Americans in swing districts, since they are the most unified and the most Democratic-leaning of any major demographic group. Because Democrat politicians could be confident that Black voters would almost always support them and because Republican politicians could be confident that Black voters would almost never support them, legislators from both parties could effectively ignore the views of Black voters. Indeed, Griffin and Newman found that Blacks were ignored more than any other group – even when they voted.

It is not only voting that matters. Subsequent research has shown that other forms of political participation—attending a political meeting, engaging in a campaign activity, displaying a sign, and especially donating money—can increase the weight that legislators place on your policy views when they are deciding which policies to support and which to oppose (Leighley and Oser 2018).

In other words:

VOTE AND ENGAGE IN YOUR DEMOCRACY!

Individual Explanations for Turnout

An enormous amount of research has gone into figuring out why some vote and others do not. Indeed, it is possible that more has been written on the subject than perhaps any other area of political science. All of that research has led to some pretty clear conclusions about the factors that drive turnout and participation. Political scientists generally agree that three sets of *individual level* factors shape democratic participation: People participate: (1) because they can; (2) because they want to; and (3) because they are asked (Verba, Schlozman and Brady 1995). Here we will review each of these explanations using data from the 2016 American National Election Study.

Individual Resources and Participation

When we say people participate because they can, we mean that individuals who have the resources and individual attributes to be able to participate and to do so easily are much more likely to engage politically than others. Generally, as socioeconomic status increases, participation increases. That is evident in Figure 7.5, where we see that those who have attained at least a college degree were much more likely to vote in the 2016 presidential election than those without a high-school degree—a difference of almost 30 percentage points. Likewise, 70 percent of those with incomes over $200,000 participated, while the rate of voting among individuals who earned less than $20,000 is 45 percent. Similarly, older Americans (over age 60) were over 40 points more likely to vote than young adults (under age 25). Each of these individual attributes not only affects the likelihood that a person will vote, but each also strongly correlates with a person's tendency to undertake other forms of participation like letter writing, campaigning, and donating money (Verba and Nie 1972; Verba, Schlozman, and Brady 1995). That is, for example, those who vote are also more likely to campaign for a candidate. But age, income, and education are not the only measure of social status that explain participation. A number of other measures, including being a homeowner, working full-time, and being married, also correlate with turnout.

Exactly why socioeconomic status impacts participation is less clear. Higher status undoubtedly tends to confer greater resources—for example, money, skills, and time—that a person can use in the political arena. A higher income, of course, makes donating to political causes much easier. A higher level of education, which correlates with higher socioeconomic status, increases knowledge and makes understanding political issues easier. Education also provides the skills needed to do things like write letters or organize community events. But higher status could also increase participation by shaping our attitudes about democracy. With education comes greater knowledge of the benefits of democracy and perhaps a greater commitment to maintaining it. Higher status may also raise the stakes for many of us. Homeowners, for example, may have more reason to get involved in local politics than renters because they cannot easily exit the community and because their well-being depends critically on housing values, which are in turn affected by local government. Finally, upper-status citizens are more likely to be surrounded by others who participate. That social context could also lead to greater political participation.

Immigration and acculturation are also critical factors shaping participation—especially for racial and ethnic minorities. Citizenship—perhaps the most important marker of incorporation—is also obviously tied to civic participation. Noncitizens are not allowed to vote and are thus dropped from most political surveys. When they are included, however, we can clearly see how citizenship correlates with different forms of participation. Naturalized citizens are about twice as likely as noncitizens to attend a political meeting or work on a campaign and about three times as likely to put up a political sign, contact a public official, or make a political donation (data from the 2018 CCES). Thus, it is problematic that nearly half of all immigrants have yet to naturalize twenty years after their arrival (Jones-Correa 2005).

For Americans who are born elsewhere, it also takes time and effort to get to know the American political system and to become comfortable navigating it. That is reflected in the voting patterns we see in Figure 7.5. In 2016, only 53 percent of foreign-born citizens voted, a rate that falls significantly below the 60.9 percent turnout rate for native-born Americans. Within the immigrant population, even more dramatic differences can be found for key markers of incorporation, such as time in the United States or English language ability. Immigrants who entered the country more recently (since 2000) voted 16.6 percentage points less often than those who arrived on American shores before 1970. Similarly, those who rely most heavily on Spanish voted much less often—15.5 percentage points—than those whose primary language is English. One notable study found that Asian Americans with more Anglicized names participate more than otherwise similar Asian Americans with ethnic names. Or put another way, Christopher Chen votes more than Shu-Wei Chen (Go 2018).

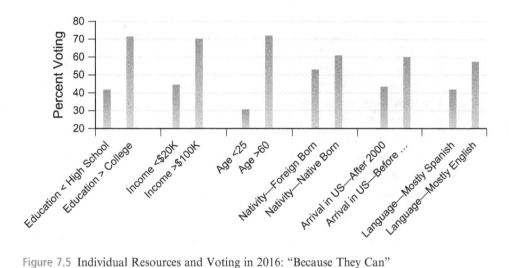

Figure 7.5 Individual Resources and Voting in 2016: "Because They Can"
Individual resources such as a college education and higher income make a big difference in voting participation.
Source: 2016 American National Election Study.

Photo 7.5 First-time voter Marwah Al Thuwayni, 18, casts her ballot in Manchester, NH, on election day. She was one of about 1,000 people who registered to vote at the Bishop Leo E. O'Neil Youth Center polling center. The Ward 9 polling station was one of the city's busiest during the 2020 presidential election on November 3, 2020.
Source: Photo Jodi Hilton © NurPhoto/Contributor/Getty Images.

Attitudes and Participation

When we say that people participate because they want to, we mean that individuals who hold more positive views of democracy and democratic participation are much more likely than others to engage politically. Some see these positive attitudes as the key to solving the paradox of participation—that being the fact that many of us participate, even though the costs of participating outweigh the benefits. If we feel better about ourselves when we participate or if we simply enjoy being involved or going to the polls, then the equation related to the benefits of voting changes in the following way:

$$V = pB - C + D$$

The added term *D* refers to citizen duty or a **psychological benefit of voting** (Riker and Ordeshook 1968). In other words, if we feel we should participate or if we enjoy participating, then we actually gain from the act of participation, and the benefits may begin to outweigh the costs. This is manifested in Figure 7.6, which shows a close relationship between attitudes and action. In particular, the more that we think voting is a duty, the more likely we are to participate. Fully 75 percent of those who strongly believe that voting is a duty cast a ballot in 2016, far surpassing the turnout figure (56 percent) for those who strongly believe that voting is a choice. Similarly, those who think they have little say in what government does participate much less (53.2 percent) than those who feel that their views have a real impact on government (71.6 percent). Indeed, a wide array of attitudes about democracy are

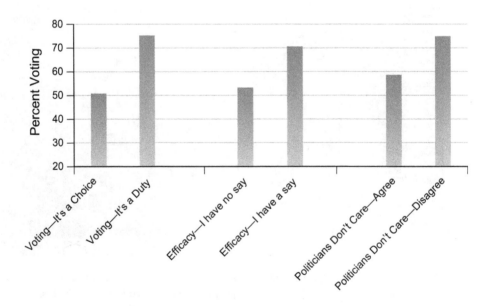

Figure 7.6 Individual Attitudes and Voting in 2016: "Because They Want To"
Individual attitudes about democracy greatly shape participation.
Source: 2016 American National Election Study.

closely correlated with turnout. Our level of political interest, our trust in government and politicians, the degree to which we think the system is fair, and the extent to which we think the system is complicated all predict whether we participate in democracy.

The real difficulty in understanding the relationship between political attitudes and political participation is that we don't know whether our attitudes cause us to participate (or not to participate) or whether having participated, we feel better about democracy. In short, we don't know whether attitudes have their own independent effect on turnout and other forms of participation.

Mobilization and Participation

The notion that people participate because someone asks them to is fairly straightforward. A range of groups and individuals—from candidates and parties on one end to social clubs, churches, and unions on the other—regularly contact individual Americans to try to get them involved in the political process. We call this **mobilization**. Mobilization efforts appear to pay off. As Figure 7.7 shows, respondents who reported being contacted by a party or related organization voted 71.6 percent of the time as compared to only 56 percent of the time for those who reported no contact. Of course, we know that parties and other organizations tend to contact people who have voted in the past and in particular people who have voted for their side in the past. They do not want to waste their time trying to mobilize someone who will never vote or, worse, mobilize someone who will vote against them. Thus, at first glance, it's hard to know whether mobilization actually does bring new voters to the polls.

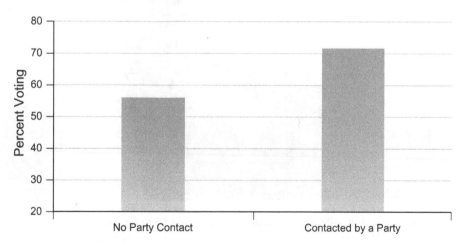

Figure 7.7 Party Mobilization and Voting in 2016: "Because They Are Asked"
Individuals who are asked to vote are much more likely to do so.
Source: 2016 American National Election Study.

TESTING THE THEORY: DOES MOBILIZATION WORK?

Concerned about low and declining turnout in local elections, two political scientists knocked on doors in New Haven, Connecticut, trying to convince people to vote (Gerber and Green 2000). They didn't knock on every door as a campaign might do. Instead, they knocked on random doors. That might sound foolish at first but they had a method behind their madness. They wanted to see whether knocking on doors and asking people to vote actually got them to vote. So they noted which doors they knocked on, and equally importantly, they noted which doors they did not knock on. Then after they were done and the election was over, they went to see who had voted and who had not. Many Americans don't know it, but whether or not you voted in each election is a matter of public record. (Of course, who you voted for is not.)

Green and Gerber found something remarkable. They found that simply knocking on someone's door and having a brief conversation about the election did, in fact, make a difference. Individuals from households they visited voted almost 9 percent more than individuals from households they did not visit. Since the visits were random and the people they visited were essentially no different from the people they didn't visit, we know for certain that the intervention worked.

Photo 7.6 Beth Kauffman, of Buffalo, gives a thumbs up to a resident, as he confirms he will be voting for Democratic presidential candidate Senator Bernie Sanders, as she goes door to door canvassing in Buffalo, NY, Saturday, April 16, 2016, for the New York primary election in 2016. The New York primary election was on Tuesday, April 19, 2016.
Source: Photo Al Drago © Al Drago/Contributor/CQ-Roll Call, Inc./Getty Images.

Determining why mobilization works is another issue altogether. The intervention in this case was remarkably limited—a two-sentence conversation about the election. Why would a short conversation with someone you don't know change your mind about voting? Could it be because we are social beings and simply want to please others? Could it be that the brief interaction convinced us that the election was important? Maybe it simply provided concrete information, such as the date and time of the election? We are still not sure which of these mechanisms made the experiment work. Remarkably, existing studies seem to find that the type of information provided at the doorstep doesn't really matter. In this particular experiment, the three different scripts they used—talking about civic duty, highlighting neighborhood solidarity, and noting the election was close—all had roughly the same effect.

What we do know is that in-person, face-to-face mobilization is more effective than a phone call or a letter in the mail. When the researchers repeated the experiment with other forms of contact, they found that both sending mailers and paying a company to contact residents by phone had a tiny impact (a less than 0.5 percent increase in voting). Something about personal contact seems to be both unique and consequential.

However, in another experiment, the same researchers used the same basic method to see whether social pressure could increase the effects of mobilization (Gerber, Green, and Larimer 2008). In this follow-up experiment, rather than knocking on doors, they sent random households a letter that provided the names of neighbors who had not voted in the last election and threatened to provide similar information in the future. That letter had an enormous impact, increasing turnout by almost ten points. According to the authors, it shows that social pressure can be a powerful force. Not voting in private is one thing. Being potentially outed for not voting in public is quite another.

Although we don't quite know why mobilization works, we now know for certain that it does. With that knowledge in hand, we wonder why political parties and other political groups aren't devoting more (or even all!) of their campaign resources to mobilizing the public.

Group Identity/Consciousness and Participation

Because members of racial and ethnic minority groups have faced widespread discrimination and exclusion in the past and continue to face significant barriers today, they tend to have a heightened sense of group identity or group consciousness. This has been especially true for African Americans, whose experiences with slavery, discrimination, and exclusion have been particularly damaging. In the 2016 American National Election Study, 81 percent of African Americans said that their racial identity was important to them, including 60 percent who indicated it was "extremely important." Past studies have found a much weaker sense of racial or pan ethnic identity among Asian Americans and Latinos. But the strength of

Latino and Asian American identities is growing sharply. In the 2016 survey, 36 percent of Latinos said their racial identity was extremely important, as did 17 percent of Asian Americans.

This notion of a collective identity can become an important resource for driving mobilization. Research shows that a heightened sense of racial or pan-ethnic group identity is associated with heightened political participation (Chong and Rogers 2005). The underlying theory is that a strong sense of group purpose and a belief that one's own fate is linked to the well-being of the rest of the group can instill a sense of purpose that can bring unusually high numbers to the polls (Dawson 1994). As such, group consciousness could potentially help minorities overcome some of the disadvantages related to lower socioeconomic status and less frequent mobilization.

Note, however, that group consciousness is no longer the exclusive purview of minorities. Ashley Jardina has shown that many White Americans increasingly express feelings of pride in their whiteness (Jardina 2018). That group consciousness, spurred in part by a growing sense that Whites are losing their dominant place in society, has in turn been linked to greater political participation by White Americans.

Explaining Turnout *within* Each Racial and Ethnic Group

When we point to the factors that shape participation, we are not claiming that each matters equally for each and every racial and ethnic group. Indeed, as Jane Junn and Natalie Masuoka have correctly noted, different factors can differently drive the turnout of each racial and ethnic group (Junn and Masuoka 2013). In response, a range of studies have tried to uncover how much the impact of factors like resources, attitudes, mobilization, and group consciousness vary by group.

In some cases, significant differences have emerged. Group consciousness, for example, likely matters more for racial minorities when predicting political engagement than it does for Whites, and it almost certainly matters more for African Americans than it does for Hispanics and Asian Americans. Immigration-related experiences appear to have a more significant impact on Latino and Asian American participation than on White or Black participation. Some social ties, including church membership, seem to have a greater impact on participation of Blacks than in other groups (Marschall 2001). One study found that feelings of alienation depress turnout more for Latinos than for other groups (Schildkraut 2005). Another study found that having served in the military may be more critical in driving participation for African Americans than for others (Parker 2009). And even within the same racial and ethnic group, researchers find differences related to time, context, or the type of survey being employed (Leighley and Nagler 2013). Lisa Garcia Bedolla, for example, found that the effect of class on Latino engagement differed greatly across two communities that she studied (Garcia Bedolla 2005). Similarly, the factors driving turnout differ significantly between the male and female racial and ethnic minorities (Brown and Gershon 2016). Minority women who are doubly disadvantaged face particularly unique barriers in life.

National origin is another important variable affecting political participation. For example, several scholars have suggested that immigrants who arrive from countries with repressive political regimes will be reluctant to participate in the United States (Cho 1999).

At the same time, researchers often find more similarities than differences across racial and ethnic minority groups. The conventional socioeconomic model discussed earlier, for example, clearly applies to African Americans, Hispanics, and Asian Americans. That is, within each racial and ethnic group, higher-status individuals participate more than group members with fewer resources. Likewise, attitudes like duty and efficacy that predict White turnout so well also predict minority turnout. And as best as we can tell, mobilization works equally well for members from each of the nation's four major racial groups.

Explanations for the Racial Gap in Turnout

We have looked at many factors that explain why many of us vote and why many of us do not. These factors also help to explain why the same individual might vote at one point in time but not at another. But does any of this actually explain why racial and ethnic minorities tend to participate less than White Americans?

We attempt to answer this question in Figure 7.8, which shows racial gaps in turnout in the 2016 presidential election. The first bar for each minority group shows turnout relative to non-Hispanic Whites without any controls. So, for example, this baseline bar simply highlights and reiterates the major gaps in voter participation between Whites and Blacks (16 percentage points more), Whites and Latinos (18 percentage points more), and Whites and Asian Americans (11 percentage points more). We then sequentially assess the extent to which three other factors explain these racial gaps. For example, the second bar in each group illustrates the

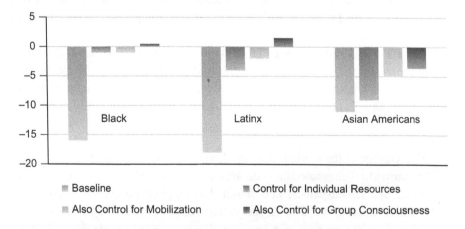

Figure 7.8 Minority Turnout Relative to White Turnout: Controlling for Different Factors. Differences in individual resources, mobilization, and group consciousness help explain racial gaps in turnout.

Source: 2016 American National Election Study and authors' calculations.

racial gap after controlling for socioeconomic resources – what we called "Because They Can" in Figure 7.5. This includes demographics like age, education, and income as well as immigration-related factors such as nativity and generation in the United States. The third bar in each set adds controls for mobilization by parties – what we called "Because They Are Asked" in Figure 7.7. The fourth bar in each set incorporates the influence of group consciousness.

DIGGING DEEPER: UNDERSTANDING REGRESSION MODELS

Here and elsewhere in the text, we will use "regression analysis" to try to determine how much a range of different factors impact a given outcome. In our current case the outcome is whether or not a given person turns out to vote. Regression analysis sounds complex and it certainly can be. But at base, regressions are a technique to estimate how changes in a given explanatory variable relate to changes in a particular outcome variable. For example, we can see if older citizens vote more often than younger citizens.

Importantly, regressions can "control" for other potential factors by including them in the model. In our voter turnout model, we might want to assess the effects of age while also controlling for income and education, since we suspect that wealthier and more educated citizens tend to vote more than poorer and less educated Americans. Indeed, in a given model we should "control" for all factors that we think could influence the outcome. In fact, our voter turnout model includes not only individual resources (e.g., age, income, and education) but also a range of other potentially relevant factors like group consciousness and voter mobilization.

What does controlling for variables in a regression mean? It means that when you assess the effect of one variable in the model, you are holding constant all of the other variables that you include in the model. That way you can assess the effect of changes in one predictor without having to worry about the effects of other predictors.

No statistical method is perfect and regression analysis should be done with knowledge of the phenomenon under study and awareness of the limitations of the regression method. But regressions are a powerful tool that help us to isolate and measure the effects of one factor, while incorporating potentially relevant factors.

You can see in the figure that individual resources (sociodemographic factors and other individual characteristics) do account for a lot of the gaps in turnout between Whites, Blacks, Hispanics, and Asian Americans, and especially for Blacks and Hispanics. Indeed, for Blacks, individual resources account for almost all of the difference, as the turnout gap between Blacks and Whites declines almost to zero once we take into account socioeconomic status and age. In other words, Blacks and Whites at similar ages and education and income levels participate at roughly the same rate. For Latinos, the estimated gap between participation of Latino and

White citizens drops by more than two-thirds after we control for both socioeconomic standing and immigrant status. In fact, the remaining 4-point difference in turnout that we see between Hispanic and White turnout in Figure 7.8 is not, statistically speaking, significant.

For Asian Americans, the story is different. As you can see in the figure, even after controlling for individual level factors, a large and significant participation gap remains. Indeed, controlling for these individual characteristics only marginally reduces the estimated turnout deficit from 11 points to 9 points. The persistent gap in this case makes no sense. Low socioeconomic status doesn't explain low Asian American turnout because most Asian Americans are relatively high status. This persistent gap between Asian American and White voter turnout remains a mystery in the literature on race and participation.

As indicated by the gray bar in Figure 7.8, lower turnout among racial and ethnic minorities is also affected by degree of mobilization. As we highlighted earlier in the chapter, mobilization works. Racial and ethnic minorities might be participating less simply because they are being asked less. Figure 7.8 shows that mobilization does, in fact, contribute to the racial skew in voting. Eliminating differences in mobilization cuts the estimated 4-point gap between Hispanic and White turnout in half and reduces the estimated 9-point gap between Asian American and White turnout from 9 points to 5 points. Moreover, that smaller 5-point gap is not statistically significant, meaning that there may actually be no Asian American– White gap in turnout after controlling for mobilization.

The reason why mobilization is so critical to understanding the racial gap in turnout is because a strongly racialized pattern determines who gets contacted and who doesn't. Every election year since 2010, the American National Election Study has asked individual Americans whether the Democratic or Republican Party contacted them about the campaign. Their responses reveal a major racial skew (see Figure 7.9). Forty-two percent of all Whites were contacted compared with 40 percent of Blacks, 31 percent of Latinos, and 24 percent of Asian Americans.

If the two major parties mobilized evenly across the population, a good share of the racial imbalance in turnout would fade away. It is worth noting that interest groups—for example, churches, labor unions, and other nonprofits—are much more racially balanced in their efforts to mobilize voters. These outside groups are becoming more and more active. The success of Stacey Abrams' Fair Fight organization in mobilizing African Americans to vote in large numbers in Georgia's 2020 and 2021 elections is just one example. But because these groups still contact far fewer Americans than the political parties do, they cannot yet compensate for the racially uneven nature of party contact.

Returning to Figure 7.8, we see that group consciousness (the fourth bar in each grouping) increases racial and ethnic minority turnout to levels that match or even surpass White turnout, especially for the Black and Latino population. The differences are small and only significant in the case of the Latino–White gap, but the analysis indicates that all else equal, Blacks who feel that their racial identity is

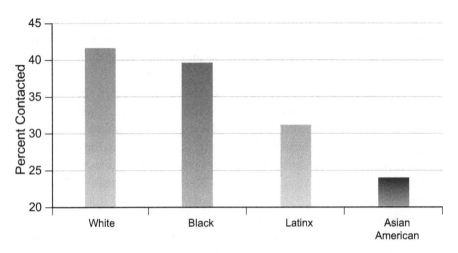

Figure 7.9 Which Americans do Political Parties Try to Mobilize?
America's political parties contact Whites more than other racial and ethnic groups.
Source: 2010–2018 American National Election Study.

important vote 0.4 percent more than Whites, while Latinos who feel that their racial identity is important vote 1.5 percent more often than Whites.

One factor we did not incorporate into Figure 7.8 is attitudes toward democracy; we have found that compared with other factors, racial differences in political efficacy, political trust, and other political attitudes do not appear to contribute all that much to racial disparities in participation. This is largely because the attitudes of Blacks, Latinos, and Asian Americans tend to align with Whites on many of these attitudinal measures. Blacks have traditionally expressed less trust than Whites in the American political system, but even that may be changing as more and more White Americans feel disenchanted with a political process that they feel ignores their views.

Institutional Explanations for Turnout

We have up to this point focused almost exclusively on individual factors shaping participation, but differences in participation cannot be explained solely at the individual level. Scholars also point to a set of institutional features that govern how elections are administered, and these can also encourage or discourage participation. Institutional features govern everything from who can vote and how those votes are added up to how easy it is to actually go to the polls and vote.

Electoral Rules on Registration and Voting

Some of the most consequential institutional factors relate to the voter registration process. Few other countries require their citizens to register on their own before

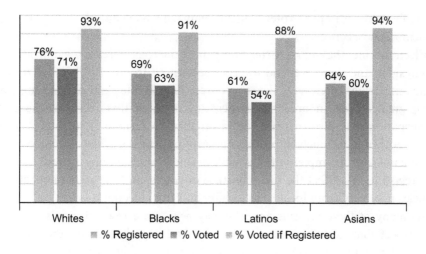

Figure 7.10 The Bottleneck of Voter Registration
Even in 2020, a year of near-record voter turnout, there is a large racial gap in turnout between
Whites (71%), Blacks (63%), Asians (60%), and Latinos (54%). There is also a significant racial
gap in registration. Once registered, a very high proportion of Americans across all racial
groups turn out to vote.
Source: Current Population Survey, November 2020. Figure shows the percentage of a group's
citizen voting age population that was registered to vote in 2020, the percentage of that
population that voted in the November 2020 election, and the percentage of those registered to
vote who voted in November 2020.

voting. Estimates suggest that the additional step of registration can decrease
participation in the United States by over 10 percentage points relative to other
countries (Jackman 1987). Other electoral rules shape the experience of voting itself.
Research shows that everything from how long voters have to travel to get to the
polls to how long those polls are open to the nature of the ballot itself can impact
turnout—sometimes dramatically.

Many of these electoral laws appear to have little connection to race. But at least
theoretically, they could impact the racial distribution of the vote. To illustrate how
election rules and institutional factors come into play in shaping racial differences in
political participation, consider the racial gap in voting. Figure 7.10 shows
2020 Current Population Survey data for U.S. adult citizens by voter registration
and turnout status. The results show that—even in 2020, a year of near-record voter
turnout—there is a large racial gap in turnout between Whites (71 percent of adult
citizens voted in 2020), Blacks (63 percent), Asians (60 percent), and Latinos (54
percent). The major difference here, however, is in getting citizens to register to vote,
with 15 percentage point and 12 percentage point differentials in vote registration
rates between Whites on the one hand and Latinos and Asian Americans on the
other. Once registered to vote, a very high proportion (between 88 percent for
Latinos and 94 percent for Asian Americans) of Americans across all racial groups
turn out to vote. These differences suggest that institutional rules and laws that

either facilitate or impede voter registration make a huge difference in participation in democratic elections.

Electoral rules that make participating more onerous increase the individual costs of engaging and therefore tend to decrease turnout for all. But because racial and ethnic minorities often have fewer resources than Whites and may be less able to incur greater costs in order to participate, anything that increases the costs of participation may also increase the racial skew to turnout. Ultimately, however, we do not yet have much empirical consensus on whether efforts to reduce some of these costs—for example, vote-by-mail, extended early voting periods, and same day registration—affect the racial balance of voters, and the actual impact of such policies may vary from locality to locality and from election to election.

As many of these reforms are relatively new, more research needs to be done. We expect that given the massive vote-by-mail experiment that the nation conducted during the COVID-19 pandemic, many new studies will soon be under way and available. Most existing studies look not at the racial skew in turnout but at the class bias in turnout—the extent to which higher-income citizens outvote lower-income citizens. That research suggests that America's electoral institutions greatly increase the class bias in turnout. One study found that of seventy-six countries studied, the United States scored the second worst in terms of class bias in turnout (Kasara and Suryanarayan 2015). Another attributed most of that class bias in turnout to America's strict registration requirements (Powell 1986). Within the United States, it is also the states with more restrictive registration requirements that tend to have the highest class bias in turnout (Highton 1997).

Electoral Rules That Suppress Votes

Another set of electoral rules and institutions—often called voter suppression—has a much clearer connection to race. Throughout American history, as we have already noted, governmental policies and controlling interests in society have systematically excluded racial minorities from the electoral process. Early on, minorities were barred from voting. But even after laws were enacted to give minorities the vote, there have often been widespread efforts at voter suppression. Today, this country still has a range of institutional features that could be construed as efforts to systematically exclude minorities. These include strict voter identification laws, felon disenfranchisement laws, and the purging of voter rolls. In each case, the impact on racial and ethnic minorities should be obvious. Racial and ethnic minorities are, for example, much less likely than Whites to have acceptable forms of government issued identification—a difference that makes them much more susceptible to being prevented from voting by strict voter identification laws which require those specific IDs (Barreto et al. 2019). Racial and ethnic minorities are also disproportionately represented in the felon population. Laws which bar felons from voting are in place in twenty-one states and have clear implications for who can and cannot vote. Nationwide, over 5 million Americans are barred from voting by these laws (Sentencing Project 2021). Additional research shows that these laws tend to have racially disparate effects (Kuk, Hajnal, and Lajevardi 2022; Manza 2006). Across the country, 6.2 percent of African American adults are ineligible to vote because of these laws. For non-Blacks, the share is only 1.7 percent (Sentencing Project 2021). In Chapter 13, we will delve much deeper into these laws and their effects.

Unconventional Participation

All the political acts—that is, voting, letter writing, campaigning, and donating—that we have examined so far can be considered **conventional acts of participation**. They occur within the confines of the normal political process and are in almost all cases viewed as just, legal, and legitimate. There are, however, unconventional acts of participation that are still generally political, but that also tend to challenge the system in more profound, more radical, and sometimes violent ways. Generally speaking, we think of demonstrations, boycotts, strikes, and occupations as unconventional acts. The line between a conventional and an unconventional political act can, of course, be a blurry one. What is viewed as just, legal, and moral by some may be viewed very differently by others. Clearly, whether any act should be considered illegitimate depends at least in part on the morality of the existing system and the fairness of its laws.

Unconventional acts are characterized by how profoundly they can challenge the current system and also by who participates in them. These acts are often viewed as weapons of the weak because they are frequently a tactic of last resort for those who have limited resources, limited power, and sometimes even limited recognition or formal inclusion within the current system. Thus, unlike with conventional forms of political participation, we tend to see higher rates of participation in unconventional acts as one moves down the socioeconomic ladder. Unconventional participation can, however, be extremely costly—resulting in imprisonment, repression, and other forms of violence. Thus, these acts tend to be relatively rare, attracting only the most motivated.

For both these reasons, unconventional political participation is often less racially skewed. The most recent U.S. data we have show that Latinos, often one of the least active groups in conventional politics, actually participate slightly more regularly in protests, demonstrations, and marches than any other racial and ethnic group. The share of Americans who protest is small for all groups, but in 2018, 9.7 percent of Hispanics reported protesting, demonstrating, or marching—a figure that slightly outpaced the 9.5 percent rate for Whites (see Figure 7.11. This activism among the Latino population appears to be relatively new. In earlier decades, Hispanics typically lagged behind both Blacks and Whites in their propensity to demonstrate, march, and protest. But the widescale immigrants' rights protests of 2006 which we will describe in greater detail in Chapter 15 may have spurred a new era of Hispanic activism. Their newfound penchant for protest may also be a sign that many in the Hispanic community feel increasingly targeted and excluded by the nation's current

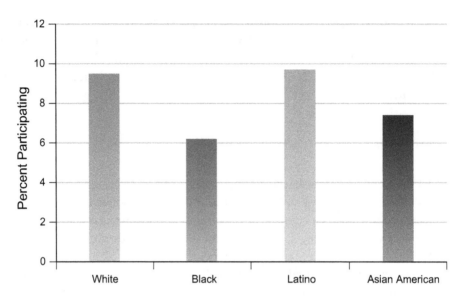

Figure 7.11 Participation by Race in Protests, Demonstrations, and Marches in 2018
Different racial and ethnic groups participate in protests and other less conventional acts at
roughly similar levels.
Source: 2018 CCES.

political regime. Perhaps not unrelated, the same 2018 survey data show that Arab
Americans were as likely or more likely than any other group to turn to demonstrations and marches. It may be that the groups that mainstream political leaders are
increasingly targeting as racial scapegoats are precisely the groups that feel the need
to stand up and protest.

Interestingly, in 2018 Blacks were the least likely to report protesting. That
represents a marked shift from the past. African Americans have typically reported
the highest level of protest activity of any racial or ethnic group. For decades,
African Americans were among the most visible marchers and protesters, most
notably during the Civil Rights Movement of the 1950s and 1960s, a subject that
we will return to in Chapter 15. The limited participation of African Americans in
protests in 2018 also contrasts with the growth of Black activism that has occurred
since 2020 as a result of the Black Lives Matter movement.

The past decade has borne witness to an explosion of protest activity across the
world. It began with the Arab Spring in 2010, in which a series of anti-government
protests, riots, and uprisings in the Middle East challenged autocratic regimes across
the region. The frequency and scope of protests was so exceptional that *Time*
magazine named "The Protester" the person of the year in 2011. Subsequent years
have seen a flourishing of protest activity in the United States. That includes the five
largest protests in American history engaging issues as diverse as women's rights, gun
violence, and the environment. Millions of Americans of all racial and ethnic stripes
protested for immigrants' rights and the Black Lives Matter movement.

Given that racial and ethnic minorities and in particular African Americans and Hispanics have engaged and are engaging disproportionately in protest, it is worth asking whether these protests actually work and ultimately translate into changes in policy. Research suggests that protest may be the one area where the actions of minorities appear to have more impact than those of the White majority.

Broadly speaking, studies assessing the effects of protest and social movements have reached mixed conclusions. But research focusing specifically on minority protest has found some consistent effects. One important study by Dan Gillion found that in congressional districts where more civil rights protests occurred over a two-year period, the Congress member representing those districts took more liberal positions on civil rights measures in the ensuing years (Gillion 2012). Moreover, the effects were large. In districts where there were 100 protests over the course of two years, the typical representative became 10 percent more likely to take liberal positions on civil rights issues. Gillion also found that representatives who were Democrats, and those who were Black, were particularly influenced by such protests. These patterns suggest that protests had more impact on legislators who were already more inclined to support pro-civil rights positions, but also that these legislators might not have done so unless they had gotten a push from politically active constituents.

Why would politicians care about protests? Gillion writes that it could be partly because they serve as a crude barometer of public concerns. "Legislators are forward-looking, concerned about future issues that could potentially endanger their seats," he writes. "They rely upon the changing political and social environment to update their understanding of issues and potentially their beliefs" (Gillion 2012: 24).

Legislators are not the only ones affected by minority protests. Other research has demonstrated substantial shifts in White opinions in response to Civil Rights Movement protests of the 1960s. Most impressive of all, those effects can last generations. One recent study found that Whites from counties where a greater number of civil rights protests occurred in the 1960s are more likely to identify as Democrats and support affirmative action today (Mazumder 2018). Other work has shown that exposure to the immigrants' rights protests in the early 2000s led to more liberal attitudes on immigration among the Latino population (Branton et al. 2015). Perhaps most remarkable of all, one recent study demonstrates that protests from low-resourced minority groups actually had greater effects on the votes of legislators than similar protests from high-resourced White groups (Gause 2022). The author of that study suggests that because minorities typically have fewer resources, their protests signals a deeper commitment to the movement that forces legislators to act.

WHAT IT LOOKS LIKE TODAY: NATIVE AMERICAN PARTICIPATION

Roughly 5 million Americans identify as American Indian or as Alaska Native. What role do they play in the political process? Comprehensive data are hard to come by, as the indigenous population is too small in most surveys to offer reliable estimates of the group's voter turnout. However, using recent data, the National

Congress of American Indians estimated that voter turnout among Native Americans falls somewhere between 5 and 14 percentage points below the national average (National Congress of American Indians 2016).

Exactly why indigenous participation falls below that of White Americans is not entirely clear. Native American participation in national politics is complicated by the fact that indigenous groups living on tribal lands often have sovereignty over their own affairs and separate political institutions. There is also, of course, a long history of repression and exclusion and plenty of evidence of ongoing discrimination against the indigenous population. New Mexico's constitution, for example, barred Native Americans from voting until 1948. North Dakota's strict voter identification law currently requires that voters present identification with a street address, something that tribal IDs generally do not include because many tribal citizens do not have residential mailing addresses—a vestige of the fact that the U.S. Postal Service does not provide residential delivery to their communities. The fact that the indigenous population is considerably younger and has lower socioeconomic status than the national population as a whole—two factors that predict political participation—also contributes to the low voting rates.

A relatively small population and low participation rates have allowed Native American issues to be ignored in the national political arena. Fortunately, some evidence indicates increased political strength in indigenous communities. The sustained protests against the Dakota Access pipeline that began in 2016 are just one sign of a growing social movement seeking to protect Native American interests and the environment in particular. And a surge in American Indian voting in Arizona likely contributed to Biden's win in that state. In 2020, over 60,000 votes were cast in Navajo and Hopi reservations in the northeastern part of the state, a figure that dwarfs the 42,500 votes cast there in 2012 (Fonseca and Kastanis 2020). One end result of this growing engagement, as we will see in Chapter 10, is that the number of American Indians in office is also growing.

Solutions to Uneven Turnout

Can we do anything to reduce racial disparities in participation and in the overall playing field of American democracy? Given that socioeconomic status explains most of the disparities, reforms that lead to greater educational attainment and higher incomes within the minority population would make a big difference. But as noble as these kinds of reforms would be, they likely require more resources than the nation is currently interested in providing. If we could instill even more positive attitudes toward democracy and voting among the African American, Latino, and Asian American populations, we could also likely narrow the racial turnout gap. But unfortunately, we don't yet know how to shift those attitudes.

Instead, we offer two avenues for change that we think are more realistic and likely to be more effective. The first is greater mobilization, and the second is institutional reform.

Increased Mobilization

We know, as we detailed earlier in this chapter, that mobilization works to increase voter participation. Experiments tell us that knocking on doors can increase the probability that a person will participate by up to 10 percent. We also know that political parties are much more likely to knock on any given White door than they are to knock on any given racial and ethnic minority door.

If we could get parties to knock on doors more equitably, we believe we could reduce the racial gap in turnout. Critically, we believe that there is every incentive for parties—or at least one party—to knock on more racial and ethnic minority doors. Experiments in which researchers randomly knocked on doors to try to get residents to vote show that mobilization works for the racial and ethnic minority populations just as much as it does for Whites (García Bedolla and Michelson 2012). Given that the vast majority of racial and ethnic minorities end up voting for the Democratic Party if and when they do vote, it is clear that the Democratic Party has a vast pool of mobilizable supporters that it can relatively easily and effectively engage. Indeed, given the success of Stacey Abrams' Fair Fight organization in mobilizing enough racial and ethnic minority voters in Georgia to ultimately win the Senate and the presidency for the Democratic Party in 2020, we suspect that the Democratic Party's efforts at mobilization will greatly expand in the future. Of course, if the Republican Party could appeal more to racial and ethnic minorities, it too could gain by mobilizing racial and ethnic minority citizens.

Regardless of whether the two major parties heed this advice, there are signs that others have begun to step up and mobilize racial and ethnic minority voters in large numbers. Turnout figures from the nation's most recent national elections in 2018 and 2020 reveal a narrowing of the racial turnout gap. Specifically as can been seen in Figure 7.12 (a and b), Latino and Asian American turnout jumped markedly in 2018 and 2020. To be sure, Latino and Asian American turnout still lagged behind White and Black turnout, but the gap in these two recent contests was much smaller. All of this is a sign that grassroots, non-partisan mobilization efforts are working and that more mobilization might eventually eliminate racial disparities in turnout.

Institutional Reform

The other potentially more practical and perhaps even more effective strategy for increasing voter participation is institutional reform. In many cases, we can make voting easier and more even, simply by passing new laws about how elections are run. A range of institutional reforms have the potential to reduce racial gaps in turnout. For one, new laws could limit or ease registration requirements. Given that the process of registering is often seen as the biggest hurdle to voting in the United States, anything that eliminates requirements for registration or that eases the burden of registration could have dramatic effects. Efforts are already underway

Figure 7.12 Turnout by Race Across
Time, 1990-2020: (a) presidential
years; (b) midterm years.
Notice how Asian American and
Latino turnout jumped in 2018
and 2020.
Source: Current Population Survey.

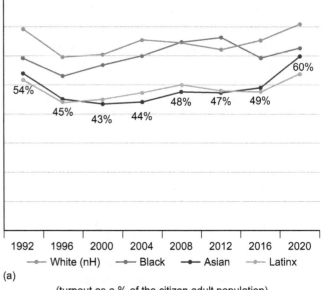

(a)

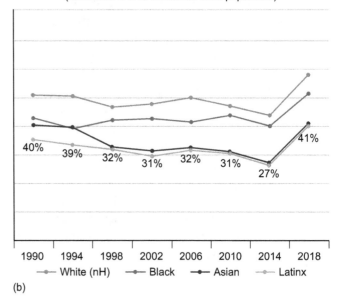

(b)

to expand automatic registration, in which eligible citizens are automatically opted
into registering when they interact with government agencies (e.g., the DMV).
Other states have moved to election day registration as an option.

Another set of reforms aims to make the voting process itself easier. This includes
extended early-voting periods, various vote-by-mail options, and more and easier
access to polling locations. Most of these measures—from mail-in voting to assur-
ance of convenient polling locations—have been found to have a positive effect on
turnout, although often smaller than expected, and less clear in their impact on the
racial balance of voters.

Thus, a more effective route might be to repeal institutional measures that critics view as racial voter suppression. For example, if we could reduce felon disenfranchisement, eliminate strict voter identification laws, eliminate biased voter purges, and ensure equal access to polls, we could likely reduce racial imbalances in turnout. Just how much those laws hurt minorities and the prospect of reforming them will be the subject of Chapter 13 on Voting Rights.

Local Electoral Reform

One seemingly small change could have dramatic effects on local democracy. The core problem with local democracy is that an extraordinarily small and unrepresentative set of residents determines how local governments allocate services and distribute the almost $2 trillion that local governments spend annually. Fortunately, scholars have found a simple solution: move the dates of local elections so that officials in cities and suburbs are elected at the same time as presidents, governors, and legislators.

The logic behind the change is straightforward. When local elections are *not* held on the first Tuesday of November with other statewide and national contests, local voters need to learn the date of their local election, find their local election polling place, and make a specific trip to the polls just to vote on local contests. That is a lot of extra work just to vote for a school board contest or a special district measure, and turnout is predictably small. By moving those elections to coincide with national elections (that is, instituting on-cycle elections), local voting is essentially costless. Citizens who are already voting for higher-level offices need only check off a few more boxes further down the ballot.

This small change in timing makes a huge difference in turnout. In 2016, Baltimore moved to on-cycle elections, and its participation soared. Registered voter turnout went from just 13 percent in the last election before the switch to 60 percent in the first on-cycle election. San Diego has on-cycle city elections and generally high turnout—76 percent turnout in November 2016. But when scandal forced the city to hold an off-cycle mayoral contest in 2013, turnout dropped to 35 percent. More broadly, research shows that participation in local elections in cities doubles when cities shift to on-cycle elections (Hajnal 2010).

Increased turnout is far from the only benefit. Research by Hajnal, Kogan, and Markarian (2021), which estimated the race and ethnicity of every voter in California over more than a decade of elections, found that the electorate also became much more racially representative when cities shifted to on-cycle elections. As Figure 7.13 illustrates, Latino voters made up only 17.8 percent of voters in off-cycle contests. That grows to 25.5 percent in on-cycle elections— still not fully representative of a state where Latinx make up 34.2 percent of the urban population but a dramatic improvement. Asian Americans also benefited, as their share of the active electorate grew from 7.7 percent in off-cycle elections in the state to 9.5 percent in local elections held the same day as a presidential contest, a figure that comes much closer to their 10.1 share of the population. African Americans benefit

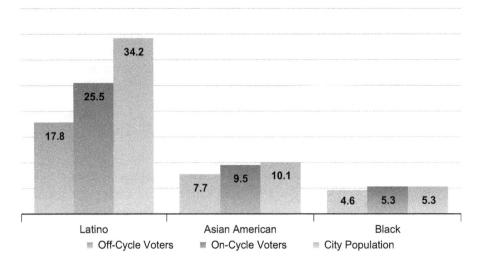

Figure 7.13 Effect of On-Cycle vs. Off-Cycle Local Elections on Racial Representation in the California Electorate
Racial and ethnic minorities make up a larger share of the electorate in on-cycle elections.
Source: Hajnal, Kogan, and Markarian (2021). Data from California, 2008–2016.

less from on-cycle elections in large part because their participation rates generally come close to matching those of Whites. Nevertheless, the Black share of the vote grew marginally from 4.6 to 5.3 percent of the vote when cities shifted from off-cycle to on-cycle elections. The net effect is that the White share of the voting population decreased from 67 percent in off-cycle contests to 56 percent in on-cycle elections, an important shift for a state where Whites make up a little less than half of the urban population.

Increasing and broadening turnout can in turn affect who wins office and the types of policies that local governments pursue. Hajnal's (2010) analysis shows that higher turnout also affected racial and ethnic minority representation on city councils. Across the nation, Hajnal found that, all else equal, cities where turnout was higher tended to elect more Latinos and Asian Americans. He estimated that large but attainable increases in turnout could eliminate about a third of the under-representation of Asian Americans on city councils and about a quarter of the underrepresentation of Hispanics on councils. Finally, Hajnal also found that cities with higher turnout and greater minority representation tended to enact policies that are more in line with the needs and preferences of all citizens, including greater social welfare spending and increased hiring of minorities in city government. In short, on-cycle elections can increase turnout, make the electorate and our elected officials more representative, and make government policy more responsive to the broader electorate.

Given that the vast majority of cities (roughly 70 percent) currently hold off-cycle elections, the potential to expand citizen participation and broaden urban democracy is very real. Critically, unlike most other reform ideas, on-cycle elections are popular, nonpartisan, and cost effective. When asked, two-thirds of Americans say they would prefer to vote in one election on one date, rather than in multiple elections on multiple dates. Remarkably, in these days of partisan polarization, Democrats and Republicans both overwhelmingly favor the same solution (73 and 61 percent, respectively). What's more, both parties have pushed this reform. In 2015, California's overwhelmingly Democratic state government passed a law mandating on-cycle local elections when local turnout falls below a certain threshold. In 2019, Arizona's overwhelmingly Republican state government passed an almost identical law. A lot of cities are shifting to on-cycle elections simply because it is cheaper to have multiple contests on the same ballot than to hold multiple elections across multiple days.

Conclusion

We began this chapter by looking at two polling places—one eerily quiet and the other overwhelmed with voters. Those two precincts epitomize the unevenness of participation in American democracy. Overall, however, our democracy is defined by relatively low participation. Only about half of us vote in major national contests. Fewer still cast ballots for lower-level offices. And even fewer engage in other civic activities like campaigning, letter writing, or donating. But as we have detailed in this chapter, participation is sharply skewed by race and ethnicity, with Whites much more involved than racial and ethnic minorities who tend to be on the outside looking in. In the context of voting and almost every other political activity, Whites are more active and therefore more influential. Within the minority population, African Americans tend to participate the most, with Hispanics and Asian Americans typically the least involved.

As we have shown in this chapter, all of this has real consequences. Those who are active and involved have substantially different preferences than those who are not active and involved. Those who vote are significantly more conservative and Republican leaning than nonvoters. If all of the nonvoters suddenly voted, policy would be likely to shift to the left, and Democrats would win many more offices. Indeed, it is not an exaggeration to say that partisan control of America's major political institutions is in no small part a function of who turns out to vote.

Why, given that so much is to be gained or lost, don't minorities participate at the same rate as Whites? Much of the answer comes down to socioeconomic resources. Once we control for those resources and factors such as immigration status, African Americans and Hispanics participate at almost exactly the same rate as White Americans. The fact that the two major parties are more likely to attempt to mobilize Whites than they are to try to engage racial and ethnic minorities also helps to explain racial disparities in participation. However, a stronger sense of group identity and linked fate within the minority population means that racial and ethnic minorities and, in particular, African Americans sometimes participate more than we would expect.

Fortunately, we can do some things to try to reduce the racial skew to participation. Broader mobilization would certainly be effective, and research supports the argument that it makes sense for political parties to devote more of their resources to contacting and mobilizing a more diverse group of Americans. A number of institutional reforms that would reduce the costs of voting also have the potential to engage a broader set of voters. Repealing voter suppression measures such as felon disenfranchisement and strict voter identification laws could do even more. One of the easiest reforms—switching the dates of local elections so that they coincide with statewide and national contests—could also increase participation while transforming local elections and local government.

KEY TERMS

Conventional acts of participation
Electoral participation
Franchise
Free riding
Gerrymandering
Group identity/consciousness
Literacy test
Logic of collective action
Mobilization
Nonelectoral participation
On-cycle election
Partisan gerrymandering
Poll tax
Psychological benefit of voting
Racial gap in turnout
Rational actor approach
Unconventional acts of participation
Voting Rights Act 1965

DISCUSSION QUESTIONS

1. What are the trends in political participation rates across racial and ethnic groups?
2. Does uneven participation matter for American democracy? How and why?
3. Why do racial and ethnic minorities tend to participate less than White Americans?
4. Should we try to broaden political participation in America? Why or why not?
5. What are some strategies for reducing racial disparities in political participation? Which groups are most likely to be affected by such changes and why?

ANNOTATED SUGGESTED READINGS

See S. Verba, Kay Lehman Schlozman, and Henry E. Brady. 1995. *Voice and Equality: Civic Voluntarism in American Politics*. Cambridge, MA, Harvard University Press, for an excellent overview of inequalities in political participation.

See J. Wong, Taeku Lee, Jane Junn, and S. Karthick Ramakrishnan. 2011. *Asian American Political Participation: Emerging Constituents and Their Political Identities*. New York: Russell Sage, for a detailed discussion of Asian American political participation that includes details on different national origin groups.

See R. A. Jackson. 2003. "Differential Influences on Latino Electoral Participation," *Political Behavior* 25: 339–366, for a deeper understanding of Latinx political participation.

See L. G. Bedolla and M. R. Michelson. 2012. *Mobilizing Inclusion: Transforming the Electorate through Get-Out-the-Vote Campaigns*. New Haven, CT: Yale University Press, to understand how mobilization works and how it works best for racial and ethnic minorities.

See K. Ramakrishnan. 2005. *Democracy in Immigrant America: Changing Demographics and Political Participation*. Stanford: Stanford University Press, for a comprehensive analysis of how immigration related factors impact participation.

See Z. L. Hajnal. 2010. *America's Uneven Democracy: Turnout, Race, and Representation in City Politics*. Cambridge: Cambridge University Press, for more information on racial and ethnic minority participation in local democracy and its causes and consequences.

CHAPTER REFERENCES

Barreto, Matt, Stephen Nuno, Gabriel Sanchez, and Hannah Walker. 2019. "The Racial Implications of Voter Identification Laws in America," *American Politics Research* 47: 238–249.

Branton, Regina, Valerie Martinez-Ebers, Tony E. Carey Jr., and Tetsuya Matsubayashi. 2015. "Social Protest and Policy Attitudes: The Case of the 2006 Immigrant Rallies," *American Journal of Political Science* 59: 390–402.

Brown, Nadia and Sarah, Gershon, eds. 2016. *Distinct Identities: Minority Women in U.S. Politics*. New York: Routledge.

Burnham, Walter Dean. 1987. "The Turnout Problem," In *Elections American Style* (ed.) A. James Reichley. Washington, D.C.: Brookings Institution.

Cho, Wendy K. Tam. 1999. "Naturalization, Socialization, Participation: Immigrants and (Non-) Voting," *Journal of Politics* 61: 1140–1150.

Chong, Dennis and Reuel Rogers. 2005. "Reviving Group Consciousness," In *The Politics of Democratic Inclusion* (eds.) Christina Wolbrecht and Rodney E. Hero. Philadelphia, PA: Temple University Press.

Citrin, Jack, Eric Schickler, and John Sides. 2003. "More Democracy or More Democrats? The Impact of Increased Turnout on Senate Elections," *American Journal of Political Science* 47: 75–90.

Dawson, Michael C. 1994. *Behind the Mule: Race and Class in African-American Politics*. Princeton: Princeton University Press.

Desilver, Drew. 2020. "In Past Elections, U.S. Trailed Most Developed Countries in Voter Turnout," Pew Research Center, www.pewresearch.org/fact-tank/2020/11/03/in-past-elections-u-s-trailed-most-developed-countries-in-voter-turnout.

Ellis, Christopher R., Joseph Daniel Ura, and Jenna Ashley-Robinson. 2006. "The Dynamic Consequences of Nonvoting in American National Elections," *Political Research Quarterly* 59: 227–233.

Flavin, Patrick. 2012a. "Does Higher Voter Turnout among the Poor Lead to More Equal Policy Representation?" *Social Science Journal* 49: 405–412.

Flavin, Patrick. 2012b. "Income Inequality and Policy Representation in the American States," *Public Opinion Quarterly* 40: 29—59.

Foner, Eric. 1984. *A Short History of Reconstruction*. New York: Harper & Row.

Fonseca, Felicia and Angeliki Kastanis. 2020. "Native American Votes Helped Secure Biden's Win in Arizona," *Seattle Times*, November 19.

Fraga, Bernard L. 2018. *The Turnout Gap: Race, Ethnicity, and Political Inequality in a Diversifying America*. Cambridge: Cambridge University Press.

García Bedolla, Lisa. 2005. *Fluid Borders: Latino Power, Identity, and Politics in Los Angeles*. Berkeley: University of California Press.

García Bedolla, Lisa and Melissa R. Michelson. 2012. *Mobilizing Inclusion: Transforming the Electorate through Get-out-the-Vote Campaigns*. New Haven, CT: Yale University Press.

Gause, LaGina. 2022. *The Advantage of Disadvantage: Costly Protest and Political Representation for Marginalized Groups*. Cambridge: Cambridge University Press.

Gerber, Alan S. and Donald P. Green. 2000. "The Effect of a Nonpartisan Get-out-the-Vote Drive: An Experimental Study of Leafletting," *Journal of Politics* 62: 846–857.

Gerber, Alan S., Donald P. Green, and Christopher W. Larimer. 2008. "Social Pressure and Voter Turnout: Evidence from a Largescale Field Experiment," *American Political Science Review* 102(1): 33–48.

Gillion, Daniel. 2012. "Protest and Congressional Behavior: Assessing Racial and Ethnic Minority Protests in the District," *Journal of Politics* 74: 950–962.

Go, Min Hee. 2018. "Does Christopher Chen Vote More Than Shu-Wei Chen? The Cost of Ethnic Retention among Asian American Voters," *Politics, Groups, and Identities* 6: 553–575.

Griffin, John D. and Brian Newman. 2005. "Are Voters Better Represented?" *Journal of Politics* 67(4): 1206–1227.

Griffin, John D. and Brian Newman. 2013. "Voting Power, Policy Representation, and Disparities in Voting's Rewards," *Journal of Politics* 75: 52–64.

Grumbach, Jacob M. and Alexander Sahn. 2020. "Race and Representation in Campaign Finance," *American Political Science Review* 114: 206–221.

Hajnal, Zoltan L. 2010. *America's Uneven Democracy: Turnout, Race, and Representation in City Politics*. Cambridge: Cambridge University Press.

Hajnal, Zoltan L., Vladimir Kogan, and G. Agustin Markarian. 2021. "Who Votes: City Election Timing and Voter Composition," *American Political Science Review*: 1–10.

Hansford, Thomas and Brad Gomez. 2010. "Estimating the Electoral Effects of Voter Turnout," *American Political Science Review* 104: 268–288.

Highton, Benjamin. 1997. "Easy Registration and Voter Turnout," *Journal of Politics* 59: 565–575.

Jackman, Robert W. 1987. "Political Institutions and Voter Turnout in Industrial Democracies," *American Political Science Review* 81: 405–424.

Jardina, Ashley. 2018. *White Identity Politics*. New York: Cambridge University Press.

Jones-Correa, Michael. 2005. "Bringing Outsiders in: Questions of Immigrant Incorporation," In *The Politics of Democratic Inclusion* (eds.) Christina Wolbrecht and Rodney E. Hero. Philadelphia, PA: Temple University Press.

Junn, Jane and Natalie Masuoka. 2013. *The Politics of Belonging: Race, Public Opinion, and Immigration*. Chicago: University of Chicago Press.

Kasara, Kimuli and Pavithra Suryanarayan. 2015. "When Do the Rich Vote Less Than the Poor and Why? Explaining Turnout Inequality across the World," *American Journal of Political Science* 59: 613–627.

Key, V. O. 1984. *Southern Politics in State and Nation.* Knoxville: University of Tennessee Press.

Kuk, John, Zoltan Hajnal, and Nazita Lajevardi. 2022. "A Disproportionate Burden: Strict Voter Identification Laws and Minority Turnout," *Politics, Groups, and Identities* 10(1): 126–134.

Leighley, Jan and Jonathan Nagler. 2013. *Who Votes Now?: Demographics, Issues, Inequality, and Turnout in the United States.* Princeton: Princeton University Press.

Leighley, Jan E. and Jennifer Oser. 2018. "Representation in an Era of Political and Economic Inequality: How and When Citizen Engagement Matters," *Perspectives on Politics* 16: 328–344.

Manza, Jeff. 2006. *Locked Out: Felon Disenfranchisement and American Democracy.* Oxford: Oxford University Press.

Marschall, Melissa J. 2001. "Does the Shoe Fit? Testing Models of Participation for African-American and Latino Involvement in Local Politics," *Urban Affairs Review* 37: 227–248.

Martin, Paul S. 2003. "Voting's Rewards: Voter Turnout, Attentive Publics, and Congressional Allocation of Federal Money," *American Journal of Political Science* 47: 110–127.

Mazumder, Soumyajit. 2018. "The Persistent Effect of U.S. Civil Rights Protests on Political Attitudes," *American Journal of Political Science* 62: 922–935.

National Congress of American Indians. 2016. "Every Native Vote Counts." www.ncai.org/initiatives/campaigns/NCAI_NativeVoteInfographic.pdf.

Parker, Christopher. 2009. "When Politics Becomes Protest: Black Veterans and Political Activism in the Postwar South," *Journal of Politics* 71: 113–131.

Powell, G. Bingham. 1986. "American Voter Turnout in Comparative Perspective," *American Political Science Review* 81: 45–65.

Riker, William and Peter C. Ordeshook. 1968. "A Theory of the Calculus of Voting," *American Political Science Review* 62: 25–42.

Rogan, Adam. 2019. "Empty Voting Booths Common on Tuesday: Turnout below 6 Percent," *The Journal Times*, February 21.

Santos, Fernanda. 2016. "Angry Arizona Voters Demand: Why Such Long Lines at Polling Sites?" *New York Times*, March 24.

Schildkraut, Deborah. 2005. *Press One for English: Language Policy, Public Opinion, and American Identity.* Cambridge: Cambridge University Press.

Sentencing Project, The. 2021. "Trends in US Corrections," In *Secondary Trends in US Corrections.* www.sentencingproject.org/publications/trends-in-u-s-corrections.

Uggen, Chris, Ryan Larson, Sarah Shannon and Arleth Pulido-Nava. 2021. "Locked out 2020: Estimates of People Denied Voting Rights Due to a Felony Conviction," *The Sentencing Project*, October 30. www.sentencingproject.org/publications/locked-out-2020-estimates-of-people-denied-voting-rights-due-to-a-felony-conviction.

Verba, Sydney, Kay Lehman Schlozman, and Henry Brady. 1995. "Race, Ethnicity, and Political Participation," In *Classifying by Race* (ed.) Paul E. Peterson. Princeton: Princeton University Press.

Verba, Sidney and Norman H. Nie. 1972. *Participation in America: Political Democracy and Social Equality.* Chicago: University of Chicago Press.

Wolfinger, Raymond E. and Steven J. Rosenstone. 1980. *Who Votes?* New Haven, CT: Yale University Press.

8   Media, Campaigns, and the Politics of Race

Researchers have demonstrated that exposure to political content through the mass media, including social media, can be remarkably persuasive—although the effects are often more indirect than direct. When these political messages also exploit racial stereotypes, their effects can be particularly effective and damaging. Several examples from the last four presidential elections help to illustrate this point.

During the 2008 presidential campaign, and for many years thereafter, critics of then-Senator Obama used the mass media and the Internet to spread false rumors about his religion and citizenship status. Specifically, these rumors held that Obama was secretly a Muslim and that he was born in Kenya. Both charges were untrue and politically explosive. Given the unpopularity of the Islamic faith following the 9/11 attacks on New York and Washington D.C., the charge that the Democratic presidential nominee was a Muslim would surely undermine his electoral support. Moreover, the false claim that Obama was born in Kenya would disqualify him from running for the presidency, as Article 2 of the Constitution explicitly states that only "natural-born citizens" are eligible for this office.

In spite of the lack of evidence to support either rumor, a significant number of Americans nevertheless believed one or both claims. According to the 2012 American National Election Study (ANES), approximately 20 percent of Americans indicated that Obama was a Muslim, and 24 percent believed that he was not born in the United States. The comparable figures for self-identified Republicans were 33 percent and 39 percent. This latter result—fueled by the so-called "birther" rumor that the president was not born in the United States—is all the more remarkable since it came several years into Obama's first administration and long after the president had posted his long-form birth certificate on the White House website in April 2011 which confirmed that Obama was indeed born in the state of Hawaii in 1961.

Donald Trump, at the time a private citizen with presidential aspirations, did not initiate these false rumors about President Obama. However, in 2011 as he considered his own possible run for the presidency, Trump played a significant role in helping to revive the rumors (Rothman 2016). The New York real estate entrepreneur and host of the NBC reality television show "The Apprentice" used his celebrity status to raise questions about the president's birth certificate and religion in a number of television appearances and in his Twitter account (Barbaro 2016).

Photo 8.1 Real estate mogul Donald Trump announced his bid for the presidency in the 2016 presidential race during an event at the Trump Tower, Fifth Avenue, New York City on June 16, 2015. Sounding already familiar themes such as his opposition to Obamacare, his perhaps most memorable comments had to do with the dangers of undocumented Mexican immigrants.
Source: © Kena Betancur/Stringer/ AFP/Getty Images.

Once Trump eventually decided to run for the Republican nomination for president, he would shift his focus to another racially tinged subject—immigration.

In June 2015, Donald Trump famously descended down the escalator in Trump Tower in New York City to announce his plans to run for president. His speech that day touched on a number of familiar themes such as trade deals with China, the war in Iraq, and his opposition to the Affordable Care Act, or "Obamacare." However, what would ultimately generate the biggest headlines were Trump's comments about immigration from Mexico. In reference to undocumented Mexican immigrants Trump declared that, "When Mexico sends its people, they're not sending their best ... They're sending people that have lots of problems, and they're bringing their problems with us [sic]. They're bringing drugs. They're bringing crime. They're rapists. And some, I suppose, are good people" (Trump 2015). Opposition to undocumented immigration soon became Trump's signature issue and, for many months, it was the only issue listed on his campaign website (Jardina 2019). Arguably, this issue helped to distinguish Trump from a crowded field of GOP presidential hopefuls and ultimately propelled him to victory in the 2016 general election.

An additional illustration of the influential role that media messages can play in American politics also centers on the presidential election of 2016. In this case, the messages were largely carried over social media and involved the Russian effort to interfere in the 2016 presidential election on behalf of the Republican nominee, Donald Trump. American intelligence agencies, from the Federal Bureau of Investigation (FBI) to the Central Intelligence Agency (CIA), concluded unanimously that the Russians engaged in a massive cyber campaign to assist Trump and undermine Democratic presidential nominee, Hillary Clinton. This campaign involved hacking into the Democratic National Committee in order to release embarrassing emails to the press and posting numerous misleading ads on Facebook. What is less well known, however, is that a central component of Russian interference into the 2016 presidential campaign involved exploiting racial divisions in America.

In fall 2019, a bipartisan Senate committee released a report on the allegations that the Russians sought to intervene in the 2016 U.S. presidential election. They found that the Russians did in fact use social media to lobby on behalf of Donald Trump. They also concluded that this cyber campaign had an "overwhelming operational emphasis on race ... [and that] no single group of Americans was targeted ... more than African Americans" (Mak 2019). The primary strategy seemed to be using fictitious accounts, ostensibly from Black activist groups, on Facebook, Twitter, Instagram, YouTube, and other outlets to criticize Hillary Clinton and urge Blacks to vote for Green Party candidate, Jill Stein—or to stay home on election day.

Lastly, the 2020 presidential contest, and its aftermath, also involved the use of subtle and not-so-subtle racial appeals publicized through the media. For example, Democratic vice presidential nominee Kamala Harris, the first woman of color to attain such a position, faced questions from partisan critics about her citizenship status and was characterized as a "monster" by President Trump (Astor 2020). After the Biden–Harris ticket won the presidential election, the Trump campaign raised unfounded allegations of election fraud in several big cities such as Detroit, Milwaukee, Atlanta, and Philadelphia—all cities with significant Black populations (Nguyen, Ruble, and Craig 2020).

These examples demonstrate how the concept of race remains the fundamental unresolved issue in this country, and therefore frequently figures prominently in political campaigns. When a Columbia and Harvard trained U.S. senator—who also happened to be of partial African ancestry—ran for the presidency in 2008, this senator's racial background was perhaps the most consequential characteristic of his candidacy for both supporters and opponents. At least in part because of his racial background, a large fraction of the electorate was receptive to unfounded rumors suggesting that Obama was ineligible to run for the presidency. One of the chief sponsors of these racially tinged rumors also sought his party's nomination for president in 2016 and did so on his signature issue of opposition to immigration from Mexico and other countries in South and Central America. The unmistakable racial implications of the 2008, 2012, 2016, and 2020 presidential campaigns highlight the subtle and not-so-subtle ways in which racial appeals are still viable strategies in contemporary American politics. Thus, it is perhaps not surprising that when the Russians sought to bolster the presidential candidacy of Donald Trump, they did so by using social media to exploit the most divisive issue in American politics—race.

In this chapter, we will focus on the various ways in which political elites use the media to inflame racial passions in order to gain electoral advantage. We will begin by defining what is meant by the term "mass media," and by explaining why freedom of the press is such an essential cornerstone of democracy. Additionally, this chapter will briefly discuss the history of the mass media and how it has historically been used by campaigns. Later in this chapter, we will focus on the various ways in which exposure to media messages can be influential in shaping the political judgments of ordinary citizens. As we will see, this influence can be both direct and indirect. In the second half of this chapter, we will explore some of the specific ways that racial appeals delivered through the media have manipulated public opinion both historically and in the contemporary political environment.

Mass Media and American Democracy

One of the cornerstones of American democracy is the ability of members of the news media to report on public affairs without government restrictions. In short, American democracy requires freedom of the press. What exactly is the media and why is its freedom from government restriction essential to democracy?

Defining the Media

Terms like "the press" or "the media" refer to the instruments by which we disseminate information on public affairs. The term mass media is used to describe communication that can reach large numbers of people in a short amount of time. At the time of the ratification of the Constitution in 1788 these terms primarily referred to printed news outlets like newspapers and pamphlets. The individuals responsible for providing the information contained in these outlets are known as journalists or political activists.

Freedom of the Press

Freedom of the press is enshrined in the First Amendment to the Constitution. "Congress shall make no law respecting an establishment of religion, or preventing the free exercise thereof; or abridging the freedom of speech, or of the press; or the right of the people peaceably to assemble, and to petition the government for a redress of grievances." In this brief passage, bedrock democratic principles such as the freedom of speech, the free exercise of religion, and the freedom to protest are all given equal weight alongside the freedom of the press. These ideals are grouped together because the framers of the Constitution recognized that the freedom of the press is indispensable to a free and open society. The media is such an essential part of a democracy because without them the citizens within the democracy would be unable to acquire the necessary information to hold their elected leaders accountable.

One of the first political observers to note the important role that the media plays in shaping public opinion was early twentieth-century journalist Walter Lippmann. As Lippmann argued in his influential book *Public Opinion*, first published in 1922, public affairs at the local, state, and national level are far too voluminous for even the most politically aware individual to absorb. Moreover, our first-hand experiences and personal interactions are much too limited to inform us of public policy matters in an advanced post-industrial society such as the United States. Citizens are therefore necessarily dependent on others—in this case, journalists and others working in the mass media—to provide them with political information that helps to shape public opinion.

Aside from simply providing political information, the media also carries out other essential duties in a democracy. For example, journalists are one of the institutions in society responsible for investigating allegations of wrongdoing within government as well as explaining and publicizing public policy. Thomas Jefferson, "Founding Father" and third president of the United States, once famously elevated the importance of the press over even that of the government. "The basis of our government being the opinion of the people, the very first object should be to keep that right; and were it left to me to decide whether we should have a government without newspapers, or newspapers without a government, I should not hesitate a moment to prefer the latter."[1]

Mass Media and Public Opinion

Information carried through the mass media is one of the chief sources of public opinion. For most of the twentieth century the term "mass media" meant hard copy newspapers, radio, and later television. Although widespread use of the Internet began in the 1990s, what we now refer to as "social media" did not emerge until the early twenty-first century with such platforms as Facebook, YouTube, Instagram, and Twitter or X. In the following sections we briefly discuss the history of the mass media and its influence on political perceptions and campaigns.

Initial Fears and Initial Findings

Although political information has been widely disseminated since the invention of the printing press in the fifteenth century, often this information did not reach a mass audience due to limitations in population literacy. All of this began to change in the 1920s and 1930s with the development of new media technologies. Specifically, with the widespread use of radio and later motion pictures, political leaders who wished to inform or mislead the public now had unprecedented access to the ear of the ordinary citizen irrespective of their educational background. This change was in some ways like the development of the printing press but in other ways even more significant, for while many citizens could not read at the advanced level of most newspapers, all could potentially understand the messages conveyed through radio or movies.

Along with the rise of mass media in the 1930s came the rise, perhaps not coincidentally, of the charismatic political leader. In Nazi Germany there was Adolph Hitler and at about that same time in Italy, the fascist leader Benito Mussolini came to power. Additionally, there was the inspiring radio presence of Winston Churchill in Great Britain. And in the United States, President Franklin

---

[1] See at: oll.libertyfund.org/titles/802.

D. Roosevelt began his famous and influential "Fireside Chats," or evening radio broadcasts to the nation.

This period also saw the rise of popular programming in the mass media, including the famous 1938 radio broadcast of *War of the Worlds* by Orson Welles. This dramatization of the H. G. Wells classic 1897 novel of the same name describes aliens from Mars attacking the United States. When listeners to the program heard the broadcast, many apparently thought the invasion was real, leading to news reports of widespread panic. The supposed frenzied reaction to the broadcast was likely overstated in the press, but many political observers nevertheless took note and worried about the undue influence that might be caused by media exposure (Memmott 2013). In short, they wondered whether a charismatic political figure might emerge and use the mass media to manipulate people into doing something they would not ordinarily do.

During the Second World War, social scientists at Columbia University first began to examine whether the public might be susceptible to large persuasion effects from exposure to media messages. In their groundbreaking book, *The People's Choice*, Lazarsfeld and his co-authors relied on the new science of survey research to examine the effects of campaign appeals—often carried through the mass media—on voter decisions in the 1940 presidential contest (Lazarsfeld, Berelson, and Gaudet 1944). The major conclusion of *The People's Choice* was what would later be referred to as "the law of minimal consequences." In other words, and surprisingly, this study found that the messages conveyed through the media were *not* especially persuasive. If anything, media messages simply strengthened political predispositions that were already in place. Essentially, this meant that exposure to campaign messages carried in the mass media simply encouraged citizens already inclined toward one candidate to support that candidate with even greater enthusiasm. Other studies followed with the same conclusion. Messages conveyed through the mass media could be effective in passing along information, but not in changing opinions.

Renewed Concerns about Media Influence

Although the "minimal effects" perspective held sway for about 15 years or so (effectively dampening scholarly interest in the topic of media effects) concern began to grow again in the late 1960s and 1970s with the rise in the popularity of television and the increasing use of this medium by presidents and presidential candidates. During this time period, the potential influence of television was undeniable. The typical American adult in the 1960s and 1970s worked about 35 hours a week thereby leaving about 6 or 7 hours a day for leisure time during the week. Researchers found that almost all of this time, over 4 hours per day, was taken up by television viewing (Graber and Dunaway 2017). Moreover, by the end of the 1970s, almost 99 percent of households had at least one television.[2] This was a

---

[2] See at: https://bit.ly/4c18VtA.

higher figure than the percentage of households with indoor plumbing. The dramatic rise in the number of households with a television set was also concerning because politicians at this time were increasingly relying on television as their preferred means of communication with voters.

Many of these renewed concerns became less important once researchers realized that many citizens appeared to pay relatively little attention to issues of public affairs in the mass media. It is common, for instance, for television sets to be on in the background without much active attentiveness from viewers. Even before the rise of cable news networks—which still draw a smaller audience than network newscasts—relatively few Americans watched the nightly news on the three major television networks (NBC, CBS, and ABC). On an average day in the 1990s, the three nightly newscasts combined to reach only about 20 percent of the American public (Graber and Dunaway 2017). In short, political programming has never been widely popular. This point is best illustrated by pointing to recent presidential elections. In 2016, 84 million Americans tuned in to watch the first presidential debate between Hillary Clinton and Donald Trump, making it the most watched presidential debate in U.S. history. In the fall election, about 139 million Americans cast votes in the presidential election indicating that about 60 percent of the electorate had seen the first debate. Still, roughly 40 percent of voters did not tune in at all. If instead of the percentage of Americans who turned out to vote for president, we consider the number of citizens who were *eligible* to vote for the president (250 million), then the 84 million tuning in to the first presidential debate in 2016 represents only about one-third of this population. During the 2020 contest, viewership of the most watched presidential debate declined to about 73 million. This represents less than half of the approximately 158 million Americans who voted in the presidential election. It seems, therefore, that exposure to political appeals via the mass media are unlikely to persuade many Americans since a large number are simply not that attentive to this information.

How the Media Indirectly Influences Public Opinion

While evidence of *direct* media persuasion seems limited, many researchers have determined that the media can be persuasive in more *indirect* ways. One such way is through a process known as agenda-setting. In the words of one scholar "... the mass media may not be successful much of the time in telling people what to think, but the media are stunningly successful in telling [their audience] what to think about" (Cohen 1963). In other words, agenda-setting is the process by which the general public comes to focus on, and regard as important, those issues that are emphasized in the media.

Political scientists Shanto Iyengar and Donald Kinder were among the first to demonstrate the power of agenda-setting in their book, *News that Matters* (1987). The authors ran a number of studies to test the agenda-setting hypothesis that media attention translates into viewer perceptions of issue importance. In one experiment they divided up a group of study participants, or subjects, and in one group of randomly assigned subjects they showed network newscasts that had been altered to emphasize the inadequacies in America's defense preparedness. In the other randomly assigned group, the control group, the network newscasts made no reference to defense issues. In both cases, the subjects were asked what they thought were the nation's most important problems before the experiment began and after it had concluded. As expected, subjects who saw the doctored newscasts (emphasizing defense issues) were much more likely to identify defense as one of the nation's most important problems after they saw the newscast rather than before. Subjects in the control group showed no change (Iyengar and Kinder 1987).

Although agenda-setting effects in the media can be quite large, their effects can also be limited by two factors: audience and message. In general, researchers have found that the politically engaged (e.g., strong partisans, individuals who are interested in politics, and the politically active) were much more likely to resist agenda-setting effects. Additionally, agenda-setting effects are most apparent with newer issues that have not been widely discussed and for issues that extend beyond one's personal experience, such as foreign policy.

Another indirect way in which the mass media can influence public opinion is through a process known as framing. With framing, the media depicts an issue or policy dispute by characterizing it in one way as opposed to another plausible way they might have covered it. Somewhat more formally, political scientist James Druckman provides the following definition. "A framing effect is said to occur when, in the course of describing an issue or event, a speaker's emphasis on a subset of potentially relevant considerations causes individuals to focus on these considerations when constructing their opinions" (Druckman 2001). For example, describing the widespread social unrest that erupted in the country following the killing of George Floyd by Minneapolis police officers in May 2020 as either "rioting" or even "anti-police demonstrations," versus "demonstrations against police brutality" can have significant implications for public opinion. The first two frames are likely to diminish support for the protests—if only because rioting or opposition to the police is unpopular in many parts of the country. Opposition to police brutality, on the other hand, especially following the widespread dissemination of video of the Floyd killing on social media, has become a far more popular political stance.

Scholars have demonstrated the impact of media-framing effects on a range of issues, including the international crisis in Kosovo, poverty, the Ku Klux Klan, and affirmative action (Berinsky and Kinder 2006; Iyengar 1991; Kinder and Sanders 1996; Nelson, Clawson, and Oxley 1997). In each of these cases and many more, scholars have shown that the manner in which an issue is covered in the media can influence the distribution of support for that issue.

As with agenda-setting, however, media framing also has important limits. In a series of articles, Druckman has argued that individuals are often exposed to multiple competing issue frames and that these competing frames can often cancel each other out (Druckman 2001; 2004). Media consumers are also not blindly receptive to issue frames and instead tend to be most sympathetic to frames provided by trusted sources (Zaller 1992). In short, context matters in terms of determining the influence of exposure to media frames.

Priming is a concept very closely related to framing. If framing involves emphasizing different, yet plausible, ways of describing an issue or political figure, then priming represents the different considerations one subsequently brings to bear on evaluating that issue or figure. For example, prior to the COVID-19 pandemic that began to seriously disrupt American society in spring 2020, the Trump administration hoped to base the president's reelection campaign on the historically low unemployment rates. That is, the Trump campaign wanted to make the upcoming election a referendum on the economy—precisely because they believed that this would cast the president in the most favorable light, thereby assuring him another term in the White House. The Democrats, on the other hand, did not want the election to be decided on the performance of the economy but instead wanted to focus on the president's recent (first) impeachment and his frequent practice of violating democratic norms. In short, when it came to the upcoming election, the Republicans wanted to prime the economy and the Democrats wanted to prime the impeachment and attitudes about Trump. To summarize these concepts, framing a political figure or issue in a particular way can influence *how* one evaluates the relevant figure or issue (i.e., priming). And, determining how an issue or event is evaluated can have important consequences for whether the evaluation is positive or negative.

Racial Priming in Political Campaigns

Just as media outlets and political campaigns can encourage voters to focus on the economy versus some other issue when evaluating political candidates, they can also determine whether racial concerns are a prominent criterion in their voting decision calculus, a phenomenon referred to as racial priming. Political campaigns can and do focus on a broad range of social groups, such as class, gender, and religion, when seeking to influence voting decisions. Although racial group appeals are not *qualitatively* different than candidate efforts to appeal to other social group cleavages, such messages are nevertheless *quantitatively* different. That is, a variety of studies have shown consistently over the past several decades that political divisions over racial matters represent the single biggest fault line in American politics (Carmines and Stimson 1989; Hutchings and Valentino 2004; Manza and Brooks 1999; Mendelberg 2001; Schickler 2016). As Abramson, Aldrich, and Rohde (2009) describe it, "political differences between African Americans and whites are far sharper than any other social cleavage" (108). Manza and Brooks (1999) present an even more sweeping conclusion when they write that, "in the history of American political development race has unquestionably been the most important of the major social cleavages, influencing virtually all political processes in one way or another" (155).

Since the passage of major Civil Rights legislation in the mid- to late 1960s, racial priming by political campaigns has mostly been subtle or implicit. In other words, modern campaigns rarely argue directly on behalf of racial segregation in principle or explicitly promote the notion of biologically superior and inferior races. Instead, contemporary politicians rely on racially neutral words and phrases that have become associated with racial minorities over time. Some common examples in recent American history involve words such as "illegal alien," "terrorist," "inner city," "welfare queen," and "thug." Simply using terms such as these can be enough to prompt voters to consider race when evaluating issues or political candidates. Additionally, scholars have found that campaign advertisements that simply pair images of racial minorities with traditional political rhetoric on crime or taxation can also succeed in priming racial considerations (Mendelberg 2001; Valentino, Hutchings, and White 2002). When the theory of racial priming was developed at the dawn of the twenty-first century, researchers believed that explicit appeals were so taboo in contemporary campaigns that even coded, or implicit, racial appeals would lose their persuasive power once critics had drawn attention to the racial subtext of the appeal (Mendelberg 2001). The quintessential example involved the infamous Willie Horton campaign, which Mendelberg found to be an effective strategy in the early and middle parts of the 1988 presidential contest but became ineffective in the latter stages of the campaign, once political elites criticized the ad as racially insensitive. (See the box, "Digging Deeper: Reagan, Bush, and the Politics of Race" later in this chapter).

Media and Politics in the Twenty-First Century

Political scientist Matthew Baum argues that when presidents and their administrations attempt to communicate to the electorate in the twenty-first century, they generally adopt one of two broad strategies: *Preaching to the Choir* and *Converting the Flock* (Baum 2011). As the names suggest, *Preaching to the Choir* refers to efforts by the administration to rally their base of true believers. That is, this strategy mostly focuses on mobilizing the administration's core supporters. What Baum refers to as *Converting the Flock*, on the other hand, involves efforts to persuade those members of the public who are not already supporters. Presidents, and other politicians, have used these two strategies for many years, but recent changes in the mass media have affected how easy it is to adopt one strategy or the other.

The New Media Environment

Matthew Baum has identified three distinct types of media in the twenty-first century: traditional news media, the "New Media," and "Soft Media" (2011). Each of these types of media can appeal to different kinds of voter, and thus influence how—or how effectively—presidents are able to *preach to the choir* or *convert the flock*. We will briefly describe each one in this section.

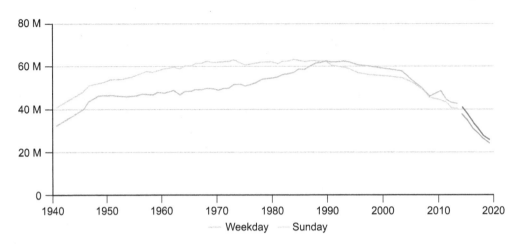

Figure 8.1 Total Estimated Circulation of U.S. Daily Newspapers, 1940–2020
Newspaper circulation reached its lowest level since 1940 in 2018.
Source: Editor and Publisher (through 2014); estimate based on Pew Research Center analysis
of Alliance for Audited Media data, 2015–2020. Pew Research Center, Newspapers Fact Sheet,
June 29, 2021, www.pewresearch.org/journalism/fact-sheet/newspapers.

The first type of media—traditional news media—is in some ways the most familiar. It refers to newscasts on the three original broadcast networks (NBC, CBS, and ABC) and major print (now increasingly online) news sources such as the *New York Times* and the *Washington Post*, as well as local city/town newspapers. The audience for network newscasts has declined substantially over the past several decades, although the evening news broadcast on the major networks did experience a significant increase during the coronavirus pandemic in spring 2020. Similarly, newspaper circulation has been declining in recent decades. In 2021, the Pew Research Center reported that newspaper circulation reached its lowest level since 1940 in 2020 (see Figure 8.1). The pandemic and economic shutdown only exacerbated a longstanding trend (Adgate 2021).

Perhaps more important than the decline in the size of the audience for traditional news media, Baum notes, is that *the partisan composition* of the audience has also changed over time. As recently as 2002, Democrats and Republicans watched network newscasts at roughly even rates (34 percent and 35 percent, respectively). However, by 2008, the Democratic figure had risen to 45 percent and the Republican percentage had declined to 22 percent (the percentage among Independents held steady). Additionally, a partisan divide has also developed for televised presidential addresses with partisans of the in-party increasingly tuning in to such events, and out-party members avoiding them (i.e., Democrats are now much more likely to watch televised addresses by Democratic presidents but not by Republican presidents and vice versa). And, with the decline of local newspapers, researchers have found that Americans have become more polarized along partisan lines. That is, in areas where local newspapers have closed individuals are somewhat less likely to engage in split-ticket voting relative to similar places that retained their local paper (Darr, Dunaway, and Hitt 2019).

In addition to the decline in the audience for traditional political news media and the partisan sorting that has accompanied it, Baum notes that *the way politics is covered* has changed. He reports that the news media is more likely to provide negative or hostile coverage of presidents and their policies, and the presidents' own words are less often used now with an emphasis instead on reporters' interpretation of what the president has said. Consequently, the average time of a presidential sound bite has declined from 40 seconds in 1968, to only 7.8 seconds in 2004. Subsequent scholarship has generally replicated this finding and extended it beyond the early 2000s (Farnsworth and Lichter 2011; Rinke 2016). This work also shows that there is a cost to the shrinking size of political sound bites: viewers are less likely to hear justifications from politicians for their policy positions (Rinke 2016). Given the more adversarial nature of traditional news media—along with their diminished coverage of presidential administrations—presidents have increasingly turned away from them as vehicles for *converting the flock*.

The second type of news media described by Baum, "New Media," refers to cable news programs and political websites. Social media platforms like Twitter, Facebook, and YouTube would also fall under this category. Unlike traditional news media, the new media does not place as much emphasis on appealing to a broad bipartisan audience. Not surprisingly, there are significant differences in the ideological spin of news stories across different political sites on the Internet and cable news networks (Baum 2011; Graber and Dunaway 2017). Additionally, the audiences that attend to these new media sources are increasingly polarized ideologically—and become even more polarized as a consequence of exposure to this content (Levendusky 2013). The significance of this pattern is that the Internet and cable news networks are not ideal venues if the president wants to *convert the flock*. That is, reaching a broad bipartisan audience is less likely here. Instead, this type of media is best for *preaching to the choir*.

Finally, the last type of political news media identified by Baum, "Soft Media," refers to programs that are primarily designed to provide entertainment rather than political information. However, in the process of providing this entertainment they may also provide *some* political information as well. In the current environment, this would include such programs as *The Tonight Show with Jimmy Fallon*, *The Late Show with Stephen Colbert*, *The View*, and *The Daily Show with Trevor Noah*. One virtue of these shows is that—again, not surprisingly—they draw a much larger audience than pure news or political programs. Also, the audiences for these shows are typically less politically engaged, less ideological, and less partisan (Baum 2011). In short, they are the kind of audiences that presidents—and other political figures—are more likely to persuade (i.e., *converting the flock*).

What are the implications of this changing media environment? There are a couple of possible negative consequences. First, as the size of the audience for network newscasts and newspapers continues to decline and as the size of the new media increases, it is possible that the voters will become insulated from opposing points of view. Second, the changing media environment may also contribute to the partisan divide by inserting ideologically skewed interpretations of news-worthy events. For example, cable news channels like Fox News and MSNBC provided markedly different coverage of President Trump's first and second impeachment trials in the Senate (Bump 2020; Hsu and Robertson 2021). Similarly, cable news channels also provided dramatically different coverage of the COVID-19 outbreak in the spring and summer of 2020 as well as the nation-wide protests following the killing of George Floyd by four Minneapolis police officers (Smith 2020).

"Fake News" and Declining Confidence in the Mass Media

The power of the news media derives at least in part from the amount of trust invested in this institution. For much of the twentieth century many Americans placed a great deal of trust in the media. However, since the mid- to late 1970s this percentage has been on the decline. One of the best sources of information on this question is the General Social Survey (GSS), a national survey conducted annually or biannually since 1972 (Smith et al. 2018). In 1976—two years after the investigative reporting of *Washington Post* journalists Bob Woodward and Carl Bernstein led to the resignation of President Richard Nixon—28 percent of Americans responding to the GSS indicated that they had "a great deal" of trust in the press. By 2018, only 13 percent of Americans expressed trust in the news media.

Given the plummeting levels of trust in the news media, it is perhaps not surprising that a media-savvy political candidate like Donald Trump would be able to capitalize on the media's unpopularity. Shortly after the 2016 election, Trump began referring to negative news coverage as "fake news" in order to assert that not only was this information inaccurate, but that the news media was often purposefully inaccurate. The president's Republican supporters, but also many Democrats, were receptive to this criticism. Analyzing survey data from December 2016, political scientists Taeku Lee and Christian Hosam (2020) reported that 88 percent of Republicans and 55 percent of Democrats agreed with the statement, "You can't believe much of what you hear from the mainstream media" (see Figure 8.2).[3] As shocking as this trend may be, Lee and Hosam also found that a belief in the prevalence of "fake news" is highly associated with anti-Muslim and anti-immigration views, opposition to affirmative action for women and racial minorities, and opposition to women's rights and LGBTQ+ rights. In short, declining trust in the media not only has implications for democratic norms but also for intergroup relations in society.

[3] By 2019, when their survey respondents answered the same questions, Lee and Hosam found that Democratic-leaning groups had become significantly more inclined to trust the mainstream media, but Republican-leaning groups remained highly skeptical of this institution.

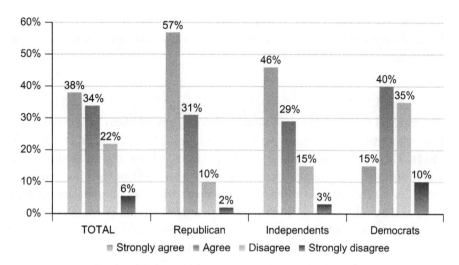

Figure 8.2 Fake News Beliefs from 2016 VOTER Survey
Survey respondents were asked whether they agreed or disagreed with the following statement:
"You can't believe much of what you hear from mainstream media."
Source: Taken from Lee and Hosam (2020), fig. 2. © 2020 Eastern Sociological Society.

Campaign Appeals to Race in Nineteenth and Twentieth Centuries

In the previous sections we have highlighted the various ways in which political campaigns, often by relying on the mass media, can indirectly influence public opinion. These campaign appeals have frequently focused on matters of race because of the central role of race in American politics. It is important to bear in mind the distinction between different kinds of race-based political appeals. At times, politicians have made overt appeals for the support of groups—typically White Americans—in an unmistakable effort to establish or preserve a system of race-based domination. As we shall see, this was fairly common throughout the nineteenth century and well into the twentieth century. Since the Civil Rights Movement of the 1950s and 1960s, such efforts have been discredited but have nevertheless survived in more covert and sophisticated forms. In more modern times, appeals of this sort can masquerade as ideological appeals that are ostensibly race-neutral but that coincidentally highlight issues popularly associated with racial minority groups. However, a more benign form of racial appeal has also been employed, increasingly so in recent years, where political candidates openly seek the support of different racial or ethnic groups in the electorate—but without the subtext that such support will lead to a race-based hierarchical society. In short, political appeals to race can be racist (i.e., attempts to impose or maintain a race-based hierarchy), and therefore disreputable, or simply racial, and hence inoffensive. In this section, we will focus more on the former with a particular emphasis on some of the overt appeals following the Civil War and during the Jim Crow era that followed the collapse of Reconstruction. Our aim here is to provide some context for understanding the evolution of racial appeals over the last several decades of American history.

Racial Appeals following the Civil War and during Jim Crow

Attempts to stoke the fires of racial animosity for political gain have a long and infamous history in America (Klinkner and Smith 1999; Mendelberg 2001; Myrdal 1944). Throughout the early years of the United States, concerns about race were either directly or indirectly implicated in political controversies involving the institution of slavery and in military engagements with the Native American populations as the country sought to acquire more territory in the West. In the aftermath of the Civil War, racial appeals became more common as a strategy for White politicians to mobilize their openly anti-Black supporters. One of the most glaring examples of this came just a few years after the Civil War when Andrew Johnson, who had ascended to the presidency following the assassination of Abraham Lincoln, vetoed a supplementary Reconstruction bill with the proclamation that:

The object of this bill ... is to put the Southern states ... in the hands of the Negroes. They are wholly incompetent to administer such a trust ... It is vain to deny that they are an inferior race—very far inferior to the European variety. They have learned in slavery all that they know in civilization. When first brought from the country of their origin they were naked savages and where they have been left to their own devices or escaped the control of the white race they have relapsed, to a greater or lesser degree into barbarism (quoted in Klinkner and Smith 1999: 78).

Such sentiments were echoed throughout the Reconstruction and Jim Crow periods in the South. One of the most notorious White supremacist politicians during this era was South Carolina governor (1890–1894) and later senator (1895–1918), Ben "Pitchfork" Tillman. Tillman regularly bragged about his role in violently overthrowing the Black Republican political leaders of his state during Reconstruction: "We took the government away. We stuffed ballot boxes. We shot them. We ain't ashamed of it" (Dray 2002: 112). This sort of overtly offensive language was common on the campaign trail even as late as the 1940s. For example in his 1946 reelection campaign, Mississippi Senator Theodore G. Bilbo boldly recommended violence to discourage Blacks from voting (presumably against him). "I'm calling on every red-blooded American who believes in the superiority and integrity of the white race to get out and see that no [N-word] votes, and the best time to do that is the night before." Bilbo, a Democrat whose statue still stands in the capital of Mississippi, was successfully elected to a third term in 1946—although the newly elected Republican majority in Congress prevented him from taking his Senate seat because of this controversial campaign (Pettus 2017). He died shortly thereafter in August 1947.

While Bilbo's violent rhetoric may have been tolerated in the South in the 1940s, it became unacceptable by the end of the decade, at least in the nation's political center. Aside from the partisan changeover in Congress, why had the racial rhetoric of Senator Bilbo suddenly become unacceptable in Washington? The allied fight

Photo 8.2 Coatless Mississippi Senator Theodore G. Bilbo, candidate for reelection, is shown here, in July, 1946, stumping for votes. An outspoken proponent of racial segregation, Senator Bilbo escalated his rhetoric of White supremacy in the 1940s, reaching a climax in his 1946 campaign.
Source: © Bettmann/Contributor/Getty Images.

against the Nazis during the Second World War represents the most likely explanation. The Nazi regime in Germany was built on the now-discredited notion of a "Master Race." With the defeat of the Axis powers in 1945, undisguised White supremacist rhetoric became a political liability—at least in elite circles.

Although it was no longer acceptable to use racial slurs on the campaign trail by the end of the Second World War, politicians committed to White supremacy still managed to court voters with similar perspectives by adopting more subtle race-based appeals. For example, when Democrat Harry S. Truman embraced racial equality in principle during his 1948 presidential campaign—most famously by desegregating the armed forces with Executive Order 9981—White southern Democrats abandoned their party and formed a third party known as the "Dixiecrats."[4] Their nominal protest slogan was the cause of "States Rights" rather than White supremacy. Nevertheless, Strom Thurmond, the Dixiecrat presidential

[4] The official name of this offshoot party was "The States' Rights Democratic Party."

candidate, made clear his position on the race issue when he indicated during the campaign that "All the laws of Washington and all the bayonets of the Army, cannot force the Negroes into our homes, schools, churches, and places of recreation" (quoted in Mendelberg 2001: 73).[5] However, Thurmond and most of his supporters insisted their opposition to federal civil rights initiatives was borne of a desire to preserve local authority and local customs, not because of any animosity toward Blacks.[6] Not all Dixiecrat politicians were as coy as Thurmond. Former Alabama Governor Frank Dixon spoke of how Truman's civil rights platform would "reduce us to the status of a mongrel, inferior race, mixed in blood, our Anglo-Saxon heritage a mockery" (quoted in Klinkner and Smith 1999: 222–223).

Racial Appeals during the Civil Rights Movement of the 1960s

In many ways, this modern strategy of fashioning racial appeals without appearing to do so overtly would achieve its greatest political significance in the presidential contest of 1964. In this contest, pitting Democrat Lyndon Johnson against Republican Barry Goldwater, the already strong support for the Democrats among African Americans began to approach unanimity. For Blacks, this contest presented one of the starkest contrasts in recent American history. Although Senator Goldwater represented the western state of Arizona, he pursued the White southern vote with a determination that, up until that time, was almost unheard of for a Republican. This novel effort had its origins in the 1950s when the Republican National Committee (RNC) initiated "Operation Dixie." The aim with this initiative was to build a moderate Republican Party in the previously inhospitable region of the South. This plan was abandoned, however, after President Eisenhower sent in federal troops to enforce school integration in Little Rock, Arkansas, in 1956. After this setback, Operation Dixie was revamped into an effort to woo Southern segregationists. As Goldwater framed it at a 1961 meeting of Southern Republican state party chairmen in Georgia, "we're not going to get the Negro vote as a bloc in 1964 or 1968, so we ought to go hunting where the ducks are" (quoted in Klinkner and Smith 1999: 262). By this phrase ("go hunting where the ducks are") he meant that Republicans should seek the votes of White Southern segregationists, who made up most of the Southern voting electorate. Indeed, one of Goldwater's high-profile segregationist supporters was South Carolina Senator, and former Dixiecrat

---

[5] Ironically, Thurmond had a Black mistress with whom he fathered a daughter (Jordan 2003). In this respect, he is similar to Thomas Jefferson who also preached against miscegenation, or "race mixing," in public but practiced it in private by fathering at least six children with Sally Hemings, a woman he enslaved at his Virginia home at Monticello (Gordon-Reed 1998).

[6] Strom Thurmond would maintain this position throughout his exceptionally lengthy political career. In 1991, Thurmond, then the senior Republican senator from South Carolina (he left the Democrats in 1964), would proclaim "that whole Dixiecrat thing in 1948 being about race, that's all wrong. It wasn't about race, it was about state's rights. Harry Truman wanted to be a dictator just like Saddam Hussein" (quoted in Klinkner and Smith 1999: 223).

presidential candidate, Strom Thurmond. The senator left the Democratic Party and switched his affiliation to the Republicans in September 1964.

In a move that would be duplicated and refined in many subsequent elections, Goldwater did not appeal openly for the segregationist vote, but he made it clear through a variety of code words and indirect references that he was the candidate of racial conservatives and outright racists. For example, in 1960 Goldwater wrote that: "It is wise and just for Negro children to attend the same schools as whites, [but] the federal Constitution does *not* require the States to maintain racially mixed schools. Despite the recent holding of the Supreme Court, I am firmly convinced—not only that integrated schools are not required—but that the Constitution does not permit any interference whatsoever by the federal government in the field of education" (quoted in Edsall and Edsall 1991: 40–41). As planned, this sentiment, although carefully withholding support for segregation in principle, reassured White supremacists throughout the South (and elsewhere) that segregation would be defended. Evidence for the success of Operation Dixie was revealed by columnist Robert Novak who, after attending the 1963 convention of Young Republicans in San Francisco, reported that there was "no doubt [the] unabashed hostility toward the Negro rights movement was fully shared by the overwhelming majority of the convention delegates. In the cocktail lounges at the Sheraton-Palace, delegates from North and South talked with a single voice on the race question ... For the Young Republicans at San Francisco, their party was now a White Man's Party" (quoted in Edsall and Edsall 1991: 43).

Goldwater made additional efforts to court the vote of racially intolerant Whites by strongly opposing the landmark 1964 Civil Rights Act and by drastically diluting the 1964 Republican platform on civil rights. He would go on appealing for the White segregationist vote through indirect racial appeals that involved the use of code words such as "states' rights," the same slogan used by the Dixiecrat Party in 1948, as well as appeals for "law and order" (Beckett 1997; Carmines and Stimson 1989; Kinder and Sanders 1996; Mendelberg 2001). Further, as O'Reilly (1995) reports, Goldwater's running mate, "William E. Miller of New York even welcomed a Ku Klux Klan endorsement, saying 'Senator Goldwater and I will accept the support of any American citizen who believes in us, our platform and our posture.'"[7] Although he lost the election to Lyndon Johnson in a landslide, Goldwater won the deep South states of Mississippi, Alabama, Georgia, South Carolina, and Louisiana. Apart from Louisiana, which voted for Republican presidential candidate Dwight Eisenhower in 1956, none of these states had voted for the Republican presidential ticket since the end of Reconstruction. With the notable exception of 1976 and the election of Jimmy Carter, most of the eleven

---

[7] After the intervention of both Eisenhower and Nixon, Goldwater eventually repudiated the endorsement of the Klan. Additionally, in the latter stages of the campaign both Goldwater and Johnson agreed, after a meeting in the White House, to "keep race out of the campaign" (O'Reilly 1995: 251). In fact, Goldwater later refused to permit his aides to publicize a campaign film using footage of Black rioters as a means to criticize the Johnson administration.

former Confederate states—or, more accurately, White citizens within these states—have remained reliably Republican since 1968.

Ironically, it was President Lyndon B. Johnson, who represented Texas in the U.S. House and Senate before ascending to the presidency, who would champion the strongest civil rights legislation since the end of the Civil War. Johnson's support for the 1964 Civil Rights Act was crucial to its passage as the still powerful southern wing of the Democratic Party worked tirelessly to defeat the bill. In the end, Johnson succeeded through a combination of legislative skill and the clever effort to link the bill to the recently assassinated President John F. Kennedy. In his first speech to the nation following the assassination, Johnson said, "no memorial oration or eulogy could more eloquently honor President Kennedy's memory than the earliest possible passage of the civil rights bill for which he fought so long ... There could be no greater source of strength to this Nation both at home and abroad" (quoted in Klinkner and Smith 1999: 272–273). As a result of both Goldwater and Johnson's appeals Black voters lined up almost unanimously behind the new president, and with slight variations across election cycles, every subsequent Democratic presidential candidate up to and including Joseph Biden.

Racial Appeals in the Post-Civil Rights Era

Barry Goldwater's efforts to appeal to Southern Whites may have failed as a strategy to win the 1964 presidential election, but it would provide a roadmap for subsequent GOP presidential candidates. Richard Nixon picked up where his fellow Republican left off in the development of his 1968 campaign for president. Nixon had previously served as a member of the U.S. House of Representatives and a U.S. senator from California from the mid-1940s until the early 1950s. When Dwight Eisenhower ran for president in 1952, Nixon served as his vice presidential running mate, and subsequently served two terms as vice president. Throughout his political career, Nixon developed a reputation as a moderate on racial issues. However, when he ran for president in 1960, then-Senator John F. Kennedy (D-Massachusetts) won the majority of the Black vote and the election. Nixon faced another electoral defeat when he ran for governor in his home state of California in 1962.

By the time that Nixon ran for president again in 1968 he had likely absorbed the lessons from his previous losses and was therefore more inclined to adopt the novel strategy of the 1964 Goldwater campaign. In 1968, Nixon ran on a platform of "states' rights." Moreover, Nixon's staff developed a campaign ad attacking the Democrats for being soft on "law and order" in the wake of widespread civil disorder following the assassination of Martin Luther King Jr. Upon reviewing the ad, Nixon reportedly said that it "hits it right on the nose. It's all about law and order and the damn Negro–Puerto Rican groups out there" (Klinkner and Smith 1999: 292). Clearly, the racial subtext of these appeals was not lost on Nixon.[8]

---

[8] Although Nixon did not adopt the relatively crude race-baiting tactics of the 1948 Dixiecrat campaign, or even the pro-segregationist appeals of George Wallace, he may have personally subscribed to the tenets of

The branding of the GOP as the party of racial conservatism did not happen by accident. It was a calculated decision by numerous entrepreneurial political figures in the Republican Party that spanned multiple election cycles. This explicit strategy was described in some detail in a 1970 *New York Times* interview with Kevin Phillips, a top political strategist for President Richard Nixon. Phillips indicated in the article that, "from now on, the Republicans are never going to get more than 10 to 20 percent of the Negro vote and they don't need any more than that ... but Republicans would be short-sighted if they weakened enforcement of the Voting Rights Act. *The more Negroes who register as Democrats in the South, the sooner the Negrophobe whites will quit the Democrats and become Republicans.* That's where the votes are" (Boyd 1970; italics added).

A 2016 article published in *Harper's Magazine* provides additional evidence on this point (Baum 2016). In the article, drawn from a 1994 interview, former Nixon aide John Ehrlichman made it clear that candidate Nixon—and later President Nixon—used his tough anti-crime stance as a thinly veiled effort to appeal to anti-Black and anti-left sentiments in the overwhelmingly White and racially conservative electorate of 1968:

The Nixon campaign in 1968, and the Nixon White House after that, had two enemies: the anti-war left and black people. You understand what I'm saying? We knew we couldn't make it illegal to be either against the [Vietnam] war or black [sic], but by getting the public to associate the hippies with marijuana and blacks with heroin, and then criminalizing both heavily, we could disrupt those communities. We could arrest their leaders, raid their homes, break up their meetings, and vilify them night after night on the evening news. Did we know we were lying about drugs? Of course we did.[9]

Lee Atwater, the Republican political strategist and campaign manager for President George Herbert Walker Bush, used even blunter language to make this point. In a 1981 interview he provided the following explanation for the racial appeals adopted by the GOP in the post-Civil Rights era. "You start out in 1954 by saying [N-word, N-word, N-word]. By 1968 you can't say [N-word]—that hurts you. Backfires. So, you say stuff like forced busing, states' rights and all that stuff. You're getting so abstract now [that] you're talking about cutting taxes, and all these things you're talking about are totally economic things and a byproduct of them is [that] blacks get hurt worse than whites" (Herbert 2005). A significant number of journalists, historians, and political scientists have also concluded that the GOP has consciously sought to recruit the support of racially intolerant Whites

---

old-fashioned racism. According to his former presidential aide John Ehrlichman, Nixon opposed social welfare policies directed at Blacks in part because he believed "blacks were genetically inferior to whites" (quoted in Klinkner and Smith 1999: 293).

[9] In a response to these comments, drawn from a 1994 interview but not published until twenty-two years later, journalist German Lopez characterized Ehrlichman's controversial claims as an oversimplification (Lopez 2016). Still, Lopez also acknowledged that, "There's no doubt that Nixon was racist, and historians told me that race could have played a role in Nixon's drug war" (see at: www.vox.com/2016/3/29/11325750/nixon-war-on-drugs).

since the early 1960s by adopting racially conservative issue positions (Edsall and Edsall 1991; Hutchings and Valentino 2004; Klinkner and Smith 1999; Mendelberg 2001; O'Reilly 1995; Valentino and Sears 2005).

DIGGING DEEPER: REAGAN, BUSH, AND THE POLITICS OF RACE

Although Goldwater and Nixon may have pioneered the "Southern Strategy," or the act of appealing to racially intolerant White voters in the South without appearing to do so, their successors in the Republican Party would continue the practice for the next several decades. Particularly effective in this regard were Ronald Reagan and George H. W. Bush. As with Nixon—and former Democratic presidents Truman and Johnson—Reagan privately endorsed some of the crudest forms of racial intolerance. In 2019, audio tapes from the Nixon White House were released revealing that in 1971 then-Governor Reagan (R-California) called the president to complain about a vote in the United Nations recognizing the People's Republic of China as the sole legitimate representative of the Chinese people. Reagan was furious, and later called President Nixon to make the following comment: "To see those monkeys from those African countries, damn them, they're still uncomfortable wearing shoes!" The president simply laughed at Reagan's outburst (Mervosh and Chokshi 2019).

On the campaign trail during the 1980 presidential campaign, Reagan was more subtle. In early August, the presidential candidate visited the Neshoba County fair in Philadelphia, Mississippi, for an overwhelmingly White campaign rally. There he declared that "I believe in states' rights." Although subtle, the subtext of this statement seemed hard to miss and was swiftly criticized by Reagan's opponent, President Jimmy Carter (Schram 1980). In addition to "states' rights" being a slogan long used by segregationists, Philadelphia, Mississippi, was also the site of the infamous 1964 murder of civil rights activists, James Chaney, Andrew Goodman, and Michael Schwerner. Several days before the rally in Philadelphia, Reagan had been endorsed by the Ku Klux Klan, although he later repudiated their support.

Reagan's vice president and successor in the White House, George H. W. Bush, also employed racial appeals to gain an electoral advantage. During the 1988 presidential contest, the Bush campaign sought to discredit his Democratic opponent, Massachusetts governor Michael Dukakis by linking him to that state's prison furlough program. This program, which was implemented before Dukakis took office, allowed convicted felons to have weekend passes outside the state prison. During one such furlough, an African American felon named William Horton— although more ominously dubbed "Willie Horton" in campaign ads—kidnapped a young White couple, stabbing the man and raping the woman. The Bush campaign, and ostensibly "independent" organizations affiliated with the Republican candidate, ran television ads linking Horton, and his unmistakably Black image, to Dukakis in the minds of the voters. Bush's campaign manager, Lee Atwater, proclaimed that "If I can make Willie Horton a household name, we'll win the election" (Baker 2018).

Our emphasis here on the ways that Republicans sought to court the support of racially conservative or racially intolerant Whites should not leave the reader with the impression that Democrats were above making racial appeals of this sort. They were not. For example, when Jimmy Carter sought the Democratic nomination for president in 1976, he reassured an audience in South Bend, Indiana, that he would not seek to dismantle all-White neighborhoods: "I'm not going to use the Federal Government's authority deliberately to circumvent the natural inclination of people to live in ethnically homogeneous neighborhoods" (Lydon 1976).[10] This effort to appeal to a segment of the White Democratic electorate was not unique to Carter. In the aftermath of the Civil Rights Movement, Democratic candidates in general have sought to distance themselves from Black constituencies and Black leaders in order to court a racially conservative White electorate. Perhaps the most adroit practitioner of this strategy was Bill Clinton, the "first Black president."[11] Throughout the primary and general election period of 1992, Clinton sent out a number of signals designed to undermine the view that he was a traditional, racially liberal Democrat. For example, Clinton, followed by a television camera crew, golfed at an all-White Arkansas country club, was photographed alongside Georgia Senator Sam Nunn at the Stone Mountain Correctional facility with a group of mostly Black prisoners conspicuously on display in the background, and personally oversaw the execution of Ricky Ray Rector, a mentally challenged African American on death row in Arkansas (O'Reilly 1995). The most prominent example of Clinton employing this strategy was his calculated denunciation of Reverend Jesse Jackson for inviting rap artist Sister Souljah to a meeting of his organization after she was accused of making anti-White remarks following the civil disturbances in Los Angeles (Page 1992). Clinton's highly publicized confrontation with Jackson over this matter was viewed by many political commentators as a cynical effort to demonstrate to Whites that he was not beholden to Black voters (O'Reilly 1995).

Obama, Trump, and Racial Appeals in the Twenty-First Century

As indicated earlier in this chapter, contemporary expressions of racial priming typically rely on *implicit* rather than *explicit* appeals. This is because societal norms and expectations have evolved since the 1960s such that the racially intolerant appeals of the recent past would now be rejected across the political spectrum. In short, the norm of racial equality has been embraced almost universally among present-day voters. Although this perspective has gone unchallenged for many years, more recent campaigns and subsequent scholarship has called this

---

[10] Two days later, Carter apologized for using the phrase "ethnic purity," but he maintained his position against using federal power to implement residential integration.

[11] Pulitzer prize-winning novelist Toni Morrison famously described Clinton as "the first Black president" in writing about the trials and tribulations of his 1998 impeachment.

Photo 8.3 Democratic presidential candidate Bill Clinton may have been one of the most astute practitioners of playing both sides of the race question. While here he joins hands with Revd. Jesse Jackson in Atlanta, in September, 1992, Jackson told reporters that he and Clinton still had differences but would soon meet to try and work them out.
Source: © Luke Frazza/Staff/AFP/Getty Images.

assumption into question (Valentino, Neuner, and Vandenbroek 2018). There are at least two reasons to reassess the unique power of implicit racial appeals. The first is that this literature has not considered that the implicit–explicit distinction might not hold for Black political candidates. The second reason is that the norm of racial equality may not be as uncontested as researchers previously thought. The presidential campaigns of Barack Obama and Donald Trump were the precipitating factors that prompted scholars to reconsider the limits of racial priming.

Racial Appeals by Black Political Candidates

The initial research on the use of racial appeals by Black candidates focused on a concept known as "deracialization." According to this theory, both White and Black Democratic candidates running in majority-White jurisdictions should avoid discussions of race or racial issues, and associations with African American constituencies, in order to diminish the influence that anti-Black stereotypes might have on their electoral prospects (Hamilton 1977; McCormick and Jones 1993; Orey and Ricks 2007; Williams 1990). Although this may be prudent advice for White Democrats, Black candidates may find that avoiding race is insufficient. After all, many White voters already assume that Black candidates will adopt liberal

Photo 8.4 Democratic presidential hopeful Senator Barack Obama participates in a church service before giving a speech about fatherhood at the Apostolic Church of God on June 15, 2008, in Chicago, IL. Obama spoke about the importance of fathers being involved in the raising of their children, something journalist Ta-Nehisi Coates claimed Obama did often, labelling him "the scold of 'black America'" in a 2013 journal article.
Source: © David Banks/Stringer/Getty Images News/Getty Images.

positions on matters of race or social welfare spending no matter what they say on the campaign trail. As a result, Black candidates are often incentivized to use more explicit racial appeals in order to court the support of a racially moderate-to-conservative White electorate. And because these candidates are also racial minorities, they have more leeway to push the boundaries of what is considered acceptable racial rhetoric in contemporary politics (Stephens-Dougan 2020). Barack Obama represents the quintessential example of this phenomenon.

During the 2008 campaign and throughout his presidency Barack Obama relied on implicit and explicit racial appeals in order to attract the support of racially conservative Whites. One strategy employed frequently by Obama was to criticize Black audiences for their presumed moral failings. A prominent early example involves Obama's June 2008 address before a predominantly Black congregation on Father's Day. The primary theme of this speech—delivered shortly after Obama had received enough delegates to ensure his position as the Democratic presidential nominee—was to criticize African American fathers (Bosman 2008). This practice of pointing out the shortcomings of Blacks became so common for Obama that journalist Ta-Nehisi Coates described him in a 2013 article as "the scold of 'black America'" (Coates 2013). Coates also pointed to the following from Obama's address to the graduating class of Morehouse College in 2013:

We know that too many young men in our community continue to make bad choices. Growing up, I made a few myself. And I have to confess, that sometimes I wrote off my own failings as just another example of the world trying to keep a black man down. But one of the things you've learned over the last four years is that there's no longer any room for excuses ... We've got no time for excuses—not because the bitter legacies of slavery and discrimination have vanished entirely; they haven't. Not because racism and discrimination no longer exist; that's still out there. It's just that, in today's hyper-connected, hyper-competitive world ... nobody is going to give you anything you haven't earned. And whatever hardships you may experience because of your race, they pale in comparison to the hardships previous generations endured—and overcame.

As Coates notes in this article, "I would have a hard time imagining the president telling the women of Barnard [an all-women's college] that 'there's no longer any room for any excuses'—as though they were in the business of making them." In response to a similar speech given before the Congressional Black Caucus (CBC) in 2011, Representative Maxine Waters, a longstanding CBC member, wondered why the president did not provide similar commentary to Hispanic audiences. The implication here is that Obama was more inclined to deliver speeches on personal responsibility to Black audiences than to other parts of the Democratic electoral coalition, such as Hispanics. When political scientist LaFleur Stephens-Dougan tested this notion by examining Obama speeches given to predominantly Black crowds, such as the NAACP, compared with primarily Hispanic audiences, such as the National Council of La Raza, she found some support for Representative Waters' intuition (Stephens-Dougan 2020). For example, as shown in Table 8.1,

Table 8.1 **The Prevalence of Personal Responsibility Rhetoric and Aspirational Rhetoric in Obama's Speeches to Ethnically Different Audiences, 2007–2012**

	Blacks vs. Whites	Blacks vs. Latinos
Personal Responsibility Rhetoric		
Responsibility	1.65 vs. 1.17**	1.65 vs. 1.28
Work	6.56 vs. 5.37**	0.34 vs. 0.17
Culture	0.22 vs. 0.28	0.22 vs. 0.35
Father	1.37 vs. 0.37***	1.37 vs. 0.64**
Excuses	0.34 vs. 0.17	0.34 vs. 0.35
Aspirational Rhetoric		
Hope	1.93 vs. 1.65	1.93 vs. 1.14*
Change	2.87 vs. 3.89	2.87 vs. 3.14

Note: Cell entries indicate the number of times a given word was used on average by type of audience. * p < .10, ** p < .05, ** *p < .01 for a z-test of proportions.
Source: Taken from Stephens-Dougan (2020).

Obama was more likely to talk about fathers when addressing Black audiences as opposed to either predominantly Latino or White audiences. He was also more likely to emphasize themes of personal responsibility and work with Black audiences, although this difference was only statistically significant when compared with Whites rather than Latinos.

In addition to criticizing the African American community in order, presumably, to demonstrate his independence from them, Obama also adopted other strategies to distance himself from this constituency. Adopting a strategy that some political scientists have labeled "Whitewashing," Obama deemphasized his association with Blacks in two ways during the 2008 presidential campaign (Hutchings et al. 2020). First, he systematically underemphasized Blacks—and overemphasized Whites—in his political ads. Although Blacks made up 13 percent of the voters in 2008, and a much larger fraction of Obama's supporters, they represented only 3 percent of the racially identifiable people in a randomly selected subset of his ads. Whites, on the other hand, were 74 percent of the voters in 2008 yet represented 93 percent of the individuals in Obama's general election campaign ads. The racial diversity in McCain's 2008 ads was much closer to approximating the actual percentage of Blacks and Whites in the population (see Figure 8.3).

The second aspect of Obama's Whitewashing campaign was to highlight his White mother and grandparents in his speeches and general election ad campaign (Hutchings et al. 2020). This point is best illustrated with his "Country I Love" ad, which was the first ad the candidate ran during the 2008 general election.[12] At first glance, this ad simply provided biographical information about the candidate's upbringing. Upon further inspection, however, the ad, which features almost no non-White individuals beyond Obama himself, appears to shrewdly associate the candidate with his mother, maternal grandparents, and "the values [they taught him] straight from the Kansas heartland where they grew up." In fact, Obama was born and raised in Hawaii and spent part of his formative years in Indonesia. Neither Hawaii nor Indonesia is mentioned in this biographical ad. Obama's African American wife, Michelle, and his two young daughters are also not present or mentioned in the ad.

Did the racial imagery in the "Country I Love" ad really influence how voters perceived candidate Obama? Hutchings and his colleagues sought to answer this question by randomly assigning their study participants to view either the authentic "Country I Love" ad (the "White Family/White Supporters ad") or an alternative version (the "Race Neutral ad") where images of the candidate's White supporters as well as his White mother and grandparents are replaced with singular images of Obama at various stages of his life. In keeping with their expectations, they found that Republican subjects assigned to view the authentic version of the ad were much *less* likely than those viewing the altered version to believe that Obama was born outside the United States or that he was secretly a Muslim (see Figure 8.4). This ad

---

[12] See at: www.c-span.org/video/?206097-1/obama-campaign-ad.

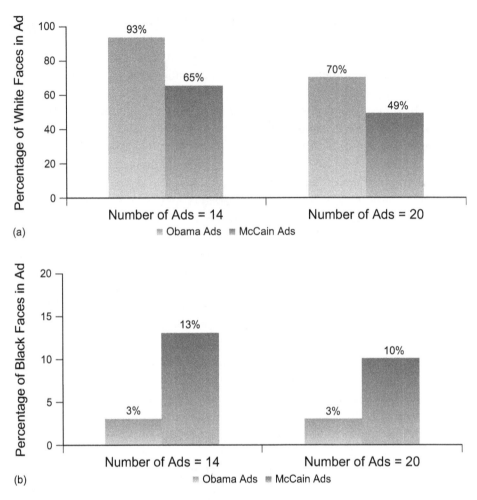

Figure 8.3   (a) Percentage of Whites in Selected 2008 Campaign Ads by Candidate; (b) Percentage of Blacks in Selected 2008 Campaign Ads by Candidate

Twenty ads were analyzed for each candidate, but six of these ads had no other people in them other than the presidential candidate or his vice presidential running mate. The two bars on the left side of the figure represent the ads with individuals other than the candidate(s). The two bars on the right side of the figure include all cases.

Source: Hutchings et al. (2020).

campaign, and similar efforts by Obama throughout his political career, helps to explain why most Whites have consistently described him as "biracial" rather than "Black" (Citrin, Levy, and Van Houweling 2014). Moreover, recent work by Stephens-Dougan (2020) has also shown that even fictitious Black candidates can employ anti-Black racial appeals without generating the kind of backlash that would emerge if the same rhetoric were used by either White Democrats or White Republicans.

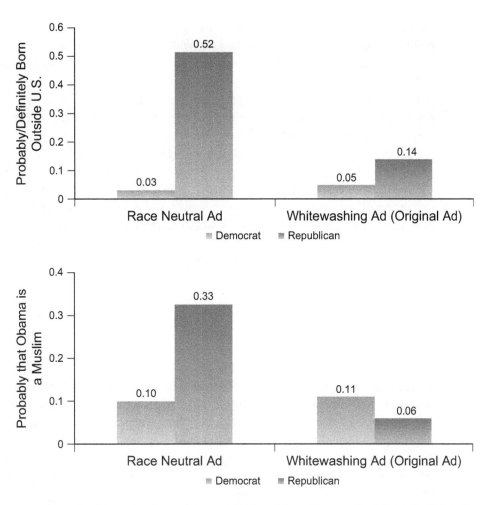

Figure 8.4   (a) Effects of Whitewashing and Partisanship on Support for "Birther"; (b) Muslim Rumors about Obama

Here the "White Family/White Supporters Ad" is the undoctored "Country I Love Ad" run in fall 2008 by the Obama campaign. The "Race Neutral" ad contains the identical narration, but removes the images of all individuals other than Obama.

Source: Hutchings et al. (2020).

Donald Trump and the Reemergence of Explicit Racial Appeals

In launching his campaign for the Republican nomination for president, Donald Trump made it clear that he was not going to play by the unspoken rules that had governed American politics since the 1970s. Explicit racial appeals were considered fair game. This was clear when Trump announced his candidacy in June 2015. Immigration was his signature issue and, in order to dispel any ambiguity about his position, he specifically denounced undocumented immigration from Mexico because, according to Trump, these individuals were drug dealers, criminals, and rapists. Shortly after making this statement the businessman and reality-television star pledged to build a wall on the U.S. border with Mexico in order to deter immigration. Trump promised that Mexico would pay for this wall.

Mexican immigrants were not the only targets of Trump's attack. He also singled out Muslims during the 2015–2016 presidential campaign. Specifically, Trump's campaign put out a press release in December 2015, "... calling for a total and complete shutdown of Muslims entering the United States until our country's representatives can figure out what's going on" (Diamond 2015). Unlike traditional politicians, who might have simply proposed a ban on travelers coming from countries with ties to suspected terrorist organizations—and effectively achieved the same outcome without being explicitly discriminatory—the Trump campaign apparently concluded that a more direct approach would be more politically beneficial.

The list of racially insensitive comments made by Donald Trump before he ran for political office, during the 2015–2016 campaign, and during his presidential administration is long and well documented. Some of the more prominent examples involve Trump questioning the impartiality of a judge because of his Mexican American heritage, describing undocumented Mexican immigrants as "animals" who would "pour into and infest our country," and describing White nationalists and neo-Confederate sympathizers at an infamous Charlottesville, Virginia, rally as "very fine people" (Leonhardt and Philbrick 2018). If Trump was seeking to court the support of the relatively fringe group of White nationalists and White supremacists, then his efforts were not in vain (Holley and Larimer 2016). Indeed, the official newspaper of the Ku Klux Klan endorsed Trump for president in 2016—although his campaign repudiated this support, as did Republican presidential candidates Barry Goldwater and Ronald Reagan when the Klan endorsed their campaigns (Holley 2016). More importantly, however, Trump's implicit and explicit racial appeals helped to solidify his support in 2016 among the much larger population of Whites who reject supremacist ideology, but nevertheless score high on measures of White identity and White racial group consciousness (Jardina 2019). Whites who fall into these categories were much more likely to support Trump over his rivals in the Republican primaries (Jardina 2019) (see Figure 8.5).

Are Explicit Racial Appeals Acceptable in the Twenty-First Century?

Donald Trump pushed the boundaries of acceptable racial discourse in the modern era as both presidential hopeful and as president. As a result, many scholars and political observers have wondered whether explicit racial appeals are now acceptable again in the current polarized political environment.

Do efforts to publicly condemn a campaign appeal for its racially implicit undertones render the appeal ineffective? One study, focusing on fictitious candidates, finds that this strategy only works for White candidates who have been targeted by such ads, but that for comparable Black candidates such a response is ineffective (Tokeshi and Mendelberg 2015). Another study examines this question by focusing on a fictitious political ad attributed to the 2016 Trump campaign (Banks and Hicks 2018). In an ad narrated by Trump where the candidate criticizes

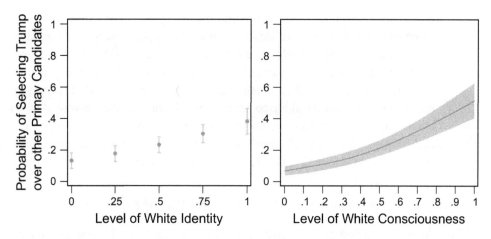

Figure 8.5 The Probability of Choosing Trump over Other Republican Primary Candidates by Levels of White Identity and White Consciousness

In these graphs, points and solid line represent the predicted probability of choosing Trump over other Republican primary candidates. The capped lines and shaded region represent the 95% confidence intervals. (White identity is measured with a single item asking how important their identity as a White person is to them. White consciousness is composed of a three-item scale including White identity importance, and two additional questions asking whether Whites should work together to change laws unfavorable to their racial group and whether Whites lose out on employment opportunities because jobs are instead given to minorities.).

Source: 2016 ANES Pilot study; estimates from full models appear in Jardina (2019: app. 8F).

a perceived crime wave in major American cities, the images in the ad show various acts of criminality committed by Black men. In keeping with the common definition of an implicit racial appeal, Trump makes no verbal reference to race in this fictitious ad. The study participants are then provided with one of four (they are randomly assigned) critiques of the ad charging it with being a shameful example of "race baiting," with two coming from prominent Republicans and two from prominent Democrats. If the expectations of the theory of racial priming are correct, then accusing an implicit racial appeal of being racially insensitive should undercut its persuasive power, even among racially conservative Whites. This is not what Banks and Hicks found. Although exposure to the criticism did reduce support among racial liberals it had no effect on racial conservatives.

The studies discussed thus far have examined whether accusing an implicit appeal of having racial undertones will render the appeal ineffective. An emerging body of research suggests that this may not be the case. But, what about *explicit* racial appeals? Are contemporary voters turned off when politicians, or their supporters, use explicit racial nouns and invoke historical stereotypes to criticize racial minorities? In a series of experimental studies, political scientists have also found that this is not the case (Valentino, Neuner, and Vandenbroek 2018). In one study, the explicit appeal involves a U.S. House candidate's opposition to the Affordable Care Act ("Obamacare") as "a giveback to African American voters." Another, more overtly offensive version of this appeal, attributes negative comments about

Blacks to supporters of this candidate including one where supporters use the N-word to describe Blacks. In this version of the appeal, the supporters also express opposition to the Affordable Care Act for Blacks because "many of these people are criminals, drug addicts, and have bad credit, so why should they get free healthcare from us?" Across four different studies, these researchers find that racially conservative Whites are just as likely to support the House candidate who relies upon an explicit appeal—for example, using terms such as "Black" rather than "inner city" and "White" rather than "suburban"—as when implicit appeals are used. In short, they find no evidence that there is a penalty for using racially explicit rhetoric.

Unanswered Questions Regarding the Use of Explicit Racial Appeals

An emerging consensus regarding the use of explicit racial appeals on the campaign trail suggests that the voters may not universally reject them, as scholars previously believed. Still if this is true, then it begs an obvious question: why aren't explicit racial appeals used as frequently today as they were throughout the nineteenth and much of the twentieth centuries? As indicated earlier in this chapter, in the late 1860s President Andrew Johnson openly referred to Blacks as "an inferior race," and as late as 1946 Mississippi Senator Theodore Bilbo described Whites as the superior race and publicly called for White men to violently prevent Blacks—although he referred to them by using the N-word—from voting. In 1948, South Carolina Senator Strom Thurmond unapologetically called for Blacks to be denied access to public accommodations, and he ran for president of the United States on this specific platform. In this final section we offer a tentative explanation for why it is unimaginable that politicians today would publicly support the notion of inferior and superior races, and openly endorse segregation in principle.

Perhaps more than any modern politician, Donald Trump has pushed the boundaries of acceptable racial rhetoric in American politics. For example, in addition to characterizing undocumented Mexican immigrants as drug dealers and rapists, he has also openly referred to them as "animals" (Davis 2018). What Donald Trump has *not* done, however, is use such sweeping and inflammatory language to describe domestic racial minority groups. Certainly, President Trump has used coarse and even offensive language against political opponents, perhaps especially if they are women or members of underrepresented minority groups. For example, he has questioned the intelligence of African American congresswoman Maxine Waters, and urged four Democratic congresswomen of Puerto Rican, Palestinian, and African heritage to "go back" to their own countries—as if they are somehow illegitimate Americans (Cummings 2018; Rogers and Fandos 2019). Still, this language targets individuals, perhaps because they are minority group members, but nevertheless avoids targeting the groups themselves. Thus, unlike with unauthorized immigrants, Trump has avoided making global unflattering comments about domestic minority groups in the abstract.

In his private comments, President Trump has not always been so careful to avoid criticizing entire (domestic) racial or ethnic groups. In a meeting with a bipartisan group of senators discussing the issue of immigration in 2018, President Trump reportedly referred to Haiti, El Salvador, and African nations as "shithole nations," and wondered aloud why the United States would want more immigrants from these countries (Vitali, Hunt, and Thorp 2018). According to reports, the president also wondered why more immigrants weren't being admitted "from places like Norway." Although the comments were widely reported at the time, and confirmed by at least one Democratic senator present for the closed-door meeting, President Trump denied making this statement. This uncharacteristic bashfulness from the president may have been motivated by electoral consider-ations. Unlike undocumented immigrants, or Muslims in foreign countries, African Americans (and Haitian Americans) can vote. Indeed, electoral considerations may also explain why President Andrew Johnson, or Senator Theodore Bilbo, or Senator Strom Thurmond felt undeterred in using explicit racially inflammatory campaign appeals: Blacks were either legally or practically denied access to the ballot box during the time these politicians were expressing their views about superior and inferior races. Additionally, open support for White supremacy in contemporary politics would likely alienate many White voters, especially women and college graduates, potentially causing them to abandon Republican candidates (Hutchings et al. 2004).

Photo 8.5 A demonstrator holds up a banner during the second annual Women's March in New York City, New York, on Saturday, January 20, 2018
Source: © Ira L. Black-Corbis Contributor/Corbis News/Getty Images.

In summary, it would seem that although the norm of racial equality is not as universally embraced as previous research suggested, there are still important constraints on the use of explicit racial appeals that were common into the 1940s. The most important constraint is the fear of an electoral backlash if one is credibly accused of categorically insulting a domestic minority group. This fear is perhaps especially potent when that group represents a significant voting bloc and when a substantial portion of voters outside this constituency are likely to react negatively to a perceived attack on this group. Even if many Americans would be undisturbed by such an attack, politicians may still be reluctant to embrace this strategy if they believe that it would bother enough voters to undermine their electoral ambitions. These concerns do not seem to extend to undocumented immigrants or nondomestic Muslims. As a result, candidates like Donald Trump can organize their campaign around demonizing these groups without fear of electoral repercussions.

Conclusion

This chapter has outlined the indispensable role that a free press plays in maintaining a functioning democracy. The framers of the Constitution recognized that without the free flow of ideas and information provided by the media, the voters would be unable to hold their elected leaders accountable. However, the impact of the mass media in a democratic society is not always so benign. Social scientists have demonstrated since the end of the Second World War that political leaders can also use the media to influence public opinion. Although direct persuasion is uncommon, political leaders can use the media to influence the public through such processes as agenda-setting, framing, and priming. Additionally, political elites have capitalized on the unpopularity of the news media to foster mistrust in mainstream journalism and to spread unfounded rumors such as questioning the citizenship of former president Barack Obama or disputing the legitimacy of the 2020 presidential contest, even when U.S. election officials have concluded unanimously that this election was the most secure in American history.

Perhaps the central theme of this chapter is that the news media is inevitably a politically neutral instrument. During the Civil Rights Movement, mainstream media exposure of protest activity was used to mobilize national sympathy for the cause of eradicating oppressive Jim Crow laws (see Chapter 15). More recently however, candidates across the partisan divide have used the media to advance their short-term political ambitions—even if this exacerbates racial, ethnic, and religious tensions in society. Ultimately, combating the seductive power of implicit racial appeals will require Americans to acknowledge that both political parties have a history of relying on this campaign strategy. And, therefore criticizing such appeals should not just be an exercise in scoring cheap political points but should instead be a consistent effort to hold Democrats and Republicans to a higher standard.

KEY TERMS

Agenda-setting
Framing
Mass media
Priming
Racial priming

DISCUSSION QUESTIONS

1. What are some of the advantages of presidents and other politicians turning away from traditional media and relying more on new media or soft news media? What are some of the disadvantages?
2. Why do you think that Americans who distrust the media are also likely to endorse negative attitudes about Muslims, immigrants, LGBTQ+ individuals, and other minorities?
3. Do you think the Obama campaign was right to deemphasize appeals to Blacks and other minorities as a way to increase his electoral opportunities? Why or why not?
4. Recent research suggests that some Americans are receptive to, or at least not turned off by, explicit racial appeals on the campaign trail. So, why do you think we haven't seen a return of the explicit campaign rhetoric that was common prior to the Civil Rights Movement?

ANNOTATED SUGGESTED READINGS

See V. Hutchings and Ashley E. Jardina. 2009. "Results from Experimentation: Racial Priming in Political Campaigns," *Annual Review of Political Science* 12: 397–402, for an overview of the classic literature on racial priming.

See LaFleur Stephens-Dougan. 2020. *Race to the Bottom: How Racial Appeals Work in American Politics*. Chicago: University of Chicago Press, for an updated examination of the use of racial appeals in the political arena, across racial and partisan groups.

See Taeku Lee and Christian Hosam. 2020. "Fake News Is Real: The Significance and Sources of Disbelief in Mainstream Media in Trump's America," *Sociological Forum* 35(51): 996–1018, to learn more about the factors driving mistrust of the media.

See Matthew S. Levendusky. 2013. "Why Do Partisan Media Polarize Viewers?" *American Journal of Political Science* 57(3): 611–623, if you would like to learn more about the link between partisan media and political polarization.

CHAPTER REFERENCES

Abramson, Paul R., John H. Aldrich, and David W. Rohde. 2009. *Change and Continuity in the 2008 Elections.* Washington, D.C.: CQ Press.

Adgate, Brad. 2021."Newspapers Have Been Struggling and Then Came the Pandemic," *Forbes*, August 20. www.forbes.com/sites/bradadgate/2021/08/20/newspapers-have-been-struggling-and-then-came-the-pandemic/?sh=1f8259ce12e6.

Astor, Maggie. 2020. "Kamala Harris and the 'Double Bind' of Racism and Sexism." *New York Times*, October 9. www.nytimes.com/2020/10/09/us/politics/kamala-harris-racism-sexism.html.

Baker, Peter. 2018. "Bush Made Willie Horton an Issue in 1988, and the Racial Scars Are Still Fresh," *New York Times*, December 3. www.nytimes.com/2018/12/03/us/politics/bush-willie-horton.html.

Banks, Antoine and Heather M. Hicks. 2018. "The Effectiveness of a Racialized Counter-Strategy," *American Journal of Political Science* 63(2): 305–322.

Barbaro, Michael. 2016. "Donald Trump Clung to 'Birther' Lie for Years, and Still Isn't Apologetic," *New York Times*, September 16. www.nytimes.com/2016/09/17/us/politics/donald-trump-obama-birther.html.

Baum, Dan. 2016. "Legalize it All: How to Win the War on Drugs," *Harper's Magazine*, April. https://archive.harpers.org/2016/04/pdf/HarpersMagazine-2016-04-0085915.pdf.

Baum, Matthew. 2011. "Media, Public Opinion, and Presidential Leadership," In *New Directions in Public Opinion* (ed.) Adam J. Berinsky. New York: Routledge, 258–270.

Beckett, Katherine. 1997. *Making Crime Pay: Law and Order in Contemporary American Politics*. New York: Oxford University Press.

Berinsky, Adam J. and Donald R. Kinder. 2006. "Making Sense of Issues through Media Frames: Understanding the Kosovo Crisis," *Journal of Politics* 68(3): 640–656.

Bosman, Julie. 2008. "Obama Sharply Assails Absent Black Fathers," *New York Times*, June 16. www.nytimes.com/2008/06/16/us/politics/15cnd-obama.html.

Boyd, James. 1970. "Nixon's Southern Strategy: 'It's All in the Charts.'" *New York Times*, May 17. www.nytimes.com/packages/html/books/phillips-southern.pdf.

Bump, Philip. 2020. "Fox Aired Only Part of the House Evidence for Impeachment. Will That Hold for Trump's Defense?" *The Washington Post*, January 27. www.washingtonpost.com/politics/2020/01/27/fox-aired-only-part-house-evidence-impeachment-will-that-hold-trumps-defense.

Carmines, Edward G. and James A. Stimson. 1989. *Issue Evolution: Race and the Transformation of American Politics*. Princeton: Princeton University Press.

Citrin, Jack, Morris Levy, and Robert Van Houweling. 2014. "Americans Fill Out President Obama's Census Form: What Is His Race?" *Social Science Quarterly* 95(4): 1121–1136.

Coates, Ta-Nehisi. 2013. "How the Obama Administration Talks to Black America," *The Atlantic*, May 20. www.theatlantic.com/politics/archive/2013/05/how-the-obama-administration-talks-to-black-america/276015.

Cohen, Bernard. 1963. *The Press and Foreign Policy*. New York: Harcourt.

Cummings, William. 2018. "Trump Slams 'low-IQ' Rep. Maxine Waters Who Called for Harassment of White House Officials," *USA Today*, June 25. www.usatoday.com/story/news/politics/onpolitics/2018/06/25/maxine-waters-trump-exchange/732505002.

Darr, Joshua P., Johanna Dunaway, and Matthew P. Hitt. 2019. "When Newspapers Close, Voters Become More Partisan," *The Conversation*, February 11. https://theconversation.com/when-newspapers-close-voters-become-more-partisan-108416.

Davis, Julie Hirschfeld. 2018. "Trump Calls Unauthorized Immigrants 'Animals' in Rant," *New York Times*, May 2016. www.nytimes.com/2018/05/16/us/politics/trump-undocumented-immigrants-animals.html.

Diamond, Jeremy. 2015. "Donald Trump: Ban All Muslim Travel to the U.S.," *CNN.com*, December 8. www.cnn.com/2015/12/07/politics/donald-trump-muslim-ban-immigration/index.html.

Dray, Philip. 2002. *At The Hands of Persons Unknown: The Lynching of Black America*. New York: Modern Library.

Druckman, James. 2001. "On the Limits of Framing Effects: Who Can Frame?" *Journal of Politics*. 63(4): 1041–1066.

Druckman, James. 2004. "Political Preference Formation: Competition, Deliberation, and the (Ir)relevance of Framing Effects," *American Political Science Review* 98(4): 671–686.

Edsall, Thomas B. and Mary D. Edsall. 1991. *Chain Reaction: The Impact of Race, Rights, and Taxes on American Politics*. New York: Norton.

Farnsworth, Stephen J. and S. Robert Lichter. 2011. *The Nightly News Nightmare: Media Coverage of U.S. Presidential Elections, 1988–2008*. Lanham, MD: Rowman & Littlefield.

Gordon-Reed, Annette. 1998. *Thomas Jefferson and Sally Hemings: An American Controversy*. Charlottesville: University of Virginia Press.

Graber, Doris and Johanna Dunaway. 2017. *Mass Media and American Politics*, 10th ed. Washington, D.C.: CQ Press.

Hamilton, Charles. 1977. "Deracialization: Examination of a Political Strategy," *First World*, March/April, 3–5.

Herbert, Bob. 2005. "Impossible, Ridiculous, Repugnant," *New York Times*, October 6. www.nytimes.com/2005/10/06/opinion/impossible-ridiculous-repugnant.html.

Holley, Peter. 2016. "KKK's Official Newspaper Supports Donald Trump for President," *The Washington Post*, November 2. www.washingtonpost.com/news/post-politics/wp/2016/11/01/the-kkks-official-newspaper-has-endorsed-donald-trump-for-president.

Holley, Peter and Sarah Larimer. 2016. "How America's Dying White Supremacist Movement is Seizing on Donald Trump's Appeal," *The Washington Post*, February 29. www.washingtonpost.com/news/morning-mix/wp/2015/12/21/how-donald-trump-is-breathing-life-into-americas-dying-white-supremacist-movement.

Hsu, Tiffany and Katie Robertson. 2021. "You Can Barely Tell It's the Same Trial in Cable Impeachment Coverage," *New York Times*, February 12 (updated March 11, 2021). www.nytimes.com/2021/02/12/business/media/cnn-fox-news-msnbc-impeachment-trial.html.

Hutchings, Vincent L., Vanessa Cruz Nichols, LaGina Gause, and Spencer Piston. 2020. "Whitewashing: How Obama Used Explicit Racial Cues as a Defense Against Political Rumors," *Political Behavior* 43: 1337–1360.

Hutchings, Vincent L. and Nicholas A. Valentino. 2004. "The Centrality of Race in American Politics," *Annual Review of Political Science* 7: 383–408.

Hutchings, Vincent L., Nicholas A. Valentino, Tasha S. Philpot, and Ismail K. White. 2004. "The Compassion Strategy: Race and the Gender Gap in Campaign 2000," *Public Opinion Quarterly* 68(4): 512–541.

Iyengar, Shanto. 1991. *Is Anyone Responsible? How Television Frames Political Issues*. Chicago: University of Chicago Press.

Iyengar, Shanto and Donald R. Kinder. 1987. *News That Matters*. Chicago: University of Chicago Press.

Kinder, Donald R. and Lynn M. Sanders. 1996. *Divided by Color: Racial Politics and Democratic Ideals*. Chicago: University of Chicago Press.

Klinkner, Philip A. and Rogers Smith. 1999. *The Unsteady March: The Rise and Decline of Racial Equality in America*. Chicago: University of Chicago Press.

Jardina, Ashley E. 2019. *White Identity Politics.* Cambridge: Cambridge University Press.

Jordan, Jacob. 2003. "Thurmond's Bi-racial Daughter Speaks Out," *NBCnews.com*, December 17. www.nbcnews.com/id/3740693/ns/us_news-life/t/thurmonds-biracial-daughter-speaks-out.

Lazarsfeld, Paul, Bernard Berelson, and Helen Gaudet. 1944. *The People's Choice: How the Voter Makes up His Mind in a Presidential Campaign.* New York: Duell, Sloane, & Pearce.

Lee, Taeku and Christian Hosam. 2020. "Fake News is Real: The Significance and Sources of Disbelief in Mainstream Media in Trump's America," *Sociological Forum* 35(51): 996–1018.

Leonhardt, David and Ian Prasad Philbrick. 2018. "Donald Trump's Racism: The Definitive List, Updated," *New York Times*, January 15. www.nytimes.com/interactive/2018/01/15/opinion/leonhardt-trump-racist.html.

Levendusky, Matthew S. 2013. "Why Do Partisan Media Polarize Viewers?" *American Journal of Political Science* 57(3): 611–623.

Lopez, German. 2016. "Was Nixon's War on Drugs a Racially Motivated Crusade? It's a Bit More Complicated," *Vox*, March 29. www.vox.com/2016/3/29/11325750/nixon-war-on-drugs.

Lydon, Christopher. 1976. "Carter Defends All-White Areas," *New York Times*, April 7. www.nytimes.com/1976/04/07/archives/carter-defends-allwhite-areas-says-government-shouldnt-try-to-end.html.

Mak, Tim. 2019. "Senate Report: Russians Used Social Media Mostly to Target Race in 2016," *npr.org*, October 8. www.npr.org/2019/10/08/768319934/senate-report-russians-used-used-social-media-mostly-to-target-race-in-2016.

Manza, Jeff and Clem Brooks. 1999. *Social Cleavages and Political Change: Voter Alignments and U.S. Party Coalitions.* Oxford: Oxford University Press.

McCormick, J.P. II and Charles E. Jones. 1993. "A Model of Racial Crossover," In *Dilemmas of Black Politics* (ed.) Georgia Persons. New York: HarperCollins, 66–84.

Memmott, Mark. 2013. "75 Years ago 'War of the Worlds' Started a Panic. Or Did it?" *npr.org*, October 30. www.npr.org/sections/thetwo-way/2013/10/30/241797346/75-years-ago-war-of-the-worlds-started-a-panic-or-did-it.

Mendelberg, Tali. 2001. *The Race Card.* Princeton: Princeton University Press.

Mervosh, Sarah and Niraj Chokshi. 2019. "Reagan Called Africans 'Monkeys' in Call with Nixon, Tape Reveals," *New York Times*, July 31. www.nytimes.com/2019/07/31/us/politics/ronald-reagan-richard-nixon-racist.html.

Myrdal, Gunnar. [1944] 1996. *An American Dilemma: The Negro Problem and Modern Democracy.* New Brunswick: Transaction (original ed., Harper & Row).

Nelson, Thomas E., Rosalee Clawson, and Zoe M. Oxley. 1997. "Media Framing of a Civil Liberties Conflict and Its Effect on Tolerance," *American Political Science Review* 91(3): 567–583.

Nguyen, Ashley, Kayla Ruble, and Tim Craig. 2020. "Anger Builds in Black Community Over Trump's Claims of Voter Fraud," *The Washington Post*, November 20. www.washingtonpost.com/national/2020/11/20/f0d11954-2b71-11eb-9b14-ad872157ebc9_story.html.

O'Reilly, Kenneth. 1995. *Nixon's Piano: Presidents and Racial Politics from Washington to Clinton.* New York: Free Press.

Orey, Byron D. and Boris E. Ricks. 2007. "A Systematic Analysis of the Deracialization Concept." *Faculty Publications: Political Science.* Paper 24.

Page, Clarence. 1992. "Bill Clinton's Debt to Sister Souljah," *Chicago Tribune*, October 28. www.chicagotribune.com/news/ct-xpm-1992-10-28-9204070622-story.html.

Pettus, Emily Wagster. 2017. "Senator: Capitol Art Should Also Show Black Mississippians," *APnews.com*, November 24 https://apnews.com/558128e7a42b49468e37f200d4763870/Senator:-Capitol-art-should-also-show-black-Mississippians.

Rinke, Eike Mark. 2016. "The Impact of Sound-Bite Journalism on Public Argument," *Journal of Communication* 66: 625–645.

Rogers, Katie and Nicholas Fandos. 2019. "Trump Tells Congresswomen to 'Go Back' to the Countries They Came from," *New York Times*, July 14. www.nytimes.com/2019/07/14/us/politics/trump-twitter-squad-congress.html.

Rothman, Lily. 2016. "This Is How the Whole Birther Thing Actually Started." *TIME.com.*, September 16. https://time.com/4496792/birther-rumor-started.

Schickler, Eric. 2016. *Racial Realignment.* Princeton: Princeton University Press.

Schram, Martin. 1980. "Carter Says Reagan Injects Racism," *The Washington Post*, September 17. www.washingtonpost.com/archive/politics/1980/09/17/carter-says-reagan-injects-racism/e7ccb250-106a-47ef-ae67-2826ba938acc.

Smith, Ben. 2020. "Record Ratings and Record Chaos on Cable News," *New York Times*, May 31. www.nytimes.com/2020/05/31/business/media/cable-news-fox-msnbc-cnn.html.

Smith, Tom W., Michael Davern, Jeremy Freese, and Stephen Morgan. 2018. General Social Surveys, 1972–2018 (machine-readable data file). Sponsored by National Science Foundation. NORC (ed.) Chicago: NORC (NORC at the University of Chicago, producer and distributor). Data accessed from the GSS Data Explorer website at: gssdataexplorer.norc.org.

Stephens-Dougan, LaFleur. 2020. *Race to the Bottom: How Racial Appeals Work in American Politics.* Chicago: University of Chicago Press.

Tokeshi, Matthew and Tali Mendelberg. 2015. "Countering Implicit Appeals: Which Strategies Work?" *Political Communication* 32: 648–672.

Trump, Donald J. 2015. "Here's Donald Trump's Presidential Announcement Speech," *TIME.com*, June 16. https://time.com/3923128/donald-trump-announcement-speech.

Valentino, Nicholas A., Vincent L. Hutchings, and Ismail White. 2002. "Cues That Matter: How Political Ads Prime Racial Attitudes During Campaigns," *American Political Science Review* 96(1): 75–90.

Valentino, Nicholas A., Fabian G. Neuner, and L. Matthew Vandenbroek. 2018. "The Changing Norms of Racial Political Rhetoric and the End of Racial Priming," *Journal of Politics* 80(3): 757–771.

Valentino, Nicholas A. and David O. Sears. 2005. "Old Times There Are Not Forgotten: Race and Partisan Realignment in the Contemporary South," *American Journal of Political Science* 49: 672–688.

Vitali, Ali, Kasie Hunt, and Frank Thorp V. 2018. "Trump Referred to Haiti and African Nations as 'Shithole' Nations," *NBCnews.com*, January 12. www.nbcnews.com/politics/white-house/trump-referred-haiti-african-countries-shithole-nations-n836946.

Williams, Linda F. 1990. "White/Black Perceptions of the Electability of Black Political Candidates," *National Political Science Review* 2: 45–64.

Zaller, John. 1992. *The Nature and Origins of Mass Opinion.* Cambridge: Cambridge University Press.

9   Race and Elections

Love him or hate him, Donald J. Trump has dominated the nation's attention for years. From his campaign for president in 2016 to his refusal to accept the results of the 2020 contest and his efforts to regain the presidency, almost every word he has uttered and every Tweet he has written has been broadcast and dissected by both the masses and the media. Through all of this, it is easy to forget that almost no one expected Donald Trump to win the presidency and to preoccupy the nation for so many years.

Less than a year before the 2016 election, few doubted that Donald Trump would lose. He had none of the credentials typically required for elevation to the nation's highest office: he had never held public office of any kind; he had exactly zero experience in dealing with national security issues; and his greatest claim to fame was as a television celebrity, but, then, he had done and said so much that seemingly would disqualify him from office. He had been caught on tape boasting about "grab[bing women] by the pussy;" also, in an exciting but checkered and uneven career in business he had filed for chapter 11 bankruptcy six times; and in multiple years he had paid no income taxes despite garnering earnings that were unimaginable to most Americans. Moreover, Donald Trump faced a deep bench of attractive and qualified opponents. In the Republican primary, he started at the very bottom of a field that included candidates with sterling resumes, dynastic family names, solid conservative records, and appealing moderate positions. In the general election, he faced perhaps the most qualified presidential nominee in the nation's history. And to top it all off, polls on the eve of the election were clear—Hillary Clinton was going to win. Yet we all now know that the polls were wrong and that Donald J. Trump ultimately won the election and assumed the presidency.

Then, four years later something almost as surprising happened. Despite his assertions to the contrary, Trump lost. He lost even though incumbent presidents almost always win their bids for a second term. Since the office of the president was established in 1789, only ten occupants of the White house have failed to win their reelection bids. What makes Trump's defeat even more remarkable is that he presided over a robust economy for most of his presidency—a pattern that usually bodes well for the incumbent.

Photo 9.1 Republican presidential nominee Donald Trump and Democratic presidential nominee Hillary Clinton participate in the first of four debates planned for the 2016 election. This one was held at Hofstra University, New York, on September 26, 2016.
Source: Photo Rick Wilking © Pool/Getty Images News/Getty Images.

How did all of this happen? Why, against all odds, did Donald Trump become president? And then why, four years later, did he lose his reelection bid to Joe Biden?

Two narratives have come to dominate our understanding of Trump's political career. One is about class and the other is about race. The class-based story argues that economic decline in working-class communities was the main factor driving support for Trump. Globalization, free trade, and the demise of manufacturing had left behind whole communities of poor and working-class Americans who were ripe for Donald Trump's populist economic message. The oft-repeated story is that Trump's guarantees to bring back manufacturing, end unfair trade deals, and generally do everything he could to help America's workers and to upend decades of growing income inequality led to a decisive shift in support for him among the working class. As NPR put it, "There's no question that one of the key issues in this election year has been the frustration of workers over wages, debt, and a sense of economic stagnation in too many households" (NPR 2016).

The other narrative is focused squarely on race. In this version, Trump won over White voters not because of his economic agenda but rather because of his racial agenda. White Americans may have been anxious about change, but the change that they were most concerned about was not fundamentally an economic one. For observers like Ta-Nehisi Coates (2017), Trump was the "First White President" whose "commitment to whiteness is matched only by the depth of popular disbelief in the power of whiteness ..." From this perspective, many Whites felt that the growing racial and ethnic diversity of the nation's population was threatening their grasp on power and privilege. Increasing immigration—especially from Mexico—and the view among many Trump supporters that the government was offering African Americans a seemingly endless expansion of rights and services was breeding more and more resentment among White Americans. Trump, this narrative asserts, appealed to these anxious White Americans by attacking Barack Obama for being an illegitimate, un-American president, by promising to reverse decades of minority giveaways, by offering a hardline anti-immigrant message, and by seeking to bar "dangerous" Muslims from entering the country.

Which version of reality best explains the success of Trump's 2016 candidacy? And, more broadly, what determines voter choice in American democracy, and how does that vary by racial and ethnic group? In this chapter we will tackle these questions in two ways. First, we will focus on the demographics of the vote. We will explore two questions: to what extent did race and ethnicity predict the vote? And to what extent did race overshadow other demographic divides like class, age, gender, or religion? We will also discuss how these patterns have changed over time and, more specifically, how the nation's political party system has transformed over the past half century. Last, we will focus on the question of why this nation is so divided politically. Are racial policies and racial attitudes at the core of the nation's partisan divide, or are economic and cultural considerations the dominant factors?

What we will find is worrying. Race sharply divides the vote. Indeed, race divides us politically more than any other demographic factor. That was true before Donald Trump arrived on the scene and it is still true today. But these divisions are also clearly getting worse. The reality is that as America becomes more diverse, it is also becoming more racially divided.

Understanding How Voters Decide

To what extent did demographics influence the outcome of Trump's two presidential bids? In Figure 9.1 we look at the demographic patterns that were on display in the vote in the 2016 and 2020 elections. The idea is simply to see which demographic factors most divide us. The figure shows the size of the gap in the vote for Donald Trump in each election by race, class, and other factors. Each bar represents the share of one group (e.g., Whites) that voted for Trump as compared with the share of a second group (e.g., Blacks) that voted for Trump. The larger the bar, the greater the gap. We will examine the specifics of each factor shown in the figure below.

Race and the Vote

When one examines the figure, one can see that race played a more significant role in the outcome of both elections than did class. Exit polls in both contests reveal

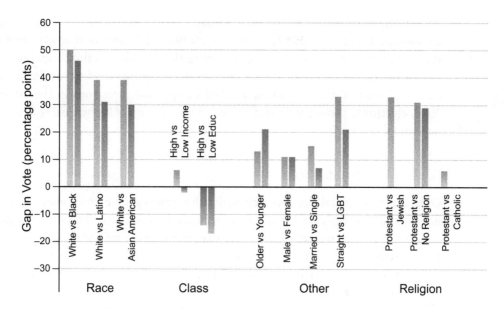

Figure 9.1 Gaps in Support for Trump in 2016 and 2020
The bars here represent the size of the gap in the vote for Donald Trump in the 2016 (in blue)
and 2020 (in red) elections, by race, class, and other factors. Each bar represents the share of one
group (e.g., Whites) that voted for Trump as compared to the share of a second group (e.g.,
Blacks) that voted for Trump. The larger the bar, the greater the gap. Some categories in
2020 are not available.
Source: Edison Research National Exit Poll, Latinos Decision (for Latino vote), and Asian
Decisions (for Asian American vote), at: www.edisonresearch.com/election-polling-2.

that large gaps existed between racial and ethnic minority voters on one side and
White voters on the other. Trump won only 8 percent of the Black vote. By contrast
he garnered 58 percent of the White. That 50-point difference, shown in the first bar
in the graph, is closer to a racial chasm than a racial gap. And we see other large
gaps related to race and ethnic votes in 2016. As Figure 9.1 illustrates, the gaps
between Whites and Latinos and Whites and Asian Americans in 2016 were both
39 points.

Moreover, despite a different outcome in 2020 and despite the movement of some
Latino and Asian American voters toward Trump in his reelection bid, racial and
ethnic identity still played a dominant role for voters four years later. Simply
judging by the size of the bars, race and ethnicity stand out as the most important
force in American electoral democracy.

Class played a role in voter decision-making in both the 2016 and 2020
presidential elections but not nearly as much as race/ethnicity did. Contrary to
much of the popular wisdom, in 2016 Trump did slightly better among higher-
income Americans than he did among lower-income Americans. And the same
was true in 2020, when he garnered 44 percent of the vote among Americans
with incomes over $250,000 compared with 40 percent of the vote among

Americans with incomes less than $30,000. When considering voters' level of education, Trump did slightly worse as individuals' education levels increased. He garnered 51 percent of the vote among those with a high-school education or less and only 37 percent among those with post-graduate degrees. Because the effects of income and education worked in opposite directions in the 2016 and 2020 elections, the overall impact of class—being a higher or lower status individual—is far from clear.

Social Class and the Vote

Over the past several decades, the nation has undergone extraordinary economic upheaval and experienced ever greater economic inequality. The three wealthiest Americans now own assets worth more than the assets of half of America's 330 million citizens combined. The typical worker now must toil over two months to match what their CEOs earn in an hour. These are massive, perhaps unprecedented, economic gaps between have and have-nots.

Yet, as shown in Figure 9.1, even in the face of these trends, class played only a *secondary* role in the 2016 and 2020 presidential elections. How can this be? Story after story following the 2016 election highlighted the fact that working-class Whites made up the bulk of voters who had once been Obama supporters but then shifted to Trump (Stern 2017). From this perspective, the lesson for Democrats would be that their chances of being elected are doomed if they do not do more to recapture the White working class.

Why did class attract so much media attention when the data clearly demonstrated that class played a marginal role in the vote? Part of the answer lies with the narrow focus of many of the media reports. Many studies focused on the narrow segment of the electorate that switched support from one political camp to another, from Obama to Trump, for example. But the reality is that less than 5 percent of the electorate switched from Obama to Trump. Although these switch voters might explain the outcome of a close election, they are not representative of the larger electorate. That is, despite the widespread focus on working-class support for Trump, lower-income Americans were no more likely than upper-income Americans to have voted for Trump.

Moreover, even when we look more closely at switchers, the argument for class as *the* central motivation is hardly convincing. If economic disadvantage was the driving force behind the Trump vote, then the most pronounced shift toward Trump should have taken place not among White voters, but among the nation's most disadvantaged populations—its racial and ethnic minorities. Blacks and Latinos are much more likely than Whites to suffer economically, and to live in neighborhoods that have been cut off from recent economic gains. Blacks and Latinos also suffered the sharpest declines in wealth, income, and employment during the Great Recession. Yet they overwhelmingly voted for the Democratic candidates in the 2016 and 2020 presidential elections. In the face of the same economic circumstances, Whites and non-Whites largely made opposite partisan choices. That should tell us something about the racial nature of our politics. It is also worth noting that several recent studies have found that racial attitudes, much more than economic concerns, predicted who would switch from Obama to Trump (Sides, Tesler, and Vavreck 2018). Economic anxiety, real as it is, has not resulted in class warfare or even class politics. This statement applies not only to the 2016 and 2020 presidential elections but also, as we will show below, across a range of recent elections.

At the same time, it is important to note that class divisions, while not all that important for the electorate as a whole, are increasingly relevant to the White vote. Over the last few presidential contests, the share of working-class White voters supporting the Republican Party has increased measurably, while the share of well-educated White Americans supporting the Democratic Party has also grown. It is fair to say that more educated White Americans, and their less educated counterparts, are more and more divided in their political preferences.

Age, Gender, Religion, and the Vote

Race and class were not, of course, the only narratives used to explain the outcome of the 2020 and 2016 elections. A lot of media attention focused on gender, age, religion, and other factors. With Hillary Clinton as the first female candidate from a major party running for president, gender was expected to be a major factor in the 2016 election. However, the final vote suggests it may not have been.[1] Female voters did favor Clinton, and male voters did prefer Trump, but neither by an overwhelming margin. In fact, the majority of White women (52 percent) supported Trump. In the end, the gender gap in 2016 and 2020 was only 11 points—although it is worth noting that women were more Democratic than men in each racial and ethnic group. Similarly, despite significant attention to the age of Trump supporters, age played relatively little role in voter choice in 2016. Older voters (those over 65) were only 13 points more likely to favor Trump in 2016 than were younger Americans (those aged 18–24). This older vs. younger gap in Trump support increased to 21 points in 2020, but age divides did vary across racial and ethnic groups with Latino voters perhaps most divided by age and Black voters the least divided by age (see Figure 9.1).

After race, the next biggest influence on the vote was social morality and religion. Figure 9.1 shows that religion played a central role in shaping both the 2016 and 2020 elections with atheists, agnostics, and Jews especially likely to support the Democratic nominee, and Evangelicals, Catholics, and Protestants particularly likely to support Trump. The increasingly central role of morality and culture is also underlined by what appear to be increasingly large divisions by sexual preference. In 2016, LGBTQ+ voters overwhelmingly supported Clinton. By contrast, straight voters were largely split between Clinton and Trump. Similar gaps by sexual orientation could be seen in 2020.

---

[1] It is, of course, possible that gender mattered in more subtle ways. Many believed that gender stereotypes shaped the coverage of the candidates and analysis of the vote itself finds that sexism among both men and women helped to shape the vote (Valentino, Wayne, and Oceno 2018).

The Racial Divide in Down-Ballot Elections

One common theme surrounding Trump's presidency was that he was unique. To offer a more general account of how much race, class, and other demographic factors can affect the vote, we need to look across a broader array of elections.

The reality, as this broader analysis demonstrates, is that the patterns we saw in the 2020 and 2016 presidential contests are far from an aberration. Indeed, 2020 and 2016 are much more accurately seen as a continuation of patterns in previous elections. Trump's tactics were a little more extreme, his rhetoric a little coarser, and his language on race and immigration a little more explicit, but the patterns behind the vote under Trump were almost identical to those in 2012, remarkably similar to patterns in the vote in previous presidential contests, and comparable with patterns in the vote for other offices from the national to the local.

Figure 9.2 shows racial- and class-based voting divides across different types of contests between 2006 and 2014, and indicates that the average Black–White gap hovers between 40 and 50 points for almost all elections between 2006 and 2014. At every level, what Whites want is generally not what Blacks want. But it is not only the Black–White divide that stands out. The gap between White voters and Latino voters is typically a little less or a little more than 20 points across the types of contests. Asian Americans and Whites differ by almost the same average margin across these elections. In almost every type of office over this recent period, the majority of Whites typically favor the candidate that the majority of Latinos, Asian Americans, and Blacks oppose.

What makes these racial divides so remarkable is not just their magnitude but also their consistency. We might have expected massive racial division in Obama's two historic presidential contests (2008 and 2012) with an African American running

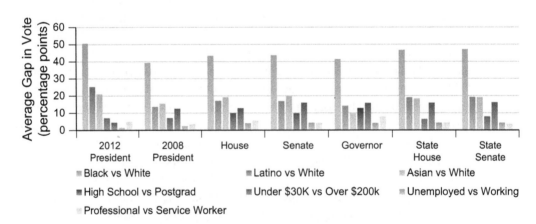

Figure 9.2 Race and Class in American Elections, 2006–2014
This figure plots the average divide in voting preferences between different groups across elections between 2006 and 2014. Presidential election data are only for 2008 and 2012. It shows that racial divides have generally been larger than class divides across all of these different types of elections.
Source: Adapted from Hajnal (2020). Data are from the 2006–2014 Cooperative Congressional Election Study, which includes over 200,000 self-reported votes across these contests.

against a White opponent. Blacks were understandably excited by the prospect of the first Black president, while Whites might have feared the historic transition to Black leadership. The fact that the majority of Whites opposed Obama in both 2008 and 2012 is probably not surprising. What is notable is that the 2012 and 2008 presidential contests do not stand out. In fact, a majority or plurality of White voters have voted for Republican candidates for president for over five decades in the United States. Further, across every type of contest we examined in the most recent elections, the average Black–White, Latino–White, and Asian American–White divides were similar. Blacks were as divided from Whites in gubernatorial contests as they were in Senate elections. Likewise, Latinos and Whites disagreed about as often in state attorney general elections as they did in House elections.

To be sure, states showed a variety of patterns in their elections. Mississippi's 2014 senatorial contest, for example, was particularly racially divided (only 16 percent of Whites voted for Democrat Travis Childers, while 92 percent of Blacks did so), while California's gubernatorial election that year was more united (54 percent of Whites, 73 percent of Latinos, and 89 percent of Blacks voted for Jerry Brown, the Democratic incumbent). But elections for the House of Representatives, the Senate, the Governor's office, the State House, and the State Senate all divide us racially to a roughly equal extent.

Moreover, as Figure 9.2 illustrates, those racial divides generally dwarf divisions by class, indicated by level of education, annual income, type of work (services vs. professional), and employment status (unemployed or working). The Americans with the highest levels of formal education—those with post-graduate degrees— only differ from those with the least formal education, defined as having less than a high-school degree, by an average of about 9 points in the typical contest. Income has a slightly larger but more variable impact on the vote. The preferences of Americans who earn less than $30,000 a year differ from the preferences of those who earn more than $200,000 a year by an average of anywhere from 4 to 16 points across the types of elections. However, regardless of how we define and measure social class, it does not seem to divide America as much as race. Differences by occupational category (professionals and managers vs. service workers and laborers), union membership, homeownership, and every breakdown of income and education that we could access in the surveys all paled in comparison with racial divides. Growing income inequality has received a tremendous amount of attention from scholars and the media, but race and ethnicity seem to have replaced class as the primary dividing line in American politics.

Still, a range of other demographic factors have small but consistent effects across all types of elections. The gap between younger (under 25) and older (over 65) Americans typically hovers around 10 points in these contests. The gender gap is roughly the same—about 12 points. Marital status plays a slightly larger role— typically, there was a little less than a 20-point gap between single and married Americans in how they voted in this range of elections.

Although not featured in Figure 9.2, the main rival for race in dividing voters is religion. Americans who describe themselves as "born again" or evangelical

Christians are about 25 points more likely to end up on the Republican side of electoral contests than are other Americans. Likewise, Americans who say that religion is very important to them are roughly 40 points more likely to favor Republican candidates for the House, the Senate, the Governor's office, and state legislative positions. Nonbelievers are about 40 points more likely to vote Democratic across the array of elections than are Catholics, and almost 50 points more likely to do so than Protestants.

Another way to assess racial divisions in voting patterns is to look at local politics, where a voter's connections to one party or the other often play a lesser role. Approximately 80 percent of all municipalities hold nonpartisan elections in which neither party's name is permitted on the ballot. Local elections also can generate unique voting patterns because the issues on the local agenda are distinct to the particular community. If racial divisions are as pronounced in election outcomes when parties are less central and when the issues are closer to home, then one can conclude that the racial divide is truly central to voting behavior.

Indeed, the data show that race dominates as a dividing factor at the local level as it does in national elections. This is confirmed in Figure 9.3, which shows the

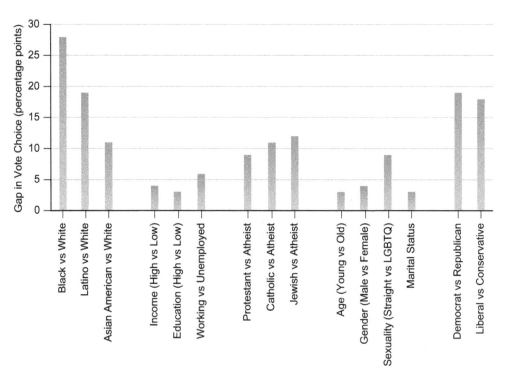

Figure 9.3 The Effect of Demographic Characteristics on Voting Patterns in Big Cities
Race has the biggest estimated effect on the vote across a range of local elections in major cities in recent years.
Source: Hajnal and Trounstine (2013). The data set includes exit poll data from sixty-three local contests across five major cities over a recent twenty-five-year period.

average estimated impact of race, other demographic factors, and political orientation on the vote for an array of big-city elections over the past few decades.

Even after controlling for a range of demographic characteristics and key political markers, race still greatly shapes the urban vote. The average estimated gap between the Black vote and the White vote is 28 points. The Latino–White divide (19 points) and the Asian American–White divide (11 points) are smaller but still substantial compared with other factors. Figure 9.3 shows once again that class plays only a secondary role in voting patterns, with relatively small class divides emerging. Critically, even when one singles out contests that involved two candidates of the same race, race still emerges as the most important demographic factor shaping the urban vote.

The rest of the local level results largely mirror what we saw in national and state contests. Factors like gender and age play a small and less consistent role. As with national contests, religion is the second most important demographic factor in local elections. Religion still strongly predicts the vote regardless of the level of the office. We also see that sexuality also matters with a 9 point predicted average gap between gay and straight voters.

What makes the role of race in the urban vote most striking is that it slightly overshadows divisions grounded in political variables such as party affiliation (19 points) and ideology—represented in the figure as liberal vs. conservative (17 points). Party affiliation and political ideology do shape the decisions of local voters, but racial difference is the dominating factor in American politics.

WHAT IT LOOKS LIKE TODAY: ARE ASIAN AMERICANS AND LATINOS COHESIVE POLITICAL GROUPS?

So far the analysis in this chapter has simply assumed that labels such as Asian American or Latino are meaningful terms that signal important distinctions about political behavior and attitudes. And, in fact, as we saw in Chapter 6, Asian American and Latino identities are growing sharply over time. That is, more and more Asian Americans and Latinos express a strong sense of connection to their group. But does that translate into political unity at the ballot box?

At first glance, the electoral contests we have looked at suggest a fair degree of cohesion. In the 2016 presidential election, for example, 79 percent of Asian Americans and 79 percent of Latinos voted for the Democratic nominee. More Latinos and Asian Americans supported Trump in 2020, but still, two-thirds of both groups ended up on the Democratic side.[2] And more broadly, two-thirds or more of Latino and Asian American voters typically ended up voting for the same candidates across most of the elections we looked at. By that metric, Latinos and Asian

[2] The American Election Eve Poll also reports that about two-thirds of Latino and Asian American voters voted for Democrats in House and Senate elections in 2020.

Americans are not as cohesive as Blacks—roughly 90 percent of whom typically vote on the same side—but they are substantially more cohesive than Whites, who might vote 60 percent on one side to 40 percent on the other side in a typical election.

Nevertheless, the Asian American and Latino populations are incredibly diverse, with wide variation related to national origin, levels of assimilation, language, and socioeconomic well-being. Should we expect two individuals from different countries, who speak different languages, have different immigration pathways, have spent different amounts of time in the United States, and who are on opposite ends of the socioeconomic spectrum, to vote alike? Should we, for example, expect Japanese Americans and Korean Americans to form a united political front in the United States even though both the Japanese and Korean nations have engaged in repeated conflict? Given the diversity within Asian American and Latino populations in the United States, it is worth delving deeper into how these divisions overlap with voting patterns. We begin with national origin, which many consider to be the primary factor that divides these groups. Figure 9.4 shows how national origin affected voting patterns in the 2016 presidential election for both Latinos and Asian Americans.

Clearly, Latinos and Asian Americans have come to the United States from many different countries, but with regard to voting patterns within these two populations, Cuban Americans and Vietnamese Americans stand out as being much less supportive of the Democratic candidate. Cuban Americans and Vietnamese Americans have traditionally been seen by the media as politically conservative and

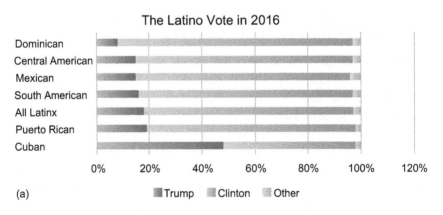

(a)

Figure 9.4 (a) and (b) Latino and Asian American Vote, by Country of Origin, in the 2016 Presidential Election
Shown here are voting preferences by national origin group among Latinos and Asian Americans in the 2016 presidential vote.
Source: Latino Decisions Poll and Asian American Legal Defense and Education Poll, at: https://latinodecisions.com/wp-content/uploads/2019/06/National_2016_Xtabs.pdf; www.aaldef.org/press-release/new-aaldef-report-the-asian-american-vote-in-2016.

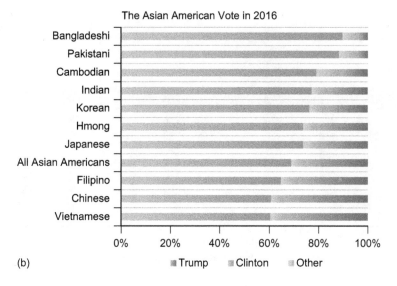

Figure 9.4 (*cont.*)

Republican—largely based on the fact that many fled a left-wing communist regime when they emigrated to the United States. But the bigger picture—at least as shown in 2016—is that there is a fair amount of agreement across all national origin groups. In 2016, none of the national origin groups identified in Figure 9.4 favored Trump, and all voted majority Democratic, though Cuban, Chinese, and Vietnamese Americans showed greater support for Trump compared with the other groups. And the 2016 presidential vote was not an aberration. In 2020, almost all of the national origin groups we could examine overwhelmingly favored the Democratic Party and only one group—Cuban Americans—was at times evenly divided between Democrats and Republicans.

With regard to other potential divisions within each pan-ethnic group, in 2016 and beyond, differences in gender, age, and class played relatively small roles in shaping Latino and Asian American voting choices. The factor that played the largest role was religion. Latinos and Asian Americans who described themselves as "born again" were 20–40 percentage points more likely to favor Republican candidates than other members of their groups.

Party Identification

We can get an even deeper look at divisions in American politics by examining party identification—the extent to which individual members of the public identify with one or the other major political party. Party identification is critical because research often shows that it structures much of our political thinking (Campbell et al. 1960; Green et al. 2002). For most Americans, party identification is their longest lasting and most fundamental political identity. It has enormous consequences not just for

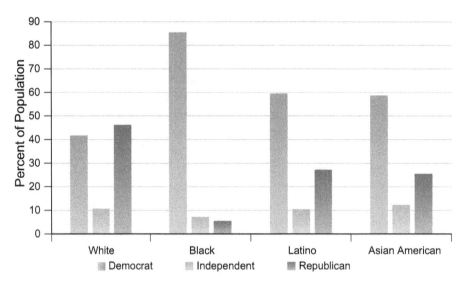

Figure 9.5 Race and Party Identification
The share of Americans who identify with each political party varies widely by race and ethnicity.
Source: 2006–2018 CCES.

how they vote but for almost any other politically motivated decision they make. Evidence even indicates that in today's world of hyper-polarization, individual Americans discriminate more against members of the other party than they do against members of other races (Iyengar and Westwood 2015).

If race and party become closely aligned—especially in a time of close elections and hyper-partisanship—then fears of deeper conflict and even violence emerge. Division may be a normal and healthy part of democracy, but if the core political identity in America is so closely tied to the racial identities of the public, then party elites on both sides have strategic incentives to campaign on race and demonize the other. Most important, if race and party are nearly synonymous with most of the White majority population on one side and most racial and ethnic minorities on the other, then the White majority has a particularly effective tool to tyrannize the minority population. In short, you have a potentially explosive mix of race, parties, and politics.

Thus, it is alarming to find that racial patterns in party identification have roughly mirrored racial patterns in the vote in recent decades. Figure 9.5 reveals that racial and ethnic minorities largely identify with the Democratic Party (84 percent of African Americans, 60 percent of Latinos, and 59 percent of Asian Americans) over the Republican Party (7 percent of African Americans, 27 percent of Latinos, and 26 percent of Asian Americans).[3] By contrast, Whites are slightly more likely to identify as Republican than Democrat (46 percent vs. 42 percent).

---

[3] In the figure, those who indicate that they "lean" toward one party are counted as partisans.

Thus, both through the candidates who are elected and patterns of political-party identification in American democracy, Whites tend to align against racial and ethnic minorities.[4] The data are surprising, disturbing, and insistent.

Why Have the Parties Aligned around Race?

How did we get here? How is it that of all the potential divisions in American society, our politics have converged on race? If we look back over U.S. history, we can see that the link between race and party has always been there. But just how much race has affected voting behavior and how much the two parties have made racial issues a core part of their platforms has varied considerably over time.

The Early Days of the Republican and Democratic Parties

Ironically, although race has always been a factor in party identification, the two parties have actually switched sides on the issue of race. The Republican Party at its founding in the middle of the nineteenth century was the party of Black interests. Indeed, the Republican Party was in no small part organized around opposition to slavery. Its first president, Abraham Lincoln, issued the Emancipation Proclamation, freeing enslaved Blacks residing in the rebellious Confederate states. Lincoln and the Republican Party also entered the Civil War in part to end slavery. In response, African Americans—when they had access to the ballot—overwhelmingly supported the Republican Party through the end of the nineteenth century and the beginning of the twentieth century.

In contrast, the Democratic Party was a more faithful servant of the Confederate South and at its founding opposed the abolition of slavery. The Democratic party solidified its hold on White Southerners and Southern politics by disenfranchising Blacks, both through legal means and through violence and intimidation. After the Civil War, Democrats were responsible for poll taxes, literacy tests, and a host of other extremely effective mechanisms that almost entirely shut out Blacks from the political process (see Chapter 7 for more about these topics). Until the middle of the twentieth century, the Democratic Party also helped to institute a broad set of Jim Crow laws that enshrined segregation in the law and that ensured that the South would be a highly unequal society for decades to come. In short, for much of American history, the Republican Party was the party of African Americans and the Democratic Party was dominated by White Americans.

The reversal in the racial orientation of the party system took a long time to develop and occurred because both parties shifted on the issue of race. The first step in that process occurred when the leaders of the Republican Party decided to reduce

---

[4] Again, it is worth noting that race better predicts partisanship than almost any other demographic factor. Divisions by class, age, and gender are very real but are much smaller than divisions by race. As with the vote, only religion rivals race in shaping partisan attachments.

Photo 9.2 Copy of Abraham Lincoln's Emancipation Proclamation, Henderson, Achert, Krebs Lith Co., Cincinnati, Ohio, 1890.
Source: © Education Images/Contributor/Universal Images Group/Getty Images.

its focus on the African American community. By the end of Reconstruction, Republican initiatives to seek racial justice and racial equality had essentially disappeared. Blacks were hardly mentioned in Republican Party agendas at the dawn of the twentieth century. As a result, African Americans became more and more disgruntled with the party, but with no attractive alternative, the Black vote remained solidly Republican.

The next critical development was the New Deal policies of the Democratic Party. With a nation facing the Great Depression, massive unemployment, and widespread poverty, President Franklin Delano Roosevelt's Democratic administration initiated an extensive program of relief measures that provided funds and jobs for those in need. Critics have rightly noted that those New Deal policies were not always race-neutral and that Whites were often favored when goods and services were distributed (Katznelson 2005). But the reality is that the New Deal benefited millions of African Americans—leading to extensive declines in Black poverty and ultimately fueling massive growth in the size of the Black middle class. Flaws aside, no administration since the Civil War was more friendly to Black interests than FDR's Democratic administration.

The net result was a period of political and racial stalemate where neither party fought vigorously for Black interests. As a result, Black voters shifted in large numbers to the Democratic Party but remained a viable target for both parties. Whites were also divided between the two parties. With Black participation both as voters and candidates still limited by poll taxes, literacy tests, intimidation, and other tactics, neither party had much incentive to appeal to the Black vote or to support a policy agenda that would aid the Black community. Over the ensuing decades, race was largely absent from the campaigns of either party. Until the 1960s, neither the Democrats nor the Republicans were particularly vocal champions of minority rights.

Racial Realignment since the Civil Rights Movement

But changing demographics, the Civil Rights Movement, and Black demands for change set in motion a process that once again radically altered the American party system. According to this racial realignment view, race has become more consequential in American politics in recent decades because Blacks mobilized for more rights and more resources and because leaders of the two major political parties chose to offer increasingly divergent positions on matters of race. For two of the best accounts of this theory, see Carmines and Stimson (1989) and Edsall and Edsall (1991).

Seeing an opportunity to secure a national majority by giving Blacks access to the vote and therefore securing those new votes, elites in the Democratic Party began to publicly embrace the basic goals of the Civil Rights Movement. Starting with President John F. Kennedy and his successor Lyndon Johnson, Democrats initiated and successfully enacted landmark legislation—in particular, the Civil Rights Act and the Voting Rights Act, both of which dismantled Jim Crow laws in the South and helped African Americans gain equal rights under the law.[5] Over time, Democrats increasingly championed policies that sought to protect and aid the racial and ethnic minority population. Then, having moved firmly to the left on race, the Democrats stayed there.

---

[5] In the conventional version of the story, elite leaders in both political parties played central roles. A more nuanced account suggests that in highlighting injustice and mobilizing in ever larger numbers, the actions of African Americans themselves played an equally critical role (Lee 2002).

Likewise, the Republican Party saw an opportunity to use race to appeal to Whites in the South, who were overwhelmingly aligned with the Democratic Party but who were also deeply concerned about Black demands for racial equality. Employing what came to be known as the Southern Strategy, a tactic to attract more White support by opposing much of the Civil Rights agenda, Republican politicians such as presidential candidates Barry Goldwater and Richard Nixon ran campaigns that criticized Blacks, disparaged violence in the minority community, and highlighted minority use of welfare and other public resources (Carmines and Stimson 1989). Typically, the message was subtle, but within a decade the Republican Party clearly had abandoned over a hundred years of racial progressivism. The party of Lincoln and emancipation was now actively seeking the support of Whites in the South and other parts of the country who resented what they viewed as special favors for Blacks. By the time Ronald Reagan highlighted an outrageous, if fictitious, Black "welfare queen," the link between the Republican Party and a platform underlined by racial concerns had been firmly established.

According to this racial realignment view, the increasingly divergent platforms of the Democratic and Republican parties on matters of race had their intended effects—that is, Blacks shifted in ever larger numbers to the Democratic Party. In his landmark study *Behind the Mule*, political scientist Michael Dawson shows that this shift largely happened because African Americans tended to believe that their individual fates were linked to the well-being of the larger Black population

Photo 9.3 Ku Klux Klan members supporting Barry Goldwater's campaign for the presidential nomination at the Republican National Convention, July 12, 1964, in San Francisco, CA, clash with an African American man pushing back.
Source: © Donaldson Collection/Contributor/Michael Ochs Archives/Getty Images.

and increasingly felt that the Democratic Party was the most likely one to advance Black interests (Dawson 1994). Dawson calls this the Black Utility Heuristic and it has come to dominate our understanding of Black political decision-making (see Chapter 6 for more detail).

Equally powerful were the campaign tactics and policy platforms of Republican leaders over the ensuing decades. Whites who held negative views of Blacks and who opposed policies designed to help Blacks achieve greater equality abandoned the Democratic Party in large numbers.

Scholars debate the exact nature of the racial concerns that have driven White voters from the Democratic Party.[6] One account holds that defections were driven by a sense of group position—that is, Whites were concerned that policies aimed at helping Blacks would undermine their privileged status in the racial hierarchy (Blumer 1958; Bobo and Tuan 2006). Other scholars assert that symbolic threats centered around things such as language, culture, or a cherished way of life drove the defections (Kinder and Sander 1996). This new racism, which is often referred to as *racial resentment*, is driven by a combination of anti-Black feelings and American moral traditionalism. According to this version, many Whites now believe that the main barriers to racial equality have been removed. As a result, they resent Black demands for what they see as special favors and extra resources.

The end result of these diverging views has been a tight relationship between how individual Americans think about race and how they think about politics, including everything from partisan identities to electoral choices and policy preferences. The evidence shows clearly that by 1980, attitudes on race were closely correlated with White party affiliation (Carmines and Stimson 1989; Valentino and Sears 2005). Perhaps most convincing of all are studies showing that how one thinks about race at any one point in time strongly predicts future defections between the parties (Kuziemko and Washington 2018; McVeigh, Cunningham, and Farrell 2014). Those who harbor racial resentment today are especially likely to become Republican tomorrow.

Racial Considerations and the Obama Vote

Although many had hoped that the election of a Black man to the Oval Office would herald the beginning of a postracial society, President Obama's tenure appears only to have hardened or increased the impact of racial sentiments on partisan politics. Studies show that racial considerations have only grown in importance and were especially prominent drivers of the vote in Barack Obama's two elections (Parker and Barreto 2013; Tesler and Sears 2012). One way to illustrate the impact of race on elections is to look at how the White vote varies with the size of the African American population in an area. In Figure 9.6 you can see the share of the White vote that Barack Obama received in 2008 in each state

---

[6] Another version of the race story was developed by psychology professors James Sidanius and Felicia Pratto (1999). This social dominance theory contends that the main motivation driving White behavior is the desire to maintain Whites' elevated position in the existing racial hierarchy.

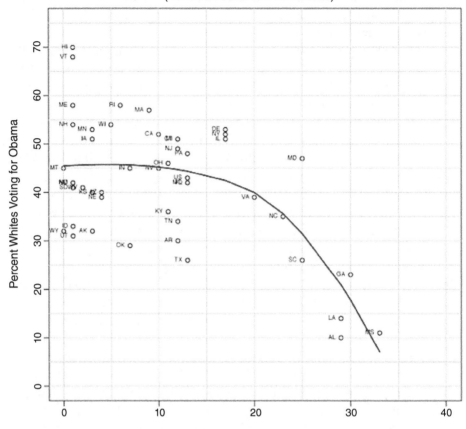

Figure 9.6 White Support for Obama by Size of African American Vote in State
The figure shows the share of the White vote that Barack Obama received in 2008 in each state against the African American share of each state's population. It shows that as the Black population increases, White support for Obama declines.
Note: Based on state exit poll results.
Source: Charles Franklin: Pollster.com and Politicalarithmetik.blogspot.com.

against the African American share of each state's population. The figure clearly shows that as the Black population increases, White support for Obama declines. In states with the smallest share of Blacks—for example, New Hampshire and Minnesota—a little over half of White voters favored Obama. By contrast, in the states with the largest African American populations—for example, Alabama and Mississippi—only about 10 percent of Whites voted for Obama.

This relationship between the size of the Black population and the candidate that White voters favor demonstrates a concept called racial threat, which was developed by V. O. Key, in his landmark 1949 study, *Southern Politics in State and Nation*. The basic theory is that the larger an outgroup, the greater the perceived threat it represents and the greater the likelihood of a backlash by the ingroup or majority. According to this theory, then, in the case of the 2008 Obama election, one can surmise that White voters felt more threatened by Blacks in places where Blacks made up a larger share of the population. The result was that White support for Obama was low in states like Alabama and Mississippi where Blacks represented as much as a third of the population. Of course, Obama's party affiliation and his policies surely also contributed to the pattern we see in Figure 9.6. But research supported this relationship between the local racial context and White support for Obama even after a range of controls were applied (Donovan 2010).

This racial threat pattern can be seen in a range of behaviors beyond voting. For example, in the context of the most extreme level of racial violence, research has found that lynchings and Ku Klux Klan activity in the South were more frequent in areas with larger concentrations of Blacks. White support for avowed segregationists like former Klan leader David Duke was also higher in counties with more Blacks (Corzine, Creech, and Corzine 1983). Other studies have shown that Whites feel more resentful toward Blacks and are less willing to provide aid to the Black community in places with larger Black populations. More recently, studies have also linked the size of the immigrant backlash to the size of the local immigrant population. All of this has two implications. The first is that race has a range of powerful effects in American politics. The second is that the effects of race may vary, depending on geography and the local context.

Racial Considerations and the Trump Vote

The impact of race and racial considerations increased during Donald Trump's presidency. Although few White Americans were willing to admit that race was the main motivating factor behind their Trump vote, studies show a close correlation between the vote in 2016 and attitudes about race (Gimpel 2017; Sides, Tesler, and Vavreck 2017). The majority of those who scored highest on racial resentment—one of the most widely accepted measures of modern-day racial attitudes—voted for Trump, while the majority of those on the opposite end of the scale supported Clinton (Enders and Small 2016). Even after taking into account party affiliation, racial views had an oversized impact on the vote. According to one analysis, Republicans who scored high on racial resentment were about 30 percentage points more likely to support Trump than their more racially liberal Republican counterparts (Tesler 2016b). Perhaps even more critically, studies show that attitudes about race—more than economic concerns—predicted which voters would switch from Obama to Trump (Sides 2017). American politics may have once conformed to the adage from Bill Clinton's campaign—"It's the economy, stupid"—but by 2016, political commentators were more likely to argue, *"It's race, stupid."*[7] Little appears to have changed since 2016. The vote in 2018 was once again closely linked to racial views (Yglesias 2018).

[7] Bill Maher as quoted in Tesler (2016b).

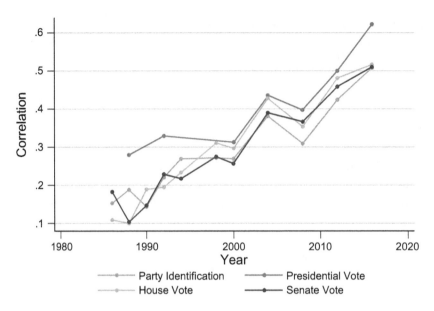

Figure 9.7 The Growing Ties Between Racial Views and the Vote, 1985–2020
Note here the size of the relationship between racial attitudes as measured by a score on the racial resentment scale and vote choice and party identification over time. For all the categories included (party identification, presidential vote, House and Senate votes), there is a clear increase in how much race matters over time.
Source: American National Election Studies.

And in 2020, the national exit poll found that 86 percent of Americans who had an unfavorable view of Black Lives Matter voted for Trump, while 78 percent of those who had a favorable view of the movement supported Biden.

The increasingly strong effects of race on the political choices of Americans are reflected in Figure 9.7, which shows the correlation between how Americans think about African Americans—as measured by their score on a racial resentment scale[8]— and their party identity and votes over time. The figure shows that the connection between attitudes about race, the vote, and party affiliation has not only grown dramatically over time but has continued to do so in the Obama and Trump eras.

New Drivers of Racial Conflict: Part One, Immigration

This racial realignment pattern has until recently been focused almost exclusively on the Black–White divide.[9] But newer studies suggest that anxiety about other groups has expanded partisan conflict over race.

---

[8] Items in the scale ask about things like whether Blacks deserve special favors, whether Blacks have gotten more than they deserve, and whether Blacks are trying hard enough.

[9] There have, however, been prolonged periods in American history during which the primary target of White ire was not Black America as exemplified by: Indian removal in the early nineteenth century; the maltreatment of Mexican landholders in the mid-nineteenth century; the widespread abuse of Chinese

The most extensive evidence relates to immigration issues, and the Latino population in particular, and their effects on the party system and the racial divide. What the researchers call the immigration backlash account (Abrajano and Hajnal 2015) argues that growth in the immigrant population and increasingly divergent Democratic and Republican positions on immigration have helped make attitudes about immigration more central to political decision-making. On one side, leaders in the Republican Party have, since the mid-1990s, increasingly seized on immigration-related concerns about jobs, crime, welfare, and American culture to attract more White support. This immigration backlash strategy was first launched by Republican Pete Wilson during his successful bid to be reelected governor of California in 1994. It was epitomized by the grainy footage of immigrant hordes crossing the border in Wilson's campaign ads and by Wilson's support of Proposition 187, a measure designed to prevent undocumented immigrants from using public services. That proposition, according to Wilson and the campaign, was designed to "Save Our State." In the ensuing decades Republican leaders have sometimes been torn between appealing to White fears on immigration and an alternate strategy of appealing to the immigrant population. But over time, the votes and rhetoric of Republican leaders have increasingly sided with the anti-immigrant approach. The strategy perhaps reached its apex with Donald Trump's 2018 comments about Mexican immigrants: "These aren't people. These are animals."[10] Either unwittingly, or by design, the Democratic Party has played into this new Republican strategy by welcoming immigrants into the Democratic fold and by campaigning on a more balanced approach to immigration.

The net result is a sharp divide between the two parties on immigration issues and close ties between individual Americans' views on immigration, their party identities, and their electoral choices. Americans who believe immigrants are a burden have flocked in ever-larger numbers to Republican candidates and the Republican Party. Likewise, those who believe immigrants benefit the nation now overwhelmingly support Democratic candidates and the Democratic cause.

Donald Trump's 2016 campaign provided ample evidence of the benefits of this anti-immigrant strategy. His meteoric rise in the 2016 presidential campaign—from the bottom to the top of the sixteen-person primary field—occurred just after he made immigration a central issue by voicing his now famous lines about Mexican immigrants: "They're bringing drugs. They're bringing crime. They're rapists. And some, I assume, are good people." In part because Trump talked about immigration more than any other subject, 58 percent of all Trump news coverage in the month after his infamous speech focused on immigration (Lamont, Park, and Alaya-Hurtado 2017).

The vote in both the primary and the general election bore out the importance of immigration for Trump's supporters. All told, 53 percent of those who preferred

---

immigrants at the end of the nineteenth century; and the internment of 100,000 Japanese Americans during the Second World War.

[10] Pete Wilson's ad showed footage of Mexican migrants racing across the border while a narrator intoned, "They keep coming."

Photo 9.4 A 2-year-old Honduran asylum seeker cries as her mother is searched and detained near the U.S.–Mexico border, June 12, 2018, in McAllen, T.X.
Source: © John Moore/Staff/Getty Images News/Getty Images.

deportation for the undocumented supported Trump in the primary. By contrast, only 26 percent of those who backed a citizenship option voted for Trump (Tesler 2016b). In the general election, three-quarters of Trump voters said that illegal immigrants were "mostly a drain" on American society. Only 11 percent of Clinton supporters agreed.

Trump's presidency did little to suggest that immigration was no longer central. From an early attempted ban on immigration from seven predominantly Muslim countries, to the repeal of Deferred Action for Childhood Arrivals (a program that gives some undocumented children a chance at work and citizenship), to the elimination of Temporary Protected Status for tens of thousands of Central Americans, a limit on the number of refugees who would be allowed into the country, and an increase in the number and scope of deportations, to the shutdown of the federal government for a record-setting 35 days to gain funds to build a wall along the entire Southern border with Mexico, Trump's presidency kept the issue of immigration front and center.

New Drivers of Racial Conflict: Part Two, Muslims

In addition to this focus on race and immigration, there are also emerging signs that attitudes about Muslims and Muslim Americans specifically may be increasingly shaping partisan attachments. With the media paying more and more attention to Muslim Americans and Muslim terrorism after 9/11 and with Republican leaders, including Donald Trump, increasingly targeting Muslims with their rhetoric and policies, attitudes toward Muslims have become increasingly central to Americans' political decisions. Studies have already shown that feelings toward Muslims helped to predict which Americans would shift their votes from Obama to Trump and that resentment toward Muslim Americans strongly shaped the presidential vote in 2016, even after considering other racial views (Lajevardi and Abrajano 2019; Sides 2017). That pattern coupled with mounting evidence of discrimination against Muslim Americans in the political sphere suggests that anxiety about Muslims could further reshape the nation's partisan politics going forward (Lajevardi 2016).

All of these developments have convinced most observers that race is increasingly central and perhaps the dominant force driving the nation's party politics.

Partisan Attachments over Time: We Are Becoming More Divided by Race

What we have described in the previous sections is the slow transformation of the American party system over the last century from one in which one's race didn't tell us much about which party we would support to the present-day system, in which one's race, more than any other demographic factor, predicts who we support. Some of that transformation is illustrated in Figure 9.8, which shows the share of each racial and ethnic group identifying with the Democratic Party over time using data from the best long-term sample of American electoral preferences—the American National Election Survey (ANES).

Beginning in the 1960s and continuing to the present day, there has been a slow and uneven shift of racial and ethnic minorities to the Democratic Party. African Americans have gone from largely Democratic in 1960 (64 percent) to overwhelmingly Democratic in recent years (81 percent in 2016). We have less data on Asian

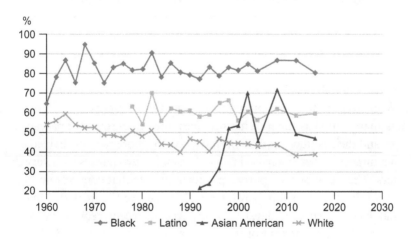

Figure 9.8 Democratic Identifiers by Race, 1960–2016
While more racial and ethnic minorities favor the Democratic Party over time, fewer Whites do so.
Source: American National Election Study Cumulative File.

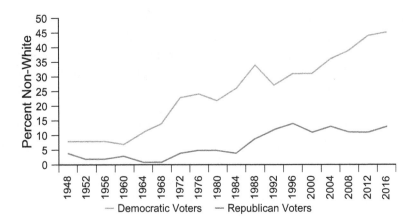

Figure 9.9 Non-White Share of the Presidential Vote by Party, 1948–2016
The figure shows that the share of all Republican voters who are non-White has stayed relatively constant over time, while the share of all Democratic voters who are non-Whites has grown dramatically over time.
Source: American National Election Study (ANES) Cumulative File.

American partisan preferences in early parts of this period, but since 1990 when more reliable data do become available, this population swung dramatically toward the Democratic Party. In the early 1990s the Republican Party held a slight edge among Asian Americans, but by 2010, Democratic identifiers outnumbered Republican identifiers by almost three to one. Asian Americans—at least those active in the political arena—now appear to be firmly in the Democratic fold. Latinos are the only minority group to see no major movement in partisanship. For all of the years for which we have reliable data, roughly 60 percent of Latinos have identified with or leaned Democratic. Overall, as more and more racial and ethnic minorities have entered the country and become engaged in the political arena, they have spoken with an increasingly clear partisan voice.

The past decades have also witnessed a substantial shift in White partisanship— with Whites moving toward the Republican Party. White America has gone from largely Democratic (54 percent Democratic in 1960) to just under 40 percent today. White Republicans now outnumber White Democrats by 48 percent to 39 percent. It is an irony that as America has become more diverse over the past six decades, its people and their political affiliations have become more racially divided.

The net impact of these increased racial divisions is two parties with very different supporters. The share of each party's presidential vote that comes from non-White voters over time illustrates this growing racial divide (see Figure 9.9). Almost all the votes that Republican candidates have received in recent years have come from White voters. About 90 percent of the vote that McCain won in 2008, that Romney won in 2012, and that Trump garnered in 2016 came from White Americans. There was a slight shift in 2020, but 82 percent of Trump's support still came from White America. The Republican Party is for almost all intents and purposes a White party.

By contrast, the share of Democratic Party votes coming from Whites has declined sharply since the 1960s. Today, almost half of all Democratic voters are non-White. Politics in America is not perfectly correlated with race, but it seems to be deeply and increasingly intertwined with race.

Alternate Accounts of Party Realignment

This chapter has focused on the increasingly central role that race plays in the American party system. At the same time, not all the movement of Whites to the Republican Party—nor all the movement of racial and ethnic minorities to the Democratic Party—is driven only by race. Scholars rightly note that economic considerations, cultural concerns, ideological conflicts about the role of government, and a range of other factors have shaped and are shaping the nation's partisan identities. Each of these factors has merits in explaining both partisan politics today and the growing racial divide over time.

As many media and scholarly accounts have highlighted, America's growing income inequality has vast political repercussions. Anxiety over wages, jobs, and long-term economic prospects is clearly a powerful political force (Abramowitz 1994; Shafer and Johnson 2005). Moreover, cultural clashes over abortion, gay rights, sexual identity, and other moral/religious issues have become increasingly relevant to the nation's partisan politics (Adams 1997; Carsey and Layman 2006). Over time, leaders of the Republican and Democratic parties have put forward increasingly divergent solutions to these cultural questions. At the same time, leaders of the Evangelical church have increasingly sided with the Republican Party and have actively tried to convince religiously conservative Americans that their home is in the Republican Party. Similarly, the core ideological divide between liberals and conservatives has increasingly sorted Americans into one party or the other. For example, divisions over the proper role and size of government seem, to many, to be a primary source of the partisan polarization that plagues the nation.

Research offers strong empirical support for the influence of each of these factors in dividing Americans. The data show very clearly that economic concerns, cultural considerations, and core liberal–conservative ideologies have all become much more closely correlated with individual partisanship over time. Moreover, each of these nonracial factors has contributed in substantial ways to America's growing racial divide.

What Is the Relative Impact of Racial Considerations?

The ultimate question is not whether racial views or economic considerations affect the vote but rather how much racial considerations matter *relative* to the other factors we have just mentioned. That is difficult, if not impossible, to answer. Part of the problem is complexity. Individuals are driven by a range of motivations and ultimately make their political decisions through uniquely complex pathways. One

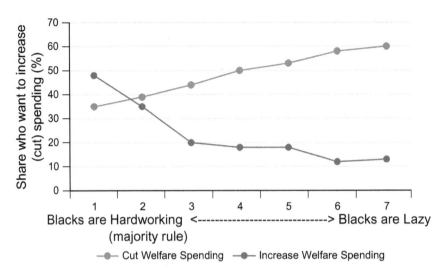

Figure 9.10 The Link Between Racial Attitudes and Welfare Views
How we think about Blacks in this country is closely related to how we think about welfare.
Source: Data from Gilens (2001).

person's motivations might even shift depending on the context, or a person might be weighing multiple considerations in one political instant.

The other reason it's hard to decipher the relative impact of race and other factors on voter decision-making and party affiliation is that race has now become closely intertwined with a range of ostensibly non-racial issues. For example, we now know that how individual Americans think about diverse policy issues—from welfare, health, and education to crime, taxes, and social security—are closely connected to how they think about race and immigration. Take welfare, for example. Surveys have shown that most Americans (wrongly) believe that most welfare recipients are Black. Surveys have also shown that many Americans view Blacks as lazy. If the two are put together, they can create powerful sentiments against welfare programs. In fact, landmark work by political scientist Martin Gilens has demonstrated that one of the best predictors of attitudes on welfare is attitudes about how lazy or hardworking African Americans are. His research, which we have partially reproduced in Figure 9.10, shows that Americans who hold positive views of work ethics among Blacks are more likely to favor increases in welfare spending. In other words, how we think about Blacks is intricately related to how we think about welfare.

Similar tests have shown that Americans' preferences regarding policies on healthcare, gun control, education, and even social security are closely linked to attitudes about racial and ethnic minorities (Filindra and Kaplan 2016; Tesler 2012; Winter 2008). Going further, Americans' attitudes about Latinos shape a number of policies related to immigration, education, and taxation (Abrajano and Hajnal 2015). Such research suggests the difficulty of disentangling attitudes about racial and ethnic groups from positions on other issues.

DIGGING DEEPER: WHY DID TRUMP GAIN MINORITY VOTES IN 2020?

One particularly puzzling aspect of the 2020 presidential election was the movement of a significant number of racial and ethnic minorities toward Donald Trump and the Republican Party. Why, despite four years of his anti-immigrant policies and his anti-minority rhetoric, did more minorities support him in 2020 than in 2016?

It is not an easy question to answer. We need first to note that the number of voters who shifted was actually relatively small. The exit poll used by most of the mainstream media, Edison Research, reported that support for Trump went up by only 4 percent among Blacks, 3 percent among Latinos, and 5 percent among Asian Americans (other election polls, such as those done by the Associated Press or the Pew Research Center, uncover somewhat different results). The same poll shows similar movement for down-ballot races for the House and the Senate. But regardless of the size of the movement, politicians will want to understand it, especially as many in the Republican Party see it as a sign of the future.

Some political observers attribute the shift to the nature of the campaign, in which Trump targeted issues that particular groups cared deeply about—for example, Cuban Americans' negative attitudes about socialism and Venezuelan Americans' concerns about authoritarianism. Others highlight the fact that Trump prioritized opening up the economy over COVID-19 concerns, a stance that may have particularly appealed to Latinos and others who were struggling economically and in danger of losing their jobs. Still others point to the idea that Trump's "machismo" appealed to Latino males. Religious and social conservatism among these minority groups may have also played a role. Perhaps most troubling of all for the Democratic Party is an argument that second-, third-, and fourth-generation Latinos and Asian Americans are increasingly identifying as working class and therefore are less motivated by racial/ethnic or immigrant-related concerns, which are the issues that have traditionally drawn people to the Democratic Party. Last, many lament that the Democratic Party has once again taken the Latino and Asian American votes for granted and failed to engage in any sort of sustained mobilization effort. Unfortunately, without much data, these arguments remain largely speculative. We do not yet know the source of Trump's growing minority support or more broadly whether racial and ethnic minority support for the Republican Party will continue to grow, or whether the GOP's performance in 2020 is simply within their traditional historical range.

Americans Who Choose Not to Engage with America's Parties

So far we have focused on the politically engaged Americans who choose a party and regularly vote. But many Americans do neither. In fact, the decision to opt out from the party system altogether is common, consequential, and at least in part connected to race and immigration.

Across the nation, some 42 percent of Americans chose not to identify with either political party in 2019. That figure has been rising over time—up from 33 percent in 1988 (Gallup 2019). And while many of these nonpartisans may, in fact, be closet partisans, the lack of partisan attachments for a large and growing segment of the population is potentially problematic.[11]

Racialized Patterns of Opting out

Moreover, research reveals racialized patterns in who does and does not identify with a party. For some Americans, choosing a party is not easy. But for immigrant Americans who were socialized in a different country and who are unfamiliar with America's parties and political system, choosing a party can be extremely challenging. Before engaging politically, these Americans need to learn what the parties stand for and how the electoral system works. The result is widespread nonpartisanship, especially among Latinos and Asian Americans, where much of the adult population is foreign-born. In fact, a slight majority of both populations in 2008— 56 percent of Latinos and 57 percent of Asian Americans—identified either as Independents or claim that they do not think in partisan terms at all (Hajnal and Lee 2011).[12] Latinos and Asian Americans may tend to vote Democratic when they do vote. But for the large share of Latinos and Asian Americans who do not vote or who are not even registered, the most common approach is to opt out of the party system altogether.

This line of research suggests that neither major party has a firm grasp on the entire Hispanic or Asian American population. At the same time, Democrats have made major inroads with minority voters in recent decades. More recent data from the 2020 Collaborative Multiracial Post-Election Survey, for instance, shows significant strides toward a crystallization of party identification, with 50 percent of Latinos and 44 percent of Asian Americans identifying as Democrats, 34 percent and 37 percent of both groups choosing not to identify in partisan terms, and only 17 percent and 19 percent identifying as Republicans. These figures, while still short of their more formidable rates of voting Democratic in elections, represent real change over a relatively short period of time.

At the same time, the hold of parties on these emerging racial minorities— particularly with respect to Latinos and Asian Americans—may yet be tenuous. Surveys of the Latino population, in particular, suggest that if Republicans change tactics on immigration, they could make major inroads with the Latino population. No similar data are available for Asian Americans, but experimental studies show that highlighting or deemphasizing racial discrimination against Asian Americans can induce large shifts in Asian American partisanship (Kuo, Malhotra, and

---

[11] Most of these nonpartisans do, when pushed, admit to leaning toward one party and these leaners often consistently support one party if they vote (Keith et al. 1992).

[12] That compares with very roughly about a third of the African American and White population.

Hyunjung 2014). All of this implies that large swaths of both pan-ethnic groups may still be up for grabs politically. As such, both parties clearly have reason to devote more resources to attracting these immigrant-based populations.

What Today's Political Parties Are Not Doing

Why have so many Latinos and Asian Americans opted out of the party system? Part of the answer, as we have already mentioned, is that the two groups are heavily immigrant based, and it is quite rational for immigrants or their children to opt out of a system that seems foreign or difficult to understand. Immigrants striving to make it in America may also have more pressing needs than politics.

But the Democratic and Republican parties also likely shoulder some of the blame. During the last major wave of immigration from the late nineteenth century to the early twentieth century local party machines actively mobilized new immigrants, wheedled favors and jobs for them, converted them into citizens, enrolled them as newly registered voters, and then ultimately schemed to manipulate their electoral choices. Given the rampant discrimination and corruption during that time, it is hard to view that era as a perfect model of inclusion and assimilation. For one thing, party leaders were engaging new immigrants for their own benefits—they wanted to win elections and new immigrants represented potentially pliably voters. But it is also absolutely clear that local political parties played a critical role in bringing new voters into the political process during that epoch.

By contrast, today's political parties do relatively little to mobilize and engage new immigrants. As scholars have documented, the share of potential voters who are contacted by political parties has declined precipitously (Rosenstone and Hansen 1993). Moreover, the limited mobilization that does occur has a clear racial tint. As we showed in Chapter 7 on "Political Participation," political parties are much more apt to contact reliable voters (read White Americans) than they are to try to activate low-propensity voters (read immigrants or Latinos and Asian Americans). In the typical election, the two major parties contacted 42 percent of the White population but only 31 percent of Latinos and 24 percent of Asian Americans.[13] The lack of a party presence in the immigrant community was highlighted by the words of a Mexican American community leader in East Los Angeles:

Stop anybody walking down the block, ask them, "Can you please tell me where is the local chapter or the local office of the Democratic Party in your neighborhood?" Everybody will look at you with bewilderment: "What is this crazy guy talking about?" (Wong 2006: 510)

It is not clear whether today's parties lack the organizational capacity, the cultural understanding, or perhaps even the political motivation to shepherd new

[13] Figures are the authors' calculations from the 2010–2018 American National Election Study.

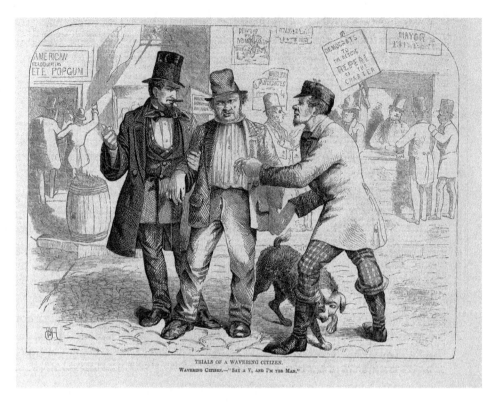

Photo 9.5 "Trials of a wavering citizen" shows a potential voter pulled in two directions by politicians. On one side, dressed in top hat and suit is a man representing the "nativists," and on the other, in plaid pants, is a man representing the Irish politician, New York City, November 1857.
Source: © Historical/Contributor/Corbis Historical/Getty Images.

immigrants into the political process and nurture secure attachments with a particular political party. What is clear is that the underwhelming presence of political parties in the everyday lives of Latinos and Asian Americans is reflected in the underwhelming rates of partisan attachments among both groups.

What Political Parties Today Could Do

To the extent that the Democratic and Republican parties are ignoring new immigrants to America, they should recognize that they do so at their peril, given the thin electoral margins that have decided recent presidential contests and the organizational imperative of both parties to sustain their membership rolls and maintain a base of party activists. Fortunately, the Democratic Party may be recognizing this. In 2020, large-scale mobilization of the Black community in Georgia and the Latino community in Arizona appear to have been decisive factors in Joe Biden's Electoral College victory.

Photo 9.6 A voting sign is seen during early voting for the June 2 primary outside the Prince Hall Masonic Temple in Ward 1, District of Columbia, Tuesday, May 26, 2020.
Source: © Tom Williams Contributor/CQ-Roll Call, Inc./Getty Images.

One other potential way for the two major parties to engage racial and ethnic minority voters is, of course, to align their policies with the stated policy preferences of minority voters. Much of the partisan history that we outlined earlier in this chapter suggests that Democrats have shifted to a variety of pro-minority policy positions and can thus now be viewed as the party of racial and ethnic minorities. But many scholars and many within the minority complain that neither party works particularly hard to favor minority interests. Paul Frymer in a landmark study argues that both parties have ignored Blacks, in particular, and that they are essentially a captured minority (Frymer 1999). According to this argument, with Democrats reluctant to appeal too much or too explicitly to minority voters for fear of losing White voters, and with Republicans trying to target White voters with an anti-minority agenda, Blacks have nowhere to go. In subsequent chapters we will look more closely at whether and how much the Democratic and Republican parties pursue policies that align with minority preferences. We will also question whether Democratic or Republican control has ultimately led to better economic outcomes for minorities. In both cases, the research suggests, minorities appear to fare better when Democrats are in charge. The Democratic Party can certainly do more to attract minority voters and to aid the minority community, but the evidence suggests that its efforts so far have made a real difference to the minority population.

WHAT IT LOOKS LIKE TODAY: THE POLITICS OF NATIVE AMERICANS, MIDDLE EASTERN AMERICANS, AND BIRACIAL AMERICANS

In studies of racial politics, Native Americans, Middle Eastern Americans, and biracial Americans typically have not received much attention. And so we cannot say precisely where each of these groups *should* fit into America's complex racial mosaic and its partisan politics. Each group is similar to Blacks, Latinos, and Asian Americans on two critically important dimensions—that is, each is a racial minority in a nation dominated by White Americans, and each faces real discrimination across a variety of contexts and circumstances. Thus, we might expect their attachment to the Democratic Party to mirror what we have seen with Blacks, Latinos, and Asian Americans. But on other dimensions, these three groups are somewhat distinct from each other. In particular, members of the three populations tend to reside at very different ends of the socioeconomic spectrum, with American Indians, at least by some metrics, more disadvantaged economically than almost any other racial and ethnic group; Middle Eastern Americans relatively well-off; and biracial Americans somewhere near the middle. To the extent that class structures our politics, those differences could be consequential. American Indians also have a special sovereign nation status that some suggest should lead to greater independence and less attachment to mainstream political parties. The question of Middle Eastern Americans' political affiliations entails other complex considerations, given uncertainty about whether Middle Eastern should even be considered a separate racial category (many in this group identify as White), whether religion rather than region of origin should be the defining feature of this group (is Muslim American a more relevant category?), and whether group identity might be more meaningfully based on national origin—for example, Syrian or Iranian or Egyptian—instead of some larger but largely fabricated pan-ethnic identity such as Middle Eastern.

Despite the complexities associated with these group identities and features, the data show quite clearly that all three closely align with the Democratic Party, though the exact figures vary from survey to survey and from election to election.[14] One study found that American Indians were almost twice as likely to identify as Democratic as they were to identify as Republican (Koch 2016). And in 2020, roughly 60 percent of the group voted for Democratic candidates at the House, Senate, and presidential levels, and only about a third favored Republican candidates in these contests. Partisan figures for Middle Eastern Americans are almost identical. Using survey data, we estimate that two-thirds of Middle Eastern

---

[14] Figures for American Indian, Middle Eastern American, Muslim American, and multiracial votes and partisanship are based on analysis of the ANES Cumulative File as well as the CCES Cumulative Files, or in the case of the 2020 American Indian Vote, the American Election Eve Poll. These figures mirror estimates from other published work on three groups. See Koch (2016) on American Indians, Pew (2018) on Muslim Americans, and Davenport (2018) on biracial Americans.

Photo 9.7 Fadima Hassan was more than happy to show off her "I Voted" sign after she voted at the Brian Coyle Center, Minneapolis, November 3, 2020.
Source: Photo Elizabeth Flores © *Star Tribune* via Getty Images/Contributor/Star Tribune/ Getty Images.

American voters checked off Hilary Clinton's name in 2016. By contrast, only a third supported Donald Trump. That same two-to-one split occurred in the 2012 presidential election as well as in recent House elections.

If we instead focus on Muslim Americans as the category of interest, we see an even sharper Democratic skew. Pew reports that in 2017, 66 percent of Muslim Americans identified as Democratic as compared with only 13 percent who said they were Republican or leaned toward Republican. Three-quarters or more of the Muslim American vote has gone to the Democratic candidate in the past three presidential elections. Multiracial Americans, too, a group that one might expect to behave slightly more like Whites, have largely affiliated themselves with the Democratic Party. Very roughly 60 percent of multiracial Americans voted Democratic in the past three presidential elections and in recent congressional contests. In this respect, American Indians, Middle Eastern Americans, and multiracial Americans all parallel the three major racial and ethnic minority groups. And following a pattern seen in Latino and Asian American populations, American Indians, Middle Eastern Americans, and biracial Americans are also substantially more likely than White Americans to identify as Independent or nonpartisan—a pattern that suggests that these groups do not feel entirely welcome in the American party system and/or that the two parties are not doing enough to attract their votes.

All in all, despite potentially different interests and motivations, all three of these smaller groups closely mirror the partisan proclivities of other larger racial and ethnic minorities.

Other Ways Race Could Impact Elections and Parties

We have described a number of obvious ways race can affect elections and parties. Now we will focus on other more subtle or more indirect factors.

To begin, one's racial or ethnic identity can shape how one votes because it leads people to prioritize different issues. For example, the experience of being a racial and ethnic minority in a largely White nation often elevates one's focus on racial considerations over class-based concerns. At least for African Americans, evidence indicates that class status does little to shape the vote and that Blacks, regardless of their economic standing, support the Democratic Party (Dawson 1994). Others have argued that Latinos and Asian Americans weigh immigration policy more heavily when they are casting their votes because of their relatively close connections to the immigration experience (Barreto and Segura 2014). It is also possible—although largely unproven—that being relatively new to America and knowing the political system less intimately means that immigration-heavy groups generally weigh policy issues and partisanship less than longer-term residents. Finally, some research indicates that being religious can matter in different ways for different racial and ethnic groups. While the connection between Evangelicalism and Republican Party identity is quite powerful among Whites, it may be less so among Asian American and Latino Evangelicals (Wong 2018).

Also, as we detailed in Chapter 7, "Political Participation," the way a party addresses racial issues can matter in many subtle ways during the campaign. For example, a range of explicitly racial and implicitly racial cues, put forward either by the campaigns or by the media, can shape attitudes about parties and candidates. Finally, the race of the candidates themselves can alter the tenor of the campaign and the final vote tally. Most of those who have studied Barack Obama's electoral contests have concluded that Obama suffered a racial penalty for being a Black man (Hutchings 2009; Parker 2016). However, as we note in Chapter 10, "Do Elected Officials Look Like Their Constituents?" the findings related to just how much Black, Latino, or Asian American candidates suffer at the ballot box are somewhat unclear.

Conclusion

When Americans vote, they divide first and foremost along racial lines. At almost every contest, at almost every level, the vast majority of African Americans, Latinos, and Asian Americans typically choose the same party or candidate. The clear majority of Whites generally choose the opposite. Race generally dwarfs other demographic factors when it comes to the vote and party identification. For example, despite decades of growing economic inequality, persistent media attention to economic insecurity among large swathes of the population, and the growing disillusionment of the White working class, class divisions are consistently overshadowed by racial divides. The nation may be experiencing an unprecedented increase in income inequality, and those on the top may be more economically and socially distant from those on the bottom, but little of that economic divide seems to be affecting political choices. At least when compared with race, social class plays a peripheral role in the electorate's choices. Age and gender are also secondary to race in determining party affiliation. And one's race is also more telling about one's political choices than is one's region of origin or sexual orientation. The one factor that has now begun to rival race as an influence on political affiliation is religion.

As America has become more racially diverse over time, racial divisions in the vote have become more pronounced. A little over a half century ago, before the Civil Rights Movement, racial divisions were relatively muted; neither party was closely associated with a racial group—an irony given the institutionally sanctioned discrimination and segregation of that day. But that party system has slowly transformed over time to the point where the Republican Party is very clearly the White party, while the Democratic Party has become closely linked with the minority vote. The way that race and ethnicity affect politics and party affiliation is also becoming more complex over time. Decades ago, the subject of race focused almost solely on the Black–White divide. But as the recent wave of immigration has transformed the demographics of the nation, it has also transformed the politics of the nation, with a White backlash against immigration pushing more and more Whites into the Republican fold and more and more Latinos and Asian Americans into the welcoming arms of the Democratic Party.

What is driving this increasingly large racial divide in the polity? Some point to economic anxiety. Others point to religion and morality. But there is little doubt that how we think about politics is increasingly and fundamentally driven by how we think about race and immigration—a fact that can and should raise alarm bells. Politics is bound to create division, but when those divisions so closely mirror racial and ethnic identity, it can lay the groundwork for more explosive conflicts tomorrow.

KEY TERMS

Linked fate model
Party identification
Racial realignment
Racial threat
Southern strategy

DISCUSSION QUESTIONS

1. Which demographic factors most divide American voters?
2. How have the coalitions behind the two parties changed over time?
3. Why have race and party identification become so intertwined?
4. Why does race dominate over class when it comes to predicting vote choice?
5. Why do so many Americans choose not to identify with either major party?
6. What do America's changing demographics imply for the future balance of power between Republicans and Democrats and more generally for the future of race in American politics?

ANNOTATED SUGGESTED READINGS

See Edward G. Carmines and James A. Stimson. 1989. *Issue Evolution: Race and the Transformation of American Politics*. Princeton: Princeton University Press, for an empirically rich account of the growing divide between Democrats and Republicans on race.

See Thomas Byrne Edsall and Mary D. Edsall. 1991. *Chain Reaction: The Impact of Race, Rights, and Taxes on American Politics*. New York: W. W. Norton, for a more descriptive history of the how race became infused in party politics.

See Michael Tesler. 2016. *Post-Racial or Most-Racial? Race and Politics in the Obama Era*. Chicago: University of Chicago Press, for the growing impact of race under President Barack Obama.

See Marisa Abrajano and Zoltan Hajnal. 2015. *White Backlash: Immigration, Race, and American Politics*. Princeton: Princeton University Press, for an illustration of the broadening impact of immigration on American party politics.

See Michael C. Dawson. 1994. *Behind the Mule: Race and Class in African-American Politics*. Princeton: Princeton University Press, for the definitive historical account of Black partisanship and vote choice.

See Zoltan Hajnal and Taeku Lee. 2011. *Why Americans Don't Join the Party: Race, Immigration, and the Failure of Political Parties to Engage the Electorate*. Princeton: Princeton University Press, for an explanation of nonpartisanship among different racial and ethnic groups.

CHAPTER REFERENCES

Abrajano, Marisa and Zoltan Hajnal. 2015. *White Backlash: Immigration, Race, and American Politics*. Princeton: Princeton University Press.

Abramowitz, Alan I. 1994. "Issue Evolution Reconsidered: Racial Attitudes and Partisanship in the US Electorate," *American Journal of Political Science* 38: 1–24.

Adams, Greg. 1997. "Abortion: Evidence of Issue Evolution," *American Journal of Political Science* 41: 718–737.

Barreto, Matt and Gary Segura. 2014. *Latino America: How America's Most Dynamic Population Is Poised to Transform the Politics of the Nation*. New York: Public Affairs.

Blumer, Herbert. 1958. "Race Prejudice as a Sense of Group Position," *Pacific Sociological Review* 1: 3–7.

Bobo, Lawrence D. and Mia Tuan. 2006. *Prejudice in Politics: Group Position, Public Opinion, and the Wisconsin Treaty Rights Dispute*. Cambridge, MA: Harvard University Press.

Campbell, Angus, Philip E. Converse, Warren E. Miller, and Donald E. Stokes. 1960. *The American Voter*. Chicago: University of Chicago Press.

Carmines, Edward G. and James A. Stimson. 1989. *Issue Evolution: Race and the Transformation of American Politics*. Princeton: Princeton University Press.

Carsey, Thomas M. and Geoffrey C. Layman. 2006. "Changing Sides or Changing Minds? Party Identification and Policy Preferences in the American Electorate," *American Journal of Political Science* 50(2): 464–477.

Coates, Ta-Nehisi. 2017. "The First White President," *The Atlantic*, October 15. www.theatlantic.com/magazine/archive/2017/10/the-first-white-president-ta-nehisi-coates/537909/

Corzine, Jay, James Creech, and Lin Corzine. 1983. "Black Concentration and Lynchings in the South: Testing Blalock's Power-Threat Hypothesis," *Social Forces* 61: 774–796.

Davenport, Lauren. 2018. *Politics beyond Black and White: Biracial Identity and Attitudes in America*. New York: Cambridge University Press.

Dawson, Michael C. 1994. *Behind the Mule: Race and Class in African-American Politics*. Princeton: Princeton University Press.

Donovan, Todd. 2010. "Obama and the White Vote," *Political Research Quarterly* 63: 863–874.

Edsall, Thomas Byrne and Mary D. Edsall. 1991. *Chain Reaction: The Impact of Race, Rights, and Taxes on American Politics*. New York: W. W. Norton.

Enders, Adam and Steven Small. 2016. "Racial Prejudice Not Populism or Authoritarianism Predicts Support for Trump over Clinton," *The Washington Post*, May 26.

Filindra, Alexandra and Noah J. Kaplan. 2016. "Racial Resentment and Whites' Gun Policy Preferences in Contemporary America," *Political Behavior* 38: 255–275.

Frymer, Paul. 1999. *Uneasy Alliances: Race and Party Competition in America*. Princeton: Princeton University Press.

Gilens, Martin. 2001. *Why Americans Hate Welfare: Race, Media, and the Politics of Antipoverty Policy*. Chicago: University of Chicago Press.

Gimpel, James. 2017. "Immigration Policy Opinion and the 2016 Presidential Vote." Center for Immigration Studies, Washington, D.C.

Green, Donald P., Bradley Palmquist, Eric Schickler, and Giordano Bruno. 2002. *Partisan Hearts and Minds: Political Parties and the Social Identity of Voters*. New Haven, CT: Yale University Press.

Hajnal, Zoltan. 2020. *Dangerously Divided: How Race and Class Shape Winning and Losing in American Politics*. Cambridge: Cambridge University Press.

Hajnal, Zoltan and Taeku Lee. 2011. *Why Americans Don't Join the Party: Race, Immigration, and the Failure of Political Parties to Engage the Electorate*. Princeton: Princeton University Press.

Hajnal, Zoltan L. and Jessica L. Trounstine 2013. "What Underlies Urban Politics? Race, Class, Ideology, Partisanship, and the Urban Vote," *Urban Affairs Review* 49(1): 63–69.

Hutchings, Vincent L. 2009. "Change or More of the Same? Evaluating Racial Attitudes in the Obama Era," *Public Opinion Quarterly* 73(5): 917–942.

Iyengar, Shanto and Sean J. Westwood. 2015. "Fear and Loathing across Party Lines: New Evidence on Group Polarization," *American Journal of Political Science* 59: 690–707.

Katznelson, Ira. 2005. *When Affirmative Action Was White: An Untold History of Racial Inequality in Twentieth-Century America*. New York: W. W. Norton.

Keith, Bruce E., David B. Magleby, Candice J. Nelson, Elizabeth Orr, Mark C. Westlye, and Raymond E. Wolfinger et al. 1992. *The Myth of the Independent Voter*. Berkeley: University of California Press.

Kinder, Donald R. and Lynn Sanders. 1996. *Divided by Color: Racial Politics and Democratic Ideals*. Chicago: University of Chicago Press.

Koch, Jeffrey W. 2016. "Partisanship and Non-Partisanship among American Indians," *American Politics Research* 45: 673–691.

Kuo, Alexander, Neil A. Malhotra, and Cecilia Hyunjung Mo. 2014. "Why Do Asian Americans Identify as Democrats? Testing Theories of Social Exclusion and Intergroup Solidarity." SSRN Working Paper.

Kuziemko, Ilyana and Ebonya Washington. 2018. "Why Did Democrats Lose the South? Bringing New Data to an Old Debate," *American Economic Review* 108: 2830–2867.

Lajevard, Nazita. 2018. "Access Denied: Exploring Muslim American Representation and Exclusion by State Legislators," *Politics, Groups, and Identities* 8(5): 1–12.

Lajevardi, Nazita and Marisa Abrajano. 2019. "How Negative Sentiment toward Muslim Americans Predicts Support for Trump in the 2016 Presidential Election," *Journal of Politics* 81(1): doi.org/10.1086/700001.

Lamont, Michele, Bo Yun Park, and Elena Alaya-Hurtado. 2017. "Trump's Electoral Speeches and His Appeal to the American White Working Class," *British Journal of Sociology* 68: 153–178.

Lee, Taeku. 2002. *Mobilizing Public Opinion*. Chicago: University of Chicago Press.

McVeigh, Rory, David Cunningham, and Justin Farrell. 2014. "Political Polarization as a Social Movement Outcome: 1960s Klan Activism and Its Enduring Impact on Political Realignment in Southern Counties, 1960 to 2000," *American Sociological Review* 79(6): 1144–1171.

National Public Radio (NPR). 2016. "Why Economic Anxiety Is Driving Working Class Voters to 'Trumpism.'" www.pbs.org/newshour/show/why-economic-anxiety-is-driving-working-class-voters-to-trumpism.

Parker, Christopher. 2016. "Race and Politics in the Age of Obama," *Annual Review of Sociology* 42: 217–230.

Parker, Christopher and Matt Barreto. 2013. *Change They Can't Believe in: The Tea Party and Reactionary Politics in America*. Princeton: Princeton University Press.

Pew Research Center. 2018. "Shifting Public Views on Legal Immigration into the U.S." www.people-press.org/2018/06/28/shifting-public-views-on-legal-immigration-into-the-u-s/#many-overestimate-the-share-of-the-immigrant-population-that-is-in-the-u-s-illegally.

Piketty, Tomas. 2018. *The Economics of Inequality*. Cambridge, MA: Harvard University Press.

Rosenstone, Steven J. and John Mark Hansen. 1993. *Mobilization, Participation, and Democracy in America*. New York: Macmillan.

Shafer, Byron E. and Richard Johnston. 2005. *The End of Southern Exceptionalism: Class, Race, and Partisan Change in the Postwar South*. Cambridge, MA: Harvard University Press.

Sidanius, Jim and Felicia Pratto. 1999. *Social Dominance: An Intergroup Theory of Social Hierarchy and Oppression*. New York: Cambridge University Press.

Sides, Jon. 2017. "Race, Religion, and Immigration in 2016," Democracy Fund Voter Study Group. www.voterstudygroup.org/publication/race-religion-immigration-2016.

Sides, Jon, Michael Tesler, and Lynn Vavreck. 2017. "The 2016 U.S. Election: How Trump Lost and Won," *Journal of Democracy* 28: 34–44.

Sides, Jon, Michael Tesler, and Lynn Vavreck. 2018. *Identity Crisis, the 2016 Presidential Campaign and the Battle for the Meaning of America*. Princeton: Princeton University Press.

Stern, Ken. 2017. "Inside How Trump Won the White Working Class," *Vanity Fair*, January 5. www.vanityfair.com/news/2017/01/how-trump-won-the-white-working-class.

Tesler, Michael. 2012. *Obama's Race: The 2008 Election and the Dream of a Post-Racial America*. Chicago: Chicago University Press.

Tesler, Michael. 2016a. *Post-Racial or Most-Racial?: Race and Politics in the Obama Era*. Chicago: University of Chicago Press.

Tesler, Michael. 2016b. "Trump is the First Modern Republican to Win the Nomination Based on Racial Prejudice," *The Washington Post*, August 1.

Tesler, Michael and David O. Sears. 2010. *Obama's Race: The 2008 Election and the Dream of a Post-Racial America*. Chicago: University of Chicago Press.

Valentino, Nicholas A. and David O. Sears. 2005. "Old Times There Are Not Forgotten: Race and Partisan Realignment in the Contemporary South," *American Journal of Political Science* 49: 672–688.

Valentino, Nicholas A., Carly Wayne, and Marzia Oceno. 2018. "Mobilizing Sexism: The Interaction of Emotion and Gender Attitudes in the 2016 US Presidential Election," *Public Opinion Quarterly* 82: 799–821.

Winter, Nicholas. 2008. *Dangerous Frames: How Ideas About Race and Gender Shape Public Opinion*. Chicago: University of Chicago Press.

Wong, Janelle. 2018. *Immigrants, Evangelicals, and Politics in an Era of Demographic Change*. New York: Russell Sage Foundation.

Wong, Janelle S. 2006. *Democracy's Promise: Immigrants and American Civic Institutions*. Ann Arbor: University of Michigan Press.

Yglesias, Matthew. "One Chart That Shows Racism Has Everything and Nothing to Do with Republican Election Wins," *Vox*, November 13. www.vox.com/policy-and-politics/2018/11/13/18080836/midterm-election-results-2018.

Part IV

Outcomes in American Democracy

10 Do Elected Officials Look Like Their Constituents?

On August 9, 2014, Michael Brown Jr., an 18-year-old unarmed Black man, was fatally shot by a White police officer in Ferguson, a suburb of St. Louis. That incident inflamed tensions in the community. For days, residents took to the streets to march and protest. Others looted businesses, vandalized vehicles, and confronted police officers. Police responded with smoke bombs, flash grenades, rubber bullets, and tear gas. At times, Ferguson looked and felt like a war zone. The violence, anger, and uproar spread throughout much of the country. Across the nation, relations between the African American community and police soured.

There are many factors that contributed to unrest in Ferguson, Missouri. But the fact that African Americans had almost no representation in city government likely drove much of what happened in that Missouri suburb. The figures are stark. At the time of the unrest, Blacks represented two-thirds of the city population, yet the mayor, five of six City Council members, six of seven school board members, and fifty of fifty-three police officers were not Black. What if the police force had more closely resembled the make-up of the city? What if African Americans had been key decision-makers in the city before or after the incident? Could the event and its aftermath have been avoided?

In this chapter, we begin to examine political representation, focusing first on descriptive representation, or the degree to which elected officials demographically resemble the voters they represent. Does the leadership of the nation physically mirror the public?

We start that investigation by looking back. How have the faces of American politics changed over time, especially since the landmark legislative victories of the Civil Rights Movement of the 1960s? Then, looking across the nation today, how close have we come to electing a government that resembles the population, writ large? What we will find is that although racial and ethnic minorities have made enormous gains in winning office, they remain greatly underrepresented. The nation's halls of power remain overwhelmingly White. This chapter attempts to explain why this is so. A number of elements play a role, including institutional barriers, financial hurdles, and the pool of candidates for office. We will examine closely the role that White voters themselves play in this underrepresentation. Close study reveals that White voters tend to favor White candidates over minority candidates. We close by looking at the impact of this underrepresentation on the politics of the nation. Or, put more succinctly: do minority leaders make a difference in governing?

Photo 10.1 Armed police confronting a protestor in Ferguson. "Hands up, don't shoot" became a symbol of the movement that the Ferguson uprising helped spawn after it was rumored that Michael Brown was shot and killed despite raising his hands and mouthing the words "Don't shoot."
Source: © Scott Olson/Staff/Getty Images News/Getty Images.

This chapter represents an important shift in our investigation of race in American democracy. In previous chapters we examined the underpinnings of America's constitutional democracy (Part I); the experience of race in America, from both institutional and individual perspectives (Part II); and inputs into our system of government, from public opinion to parties and elections (Part III). All of this has helped to inform us about the openness of our democracy and about the desires of the public. But what we have looked at so far represents only the beginning of the democratic process. For many interested in race and American democracy, their primary concerns relate to the outputs of the democratic process. Who wins office? What policies do they pursue? Who gets represented? What interests get represented? We agree that these questions are of tantamount importance in judging our democracy. Thus, these questions of representation are the subject of the next two chapters.

Tyranny of the Majority?

Democracy is not a game that we engage in purely for the fun of it. There are immense consequences to outcomes. After the campaign is over and the votes have been tallied, winners will have access to the halls of power. They will have control over vast economic resources. And they will be able to make policy decisions that deeply affect the well-being of every citizen and resident in the nation. On the other side of the contest stand the losers. These losers will be on the outside looking in. Their interests and wishes may or may not be ignored. Their pocketbooks may or may not be filled. The simple truth is that in a majoritarian democracy, where those in the numerical majority have the final say about an issue, there will be winners and losers.

All of this is a normal and perhaps even a healthy aspect of democracy. But what if some win consistently and others lose consistently? What if those from a particular social class or a specific racial group end up as losers over and over again? And what if the advantaged class or the advantaged race begins to trample the rights and interests of the disadvantaged class or the disadvantaged race? In short, with democracy comes the possibility of a majority using its numbers and power to repeatedly overrun the interests and preferences of a minority—an outcome we often call tyranny of the majority.

This is, of course, not a new concern. Anxiety about the fate of minorities in this nation goes back to the Founders and James Madison's concerns about "the superior force of an interested and overbearing majority" (Hamilton, Madison, and Jay 1961: 77). That is in part why the drafters of the U.S. Constitution created a set of institutional features, such as the judiciary, that serve as checks and balances on the will of the people. Thus, the courts could, for example, step in and rule same-sex marriage constitutional at a time when the public had made it clear that it wanted to outlaw same-sex marriage in multiple states.

Nevertheless, the fact that almost every election in the United States is conducted under "winner takes all" majoritarian rules—in which the candidate with the most votes wins full power—only serves to heighten concerns about the welfare of losers in American democracy. Indeed, there are plenty of cases where mayoral candidates win office with roughly half or even less of the vote. They win in our system because they get more votes than any other candidate. But does support from half of all voters and in some cases far less than half of city residents (when many candidates are on the ballot and turnout is low, half of the votes can equate to a tiny share of the total city population) really mean that a single person should be able to decide and enact policy?

At least in theory, a slim majority of voters could be electing candidates and passing laws that a large minority strongly opposes. Pushing the last example a little further, after getting elected those same mayors can choose to ease gun restrictions in their cities even if the residents of their cities strongly favor stronger gun control. Comparative cross-national data add fuel to this anxious fire. Research suggests that majoritarian systems like the United States tend to be less friendly to minority interests than proportional representation systems that distribute electoral offices and political power roughly in proportion to the vote (Lijphart 1996). In these proportional representation systems—which are in place in most European countries—the share of votes that each party gets from the public translates into that party's share of seats in the legislature. Thus, for example, under proportional representation, environmental parties like the Green Party that are often supported by only a small minority of the electorate can still win seats in the legislature and can thus have real influence over how countries choose to address climate change. By contrast, in the United States, a small minority party that cared deeply about global warming would have almost no chance of winning an election and thus would likely have little influence over policy. If there is going to be tyranny of the majority in any democracy, a majoritarian system like the United States is a likely candidate.

Although these concerns are not new, they may be especially relevant today. As America has become more unequal economically, with the latest figures revealing that 30 percent of the nation's wealth is held by the richest 1 percent of the population, concerns about a lack of representation among the have-nots have grown. Moreover, with wealthy people funneling almost unimaginable quantities of money into the political process, there is increasing concern among many Americans that the rich rule America.

All of these questions about uneven governance gain new urgency as America becomes more racially diverse. A "White" nation may not be majority-White for much longer, which puts the country at a tipping point: this greater mix of people could encourage greater collaboration and engender greater compromise; but it could also spark greater conflict and greater upheaval. The probability that Whites will be a minority in the United States within the next fifty years; the calls by African Americans for the nation to once and for all address racial inequities going back 300 years, to the start of the slave trade in the North American colonies; and the efforts of America's new immigrants to become full-fledged Americans with equal rights and equal access to government resources all raise the stakes for our democracy.

The racial divisions and inequities that we have seen in previous chapters raise even more concerns about American democracy and the degree to which it represents all racial and ethnic groups. We have seen that when America votes, there is a clear racial pattern to that vote. In most elections, the majority of White America ends up on one side of the vote, while the overwhelming majority of racial and ethnic minorities end up on the other.

The potentially negative consequences of this large racial divide are not hard to imagine. Indeed, the math is quite simple. Although America is becoming more and more racially diverse, it is still a nation in which Whites dominate the political process. Non-Hispanic Whites still represent 61 percent of the population. And, more critically, they still account for roughly 70 percent of the active voters in the country.[1] Given that most Whites oppose candidates favored by most racial and ethnic minorities, the chance of minorities losing out in American democracy is very real. Does the White majority shut racial and ethnic minorities out of most aspects

---

[1] Data on the population are from the 2017 American Community Survey and data on the share of voters who are White are from the National Exit Poll.

of the democratic process? That is a question we will address later in this chapter and in the chapter that follows.

Measuring Representation

What is the reality of representation in the United States today? Is there, in fact, tyranny of the White majority? Are Whites using their numerical dominance to trample racial minorities in the electoral arena?

Measuring representation is not easy.[2] Over the course of the next two chapters, we will focus on a number of different measures of representation. By looking at a range of standard measures as well as at some new ways of gauging minority representation, we hope to ultimately present a fairly complete and accurate picture of minority representation in American democracy. But for now we focus on *descriptive representation*—the degree to which elected officials demographically resemble the voters they represent. We start here because when scholars and others seek to understand how well a group is incorporated into a democracy or how much influence they have, descriptive representation is the first measure to which they almost always turn.

Counting up the number of racial and ethnic minorities in office makes sense. If minorities are shut out of the halls of power, they are at a severe disadvantage. Holding the levers of power and having a voice in the deliberations that determine policy is likely to be critical. Black, Latino, Asian American, and Native American leaders almost certainly need to be in office if there is going to be meaningful policy change.

The election of minorities to office might also be important to minority communities for other less concrete reasons. Having minorities in office might also aid in more symbolic ways. Seeing someone in an elected office who looks like you could be a powerful signal about the openness and legitimacy of a political system. That signal could, in turn, lead to greater confidence that the system works, greater trust in government, and higher political participation within the racial and ethnic minority population.

Another reason to focus on descriptive representation is that a wide range of studies have shown that minority voters tend to favor minority candidates. One such study showed quite definitely that Blacks and Hispanic Americans both greatly value having representatives from their own racial and ethnic group governing in their districts (Casellas and Wallace 2014). Others have shown that in biracial elections pitting White and non-White candidates against each other, racial and ethnic voters generally choose the racial and ethnic minority candidate—and often in overwhelming numbers (Hajnal 2010).

---

[2] For excellent summaries of the different dimensions of representation, see Mansbridge (1999); Phillips (1998).

It is clear that the election of minorities to office is a major marker of minority empowerment. As such, an assessment of descriptive representation is an important first step in gauging the fate of minorities in American democracy.

Counting Minorities in Office

When we count up the number of racial and ethnic minorities in office across the nation, we see tremendous growth in minority representation in the 70 years following the Voting Rights Act of 1965, which provided unprecedented protection of the vote for African Americans. As illustrated by Figure 10.1, there has been a steady and dramatic increase in empowerment for Blacks, Latinos, and Asian Americans. Each of these groups has gone from having almost no representation in elected office to holding a large and varied array of offices. African Americans were almost entirely shut out of the governing process well into the 1960s. As late as 1965 there were only 500 Black elected officials. But that number has steadily grown since then. Today African Americans preside over 10,000 offices at the local, state, and federal levels across the county. Likewise, Latinos have grown from a small number of elected positions—just over 1,000 in 1973—to over 6,000 today. And Asian American representation grew from under 250 documented cases in 1980 to over 1,000 offices today. Racial and ethnic minorities are an increasingly large presence in the nation's halls of power.

Moreover, these gains have occurred at almost every level of representation. In particular, the list of African American success stories in the last half century has been long and notable. Over that time, African Americans have won office at every conceivable level. Carl Stokes became the first Black mayor of a major city in 1967. His victory in Cleveland was eventually followed by Black mayoral victories in almost every major American city. African Americans have served as mayor in New York City, Los Angeles, Chicago, Houston, Philadelphia, Dallas, San Francisco, and many others. A similar pattern is evident in Congress. In the early

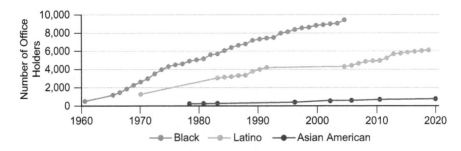

Figure 10.1 Increasing Descriptive Representation, 1965–2020

Notice here both that there were almost no racial and ethnic minorities in office in the 1960s and that the number of minorities in offices rises sharply and fairly evenly over time. However, as the figure also shows, the growth of Asian American elected officials, while steady, has not been as sharp.

Source: Hajnal (2020).

1960s, there were only four African American members of Congress. Today there are fifty-nine.[3] African Americans have also won office as governors, state legislators, city council members, and every other elected office imaginable. The highest hurdle was overcome when Barack Obama was elected president in 2008, and Kamala Harris was elected the first African American, first Asian American, and first female vice president in 2020. Even today, African Americans are winning offices for the first time. Recently, St. Paul, Minnesota, Helena, Montana, and Milledgeville, Georgia elected their first Black mayors.

WHAT IT LOOKS LIKE TODAY: WHO FITS INTO WHICH RACIAL CATEGORY?

One issue with counting up racial and ethnic minorities in office is determining who fits into which category. President Barack Obama is a prime example. His father, Barack Obama Sr., was Black and was born of Luo ethnicity in Kenya. His mother, Ann Dunham, was White and was born in Wichita, Kansas. Obama also lived for a brief period in Indonesia with his stepfather, Lolo Soetoro, who was born in Indonesia. Obama recognized the diversity of his extended family: "It's like a little mini-United Nations," he said. "I've got relatives who look like Bernie Mac, and I've got relatives who look like Margaret Thatcher."[4] Given this background, should we say that Barack Obama is Black, White, multiracial, or some other category?

Perhaps the best way to answer the racial identity question in this case—or any other case—is to ask the person directly. Obama self-identifies as Black. Or, at least, we know that he checked the category "Black, African American, or Negro" on the 2010 Census questionnaire. For any politician, the perceptions of voters are also key. A slim majority of Americans—52 percent—label him as mixed race, while a little over a quarter describe the former president as "Black." Complicating matters even more, different groups within American society viewed him differently. The same survey found that a majority of African Americans (55 percent) see Obama as Black. By contrast, Whites and Hispanics were more likely to call him mixed-race (Gonzalez-Barrera and Hugo Lopez 2015).

Barack Obama was certainly not the first politician to raise issues of identity. In fact, the very first African American in Congress, Hiram Rhodes Revels, was also Scottish and Croatan Indian, making him possibly one of the first American Indians in the Senate as well. Likewise, Elizabeth Warren's 2020 presidential campaign and her claims of being Native American have reintroduced questions of who can or should be considered Native American.

The folly of trying to identify the race of these politicians lays bare the deep problems with racial categories and racial identities. There are any number of

---

[3] That includes three Black senators (Raphael Warnock, Cory Booker, and Tim Scott) and fifty-six Black House members.

[4] Quoted in "Keeping Hope Alive: Barack Obama Puts Family First," *The Oprah Winfrey Show*, October 18, 2006.

Photo 10.2 A family portrait including Barack Obama hangs in the Obama family home in Kogelo, western Kenya, January, 2008, before Barack Obama was elected the 44th President of the United States. Obama's father, Barack Hussein Obama, was born and raised in Kogelo. Obama's parents separated when he was young, and he was raised by his mother, Stanley Ann Dunham—and later, his maternal grandparents—in Hawaii.
Source: Photo Peter Macdiarmid © Peter Macdiarmid/Staff/Getty Images News/Getty Images.

complications with our existing racial categories. Is Hispanic a race or a separate ethnic category? The Census considers "Hispanic or Latino" a separate ethnic category defined "as a person of Cuban, Mexican, Puerto Rican, South or Central American, or other Spanish culture or origin regardless of race," but survey data show that around 70 percent of the Latino population would choose "Hispanic" as their race if given the choice (Cohn 2017). Another complication is that most of the Hispanic population would actually identify with their national origin group if given that choice, suggesting that the group might not even be a single category (Taylor et al. 2017).

Likewise, how does one classify a group like Filipinos who often have Spanish names and who retain many aspects of Hispanic culture but hail from Asia? What about Indians and others from South Asia who have at times been categorized by the Census as White and at others as non-White? We tend to consider race as fixed, solid, and clear, but as a socially constructed category, it is anything but clear. In short, it is difficult to know who fits where.

Latino and Asian American elected officials have had a growing impact on almost every level of American politics. Latino electoral victories often started later than those of African Americans. The first Latino mayor of a major city—Henry Cisneros in San Antonio—was not elected until 1981. But since that time the number of Hispanics in office has grown rapidly at almost all levels. Latinos have since garnered the governor's office in four states, they have won increasing numbers of seats in the House and Senate, and they have held office at every state and local level. Likewise, Asian Americans lacked substantial representation until well into the 1970s. But the last four decades have seen a rise in the number and stature of Asian American leaders. The first Asian American state governor, George Ariyoshi, took office in Hawaii in 1974 and was followed by increasing numbers of Asian Americans elected to the Senate, House, and state legislatures. The nation has never elected an Asian American or Latino president, but the 2016 crop of Republican presidential hopefuls contained two Asian American contenders: Bobby Jindal and Nikki Haley. In 2020, an Asian American—Andrew Yang—and a Pacific Islander—Tulsi Gabbard—ran in the 2020 Democratic primaries. Kamala Harris' ascension to the vice presidency marked the first time that a woman of Asian American and African American ancestry has held that office.

A more systematic look at the numbers confirms the enormous gains each racial and ethnic minority group has made at every level over the last half century. At the federal level, there were—as Table 10.1 indicates—only eleven African Americans in the U.S. House and Senate combined in 1970. In 2021, there were sixty-one—including fifty-six members of the House and three Senators. Growth for Latinos has been similarly impressive. Until 1973, Latinos seldom held more than five seats in Congress. That figure has since increased more than tenfold. In 2022, there were six Hispanic Senators and forty-six Hispanic U.S. House members. Growth for Asian Americans at the federal level has been less robust but it is still evident. The number of Asian Americans in the U.S. House and the Senate has more than quadrupled, from five in the early 1970s to twenty-one in 2022 (nineteen House members and two U.S. Senators).

In terms of raw numbers, growth has been even more remarkable at the state level. As Table 10.1 illustrates, over the last fifty years, the nation's fifty legislatures have been transformed from institutions that were almost completely White

Table 10.1 **Minority Representation Then and Now**

	African American		Latino		Asian American	
	1970	2022	1973	2022	1978	2022
U.S. Congress	11	61	5	52	5	21
State Legislatures	169	760	68	444	63	169
Local offices	715	5,753	899	2,313	52	441

Source: Hajnal (2020).

to more diverse bodies that have begun to reflect their respective populations. The number of African American legislators rose from under 200 in the late 1960s to well over 700 today. Latinos started at a lower base—there were only sixty-eight Hispanic state legislators in 1973—but they have experienced growth at a roughly equal pace over time. In 2022, across the fifty states, there were 444 Hispanic state legislators as well as two Latino governors. Again, we see growth in the number of Asian American elected officials but at a slightly slower pace. The number of Asian American state legislators has grown from sixty-three in 1968 to 169 today. Particularly noteworthy is the fact that there have been three recent Asian American governors: Nikki Haley, R-South Carolina; Bobby Jindal, R-Louisiana; and David Ige, D-Hawaii.

All three groups have experienced substantial gains in representation at the local level as well. Blacks, in particular, held only 715 local elected offices around the country in 1970 but by 2015 represented nearly 6,000 local offices. Similarly, Latino local office-holding expanded from only 899 positions in 1983 to 2,313 offices in 2015. For Asian Americans the total grew from fifty-two in 1978 to 441 in 2015.

Judging by the enormous growth in minority elected officials, it is hard not to conclude that minorities have made it in American democracy. Just as there is no doubt that racial and ethnic minorities were almost totally shut out of office before the 1960s, there is also no doubt that minority empowerment is real. These numbers and all of the faces and stories behind the numbers may be why so many—including perhaps the U.S. Supreme Court—believe that there is little ongoing racial discrimination and that minorities are well represented in American democracy. But is this really the case?

HOW IT HAPPENED: HOW BLACK REPRESENTATION GAINS WERE WIPED OUT AFTER RECONSTRUCTION

American history teaches us that minority gains in representation are fragile and that the potential for a backlash always lurks. The current gains in minority descriptive representation actually represent a return to prominence of sorts. African Americans were also well represented in office in the period immediately after the Civil War. Extensive mobilization by Blacks and effective coalition-building with White Republicans in the South led to the election of almost 1,500 Black officials over the course of Reconstruction. At the height of this movement in 1872, 324 Blacks were elected to state legislatures and Congress in the former Confederate states.

However Whites—especially Southern Whites—mobilized in large numbers and used an array of violent and nonviolent tactics to suppress Black voting and reduce the number of Black elected officials (Foner 1984). In Louisiana, for example, in less than a year, Democrats killed over 1,000 people in their effort to regain control of the political process. Within 30 years, White Southerners had wiped out virtually all the gains made by Black voters. By 1900, only five Blacks still held power in state legislatures or Congress (Kousser 1992).

Photo 10.3 The first Blacks elected to Congress are shown here in a print that was published around 1872 and include Senator Hiram Revels of Mississippi, Benjamin S. Turner of Alabama, Robert DeLarge of South Carolina, Josiah Walls of Florida, Jefferson Long of Georgia, and Joseph Rainey and Robert B. Elliott of South Carolina.
Source: Currier and Ives, all Republicans, 1872.

   This White counter-mobilization underlines both how much of a threat descriptive representation can be to the existing power structure and how quickly it can be undermined.

The Stories behind the Early Victories

Racial and ethnic minority gains in public office have not been easily achieved. Particularly early on, opposition to minority empowerment was intense. That opposition is perhaps most clearly illustrated by the fear generated among Whites by early Black challengers for mayor in America's big cities. Their opponents—White incumbents and candidates—repeatedly highlighted the potentially disastrous consequences of a Black victory. For example, in Los Angeles Sam Yorty, the White incumbent, ran against Tom Bradley, the African American challenger in 1973, by asking: "You know what kind of city we've got. We don't know what we might get. So we'd be taking quite a chance with

Photo 10.4 Tom Bradley, with his wife beside him, takes the Los Angeles mayoral oath of office delivered by former Chief Justice of the United States, Earl Warren.
Source: © Bettmann/Contributor/Bettmann/Getty Images.

this particular kind of candidate ... Will your city be safe with this man?" (Hajnal 2006). Yorty even suggested that much of the police force would leave the city if Tom Bradley—a member of the Los Angeles police for 21 years— were elected. Similarly in 1987, Chicago mayoral candidate Eddie Vrdolyak highlighted White concerns about a Black man running the city: "It's a racial thing. Don't kid yourself. I am calling on you to save your city, to save your precinct. We're fighting to keep the city the way it is" (Rivlin 1992: 155). In Newark, the White police chief was even more dramatic, "Whether we survive or cease to exist depends on what you do on [election day]" (Eisinger 1980: 15). In Atlanta, when Maynard Jackson ran in 1973, the slogan of the White candidate was, "Atlanta is too young to die." Jackson's White opponent, Sam Massell, stated that a Black victory would mean "an end to progress, an end to opportunity, an end to faith." In almost every case, this kind of fear-mongering led most Whites to support the White candidate.

When African Americans did win, it was typically only after a period of pro-longed electoral struggle. The first Black candidates to win office faced almost insurmountable White opposition. Early Black challengers who won the mayoralty for the first time in their cities often had to overcome record White turnout and near-unanimous opposition by White voters. Black mayoral challengers who won office in their cities for the first time in the 1960s and 1970s confronted turnout that averaged over 70 percent—unheard of for local elections that typically average 20–30 percent turnout. They also faced a united White vote—over 80 percent of White voters opposed them on average (Hajnal 2006). When, for example, Willie Herenton became the first Black mayor of Memphis in 1991, he overcame the opposition of 97 percent of White voters and record White turnout. Successful Black challengers were able to win only by turning out African American voters in equally high numbers and by forging an equally unified Black vote (Hajnal 2006). Herenton won—where a dozen other Black candidates had failed before him—because African Americans had grown to become the majority of the population in Memphis, because Blacks turned out in historically high numbers, and because Blacks gave Herenton 98 percent of their votes.

A Fair *Share* of Offices?

The fact that enormous change has occurred in recent decades is undeniable. Each electoral victory is meaningful. But viewed from a different lens, the gains that minorities have made can be seen as much less significant. Ultimately, we may be less interested in the *number* of minority elected officials than in the *share* of all offices that minorities hold. There are, after all, hundreds of thousands of elected offices across the nation—roughly 511,000 according to the U.S. Census. Thus, the more critical question becomes: do minorities hold their fair share of offices?

The Picture for Blacks, Latinos, and Asian Americans

If we compare the number of racial and ethnic minorities in office to the number of Whites in office, it becomes abundantly clear that the political leadership of the nation remains overwhelmingly White and that racial and ethnic minorities are greatly underrepresented at almost every level of government relative to their share of the population. Figure 10.2 provides a telling picture of minority underrepresentation in American politics. It shows both the share of minorities in the national population and the share of minorities in various offices from the U.S. Senate to city councils.

It is clear from Figure 10.2 that despite all the gains, racial and ethnic minorities remain grossly underrepresented at every level of American democracy. According to the latest (2020) Census figures, Latinos represent 18.7 percent of the national population, yet they hold only 2.7 percent of city council positions, 4.5 percent of all state legislative offices, 4 percent of the Senate, and 9 percent of the seats in the House. Asian Americans fare no better. The Asian American share of the

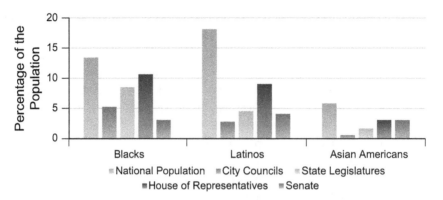

Figure 10.2 Minority Representation in Office
Each group's representation falls far short of its share of the national population at every level of office. For example, Blacks comprise around 13 percent of the U.S. population but they hold only 5.2 percent of city council seats. Blacks and Latinos are, however, closest to their share in the House.
Note: All data except the city council (2015) and state legislatures (2015) are from 2018.
Source: Hajnal (2020).

population (5.9 percent) greatly eclipses the share of Asian Americans in city councils (1 percent), state legislatures (1.6 percent), in the Senate (3 percent), and in the House (3 percent). African Americans, as the group that has had the longest and most sustained presence in American politics, are somewhat closer to parity in office but they are still greatly underrepresented at almost every level. Blacks represent roughly 12 percent of the population nationwide, but they hold only 5.2 percent of all city council seats, 8.5 percent of all state legislative districts, 1 percent of the Senate, and 10.6 percent of House seats. In no case does a minority group's representation match its population size.

The underrepresentation of racial minorities in elected offices is reflected in the overrepresentation of Whites, who in 2020 make up 58 percent of the population and yet hold 90 percent of all city council seats, 85 percent of state legislative seats, 90 percent of the Senate, and 77 percent of Congress. Political decisions at every level continue to be made overwhelmingly by Whites.

One important set of offices not included in Figure 10.2 are members of the cabinet. They are appointed rather than elected and therefore very much subject to the preferences and priorities of the sitting president. Donald Trump's cabinet hardly reflected the diversity of the nation. Only three of twenty-three cabinet members were racial and ethnic minorities: Transportation Secretary Elaine Chao (Asian American), Housing and Urban Development Secretary Ben Carson (African American), and Labor Secretary Alex Acosta (Latino). That differs dramatically from both his predecessor's cabinet and his successor's cabinet. Under Barack Obama, there were nine minorities in the cabinet representing almost 40 percent of the entire body. Joe Biden's first cabinet has been described by some as the most diverse ever, with three Latinos and the first Native American cabinet secretary (Deb Haaland), the first Black Pentagon Chief (Lloyd Austin), and the first openly gay cabinet member (Pete Buttigieg).

Figures for the federal bureaucracy—important in terms of the implementation of the laws and policies of the land—are substantially better than they are for most elected offices. As of 2016, 18 percent of the roughly 2 million federal employees were Black, a number that means that Blacks are overrepresented in the federal government. Hispanics made up 9 percent of the federal workforce. For Asian Americans it was 6.3 percent (OPM 2016). The hiring process at the federal level appears to be more race-neutral than the electoral process.

DIGGING DEEPER: SUCCESS IN THE JUDICIARY

Perhaps surprisingly, one of the places where racial and ethnic minorities and other disadvantaged groups appear to be the most well represented is in the judiciary—or at least some of the upper reaches of the judiciary. In some respects, the nine justices currently on the Supreme Court roughly reflect the U.S. population. With one Latino judge, Justice Sonia Sotomayor, and two African American judges, Justice Clarence Thomas and most recently appointed Justice Ketanji Brown Jackson, both Hispanic Americans and African Americans have reached near parity in the nation's highest court.

Recent data from U.S. federal appeals and district courts also reveal relatively high minority representation in the judiciary at those levels. African Americans hold 13 percent of these offices—a figure that puts them on par with their share of the population. With Latino judges holding 10 percent of these office, Hispanics are also close to achieving proportional representation. Asian American judges (3.7 percent) are also relatively well represented here. Native Americans (0.1 percent) and LGBTQ+ Americans (1.2 percent) are, however, relatively rare at this level of the judiciary.[5]

One wonders whether the fact that these judges are appointed rather than elected is part of the explanation for the higher level of minority representation. If voters—especially White voters—are leery of selecting racial and ethnic minorities for the judiciary, then getting appointed to the judiciary might be a much easier pathway to a judicial position. On this point, it is worth noting that racial and ethnic minorities and other disadvantaged groups are much less well represented on state supreme courts around the country—typically an elected office. The research examining whether one system or the other—elections versus appointments—is more advantageous to minorities is, however, far from conclusive.[6]

[5] Data from Herick (2017).
[6] See Bratton and Spill (2002); Hurwitz and Lanier (2003).

Photo 10.5 Members of the Supreme Court sit for a group photo at the Supreme Court building on Friday, October 7, 2022. Bottom row, from left, Associate Justice Sonia Sotomayor, Associate Justice Clarence Thomas, Chief Justice of the United States John Roberts, Associate Justice Samuel Alito, and Associate Justice Elena Kagan. Top row, from left, Associate Justice Amy Coney Barrett, Associate Justice Neil Gorsuch, Associate Justice Brett Kavanaugh, and Associate Justice Ketanji Brown Jackson.
Source: Photo Jabin Botsford © *The Washington Post*/Contributor/Getty Images.

The Picture for Other Minorities

We have much less data on other racial and ethnic minority groups, but the limited data that we do have suggest that other minorities are also severely underrepresented in office. Native Americans represent 2 percent of the national population but hold relatively few elected offices. In 2009, the last year for which we have systematic data, Native Americans held only 1 percent of state legislatures seats across the country (seventy-seven seats) (NCSL 2010). Moreover, that representation was concentrated in a small number of states with higher Native American populations. In fact, over a quarter of all Native American state legislators were from Oklahoma, where 13 percent of the population is Native American.

The number of Native Americans in office does, however, appear to be growing. Recently, the number of Native Americans serving in Congress doubled. In 2019, Kansas' Sharice Davids, a member of the Ho-Chunk people who is also openly gay and New Mexico's Deb Haaland, of the Laguna Pueblo people (who later became the nation's first Native American Interior Secretary in Joe Biden's administration), became the first Native American woman to serve in Congress in its 230-year history. With five Native Americans now serving, the 116th Congress represents the high point of Native American representation in Congress. That high point is, however, still well below parity. Those five seats represent only about 1 percent of the seats in Congress. Over the course of the nation's history, only four Native Americans have served in the Senate, including Hiram Rhodes Revels, who also happens to be the first African American Senator to serve in the office. In the same 2018 election cycle, Peggy Flanagan of the White Earth Nation became the first Native woman elected to statewide office by winning the lieutenant governor's race in Minnesota. In 2018, Oklahoma elected Kevin Stitt, a Cherokee tribal member, as governor, and Montana moved to near parity in Native American representation in the state legislature (Woodard 2019). According to a tally by *Indian Country Today*, most of the Native officeholders elected across the country in 2018 were Democrats and almost half were women.

Despite a population of 3.5 million, Muslim Americans have until recently largely been absent from American politics. But perhaps in response to increasingly anti-Muslim rhetoric in political campaigns and a 600 percent increase in anti-Muslim hate crimes since 2014, more and more Muslims are running for office and winning.

Photo 10.6 U.S. President Joe Biden hands a pen to Secretary of the Interior Deb Haaland after signing an executive order to expand the areas of three national monuments that former President Donald Trump had opened to mining, drilling, and development during his time in office. The Biden administration restored the areas of two Utah parks (Bears Ears National Monument and the Grand Staircase-Escalant) with lands held sacred by several Native American tribes, along with the Northeast Canyons and Seamounts off the New England coast.
Source: Photo Chip Somodevilla © Chip Somodevilla/Staff/Getty Images News/Getty Images.

The number of Muslims running across the country is estimated to have increased from just a dozen in 2016 to 128 in 2018 (Raphelson 2018). That increase led to major inroads. The first two Muslim women in Congress, Rep. Ilhan Omar (D-Minnesota) and Rep. Rashida Tlaib (D-Michigan), were elected to great fanfare. That same year, Keith Ellison, formerly a Congressman, became the first Muslim to win election in a statewide office, winning the position of Attorney General in Minnesota. North Carolina also saw its first Muslim American ever elected to the state Senate. All told, a record fifty-five Muslims won office in that 2018 election cycle. Almost all of these Muslim winners were Democrats. Muslim Americans still hold fewer than 300 elected offices at all levels across the country, but their potency as a political force appears to be growing.

The Picture for Other Disadvantaged Groups

Throughout this book we often compare outcomes along race with outcomes along other potentially important demographic dimensions like class, gender, age, and religion. The data on descriptive representation do not lend themselves to a systematic test of the relative contributions of race, class, and other factors. But we can convey how descriptive underrepresentation varies across the different dimensions.

A straightforward tally tells us that racial and ethnic minorities are not the only population that is disadvantaged in American democracy. Working-class Americans are also starkly underrepresented in office. The working class—those employed in manual labor, service industries, clerical, or informal sector jobs—make up over half of the labor force but occupy less than 2 percent of the seats in the U.S. Congress.[7] By contrast, more than 75 percent of Congress is comprised of former lawyers and business people even though only about 10 percent of the overall population fits into those categories. And it is not just Congress. Comparable figures are not available for every level of office but data at the city council level indicate that about a third of all council members in the country have backgrounds as lawyers or as business professionals. The people making the nation's laws are much more privileged than the nation as a whole. The skew by gender is similarly severe. Despite accounting for half of the population—51 percent to be precise—women hold a small fraction of all the elected offices in the country. Men hold 80 percent of the seats in Congress, they occupy the governor's mansion in forty-four of fifty states, they run 78 percent of the nation's cities, and they account for 75 percent of the state legislative positions in the nation (Center for Women in Politics 2021). Figures for religion and age are less readily available, but we do know that in Congress, Catholics, Jews, and Protestants are overrepresented while Buddhists, Muslims, and the nonreligious are underrepresented. More than one in four (26 percent) Americans describe themselves as atheist, agnostic, or not religious but only one of 533 members of the Senate and House does not identify

---

[7] See Carnes (2021) for a thorough analysis of the representation of working-class Americans.

Photo 10.7 Newly elected incoming members of the Congressional Progressive Caucus, including Rep.-elects Maxwell Frost (D-Florida), Robert Garcia (D-California), and Delia Ramirez (D-Illinois), take a selfie with Chair Rep. Pramila Jayapal (D-Washington). and Rep. Ilhan Omar (D-Minnesota), after a news conference days after the 2022 election. While the Senate's median age continues to rise, the House of Representatives is getting younger, with the median age of voting House lawmakers in the 118th Congress at 57.9 years, down from 58.9 in the 117th Congress (2021–2022). Maxwell Frost is the first Generation Z member elected to the House.
Source: © Tom Williams/Contributor/CQ-Roll Call, Inc./Getty Images.

with a particular religion (Pew 2021). We also know that elected officials skew older than the American public at large. For the 117th Congress, the average age of members of the Congress was 59 years old and the median age is 60 years old. Ages in the 118th Congress skewed slightly lower. According to the U.S. Census Bureau, the median age in the United States in 2019 was 38 years old.

All of this is to say that gender, class, religion, and age may even rival race in shaping who does and who does not win office. This does not limit our concern for the plight of racial and ethnic minorities in American democracy. But it does tell us that American democracy is tilted along all sorts of dimensions.

Why Are Minorities Underrepresented?

How can we explain the disparity in representation? Answering that question is not easy. Minority underrepresentation in office is a complex real-world problem with many contributing factors, including institutions, candidate supply, resources, and voters. We know that each of these factors plays a role. We are less certain about which of them is most important.

Institutional Barriers and Minority Vote Dilution

The link between institutional structure—essentially the rules that determine how votes are compiled and the winner is chosen—and minority representation has probably been more closely studied than any of the other factors that contribute to underrepresentation of minorities in elected office. And based on this extensive research, there is little doubt that institutions have served and continue to serve as significant barriers to minority representation. Some also believe that institutional reform could serve as a catalyst for greater minority representation in the future.

The Plurality Vote

Within the broader context of American democracy, the institutional feature perhaps most often cited as limiting minority success is the plurality vote. In the American electoral system almost every election is conducted under "winner takes all" plurality rules: the candidate with the most votes wins the election and garners all the power. That means that the plurality—sometimes just over half of the voters and occasionally even less than half of the voters—can control 100 percent of the electoral outcomes. Donald Trump, for example, received less than half of the presidential vote (46 percent) in 2016, but he still won the election and control of the presidency for four years. At least theoretically, this plurality structure could give the White majority excessive influence over outcome. That concern is perhaps best epitomized by legal scholar Lani Guinier who argues that "In a world of bloc voting, with one candidate per bloc, the minority is *completely shut out*. Not only can it not elect one of its own; it cannot even influence whom the majority elects" (Guinier 1994).[8] Comparative cross-national data show, in fact, that *proportional representation systems* that allocate legislative seats roughly in proportion to the share of votes received by each political party tend to be more friendly to minority interests. As we noted earlier, proportional representation systems are common in Europe, and they often lead to the election of more liberal and left-leaning policymakers.

Although very few elections in the United States are conducted under anything other than plurality rules, there are some exceptions in a handful of localities across the country. Studies of those exceptions show quite convincingly that alternative electoral rules can greatly expand minority representation. Cumulative voting—when voters get several votes to choose several positions at the same time and can

---

[8] This is in contrast to a model of the vote put forward by Downs (1957) in which outcomes respond to the preferences of all voters. In this median voter model, each new minority shifts the median vote and alters the equilibrium toward their preferences.

use all of those votes to support the *same* candidate *multiple* times—which has been used regularly in parts of Alabama has resulted in significant gains in minority representation. For example, when cumulative voting was used for the first time in elections for the Chilton County Commission in 1988, Black voters cumulated their votes on one candidate, Bobby Agee, who became the first African American elected to the commission since Reconstruction. Likewise, examinations of limited voting around the country—where voters have fewer votes than there are seats up for election—have found that it often leads to the election of more racial and ethnic minorities (Bowler, Donovan, and Brockington 2003).

Civil rights campaigners and others have also advocated for ranked choice voting—where voters rank their preferences across all of the candidates—but there is, as of yet, little empirical evidence showing how this reform impacts minority representation.

Racial Gerrymandering and Other Electoral Structures

Racial gerrymandering, the process of drawing district lines to limit minority gains, has also been cited as a major barrier to descriptive representation. Drawing district lines so that African American communities are apportioned across several different districts and no single district has a Black majority has been extremely effective in the past, particularly in the South. But it is less clear how much racial gerrymandering limits the election of minorities to office today. Thanks in part to the courts and in part to the electoral interests of the Republican Party, lines today are often drawn to create more rather than fewer majority-minority districts ("packing"). The fact that the minority underrepresentation we saw in Figure 10.2 was less severe in the House where districts can be gerrymandered than it was where boundaries cannot be altered (e.g., in the Senate) suggests that drawing lines to elect minorities can be very effective. Whether this ultimately hurts minorities by putting lots of minorities into one district and creating more Republican minority districts elsewhere, however, is a matter of debate (see Cameron, Epstein, and Halloran 1996; Washington 2012) for more on this debate). Chapter 13, "Voting Rights", discusses "cracking" and other forms of racial gerrymandering in more detail.

A range of electoral structures at the local level have also been linked to the number of minorities in office. Chief among these are at-large elections where candidates run jurisdiction-wide (e.g., for an entire city or county) rather than in separate districts. In at-large contests, voters elect several candidates at once to the same office and voters are allotted as many votes as there are seats. If the majority vote cohesively chooses the same set of candidates, it can win all of the seats and effectively shut out a minority. The evidence showing that at-large elections reduce Black and Latino representation in office is vast (Molina and Meier 2018; Trounstine and Valdini 2008). As a result, the courts have outlawed at-large elections under a range of contexts. As part of that reform the California legislature passed the California Voting Rights Act (CVRA) in 2002 making it easier for minorities to sue localities running at-large elections. Across the 335 local jurisdictions that were eventually forced to shift from at-large to district elections, Latinos increased their share on the school board by an average of 64 percent. By contrast, in places that maintained at-large elections, Latino representation was flat (ACLU 2022). Still, today roughly 64 percent of U.S. cities and 68 percent of all school boards use at-large elections (Molina and Meier 2018).

Other local electoral features associated with diminished minority representation include the following (although the evidence is less clear in the last two cases):

- Off-cycle elections: most cities in America hold elections on dates that do not match up with state and federal contests. That generally means lower and more racially uneven turnout, a pattern that leads to less minority representation.
- Reductions in the number of seats on the city council: reducing the total number of available seats often limits the number of chances that minorities have to win and enter office.
- The absence of term limits: since Whites currently control most offices, term limits—which force incumbents out of office after a set term—help open up more competitive seats that minorities can compete for.
- Staggered terms: in staggered elections residents vote on half of the local elected offices in one year and half in another year. That makes each election less consequential and tends to significantly lower voter turnout.
- Nonpartisan elections: by preventing party labels from appearing on the local ballot, cities effectively limit the role of parties in local democracy, a reform that reduces partisan mobilization and makes local politics less accessible for racial and ethnic minorities—many of whom are immigrants and new to American politics.

In different ways all of these institutional barriers touch on the concept of minority vote dilution: racial and ethnic minorities have access to the vote but the effectiveness of that vote is curtailed by structures that limit minority influence. Minority vote dilution has been increasingly central to voting rights and its enforcement. When the Voting Rights Act of 1965 was first passed, the primary focus was on garnering access to the vote but as minority voter participation has increased, advocates and the courts have paid increasing attention to the influence of that vote, and have in some cases outlawed electoral institutions that limit that influence.

Limiting Access to the Vote

While some attention has been given to the problem of minority vote dilution, scholars and members of the minority community remain especially attentive to concerns about *access* to the vote. Democrats and progressives have been touting a host of institutional reforms that they hope will expand access to the vote, while several Republican-led initiatives aimed at institutional change have, according to critics, impinged on minority participation. At the state level a host of electoral rules that in different ways govern access to the vote have been purported to impact minority representation. Minority rights advocates argue that any additional hurdle to participating will reduce participation among the disadvantaged—often racial and ethnic minorities—more than it will impact the advantaged—often wealthy Whites.

Registration requirements represent one of the biggest potential factors along these lines. Research has shown that the later the deadline to register to vote, the higher the turnout (Highton 2004). Voting rights advocates believe that automatic voter registration—where citizens who interact with government agencies are registered to vote unless they choose to opt out—can greatly increase participation and expand the influence of less advantaged segments of the electorate, although the latter relationship has not yet been proven.

There is increasingly clear evidence that strict voter identification laws discriminate against racial and ethnic minorities (Barreto et al. 2019; Kuk, Hajnal, and Lajevardi 2020). For example, North Dakota's strict identification law requires voters to present an identification with a conventional mailing address, a requirement that is difficult to comply with for Native Americans who live on reservations without street addresses. There is also no doubt that felon disenfranchisement laws have had a disproportionately negative impact on racial and ethnic minority voting (Manza 2006). Under many of these laws, people who have been convicted of a felony are unable to vote in any election. Given that a higher percentage of minorities are convicted, these laws bar a higher share of racial minorities from the electoral process. Civil rights backers are concerned that cuts in early voting, reductions in polling hours and locations, new identification requirements for voter registration, and efforts to purge voter files by dropping residents who have changed addresses or have not voted in recent elections (both groups are disproportionately made up of racial minorities) will all ultimately reduce minority participation and influence. Time will tell how much North Carolina's decade-long effort at reform—including eliminating same-day registration (used primary by Black and student voters), ending pre-registration for 16 and 17 year olds (the minority population skews younger), outlawing Sunday voting prior to elections (a day when Black churches tend to bring out lots of voters), and drastically cutting the number of early voting locations, will reshape the electorate in that state and how much that will alter the makeup of North Carolina's elected officials.

The notion that a supposedly race-neutral law could negatively impact minority turnout and affect the outcome of the vote is, of course, not new. Today's battles over strict voter identification laws, polling locations, registration laws, and the like echo past fights over poll taxes and literacy tests. A poll tax—which at least theoretically should be applied to everyone equally—had disastrous consequences for minority participation in the South and was ruled unconstitutional by the Supreme Court, but not until 1966. Southern state legislatures also employed literacy tests—purportedly to ensure that voters were literate—until the passage of the 1965 Voting Rights Act forced them to abandon these laws. These tests had been extremely effective at disenfranchising African Americans (Parker 1990).

Limited Minority Candidate Supply/Financial Resources

Candidate supply is also critical to racial and ethnic minority success at the ballot box. If minorities do not run for office—and there is clear evidence that they run at lower rates than Whites—they cannot get elected (Fraga, Juenke, and Shah 2020). This mirrors work on female representation where research shows that a major factor behind the underrepresentation of women in office is the greater willingness of men to run for office (Fox and Lawless 2010). Fortunately, we are also seeing more women running and winning—a pattern that was especially pronounced in the 2018 midterms where the number of women in Congress jumped from 107 to 133 in one election cycle. In 2020, that number increased again to 145 of 535 seats in Congress being held by women, and after the 2022 midterms, 149 women (107 Democrats and 42 Republicans) were set to serve in the 118th Congress (CAWP n.d.). Underpinning every aspect of the electoral process including the decision to run are the resources of the minority community. As we have already highlighted, racial and ethnic minorities on average fall lower on the socioeconomic spectrum than do Whites. Lower incomes and less wealth are critical factors when it comes to fundraising and candidate viability. Given the enormous outlays of money that are often required to run and win in the electoral arena, it is perhaps not surprising that the limited availability of financial resources within the minority community has been shown to drive down the descriptive representation of racial and ethnic minorities. Organizational capacity and the degree to which minority communities are concentrated in one location have also been linked to minority representation.

The Role of White Voters

Of all of the factors that contribute to the dearth of minorities in office, there is one likely suspect—White voters—that bears a closer look. In Chapter 9, "Race and Elections," we saw racialized patterns in voting. In almost every type of election a majority of White Americans favored one side while a clear majority of non-Whites favored the other. Logic suggests that if Whites are the majority—and even today Whites represent roughly 70 percent of all active voters—White voters could be the main barrier to minority underrepresentation. Put simply, Black, Latino, and Asian American candidates could be losing because so many White Americans are not voting for them.

Of course, it is difficult to determine the degree to which White voters object to African American, Latino, and Asian American candidates on race alone. White voters who dislike racial and ethnic minorities are unlikely to be honest about their views or their intentions in the voting booth. That problem is perhaps most clearly illustrated when one simply asks individual Americans about their own willingness to vote for minority candidates. As Figure 10.3 illustrates, the share of Americans who claim to be willing to vote for a racial and ethnic minority candidate has grown enormously over time to the point where almost everyone now maintains that they would not use race to discriminate. The last time Gallup surveyed the population,

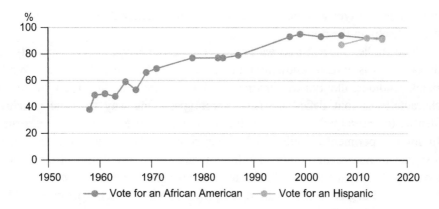

Figure 10.3 Percentage of Americans Who Say They Will Vote for a Minority Candidate, 1958–2020
The share of Americans who indicate that they would be willing to vote for a "qualified" Black candidate and a "qualified" Hispanic candidate has increased over time. As of 2015, almost all Americans claim that they would vote for a minority candidate.
Source: Gallup Polls.

92 percent of Americans indicated that they would vote for "a generally well-qualified person ... who happened to be Black" (Gallup 2015). Fully 91 percent said they would do the same for a Hispanic candidate. Judging by these answers, resistance to minority candidates has largely disappeared.[9]

When asked about the behavior of *other* Americans, individual Americans are much less sanguine about the color-blind nature of the vote. In fact, in another Gallup poll just over half (54 percent) of Americans admitted that in a biracial election "most White voters will tend to vote for the White candidate regardless of qualifications." Only about a third of Americans felt that White Americans would vote for the most qualified candidate regardless of race.[10] Based on these two very different responses, it is hard to know where the truth lies.

Researchers have used a variety of tests and tools to try to get closer to the truth. One insightful technique has been to compare Whites' evaluations of a "typical Black candidate" with their evaluations of a "typical White candidate" (Schneider and Bos 2011). These studies reveal deep-seated stereotypes of Black candidates. Without knowing anything about a candidate other than his or her race, Whites rated the typical Black candidate as less intelligent, less likely to have good judgment in a crisis, less likely to be a strong leader, less hardworking, less trustworthy, and less fair. Black candidates are also stereotyped as being overly liberal. The only

[9] The share of Americans willing to support a qualified minority candidate is now roughly on par with the share willing to support a qualified female candidate (92 percent in 2015). The one group most like a racial/ethnic group that many Americans are still willing to openly discriminate against is Muslims. In 2015, Gallup found that only 60 percent of Americans said they would vote for a qualified Muslim candidate for president.

[10] Unfortunately this latter question was only asked once, in 1987.

area where the typical Black candidate was rated higher than the White candidate was in "helping the poor."

These studies suggest that we hold troubling stereotypes about minority candidates. But it is hard to know how those views translate into the vote.[11] What if a Black candidate like Barack Obama or a Latino candidate like Ted Cruz displayed characteristics that defied negative stereotypes? One way to more conclusively identify the causal link between attitudes on race and the vote is to run experiments. In some experiments, adults read about fictitious candidates and are randomly assigned to assess candidates of different races or skin colors who are otherwise identical. In recent years political scientists have relied increasingly on this method to assess the degree to which the race of the candidate affects vote choice. There is some variation in the results across different experiments but the bottom line here once again is that race matters—although the effects are typically not that large (Visalvanich 2017). White and light-skinned candidates typically do a few percentage points better than identical Black, Latino, or dark-skinned candidates. Interestingly, more recent experiments reveal a larger bias against African American candidates, a smaller bias against Hispanic candidates, and perhaps even a racial advantage for Asian American candidates (Visalvanich 2017).

But again, what happens in a real-world context when candidates are actual people with different personalities, narratives, and policy positions? When voters have a lot more information than simply the race of the candidates, do these racial effects endure? Or do they fade away? Experiments that provide voters with more nonracial information about the candidates (such as their political affiliation and policy positions) tend to find that discrimination declines as information increases. Ultimately, to know how much race matters in the real world, we need to examine real-world elections. When one researcher looked into whether being Black, Latino, or Asian American hurt a candidate's chances of being elected after controlling for a range of controls like political party, experience, fundraising, and endorsements, he found no effect (Highton 2004). Black candidates for Congress did just as well among White voters as equally qualified White candidates. That suggests that race is irrelevant in the real world and that White voters are not the problem. But the real world is complicated and it is difficult to disentangle race from other factors.

The issue with all of these studies—experimental or real-world—is that they may be asking the wrong question. Each of these studies is essentially testing to see if Whites are racially biased against Black or minority candidates. Do they vote against minority candidates *because* of their race? But for minority candidates and for the well-being of minority communities, that may be of secondary importance. The first and most important question is whether White voters vote for minority

---

[11] We can, however, look to see how racial prejudice predicts vote choice in real-world elections as several studies have done. There is little doubt that Whites' racial attitudes greatly shape the vote in biracial contests. Every study that looked at the Obama vote, for example, found the more prejudiced White Americans were a lot less likely to vote for Obama (Kinder and Dale-Riddle 2011; Tesler and Sears 2010).

candidates at all. Regardless of their reasons, will White Americans support candidates put forward by the minority community?

The simplest and most direct way to answer this question is to look at the White vote in biracial contests. When White voters have a choice between a White candidate and a non-White candidate, who do they choose? The answer to this question is clear. Given a choice, a majority of White voters favor the White candidate most of the time. At the local level the results are particularly stark. A study of the White vote in mayoral elections in the nation's thirty largest cities over a twenty-year period between 1989 and 2009 showed that Whites voted heavily against Black, Latino, and Asian American candidates. On average across the forty-one Black–White contests for which the vote by race was acquired, fully 80 percent of all White voters opposed the Black mayoral candidate. In only one of these forty-one elections did a majority of Whites favor a Black candidate. In Detroit in 2005, 56 percent of Whites voted for Freeman Hendrix, an African American who was one of four candidates in the contest. But even this one exception proves troubling. In that election, most Whites did not support Kwame Kilpatrick, the African American candidate favored by the majority of the Black community. The upshot is that White voters generally do not support Black candidates.

White voters were almost as likely to oppose Latino candidates for mayor. Across the twenty-six Latino–White contests in the data set, on average, 75 percent of White voters voted for the White candidate. There were many fewer Asian American–White mayoral contests, but in the three elections for which data are available, 81 percent of Whites voted against the Asian American candidate.

We have systematic data on the vote by race at one other level: U.S. congressional elections. Although the congressional-level patterns are not nearly as extreme as at the mayoral level, once again we find that most Whites do not vote for most minority candidates. Between 2010 and 2012 there were ninety African American candidates running for Congress against White opponents. On average, 59 percent of White voters voted for the White candidate rather than the Black candidate. That figure is the same in Latino–White contests—59 percent—and only drops slightly to 56 percent in Asian American–White contests. There are times when the majority of Whites support racial and ethnic minority candidates for Congress, but these exceptions usually occur when that minority candidate is a Republican who garners little support from racial and ethnic minority voters. For example, when Republican Tim Scott was elected as the first Black senator of South Carolina in 2014, he won with 88 percent of the White vote but only 10 percent of the Black vote.

Ultimately, White opposition to minority candidates can perhaps best be illustrated by looking at the geographic distribution of minority elected officials. Across the nation at almost every level of office, minority candidates generally win office in majority-minority localities—political districts where Whites represent a minority of the population. At the congressional level, 89 percent of Black representatives, 91 percent of Latino representatives, and 70 percent of Asian American representatives in office today are elected in majority-minority districts. For example, in 2020 Hakeem Jeffries, an African American, was elected in New York's 8th congressional district—a district where Blacks make up 55 percent of the voting population. At the local level, the figures are equally remarkable. In our data set, 81 percent of Black mayors and 77 percent of Latino mayors win office in cities where Whites are the minority.[12] When minorities win, they tend to win largely or exclusively in majority-minority places.

Equally illuminating are the patterns in areas where Whites are the majority. When Whites make up most of the voters and can essentially control the outcome of the vote, who do they choose? Here the data are equally unequivocal. In Congress today, 96 percent of all of the majority-White districts are governed by White legislators. That figure is worth pondering more closely. When Whites have the power to elect whomever they want, 96 percent of the time they choose White. The number at the mayoral level is not nearly as severe. Eighty percent of the majority-White cities in our data set elect White mayors. That means that Whites choose White the vast majority of the time, but it also means that White-majority cities appear to be slightly more open to minority leadership. In some notable elections, Whites helped to elect a minority mayor. Norm Rice was mayor of Seattle, Washington, from 1990 to 1997, and Michael Coleman was mayor of Columbus, Ohio, from 1999 to 2015.

All of the other factors that we have mentioned, including institutional barriers, a limited supply of minority candidates, and meager financial resources for campaigns in minority communities, undoubtedly contribute to the stark underrepresentation of minorities in American democracy. But the distribution of minority elected officials tells us emphatically that White opposition to non-White candidates is a major factor. A lot of this opposition is driven by partisanship—that is, the many White Americans who identify as Republican favor Republican candidates who often happen to be White. It is far from clear how much of a role the race of a candidate plays but the reality is that most White Americans are not helping minorities to achieve better descriptive representation across the United States at all levels of office.

One result of these barriers is that minority candidates are generally heavily dependent on the minority vote. There is little doubt that racial and ethnic minorities support their own in large numbers. Our data set on mayoral candidates reveals that on average 71 percent of Black voters, 56 percent of Latino voters, and 52 percent of Asian American voters favored candidates from their own racial or ethnic group when given the opportunity. Likewise, at the city council level, an extremely close correlation between the share of non-Whites in the city and minority representation in the city suggests that minority city council members rely heavily on minority voters.[13] The reliance of minority candidates on minority voters is so strong that almost every study of descriptive representation finds that the size of the minority population is the single largest determinant of minority success (Ocampo 2017).

---

[12] No Asian American mayors won office in the data set. But many of the big-city Asian American mayors (such as Edwin Lee in San Francisco and Jean Quan in Oakland) won office in majority-minority cities.

[13] This analysis used data on city council representation from a recent ICMA survey and city demographics from the Census.

Do Minority Leaders Make a Difference?

America, a racially diverse nation, is still governed largely by Whites. At first glance, that imbalance is disturbing. But is it consequential? Are racial and ethnic minorities more effective in representing racial and ethnic minorities than their White counterparts?

The answer appears to be a qualified yes. The qualified part of the answer comes from the difficulty of disentangling the effects of having a minority representative in office from the effects of having a lot of racial and ethnic minority voters in a district. The two tend to go hand in hand. Studies from 25 years ago revealed little difference between the voting patterns of Black and Latino members of Congress and their White counterparts (Hero and Tolbert 1995; Swain 1995). In these studies, Black and Latino elected officials were no more or less likely to support liberal policies and no more or less likely to support civil rights legislation. At the mayoral level, several studies have found that there was little indication that having a racial and ethnic minority mayor altered the economic trajectory of the city (Kerr and Mladenka 1994). Some went so far as to call these Black electoral victories "a hollow prize" (Smith 1996). In part, as a result, many argued that efforts to create majority-minority districts to elect more minorities were misguided.

Major shifts in policy and outcomes as a result of one or two minorities holding office may, however, have been too much to expect. Other studies looking at smaller, more defined policies have identified areas where descriptive representation clearly does matter (Grose 2011). Black and Latino office-holding has, for example, been closely linked to more Blacks and Hispanics in the local bureaucracy and greater citizen oversight of the police. Other research demonstrates that Blacks and Latinos in Congress and in state legislatures spend more time advocating on racially focused bills and keeping minority interests on the agenda. They also direct more government spending to minority districts. Having African American and Latino judges also leads to more favorable outcomes for minorities across a range of judicial decisions.

In addition, as the numbers of minorities in office have grown and as researchers have employed more sophisticated research designs, there has been growing evidence that descriptive representation does lead to real, if relatively small, shifts in legislative voting behavior. Minority members at the congressional level are more likely to support legislation deemed to be helpful to minorities than are their White counterparts (Griffin and Newman 2007).

One area where minority representation in office seems to lead to significant and favorable outcomes for minorities is in state legislatures. One recent study found that Black and Latino Democrats were much more liberal than White Democrats, and that in majority-minority districts, Black and Latino Democrats were significantly more liberal than White Democrats (Juenke and Preuhs 2011). Although descriptive representation is not a panacea for all that ails the minority population, the bottom line is that it does represent a significant step forward for minority interests in the policy realm.

Where minority elected officials appear to have had the most impact is in terms of symbolic value—what political scientists refer to as symbolic representation. Symbolic representation refers to the intangible or psychological benefits that accrue to constituents who have members of their own group in power. The underlying idea is that seeing a member of one's own racial or ethnic group in power could lead to a greater sense that democracy is open and legitimate, thereby increasing feelings of inclusion for groups that are often excluded or disadvantaged.

Scholars who look at these sorts of symbolic effects have found clear evidence that having a leader of the same race or ethnicity in office can lead to increases in Black and Hispanic trust and efficacy, more positive views of government, increased political knowledge, reduced political alienation, and a greater willingness to vote and contact elected officials (Gay 2001). Significantly, the impact of having minority leadership extends to the White population. One study found that experience under Black mayors led to reductions in White racial animosity (Hajnal 2001). According to that study, experience under Black leaders taught many Whites that Black empowerment was less of a threat than they originally feared.[14] While all of these benefits may not lead directly to shifts in policy, they are, nevertheless, critically important in a nation where racial and ethnic minorities have often been politically marginalized.

TESTING THE THEORY: AN EXPERIMENT ON SYMBOLIC REPRESENTATION

Is there something unique about having racial and ethnic minorities in office? Is there something about shared experiences as a minority that changes these representatives and their actions? One scholar, David Broockman, set out to find out. He ran an experiment in which he emailed 6,928 U.S. state legislators to see how they reacted to contact from racial and ethnic minorities. Some of those emails were from an African American who claimed to be from the legislator's district and some were from an otherwise identical African American who claimed not to be in the district. Crucially, Broockman randomly varied which legislators got which message. In the end, the results were clear. Non-Black legislators were much less responsive to emails from outside their own district—presumably because people outside their district are unlikely to affect their reelection chances. Black legislators were different. Black legislators were as responsive to emails from African Americans outside the district as they were to emails from African Americans inside the district—even when doing so promised little political reward. This can be interpreted as "surrogate representation"—the desire of minority elected officials

---

[14] Of course, heightened racial animosity among Whites under Barack Obama, the nation's first African American president, suggests that these psychological benefits do not always accrue when minorities are in office.

to serve the needs of a group of people who are not their voters. Essentially, minorities in office feel that they have a duty or an intrinsic motivation to represent minorities all around the country—not just those in their district. This is another way in which descriptive representation can play a crucial role in advancing minority political interests.

Conclusion

The portrait of descriptive representation that emerges in this chapter is a troubling one. Although racial and ethnic minorities have made enormous gains in winning office, they remain greatly underrepresented. Moreover, there are signs that White voters are responsible for much of this underrepresentation. An analysis of the vote reveals that White voters tend to favor White candidates over minority candidates. Further analysis of geographic patterns in minority representation indicates that the gains that minorities have made have occurred disproportionately in areas where Whites are the minority. Where Whites are the majority, they almost always choose to elect White representatives. As a result, the nation's halls of power remain overwhelmingly White.

KEY TERMS

At-large districts
Automatic voter registration
Cumulative voting
Descriptive representation
Majority-minority localities
Minority vote dilution
Plurality rules
Proportional representation systems
Racial gerrymandering
Ranked choice voting
Representation
Staggered elections
Symbolic representation
Tyranny of the majority

DISCUSSION QUESTIONS

1. To what degree have racial and ethnic minorities attained fair representation in American democracy?
2. How does the descriptive representation of racial and ethnic minorities compare with the representation of other groups?
3. What are the main barriers to expanding minority representation?

4. Should we try to elect more minorities to office? Why?
5. What are the symbolic effects of descriptive representation?
6. Do the use of majority-minority districts advance the greater interests of Black and Latino constituents, or work against them? Discuss.

ANNOTATED SUGGESTED READINGS

See Neil Visalvanich. 2017. "When Does Race Matter? Exploring White Responses to Minority Congressional Candidates," *Politics, Groups, and Identities* 5(4): 618–641, to learn more about whether White voters are willing to support minority candidates.

See Michael Minta. 2011. *Oversight: Representing the Interests of Blacks and Latinos in Congress*. Princeton: Princeton University Press, to see the efforts of minority legislators on behalf of the minority community.

See Eric Juenke. and Robert Preuhs. 2011. "Irreplaceable Legislators? Rethinking Minority Representatives in the New Century," *American Journal of Political Science* 56(3): 705–715, to understand the broader impact of minority representatives.

CHAPTER REFERENCES

ACLU (American Civil Liberties Union). 2022. "The California Voting Rights Act in 2018." www.advancingjustice-alc.org/media/CVRA-Fact-Sheet-12-2018.pdf.

Barreto, Matt A., Stephen Nuño, Gabriel R. Sanchez, and Hannah L. Walker. 2018. "The Racial Implications of Voter Identification Laws in America," *American Politics Research* 47: 238–249.

Bowler, Shaun, Todd Donovan, and David Brockington. 2003. *Electoral Reform and Minority Representation: Local Experiments with Alternative Elections*. Columbus: Ohio State University Press.

Bratton, Kathleen A. and Rorie L. Spill. 2002. "Existing Diversity and Judicial Selection: The Role of the Appointment Method in Establishing Gender Diversity in State Supreme Courts," *Social Science Quarterly* 83: 504–518.

Cameron, Charles, David Epstein, and Sharyn Halloran. 1996. "Do Majority-Minority Districts Maximize Substantive Black Representation in Congress?" *American Political Science Review* 90: 794–812.

Carnes, Nicholas. 2013. *White-Collar Government: The Hidden Role of Class in Economic Policy Making*. Chicago: University of Chicago Press.

Casellas, Jason P. and Sophia J. Wallace. 2014. "The Role of Race, Ethnicity, and Party on Attitudes toward Descriptive Representation," *American Politics Research* 43(1): 144–169.

CAWP (Center for American Women in Politics). n.d. "Women in Elective Office: 2008," Center for American Women in Politics. www.cawp.rutgers.edu/fast_facts/levels_of_office/documents/elective.pdf.

Cohn, D'Vera. 2017. "Seeking Better Data on Hispanics, Census Bureau May Change How It Asks about Race," Pew Research Center, April 20. www.pewresearch.org/fact-tank/2017/04/20/seeking-better-data-on-hispanics-census-bureau-may-change-how-it-asks-about-race.

Currier & Ives. 1872. "The First Colored Senator and Representatives—in the 41st and 42nd Congress of the United States. United States, 1872," New York: Currier & Ives.

Downs, Anthony. 1957. *An Economic Theory of Democracy*. New York: Harper & Row.

Eisinger, Peter K. 1980. *Politics and Displacement: Racial and Ethnic Transition in Three American Cities*, Institute for Research on Poverty Monograph Series. New York: Academic Press.

Foner, Eric. 1984. *A Short History of Reconstruction*. New York: Harper & Row.

Fox, Richard and Jennifer Lawless. 2010. *It Still Takes a Candidate: Why Women Don't Run for Office*. New York: Cambridge University Press.

Fraga, Bernard. 2018. *The Turnout Gap: Race, Ethnicity, and Political Inequality in a Diversifying America*. New York: Cambridge University Press.

Fraga, Bernard L., Eric Gonzalez Juenke, and Paru Shah. 2020. "One Run Leads to Another: Minority Incumbents and the Emergence of Lower Ticket Minority Candidates," *Journal of Politics* 82: 771–775.

Gallup. 2015. "In U.S., Socialist Presidential Candidates Least Appealing." https://news .gallup.com/poll/183713/socialist-presidential-candidates-least-appealing.aspx.

Gay, Claudine. 2001. "The Effect of Black Congressional Representation on Participation," *American Political Science Review* 95(3): 603–618.

Gonzalez-Barrera, Ana and Mark Hugo Lopez. 2015. "Is Being Hispanic a Matter of Race, Ethnicity, or Both?" Pew Research Center, June 15. www.pewresearch.org/fact-tank/ 2015/06/15/is-being-hispanic-a-matter-of-race-ethnicity-or-both.

Griffin, John D. and Brian Newman. 2007. "The Unequal Representation of Latinos and Whites," *Journal of Politics* 69: 1032–1346.

Grose, Christian R. 2011. *Congress in Black and White*. New York: Cambridge University Press.

Guinier, Lani. 1994. *The Tyranny of the Majority: Fundamental Fairness in Representative Democracy*. New York: Free Press.

Hajnal, Zoltan L. 2001. "White Residents, Black Incumbents, and a Declining Racial Divide," *American Political Science Review* 95: 603–617.

Hajnal, Zoltan L. 2006. *Changing White Attitudes toward Black Political Leadership*. New York: Cambridge University Press.

Hajnal, Zoltan L. 2010. *America's Uneven Democracy: Turnout, Race, and Representation in City Politics*. Cambridge: Cambridge University Press.

Hajnal, Zoltan. 2020. *Dangerously Divided: How Race and Class Shape Winning and Losing in American Politics*. Cambridge: Cambridge University Press.

Hamilton, Alexander, James Madison, and John Jay. 1961. *The Federalist Papers: A Collection of Essays Written in Support of the Constitution of the United States* (ed.) Roy P. Fairfield. Garden City, NY: Anchor Books.

Hero, Rodney E. and Caroline J. Tolbert. 1995. "Latinos and Substantive Representation in the U.S. House of Representatives: Direct, Indirect, or Non-Existent?" *American Journal of Political Science* 39: 640–652.

Highton, Benjamin. 2004. "White Voters and African American Candidates for Congress," *Political Behavior* 26: 1–25.

Hurwitz, Mark S. and Drew Noble Lanier. 2003. "Explaining Judicial Diversity: The Differential Ability of Women and Minorities to Attain Seats on State Supreme and Appellate Courts," *State Politics & Policy Quarterly* 3: 329–352.

ICMA. 1986–2011. "Form of Government Survey."

Juenke, Eric Gonzalez and Robert R. Preuhs. 2011. "Irreplaceable Legislators? Rethinking Minority Representatives in the New Century," *American Journal of Political Science* 56: 705–715.

Kerr, Brinck and Kenneth R. Mladenka. 1994. "Does Politics Matter? A Time-Series Analysis of Minority Employment Patters," *American Journal of Political Science* 38: 918–943.

Kinder, Donald R. and Allison Dale-Riddle. 2011. *The End of Race? Obama, 2008, and Racial Politics in America*. New Haven, CT: Yale University Press.

Kousser, J. Morgan. 1992. "The Voting Rights Act and the Two Reconstructions," In *Controversies in Minority Voting: The Voting Rights Act in Perspective* (eds.) Bernard Grofman and Chandler Davidson. Washington, D.C.: Brookings Institution, 135–176.

Kuk, John, Zoltan Hajnal, and Nazita Lajevardi. 2020. "A Disproportionate Burden: Strict Voter Identification Laws and Minority Turnout," *Politics, Groups, and Identities* 10(1): 126-134.

Lijphart, Arend. 1997. "Unequal Participation: Democracy's Unresolved Dilemma," *American Political Science Review* 91: 1–14.

Mansbridge, Jane. 1999. "Should Blacks Represent Blacks and Women Represent Women? A Contingent Yes," *Journal of Politics* 61: 628–657.

Manza, Jeff. 2006. *Locked Out: Felon Disenfranchisement and American Democracy*. Oxford: Oxford University Press.

Molina, Angel Luis and Kenneth J. Meier. 2018. "Demographic Dreams, Institutional Realities: Election Design and Latino Representation in American Education," *Politics, Groups, and Identities* 6: 77–94.

NCSL (National Conference of State Legislatures. 2019–2011. "Women in State Legislatures." www.ncsl.org/legislators-staff/legislators/womens-legislative-network/women-in-state-legislatures-for-2019.aspx.

Ocampo, Angela X. 2017. "The Wielding Influence of Political Networks: Representation in Majority-Latino Districts," *Political Research Quarterly* 71: 184–198.

Parker, Frank R. 1990. *Black Votes Count: Political Empowerment in Mississippi after 1965*. Chapel Hill: University of North Carolina Press.

Pew Research Center. 2012. "Faith on the Hill: The Religious Composition of the 113th Congress." www.pewforum.org/2012/11/16/faith-on-the-hill-the-religious-composition-of-the-113th-congress.

Pew Research Center. 2021. "Faith on the Hill: The Religious Composition of the 117th Congress." www.pewresearch.org/religion/2021/01/04/faith-on-the-hill-2021.

Phillips, Anne. 1998. "Democracy and Representation: Or, Why Should It Matter Who Our Representatives Are?" In *Feminism and Politics* (ed.) Anne Phillips. Oxford: Oxford University Press, 224–240.

Raphelson, Samantha. 2018. "Muslim Americans Running for Office in Highest Numbers since 2001," *NPR*, July 18. www.npr.org/2018/07/18/630132952/muslim-americans-running-for-office-in-highest-numbers-since-2001.

Rivlin, Gary. 1992. *Fire on the Prairie: Chicago's Harold Washington and the Politics of Race*. New York: Henry Holt.

Schneider, Monica C. and Angela L. Bos. 2011. "An Exploration of the Content of Stereotypes of Black Politicians," *Political Psychology* 32: 205–233.

Smith, Robert C. 1996. *We Have No Leaders: African Americans in the Post-Civil Rights Era*. Albany: University of New York Press.

Swain, Carol M. 1995. *Black Face, Black Interests: The Representation of African Americans in Congress*. Cambridge, MA: Harvard University Press.

Taylor, Paul, Mark Hugo Lopez, Jessica Martínez, and Gabriel Velasco. 2012. "When Labels Don't Fit: Hispanics and Their Views of Identity. www.pewresearch.org/hispanic/2012/04/04/when-labels-dont-fit-hispanics-and-their-views-of-identity.

Tesler, Michael and David O. Sears. 2010. *Obama's Race: The 2008 Election and the Dream of a Post-Racial America*. Chicago: University of Chicago Press.

Trounstine, Jessica L. and Melody Ellis Valdini. 2008. "The Context Matters: The Effect of Single Member vs At-Large Districts on City Council Diversity," *American Journal of Political Science* 68(4): 554–569.

Visalvanich, Neil. 2017. "When Does Race Matter? Exploring White Responses to Minority Congressional Candidates," *Politics, Groups, and Identities* 5: 618–641.

Washington, Ebonya. 2012. "Do Majority Black Districts Limit Blacks' Representation? The Case of the 1990 Redistricting," *Journal of Law and Economics* 55: 251–274.

Woodard, Stephanie. 2019. "Native Americans Take Power: The New Wave of Indigenous Elected Officials," In *Native Americans Take Power: The New Wave of Indigenous Elected Officials*, January 16. https://inthesetimes.com/features/native-american-voters-government-political-revolution.html.

11   Does Government Carry Out the Will of the People?

The 2016 victory of Donald Trump as president was a loss for the descriptive representation of racial and ethnic minorities. The country had been led by a Black man—for the first time ever—during the eight years prior to Trump's election. But what if Trump had lost? A number of non-White candidates had been in the running, and the election of one of them would theoretically have led to greater descriptive representation for various racial minority groups. What if Ben Carson, the African American neurosurgeon, author, and Republican candidate, had gone on to win the Republican nomination and ultimately the presidency? An African American would have once again held the nation's most powerful office. But would his presidency have truly signaled a shift toward greater Black representation? Given that the overwhelming majority of African American voters are not Republican and therefore in all likelihood would not have voted for him in the general election, and given that the policies Carson has espoused often aligned poorly with the stated views of African Americans in national surveys, it is hard to see a Carson presidency as a strong sign of minority incorporation and influence.

Much the same argument could be made for Ted Cruz and Marco Rubio, the two Hispanic candidates for the Republican nomination in 2016. As Cuban Americans, both men are Latino and would count as Hispanic in any measure of descriptive representation. But would a Cruz or Rubio presidency have marked a historic watershed in Latino representation? Neither appears to match up all that well with the bulk of Hispanic voters, either in terms of party affiliation—Latino Democrats outnumber Latino Republicans by two to one—or in terms of policy. Likewise, a victory for Bobby Jindal, the Indian American former governor of Louisiana and candidate for the Republican nomination, would have led to an Asian American presidency, but it is hard to argue that a Jindal win would represent a victory for Asian American voters, most of whom voted on the Democratic side.

In each of these cases, victory by a racial and ethnic minority candidate would count toward minority descriptive representation but it would not necessarily mean that minority citizens were better represented. Racial and ethnic minority elected officials may not always represent the interests of racial and ethnic minority voters.

The other potential problem with using the race of the candidate as the marker of representation is that it implicitly assumes that members of the White majority cannot represent minority interests. This is an important assumption in a nation

Photo 11.1 Republican presidential candidates (left to right): Ben Carson, Senator Marco Rubio (R-Florida), Donald Trump, Senator Ted Cruz (R-Texas), and Ohio Governor John Kasich stand ready to debate at the University of Houston, February 25, 2016. This was the last primary debate before the March 1 Super Tuesday primaries.
Source: Photo Michael Ciaglo © Pool/ Pool/Getty Images News/Getty Images.

where, as we saw in the last chapter, roughly 90 percent of all elected officials are White. Is it possible that of the thousands and thousands of White elected officials across the country, none seeks to represent minority constituents?

Turning back to the 2016 election, what if Hillary Clinton had won the election? As we saw in Chapter 9, "Race and Elections," Clinton garnered the support of the overwhelming majority of African American, Hispanic, and Asian American voters. By many accounts, her policy priorities and issue platform accorded well with the preferences of large shares of the racial and ethnic minority population. Her victory as a White woman would not count toward minority descriptive representation but one could reasonably argue that her victory would have better reflected the preferences and interests of most racial and ethnic minority group members than the victory of Donald Trump. In short, the 2016 election suggests that a simple count of minority elected officials may offer an incomplete picture of the representation story. In this chapter we dig deeper into the representation of racial and ethnic minorities in American democracy.

As the introduction to this chapter suggests, simply counting up the number of racial and ethnic minorities in office as we did in the last chapter may not be sufficient. In this chapter we will think a little bit about what it means for our government to represent its peoples by introducing two additional ways to measure minority representation—electoral representation and substantive representation. By electoral representation, we mean the degree to which voters from different groups vote for candidates that ultimately win their electoral contests. For example, in the 2020 presidential contest, Blacks scored well on this electoral representation measure because the vast majority of Black voters (approximately 90 percent) voted for Joe Biden, the candidate who won the contest (Hajnal and Horowitz 2014). By contrast, only about 10 percent of Black voters ended up 'losing' the contest by supporting Donald Trump, the losing candidate. In substantive representation, the focus is squarely on policy and the degree to which policies of elected officials favor the interests of some groups more than others. For example, Senator Cory Booker of New Jersey advocates and votes for reparations for slavery, making lynching a hate crime, raising the minimum wage, banning assault weapons, and Medicare for all—policies that are aimed at helping disadvantaged African Americans and reducing Black–White inequality.

We will spend most of this chapter examining the empirical record related to electoral and substantive representation. Do the outcomes of our democratic process, in fact, match the will of the people? And even more critically for a textbook on race and democracy, do the outcomes match the will of *all* of the people or just some of the privileged few? At the end of the day, does our government really represent us?

We will learn that there is a significant racial component to electoral representation in the United States. Across the nation, most members of most groups—racial or otherwise—end up voting for candidates that ultimately win. There is, however, one exception—African Americans. For most of the offices we look at here, the majority of Black voters end up on the losing side of the vote. This is a disparity that we should be concerned about because these repeated losses mean that Blacks get less representation and are likely to be less satisfied with and more angered by American democracy.

The polices that we, as a nation, implement are also skewed. Congress and the President listen to the public when they make decisions about policy, but some voices are louder than others. Race, more than class, age, gender, or any other demographic factor, determines who wins and who loses in the policy arena. On important matters of policy, African Americans are again the biggest losers in our democracy.

At the same time, we will be quick to point out that American democracy is not nearly as uneven as it could be. There is nothing in this chapter that will show that every racial and ethnic minority is a loser when it comes to the vote or to policy. Likewise, not all Whites are winners. There is no absolute tyranny of the racial majority. The racial gaps, although substantial, are relatively small.

Electoral Representation

Our initial foray into the races and ethnicities of the candidates in the 2016 presidential contest suggests that we might get a clearer picture by shifting the focus of our attention away from the candidates and onto the voters themselves. Electoral representation provides a measure of how successful voters from different groups are at getting their favored candidates into office.

Measuring Electoral Representation

Electoral representation can be measured by asking any given voter in any given election: Did your favored candidate win the election or lose the election? A count of how many voters from different racial or demographic groups end up voting for a candidate who eventually wins and how many voters from different groups end up voting for a candidate who eventually loses can help us assess electoral representation. If this count is repeated for a wide range of elections, we begin to attain a more global assessment of how well members of different groups are faring in democracy. After the tabulations are complete, one can compare the proportion of winners and losers across a range of key demographic characteristics that regularly divide the electorate. When all is said and done, are racial minorities regularly and repeatedly ending up on the losing side of democracy? And, are outcomes more skewed by race than by other dimensions?

Counting winners and losers this way has several advantages over existing measures of representation. It requires no subjective evaluation of minority interests—that is, we do not have to posit that one candidate is better than another candidate for a minority group. Minorities themselves choose which side they are on. The advantage of this count is that it also incorporates the preferences of every member of a given group, regardless of whether they vote with or against the group's majority preferred candidate.

At the same time, it is important to recognize that counting winners and losers is by no means a perfect test of representation for several reasons:

• If minority voters have no good option among the available candidates, then it does not matter which candidate wins. African American voters, for example, may have no real choice in a Republican Party primary in the South featuring two candidates who support Confederate flags and monuments, repeal of Obamacare, retrenchment on education and welfare, and other policies that are strongly opposed by the clear majority of African American voters. In this case, regardless of who wins, Black voters lose. Of course, African Americans rarely vote in Republican primaries in the South. But other similarly limited choices can and do occur at different levels of office in different parts of the county. What this means is that even if minorities win at the same rate as Whites, outcomes may not be equal because they sometimes have to choose between two poor candidates.
• A count of winners and losers in the vote also assumes that voters make reasonable choices that reflect their interests. But political scientists know that voters often have limited knowledge about the candidates and that as a result they can and do make mistakes. Winning and losing should give us a rough sense of the balance of power in American democracy but it will not tell us exactly how well represented each group is in the system.

Who Loses the Vote?

After the vote is counted, who tends to lose in American elections? To answer that question, we have to look across an array of different types of offices, elections, and years. To get that broader look at American democracy, we turn to a unique study by one of this text's authors that computed losers and winners for over two decades of elections for presidential, House, Senate, gubernatorial, and mayoral elections.[1] These elections do not offer a complete picture of democracy in America. There are, for example, no state legislative contests in the data set and no local offices below the mayoralty. But they represent a broad enough set of cases that the patterns they expose cannot be dismissed as mere anomalies.[2]

Table 11.1 summarizes that data. It shows the proportion of voters who end up supporting losing candidates in presidential, senatorial, gubernatorial, congressional, and mayoral elections broken down by voter characteristics. We look not just at the race and ethnicity of the voters but at an array of other demographic dividing lines like class, gender, age, religion, and sexuality that shape the American public. We want to know if racial minorities lose regularly, but crucially we also want to know if racial minorities lose more or less often than other potentially disadvantaged groups.

The first and probably the most obvious conclusion from the table is that no one group is totally shut out from the winning side of electoral democracy. For example, the table reveals that of all the low-income voters surveyed in these elections—a group that is often viewed as disadvantaged in American democracy—53 percent chose the losing candidate in presidential elections, 46 percent voted for the losing candidate in U.S. Senate contests, 46 percent favored losing House candidates, and 47 percent wound up on the losing side of gubernatorial elections. All of these numbers are quite close to 50 percent, which tells us that low-income voters were almost as likely to win as they were to lose in American democracy.

Across all of the demographic groups and all of the different elections, the worst outcome for any single group is to end up on the losing side of the vote 65 percent of the time. For example, both people who live in cities and those who state they are not religious supported losing candidates in presidential elections 65 percent of the time. However, there is a fair amount of winning in American democracy—perhaps what you would expect in a majoritarian democracy. In most cases, the majority of voters from each group end up on the winning side of the vote. America's democracy may be divided, but it is not the case that an overwhelming majority consistently wins out against a united minority voting bloc.

---

[1] Specifically, Hajnal (2020) assessed winners and losers for all elections that are represented in the Voter News Service Exit Poll series from 1994 to 2006 which included the following contests: three presidential, 139 gubernatorial, 198 for the U.S. Senate, and 919 for congressional seats. For the mayoral vote, Hajnal included all available data on any contested primary or general election that occurred in the nation's twenty largest cities between 1989 and 2009.

[2] To some extent the presidential results are skewed by the fact that they include two Republican victories and only one Democratic victory.

Table 11.1 **Who Loses in American Democracy?**

	President	Senate	House	Governor	Mayor
	\multicolumn{5}{c}{Percent of Voters on the Losing Side of Elections}				
Race					
African Americans	59	55	29	52	53
Whites	50	42	43	44	47
Latinos	54	55	32	52	52
Asian Americans	59	34	31	42	53
Income					
Low	53	46	46	47	–
Middle	51	43	43	46	–
High	50	41	40	44	–
Education					
High school or less	51	46	47	45	–
Some college	50	46	45	45	–
College Graduate	54	43	47	45	–
Gender					
Men	51	44	44	45	–
Women	52	43	38	45	–
Age					
18–29	52	44	40	47	–
30–49	51	43	41	45	–
50+	51	43	39	45	–
Religion					
Catholic	51	42	45	43	–
Protestant	46	42	47	45	–
Jewish	62	37	47	49	–
Not Religious	65	47	37	48	–
Urbanicity					
City	65	48	42	47	–
Suburb	52	43	46	48	–
Non-Urban	47	46	–	46	–
Orientation					
Gay/Lesbian	–	48	–	43	–
Heterosexual	–	41	–	45	–

Source: Adapted from Hajnal (2020). Underlying federal election data from Voter News Service Exit Polls (1994–2006) and for mayoral elections from surveys in the twenty largest cities from 1989 to 2009.

This does not mean that all groups win equally often. The first four rows of the table reveal a racial hierarchy, with African Americans clearly on the bottom. During this period, Blacks are the least successful group in American elections. Blacks are the only group that loses more than half the time in most contests. A majority of all Black voters ended up on the losing side in Presidential elections (59 percent), Senatorial elections (55 percent), gubernatorial elections (52 percent), and mayoral elections (53 percent). The one exception where Black voters did well is in House elections, where 71 percent of Black voters end up getting their favored candidate into office. We discuss the distinctive elements of House elections in more depth below. But overall, African Americans stood out compared to every other group—be it racial, political, or demographic. No other group, aside from Latinos, lost more than half the time in more than one type of contest.

The other racial and ethnic minority group that fares poorly is Latinos. In four of the five types of contests, a slim majority of Latino voters ends up on the losing side and in two sets of these elections, Latinos lose just as often as Blacks. Asian Americans are the most difficult racial group to characterize since they have the most mixed outcomes—sometimes surpassing Whites and sometimes losing more than any other racial group.

At the far end of the racial spectrum, White voters stand out for their consistent success. In particular, for four of the five different kinds of contests, White voters are substantially more likely than Black and Hispanic voters to end up voting for winning candidates. Whites win half or more of the time in every contest, and in most cases close to 60 percent of White voters end up winners.

Class and Other Demographics

It is significant that none of the demographic factors other than race seems to have a consistent impact on winning and losing in American elections. Looking more closely at class, one sees little indication that lower-class Americans are particularly disadvantaged in these electoral contests. Members of the lower class—as measured by income and education—win more than half of the time in at least three of the four types of contests. Class may be an important factor in other aspects of American democracy, but it appears to play little role here.

Indeed, we could find no group other than racial minorities that tended to lose more often than they won. Members of every nonracial group in the table win more than half of the time in most types of elections. In terms of losing, there is no consistent pattern in outcomes for age, gender, religion, urbanicity, or sexual orientation. City residents, for example, may have fared worse than any other group in the three presidential contests but they ended up as regular winners in the other three types of contests. When we dug deeper, we could also find no connection between region and electoral victory.

Is It Really Party Rather Than Race?

It is interesting to note that the two biggest losers in Table 11.1, Blacks and Latinos, are more likely than most other groups to support Democrats. It could be that party and politics rather than race are driving much of these patterns. Black and Hispanic voters could lose more than others simply because they happen to be liberal and Democratic in a time when conservatives and Republicans are more frequently coming out on top.

To assess this possibility and more broadly to isolate the independent effect of each demographic characteristic, the study estimated the effect of race on losing *after* controlling for each individual's political preferences—party identification and ideology—and all of their other demographic characteristics. The results were clear. Even after taking into account political views and party identification and other factors, African American voters were substantially more likely than Whites to end up on the losing side for every type of election. Blacks were 11 percent more likely than Whites to end up losers in Senate contests, 5 percent more likely to do so in gubernatorial elections, 3 percent more likely to lose in congressional contests, and 4 percent more likely to lose in presidential elections. After controls, outcomes were more mixed for Latinos. In two cases (Senate and House elections), Latinos are substantially more likely than Whites to end up losers (2 and 12 percent more likely, respectively) and in another (presidential elections) they win slightly less often than Whites. For Asian Americans, the pattern is one of sometimes winning disproportionately (Senate and president) and sometimes losing at about the same rate as White (governor).

All of this suggests that there is a racial hierarchy to American elections. Whites appear to be the most privileged voters in American democracy. When election results have been posted, their preferences are more likely to triumph than to be defeated. The story changes as one moves down the racial hierarchy. Asian Americans, the other racial group that maintains a relatively privileged economic status, tend to fall somewhere near the middle of the spectrum. Latinos are not consistent losers, but they are clearly more likely than Whites and Asian Americans to lose in most American elections. Then there are African American voters. They reside at the bottom end of the spectrum.

Once the study controlled for politics and all of the other demographic factors, none of the other demographic characteristics predicted losing as consistently as being Black. Class, in particular, had little clear impact on winning or losing the vote. Across income levels and education levels, there were no big winners or losers. At least by this test, class makes little difference in shaping who loses in American democracy. Critically, politics also plays no consistent role here. Democrats are more likely than Republicans to end up on the losing side of presidential democracy. But the effects are not particularly large (3 percent more likely to lose). And in one case (House elections) Democrats fare marginally better than Republicans (5 percent less likely to lose), all else being equal. In the other two types of elections (Senator and gubernatorial), Democrats were no more or less likely than Republicans to lose.

This study points to the conclusion that Blacks are distinctively disadvantaged in American democracy and that disadvantage is not simply due to their liberal or Democratic tendencies. There is something unique about their place in American society or American politics that singles them out as the biggest losers when votes are tallied.

Consistent Losers

In some ways, the numbers in Table 11.1 understate the depth of America's racial hierarchy. We certainly care who wins and who loses in each individual

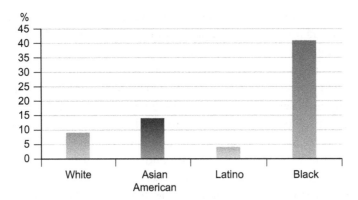

Figure 11.1 Consistent Losers: Percent of Each Group Losing in All Three Elections in the Same Year
The data here show that Black voters lose much more consistently than all other racial groups.
Notes: Underlying data from Voter News Service Exit Polls, 1994–2006; includes presidential, senatorial, and gubernatorial elections.
Source: Adapted from Hajnal (2020).

contest. But what we might be most concerned about are individual voters who lose consistently across multiple elections. Losing once might be okay but losing all of the time is more problematic. The data do not allow us to look at the same individual over time, but we can see if the same *individual* voter lost across three elections (president, Senate, and governor) in the same year. We refer to people who lose in all three contests at the same time as consistent losers. Figure 11.1, which shows the share of each racial group that ends up as losers, reveals an even more severe racial hierarchy. Overall, 41 percent of all Black voters can be characterized as consistent losers. By contrast, only 9 percent of Whites, 4 percent of Latinos, and 14 percent of Asian Americans ended as losers. By this measure, Blacks stand out from every other demographic group in America.

Substantive Representation

While philosophers may debate the virtues of descriptive, or mirror, representation, most ordinary citizens are concerned foremost with *substantive representation*—the degree to which the policies that a government enacts match what its citizens want. We may care about who is elected but we should care even more about the policies those officials pass. At the end of the day, if we are concerned about the inclusion and belonging of minority groups in a democracy, we need to know if the policies that a government enacts favor or ignore their preferences. Thus, in this next section, we shift the focus from who wins office and the outcome of the election to the substance of what a government does.

Substantive representation may have a clear advantage over the other measures. However, it also has a clear disadvantage: it is hard to measure. We often have exacting measures of policy outcomes, but we rarely have good measures of the views of different segments of the public on those specific policies. Thus, it is difficult to accurately assess the fit between minority preferences and policy outcomes. For example: we have great detail on all of the different gun restriction laws that each state has passed in the last few decades, but we know much less about how members of each racial and ethnic group in each state felt about these laws at the time they were passed. In the past, this difficulty has often led to relatively narrow studies that focused on a specific locality or a single policy. For example, we have compelling case studies of substantive representation in a particular city; we have insightful analysis of outcomes across a number of school districts; we have telling assessments of direct democracy in a particular state; or we have data on the responsiveness of bureaucrats in a particular policy arena.[3] These kinds of studies have provided real insight into an office, a location, or an aspect of policy but it is hard to piece them together to get an overall evaluation of minority representation. Fortunately, new data and new means of compiling that data has resulted in an explosion of recent research on substantive representation.

Most of these newer studies, going back to the 1990s, have focused on class. We now have considerable evidence that the rich get more of what they want on policy than do the poor.[4] In perhaps the most encompassing study of public preferences and policy change, Martin Gilens offered this bleak conclusion about American democracy: "What I find is hard to reconcile with the notion of political equality... responsiveness is strongly tilted toward the most affluent citizens. Indeed, under most circumstances, the preferences of the vast majority of Americans appear to have essentially no impact on which policies the government does or does not adopt" (Gilens 2012: 1).

Larry Bartels' seminal study of class and the voting patterns of senators likewise finds that "the views of constituents in the bottom third of the income distribution received no weight at all in the voting decisions of their Senators" (Bartels 2008: 254). Perhaps the most egregious example was on a vote to raise the minimum wage, where the voices of the poor were essentially ignored even though they were the ones most directly impacted by the proposed measure. These are eye-opening and deeply troubling findings, representing patterns that individual Americans have witnessed and been angered by. Inequality in responsiveness is in part what drove many Americans to unite under the Occupy Wall Street movement—a protest movement

---

[3] These more focused studies include work on school districts (Meier, Stewart, and England 1991, individual cities (Browning, Marshall, and Tabb 1984), direct democracy (Hajnal, Gerber, and Louch 2002), public housing (Einstein and Glick 2016), and many more specific outcomes or localities. The broadest of this work has looked at the correspondence between the votes of individual legislators and their constituents (Griffin and Newman 2007).

[4] A number of methodological critiques have, however, raised some doubt about the extent to which the rich dominate. One important critique is that the rich and the poor generally agree on policy and that it is therefore almost impossible to say which has more say.

Photo 11.2 In October, 2011, the Occupy Wall Street protestors took their "Millionaires March" to the front of the homes of some of New York City's wealthiest residents, including News Corp. CEO Rupert Murdoch, JP Morgan Chase CEO Jamie Dimon, and oil tycoon David Koch.
Source: Photo Emmanuel Dunand © Emmanuel Dunand/ Staff/AFP/Getty Images.

against the undue influence of corporations that began in New York City in the early 2010s. When they chanted, "We are the 99 percent," and asked for "A government accountable to the people, freed up from corporate influence," it was clear that they keenly felt this inequality in responsiveness.[5]

Who Wins in the Policy Process?

The problem with these existing studies is that none have incorporated race. Yet we know that race and class are closely connected. Just to cite two figures: 66 percent of the poor in this country are non-White, while only 9 percent of the wealthy are non-White (Keister 2014). Because racial and ethnic minorities tend to be less well-off than Whites, it is quite conceivable that differences in responsiveness by class are, in fact, driven by differential responsiveness by race. As we saw in Chapter 6, "Public Opinion," we also know that racial differences in opinion are sometimes quite large, so there is a real possibility that minority citizens' views are regularly losing in a policy world dominated by the White majority.

[5] The quote is from Amin Husain, one of the organizers of the protest as quoted in Greenberg (2012).

For that reason we highlight here the results of one recent study that looked not only at responsiveness by race across a wide range of policy areas but also compared the effects of race, class, and other demographic factors. That study by a group of scholars including one of the authors of this textbook examined the spending preferences for almost half a million Americans on eleven major national policy areas (welfare, national defense, education, foreign aid, parks and recreation, law enforcement, improving and protecting the nation's health, solving the problems of big cities, improving and protecting the environment, the space exploration program, and highways and bridges) over almost four decades (Griffin et al. 2019). These eleven areas do not cover all issues of concern to the public or even all major government spending areas, but they do cover half of the federal budget.

For each policy area, individual Americans were asked whether they think the government should increase spending in that area, decrease spending, or keep spending at about the same level. Individual policy preferences are then matched with actual federal government spending outcomes in each area to determine whose preferences are followed and whose are not. If, for example, a particular individual favored a decline in federal welfare spending and the federal government chose to significantly decrease welfare spending in the following year, that individual is a "policy winner." That one-year time gap is important because we want to know if public opinion actually drives future policy changes.

Figure 11.2 provides an overall sense of winners and losers on federal spending policy. The figure shows the share of each group that ended up policy winners across the four decades of the data. Looking across the entire figure, a perceptive reader might notice that responsiveness to all groups is relatively low. For every group in the figure, fewer than half end up policy winners. This may at first be somewhat surprising, but it actually matches up with other studies of government

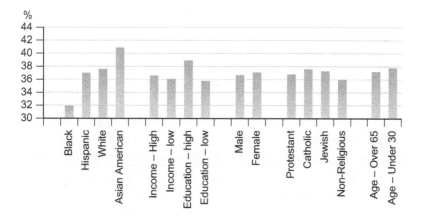

Figure 11.2 Policy Winners
The figure shows the share of each group that are policy winners. For example, people over the age of 65 were policy winners 37.2% of the time, while those under the age of 30 were policy winners 37.8% of the time. *Note*: Data on Hispanics and Asian Americans are limited to 2000–2010 and are not strictly comparable to the other figures in the table.
Source: General Social Survey (1972–2010) and Federal Budget. Adapted from Griffin (2019).

responsiveness. A landmark study in 1963 showed that while the voting records of members of Congress did align closely with opinions of voters in their districts, the fit between the two was far from perfect and varied from issue to issue (Miller and Stokes 1963). A few years later, Ben Page and Robert Shapiro showed that large shifts in national public opinion on a particular issue were more often than not followed by a similar shift in federal government policy. They found, for example, that the Civil Rights Act was passed shortly after public opinion shifted and a clear majority of the public favored a law giving Blacks "the right to be served in public places." At the same time, they found that in up to a third of the cases, policy moved in the opposite direction to the public's views (Page and Shapiro 1983).

More recent research at the state level has similarly found substantial but far from complete policy responsiveness. One study in particular found that while state "policy is highly responsive to policy-specific opinion... policy is congruent with majority will only half the time" (Lax and Phillips 2011: 148). These initial results offer an encouraging if not an overwhelmingly positive statement on the functioning of American democracy.

Also reassuring is the fact that when one looks across all of the different demographic groups in Figure 11.2, the overall picture that emerges is one of relatively even responsiveness. Most of the group level differences are relatively small—often less than 1 percentage point. Women, for example, win in the policy realm 37.1 percent of the time, a figure that differs only marginally from the 36.7 percent success rate for men. All of this confirms that there is no overwhelming tyranny of the majority. No group is getting what they want all of the time, and no group is losing every time. American democracy may not be perfect—a claim we will make time and again—but it is not totally shutting out the voices of its minorities.

There are, however, real differences in responsiveness, and the pattern to those differences is a familiar one. Race, more than anything else, shapes who wins and who loses in American democracy. Blacks are the least advantaged group in the policy world and by a considerable margin. Blacks are winners in only 31.9 percent of cases. The next biggest policy loser is Americans without a high-school education, who win just 35.8 percent of the time. Blacks stand out as policy losers, and they very much stand out compared to Whites who get their favored policy enacted 37.6 percent of the time.

The Black–White gap may not be massive—an important point to reiterate—but it does dwarf every other group factor that we could examine. Race clearly trumps class. The 5.7 point difference between Blacks and Whites in winning rates is almost twice as large as the 3.1 point difference between college graduates and high-school dropouts and roughly ten times larger than the 0.5 point difference between high- and low-income earners. Class may work in the way we would expect it to. The well-educated get what they want more than the poorly educated and the rich do better than the poor. But at the end of the day, class gaps are much smaller than the race gaps.

Even if we look at more extreme categories like the top 10 percent of earners, or the top 1 percent of earners, class still fails to drive policy responsiveness to any great degree. The top 10 percent of earners win on policy 37.9 percent of the time while the top 1 percent win 36.8 percent of the time. Top earners thus do better than the poor in terms of responsiveness to their policy preferences—but not by much. Analysis of other potential markers of class, such as being unemployed (35.4 percent winners) also does not reveal major differences in responsiveness.

The measures of religion that have been looked at in these studies are limited in that they do not single out key groups like White Evangelicals. But we do find that race also trumps religion. The biggest gap for religious groups that is visible, between the nonreligious and Catholics, is just 1.6 points (i.e., 37.6 percent of Catholics and 36.0 percent of the nonreligious see their policy preferences come to pass). Differences across other religious groups are even less pronounced.

We have not mentioned Latinos and Asian Americans yet because the data for these groups are unfortunately quite limited. The surveys used in this analysis asked about Latino and Asian American identities only after 2000. As such, it is difficult to compare the success rates of these two racial minorities to other demographic groups who have been analyzed over a much longer period of time.

At best, we can offer some preliminary conclusions about these two groups. Over the ten-year period for which we have data for all four racial groups, Latinos won in terms of their policy preferences coming to pass in 37.0 percent of cases, just slightly below the figure for Whites for the same period (38.1 percent), suggesting that Hispanics could have less influence than Whites over policy. By contrast, Asian Americans won at higher rates than Whites (40.9 percent) and might therefore be viewed as privileged in the political system.

Is It Really Race?

The results of studies up to this point suggest that Black voices are not equal to others when it comes to policy. But there are reasons to think that differences among races in terms of policy success may not ultimately be about race. Blacks could be especially likely to lose because their political preferences are distinctive relative to other groups. Blacks tend to be more Democratic than almost any other group, they tend to be more liberal and to favor a more active and involved government than other groups. Blacks may be losing more than others simply because they are Democratic and liberal in a polity that favors Republicans and conservatism. Similarly, they could be losing because they regularly favor spending increases in a budget environment that favors constraints on spending. It is also possible that race is correlated with other demographic factors like class, age, gender, and religion that are actually driving responsiveness.

However, when the authors of the study looked at a more complex model that controlled for not only race and ethnicity but also political preferences (whether you are a Democrat, a Republican, a liberal, or a conservative) and a host of demographic characteristics, they found that the effects of race persisted. Figure 11.3 shows the differences in the level of responsiveness between two groups (e.g., Whites vs. Blacks) while simultaneously considering all of the other factors in the figure.

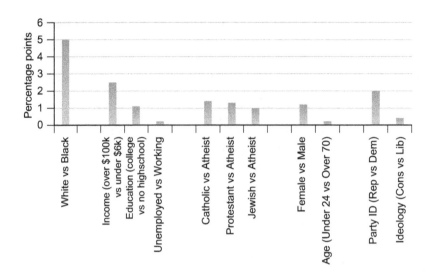

Figure 11.3 Predicted Gaps in Being a Policy Winner
The data summarized here show that race plays by far the largest role in shaping political responsiveness.
Source: General Social Survey, 1972–2010, and Federal Budget. Adapted from Griffin et al. (2019).

Figure 11.3 illustrates the uniquely powerful role of race in shaping political responsiveness. All else being equal, the federal government is 5 points more likely to follow the preferences of a White respondent than a Black respondent. That 5-point gap is not enormous, but it is by far the largest impact on government responsiveness in the figure. Race is twice as powerful as income or education in explaining who wins in the policy arena. Race also overshadows the impact of religion and every other demographic characteristic. And perhaps most importantly, race even outweighs politics in structuring policy responsiveness. Republicans win on policy more than Democrats over the time period of the study, but the gap is a relatively small 2.0 points. If we really want to explain inequality in American politics, we need to begin with a focus on race. Other factors like class are certainly relevant but the biggest part of why some Americans get what they want from government and others do not is a function of race.

The prominent role of race in Figure 11.3 tells us that the connection between race and policy responsiveness cannot be easily explained away. African Americans are not losing in the policy arena because of their socioeconomic status or their political orientation, because they are poor or less well educated than others. They are not losing because they are more liberal or more Democratic than others, because they favor more spending increases.

The disadvantage Blacks face in the American policy world seems much deeper. One real possibility is that racial discrimination is at play here. Perhaps politicians simply heed Black voices less. We have already seen that when White and Black constituents try to contact their legislators via email, legislators respond to White-sounding names more than they respond to names they perceive as Black or Hispanic (Butler and Broockman 2011). Moreover, as we saw in Chapter 10, roughly 90 percent of all elected officials are White. Would it be that surprising if White elected officials were slightly more likely to listen to White voices and slightly more likely to heed their calls for policy? Institutional structures might also be impeding Black interests in American democracy. In particular, Black interests could be undermined through gerrymandering—a subject we will return to in later chapters. The malapportionment of the Senate could also be a factor as Blacks tend to live in the most populous states that have, relatively speaking, the worst representation in the Senate (Malhotra and Raso 2007).

Intersectionality: Who Is "Doubly Disadvantaged"?

What Figure 11.3 does not tell us is whether different dimensions like race and gender interact with each other to shape responsiveness. Does disadvantage on one dimension reinforce disadvantage on the other? As we noted in Chapter 4, inequality is often the result of intersectional disadvantages – that is, where multiple, interacting dimensions of an individual's identity or status may combine to put them in a unique unfair or unfavorable position (Marie-Hancock 2016). Whereas the intersection of "older," "White," and "male" puts a person, at least statistically, in a uniquely advantaged position for many outcomes in American society, other intersections like "young," "Latinx," and "LGBTQ+" or "immigrant," "Arab," and "Muslim" may combine to uniquely disadvantage someone in American society. Research on intersectionality has paid particular attention to racialgendered identities and outcomes (e.g., Brown and Gerson 2016; Hardy-Fanta et al. 2016; Phillips 2021). We do, in fact, find that Black women are doubly disadvantaged as women and as racial minorities when it comes to federal government policy responsiveness. The gaps in policy responsiveness are small but our study nevertheless reveals that when government chooses policy, Black women are about 1 percentage point less likely than Black men to have their preferences translate into federal government spending decisions.

We also find that race and class interact to impact Blacks and Whites differently. Essentially, we find that the effect of class works in the opposite direction for Whites and Blacks. Whereas, higher-income Whites are 1.9 percentage points more successful on policy than low-income Whites, higher-income Blacks are actually marginally less likely than lower-income Blacks to get the policies they want (0.9 percent). In other words, this research suggests that attaining higher status does not appear to be an avenue through which Blacks can narrow the responsiveness gap.

Variation across Issues

Looking at all of the different policy areas together in one big analysis—as we have done up to this point in this chapter—is important to get an overall evaluation of

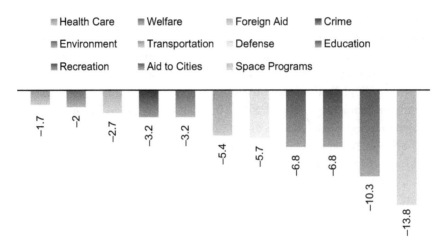

Figure 11.4 The Black–White Gap in Responsiveness by Area
This figure shows the degree to which Black views have less influence than White views on eleven different federal government spending areas: Blacks get less of what they want than Whites across every one of the policy areas, with healthcare the area where Blacks and Whites are closest in getting what they want.
Source: General Social Survey, 1972–2010, and Federal Budget. Adapted from Griffin et al. (2019).

policy responsiveness. By incorporating the views of many Americans across many different policies, we get a broad window into policy responsiveness in American democracy. But this larger picture could conceal enormous variation. We also want to know how policy winners and losers change from policy to policy. In particular, to get a true sense of how disadvantaged African Americans are in the policy arena, we want to know if they are consistent losers. Compared with other groups, do they lose on policy after policy? Or are losses on some policies offset by victories on others?

To answer these questions, the authors separated out the eleven different policy areas and repeated the analysis. Those results are displayed in Figure 11.4, which shows the size of the racial gap in responsiveness for each of the 11 policy areas— again after controlling for all of the other factors.

First and foremost, we learn from this analysis that African Americans are significantly disadvantaged on *every issue*. Regardless of the government's policy focus, Black opinions hold significantly less sway than White opinions. There is, however, some interesting variation across issues in the degree to which African Americans are disadvantaged. The size of the Black disadvantage diminishes somewhat on policy areas that appear to be particularly important to the Black community. Specifically, the degree to which Blacks fall behind Whites appears to be somewhat smaller on welfare (-2.0 percent), healthcare (-1.7 percent), and crime (-3.2 percent) than it does on other policy areas. This is slightly encouraging in that Blacks are getting a little more responsiveness on the policies they want on the issues that are especially critical to their community—a pattern of results that matches studies of other minorities (Bishin 2009). Whether it is because African Americans are pushing particularly hard and are making their voices heard on these particular policy areas or because leaders in the federal government simply recognize that these are areas where Black voices should hold greater sway, this is a positive pattern.

The figure does not show the results for class, but the analysis revealed that class has a much less consistent impact on policy responsiveness. In more than half of all policy areas, income has no significant effect on who wins or loses. That suggests that for much of what government does, income plays little part in shaping whose voices are heard. Higher-income Americans, for the most part, have no better political megaphones that allow their voices to be heard more than lower-income Americans. On issues in which income does matter—on crime, aid to cities, space, and defense—lower-income Americans were significantly less influential than were wealthier Americans. The effects of education are similarly uneven across the eleven policy areas. Put succinctly, the effects of class are highly variable. We sometimes see a bias toward the voices of the well-off, but we occasionally see a bias against those voices, and we also see cases where class status is largely irrelevant. What all of this tells us is: *race is much more of an ever-present barrier than class.*

At the same time, it is important to recognize the limitations of this study. The method we have used assumes that individual Americans know what they want in terms of federal government spending. Yet studies of public opinion have shown that individual views on policy can be highly variable and error-prone. The patterns we uncover could also be very different if we were to shift from an examination of government spending to other aspects of policy, if we were to focus on state or local government policy, or if we were to look at different time periods.

Interpreting the Patterns in Electoral and Substantive Representation

To be fair, there are different ways of interpreting the patterns we have seen throughout this chapter. One read of the data is that American democracy is fairly open. No single group appears to wield total control of the process. And at the other end of the spectrum, no single group loses all of the time. When the votes are counted, some groups lose more than others, but no groups win all of the time and American democracy today often finds a way to incorporate the voices of its minorities. In short, things could be a lot worse. This is a core tenet of pluralism as a form of democracy which James Madison and his fellow Federalists foreshadowed—namely, that in the face of factions in society, the "principal task of legislation" is to regulate competing factions such that no one group's interests would dominate (see Dahl 1961).

A second view might see differences in representation as real but argue that they are both unsurprising and justified. They are unsurprising and justified because the group that loses more than all others, African Americans, represents a small minority of the population. It is little wonder that their candidates lose more frequently and that they win on policy less than the White majority. Moreover, in this view the inequalities are seen as justified because Blacks, as a minority, should have less say than the majority-White population. Put simply, the median voter is White and politicians should represent the median voter, both strategically and normatively.

In this second case, we would push back more forcefully. We would counter that while that majoritarian logic may be reasonable, it does not explain why Blacks—and to a lesser extent Latinos—stand out even among small minorities. Blacks are the *only* group singled out in this way in American democracy. The poor, the young, the unemployed, Jews, and Catholics, and even Asian Americans—a much smaller minority than African Americans—all win more often than they lose on the vote and all get roughly equal influence on policy. In some cases, in fact, some of these groups wield more influence than their numbers would suggest. Moreover, the smallest minority we examine, the wealthiest 1 percent, fare the best in policy terms, and no one would argue that the wealthiest 1 percent are "the median voter." Other minorities do not lose disproportionately in the way that African Americans do, according to the evidence we have shown in this chapter. Only Black voices are consistently ignored. Those who are in some ways most in need of representation get it the least.

It is not just that African Americans lose more in the vote and in the policy world than any other demographic group. Critically, Blacks' disadvantage cannot be easily explained away. African Americans are not losing out on the vote or in the policy world because they identify overwhelmingly as Democrats or liberals. Blacks are not losing on policy because they are more liberal and prefer greater spending. Even after we control for party identification, ideological orientation, and a tendency to favor spending increases, Blacks still lose significantly more than any other group. Moreover, even when Blacks make it to the middle class, they still end up with limited policy influence. Middle-class Blacks actually have, by our estimates, less influence than poorer Blacks.

The other issue regarding the lack of influence in policy is the consistency with which African Americans lose in American democracy. It is not just that they lose more than others when the votes are counted and that they lose more than others when policy decisions are made. It is also how consistently they lose. This is the scenario that has vexed political philosophers at least since Jean-Jacques Rousseau forcefully articulated the dangers of a "tyranny of the majority" that might result from societies that govern solely based on majority rule, even in the face of inequalities of power and privilege that would result in a "permanent majority."

Black voters are substantially more likely than White voters to lose across almost every type of electoral contest we looked at. Fully 41 percent of Black voters could be labeled as losers, having lost in every contest in the same year. Blacks are also substantially more likely than Whites to lose across every type of policy we could examine. It is natural to lose in a majoritarian democracy. There will always

Photo 11.3 Protesters hold up signs outside the U.S. Chamber of Commerce Headquarters, August 26, 2021, in Washington, D.C. The demonstration was held in partnership with Black Voters Matter, Greenpeace, and other organizations who claimed that the Chamber of Commerce opposed the For The People Act, a bill to expand voting rights. That bill was passed by the 117th House of Representatives in March 2021, but was held up in the Senate, where it was blocked by the threat of a Republican filibuster.
Source: Photo Anna Moneymaker © Anna Moneymaker/Staff/Getty Images News/Getty Images.

be winners and losers. But it becomes much more problematic when the same group loses all the time. These patterns raise a legitimate question of whether groups that lose regularly have enough of a say in the political arena.

The bottom line is that the differences we see in electoral and substantive representation are both real and concerning. All of this suggests that racial equality remains an elusive goal in the American political landscape. Political equality—a fundamental ideal for any democracy—is undercut if the color of one's skin is the most important determinant of whether one wins or loses in a democracy.

It should, therefore, come as no surprise that African Americans and to a lesser extent Latinos feel substantially more dissatisfied with American democracy. There are wide gaps in the degree to which members of different racial groups feel they are represented. Study after study has shown that minorities—and most emphatically African Americans—are much less satisfied than White Americans with government. Blacks and other minorities also express less trust in the political system and are more apt to report that what they say does not matter in the political sphere. More worrying is the fact that a high share of the Black population expresses little hope for the future of American democracy. Only 20 percent of Blacks believe that existing inequities will be erased in their lifetime (Dawson 2011). Of course, a range of factors beyond winning and losing elections is driving these sentiments among minorities. But if Blacks, and to a lesser extent, Latinos, feel dissatisfied, disengaged, and powerless because they feel their votes and their voices do not count, then American democracy has a real problem.

Is There Anything We Can Do?

Recognizing a problem is one thing. Solving it is quite another. One of the most obvious ways to look for potential solutions is to look at variation in outcomes. If we can identify times or contexts when African Americans fared relatively less poorly and find out why those exceptions occurred, we may be able to come up with pathways to more equitable representation in the future.

Improving Electoral Representation

In terms of electoral representation, a look at variation in the data immediately points to House elections, where Black voters fare relatively well. Recall that African American voters fared worse than voters from other groups everywhere except House elections. By contrast, when Blacks voted in House contests, they ended up voting for the winning candidate 71 percent of the time—an extremely successful rate compared to other groups.

What is about the House that leads to greater Black success? It is the only type of election that we looked at where the lines separating out one district from another are regularly redrawn. In other words, politicians, judges, and redistricting commissions have control over the shape and demographics of the district. For the senatorial, gubernatorial, presidential, and mayoral elections—the other contests we focused on—there is no line-drawing. All of this suggests that gerrymandering—the process of drawing district lines—can make a real difference. In the case of the House, district lines have often been drawn to create majority-minority districts in which African Americans are placed with other African Americans and other racial and ethnic minorities. The positive outcomes for Black voters in House elections suggest that putting minorities together and at times grouping them with like-minded White Democrats can lead to minority voters winning more regularly and ultimately getting the candidates they want into office more frequently. Of course, the potential drawback here is that creating more majority-minority districts might mean fewer liberal or Democratic districts overall. If racial and ethnic minorities are bunched together into a small number of majority-minority districts, then the rest of the districts— the overwhelming majority of districts—will end up being majority-White and quite possibly disproportionately Republican and conservative. We will examine an academic debate about whether and how much this happens in Chapter 13, "Voting Rights."

The other interesting variation in electoral representation is from state to state. Additional analysis of the state-level contests—gubernatorial and senatorial elections—suggests that Black voters are more successful when they live in states that are more Democratic, more liberal, and less Republican. Indeed, the estimated effects at the state level are dramatic.[6] Black voters in more liberal Democratic states were 74 percent less likely to lose in Senate elections and 38 percent less likely to lose in gubernatorial contests than Black voters in more conservative Republican states. That same analysis shows that Black voter success in statewide contests depends a lot on the size of the Black population—although the relationship is somewhat complex.

Since we cannot change state boundaries, we cannot point to concrete reforms. But this analysis does imply that Black success in American democracy rests substantially on the willingness of the non-Black neighbors of African Americans to support a liberal Democratic agenda. Analysis of the statewide contests also shows that Black success rates were significantly lower in states covered under the 1965 Voting Rights Act, section 5; these are states that were identified by the landmark civil rights legislation as having a history of disenfranchising African Americans. In other words, states with a prior history of racial disenfranchisement continue to have reduced Black representation today. This is an important finding in light of the U.S. Supreme Court's decision in *Shelby* v. *Holder* in 2013. In that landmark case, the Supreme Court effectively invalidated core elements of the Voting Rights Act because it claimed that there was little recent evidence of covered jurisdictions limiting minority representation. These results suggest that minority representation continues to be hindered in states covered by the Voting Rights Act.

Improving Substantive Representation

Our analysis of responsiveness on federal government spending did not reveal a lot of variation in substantive representation. Blacks lost disproportionately on every policy area that we were able to examine. But that was only one kind of decision—how to allocate dollars—and only one context—federal spending. There is little doubt that racial and ethnic minorities have fared worse at some points in American history and equally little doubt that minorities have done better on policy in some localities and under some circumstances than others. What are the factors that help explain that variation and that might help lead to better substantive representation for racial and ethnic minorities?

Scholars have identified an array of factors that can improve minority representation. One of the first and most obvious is the size of the minority population itself. In areas where the minority population represents a majority of the local population, policy outcomes tend to favor minority interests. This has been demonstrated at almost every level of American democracy including across states, congressional districts, cities, and school districts.

---

[6] See Hajnal (2020) for details on the analysis.

Racial Context and Minority Representation

Do more minority residents mean more favorable policy? Given that America is a democracy, one might expect that as the size—and thus the political power—of the minority population grows, so too should its influence. But there is a countervailing force potentially at work. As we noted in Chapter 6, "Public Opinion," it is also possible that as the size of the minority population grows, the perceived threat it poses to the majority (White) population increases. Thus, more minorities would mean more of a (White) backlash. The end result would then depend on the balance of these two countervailing forces.

At least theoretically, we could see different patterns to changes in minority representation as racial demographics change. Figure 11.5 illustrates some of the possibilities:

- **Influence model**. This is a simple linear model: As the share of minorities in the district population increases, their influence also increases, and policy shifts more and more in a pro-minority direction. This assumes little or no White backlash.
- **Curvilinear model**. In this model, where the minority population of the district is small, it has some influence. But as the minority population grows, the White majority mobilizes to oppose minority interests. This backlash dominates more and more until the point where the minority becomes the majority in the district and gains control over policy.
- **Majoritarian model.** In this model, minorities have little influence until they become the majority in the district and can greatly determine policy.

How closely do these models represent the real world? One seminal study that looked at how much individual members of Congress vote for pro-minority legislation found that congressional districts outside the South tended to fit the *influence model* (Figure 11.5): the more minorities in the district, the more their congressional representative voted for policies that Civil Rights group favored. In essence, this pattern suggests that there was not a lot of backlash outside the South. However, the same study found that the *majoritarian model* (Figure 11.5) tended to apply in the South. Legislators were largely unresponsive to minority preference but that changed dramatically in majority-minority districts. In yet another context, when Hajnal (2020) looked at the extent to which minorities win the vote across states, he found more of a *curvilinear* pattern. Specifically, Black voters in Senate and gubernatorial elections are quite successful when the Black population is relatively small, but once the Black population grows beyond a certain level, White resistance to Black interests grows. Black failure peaks at the topmost point of the curve. Then, as Blacks become a more numerous and decisive voting bloc, the likelihood of Blacks ending up on the losing side of the vote declines. All of this resembles the relationship highlighted in Figure 11.5.

Institutional Structure and Minority Representation

Another factor that can help or hurt minority representation is institutional structure. Several institutional features within American democracy have been linked to

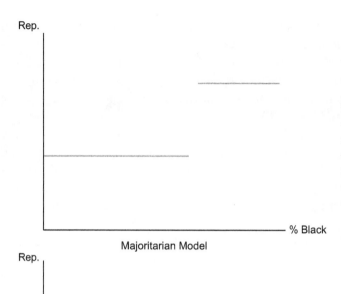

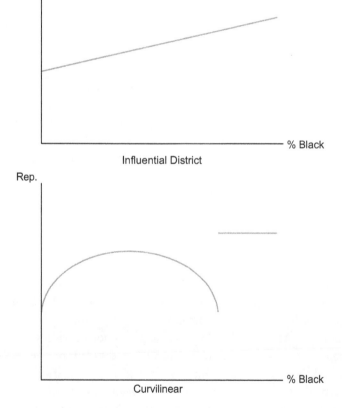

Figure 11.5 Possible Relationships between Minority Population Share and Minority Representation
The figure shows three different patterns of how minority influence and representation in a district might change as racial demographics in that district change.
Source: Cameron, Epstein, and Halloran (1996).

minority success in policy representation. We discuss these in Chapter 13, "Voting Rights," but we highlight a few here:

- **Senate Malapportionment**. Because racial and ethnic minorities live disproportionately in more populous states and the Senate gives every state the same level of representation—two senators—racial and ethnic minority voices are weighted much less heavily than White voices.

- **Racial Gerrymandering.** There is little doubt that minority interests have been significantly impacted by racial gerrymandering in a number of states. Just how much line-drawing has hurt minority interests overall, however, is a debate that we will explore in Chapter 13.
- **At-large Election model.** We discussed at-large elections in Chapter 10 on representation. Critics of local government structure often emphasize the deleterious effects of at-large elections where all of the members of a body like the city council are elected in one contest, allowing a White majority to effectively control every office. At-large elections are cited as impacting everything from minority student outcomes to local government spending.
- **Direct Democracy.** Some have pointed to direct democracy—where individual citizens directly determine policy by voting on ballot initiatives—both as a savior and as a villain in the process of protecting minority rights (see box, "Digging Deeper: Minority Representation in Direct Democracy," below).

DIGGING DEEPER: MINORITY REPRESENTATION IN DIRECT DEMOCRACY

Could direct democracy be a solution to inequalities in American democracy? Our current system of representative democracy in which elected officials are entrusted to make most of the important policy decisions certainly has lots of detractors. Many feel that elected officials work too closely with and on behalf of special interest groups (such as oil companies) who contribute to their campaigns. Other critics lament outright corruption among office holders. Still others worry about the incompetence of elected officials. All of this may be why public trust in the nation's political elites is at an all-time low. As a result, many wonder if the public would do a better job. After all, who is better able to determine what is best for the people than the people themselves? For supporters of expanding direct democracy, there is no more democratic system than one that places power directly and clearly in the hands of the people.

But there are dangers to direct democracy as well—particularly when it comes to minority representation. Perhaps the biggest concern is tyranny of the majority. Direct democracy affords the majority an opportunity to trample the rights and interests of the minority. As James Madison so long ago noted, with direct citizen involvement in policy making, "measures are too often decided, not according to the rule of justice and the rights of the minor party but by the superior force of an interested and overbearing majority" (Hamilton, Madison, and Jay 1961: 77).

So is direct democracy a solution? There is no doubt that a significant number of clearly anti-minority measures have been passed through direct democracy. In just one state—California—direct democracy led to laws that legalized housing discrimination (Prop. 14), mandated English as the official language (Prop. 63), denied social services to the undocumented (Prop. 187), eliminated affirmative action programs (Prop. 209), dismantled bilingual education (Prop. 227), and outlawed same-sex marriage (Prop. 8). More generally, studies have shown that when explicitly anti-minority measures are on the ballot, they pass regularly (Lewis 2011).

But is this better or worse than representative democracy? It is likely that the results under representative democracy would not be much better. One study of direct democracy in California over an almost thirty-year period found that Black, Latino, and Asian American voters all lost on ballot measures between 4 and 5 percent more often than White voters. That racial deficit in direct democracy is similar in size to what we found earlier in this chapter for federal government policymaking. In other words, minorities are more apt than Whites to lose whether under direct democracy or representative democracy. Looking more broadly across all of the states, another study found there was no real difference between direct-democracy states and other states in terms of how much state policy supported gay rights (Lax and Phillips 2011).

Ultimately, what direct democracy may do that is different is simply amplify or exaggerate the voice of the majority, whatever that voice may be. When the majority is sympathetic to minority interests, direct democracy may help ensure those minority interests are fully represented. But when the majority is hostile toward the local minority, direct democracy probably helps the majority to target the minority (Gerber 1999).

Descriptive Representation and Policy Outcomes

As we noted in the last chapter, descriptive representation can have wide-ranging effects on policy outcomes. Studies have shown that electing more minorities to office can lead to measurable policy shifts in favor of minority interests at the federal, state, judicial, municipal, and school-district levels. Actions or inaction of minorities themselves can also play a role. Research has linked minority turnout to policy representation (Griffin and Newman 2007). That is, when minorities turn out to vote, the policies they support are more likely to be implemented. One study demonstrates a connection between protest activity by minority groups and the extent to which legislators favor minority interests (Gillion 2012). Finally, resources and, in particular, money, are key to fostering greater representation. Minorities, for example, appear to have more influence over policy in cities where the minority population is more educated and has greater financial might (see box "What It looks Like Today," below).

WHAT IT LOOKS LIKE TODAY: REDUCING BIAS IN RESPONSIVENESS—THE CASE OF LOCAL FINES

City governments, like just about every type of government, are often cash-strapped and looking for new sources of revenue. One solution that cities have put forward to raise much-needed revenue is the use of fines and court fees. One estimate is that cities raise roughly $8 per person per year from fines and fees. The problem is that these fines and fees are highly racialized.

A recent study found that the degree to which cities rely on fines and fees is closely related to the size of the local Black population (Sances and You 2017). The study found that reliance on fees and fines more than doubled (up to $20 per person per year) in cities with the highest concentrations of Blacks. This is especially troubling given that African Americans are often the least able to pay the fines and can ultimately be imprisoned for failing to do so. Interestingly, if a city had at least one Black city council member, there was a sharp reduction in the connection between the size of Black population and revenue from fines.

A similarly powerful example is the cash bail system. In the United States today, there are more than 10 million arrests each year, mostly for minor offenses. After an arrest, judges (and sometimes other legal actors) have the authority to determine whether the defendant accused of a crime has to remain incarcerated as they await trial or if they can be released pretrial. Cash bail is one of the most common practices used in pretrial release, where a defendant is required to pony up a determined amount of money held as collateral by the courts to ensure that the individual returns for their trial date and steers clear of further arrests. This seemingly race-neutral practice results in enormously disparate outcomes: Blacks and Latinos are not only more likely to be denied bail, but they are also more likely to be levied higher bail amounts and more likely to be unable to afford cash bail (Arnold, Dobbie, and Yang 2018).

The lessons? First, policies that are race-blind on the surface can be applied and implemented in racially uneven ways and can ultimately have deeply concerning racial consequences (see Chapter 5). As we will see later, voter identification laws—another policy that is on its face not about race—are passed in states with higher concentrations of minorities, are often implemented by local administrators in racially disparate ways, and ultimately have racially disparate consequences for who does and does not turn out to vote. Second, descriptive representation matters. Electing more minorities into office can begin to alter these racialized patterns and can ultimately reduce racial bias in policy.

Political Parties and Minority Representation

What about political parties? Do they have an impact on the degree to which minorities are heard and their interests represented? One might think that minorities are better represented when Democrats are in charge. The Democratic Party certainly makes claims that it is the party of minority interests. As the party of greater redistribution of resources, increased affirmative action, and tougher anti-discrimination measures, Democrats assert that their agenda is pro-minority. Democrats also maintain that their more liberal policies on race, welfare, education, poverty, and crime are bound to help minorities who fall disproportionately on the lower half of the socioeconomic spectrum. And judging from the fact that the overwhelming majority of racial and ethnic minority voters vote Democratic, most minorities appear to agree. The fact that Whites tend to favor Republican candidates reinforces the notion that the two parties serve different racial interests. Surely, all of these Americans—both White and non-White—cannot be wrong in their view of the two major parties.

But it is important to note that the Republican Party makes almost identical claims about how much their policies help minorities. In particular, Republican leaders contend that greater efficiencies associated with more conservative policies and smaller government ultimately lead to more growth and higher incomes for all. During the 2016 presidential debates, Donald Trump claimed "I will do more for African Americans and Latinos than [Hillary Clinton] can ever do in ten lifetimes. All she has done is talk to the African Americans and to the Latinos." Trump's comments echo a Republican theme that goes back to Ronald Reagan and beyond. Republicans also argue that the absence of policies targeting minorities reduces race-based stigmatization and results in a more just, color-blind society. Finally, Republicans can also claim to offer a more socially conservative policy agenda that fits with the views of many highly religious minority voters.

There are scholars who claim that neither party has been especially good about enacting minority-friendly policies. Paul Frymer, in particular, argues that because Blacks tend to fall on the liberal fringe of the Democratic Party, they essentially have nowhere else to turn for a political party affiliation, because the Democrats are the most liberal of the two major parties. The conventional logic of politics suggests that, under competitive electoral systems, political parties will always have an incentive to bring in and to represent groups that can increase the size of their coalition. Because Blacks typically fall so far on one end of the policy spectrum, both Democratic and Republican parties have to weigh the gains of representing their interests against offsetting losses in potential voters whose political views are not so liberal. Frymer argues that in such situations, the logic of electoral competition dictates that it is in the interest of both parties to ignore the interests and demands of Blacks and to render them more or less invisible in campaigns. Other scholars have made similar claims about Latinos and Asian Americans being ignored by both parties (Espino, Leal, and Meier 2007; Fraga and Leal 2004; Kim 2006). In the case of Latinos and Asian Americans, the calculus facing political parties is the potential gains from including these new voters into their party coalition weighed against potentially larger offsetting losses from other voters if they are persuaded to see outreach to these heavily immigrant groups as "un-American."

To test these different claims, we return to the data on responsiveness in federal government spending to see whether shifts in the party in power leads to shifts in the pattern of responsiveness. Remember that the data show that Blacks lose more on policy than other groups, and they lose more than Whites on the eleven policy areas that we examined. But one thing we did not do is look to see how responsiveness varies from year to year. A look at variation over time suggests that who is in power might matter.

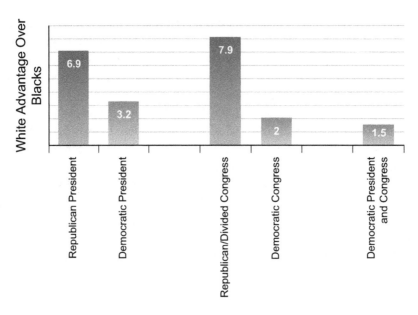

Figure 11.6 Gaps in Policy Responsiveness by Race under Democrats and Republicans, 1972–2010
Having Democrats in office reduces racial disparities in policy responsiveness by the federal government.
Source: General Social Survey, 1972–2010, and Federal Budget. Adapted from Griffin et al. (2019).

And that is exactly what Griffin and his co-authors found. When one breaks down the data about policy responsiveness based on which party controls Congress and the presidency, as we do in Figure 11.6, it is clear that racial imbalances largely fade away when Democrats are in charge. When Republicans control the White House, White Americans are almost 7 points more likely than Blacks to see their preferences met on policy. But more than half of that racial gap fades away when the nation has a Democratic president. Likewise, the racial gap in responsiveness drops from an average of 7.9 points when Democrats do not control the House and Senate to 2.0 points when Democrats control both houses of Congress. And it drops even further when Democrats control both Congress and the presidency. In fact, the more complex models estimate that all else equal, policy follows the preferences of individual African Americans just as much or even slightly more than Whites in years when Democrats are in the White House and in the majority in Congress. In short, under Democrats, African Americans receive a full and fair say in the policies that our government pursues.

Latino and Asian American policy preferences are only available for a small subset of the years in this study, but analysis of those years provides some minimal evidence that Democratic control also leads to greater policy responsiveness for Latinos and Asian Americans. Judged at least by this test, partisan control is a

Photo 11.4
Source: © MHJ/DigitalVision Vectors/Getty Images.

critical factor shaping who wins and who loses in the policy arena. Under Democrats the racial imbalance in responsiveness all but disappears and American democracy becomes more even-handed.

One cannot know if this partisan pattern will persist. It is worth noting, however, that recent developments in American politics do not herald major changes in the extent to which each major party advances policies favored by racial and ethnic minorities. President Trump pushed to repeal Obamacare and sought deep cuts in welfare and sharp increases in military spending. That is essentially the opposite of what most African American survey respondents say they want. By contrast, President Biden has tried to expand education funding, increase support for Obamacare and Medicare, and limit military spending—all policies favored by most racial and ethnic minorities.

Partisan Politics and Economic Well-being

As members of a democracy, we care about whose voices are heard when policy decisions are made. But at the end of the day, none of this really matters unless it impacts the lives of individual Americans. This chapter has evaluated important aspects of representation, but all of them are, in some sense, of second-order concern. We have not yet addressed the outcome that citizens may be most likely to care about: their well-being.

As we have already highlighted, there are large racial disparities in economic well-being across the country, with Whites more likely to be on the top and racial and ethnic minorities more likely to be near the bottom. The statistics are telling. Blacks and Latinos earn only two-thirds of what Whites earn, they are twice as likely as Whites to be poor, twice as likely to be unemployed, between three and five times more likely to be arrested, and they accumulate roughly one-tenth of the wealth that Whites acquire (Bhutta et al. 2020; Lewis and Burd-Sharps 2010).

In this section, we take the next and arguably the most critical step of assessing the effects of different governing regimes on this racial hierarchy. Can control by one party or the other impact these severe racial inequities in economic well-being?

The empirical test is straightforward. The idea is to trace the well-being of racial and ethnic minorities over the last half century using objective, empirical measures of income, poverty, and unemployment and then compare the relative annual progress of each racial and ethnic group under different partisan regimes. The data for this test come from Hajnal (2020).

Charting the economic well-being of different racial groups under Democratic and Republican presidencies over more than half a century reveals a stark pattern, as we see in Figure 11.7, Democratic Party control does make a real difference on objective indicators of economic status. When the nation is governed by Democratic presidents, racial and ethnic minority well-being improves dramatically. Under Democratic presidents, Black, Latino, and Asian American annual incomes grew by an average of almost $900, $600, and $1,000 respectively. Having a Democrat in the White House was also associated with declining poverty for all three groups and declining unemployment for Blacks and Latinos.

By contrast, under Republican administrations, Blacks, Latinos, and Asian Americans generally suffered economic losses. These partisan differences are substantial and they hold up even when controlling for a range of other factors that could impact economic trends.[7] Even more telling is the fact that partisan differences are more pronounced in second-term presidencies. Democrats are not just getting lucky and inheriting robust economies.

The cumulative effects of these partisan differences are immense. Across 26 years of Democratic administrations in the data set Black incomes grew by a total of $23,281.[8] Black incomes also grew under Republicans, but much more slowly—less than $4,000 across 28 years. The figures for unemployment and poverty are equally pronounced. Across all years of Democratic leadership in the data, the Black

---

[7] The greater gains for minorities under Democrats persist even after controlling for changes in overall economic conditions (including inflation, GDP growth, oil prices), changes in the labor force, and longer-term trends like increasing globalization and increasing single parenthood.

[8] Figures are in constant 2008 dollars.

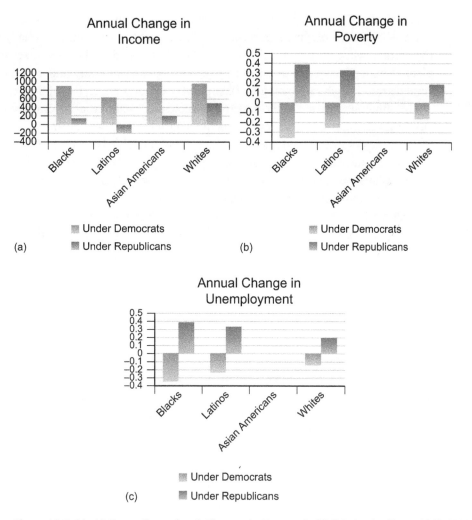

Figure 11.7 (a)–(c) Party Control and Changes in Economic Well-being by Race, 1948–2010
These graphs compare average annual changes in Black, Latino, Asian American, and White
economic well-being (annual changes in income, poverty, and unemployment) under
Democratic and Republican administrations. The results show that outcomes for Blacks such as
earnings have improved much faster under Democrats (gaining almost $900 per year) than
under Republicans (gaining a little over $100 per year).
Source: U.S. Census Bureau (American Community Survey), 1948–2010. Adapted from Hajnal
(2020).

poverty rate declined by 38.6 percentage points. By contrast, over all of the
Republican presidencies, the rate of poverty for Blacks grew 3 points. Likewise,
the Black unemployment rate fell by a total of 7.9 percentage points under
Democrats but grew by an alarming 13.7 points under Republicans.

Importantly, the underlying data show that minorities did not just do better, they
also made gains relative to Whites. Minorities—especially African Americans—
were much more apt to catch up to Whites economically under Democratic

administrations than they were under Republican administrations. For example, the Black–White unemployment gap declined by on average 0.20 points annually under Democrats, while it grew by 0.21 points annually under Republicans. Likewise, the Black–White poverty gap declined by just over 2 points annually under Democratic administrations, while growing by 0.23 points annually under Republicans.

This finding mirrors other research which has found that overall economic inequality declines faster under Democrats (Bartels 2008). All of this suggests that Democratic control can do a lot to reduce racial inequities in well-being.

Critically, the data also show that *these minority gains do not come at the expense of Whites*. White incomes also grew and White joblessness and poverty also declined under Democratic administrations—although it is not clear from the study whether White gains under Democrats are statistically greater than White gains under Republicans.

There are some caveats with the study. For one thing, there are relatively few years of data for Latinos and Asian Americans, so the impact of partisan control on their well-being is much less certain.[9] For another, the data are largely limited to economic outcomes.[10] If individual citizens care more about the environment or cultural and moral outcomes like abortion or divorce rates or even foreign policy, then these economic measures will not be as important to their assessments of the Democratic and Republican parties. Finally, the study did not identify the specific policies that Democrats passed that might have been responsible for the gains that minorities experienced under Democrats. Until the gains that are made under Democrats can be definitively tied to specific policy changes, it is likely that some will remain skeptical about the ability of Democratic control to alleviate racial inequality (Blinder and Watson 2016).

Conclusion

When Donald Trump won in 2016, the racial and ethnic minority population "lost" in multiple ways. As this chapter has outlined, representation can be thought of and measured in different ways. In one of those ways—*descriptive representation*—the minority population lost when Donald Trump was elected because a White man replaced a Black man in the Oval Office. In another way—*electoral representation*—the minority population lost because Hillary Clinton, the candidate that they overwhelmingly supported, lost the election. And in yet another way—*substantive representation*—racial and ethnic minorities lost because Trump pursued a range of policies that they did not favor. Trump's signature policies—lowering taxes for the wealthy,

---

[9] Likewise, it is hard to assess the impact of congressional control on minority well-being because there are relatively few shifts in which party controls Congress during this period.

[10] The study by Hajnal (2020) did, however, find that partisan control also impacted outcomes in the criminal justice system. Arrest rates for African American declined significantly faster under Democratic presidents than they did under Republican administrations.

ending Obamacare, ending the Dreamers Act, building the wall—are all policies that clear majorities of the Black, Latino, and Asian American population opposed.

But 2016 is just one election and Donald Trump is just one elected official. This chapter has endeavored to look more broadly at these different forms of representation and to systematically assess how well minorities fare on each. What we have found is somewhat mixed. On basic measures of electoral representation and substantive representation, there is no overwhelming tyranny of the majority. Most members of most groups end up on the winning side of American democracy most of the time. But at the same time, there appears to be a clear racial hierarchy to American democracy. Whites often end up on the top and African Americans often wind up on the bottom with Latinos and Asian Americans often in the middle.

This is true for electoral representation. African Americans, more than any other racial or demographic group, are consistently more likely to end up losers when the votes are tallied. Blacks are, in fact, the only group that loses more than half of the time across most of the electoral contests we examined. Critically, this racial disadvantage holds even after controlling for a range of other demographic characteristics. Race, more than class or any other demographic factor, determines who loses in the vast array elections in American democracy. Moreover, it is not just the partisan and ideological leanings of Blacks that drive these outcomes. Blacks are still uniquely disadvantaged after taking into account the political views and party identification of each voter.

Similarly, our analysis of substantive representation and policy "winners" and "losers" demonstrated the uniquely powerful role of race in shaping political responsiveness. Class does matter as past studies have indicated. Lower-class Americans are slightly less likely than the upper class to win on policy. But these class-based inequities, as well as gaps by age, gender, and religion, are all small compared with racial inequalities. Blacks stand out among all of the groups we looked at. Blacks lose more on policy than any other group, they lose more consistently across all of the policy areas, and they lose more consistently over time. Blacks, the group that by many metrics needs the most, gets the least.

Critically, this differential policy responsiveness by race cannot be easily explained away. African Americans are not losing in the policy arena because they are poorer or less well educated than others. They are not losing because they are more liberal or more Democratic than others. They are not losing because they favor more spending increases or oppose the public's favored position more than others. The disadvantage Blacks face in the American policy world seems much deeper. All of this raises real questions about equity in American democracy.

Is there anything we can do about it? By looking at variation in representation across different years and different contexts, researchers have been able to identify a range of factors that might help to foster greater minority representation. These include institutional reforms (such as district elections and redistricting to reduce racial gerrymandering), to greater minority turnout, and electing more minorities in office. We found that Democratic party control of the nation's levers of power, the one factor that we examined in greater detail, tends to reduce racial inequities in policy responsiveness and may ultimately reduce disparities by race in economic well-being.

KEY TERMS

Electoral representation
Intersectionality
Substantive representation

DISCUSSION QUESTIONS

1. How should we characterize the electoral representation of racial and ethnic minorities in American democracy?
2. How well represented are racial and ethnic minorities in terms of policy in American democracy?
3. What measure(s) of representation best reflect minority influence in American democracy?
4. What can or should we do to improve the representation of racial and ethnic minorities in American democracy?
5. What impact does Democratic Party control have on the policy interests and economic well-being of the racial and ethnic minority population?

ANNOTATED SUGGESTED READINGS

See J. D. Griffin and B. Newman. 2008. *Minority Report: Evaluating Political Equality in America*. Chicago, University of Chicago Press, to see how well different racial groups are represented through the voting behavior of individual legislators.

See K. Einstein and D. Glick. 2016. "Does Race Affect Access to Government Services? An Experiment Exploring Street-Level Bureaucrats and Access to Public Housing," *American Journal of Political Science* 61(1): 100–116, for an in-depth look at the role that race plays for representation in the bureaucracy.

See P. Frymer. 1999. *Uneasy Alliances: Race and Party Competition in America*. Princeton: Princeton University Press, for a compelling argument about the lack of responsiveness to African American interests in the American party system.

See M. Gilens. 2012. *Affluence & Influence: Economic Inequality and Political Power in America*. Princeton, Princeton University Press, for one of the most systematic studies of how representation varies across class lines.

See M. Gilens and B. I. Page. 2014. "Testing Theories of American Politics: Elites, Interest Groups, and Average Citizens," *Perspectives on Politics* 12(3): 564–581, for one of the best assessments of the role of class and interest groups in shaping policy.

See E. R. Hansen and S. A. Treul. 2015. "The Symbolic and Substantive Representation of LGB Americans in the US House," *Journal of Politics* **77**(4): 955–967, for the representation of LGB Americans in the House.

CHAPTER REFERENCES

Arnold, David, Will Dobbie, and Crystal S. Yang. 2018. "Racial Bias in Bail Decisions," *Quarterly Journal of Economics* 133: 1885–1932.

Bartels, Larry M. 2008. *Unequal Democracy: The Political Economy of the New Gilded Age*. Princeton: Princeton University Press.

Bhutta, Neil, Andrew C. Chang, Lisa J. Dettling, and Joanne W. Hsu. 2020. "Disparities in Wealth by Race and Ethnicity," Board of Governors of the Federal Reserve System. www .federalreserve.gov/econres/notes/feds-notes/disparities-in-wealth-by-race-and-ethnicity-in-the-2019-survey-of-consumer-finances-20200928.htm.

Bishin, Ben. 2009. *Tyranny of the Minority: The Subconstituency Politics Theory of Representation*. Philadelphia, PA: Temple University Press.

Blinder, Alan and Mark Watson. 2016. "Presidents and the US Economy: An Econometric Exploration," *American Economic Review* 106: 1015–1045.

Brown, Nadia and Sarah Gershon (eds.). 2016. *Distinct Identities: Minority Women in U.S. Politics*. New York: Routledge.

Browning, Rufus R., Dale Rogers Marshall, and David H. Tabb. 1984. *Protest Is Not Enough*. Berkeley: University of California Press.

Butler, Daniel M. and David E. Broockman. 2011. "Do Politicians Racially Discriminate against Constituents? A Field Experiment on State Legislators," *American Journal of Political Science* 55: 463–477.

Cameron, Charles, David Epstein, and Sharyn Halloran. 1996. "Do Majority-Minority Districts Maximize Substantive Black Representation in Congress?" *American Political Science Review* 90: 794–812.

Dahl, Robert A. 1961. *Who Governs? Democracy and Power in the American City*. New Haven, CT: Yale University Press.

Dawson, Michael. 2011. *Not in Our Lifetimes: The Future of Black Politics*. Chicago: University of Chicago Press.

Espino, Rodolfo, David L. Leal, and Kenneth J. Meier (eds.). 2007. *Latino Politics: Identity, Mobilization, and Representation*. Charlottesville: University of Virginia.

Fraga, Luis Ricardo and David L. Leal. 2004. "Playing the 'Latino Card': Race, Ethnicity, and National Party Politics," *Du Bois Review* 1: 297–317.

Gerber, Elisabeth R. 1999. *The Populist Paradox: Interest Group Influence and the Promise of Direct Legislation*. Princeton: Princeton University Press.

Gilens, Martin. 2012. *Affluence & Influence: Economic Inequality and Political Power in America*. Princeton: Princeton University Press.

Gillion, Daniel. 2012. "Protest and Congressional Behavior: Assessing Racial and Ethnic Minority Protests in the District," *Journal of Politics* 74: 950–962.

Greenberg, Michael. 2012. "What Future for Occupy Wall Street?" *New York Review of Books*, February 9. www.nybooks.com/articles/2012/02/09/what-future-occupy-wall-street/

Griffin, John, Zoltan Hajnal, Brian Newman, and David Searle. 2019. "Political Inequality in America: Who Loses on Spending Policy? When Is Policy Less Biased?" *Politics, Groups, and Identities* 7: 367–385.

Griffin, John D. and Brian Newman. 2007. "The Unequal Representation of Latinos and Whites," *Journal of Politics* 69: 1032–1046.

Hajnal, Zoltan. 2020. *Dangerously Divided: How Race and Class Shape Winning and Losing in American Politics*. Cambridge: Cambridge University Press.

Hajnal, Zoltan and Jeremy Horowitz. 2014. "Racial Winners and Losers in American Party Politics," *Perspectives on Politics* 12: 100–118.

Hamilton, Alexander, James Madison, and John Jay. [1787–1788] 1961. *The Federalist Papers: A Collection of Essays Written in Support of the Constitution of the United States* (ed.) Roy P. Fairfield. Garden City, N.Y: Anchor Books.

Harty-Fanta, Carol, Pei-te Lien, Dianne Pinderhughes, and Christine Marie Sierra. 2016. *Contested Transformation: Race, Gender, and Political Leadership in 21st-Century America*. Cambridge: Cambridge University Press.

Keister, L. 2014. "The One Percent," *Annual Review of Sociology* 40: 347–367.

Kim, Thomas. 2006. *The Racial Logic of Politics: Asian Americans and Party Competition*. Philadelphia, PA: Temple University Press.

Lax, Jeffrey and Justin Phillips. 2011. "The Democratic Deficit in the States," *American Journal of Political Science* 56: 148–166.

Lewis, Daniel C. 2011. "Bypassing the Representational Filter?: Minority Rights Policies under Direct Democracy Institutions in the U.S. States," *State Politics & Policy Quarterly* 11: 198–222.

Lewis, Kristen and Burd-Sharps, Sarah. 2010. "A Century Apart: New Measures of Well-being for U.S. Racial and Ethnic Groups." SSRN report.

Malhotra, Neil and Connor Raso. 2007. "Racial Representation and U.S. Senate Apportionment," *Social Science Quarterly* 88: 1038–1048.

Marie-Hancock, Angie. 2016. *Intersectionality: An Intellectual History*. New York: Oxford University Press.

Meier, Kenneth J., Joseph Stewart Jr., and Robert E. England. 1991. "The Politics of Bureaucratic Discretion: Educational Access and Urban Service," *American Journal of Political Science* 35: 155–177.

Miller, Warren and Donald Stokes. 1963. "Constituency Influence in Congress," *American Political Science Review* 57: 45–57.

Page, Benjamin I. and Robert Y. Shapiro. 1983. "Effects of Public Opinion on Policy," *American Political Science Review* 77: 175–190.

Phillips, Christian Dyogi. 2021. *Nowhere to Run: Race, Gender, and Immigration in American Elections*. Oxford: Oxford University Press.

Sances, Michael W. and Hye Young You. 2017. "Who Pays for Government? Descriptive Representation and Exploitative Revenue Sources," *Journal of Politics* 79: 1090–1094.

12   Race and Criminal Justice

Just after midnight, the hail of bullets began. Plainclothes Louisville Metro Police Department officers used a battering ram to force open the green door of Apartment No. 4, St. Anthony Gardens complex. Inside, Breonna Taylor and her boyfriend Kenneth Walker awoke to what they were certain was a home invasion. Walker, who was a licensed gun owner with no criminal record, tearfully pleaded to 911 for help. To try to protect himself and his girlfriend, Walker fired one shot that struck one of the police officers in the thigh. In return, three officers discharged more than twenty-five bullets into the apartment. Breonna Taylor, a licensed EMT who had worked on the front lines of the pandemic for the city of Louisville and whom friends described as "full of life," was now dead—fatally struck by at least eight bullets (Carrega and Ghebremedhin 2020). In the end, the actions of three White police officers resulted in the death of one Black woman.

Breonna Taylor's story is, unfortunately, not unique. The death of young African Americans at the hands of police is now an all-too-familiar story. George Floyd, Eric Garner, Sandra Bland, Freddie Gray, Daunte Wright, and Philando Castile— the list goes on and on—each name representing a tragic, far-too-early end. According to tracking by *The Washington Post*, police in the United States kill more than 1,000 people every year, and Black Americans are killed at a much higher rate than White Americans. As of May 1, 2023, according to the *Post* data, police have killed nearly 2,000 Black Americans—a victimization rate that is twice as high as it is for White Americans (*The Washington Post* 2023). Police violence is a leading cause of death for young Black men in the United States. Over the course of their lives, about 1 in every 1,000 Black men can expect to be killed by police—a rate that is about 2.5 times greater than the probability of such outcomes for White men (Edwards, Lee, and Esposito 2019). As one young Black man so aptly put it, "the people who are supposed to protect us are killing us" (Moore 2020).

Breonna Taylor's story and the long list of African Americans killed by the police raise deep questions about the criminal justice system—the subject of this chapter. The fact that so many of the victims in fatal police encounters are Black, unarmed, and subject to what appears to be excessive force raises real questions about bias. Are the actions of police officers driven in part by racial stereotypes and implicit bias? And more broadly, what roles do race and racial discrimination play in the larger criminal justice system? The fact that so many of these deaths are occurring in largely Black neighborhoods with a largely White police force targeting largely Black suspects also raises questions about how much the criminal justice system is living up to its motto—to protect and serve.

There is no denying that crime is real. Every year millions of Americans are the victims of crime. In 2019, the FBI reports that almost 7 million Americans were the victims of property crime. More than a million more were victims of violent crime. We need the police and the larger criminal justice system to protect us. We need a criminal justice system that prevents crime and punishes criminals. But questions abound about how well those who enforce the laws are actually achieving these goals. Questions also abound about the laws themselves. How well are criminal justice policies and legal statutes doing at both preventing crime and protecting the innocent? And, the reaction of Americans to Breonna Taylor's case and to other similar incidents raise questions about the public's role in reforms of the current system. The "Say Her Name" campaign that forces Americans to think about and ask questions about the numerous Black women who have been victims of police violence gained increased prominence with Breonna Taylor's death; the massive protests generated by these events and the broader Black Lives Matter movement all suggest that Americans may well be ready for reform. But should we really expect things to change? These are the questions that this chapter will attempt to answer.

Photo 12.1 Protesters march against police brutality in Los Angeles, September 23, 2020, following a Louisville, KY judge's announcement that charges would be brought against Detective Brett Hankison, one of three police officers involved in the fatal shooting of Breonna Taylor in March 2020. A jury ultimately acquitted Hankison a year later.
Source: Photo Apu Gomes © Apu Gomes/Contributor/AFP/Getty Images.

The reality, as we will see, is complex. There is incontrovertible evidence that race shapes the criminal justice system. At every level of the system, from the initial decision of police officers to engage with the public to the trial and the sentencing phases as well as the laws themselves, we will find clear evidence that both bias (implicit and explicit) as well as structural discrimination play major roles. Thanks in part to this bias and discrimination, racial disparities within America's incarceration state are now staggering. African Americans make up about 13 percent of the national population, but they account for fully 39 percent of all federal inmates (FBP 2021). Indeed, America imprisons a larger percentage of its Black population than South Africa did at the height of apartheid (Alexander 2012). Likewise, Latinos represent about 17 percent of the population nationwide but make up 30 percent of federal inmates. Native Americans are equally overrepresented, while Whites and Asian Americans are greatly underrepresented.[1]

Ultimately, it is hard to find an area within American society where racial disparities are greater or more consequential. That is why some refer to the criminal justice system as the "New Jim Crow" and why we devote an entire chapter to this particular subject. On the other hand, it is also clear that a criminal justice system is needed. Our system does often serve to protect the innocent and to punish the guilty. In short, the criminal justice system simultaneously protects and victimizes. At the end of the day it is clear that major reforms are necessary.

It also clear that American attitudes on race and policing have shifted as awareness of systemic discrimination in the criminal justice system has grown among the general public. But it is not at all clear whether we have reached any sort of consensus on where we should go. We will close this chapter by discussing different policy options and by thinking about ways in which we can reduce these racial disparities and perhaps also shift the balance toward more protection and less victimization.

America's Carceral State

When the 1st Congress of the United States passed the Bill of Rights in 1791, it had lofty goals. The Bill of Rights was designed to protect all citizens from improper government intrusion. At the heart of the bill was a series of constitutional amendments designed to protect the innocent by ensuring that our government would have to meticulously observe a series of procedures shielding the accused. More specifically, the Fifth Amendment states that no person in this country shall "be deprived of life, liberty, or property without due process of law." Americans were "innocent until proven guilty" and their government had to treat them that way. But, as we have seen throughout this textbook, America has frequently failed to live up to its

---

[1] Asian Americans represent 5 percent of the population and 1.5 percent of federal inmates. The figures for Native Americans are 1.6 percent of the population and 2.4 percent of the prison population. Non-Hispanic Whites make up 61 percent of the nation and an estimated 30 percent of the inmate population.

lofty goals. The criminal justice system is yet another case where goals and reality sometimes clash.

The reality is that America is like no other nation in the world when it comes to incarceration. Our nation has only about 5 percent of the world's population, but we house one-quarter of the world's prison population. With over 2 million people behind bars, we have by far more people imprisoned than any other country in the world (World Prison Brief 2021). We also have the highest incarceration rate in the world. Indeed, the rate at which we put our citizens behind bars dwarfs that of every other industrialized democracy and even surpasses those in highly repressive regimes like Russia and China.

The Rapid Expansion of the Carceral State

It was not always this way. Over the last half century, there has been enormous growth in the reach of the carceral state. By the carceral state, we mean not only the law enforcement officers who patrol the streets but also the lawyers, judges, parole offices, and all of the other correctional officials. The carceral state also very much includes the jails (ostensibly for those awaiting sentencing and those convicted of more minor crimes, but frequently for those merely awaiting trial and thus still presumed innocent) and prisons (often for criminals convicted of more serious crimes). Basically, the carceral state includes all of the individuals and formal entities and organizations that define the criminal justice system.

As Figure 12.1 illustrates, the jail and prison population in the United States was relatively small and its growth relatively limited until 1970. It has ballooned since then. There were fewer than 200,000 Americans in federal and state prison in 1970—less than 0.1 percent of the adult population. By 2008, there were over 1.5 million—roughly 0.6 percent of all adults. That is a more than 700 percent increase. And despite a dip in incarceration after 2008, if you add jail inmates to the state and federal prison population, America currently has well over 2 million people behind bars (Maruschak and Minton 2020). Adding in those on parole or probation brings the number of Americans in the criminal justice system to well over 6 million. We have, in just a few short decades, become the world's largest carceral state.

The Costs of Policing and Incarceration

The nation's high incarceration rate and the enormous growth in incarceration in recent decades raise a number of questions and concerns. One concern stems from the potential costs to all of those involved in the criminal justice system. The Breonna Taylor case and all of the videos of African Americans being beaten or killed by the police vividly attest to those costs. The fact that violent encounters with police is a leading cause of death for young Black men makes those costs even more apparent.

But the costs of being enmeshed in the criminal justice system are not just physical injury or death. Prison itself can cause harm. There is growing evidence that

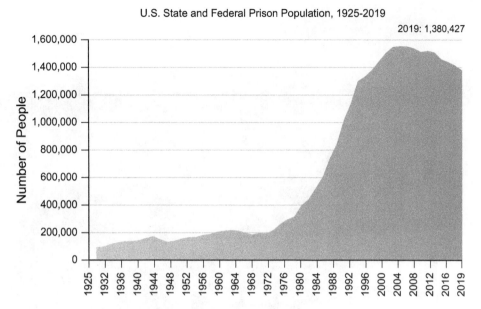

Figure 12.1 U.S. State and Federal Prison Population, 1925–2018
Looking at the prison population in the United States from 1925 to 2018, it is clear there has
been an enormous and unprecedented growth since 1980.
Source: Bureau of Justice Statistics, www.sentencingproject.org/research/us-criminal-justice-
data.

spending time in prison increases one's propensity to commit crimes in the future.
In the United States, almost half of all criminals released from prison return to
prison within five years (World Population Review 2021).

The mark of a criminal record can also profoundly shape lives after prison. There
are automatic consequences of having a criminal record. Ex-felons cannot vote in
many states. They are excluded from juries. More importantly, they cannot hold a
range of jobs. Often they cannot receive government benefits like welfare and they
can be barred from living in public housing. But even when ex-felons are not
explicitly barred from work or other opportunities, a record of prison time greatly
reduces their chances of succeeding and of supporting themselves and their families.
One study by Devah Pager (2003) sent otherwise identical individuals to look for
jobs. Pager found that, regardless of racial background, those who were randomly
assigned to have a criminal record on their resumes were about half as likely to get a
call-back as those with no criminal record. Blacks who were randomly given a
criminal record on their resume suffered from even lower call-back rates—indeed,
Blacks with no criminal record fared slightly worse in terms of call-backs than
Whites with a criminal record. Researchers who study people over the course
of their lives have found that men who have spent time in prison tend to end up
with much lower wages and employment rates than similar men without criminal
records (Western 2006). All of this means that those with a criminal record face

Photo 12.2 A group of prison inmates start boot camp by marching in line at the Sumter County Correctional Institution in Bushnell, FL.
Source: © Bettmann/Contributor/Getty Images.

what Michelle Alexander calls "a cruel new phase of stigmatization and control" that confines them "to the margins of the mainstream society and economy" (Alexander 2012: 5, 17). For the children of convicted criminals—a situation in which one in ten Black children have found themselves, prison means the loss of a father or a mother for an extended period of time as well as the loss of family income—all of which can perpetuate a cycle of broken families, poverty, and crime (Western 2006).

And we have not yet even considered the enormous costs to taxpayers of housing all these prisoners, paying for all of the nation's policing efforts, and supporting the court system—a figure that approaches nearly $300 billion annually (Hyland 2019).

Of course, all of these costs have to be balanced against the potential benefits of police protection and crime deterrence. Innocent citizens need protection from those who would do them harm. Crime itself can cause an enormous toll. Researchers estimate the annual costs of crime at somewhere between $1 and $3 trillion dollars (Government Accountability Office 2019). Just as damaging are the emotional and physical tolls of being victimized by crime. In short, there are legitimate reasons to have a criminal justice system. Thus, the criminal justice system must walk a tightrope between being too invasive and predatory on the one hand and being too permissive and not protective enough on the other.

How Did We Get Here?

How is it that our nation imprisons more people than any other? Why have incarceration rates gone up so much in the last few decades? If the patterns we have seen so far are a response to trends in crime itself, then they may be justified. If, however, they are largely unrelated to conditions on the ground and if they are conducted in a biased or uneven manner, then we have to ask deeper questions about our courts and policing practices.

The most obvious and the most reasonable explanation for increased incarceration in the United States would have to be that Americans have been committing more crimes. But the numbers simply do not bear that out.

The reality is that crime rates and incarceration rates in the United States are largely uncorrelated. Data on crime rates over time—both for violent crime and for property crime—shows a steep increase in crime from 1960 through to the 1980s and then an equally sharp decrease in crime after 1990 (see Figure 12.2). This pattern holds whether we measure crime rates by crimes reported to the police (as is in the case in Figure 12.2) or by national surveys that ask about crime victimization. Today, crime rates in the United States have fallen to the point that we are as a nation below the norm in Western countries (Beauchamp 2018). Yet we still imprison more people and a higher share of our people than just about any nation on earth.

If we compare Figure 12.1 with Figure 12.2, it becomes clear that incarceration rates do not track crime rates. The imprisonment rate grew steadily through periods of increasing crime (1960s–1980s) as well as through periods of decreasing crime (1990s–today). The reality is that most of the growth in incarceration in America came while crime rates were decreasing. Fewer crimes were being committed but more and more people were being put behind bars. It is difficult to tie the explosion in the prison population to increases in criminality.

Of course, that does not mean that there is absolutely no link between crime rates and incarceration. It is possible that the steep increase in incarceration early in this period (1960–1990) directly caused falling crime in the second half of this period (1990–today). Stiffer penalties could have deterred would-be criminals. Alternatively, putting more people behind bars could have meant that fewer would-be criminals were on the street where they could commit additional crimes. Whether increased incarceration actually deterred crime in these ways is a question we address later in the chapter.

Law and Order and the Growth of Incarceration

Rising crime could be connected to rising incarceration in yet another way. Indeed, it seems quite clear that major increases in crime in the 1960s, 1970s, and 1980s—coupled with more and more attention to those crimes from politicians and the media—led to a sharp public reaction. In response to rising crime and the fear that it generated, Americans made a collective decision to be more punitive and to increase penalties for crime. The result, quite logically, was more Americans in prison.

Figure 12.2 Trends in Crime
Over Time, 1960–2018
Crime rates skyrocketed in
the last part of the twentieth
century and fell almost as
much in the 2000s.
Source: FBI Uniform Crime
Reports, UCR Online
Database and 2018 Report,
https://cdn.factcheck.org/
UploadedFiles/violent-crime-
rate.jpg.

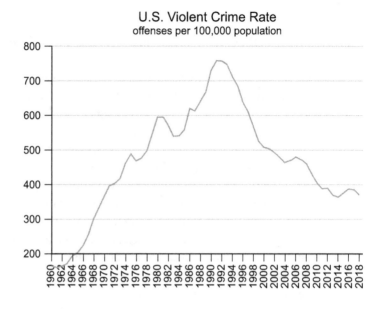

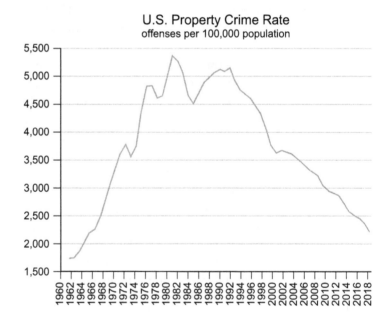

For many, the real origins of America's expansive prison state are political.
Responding to the increased disorder of the 1960s—which included not only
increased crime but also greater Black militancy and riots or rebellions in a number
of American cities—key candidates in the Republican Party initiated a series of "law
and order" campaigns that played on White Americans' unease. These politicians
criticized the violence, vowed to increase criminal penalties, and promised to lock up
perpetrators. President Richard Nixon, in particular, devoted seventeen speeches to

Photo 12.3 President Nixon, in his first State of the Union message delivered on January 22, 1970, called for the most expensive program of crime prevention in the nation's history. *Source*: © Bettmann/Contributor/Getty Images.

the topic of law and order during his 1968 presidential campaign. In his first State of the Union address he declared war on "the criminal elements which increasingly threaten our cities, our homes, and our lives." Later in 1971 he officially declared a "War on Drugs" maintaining that drug abuse was "public enemy number one."[2] As we discussed in Chapter 8, at least one Nixon administration official has admitted to the racial subtext behind this anti-drug appeal. That message was refined by successive Republican candidates over the 1970s and 1980s, with Ronald Reagan expanding the "war on drugs" and George H. W. Bush offering his strong support for the death penalty. Democrats, who felt that their more sympathetic policies were losing them votes, followed suit. President Bill Clinton, in particular, helped to pass the 1994 Violent Crime Control and Law Enforcement Act—a law that instituted life terms in prison for three-time felons and earmarked billions of dollars for prisons. Over a relatively short period, America's main motivation for the criminal justice system had shifted from rehabilitation to punishment and confinement.

[2] The early model for the war on drugs was the drug laws enacted in New York in 1973 under then-Governor Nelson Rockefeller which called for harsh sentencing and which often included mandatory minimum sentences. These laws were among the first to try to address drug abuse through the criminal justice system rather than through medical health systems.

While these law-and-order campaigns were ostensibly race-blind, they were often accompanied by racial imagery. Nixon's ads featured violent Black militants, while Reagan subtly combined welfare, drugs, and crime into a potent mix of topics that conjured up Black images and fostered White fear and resentment. Illustrative of this strategy was the story of a Chicago "welfare queen" who had eighty names, thirty addresses, and twelve Social Security cards—a story that Reagan regularly repeated. But perhaps the most famous of these racially tinted campaigns was George H. W. Bush's tough-on-crime ad that never mentioned race but that highlighted Willie Horton, a menacing-looking African American murderer. Later, Donald Trump would make this strategy more explicit and more focused on Latino immigrants with his anti-immigrant campaign and in particular his comments about Mexicans bringing drugs and crime and being rapists. Adding fuel to the prison-building business were the enormous financial incentives of the prison industry itself. Prisons are big business. Large private prison companies with the prospect of lucrative government contracts lobbied and likely helped to push the nation ever further toward incarceration.

The media did not help. Over the years, crime was presented with an overwhelmingly minority face. Even though most crimes in the mid- to late twentieth century were committed by Whites, most of the local and national news coverage focused on African Americans (Entman and Rojecki 2000). Similarly, when Latinos were portrayed in the news, the stories and images were overwhelmingly negative and often focused on illegality (Abrajano and Hajnal 2015). Experiments have since shown that racially focused crime scripts do, in fact, alter our perceptions. Randomly exposing individual Americans to a news segment about a violent crime involving a Black suspect significantly increases support for punitive approaches to crime (Gilliam and Iyengar 2000). Likewise, studies show that portrayals of the immigrant threat narrative in the media—essentially stories that highlight immigrants committing crimes or performing other negative or costly actions—can lead to more negative attitudes toward Latinos and more repressive policy choices (Abrajano and Hajnal 2015). The end result is a close association between crime and race in the minds of many White Americans (Hurwitz and Peffley 1998).

Public Beliefs about Increasing Crime

Many of the changes in the criminal justice system in the United States are mirrored in the public's changing views on crime. As late as 1980, most Americans (53 percent) thought the primary purpose of prison was to rehabilitate. But years of law-and-order campaigns, increasing crime rates, and negative media coverage led to much less support for rehabilitation and much more support for punishment. By 1993, only 25 percent of Americans felt that rehabilitation was the main reason for imprisonment. Over the same period, the share of Americans who thought the primary purpose of prison was punishment almost doubled, from 32 percent to 61 percent.

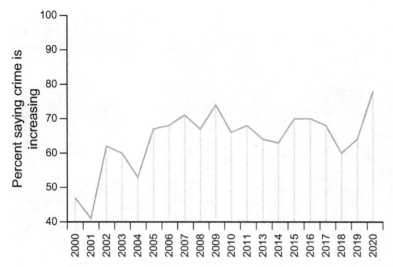

Figure 12.3 Americans'
Beliefs about Crime,
2000–2020
From 2000 to 2020, more
and more Americans
believed that crime was
increasing, even as crime
rates were
trending down.
Source: Gallup Survey,
https://news.gallup.com/
poll/323996/perceptions-
increased-crime-highest-
1993.aspx.

The continuation of law-and-order campaigns and the ever-expanding war on crime have since led to widespread public misperceptions about crime. Despite the fact that crime rates plummeted after 1990, Figure 12.3 shows that the public is often not aware of those declines. Indeed, as the figure reveals, public views moved in the opposite direction. During the last two decades of sharply declining crime, more and more Americans actually believed that crime was increasing. The share of Americans that felt that crime had increased from the previous year almost doubled, from 41 percent in 2001 to 78 percent in 2020. While crime rates were plummeting, the public's perceptions of crime were on the rise.

The War on Crime

As a consequence of the law-and-order campaigns and the public's increasingly negative views about crime, the nation moved to much more active policing and much more punitive criminal sentencing after the 1970s. One of the most significant developments was President Richard Nixon's War on Drugs. That initiative included the creation of the Drug Enforcement Administration (DEA), a force dedicated to targeting illegal drug use, mandatory prison sentencing for drug crimes, and major increases in federal funding for drug-control efforts. Reagan expanded those efforts with the Anti-Drug Abuse Act of 1986, which mandated minimum sentences for many drug crimes and allocated yet more funds for new prisons. The net effect was a 1,100 percent increase in the number of people in prison or jail for a drug offense between 1980 and 2010. All told, FBI Crime Reports indicate that almost 40 million people have been arrested for drug offenses since the war on drugs began.

The nation's stricter attitudes were also reflected in the Crime Sentencing Reform Act of 1984 and more generally with the introduction of tougher sentencing laws at both the federal and state level throughout this period. Emblematic of this

Photo 12.4 A man is arrested on January 1, 1994, in Bridgeport, CT. At the height of America's crack epidemic, many cities received federal funds to increase their police forces with narcotics police and make more drug arrests, often arresting small-time street dealers and their customers who were buying and selling crack cocaine, but not often addressing any of the social, political, or economic issues that brought the drugs into the community.
Source: Photo Andrew Lichtenstein © Andrew Lichtenstein/Contributor/Corbis News/Getty Images.

tough-on-crime attitude was the passage or strengthening of three-strikes laws in twenty-four states in the early 1990s. These measures mandated life or extended imprisonment for a third felony conviction. Georgia's two-strikes laws, which allowed prosecutors to impose life imprisonment for a second drug conviction, was for many the pinnacle of the nation's penchant for punishment. Several states also opted to relegalize the death penalty, several others limited or eliminated parole in some circumstances, and throughout the country police forces were upgraded with military-style equipment. The net effect was that more people were sentenced to prison and those that went spent more time there. As Devah Pager put it, "incarceration has changed from a punishment reserved primarily for the most heinous offenders to one extended to a much greater range of crimes and a much larger segment of the population" (Travis and Western 2014: 108). All of this helps explain how lower crime rates could translate into more incarceration.[3]

---

[3] One consequence of higher incarceration rates was that total spending on corrections more than quadrupled from 1980 to 2010 (Kearney et al. 2014). State expenditures on corrections exploded from just $6.7 billion in 1985 to $60.9 billion in 2018 (Sentencing Project 2021).

To be fair, the war on drugs and the larger effort to be tougher on criminals has lagged somewhat in recent years. Since 2000, the federal government and multiple state governments have enacted a number of laws that reduce criminal penalties and instead seek to rehabilitate. In 2008, President Bush signed the Second Chance Act, a prison rehabilitation initiative that allocated $362 million that in part expanded job training and housing for newly released prisoners. The Obama administration followed in 2010 by passing the Fair Sentencing Act which reduced the disparity in sentences between crack and powder cocaine. The recent legalization of marijuana in a number of states and the District of Columbia has also led to a more tolerant political view on recreational drug use. These and other efforts have slowed and, in some cases, even reversed the growth in U.S. incarceration since 2014.

The Effects of Increased Incarceration on Racial Disparities in the Criminal Justice System

Although none of the new tough-on-crime laws and tactics had an explicitly racial component, the racial consequences have been dramatic. A prison population that was mostly White at mid-century has been transformed into one that is almost 70 percent Black and Latino in the present day (Sentencing Project 2021; Waterman 2016). The war on drugs likely played the biggest role in putting minorities behind bars and in increasing racial disparities in outcomes. Between 1983 at the onset of the war on drugs and 2000, the rate at which Blacks were admitted to prison for drug crimes increased twenty-six-fold. The comparable rate of increase for Latinos was twenty-two times, and for Whites it was only eight times (Alexander 2012).

The net effect is that Blacks and Latinos are profoundly impacted by the criminal justice system. Based on data drawn from the U.S. Bureau of Justice Statistics, the Sentencing Project estimates that an African American male born in 2001 has a 1 in 3 likelihood of being imprisoned. This figure is 1 in 6 for Latino men. For comparable White men, the figure is 1 in 17. All of this is even worse for poor and less educated racial and ethnic minorities. Almost 60 percent of Black male high-school dropouts have spent time in prison before turning 40 (Western 2006). Women are much less likely than men to be imprisoned, but even here there are large racial differences. The likelihood that a woman born in 2001 will be imprisoned at some point in their life is 1 in 18 for Black women, 1 in 45 for Hispanic women, but only 1 in 111 for White women. Mirroring much of what we have seen in this text, a system with lofty ideals and one that—at least since the passage of landmark civil rights legislation in the 1960s—is explicitly color-blind nevertheless ends with outcomes that are anything but racially even.

Understanding Racial Disparities in Incarceration

A number of factors drive and compound the existing racial disparities in incarceration. Structural factors like poverty, education, and distressed neighborhood conditions all help to shape crime and to drive racial disparities. Because Blacks and Latinos are more likely to grow up in poverty, more likely to leave school earlier, and more likely to live in poor, environmentally dangerous and racially segregated neighborhoods, they are also more likely to be involved in criminal activities.

But even after accounting for these and other factors, racial disparities persist. Although it is impossible to come up with a precise breakdown of the population that commits crimes, victimization surveys suggest that minorities are arrested at a higher rate than their criminal behavior warrants. In 2018, for example, victims of violent crimes reported that Blacks accounted for 29 percent of the offenses nationwide (Beck 2021). But that same year, the FBI's Uniform Crime Report indicated that African Americans accounted for 33 percent of all arrests for violent crime. Similarly, victims reported that Latinos made up 14 percent of offenses, but in that same year Latinos made up fully 18 percent of arrests. By contrast, Whites were underrepresented in arrests. Victims reported that Whites were responsible for 52 percent of all violent crimes. But Whites accounted for only 46 percent of all arrests for violent crime.

The disparities are clearer and more dramatic for drug crimes. Despite the fact that surveys, hospitalizations, and other sources indicate that drug use and the sale of drugs is relatively even across racial groups, Black men have been admitted to state prison on drug charges at a rate that is more than thirteen times higher than White men (Alexander 2012). Given that almost half of all federal prisoners were convicted for a drug crime, this dramatic racial disparity is alarming.

Race seems to matter all the way through the criminal justice system, from the initial arrest stage to final sentencing. Although much of the racial disparity in sentencing can be explained "by the initial case and defendant characteristics, including arrest offense and criminal history," these legally permitted factors do not explain all of the difference. A comprehensive analysis of federal cases from the arrest phase through to sentencing revealed that Blacks are more harshly sentenced by juries and judges than Whites when the underlying facts and circumstances of the cases are similar (Rehavi and Starr 2014). The effect of being Black on sentences also had national economic consequences. The authors of the study estimated that eliminating the Black "premium" in sentencing would reduce the number of Blacks in federal prison by around 10,000 and would save the government roughly a quarter of a billion dollars per year in direct costs. Race probably plays an even larger role in juvenile sentencing. One 2000 report found that among youth who had never been to prison before, Black youth were six times as likely as White youth to be sentenced to prison for identical crimes (Poe-Yamagata and Jones 2020). The overrepresentation of minorities and the underrepresentation of Whites in the criminal justice system varies by year and by the type of crime, but it is readily apparent that more racial and ethnic minorities are being caught up in the criminal justice system than need be or should be.

How does a formally race-neutral system manage to achieve such racially disparate outcomes? The answer, unfortunately, is that race matters at every stage of the criminal justice process. How race matters at each stage is complex. There is both individual bias and institutional discrimination. At the individual level, there are certainly those involved in the process who intentionally discriminate. But there may also be implicit bias by those who may not know or think that race is affecting their actions. And then at the institutional level, there are a range of ostensibly race-neutral rules that play out very differently for America's different racial and ethnic communities. In the next few pages, we detail how race impacts each stage of the criminal justice process to ultimately lead to the severe racial disparities that we see today.

The Arrest Phase

Even before a police officer engages with a member of the public, there are a range of highly consequential decisions that that officer and her or his superiors have to make. Although the Fourth Amendment asserts that law enforcement cannot stop, search, or harass Americans without reasonable suspicion of wrongdoing, the reality is that law enforcement officials have extraordinary discretion about who to target and where to focus their efforts. Does that discretion have racial consequences? Do police officers use race and ethnicity as factors to help estimate the likelihood that an individual citizen will commit or has committed a crime—a practice often referred to as racial profiling? The simple answer is yes.

Driving While Black

One area where police officers have considerable discretion is in whether or not to pursue traffic violations. Because drivers commit so many traffic violations so regularly (such as failing to come to a complete stop at a stop sign, exceeding the speeding limit, failing to signal a turn—and even, in some states, hanging an air freshener from the rearview mirror), law enforcement officials cannot possibly stop every motorist who violates some aspect of the traffic code. As a result, police officers pick and choose which particular motorists to pull over. To determine whether race played a factor in these kind of traffic stops, several researchers examined every traffic stop in the state of North Carolina from 2002 through 2016—more than 20 million stops (Baumgartner, Epp, and Shoub 2018). Their database included information about the race of the driver being stopped, as well as other relevant details such as why the officer pulled the driver over, whether the driver or vehicle was searched, and whether the stop resulted in an arrest.

The authors found that African Americans were about twice as likely as Whites to be stopped. Hispanics were about 25 percent more likely to be stopped than Whites. Even after accounting for factors that may have contributed to the stop (such as time of day or whether the driver was speeding) the researchers found that Hispanic drivers were 68 percent more likely than Whites to receive a ticket once they had been stopped. They also report that both Blacks and Latinos are 40–50 percent more likely to be arrested after a traffic stop, compared with similarly situated Whites. Whites who were searched were actually more likely to carry contraband than Blacks and Hispanics—a pattern that suggests that Whites should have been targeted more.

North Carolina is not alone in demonstrating racial bias in policing. Data from New Jersey show that while only 15 percent of drivers in the state are Black, fully 42 percent of all stops and 73 percent of all arrests were of Black motorists (Alexander 2012). Blacks were targeted even though the data show that Blacks and Whites violated traffic laws at almost exactly the same rate. Interestingly, when stops were initiated because a radar gun registered a speed violation—an objective measure—there was no racial disparity. But when stops were made by officers involved in drug interdiction who often had to make judgment calls, minorities were twice as likely as Whites to be targeted. Unfortunately, these patterns have since been confirmed across the nation with a recent study of nearly 100 million traffic stops nationwide (Pierson et al. 2020). Racial profiling of drivers led to the now well-known ironic phrase "driving while Black."

Racial profiling is also not limited to traffic violations. Pedestrians are targeted in much the same way. Of more than a half a million stops initiated through New York City's "stop and frisk" program in 2008, fully 80 percent of those who were stopped were African American or Latino (Baker and Vasquez 2007). Blacks alone made up 85 percent of those who were ultimately frisked. All of this in a city where Blacks and Hispanics combined make up just under half of the population. And it

Photo 12.5 Dozens of protesters on the steps of San Francisco City Hall call on Mayor Ed Lee to put a stop to the city's controversial Stop and Frisk policing proposal, July 17, 2012.
Source: Photo Michael Macor © *San Francisco Chronicle*/Hearst Newspapers via Getty Images/ Contributor/Hearst Newspapers/Getty Images.

continued even though it was demonstrated that guns and other contraband were ultimately seized less often in stops involving Blacks and Hispanics.

Another study that focused explicitly on the police use of force around the country demonstrated that Blacks and Hispanics were more than 50 percent more likely than comparable Whites to experience some form of force in their interactions with police (Fryer 2019). Moreover, adding controls for the context of the interaction and the behavior of the civilian reduced but did not fully explain these racial disparities.

One factor that shaped and could ultimately reduce this bias is Black political power. Even after accounting for crime and poverty rates across cities, the authors of the North Carolina traffic stop study found that in cities where Blacks wielded greater political influence, racial disparities in traffic stops declined. This suggests that a core reason for racial bias in policing is the relative lack of political power in minority communities.

Another reason for these racial disparities may be the overrepresentation of White police officers across the nation. Although findings have been somewhat mixed, several researchers have found that the race of a police officer does matter. In particular, a 2019 study which factored in the race of every U.S. sheriff over a period of 25 years concluded that the "ratio of black-to-white arrests is significantly higher under white sheriffs" and that these effects appear to be driven by arrests for less serious offenses in which Blacks are often targeted (Bulman 2019). Similar results were uncovered in the city of Chicago (Ba et al. 2021). These researchers studied nearly 7,000 officers from 2012 to 2015 in Chicago and found that White officers were more likely than Hispanic and especially Black officers to stop, arrest, and engage in the use of force against Chicago civilians, particularly Black and Hispanic city residents.

Police Discretion, Stereotypes, and Racial Profiling

A range of different factors undoubtedly plays a role in helping to drive racial disparities in police stops and arrests, but even after controlling for all known factors, study after study have found that major racial disparities still remain. If racial disparities in stops and arrests cannot be explained by underlying patterns in crime, why is it that police officers disproportionately target minorities when patrolling?

Few believe that police officers are all driven primarily by the kind of crude racial hostility that was present in earlier eras of American history. But, aside from institutional discrimination embedded in recent judicial decisions as described below, many suspect that a subtler form of racial animus that relies on deep-seated racial stereotypes underlies at least some of these racial disparities.

As we saw in Chapter 5 on Public Opinion, Americans tend to hold deep-seated stereotypes about racial minorities. A large share of the public believes that African Americans and, to a slightly lesser extent, Latinos are prone to violence and criminality. Indeed, a 1995 study found that people automatically associate drug users with Black men. Study participants were asked, "Would you close your eyes for a second, envision a drug user, and describe that person to me?" Ninety-five percent pictured a Black man. Obviously, this is wildly inaccurate as Blacks make up only about 13 percent of the U.S. population and—as indicated previously—Blacks do *not* use or sell drugs more than other racial groups in society. The truth is that most people in this country are White and therefore most illegal drug users and illegal drug dealers are also White.

Unfortunately, these racial stereotypes have obvious implications for police decision-making given that law enforcement officials are far from immune to stereotypes and biases (Eberhardt 2019; Goff et al. 2014; LeCount 2017; Voigt et al. 2017). The fact that the largest study of traffic stops found that racial disparities in stops declined markedly at night—when darkness often prevents police officers from identifying the race of the driver—helps confirm the role of implicit bias (Pierson et al. 2020).

Of course, this implicit bias can impact not only the decision to initiate a stop, but also what happens after the officer engages a citizen including whether or not to charge the individual. For example, the courts have given police officers wide discretion in carrying out drug arrests (Alexander 2012). In *Whren* v. *United States* (1996) the Supreme Court held that police are permitted to use minor traffic violations as an excuse to stop drivers for drug investigations. According to the *Whren* decision, the police do not need any evidence or probable cause once they have made the traffic stop—and as we discussed earlier, the decision to make the traffic stop can often be influenced by racial bias. This same bias can also influence whether an officer is likely to be more fearful and ultimately can lead to a decision to pull their gun and use violence.

It is also difficult to seek legal remedies when police officers are accused of misconduct. The case most responsible for this outcome is *City of Los Angeles* v. *Lyons* (1983). In this case, a 24-year-old Black motorist (Lyons) was pulled over by police for a burned out taillight (Alexander 2012). After being ordered to exit his vehicle, Lyons was subsequently placed in a chokehold—even though he had complied with all requests. He lost consciousness and awoke "spitting up blood and dirt, had urinated and defecated, and had suffered permanent damage to his larynx." He sued the city of Los Angeles, attempting to get them to ban the use of the infamous chokehold. The Supreme Court dismissed the case arguing the Lyons lacked "standing," or the right to bring suit in court, because he needed to show that he was highly likely to be subject to the chokehold again in order for his case to be considered. Racial bias can seep into any stage of the criminal justice process and can impact prosecutors, judges, and juries as well as police officers.

Racial Profiling and Immigration Enforcement: Walking While Hispanic

Are there situations in which racial profiling is warranted? Some believe that immigration enforcement is one of those cases. The fact is that three-quarters of undocumented immigrants in this country are from Mexico or other parts of Latin America (Migration Policy Institute 2021). Would it not make sense to target Hispanics when trying to identify the undocumented?

That is essentially what Arizona and several other states have done in their efforts at immigration enforcement. In 2010, Arizona passed its "Support Our Law Enforcement and Safe Neighborhoods Act" (known mainly as SB 1070), a law that requires that police officers determine the immigration status of a person "where reasonable suspicion exists" that the person is in the country illegally. Given that the overwhelming majority of the undocumented in the state are Hispanic, critics believe that law enforcement officers will naturally single out Hispanics when they attempt to determine who might be undocumented. Based on that fear, Arizona's law and several copycat laws passed in other states have been widely condemned. But the U.S. Supreme Court ultimately ruled that the main provision was constitutional. That decision confirmed a 1975 U.S. Supreme Court ruling in *United States* v. *Brignoni-Ponce* in which the court indicated that the likelihood that any person of Mexican ancestry is alien is high enough to make Mexican appearance a relevant factor (Alexander 2012).

The Arizona law appears to have been effective. One study found that the legislation "significantly reduced the flow of illegal workers into Arizona from Mexico by 30 to 70 percent" (Hoekstra and Orozco-Aleman 2017). But at what cost? While it is true that the vast majority of the undocumented are Latino, it is also true that the vast majority of the Latino population—upwards of 85 percent—is documented. To the extent that the law does lead police officers to target Latinos, it will draw more Latinos into the criminal justice system. That will clearly have a discriminatory effect. All of this raises a deeper question about whether the benefits of racial profiling outweigh the costs. It also raises the question of whether being undocumented should be considered a crime at all. (See box, below.)

WHAT IT LOOKS LIKE TODAY: PROFILING TERRORISTS

Every single one of the 9/11 attackers was Middle Eastern and male. For a period of time the threat of terrorism in the United States came almost exclusively from the Arab world and in particular from Arab men. For that reason, it often made sense to use ethnicity and gender to help identify potential terrorist threats. Airport screeners, for example, had to pick and choose who to approach. If airport screeners randomly selected passengers for questioning, much time and energy would be spent screening groups like young children and elderly women—two groups that we think pose essentially no threat. Thus, many felt that it made sense to use ethnicity and gender to narrow the target population and use resources more efficiently.

But as we just noted with the immigration enforcement case, the practice is clearly discriminatory. Undeniably, almost no Middle Eastern males are terrorists. A strategy of using ethnicity and gender would entangle thousands, if not millions, of innocent people. And, conceivably, this targeting could even radicalize one or two of them—exactly the opposite of what the practice of targeting is trying to accomplish. Moreover, singling out "Arab looking" men is undoubtedly going to entrap lots of individuals who are not Middle Eastern. Equally likely, lots of men who are in fact Middle Eastern will not be perceived as such and will be missed by this process. In response to these kinds of tactics, terrorist groups adjusted accordingly and increasingly recruited women as suicide bombers (Thomas and Bond 2015).

For anyone who might think that the efficiency of targeting by race or ethnicity outweighs the discrimination that such policies necessarily create, it might be worth thinking about America's current terrorist threats. Of those who stormed the U.S. Capitol Building on January 6, 2021, almost all were White supporters of Donald Trump. More broadly, the Department of Justice has found that some 70 percent of all domestic terrorist acts committed in the United States between 2008 and 2017 were committed by members of far-right and White supremacist groups. Members of those groups also disproportionately support Donald Trump. The source of the major domestic terrorist threat is clear. Should we therefore single out and target all Americans who wear MAGA hats for additional screening?

The Prosecutorial Phase

Knowledgeable observers of the criminal justice system tend to believe that no individual has more power to impact the course of a criminal case than the prosecutor. Prosecutors have wide-ranging discretion not only to decide whether or not to pursue a particular case, but also to determine what the charges are. Because the criminal code is vast and the definitions of different crimes overlap, prosecutors often have a wide array of charging options. Prosecutors can also devote more or fewer resources to a particular trial. And finally, prosecutors can play a decisive role in the plea-bargaining process.

The unfortunate reality is that this discretion has exacerbated racial disparities in the criminal justice system. One of the starkest examples is the decision of district attorneys in Georgia over whether or not to charge defendants under the state's "two strikes and you're out" law—a sentencing scheme that imposes life imprisonment for a second drug offense. District Attorneys, who have essentially unilateral decision-making authority over whether to apply the law for second drug offenses, invoked it against only 1 percent of White defendants facing a second drug conviction. For Black defendants in the same situation, they invoked it 16 percent of the time. The net result was that 98 percent of those serving life sentences in the state under that sentencing scheme were Black (Anderson 2012).

And Georgia is certainly not an isolated case. Across the nation, a comprehensive study of the federal justice system found that Black men are 1.75 times more likely to be charged under mandatory minimum laws than White men who are arrested for similar crimes and who have essentially identical criminal records (Rehavi and Starr 2014). Indeed, that decision by prosecutors to bring charges carrying "mandatory minimum" sentences is perhaps the single most important factor driving racial disparities in the criminal justice system. The same study found that the decision to use or not use mandatory minimum sentencing schemes accounts for most of the racial disparities in sentencing that are not due to the original arrest or the defendant's criminal history (Rehavi and Starr 2014).

Similar racial disparities emerge in the plea-bargaining process. One study that assessed 700,000 criminal cases found that Whites were much more successful in obtaining reduced sentences through plea bargains than either Blacks or Latinos with similar criminal histories who were accused of similar crimes (Schmitt 1991). Another found that White defendants are 25 percent more likely than Black defendants to have their principal initial charge dropped or reduced to a lesser crime. That racial disparity was most pronounced for defendants who had no criminal history and who were charged with misdemeanors or minor felonies (Berdejo 2018). Given that the overwhelming majority of criminal cases in the United States are resolved through plea deals, these racial disparate decisions raise alarms.

The Trial Phase

Racial disparities do not end when trials begin. The Sixth Amendment to the U.S. Constitution guarantees that, "In all criminal prosecutions, the accused shall enjoy the right to a speedy trial, by an impartial jury ... and to have the Assistance of Counsel in his defense." But those protections are not always extended equally to all Americans. Race, once again, bleeds into the process.

Legal Counsel

The process begins with legal counsel. Roughly 80 percent of criminal defendants are indigent and must rely on public defenders who have large caseloads and who are often not able to devote sufficient resources to adequately defend their clients. Racial minorities are once again more likely than Whites to be in that situation.

Race can enter into the equation in other more subtle ways. An experiment that sent requests for representation to lawyers found that lawyers are less likely to take on clients with Black-sounding names than White-sounding names (Libgober 2020). Moreover, the fact that Black lawyers did not discriminate against potential Black clients, while White lawyers did, suggest that racial preferences are driving this disparate behavior. Given that roughly 85 percent of all lawyers are White, minorities seeking legal representation clearly face an uphill battle (American Bar Association 2020).

Juries

Juries can also contribute to racial disparities. While overarching statements about jury bias are difficult to make given available data, it is clear that jury race can impact outcomes for criminal defendants. A widely cited study found that all-White juries convict Black defendants significantly more often than White defendants (16 percentage points). But that same study found that adding at least one Black juror entirely eliminates that racial disparity (Anwar, Bayer, and Hjalmarsson 2012).

That is problematic because the Supreme Court has indicated that non-White potential jurors can be dismissed from the jury pool for almost any pretext (Alexander 2012). The relevant court decision came in *Purkett* v. *Elm* (1995). In this case, the Court found that prosecutors could provide virtually any rationale for removing Blacks from the jury as long as they (the prosecutor) did not admit that it was because of race. In *Purkett*, the prosecutor claimed that African Americans were removed because of "long hair," "a mustache and a goatee," and because he "didn't like the way they looked." The Court found this rationale acceptable, arguing that prosecutors were not required to provide "an explanation that is persuasive, or even plausible," if the trial judge found it to be acceptable.

Judges

Given their discretion over sentencing, judges can also play an important role in the outcome of a case. Again, assessing overall bias against minority defendants on the part of judges is difficult. But at least in one context—bail hearings—there is compelling evidence that judges are biased against Black defendants. In a study of bail hearings across two states, researchers found that Black defendants were 11.2 percentage points more likely to be required to pay for bail and that once assigned monetary bail, Black defendants had to pay on average $14,376 more than White defendants (Arnold, Dobbie, and Yang 2018). That, of course, is not evidence of bias in and of itself. But in an ingenious twist, the authors looked at the pretrial behavior of both the Black and White defendants. If judges were evenhanded, then pretrial misconduct—things like failing to appear for a hearing or failing a drug test—would have exactly the same consequences for the amount of bail that Black and White defendants were required to pay. The reality was that Black defendants required to pay bail were much less likely than their White counterparts to engage in misconduct pretrial. In effect, judges let Whites get away with more before they were deemed a risk and required to pay bail. Inexperienced and part-time judges were especially biased. (See box, "What It Looks Like Today: Does a Judge's Race Matter?" for more on this topic.)

Why are judges and their prison sentences so racially disparate? We have already outlined a number of ways in which race influences the outcome. But it is important to return to the topic of negative racial stereotypes. Judges' decisions and indeed those of almost any official involved in the judicial system can be impacted by subtle racial considerations—perhaps considerations that those officials do not even fully recognize.

Probably the best evidence that negative racial stereotyping is common throughout the criminal justice system involves the far-reaching effects of skin tone bias. In particular, study after study has shown that darker skinned African Americans face worse treatment than lighter skinned African Americans—even after controlling for the circumstances of the case (Hochshild and Weaver 2007). One study that focused on Black and White men in Georgia revealed that medium- and dark-skinned African Americans received 4.8 percent longer sentences than Whites (Burch 2015). By contrast, light-skinned Blacks received sentences of about the same length as Whites. A different study of women also found that Black women with lighter skin tone tend to receive more lenient sentences that mirror those of

Whites (Viglione, Hannon, and DeFina 2011). All of this is perhaps not so surprising given that the vast majority of judges are White. And because most federal judges serving today were appointed by White Republican presidents, these judges are not only apt to be White, they may also be on the conservative side. Donald Trump, for example, elevated more people to the federal bench during his four years than Clinton and Obama did across all of their years in the presidency.

WHAT IT LOOKS LIKE TODAY: DOES A JUDGE'S RACE MATTER?

Despite America's increasing racial diversity, its court personnel and its judges remain overwhelmingly White. At the federal level, fully 85 percent of judges are White (American Bar Association 2020). Latinos, Blacks, and Native Americans, by contrast, are greatly underrepresented in the ranks of federal judges. Does the Whiteness of the judiciary drive the racial disparities that we so often see in the criminal justice system? Studies that seek to assess the implications of a judge's race have reached somewhat mixed conclusions. Some of the most rigorous studies have found that African American judges are more liberal and tend to be more supportive of Black causes like the 1965 Voting Rights Act (Cox and Miles 2008; Kastellec 2013). Scholars have also found that having a minority judge on a multi-member judicial panel can influence the decisions of White judges leading to more support for affirmative action (Kastellec 2013). But others focused on different levels and decisions have uncovered few differences in judicial decision-making by race (Farhang and Wawro 2004). A reasonable conclusion from these mixed results is that a judge's race can affect her actions but that the extent of the racial differences may be limited. That limited impact makes sense given that judges, regardless of race, receive similar legal training and that judges, regardless of race, need to follow the law and base their decisions on the facts of the case at hand.

The Punishment Phase

Racial disparities can also be reinforced after conviction, in the prison experience itself, and prior to conviction in the decision to use the death penalty.

Prison

Studies have shown that race can have an impact on a convicted person's treatment in prison. For example, a *New York Times* study found that across tens of thousands of disciplinary hearings against inmates in New York, Black and Latino inmates were sent more frequently to solitary confinement and held there for longer durations than Whites. Again, this is not necessarily evidence of racial discrimination. But the fact that racial disparities were much higher for violations where prison guards had considerable discretion in whether to send a prisoner to solitary confinement (such as disobeying a guard's order to get in a line) than they were for violations that required physical evidence (such as possessing contraband) implies that racial bias likely played a significant role. All of this suggests that race may also be embedded within the prison experience. The box below considers the use of prison labor and its relation to racial disparities.

WHAT IT LOOKS LIKE TODAY: THE USE OF PRISON LABOR

Over 30 percent of federal prisons employ incarcerated people (Littletree-Holston 2019). Most prisoners who work volunteer to do so, but at some facilities labor is forced. The most common form of this forced labor involves work inside the correctional facility—including custodial work, grounds-keeping, and food service. Average wages are abysmal—ranging from 14 cents to 63 cents per hour in 2017 (Garcia 2020). But even worse are states like Alabama, Arkansas, Florida, Georgia, Mississippi, Oklahoma, South Carolina, and Texas where labor within government-run prisons can go unpaid. Most recently, states have relied on prisoners to fight fires in California or to manufacture hand sanitizer, protective gowns, and toilet paper during the COVID-19 pandemic. A loophole in the Thirteenth Amendment, which abolished slavery, is that it nevertheless allows incarcerated persons to be forced into work as punishment for their crimes. Proponents claim that prison labor can help with rehabilitation, but detractors firmly believe that it should be viewed as cruel and unusual punishment.

Photo 12.6 Delta Crew 5, a Cal Fire inmate hand-crew from Suisun City, CA, work on a fuel reduction project in Solano County, CA, July 31, 2012.
Source: Michael Macor © *San Francisco Chronicle*/Hearst Newspapers via Getty Images/Contributor/Hearst Newspapers/Getty Images.

The Death Penalty

Most countries do not allow the death penalty, and only a handful of countries (all nondemocratic countries like China, Saudia Arabia, and Iran) use the death penalty more often the United States (BBC News 2022). America's unique reliance on the death penalty as well as deeper concerns about whether it is morally and ethically just for the government to kill one of its citizens has led many to wonder whether the death penalty is excessive and should be considered "cruel and unusual punishment." Supporters counter that it serves as an effective deterrent. But empirical studies tend not to find a link between the death penalty and homicide rates (Nagin 2013).

Putting aside these core questions, it is also important to consider the racial implications of the death penalty. Of all of the defendants sentenced to death between 1995 and 2000, fully 48 percent of the defendants were Black and 29 percent were Hispanic—figures that dwarf the two groups' share of the population at large (Snell and Maruschak 2002). Moreover, there is considerable evidence that the racial disparity stems at least in part from racial bias, especially in relation to the race of the victim.

Much of that evidence was brought to light in the Georgia death penalty case of *McCleskey* v. *Kemp* (1987). McCleskey, a Black man, appealed his conviction for killing a White police officer up to the U.S. Supreme Court. His defense provided one of the most thorough statistical investigations on record of racial bias in the imposition of the death penalty. They demonstrated that even when accounting for the circumstances of the crime and other extenuating factors, defendants charged with killing White victims in the state of Georgia received the death penalty over four times more often than defendants charged with killing Blacks. Blacks who were found guilty of killing Whites had the highest probability of all of receiving the death penalty. In short, McCleskey's lawyers, relying on the work of Baldus, Pulaski, and Woodworth (1983), had uncovered dramatic evidence of racial bias in the imposition of the death penalty in Georgia. The Supreme Court nevertheless rejected the claim that this pattern of racial bias constituted a violation of the equal protection clause of the Fourteenth Amendment. In a narrow 5–4 decision, the Court held that in spite of the statistical evidence—which it did not dispute— McCleskey needed to show that there was "intentional and conscious racial bias in his individual case." McCleskey was executed in 1991.

An updated examination of all U.S. executions from 1976 (when the death penalty was reinstated in the United States) until 2013 found additional evidence, at the national level, of racial bias in the imposition of the death penalty (Baumgartner, Grigg, and Mastro 2015). The new study found once again that the death penalty is much more likely to be carried out on individuals convicted of killing Whites, especially if the killer is Black. What is even more noteworthy about this pattern is that the odds of a White person being murdered are much lower than the odds of a Black person being murdered. African Americans make up almost half of all homicide victims in the United States, even though they represent only about

13 percent of the national population. In other words, Blacks are much *more* likely than Whites to be murdered, but their killers are much *less* likely to receive the death penalty. That racial bias was further tested in a study that looked at reversals—cases where the death penalty was eventually thrown out. Those cases show that convictions in which minorities kill Whites are much more likely to be reversed than are other death penalty convictions—a pattern which suggest more "errors" or more bias against Blacks who kill Whites (Alesina and Ferrara 2014).

Legal Statutes

In addition to all of the different factors that impact the application of the law, we also have to consider the laws themselves. What we choose to criminalize and how severely we penalize different illegal acts can all have broad racial implications. The most egregious and well-known example is the differential rate at which crack and powder cocaine have been penalized. For years, the penalty for the sale of 5 grams of crack triggered the same penalty as the sale of 500 grams of powder cocaine. This 100 to 1 sentencing ratio meant that White Americans who were much more likely than African Americans to possess and sell powder cocaine were relatively lightly penalized while Blacks, who tended to favor crack cocaine, were severely punished.[4] Recognizing the unfairness, President Obama signed the Fair Sentencing Act into law in 2010. That measure dramatically reduced the disparity in sentencing between crack and powder cocaine from 100 to 1 to 18 to 1 and eliminated the five-year mandatory minimum sentence for simple possession of crack cocaine. President Biden is seeking to further reduce those disparities.

But racial imbalances still exist for all sorts of criminal policy. Criminalizing behaviors such as vagrancy or loitering has real racial consequences in a nation where racial and ethnic minorities tend to fall further down the socioeconomic ladder and are more likely to end up homeless. More broadly, harsher sentences for street crimes and more lenient rules for white-collar crimes like tax fraud and securities fraud tend to favor relatively more well-off White Americans over less well-off racial and ethnic minorities. Criminalizing undocumented immigration is another policy with sharply racial consequences. Indeed, in 2020, fully 16 percent of all Hispanic federal prisoners were serving time for immigration offenses (Carson 2020).

Even something as innocuous as instituting fines for petty infractions can shape the racial contours of the criminal justice system. Cities and police departments often view fines as a means to make money and pay for expenses, but these fees, which tend to fall overwhelmingly on residents of poor, minority neighborhoods, can be debilitating for working-class Americans who often cannot afford to pay them. One comprehensive study of fines in the Washington, D.C. region, for

---

[4] Of course, the racially disparate effect of these laws was also due to their application. Almost all crack arrests are made at the street level, while powder arrests generally happen off the street and are usually the result of lengthy sting operations that take longer and are more cumbersome than street-level frisks.

example, found that 62 percent of all the fines were issued in poorer, largely Black neighborhoods—even though these neighborhoods represent less than a third of the city's population (Harden 2021). By contrast, in overwhelmingly White and financially well-off census tracts where fines are relatively easy to pay off, the city issued few infractions. The Justice Department's review of policing in Ferguson, Missouri, likewise found that more than 90 percent of fines for petty offenses—such as walking in the roadway or disturbing the peace—were handed out to African Americans even though Blacks made up only 67 percent of the city population (Department of Justice 2015).

Critics of the heavy use of fines contend that it not only targets Blacks and other minorities but also effectively criminalizes poverty. In D.C., for example, when someone cannot pay their fines, the fees double. The city blocks residents from renewing a driver's license or almost any license if they owe the city more than $100. All of this means that the most disadvantaged citizens are the most hurt by these fees.

The Consequences of Racial Disparities in the War on Drugs

The racially disparate actions at all phases of the criminal justice process combine to have enormous consequences for America's racial and ethnic minority population. Those consequences are perhaps most pronounced in the nation's war on drugs, where Blacks, more than any other group, are caught up in the criminal justice system.

The numbers, as Figure 12.4 illustrates, are both impressive and alarming. African Americans represented only about 12 percent of the nation's population when these numbers were compiled. Their share of drug users is roughly on par with

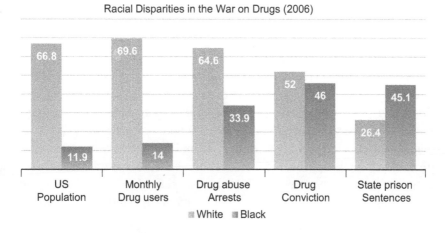

Racial Disparities in the War on Drugs (2006)

White | Black

US Population | Monthly Drug users | Drug abuse Arrests | Drug Conviction | State prison Sentences
66.8 / 11.9 | 69.6 / 14 | 64.6 / 33.9 | 52 / 46 | 26.4 / 45.1

Figure 12.4 Racial Disparities in the War on Drugs, 2006
African Americans are frequently targeted by the war on drugs even though their drug use is roughly on par with the rest of the nation.
Source: Adapted from Bobo and Thompson 2010.

their numbers in the population. But the anti-crime agencies of the government target them disproportionately. Blacks make up a third of those arrested for drugs (more than twice their share of users). Convictions are even worse. African Americans account for 46 percent of all individuals convicted for drug use—in this case a figure that is more than three times their proportion of users. And they are just as targeted and disadvantaged at the sentencing level where Blacks unfortunately make up 45 percent of all Americans sentenced to state prisons on drug sentences—roughly three times their proportion of users.

Reforming the Criminal Justice System

The debate over how we should reform the criminal justice system in the United States often boils down to two deeply opposed viewpoints. On the one hand are conservatives who believe that police action and tough sentencing deters crime. They tend to argue in favor of greater policing and ever more stringent penalties for those who commit crimes. On the other side are liberals who lament the discriminatory actions of police officers and who are skeptical of the deterrent effects of most criminal justice policies. They are inclined to call for steep reductions in policing and sentencing.

This discussion will not assess the entire list of reforms recommended by either side. There are simply too many different proposals for us to give each sufficient attention. Moreover, even sustained attention often does not lead to clear answers. Systematic evidence assessing the effectiveness of those reforms is often limited. Knowing what works and what does not work is often impossible. Nevertheless, we will highlight some of the main proposals and offer brief assessments of their viability.

Prison Reform

Given that America incarcerates more of its citizens than just about any other nation in the world, one of the first and most important decisions is whether to increase or decrease those high rates of incarceration. Those in favor of incarceration often point to incapacitation (rendering criminals incapable of committing another crime because they are behind bars) and deterrence (the threat of punishment deters people from committing criminal acts), the two potentially positive effects of putting people behind prison walls, as the main motivation for high levels of imprisonment. The logic in each case is relatively straightforward. But does imprisoning people really reduce crime through incapacitation or deterrence?

Incapacitation

The evidence in favor of incapacitation is clearer (Levitt 1996; Nagin 2013). While it is certainly not impossible to commit a crime while in prison, the odds are reduced by the significant level of control that the correctional system exerts over prisoners. As such, there is little doubt that the sustained increase in imprisonment since 1970 reduced crime by incapacitating more and more prisoners.

At the same time, it is also clear that the size of the incapacitation benefit can vary. The effects of incapacitation are larger for policies that tend to incarcerate high-rate offenders (those who tend to commit frequent criminal acts) and smaller for policies that incarcerate low-rate offenders (those who rarely commit crimes). Thus, it should come as no surprise that the incapacitation effect has tended to decline as the scale of imprisonment in the United States has increased and more and more low-rate offenders (including those who commit nonviolent drug offenses) are apprehended and incarcerated (Johnson and Raphael 2016). Given these patterns, the movement to reduce our exceedingly high rate of incarceration has been gaining momentum.

The Threat of Imprisonment and Deterrence

The *threat* of imprisonment can also deter crime, although the effects are less clear than those for incapacitation. The core logic is that the fear of arrest should be enough to deter would-be criminals from offending in the first place. But the reality is often more complex. Studies seeking to assess the deterrent effect of potential incarceration have reached decidedly mixed findings. One interesting study found that individuals who faced an imminent threat of imprisonment for unpaid fines were more likely to pay their fines than others who were not threatened with incarceration (Weisburd, Einat, and Kowalksi 2008). Likewise, an examination of California's famous "three strikes and you're out" law found that individuals who had been convicted of two strikes and were thus facing a potential life sentence for another crime were much less likely to commit a crime than similar individuals who had only had one strike and were not facing life in prison for their next crime (Helland and Tabarrok 2007). But others find little deterrent effect from the threat of incarceration. For example, there is little sign that teenagers commit fewer crimes after they turn 18 and face much stiffer penalties as adults (Lee and McCrary 2017).

The Experience of Prison and Deterrence

The other way in which imprisonment can potentially change behavior and deter crime revolves around the experience of prison itself. The overwhelmingly negative nature of time spent behind bars should, the argument goes, motivate ex-prisoners to build a better life and avoid returning to prison in the future. However, it is important to note that there are many reasons to suspect that the experience of punishment can increase, rather than decrease, future offending. Prison exposes individuals to other criminals, it can teach individuals more about criminal enterprise, and it can build resentment and anger. A prison record also greatly reduces opportunities and life chances after prison. Thus, it should come as no surprise that the clear majority of studies find that the experience of punishment actually increases the likelihood of offending in the future (Nagin 2013). Indeed, studies of recidivism in the United States find exceedingly high rates of reoffending. Nationwide, the Bureau of Justice found that about six in ten prisoners released from prison in 2012 were re-arrested within three years, and seven in ten were re-arrested within five years. As the National Advisory Commission on Criminal Justice long ago noted, "the prison, the reformatory, and the jail have achieved only a shocking record of failure. There is overwhelming evidence that these institutions create crime rather than prevent it" (National Advisory Commission on Criminal Justice Standards and Goals 1973: 358).

Alternatives to Incarceration

America's exceedingly high rates of incarceration are concerning not just because prison often leads to more prison, but also because prisons are expensive—as a nation we pay nearly $300 billion annually to house our prisoners and to support the criminal justice system (Hyland 2019). The mark of a criminal record can also profoundly and negatively shape lives after prison. Ex-felons face discrimination, greatly reduced job opportunities, limited government benefits, and often disenfranchisement from American democracy.

In light of these concerns, many reformers are pushing for alternatives to prison. In some cases these reform efforts focus on reducing prison sentences. Dropping mandatory minimum sentences is often cited as one of the keys to reducing both imprisonment and racial disparities in imprisonment. By dropping those mandatory minimums, we give judges a chance to lower sentences when warranted and we eliminate some of the racial bias when racial minorities are targeted through these laws. In other cases, these reform efforts focus primarily on the early release of existing prisoners. Either way, the goal is to have fewer Americans in prison. (See box below.)

TESTING THE THEORY: WHAT HAPPENS WHEN WE REDUCE THE PRISON POPULATION?

After decades of growth in California's prison population, the state's prisons were desperately overcrowded. By 2009, the state held twice as many inmates as its prisons were designed to hold. Litigation led to a federal court order to reduce prison overcrowding. The state responded with a wide-ranging effort to reduce the number of inmates in the system. That effort included early parole, early release, reduced penalties for non-violent offenses, and transfers to county prisons.

Reforms reduced the total prison population by almost 30,000 in the first year and much more since then. That rapid decline has given scholars a unique situation to test the effects of reduced incarceration. Almost a decade after the state's

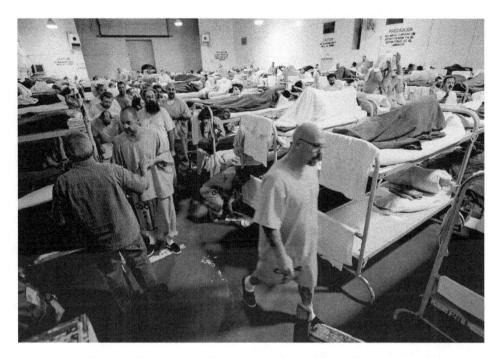

Photo 12.7 This gymnasium was turned into a temporary prison in Chino, California in 2010—
the type of situation that led to lawsuits requiring the state to reduce prison overcrowding.
Source: Kevork Djansezian © Kevork Djansezian/Staff/Getty Images News/Getty Images.

program began, the results are largely positive. Violent crime rates did not
increase—they remain at or near historic lows. As well, recidivism rates—the rate
at which released prisoners commit new crimes once they are free—have remained
largely unchanged. Perhaps the only negative is that state spending on corrections
remains stubbornly high (Lofstrom and Martin 2015).

Other reformers are pushing for the nation to reimagine incarceration by making
the experience more humane and by offering more services to help inmates develop
skills to succeed in life after prison. Given that almost all prisoners will leave prison
and eventually return to their communities, many are pushing for greater educational opportunities while in prison and more sustained job training and job
preparation upon release. Still others are focused on the expansion of drug treatment and mental health services. Unfortunately, while the impetus behind these
reforms is strong, the number and size of such programs is still relatively limited and
their impact relatively untested.

Policing Reform

In light of the growing number of Americans who have been killed or mistreated by
police and the widespread attention that these cases have generated, many in

America are demanding police reform. Some have even called for the nation to "defund the police." The voices seeking to reduce the number of police officers patrolling the streets are often loud and forceful. But calls for police reform require us to understand more about whether and how policing works in the first place.

Does Policing Work?

Do police actions actually deter crime? Or, put another way, does having police on the street deter potential offenders from carrying out criminal acts? The short answer is yes. Studies that investigate the effects of abrupt changes in police presence—often due to large budget cuts or lawsuits—conclude that major decreases in policing are usually followed by substantial increases in crime (Nagin 2013). Similarly, research assessing the impact of large increases in police resources due to new terrorist threats finds that these increased resources are associated with decreased crime. Even analysis based on the location of policing finds significant effects (Braga and Bond 2008). In one experiment, crime dropped by 6–13 percent in high-crime areas where police patrols were doubled compared to the same period in similarly high-crime areas that did not receive an increased police presence (Sherman and Weisburd 1995).

The Move toward Better Policing

If police tend to be helpful in preventing crime, it is hard to argue in favor of totally defunding the police. But even if we choose to maintain a police presence, we may, nevertheless, seek to alter *how* officers police our communities. Thus, many reformers are asking for changes in police tactics, training, and oversight in an effort to improve policing.

A lot of the current conversation revolves around enhancing oversight and accountability to reduce police transgressions. At the federal level, many applaud the Biden administration's call to resume and reinvigorate Department of Justice investigations into systematic problematic behavior by police departments around the country. Others contend that we need to lower the burden of proof in cases where police officers have been accused of wrongful behavior. And still others call for clearer restrictions on police use of force—especially the use of deadly force. Reformers have also called for more civilian oversight and greater transparency on the part of police forces. Perhaps the most popular aspect of this push for increased transparency has been mandates for the use of body-worn cameras by police around the country.

The net result of the public's concern and engagement has been widespread change in policy. Since George Floyd's death, more than thirty states have passed police oversight and reform laws. Many of these laws have given states greater ability to monitor and control the police. Complete assessments of these relatively new laws will, however, require more time.

Another major part of the current debate focuses more directly on police behavior while performing their duties. In response to the steady militarization of police forces in the last few decades, many people support bans on military-style gear like explosives and armored vehicles. The hope is that these bans will reduce police excesses which will in turn reinforce the public's trust in the police.

For others, the core hope for better protection and better police–community relations is a shift from rapid and limited police interventions in response to ongoing crimes to more sustained community policing where officers engage in more positive and longer-term interactions with organizations and individuals in the community.

Finally, many argue in favor of aiding both the public and the police by hiring and incorporating more community and social service workers so that the police are not forced to respond to so many noncrime-related calls and so that individuals with the skills and compassion to assist in such situations are available and ready to help as most needed.

Restricting Gun Ownership

Another area of potential criminal justice reform where Americans are deeply divided is gun control. Almost every time guns are used to kill Americans in mass shootings around the country, a major segment of the population laments the widespread availability of guns in this country and demands new laws to restrict access to gun ownership. But another group of Americans makes equally strong claims that guns are not the problem and focuses instead on our constitutional right to bear arms.

The data, however, tend to fall very clearly on one side. Across countries, it is clear, as Figure 12.5 reveals, that countries with more guns have more gun deaths (Lopez 2021). Indeed, the United States stands out on both counts. We have many more guns per person than any other nation in the study and we also have many more gun deaths per capita than any other country.

It is also clear, as Figure 12.6 shows, that states with more guns have more gun-related deaths. In other words, the mere presence of firearms often appears to make a potentially tense situation turn more deadly (Lopez 2021).

Confronting Racial Bias in Criminal Justice

For many Americans the primary focus of reform is to try to address the role of racial bias in the criminal justice system. Research suggests that one of the first and perhaps one of the most important steps is to eliminate mandatory minimum sentences that tend to disproportionately target minority citizens (Rehavi and Starr 2014). Likewise, the clear racial inequities in the use of the death penalty that we outlined earlier in the chapter suggest that efforts to abolish the death penalty could be particularly helpful for racial and ethnic minorities, given the undeniable bias in death penalty decisions. Another critical step is likely to provide anti-racism training for federal, state, and local law enforcement officers. The fact that Blacks

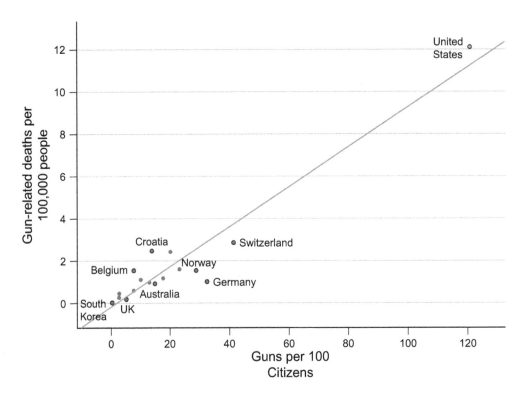

Figure 12.5 Gun Ownership vs. Gun Deaths in Selected Countries
When looking at gun ownership and gun-related deaths across countries, the evidence is clear that countries with more guns have more gun deaths; and the United States far surpasses other countries on both counts.
Source: Data from Gunpolicy.org, created by Vox: www.vox.com/policy-and-politics/23141964/america-gun-violence-epidemic-chart.

and Hispanics are disproportionately targeted, stopped, and sentenced suggests that racial stereotypes can play a major role in police actions. Training is unlikely to eliminate these biases, but by raising consciousness about them, it is possible that they may be significantly reduced.

Increasing the racial diversity of police forces could also reduce biases and lead to more equitable policing. Although local police officers around the country are relatively representative of the national population, the share of White officers (71 percent) still outweighs the share of White residents. Moreover, given research that shows that Hispanic and Black officers make fewer stops and use less force than White officers - especially against Black civilians – there is reason to believe that hiring more minorities could diminish racial disparities in outcomes (Ba et al. 2021). There is also reason to believe that eliminating or substantially decreasing the use of fines and fees could lessen racial inequities. These fines and fees tend not only to fall disproportionately on minority communities but also to have a bigger impact on the poorer members of these communities who often cannot afford to pay them (Harden 2021).

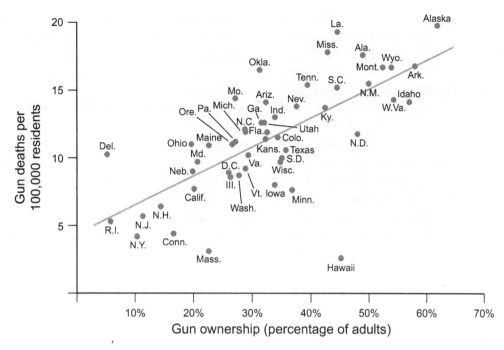

Figure 12.6 Gun Ownership and Gun Deaths in Selected States, 2021
Looking at individual states, the states with the lowest percentage of gun ownership (such as
Rhode Island, New York, and New Jersey), tend to have the lowest number of gun deaths per
100,000 residents and states with the highest percentage of gun ownership (such as Arkansas,
Wyoming, and Alaska, tend to have the greatest number of gun deaths.
Sources: Centers for Disease Control and Kalesin et al. (2015).

Conclusion

Throughout this chapter we have seen powerful statistical evidence that race is a
strong determinant affecting how people are treated by and within the American
criminal justice system. At every level of the system, widespread endorsement of
negative stereotypes about racial and ethnic minorities as well as structural discrimination play major roles in creating these disparities. All minority groups except for
Asian Americans are overrepresented relative to their population shares at every
phase of the criminal justice process, from arrest to punishment. Reform is clearly
needed, but can reform really succeed in a nation where the public often fears crime,
often believes that crime is on the rise, and often thinks that racial minorities are
disproportionately to blame?

Public views, perhaps more than anything else, may be the biggest barrier to real
reform of the criminal justice system. All of the attention to police killings that we
highlighted at the beginning of this chapter has certainly raised the nation's awareness of racial inequities in our crime fighting efforts. The Black Lives Matter
movement and the actions of political progressives and even some conservatives

have forced many Americans to recognize that racial discrimination in policing exists and that we need to do something about it. Two-thirds of all Americans now believe that Blacks are treated less fairly than Whites by the police (Desilver 2020). There is, in short, burgeoning recognition of the problem, growing activism on the problem, and even some small signs of change.

Unfortunately, relatively widespread agreement that there *is* a problem is unfortunately not matched with any agreement over how to solve the problem. There are, as well, profound differences in the preferences of White Americans and racial and ethnic minorities on how to address these issues. White Americans are much more likely than racial and ethnic minorities to have confidence in the police, and they are much more likely as a group to favor the continuation of current policies like the death penalty and relatively unrestricted access to guns.

Moreover, despite all of the attention paid to the police killings of George Floyd, Breonna Taylor, and countless others, the resistance to change among the majority-White population and the sharp racial divide in views does not appear to be declining all that much. With America still very much divided and with many still strongly in favor of more punitive criminal justice policies, hopes for radical change and a sharp reduction in racial inequities in the criminal justice system should be muted. The criminal justice system, as flawed as it now is, is both complex and deeply entrenched. It remains to be seen how much things on the ground will really change in the years going forward.

KEY TERMS

Deference
Implicit racial bias
Incapacitation
"Law and order" campaigns
Racial profiling
Three-strikes laws
War on Drugs

DISCUSSION QUESTIONS

1. How does race shape outcomes in the criminal justice system?
2. Why are African Americans and Latinos more likely than Whites to be caught up in the criminal justice system?
3. What is the War on Drugs and why has it been so important in shaping racial inequities in the criminal justice system?
4. How and why has the prison population grown so much since the 1960s?
5. What are the best policies for reducing racial disparities in the criminal justice system?
6. Do you think the death penalty should be abolished? Why or why not?
7. How likely are we to see major reforms in the criminal justice system and what will those reforms look like?

ANNOTATED SUGGESTED READINGS

See Michelle Alexander. 2012. *The New Jim Crow: Mass Incarceration in the Age of Colorblindness*. New York: New Press, for one of the most comprehensive and convincing accounts of how race shapes outcomes in the criminal justice system.

See Michael Tonry, 2012. *Punishing Race: A Continuing American Dilemma*. Oxford: Oxford University Press, for another excellent explanation of racial disparities in criminal justice as well as for a deeper understanding of the historical, political, and sociological roots of those inequities.

See Jennifer Eberhardt. 2019. *Biased: Uncovering the Hidden Prejudice That Shapes What We See, Think, and Do*. New York: Viking, for those interested in a deeper understanding of how implicit racial biases alter the actions of police officers and others.

See Jeffrey Manza. 2006. *Locked Out: Felon Disenfranchisement and American Democracy*. Oxford: Oxford University Press, for the most complete and most compelling account of the impact of felon disenfranchisement in America today.

See Mark Peffley and Jon Hurwitz. 2010. *Justice in America: The Separate Realities of Blacks and Whites*. New York: Cambridge University Press, for not only one of the best overviews of the public's views on crime, but which also helps us to understand the sources of the starkly different views of White and Black Americans on crime.

See Alex Kotlowitz. 1991. *There Are No Children Here: The Story of Two Boys Growing up in the Other America*. New York: Anchor Books, to help us understand the plight of poor, minority children by offering a moving story of two African American children growing up in poverty in one of Chicago's most disadvantaged neighborhoods.

CHAPTER REFERENCES

Abrajano, Marisa and Zoltan Hajnal. 2015. *White Backlash: Immigration, Race, and American Politics*. Princeton: Princeton University Press.

Alesina, Alberto and Eliana La Ferrara. 2014. "A Test of Racial Bias in Capital Sentencing," *American Economic Review* 104: 3397–3433.

Alexander, Michelle. 2012. *The New Jim Crow: Mass Incarceration in the Age of Colorblindness*. New York: New Press.

American Bar Association. 2020. "Profile of the Legal Profession." www.americanbar.org/content/dam/aba/administrative/news/2020/07/potlp2020.pdf.

Anwar, Shamena, Patrick Bayer, and Randi Hjalmarsson. 2012. "The Impact of Jury Race in Criminal Trials," *Quarterly Journal of Economics* 127: 1017–1055.

Arnold, David, Will Dobbie, and Crystal S. Yang. 2018. "Racial Bias in Bail Decisions," *Quarterly Journal of Economics* 133: 1885–1932.

Ba, Bocar A., Dean Knox, Jonathan Mummolo, and Roman Rivera. 2021. "The Role of Officer Race and Gender in Police–Civilian Interactions in Chicago," *Science* 371: 696–702.

Baker, Al and Emily Vasquez. 2007. "Number of People Stopped by Police Soars," *New York Times*, February 3.

Baldus, David., Charles Pulaski, and George Woodworth. 1983. "Comparative Review of Death Sentences: An Empirical Study of the Georgia Experience," *Journal of Criminal Law and Criminology* 74: 661.

Baumgartner, Frank, Derek Epp, and Kelsey Shoub. 2018. *Suspect Citizens: What 20 Million Traffic Stops Tell Us about Policing and Race*. New York: Cambridge University Press.

Baumgartner, Frank R., Amanda J. Grigg, and Alisa Mastro. 2015. "#Blacklivesdon'tmatter: Race-of-Victim Effects in US Executions, 1976–2013," *Politics, Groups, and Identities* 3: 209–221.

BBC News. 2022. "Death Penalty: How Many Countries Still Have It?" *BBC News.* www.bbc.com/news/world-45835584.

Beauchamp, Zack. 2018. "America Doesn't Have More Crime Than Other Rich Countries. It Just Has More Guns," *Vox*, February 15. www.vox.com/2015/8/27/9217163/america-guns-europe

Beck, Allen. 2021. "Race and Ethnicity of Violent Crime Offenders and Arrestees, 2018," U.S. Department of Justice. https://bjs.ojp.gov/content/pub/pdf/revcoa18.pdf.

Berdejo, Carlos. 2018. "Criminalizing Race: Racial Disparities in Plea-Bargaining," *Boston College Law Review* 59: 1187–11250.

Bobo, Lawrence and Victor Thompson. 2010. "Racialized Mass Incarceration: Poverty, Prejudice, and Punishment," In *Doing Race: 21 Essays for the 21st Century* (eds.) Hazel Rose Markus and Paula Moya. New York: W. W. Norton.

Braga, Anthony A. and Brenda J. Bond. 2008. "Policing Crime and Disorder Hot Spots: A Randomized Controlled Trial," *Criminology* 46: 577–607.

Bulman, George. 2019. "Law Enforcement Leaders and the Racial Composition of Arrests," *Economic Inquiry* 57: 1842–1858.

Burch, Traci. 2015. "Skin Color and the Criminal Justice System: Beyond Black–White Disparities in Sentencing," *Journal of Empirical Legal Studies* 12: 395–420.

Carrega, Christina and Sabina Ghebremedhin. 2020. "Timeline: Inside the Investigation of Breonna Taylor's Killing and Its Aftermath," *ABC News*, November 17.

Carson, E. Ann. 2020. "Prisoners in 2019," Bureau of Justice Statistics. https://bjs.ojp.gov/content/pub/pdf/p19.pdf.

Cox, Adam and Thomas Miles. 2008. "Judicial Ideology and the Transformation of Voting Rights Jurisprudence," *University of Chicago Law Review* 73: 1493–1539.

Department of Justice. 2015. "Investigation of the Ferguson Police Department." www.justice.gov/sites/default/files/opa/press-releases/attachments/2015/03/04/ferguson_police_department_report.pdf.

Desilver, Drew. 2020. "In Past Elections, U.S. Trailed Most Developed Countries in Voter Turnout." Pew Research Center, March 11. www.pewresearch.org/fact-tank/2020/11/03/in-past-elections-u-s-trailed-most-developed-countries-in-voter-turnout.

Eberhardt, Jennifer. 2019. *Biased: Uncovering the Hidden Prejudice That Shapes What We See, Think, and Do.* New York: Viking.

Edwards, Frank, Hedwig Lee, and Michael Esposito. 2019. "Risk of Being Killed by Police Use of Force in the United States by Age, Race–Ethnicity, and Sex," *Proceedings of the National Academy of Sciences* 116: 16793.

Entman, Robert and Andrew Rojecki. 2000. *The Black Image in the White Mind: Media and Race in America.* Chicago: University of Chicago Press.

Farhang, Sean and Gregory Wawro. 2004. "Institutional Dynamics on the U.S. Court of Appeals: Minority Representation under Panel Decision Making," *Journal of Law, Economics, and Organization* 20: 299–330.

FBP (Federal Bureau of Prisons). 2021. "Inmate Race." www.bop.gov/about/statistics/statistics_inmate_race.jsp.

Fryer, Roland G. Jr. 2019. "An Empirical Analysis of Racial Differences in Police Use of Force," *Journal of Political Economy.* 127(3): 1210–1261.

Garcia, Tess. 2020. "People are Calling to Abolish Prison Labor. Here's What That Actually Means," Bustle.com, June 30. www.bustle.com/rule-breakers/what-does-prison-labor-really-mean-should-we-abolish-it-27626108

Gilliam, Franklin D. and Shanto Iyengar. 2000. "Prime Suspects: The Influence of Local Television News on the Viewing Public," *American Journal of Political Science* 44: 560–573.

Goff, Phillip Atiba, Matthew Christian Jackson, Brooke Allison Lewis Di Leone, Carmen Marie Culotta, and Natalie Ann DiTomasso. 2014. "The Essence of Innocence:

Consequences of Dehumanizing Black Children," *Journal of Personality and Social Psychology* 106(4): 526–545.

Government Accountability Office. 2019. "Costs of Crime: Experts Report Challenges Estimating Costs and Suggest Improvements to Better Inform Policy Decisions." www.gao.gov/products/gao-17-732.

Harden, John. 2021. "D.C. Parking, Traffic Tickets Snowball into Financial Hardships," *The Washington Post*, August 6. www.washingtonpost.com/dc-md-va/2021/08/06/dc-traffic-parking-tickets-black-neighborhoods/

Helland, Eric and Alexander Tabarrok. 2007. "Does Three Strikes Deter? A Nonparametric Estimation," *Journal of Human Resources* 42: 309–330.

Hochschild, Jennifer L. and Vesla Weaver. 2007. "The Skin Color Paradox and the American Racial Order," *Social Forces* 86: 643–670.

Hoekstra, Mark and Sandra Orozco-Aleman. 2017. "Illegal Immigration, State Law, and Deterrence," *American Economic Journal: Economic Policy* 9: 228–252.

Hurwitz, Jon and Mark Peffley (eds.). 1998. *Perception and Prejudice: Race and Politics in the United States.* New Haven, CT: Yale University Press.

Hyland, Shelley. 2019. "Justice Expenditure and Employment Extracts, 2016—Preliminary," Bureau of Justice Statistics. https://bjs.ojp.gov/library/publications/justice-expenditure-and-employment-extracts-2016-preliminary.

Kalesin, Bindu, Marcos D. Villareal, Katharine M. Keyes, and Sandro Galea. 2015. "Gun Ownership and Social Gun Culture." https://injuryprevention.bmj.com/content/injuryprev/early/2015/06/09/injuryprev-2015-041586.full.pdf.

Kastellec, Jonathan P. 2013. "Racial Diversity and Judicial Influence on Appellate Courts," *American Journal of Political Science* 57: 167–183.

Kearney, Melissa S., Benjamin H. Harris, Elisa Jácome, and Lucie Parker. 2014. "Ten Economic Facts about Crime and Incarceration in the United States," Brookings Institution. www.brookings.edu/wp-content/uploads/2016/06/v8_thp_10crimefacts.pdf.

Johnson, Rucker and Steven Raphael. 2012. "How Much Crime Reduction Does the Marginal Prisoner Buy?" *Journal of Law and Economics* 55: 275–310.

LeCount, Ryan Jerome. 2017. "More Black Than Blue? Comparing the Racial Attitudes of Police to Citizens," *Sociological Forum* 32 (S1): 1051–1072.

Lee, David S. and Justin McCrary. 2017. "The Deterrence Effect of Prison: Dynamic Theory and Evidence," In *Regression Discontinuity Designs, vol. 38, Advances in Econometrics.* Leeds, UK: Emerald Publishing, 73–146.

Levitt, Steven D. 1996. "The Effect of Prison Population Size on Crime Rates: Evidence from Prison Overcrowding Litigation," *Quarterly Journal of Economics* 111: 319–351.

Libgober, Brian. 2020. "Getting a Lawyer While Black: A Field Experiment," *Lewis and Clark Law Review* 24: 53–108.

Littletree-Holston, Kamau. 2019. "Prison Labor in the United States." https://confluence.gallatin.nyu.edu/context/interdisciplinary-seminar/prison-labor-in-the-united-states.

Lofstrom, Magnus and Brandon Martin. 2015. "Corrections Realignment Largely Successful but Challenges Remain," Public Policy Institute of California. www.ppic.org/press-release/corrections-realignment-largely-successful-but-challenges-remain.

Lopez, German. 2021. "America's Unique Gun Violence Problem, Explained in 16 Maps and Charts," *Vox*, April 16. www.vox.com/policy-and-politics/2017/10/2/16399418/america-mass-shooting-gun-violence-statistics-charts

Maruschak, Laura M. and Todd D. Minton. 2020. "Correctional Populations in the United States, 2017–2018," U.S. Department of Justice. https://bjs.ojp.gov/content/pub/pdf/cpus1718.pdf.

Migration Policy Institute (MPI). 2021. "Profile of the Unauthorized Population: United States." www.migrationpolicy.org/data/unauthorized-immigrant-population/state/US.

Moore, Tre. 2020. "On the Murders of George Floyd and Ahmaud Arbery: 'That Could Be Me'." *New Jersey Star-Ledger*, June 4.

Nagin, Daniel S. 2013. "Deterrence: A Review of the Evidence by a Criminologist for Economists," *Annual Review of Economics* 5: 83–105.

National Advisory Commission on Criminal Justice Standards and Goals. 1973. *Task Force Report on Corrections*. Washington, D.C.: Government Printing Office.

Pager, Devah. 2003. "The Mark of a Criminal Record," *American Journal of Sociology* 108: 937–975.

Pierson, Emma, Camelia Simoiu, Jan Overgoor et al. 2020. "A Large-Scale Analysis of Racial Disparities in Police Stops across the United States," *Nature Human Behaviour* 4: 736–745.

Poe-Yamagata, Eileen and Michael A. Jones. 2020. "And Justice for Some." www.nccdglobal.org/sites/default/files/publication_pdf/justice-for-some.pdf.

Rehavi, M. Marit and Sonja B. Starr. 2014. "Racial Disparity in Federal Criminal Sentences," *Journal of Political Economy* 122: 1320–1354.

Schmitt, Christopher. 1991. "Plea Bargaining Favors Whites, as Blacks, Hispanics Pay Price," *San Jose Mercury News*, December 8.

Sentencing Project. 2021. "Trends in US Corrections," www.sentencingproject.org/publications/trends-in-u-s-corrections.

Sherman, Lawrence W. and David Weisburd. 1995. "General Deterrent Effects of Police Patrol in Crime 'Hot Spots': A Randomized, Controlled Trial." *Justice Quarterly* 12: 625–48.

Snell, Tracy L. and Laura M. Maruschak. 2002. "Capital Punishment, 2001," Bureau of Justice Statistics. https://bjs.ojp.gov/library/publications/capital-punishment-2001.

Thomas, Jakana L. and Kanisha D. Bond. 2015. "Women's Participation in Violent Political Organizations," *American Political Science Review* 109: 488–506.

Travis, Jeremy and Bruce Western. 2014. *The Growth of Incarceration in the United States: Exploring Causes and Consequences*. Washington, D.C.: National Academies Press.

Viglione, Jill, Lance Hannon, and Robert DeFina. 2011. "The Impact of Light Skin on Prison Time for Black Female Offenders," *Social Science Journal* 48: 250–258.

Voigt, Rob, Nicholas P. Camp, Vinodkumar Prabhakaran, William L. Hamilton, Rebecca C. Hetey, Camilla M. Griffiths, David Jurgens, Dan Jurafsky, and Jennifer L. Eberhardt. 2017. "Language from Police Body Camera Footage Shows Racial Disparities in Officer Respect," *Proceedings of the National Academy of Sciences* 114: 6521.

Washington Post. 2023. "Fatal Force," Database. www.washingtonpost.com/graphics/investigations/police-shootings-database, last accessed May 2, 2023.

Waterman, Morgan. 2016. "Race, Segregation, and Incarceration in the States, 1920–2010." https://journeys.dartmouth.edu/censushistory/2016/10/31/rough-draft-race-segregation-and-incarceration-in-the-states-1920-2010.

Weisburd, David, Tomer Einat, and Matt Kowalski. 2008. "The Miracle of the Cells: An Experimental Study of Interventions to Increase Payment of Court-Ordered Financial Obligations," *Criminology and Public Policy* 7: 9–36.

Western, Bruce. 2006. *Punishment and Inequality in America*. New York: Russell Sage Foundation.

World Population Review. 2021. "Recidivism Rates by Country 2021." https://worldpopulationreview.com/country-rankings/recidivism-rates-by-country.

World Prison Brief. 2021. "Highest to Lowest: Prison Population Total." www.prisonstudies.org/highest-to-lowest/prison-population-total?field_region_taxonomy_tid=All.

13 Voting Rights

Dorothy Guilford knew all about the hardships that African Americans have faced in order to vote in America. Born in 1920 in Montgomery, Alabama, she lived through it all. In order to cast her first ballot, she had to pay a poll tax. The $1.50 sum might seem small today, but for a poor African American struggling to make it in the South at the time, it was a princely sum. And it was not just a one-time payment. That tax accrued every year. If she couldn't afford to pay it, she couldn't vote. Dorothy also had to pass a literacy test. Despite the barriers, she persisted and made sure her vote counted and her voice was heard.

Decades later, she walked to work every day for over a year to support the Montgomery Bus Boycott—a fight to ensure that Blacks could sit in any seat they chose on a city bus. She was also nearby when a bomb exploded on the front porch of Dr. Martin Luther King Jr.'s parsonage, and she was there when the Freedom Riders arrived in her city to register Blacks to vote. She watched in horror as those Freedom Riders—many of whom were college students on summer break—were viciously beaten by Ku Klux Klansmen while police looked away.

Because of all she saw and endured, Dorothy cherished the right to vote. That is why on the fiftieth anniversary of the Voting Rights Act in 2015 she expressed dismay at voter identification laws, felon disenfranchisement, and other ongoing efforts to limit access to the vote. Her simple message for politicians who enact laws that make it harder for racial and ethnic minorities and the poor to vote: "I don't think that's right" (Gunter 2014).

Dorothy's travails and triumphs are emblematic of the story of voting rights in America. They also mirror the themes of this chapter. Despite the fact that the United States was founded explicitly on the notion of equality for all, voting rights in this country have been anything but universal. For much of our history, most of the residents of this country have been effectively barred from voting, a situation referred to as **disenfranchisement**. Moreover, for those who have been excluded, inclusion has come from hard-fought battles. Time and time again, the extension of basic voting rights required protest and struggle. And even after basic rights were extended, those on the inside—privileged Americans who already had the franchise—often fought back, sometimes violently, to repeal or diminish those hard-fought victories. Thus, the history of voting rights is one of ebb and flow.

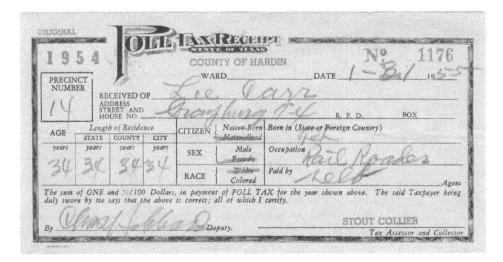

Photo 13.1 During the era of segregation in the United States, voting rights were denied to African Americans in the form of discriminatory taxation. This poll tax receipt, issued in 1955, proves that the voter has paid the $1.50 poll tax in Hardin County, Texas.
Source: Photo Heritage Art © Heritage Images Contributor/Hulton Archive/Getty Images.

Gains are won slowly and painfully over time and are often followed by periods of backlash and retrogression.

Disenfranchisement and voting rights have come up in this book multiple times, and that is because the free and fair right to vote lies at the heart of our political system. We will review the history of voting rights again here, and then we will then focus on the debates of our own times. Many of those debates continue to center on *access* to the vote and barriers such as voter identification laws, felon disenfranchisement, the purging of voter rolls, and registration requirements. Other voting rights-related topics—for example, gerrymandering, Senate malapportionment, and the Electoral College—focus on the *quality* of the vote and the ability of minority groups to influence who wins elections and what policies they pass once in office. Moreover, while much of the conversation continues to spotlight African American rights, debates have increasingly focused on the representation of immigrants and the Latino and Asian American populations. There is no such a thing as a perfect democracy, but it is clear that America's experiment with democracy is still far from complete. Real barriers to full inclusion persist.

We cannot overstate the importance of voting rights. Voting is the bedrock of democracy. Access to the vote equals access to power, and to all the other rights and privileges that can be bestowed on citizens. Without the vote, protecting one's rights is nearly impossible. As Supreme Court Justice Hugo Black wrote, "No right is more precious in a free country than that of having a voice in the election of those who make the laws under which, as good citizens, we must live. Other rights, even the most basic, are illusory if the right to vote is undermined" (*Wesberry* v. *Sanders* 1964).

What makes voting rights all the more contentious is that there are no best practices for democratic institutions. Any rules or procedures will be biased in favor of one interest or another. And perhaps most centrally, there will always be an inherent tension between majority rule and minority rights. In a democracy we want the majority to be heard and heeded. But in a democracy, we also want the minority to have a say and to have its fundamental rights protected. Indeed, much of the modern-day debate on voting rights focuses squarely on how much influence minorities should and do have.

What makes voting rights and its history particularly compelling is that the privileged few with voting rights generally get to decide whether to enfranchise previously excluded groups. Often the majority determines whether to confer rights on an excluded minority. The ability of those with existing power to shut out those without rights makes *any* expansion of voting rights remarkable. Of course, as we will see in this chapter, the courts, as the third branch of power and one that is not beholden to the people, have also often played a pivotal role in the expansion or restriction of voting rights.

America's Voting Rights History

From the moment this nation declared its independence, equality has been its mantra. As the Declaration of Independence so boldly proclaims: "We hold these truths to be self-evident, that *all men are created equal*, that they are endowed by their Creator with certain unalienable Rights, that among these are Life, Liberty and the pursuit of Happiness." But the history of voting rights in this country tells an entirely different story. It is one of stark inequality and extensive exclusion. It is a history in which many have had to fight hard and long to garner rights—rights which are only begrudgingly given and then often-times taken back. It is a history in which tremendous gains have been made but with many reversals. Clearly, further work is required.

The Nation's Founding

Although the Constitution did not explicitly define who could and could not vote, by the time of the first presidential election in 1778, only propertied White men held that privilege. Everyone else—about 95 percent of the population—was effectively powerless. That exclusion set in motion a more than 300-year-long effort to extend the franchise to all Americans regardless of race, gender, religion, or other personal characteristics.

For the better part of a century, Blacks were explicitly excluded from voting in almost all states. So too were women. Most non-European immigrants were also left out. Latinos with citizenship had a tenuous hold on the vote—meaning that they were often discriminated against and excluded by practice, if not law. When Asian Americans began to arrive in significant numbers, the 1790 Naturalization Act denied them citizenship and the vote. The role of Native Americans in American democracy was not immediately codified, but by 1856 the determination of American Indians as "subjects" rather than "citizens" effectively ruled out the vote for most of them. The only major change over the next hundred years was a gradual diminishing of property requirements, which expanded the franchise only among White men.

HOW IT HAPPENED: GROWTH AND BACKLASH—A REVERSAL ON BLACK VOTING RIGHTS

A part of the voting rights story that is not well known relates to the status of *free* Black men in America's early democracy. By the time the Constitution was ratified, free men of color actually had the right to vote in all of the thirteen original colonies except South Carolina and Georgia. But over the decades, as the number of free Blacks began to grow, efforts to curtail their vote grew as well. By the time of the Civil War, laws had been enacted to ensure that free Black men could *not* vote in any Southern state as well as in all of the newer western states. Moreover, the voting rights that Blacks had previously enjoyed in some Northern states were also being limited. When the Civil War began, Black men could vote in only five states in the Union, and all were in New England where few Blacks actually lived.[1] The backlash against the right to vote for free Black men is not unique to that era. It was not the first and it certainly wouldn't be the last time that America chose to limit voting rights.

Civil War, Reconstruction, and Its Aftermath

The first major expansion of voting rights to racial and ethnic minorities required a war. Although many Northerners found the practice of slavery abhorrent and the exclusion of Blacks from politics objectionable, a compromise between North and South kept the status quo in place until the Civil War. With the secession of southern states and the initiation of war, that compromise failed. In rapid succession, the Thirteenth Amendment formally abolished slavery, the Fourteenth Amendment extended citizenship to the formerly enslaved, and the Fifteenth Amendment proclaimed that "the right of citizens of the United States to vote shall not be denied or abridged by the United States or by any State on account of race, color, or previous condition of servitude." Just under one hundred years after its birth, the nation had finally provided African American men with access to the vote. The impact of these measures was massive. At the height of post-Civil War Reconstruction, estimates suggest that two-thirds of eligible Black men voted in

---

[1] Blacks could still vote in New York, but they faced property restrictions.

federal elections in the South (Davidson 1999). By 1872, 324 Blacks had been elected to state legislatures and Congress in former Confederate states.

But as noted above, each expansion of voting rights in America has generally been met with swift and decisive efforts at disenfranchisement. As discussed in Chapter 5 on institutional discrimination, the Compromise of 1877—an informal and unwritten deal that settled a dispute over the 1876 presidential election—led to the removal of the last federal troops from the South. Whites in the South then engaged in a vigorous and effective campaign to stamp out Black political participation. The campaign began with intimidation and violence. Rioters in cities targeted and threatened politically active Blacks. And in rural areas members of the Ku Klux Klan, a secret society of White supremacists, lynched Blacks who dared to vote or speak up. In Louisiana, for example, in less than one year, Democrats—the party typically aligned with White former Confederates—killed more than 1,000 people in their effort to regain control of the political process from the multiracial and more politically progressive Republican Party (Kousser 1974). (See Chapter 4 on individual discrimination and Chapter 5 on institutional discrimination for a fuller discussion of the violence directed against Blacks during this period.)

The most effective measures of exclusion were a series of ingenious changes to Southern state constitutions. Because constitutions could no longer explicitly bar Black participation, state legislatures developed a series of tools including poll taxes, literacy tests, and increased registration requirements to effectively reduce the Black vote. All of these measures appeared to be race-neutral and could be justified on nonracial grounds. Poll taxes, which had to be paid in order to vote could be framed as a way of generating revenue for the state. But in each case, the tool was fashioned in such a way that it primarily affected Blacks, restricting them from voting, often because the policy was applied in a discriminatory fashion or because it included grandfather clauses that Blacks could not meet. For example, if people could prove that their father or grandfather had voted prior to the abolition of slavery (when no Black person would have qualified to vote), they were exempt from paying the poll tax. In addition, the Democratic Party in Southern states barred Blacks from voting in the Democratic Primary. The measure excluded Blacks from the only meaningful election in a region that, after the end of Reconstruction, was dominated by the Democratic party.

The end result was a precipitous drop in Back turnout, which fell from a high of 61 percent in the eleven former Confederate states in 1880 to 17 percent in 1900 and 2 percent in 1912 (Fraga 2018). Over a thirty-year time span White Southerners wiped out virtually all the gains made by Black office-holders. By 1900, only five of the 324 Black elected officials in the South were still in power (Kousser 1992). In a far from rare pattern, America had once again effectively curbed the voting rights of its racial minorities.

These discriminatory electoral laws were supplemented with a broader set of rules that enforced racial segregation in schools, housing, hospitals, restaurants, and other aspects of daily life. Combined, they created a severely unequal society that defined the Jim Crow South where Blacks lived under enforced segregation from Whites for generations. The Supreme Court weighed in on these laws in 1896 in the landmark case of *Plessy* v. *Ferguson*, essentially declaring the practice of "separate but equal" to be constitutional. The Jim Crow era remained in place essentially unchanged until the middle part of the twentieth century.

TESTING THE THEORY: TAKE A LITERACY TEST

We encourage you to take the following literacy test from the state of Louisiana. Literacy tests like this one were in effect in the South until the passage of the Civil Rights Act in 1965. If you get a single answer wrong, you fail the test and you would not have been allowed to vote. (The real test was actually twice as long, but we thought we would give you a fighting chance to qualify to vote.) The tests were ostensibly race-neutral and were, it was claimed, used simply to test voter competence. But in reality, they were generally designed to weed out as many Black voters as possible. White voters were often given easier tests. Other Whites were grand-fathered in. Answers can be found at the end of the chapter.

1. Which of the following is a right guaranteed by the Bill of Rights?
_____ Public Education
_____ Employment
_____ Trial by Jury
_____ Voting

2. The federal census of population is taken every five years.
_____ True
_____ False

3. If a person is indicted for a crime, name two rights which he has.
_____
_____

4. A U.S. senator elected at the general election in November takes office the following year on what date?
_____

5. A president elected at the general election in November takes office the following year on what date?
_____

6. Which definition applies to the word "amendment"?
_____ Proposed change, as in a constitution
_____ Making peace between nationals at war
_____ A part of the government

7. A person appointed to the U.S. Supreme Court is appointed for a term of _____.

8. When the Constitution was approved by the original colonies, how many states had to ratify it in order for it to be in effect?
_____

9. Does enumeration affect the income tax levied on citizens in various states? _____

10. A person opposed to swearing in an oath may say, instead: I (solemnly) _____

11. To serve as President of the United States, a person must have attained:
    _____ 25 years of age
    _____ 35 years of age
    _____ 40 years of age
    _____ 45 years of age

12. What words are required by law to be on all coins and paper currency of the U.S.?
    _____

13. The Supreme Court is the chief lawmaking body of the state.
    _____ True
    _____ False

14. If a law passed by a state is contrary to provisions of the U.S. Constitution, which law prevails?
    _____

15. If a vacancy occurs in the U.S. Senate, the state must hold an election, but meanwhile the place may be filled by a temporary appointment made by
    _____.

16. A U.S. senator is elected for a term of _____ years.

17. Appropriation of money for the armed services can be only for a period limited to _____ years.

18. The chief executive and the administrative offices make up the _____ branch of government.

19. Who passes laws dealing with piracy?
    _____

20. The number of representatives which a state is entitled to have in the House of Representatives is based on
    _____.

21. The Constitution protects an individual against punishments which are _____ and _____.

Text courtesy of Kids Voting USA.

The Civil Rights Era

Despite the ever-present threat of retaliation and violence and despite relatively limited resources, Blacks organized in massive numbers to protest against the injustices they faced. In 1955, when Rosa Parks refused to move to the Black section of a bus in Montgomery, Alabama, she helped launch a sustained period of mass demonstrations and marches that altered the public's views on race and ultimately led to the end of Jim Crow laws. Images of nonviolent Black marchers attacked by police dogs and fire hoses convinced many Americans that something needed to be done. When Democratic politicians, including Presidents Kennedy and Johnson, realized that a new electoral strategy that incorporated racially sympathetic Whites and African Americans could garner a majority nationwide, they moved forward with the passage of several key civil rights measures including the 1964 Civil Rights Act and the 1968 Fair Housing law. The biggest of these—at least in terms of its impact on the democratic process—was the 1965 Voting Rights Act. The Act explicitly outlawed many of the tactics Whites in the South had used to limit the participation of racial and ethnic minorities, including both literacy tests and poll taxes. Importantly, section 5 of the Act included **preclearance provisions**, which required states and local jurisdictions covered by the Act to acquire the approval of the U.S. District Court before enacting new voting laws. For the first time, jurisdictions had to prove that any new procedures they implemented would not have a discriminatory impact. The Act also authorized federal examiners to go to the South to directly supervise voter registration and actively enforce these laws. These measures had an immediate and impressive impact. Black voter registration in the South increased from only 38 percent in 1965 to 65 percent by 1969. New rights had taken a long time to acquire and they came only after sustained effort, but people like Dorothy Guilford could now vote, largely unimpeded. Interestingly, the data also reveal that White turnout also grew dramatically at this time, so the ability of Blacks to influence the outcome of elections grew more marginally (Fresh 2018).

Photo 13.2 A group of voters lining up outside the polling station, a Sugar Shack small store, in Peachtree, Alabama. The Voting Rights Act was passed the previous year, May 3, 1966.
Source: Photo MPI © MPI/Stringer/Archive Photos/Getty Images.

HOW IT HAPPENED: MISSISSIPPI BURNING

One of the key events of the Civil Rights era was the Freedom Summer of 1964. Over 1,000 volunteers—most of whom were college students like yourselves—traveled to Mississippi to register as many African American voters as possible. The campaign was met with what Frank Parker in his book *Black Votes Count* has called "a reign of terror." Over the course of the ten-week campaign, Mississippi's deeply resentful White residents arrested over 1,000 volunteers as well as local Blacks trying to register, bombed or burned thirty-seven Black churches, beat at least eighty volunteers, and murdered three White volunteers and at least four Black Mississippians (McAdam 1988). The violent White reaction is an alarming illustration of how important the vote is and how far those with the vote will sometimes go to prevent others from obtaining it.

Photo 13.3 The charred remains of a station wagon which belonged to three civil rights workers—James Cheney, Andrew Goodman, and Michael Schwerner—who were murdered by men from Meridian, Mississippi. It took 41 years to obtain a conviction in that case. *Source*: © Bettmann/Contributor/Getty Images.

White Resistance to the Voting Rights Act in the 1960s and 1970s

As has been the case so many times in American history, rights given were once again taken away. As soon as the Voting Rights Act was passed, legislatures throughout the South enacted a range of inventive measures designed to reduce the influence of the minority vote. We have discussed many of these measures in previous chapters, as their legacy has in some cases lived on. For example, within a year, Mississippi's legislature passed laws that moved from single district elections in areas where Blacks were the majority to larger at-large elections where Whites were the majority and could determine the winners; gerrymandered (or re-shaped) district boundaries to maintain as many White majorities as possible; eliminated electoral offices in areas with Black majorities; required separate registration for municipal and federal elections; increased candidate requirements in ways that disproportionately barred Blacks from running; annexed outlying areas to create majority-White cities; and shortened poll hours and shifted polling locations in key sites. At times, the majority-White legislature was highly creative. For instance, in Mississippi, where the state constitution prohibits singling out individual counties in election legislation, the legislature passed a new law that required the school superintendent to be appointed rather than elected in "ANY class four county having a land area of 695 square miles, bordering on the state of Alabama, wherein the Treaty of Dancing Rabbit was signed and wherein US highway 45 and Mississippi highway 14 intersect." The area described in that law turns out to be Noxubee County, a majority-Black county that might have elected a Black super-intendent. In Mississippi and throughout the South, these measures could not prevent Blacks from voting, but they effectively reduced the influence of that Black vote.

At-Large Elections

As we highlighted in Chapter 10, one of the most effective tools used to limit voter access was and in many places still is a move to at-large elections to try to control the outcome of local elections. Instead of candidates running in their own separate districts, all candidates run in one contest that elects several officials "at-large." For example, a city might shift from a city council election in which its five members are elected by voters from five separate districts (several of which are likely to be majority-Black and therefore likely to elect Black city council members) to an at-large contest in which all the candidates run in a single citywide election. If White voters are the majority citywide, as they often were in the South, they could control the outcome of all city council seats by all voting for the same candidates. Even if African Americans made up 40 percent of the voters and voted cohesively for Black candidates, they would not have enough votes to elect a single Black council member. The same tool could be used for county boards, school boards, and other types of contests. Research shows that even today, at-large systems remain an effective tool for reducing minority representation, especially in segregated cities (Trounstine and Valdini 2008). See box, "How It Happened: The California Rights Act," for an example of the power of legislation aimed at removing at-large systems.

Racial Gerrymandering

Racial gerrymandering has been another valuable tool in the effort to suppress or undermine the Black vote. Recall from Chapter 10 that racial gerrymandering is the process of drawing district lines to limit minority gains. Figure 13.1 illustrates a racial gerrymander devised by the Mississippi state legislature to prevent the election of Black county board members. In this case, the largely Black city of Jackson was divided into five separate districts, each of which was combined with predominantly White rural areas outside the city limits to create a new majority-White district. In all five districts, White voters were able to elect White county board members. This process of splitting apart majority-Black areas to create several majority-White districts is called *cracking*. Cracking was also used to create majority-White congressional districts in the state. Even though Blacks made up about 35 percent of the state population, no Blacks were elected to Congress from 1966 to 1982.

Another means of racial gerrymandering is packing, whereby Black voters are packed together into a single overwhelmingly Black district in which many of the Black votes are wasted. Any remaining Black voters are spread across a number of other districts—all with White majorities. The result is generally that only one Black representative is elected, in the packed district, when, based on the total number of Black voters in the area, there could have been many more. Figure 13.2 illustrates both cracking and packing and how they differ from competitive districts. More specifically, the figure shows how a population that has an equal number of Democrats (represented by blue dots) and Republicans (red dots) can be

Figure 13.1 An Example of Racial Gerrymandering by Cracking, Hinds County, Mississippi.
The shaded area in this map is the city of Jackson, largely Black, which was combined with White rural areas outside the city to create five majority-White districts for the county board.
Source: Parker (1990).

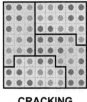

CRACKING

COMPETITIVE

PACKING

Figure 13.2 Competitive Districts Compared with Gerrymandered Districts Using Cracking and Packing

All three examples here have an equal number of Democrats (blue dots) and Republicans (red dots), but each is likely to elect a different number of Democratic and Republican officials. In the Competitive example, Republicans and Democrats have an equal chance of winning each district. In the packing example, Democrats are likely to win three districts and Republicans one. Finally, in the cracking example, Democrats are likely to win one district and Republicans the other three.

Source: The Princeton Gerrymander Project.

gerrymandered to lead to widely different electoral outcomes. The competitive map creates four districts in which either party has a fair chance of winning. The packing map groups half of the Democrats into one district (the blue area) such that the other three districts (the pink areas) are all dominated by Republicans. Finally, the cracking map splits apart Republican voters and distributes them to create three majority-Democrat districts. So, as you can see, with the same underlying population, one can create four competitive districts, three Democratic districts and one Republican district, or three Republican districts and one Democratic district. In short, how districts are drawn matters.

Gerrymandering measures have proven extremely effective over the years. Although the number of Black voters soared after the passage of the Voting Rights Act in 1965, Blacks won relatively few electoral victories as a result. In Mississippi, for example, the share of voting-age African Americans who were registered skyrocketed from just 7 percent in 1964 before the Voting Rights Act to 60 percent three years later. But the number of Black elected officials hardly changed. As late as 1976, Blacks held only 4 percent of the elective offices in a state where Blacks made up roughly 35 percent of the population (Parker 1990). Blacks remained grossly underrepresented in elective offices in all areas of the South for decades.

The Modern Struggle for Voting Rights: Minority Vote Dilution

The struggle for voting rights after 1965 was less about getting access to the vote and more about the *quality* of that vote. That is, although Blacks now had the right to vote, there were real concerns about how much their votes could actually affect election outcomes in a system that was rigged by racial gerrymandering and other factors that favored White voters. A critical development in that battle was the 1982 Amendment to section 2 of the Voting Rights Act (VRA). Congress' extension of the VRA that year did two things. First, it prohibited any voting law that had a discriminatory effect regardless of whether the law was intended to discriminate. This shift from discriminatory intent to discriminatory results made it much easier to challenge discriminatory laws. Section 2, as amended, also changed the ultimate goal of voting rights. The amended law granted minorities the right to have a fair chance "to elect representatives of their choice." That shifted the focus from access to the vote to the quality of vote. Moving forward, efforts at minority vote dilution—essentially anything that reduced the impact of the Black vote on electoral outcomes—would be actionable in court. With these legislative tools in hand, African American activists shifted the focus of the battle to the courts.

Pursuit of Voting Rights for Latinos, Asian Americans, and American Indians

While the discussion above has focused primarily on the history of voting rights for Blacks in the United States, this text has made it clear that all minority groups have been affected by voting rights issues. Women were denied the right to vote until the passage of the Nineteenth Amendment in 1920. And, as we've seen, Native Americans, Latinos, and Asian Americans have also been denied the franchise at different points in our history. Over time, each group has gained greater access to the vote in a variety of ways.

In 1924, the Indian Citizenship Act gave Native Americans citizenship and the right to vote—although many had already qualified via the Dawes Act of 1887. Asians lost the right to vote almost as soon as they arrived on American shores. They were barred from citizenship by the Naturalization Act of 1790. And the Naturalization Act of 1870 and several subsequent court cases reaffirmed their non-White status and lack of citizenship. The Chinese Exclusion Act of 1882 then barred Chinese immigration entirely. But an 1898 court case (*United States* v. *Wong Kim Ark*) concluded that native-born Chinese were, in fact, citizens (even if their immigrant parents could not be). And in 1952 the McCarran–Walter Act, which made all legal residents eligible for the naturalization process, ended legally recognized restrictions on access to the franchise for the group.

The story for Latinos has been more varied, with some obtaining official status and rights but with many attempts at exclusion. Officially, the Treaty of Guadalupe Hidalgo, the California constitution, and Texas laws proffered citizenship to the original Mexican inhabitants and their descendants within these territories. But efforts at disenfranchisement were not uncommon. In Texas, White natives called Mexican Americans "unfit to have the vote" and sought to reduce their influence by barring them from voting in the White Primary.[2] Mexican immigrants with indigenous ancestry were, for a time, denied the franchise on the basis of the Naturalization Act of 1870, which allowed Whites and "persons of African descent" to become citizens but barred other non-Whites from doing so. The Supreme Court's decision to end the White Primary—Primary contests in which only Whites were allowed to vote—in 1944 and the McCarran–Walter Act of 1952, which also confirmed that all legal Latino residents were eligible for naturalization, effectively ended the legal exclusion of Latinos from the vote.

But the end of official legal disenfranchisement did not mean the end of de facto disenfranchisement for members of either pan-ethnic group. In response to those exclusionary efforts, minority organizations such as the Mexican American Legal Defense and Education Fund (MALDEF) pushed for and won the inclusion of protections for Latinos and Asian Americans in the 1975 extension of the Voting Rights Act. By this time, the VRA also included provisions requiring that election materials be provided in a variety of languages. Subsequent research has shown that language provisions have real impacts on voter turnout and representation (Hopkins 2011; Marschall and Rutherford 2016). Also, the 1982 VRA extension gave Latinos and Asian Americans the right to bring cases of minority vote dilution. That did not stop more than twenty states from passing "English Only" laws in the 1980s, but it did help both communities increase their representation in elective offices around the nation.

HOW IT HAPPENED: THE CALIFORNIA VOTING RIGHTS ACT

Despite the passage of the Voting Rights Act in 1965, at-large elections remained commonplace. In fact, roughly two-thirds of all cities around the country continued to use at-large elections. In 2002, the California legislature attempted to rectify the problem in that state. The California Voting Rights Act (CVRA) made it easier for minorities to sue local governments because they no longer needed to demonstrate that they were large enough and concentrated enough to represent the majority of voters in a well-drawn council district. It didn't hurt that cities that lost such lawsuits would have to pay the plaintiff's court costs and damages.

The California Voting Rights Act has shown how powerful voting rights legislation can be. To date at least 335 local jurisdictions in California—city councils, school boards, and special districts—have shifted from at-large to district elections. And the gains in minority representation have been substantial (see Figure 13.3). In places that switched to district elections, Latinos increased their share of school board seats from 10.2 percent to 16.7 percent—a 64 percent growth in

---

[2] The quote is from Montejano (1987: 130–131). For more on the White Primary in Texas, see Brischetto (1987).

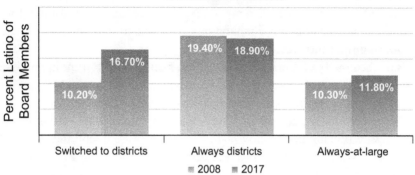

Figure 13.3 The Effect of the 2002 California Voting Rights Act on the Share of
Latino Representation
The percentage of board offices held by Latinos shows a large increase between 2008 and 2017
where elections shifted from at-large to district elections.
Source: ACLU, the California Voting Rights Act in 2018, www.advancingjustice-alc.org/wp-content/uploads/2012/11/CVRA-Fact-Sheet-12-03-2018.pdf.

representation. By contrast, Latino representation was flat in places that had always held district elections or that continued to maintain at-large elections. More sophisticated analysis confirms the impact of the CVRA on minority representation both on school boards (Abott and Magazinnik 2020) and city councils (Collingwood and Long 2019). Given that higher levels of Latino representation on school boards are associated with increases in Hispanic teaching staff, which have in turn been linked to higher graduation rates, improved test scores, and lower dropout rates for Hispanic students, the CVRA appears to have made a meaningful difference in the lives of minorities in the state.

Over time as the immigrant, Latino, and Asian American populations have grown, the nation's voting rights debates have increasingly focused on these groups. Widespread attention to unsubstantiated concerns over undocumented immigrant voting and subsequent efforts to require individuals to prove their citizenship both to register and to vote are part of that focus. There has also been debate over whether to count noncitizens in redistricting and whether to expand minority language provisions. More broadly, resentment toward Latinos and immigration is increasingly driving White's policy views on voting rights (Ramirez and Peterson 2020).

DIGGING DEEPER: NONCITIZEN VOTING

During much of U.S. history, citizenship has been one of the biggest barriers to voting rights for the Latino and Asian populations. It continues to be so today. But it does not have to be. The Constitution did not explicitly indicate who could vote.

Thus, in the early years of the Republic, individual states could determine who could and could not vote. As mentioned earlier in the chapter, most limited the vote to propertied White males. But not all. New York State's constitution, for example, proffered the vote to all male inhabitants. That meant that noncitizens had the right to vote—a right they retained for over forty years.

But when the New York state population swelled with European immigrants, residents voted to authorize a convention to revise the constitution. That new constitution, enacted in 1821, restricted the vote to citizens. Later, around the turn of the twentieth century, when immigration was peaking and not coincidentally anti-immigrant sentiments were running particularly high, noncitizens were disenfranchised in Alabama, Colorado, Wisconsin, and Oregon. Nationalism around the First World War also caused a broad retreat from noncitizen voting when seven states ended the right of aliens to vote between 1918 and 1921. All of this is yet another example of backlash and disenfranchisement in response to a growing minority or immigrant population.

Noncitizen voting has not, however, been completely eliminated. Noncitizens have had and continue to have the ability to vote at the local level in certain parts of the country. Currently, eleven local governments allow noncitizens to vote in local contests. In San Francisco, for example, noncitizen parents can vote in school board elections—a setting where noncitizen voting seems particularly justified. Noncitizen parents have children who are deeply affected by school board policies but who are too young to vote even though they may themselves be citizens. Many have called for further expansions of the right of the undocumented to vote.

Current Controversies Surrounding Voting Rights

As we saw in Chapter 6, "Public Opinion," most Americans now claim to believe that racial minorities should have a fair chance to vote and elect representatives of their choice. But exactly what fair means is very much a matter of interpretation and a source of dispute. The debates over current policy echo historical conflicts over voting rights, with one side putting forward what they claim are reasonable, race-neutral policy measures, while the other side claims that these measures are, in fact, intended to reduce minority influence. Critics also frequently demonstrate that these ostensibly race-neutral levers have racially disproportionate effects.

Whither the Voting Rights Act?

One of the biggest questions about voting rights in America today concerns the Voting Rights Act itself. In 2013, in *Shelby* v. *Holder*, the U.S. Supreme Court's conservative majority ruled that the government was using an outdated and unconstitutional process to determine which states and jurisdictions were required to get preclearance for voting rule changes. The conservative justices argued that because the Act had effectively reduced discrimination, it might no longer be needed. However, in her dissent, Justice Ruth Bader Ginsburg countered that "throwing out preclearance when it has worked and is continuing to work to stop discrimin-atory changes is like throwing away your umbrella in a rainstorm because you are not getting wet."

The differences between the Supreme Court justices as well as between politicians and advocates on both sides are essentially over how much protection minorities should have in America today. A secondary question centers on where protections are needed and whether the states and jurisdictions covered by the VRA are, in fact, still the areas most likely to seek to dilute minority vote strength. Prominent critics of the VRA, such as scholar Abigail Thernstrom, claim that the VRA goes too far (Thernstrom 1987). Thernstrom argued, like the conservative justices, that racial barriers have largely dissipated and thus the Act is no longer needed. But she goes further. In her view, the act confers special privileges on minorities and as such is not only unconstitutional but also promotes a color-conscious society.

On the other side, supporters of the VRA note that almost immediately after the *Shelby* ruling effectively removed much of the ability to enforce the VRA, states initiated a flood of new laws that could be seen as limiting the vote. Within 24 hours, Texas announced it would implement a strict photo ID law. Almost as quickly, Mississippi and Alabama began to enforce ID laws that had previously been barred though preclearance. Supporters of the VRA also maintain that the data show clearly that minorities are still disadvantaged in American democracy (Hajnal 2020). Some of the data we presented earlier in this book confirm this view. As discussed in Chapter 9, "Parties and Elections," racial and ethnic minorities still vote less than Whites. And as we showed in Chapter 11, "Does Government Carry Out the Will of the People?", when Blacks do vote, they are more apt than Whites to end up on the losing side of the vote. Perhaps, even more important, as Chapter 10 demonstrated, racial and ethnic minorities remain greatly underrepresented in elective offices nationwide. Roughly 90 percent of elected leaders are White even though only 60 percent of the population is White. Nothing in the Constitution says that minority groups are entitled to proportional representation, but the fact that minorities are still largely on the outside of the halls of power looking in raises concerns about the ongoing fairness of our democracy.

Redistricting

Another ever-present debate concerns the drawing of electoral district lines. Decisions about how boundaries are drawn—the process of redistricting—are critical to the outcome of elections. How we draw the lines and who we include and exclude can have dramatic implications for who wins and who loses—both in terms of race and partisanship. Decisions about redistricting are also unavoidable. The Constitution and subsequent court rulings have determined that district lines need to be redrawn every ten years (after the Census) to ensure that districts have equal populations.

Many factors go into redistricting decisions, with a number of goals in mind. For instance, legislators could draw lines to maximize the number of racial and ethnic minorities in office by creating as many majority-minority districts as possible. The data show that 95 percent of all Black state legislators elected in the South come from majority-minority districts (Lublin 2018). Given the effectiveness of majority-minority districts at increasing the representation of minorities in elective office, it is important to look at their constitutionality. In 1986 in *Thornburg* v. *Gingles*, the Supreme Court ruled that district lines cannot be established to dilute minority representation, but at the same time, they cannot be drawn with race as the predominant consideration. That leaves a fair amount of leeway for interpretation. But in practice, courts have supported majority-minority districts as long as the boundaries are not too irregular. Figure 13.4 shows one district that went too far. In 1996, the Supreme Court in *Bush* v. *Vera* ruled that the bizarre shape of the 30th District in Texas was unconstitutional. As Justice Sandra Day O'Connor wrote, the district "is so extremely irregular on its face that it rationally can be viewed only as an effort to segregate the races for purposes of voting, without regard for traditional districting principles."

Figure 13.4 A Black-Majority District in Texas
This image shows the boundaries of the proposed 30th Congressional District in Texas, part of the plan that was struck down by the Supreme Court in 1996.
Source: Supreme Court of the United States: 517 U.S. 952, https://en.wikipedia.org/wiki/Bush_v._Vera#/media/File:Texas_30th_CD_1991_-_1996.gif.

Alternatively, when legislators draw district lines, they might have the goal of maximizing the substantive or policy representation of racial and ethnic minorities. Academics have long debated whether majority-minority districts help or hurt Black policy interests. (For differing perspectives on redistricting to maximize Black substantive interests, see Washington (2012), Lublin (1997), and Cameron, Epstein, and Halloran (1996)). Some maintain that creating majority-minority districts can concentrate too many minority voters in one district and lead to the election of more Republicans elsewhere—Republicans who generally support more conservative polices than African Americans favor. In all probability, the goal of maximizing Black policy interests in a legislature is likely to encompass different strategies in different regions for different minority groups. In the South, for example, one study found that drawing as many districts as possible that are just barely over the threshold of being majority-minority districts maximized the degree to which the legislature pursued Black policy interests. But in other regions of the country, the same study found that an even distribution of the Black population across districts served the same purpose. We do not yet really know how to draw lines to maximize Latino or Asian American policy interests.

But what if legislators or the public were seeking an entirely different goal? What if the goal was to try to totally ignore race in drawing districts? That may not be easy at all. Because race is correlated with so many other factors that we could consider in redistricting, it is not at all clear how we could ignore race. On this point it is instructive to look back at Figure 13.1, which illustrates a severe racial gerrymander in Mississippi. In that gerrymander, the White majority legislature drew lines that "cracked" the primarily Black city of Jackson into five pieces and added heavily White rural areas to each of those five pieces to create five majority-White districts that ultimately elected five White county board members. But looked at another way, that racial gerrymander is not racial at all. One primary job of the five county board members was highway maintenance. By splitting up the city of Jackson, which contains relatively few highway miles, a severe racial gerrymander also evened out the highway mileage that each county board member needed to maintain. Indeed, that is what the majority-White legislature claimed as justification. In a sense, then, this could be seen as a case of race-neutral redistricting. But given that race is correlated with socioeconomic status as well as policy views and policy interests, it is hard to come up with a truly color-blind redistricting strategy.

Of course, as states redraw lines after the 2020 Census, the main motivation is often partisan interests. Partisans typically gain advantage the same way Whites racially gerrymandered Blacks out of offices—by packing their opponents into as few districts as possible so that many votes are wasted in extremely lopsided victories. *Rucho* v. *Common Cause*, a 2019 Supreme Court ruling, reaffirmed that there are essentially no limits on how far this kind of partisan gerrymandering can go. The end result of all of this is a new congressional map in this country that will have fewer competitive districts and more secure Republican and Democratic districts. In Texas, for example, the enumeration from the 2020 Census resulted in the state gaining two additional congressional seats, growing from 36 to 38 seats.

Fully 95 percent of the state's population growth is attributable to growth in the number of people of color—nearly half of the growth due to an increase in the Latino population in Texas. Yet the districts appear to be drawn not only to limit the success of Democratic candidates for Congress, but also to limit the number of districts that are likely to produce a Latino member of Congress.

The point to remember here is that any party that controls the redistricting process can have a massive impact on the outcome of elections in that state—especially in a closely divided state. Take North Carolina, for example. Since 2008, the statewide vote has been reasonably closely divided between Democrats and Republicans. But the actual delegation elected to Congress has varied anywhere from eight Democrats and five Republicans when Democrats controlled the maps, to ten Republicans and three Democrats when Republicans drew the lines. Those different sets of lines have been heavily litigated. Four are illustrated in Figure 13.5, which includes the 2008 Democratic-controlled map that elected mostly Democrats; the 2016 Republican-controlled map that elected mostly Republicans; as well as two more moderate alternates proposed in litigation, one of which was used in 2020.

Of course, the fact that race and party are now deeply intertwined complicates all of this. With racial and ethnic minorities voting overwhelmingly for Democrats and most Whites voting for Republicans, any partisan gerrymander is also going to be a racial gerrymander. Because Republicans have controlled more state legislatures than Democrats, they have increasingly won the gerrymandering war. As a result, in recent years redistricting across the country has more often than not hurt the representation of racial and ethnic minorities.

TESTING THE THEORY: DO-IT-YOURSELF REDISTRICTING

Visit the following website for additional information about redistricting: https://projects.fivethirtyeight.com/redistricting-maps.

Once you are there, look at the current boundaries in your own state. Then, see how subtle changes in congressional boundaries can maximize one goal over another, such as promoting competitive elections or making the districts as compact as possible, and as a result radically changing the balance of power in your state. The website also provides data on an important redistricting metric—the efficiency gap, which is a measure of how many more votes of one political party are wasted by voting for candidates that ultimately lose. Without a doubt, redistricting is complex, subtle, contentious, and important.

Felon Disenfranchisement

Felon disenfranchisement is the loss of voting rights due to a conviction for a criminal offense. It is widespread in the United States. Felon disenfranchisement laws vary widely across states, but nationwide just over 6 million Americans are currently disenfranchised for having committed a felony. The racial implications of

The Power of Redistricting: One State, Four Outcomes

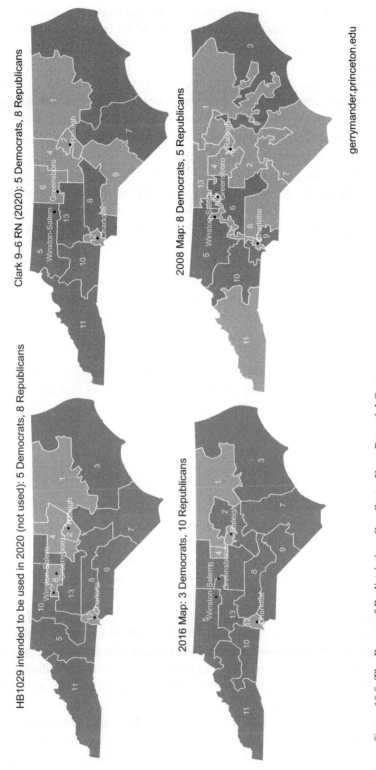

HB1029 intended to be used in 2020 (not used): 5 Democrats, 8 Republicans

Clark 9–6 RN (2020): 5 Democrats, 8 Republicans

2016 Map: 3 Democrats, 10 Republicans

2008 Map: 8 Democrats, 5 Republicans

gerrymander.princeton.edu

Figure 13.5 The Power of Redistricting: One State, Four Potential Outcomes

These four maps show the differences between the districts in North Carolina relied on in 2008, 2016, and 2020, plus an alternate proposed for 2020 that was not used.

Source: The Princeton Redistricting Project and www.newsobserver.com/latest-news/article237976679.ece/BINARY/Princeton-gerrymander-NC-maps-Wang-2dec2019.pdf.

these laws are readily apparent. While only 1 in 40 Americans is disenfranchised, the figure for African Americans is 1 in every 13 adults. Latinos are also disproportionately affected. (We documented some of the reasons for the racial disparities in the criminal justice system in Chapter 12.)

The United States stands out internationally in terms of felon disenfranchisement, both because our incarceration rates are relatively high and because our laws are relatively harsh. About half of all democracies put no voting restrictions on felons, and in all but one or two countries, felons who have completed their sentence have their voting rights restored (Sentencing Project 2021).

The debate about whether felons should be disenfranchised is heated. Proponents contend that felons have broken the social contract and have therefore forfeited their right to participate in democracy. One set of critics counters that voting rights are universal and should never be lost. Other critics agree that felons should be punished but argue that all voting rights should be restored once felons have served their time. This latter group is particularly troubled by the fact that roughly half of the disenfranchised in America have already paid their debt to society and are now out of prison. They believe that restoring voting rights for these ex-felons is not only fair and just but would also help with their reentry to society.

The arguments against felon disenfranchisement appear to be slowly winning out both in public opinion and in policy. More than two-thirds of Americans now believe convicted felons should be allowed to vote after serving their sentences (Bialik 2018). Since 2000, seventeen states have passed laws that have relaxed or eliminated felon disenfranchisement laws, while only two states have enacted more punitive laws.

WHAT IT LOOKS LIKE TODAY: FELON DISENFRANCHISEMENT LITIGATION IN FLORIDA

Nowhere is the issue of felon disenfranchisement more contentious or potentially more impactful than in Florida. Approximately one-quarter of all the disenfranchised reside in Florida. Moreover, the state's law leads to stark racial disparities. Fully 21 percent of African Americans in Florida are disenfranchised. That dwarfs the 1 in 10 adults who are disenfranchised statewide.

The number and share of Blacks disenfranchised in the state are particularly noteworthy given that Florida is such an important swing state. When Florida provided the decisive electoral votes in the 2000 presidential election, the margin of victory was 537 votes. At the time, an estimated 600,000 disenfranchised felons resided in the state. Given that most of the felons were Black or Hispanic—groups that overwhelmingly vote Democratic—it seems likely that the state's felon disenfranchisement law won the election for George W. Bush and the Republican Party.

In 2018, 65 percent of Floridians voted in favor of an amendment to allow all persons convicted of a felony (except murder or sexual abuse) to regain their voting rights after completing their sentence. Previously, felons in the state faced a lifetime

Photo 13.4 Michael Monfluery stands in a Miami-Dade courthouse corridor following a special court hearing aimed at restoring the right to vote under Florida's Amendment 4, passed in November 2018. In March 2019, a state law was passed that limited Amendment 4, requiring former felons to either pay all fees that they owe as part of their case or get their sentence modified in order to register to vote, effectively disenfranchising potentially thousands of eligible voters simply because they are too poor to pay such fees.
Source: Photo Zak Bennett © Zak Bennett/Contributor/AFP/Getty Images.

ban from voting. However, the state legislature subsequently passed a law, SB7066, which required ex-felons to pay off existing fees, which were difficult to determine, before regaining their right to vote. Critics liken this extra step to the poll taxes that were used to disenfranchise Blacks in former Confederate states. Felons' rights advocates sued the state over SB7066, but the case is still ongoing. All the while Florida continues to be a critical swing state.

Voter Identification Laws

Voter identification laws—that is, laws that request or require people to provide identification in order to vote—represent another seemingly race-neutral mandate that can have a widely disproportionate racial impact. But unlike felon disenfranchisement laws, voter ID laws are proliferating. In 2006, only one state required photo identification to vote on election day. Today, eleven states require identification, and thirty-five states, with more than half the nation's population, have some version of voter identification rules.

Opinions vary about these fast-multiplying laws. Proponents claim that ID laws are necessary to reduce fraud and to restore trust in the democratic system. Backers also note that these laws are popular among the public and also claim that they do not preclude legitimate voters from participating. According to these supporters, the laws raise no new barriers for the vast majority of Americans because they have identification. Moreover, they represent a small, easily surmounted hurdle for the subset of Americans who do not have identification.

On the other side, critics claim that voter ID laws limit the legitimate participation of racial and ethnic minorities and other disadvantaged groups who often do not have the correct IDs. Critics also note that there is little documented evidence of voter fraud (more on that below) and thus little reason to enact these laws in the first place. They contend that Republican leaders are passing these laws to hijack the democratic process and bias outcomes in their favor.

Racial minorities are undoubtedly being targeted by voter ID laws. First, strict photo ID laws are passed almost exclusively in states controlled by Republicans, and they tend to emerge in states where minorities represent a larger share of the population (Biggers and Hanmer 2017). Moreover, in some cases the laws appear to be designed to target one particular minority group. For example, North Dakota's voter identification law is the only ID law to require identification with a street address. Given that tribal IDs generally do not include a street address, and given that many Native Americans only have tribal IDs, the law seems tailored to exclude Native Americans. Studies also show that racial and ethnic minorities are less likely than Whites to have ready access to valid identification (Barreto et al. 2018). And evidence indicates that these laws are unevenly implemented. For example, research reveals that poll workers disproportionately ask minorities for identification (Atkeson et al. 2010). Finally, while research on the effects voter identification laws have on turnout has reached mixed conclusions, the emerging evidence indicates that racial and ethnic minority turnout often falls disproportionately when these laws are passed but that mobilization efforts against these laws can also at times spur increased turnout (Kuk et al. 2020; Valentino and Neuner 2017).

WHAT IT LOOKS LIKE TODAY: THE MYTH OF VOTER FRAUD

Allegations of voter fraud tend to attract attention, and President Trump attracted a lot of attention by making claims of widespread voter fraud. First, he asserted that millions of illegal votes cost him the popular vote in 2016. He later lamented that the "Republicans don't win and that's because of potentially illegal votes … Sometimes they go to their car, put on a different hat, put on a different shirt, come in and vote again" (Rupar 2018). And it was not just Donald Trump. For years, Republican elites around the country have made similar comments about widespread electoral fraud to justify strict voter identification laws, voter roll purges, and other steps to limit the vote.

Photo 13.5 An election worker verifies signatures on mail-in ballots on the day of the Recall election at the Orange County Registrar in Santa Ana, CA.
Source: © Gina Ferazzi/Contributor/*Los Angeles Times*/Getty Images.

However, the overwhelming scholarly and legal consensus indicates that voter fraud is extraordinarily rare. When legal scholar Justin Levitt tracked allegations of in-person voter fraud—the only kind of fraud that voter identification laws can combat—he found only thirty-five credible cases across a period when over 800 million votes were tallied. As he noted, "It is more likely that an individual will be struck by lightning than he will impersonate another voter at the polls" (Levitt 2007). Another study used an experiment that allowed individual Americans to admit to voter fraud without getting caught. They then used the same type of experiment to determine how many Americans thought they had been abducted by extraterrestrials. Their conclusion: "The population reporting voter impersonation is indistinguishable from that reporting abduction by extraterrestrials" (Ahlquist, Mayer, and Jackman 2014). Fraud rarely, if ever, affects American elections, yet it is regularly used as a justification for altering electoral laws.

The fact that research has demonstrated that fraud is rare and inconsequential has not, unfortunately, put this issue to rest. In fact, accusations of fraud and electoral irregularities have only grown more central to American democracy and have made the future of our democracy all the more perilous. Donald Trump's claims that the 2020 presidential election was stolen from him, his efforts to overturn the results of the contest, and his reluctance to support a peaceful transition of power—a hallmark of every true democracy—have led to a constitutional crisis that threatens the future of our democracy. Even though there is no evidence of widespread fraud in 2020, Trump's false claims have resonated with large segments of the public and have been echoed repeatedly by Republican elites around the country. These false claims and the intense divisions they have helped to create have put our democracy more at risk than at almost any other time in our history.

Other Means of Controlling Voting

Disputes over voting have also recently focused on a set of measures that make the process of voting either easier or harder. The list of convenience voting measures—laws that make the process of voting easier—includes everything from offering mail-in ballots and more ballot drop boxes, to early voting, to more polling locations and longer poll hours. Studies suggest, however, that most of these measures have only a limited impact on overall turnout. But the concern has often been that restricting these measures can reduce minority turnout. For example, in 2018, a set of North Carolina measures placed limits on early voting, ended a policy of preregistering high-school students, stopped same-day registration, and created a new strict photo identification law. In response to a lawsuit an appeals court struck the law down, noting that the legislators had acted with "discriminatory intent." In addition, the court found that the changes "target African Americans with almost surgical precision" (Domonoske 2016). As many of these measures—both restrictive and expansive—are relatively new, more research needs to be done before we can assess their impact on the racial balance of voters. However, in the following sections, we will take a closer look at four controversial voting measures.

Poll Closures and Unequal Wait Times

Poll closures appear to have been particularly problematic for racial and ethnic minority voters. A report issued in 2019 by the Leadership Conference on Civil and Human Rights analyzed voting location closures in the states that fall under the jurisdiction of the Voting Rights Act (Leadership Conference Education Fund 2019). They found that in those states more than 1,600 polling places had closed since the *Shelby* decision—most of them in minority communities.

A disparity in voting wait times also presents a potential avenue for discrimination. Recent research found substantial racial disparities in voter wait times during the 2016 U.S. presidential election (Chen et al. 2019). Studying smartphone data, the researchers determined that "residents of entirely-black neighborhoods waited 29 percent longer to vote and were 74 percent more likely to spend more than 30 minutes at their polling place" compared with residents of entirely White neighborhoods. The disparity holds when comparing predominantly White and Black polling places within the same states and counties.

Purging of Voter Rolls

A new battle is also emerging over the purging of voter rolls, a process by which inactive or ineligible voters are dropped from voter registration lists. Every election cycle, millions of Americans are dropped from these voter lists—most because they have moved, died, or are otherwise ineligible. Voter roll maintenance is required by federal law. But if the process is done unevenly or overly aggressively, it can be used as voter suppression. Voters who are mistakenly dropped from the list cannot vote until they re-register. One of the most contentious cases occurred in Georgia, where the then Secretary of State, Brian Kemp, purged over a million voters, employing the catch phrase "Use it or lose it." When one batch of purged names turned out to be 70 percent Black in a state that is only 32 percent Black, Kemp was accused of deliberately disenfranchising Black voters. This was particularly troubling because Kemp was running for governor at the time and was essentially purging Black voters who were likely to vote for his opponent, Stacey Abrams. With more states pushing to more aggressively remove voters, the chance of a voter purge altering the outcome of an election is increasing.

Registration Laws

Electoral laws that govern registration often stand out for their impact on turnout. As we noted in Chapter 7, "Political Participation," the United States is relatively rare in that it requires voters to go through a process of registration. That extra hurdle has in the past reduced turnout by as much as 10 percentage points relative to other countries (Jackman 1987). Similarly, states with the easiest registration processes (including election-day registration) have turnout that is higher than states with more arduous registration rules. In an effort to expand turnout, a number of states have implemented measures to make registration almost costless, including same-day registration and opt-out motor voter registration, which automatically registers citizens when they interact with government agencies unless the individual chooses to opt out. It is not yet clear how much impact these registration laws have on the racial composition of the electorate.

Senate Malapportionment

One voting rights issue that gets relatively little attention but, nevertheless, has substantial racial implications is senate malapportionment. By that, we mean that states with small populations get the same representation in the Senate—two senators—as states with large populations. That malapportionment was actually the result of a Great Compromise between smaller and larger colonies at the founding of the nation. Smaller colonies feared their voices would be drowned out if Senate representation was proportional to population size. In order to get the Constitution passed, larger colonies had to compromise.

Today, that compromise puts vastly different weights on different votes. Wyoming, with half a million people, gets exactly the same representation—two senators—as California, a population with 41 million people. Thus, the voting power of a citizen in Wyoming is about sixty-seven times that of a citizen in California.

This creates stark racial disparities, as African Americans and Latinos disproportionately live in states with larger populations and Whites disproportionately reside in states with smaller populations. As a result, studies have shown, African Americans and Latinos have less influence than Whites over governmental policy (Griffin 2006; Malhotra and Raso 2007). Demographic projections suggest that this problem will become even worse for Latinos in the future.

The Electoral College

The Electoral College consists of a complex system of constitutional provisions, political party rules, and state and federal laws. But at its heart, its effect is that American voters only elect the president indirectly and that the state-level Electoral College vote, not the popular vote, ultimately determines who wins. Given that the candidate who won the popular vote in both 2000 and 2016 ended up losing the election, and given real concerns that this could happen again, there have been increasing calls to abolish the Electoral College and to instead let the voters directly elect the president. Also, given that the party that racial and ethnic minorities tend to favor—the Democratic Party—was on the wrong side of the Electoral College in both 2000 and 2016, the issue can be viewed as a racial one. Amending the Constitution in this case is unlikely, but the National Popular Vote Interstate Compact, an agreement by states to award all their electoral votes to whichever presidential candidate wins the overall popular vote, has already been adopted by fifteen states representing 36 percent of the Electoral College. If a few more states sign on and the compact passes the 50 percent Electoral College threshold, the Electoral College will be a vestige of history.

The net effect of many of these disenfranchising laws—from the Electoral College to Senate malapportionment to voter identification laws and felon disenfranchisement—may be to foster minority rule. Specifically, many worry that these laws have been and will continue to allow a declining White majority to retain political power long after they lose their majority status and the United States becomes a majority-minority nation. Exactly how the fight over voting rights will proceed as America changes demographically is a fascinating and foreboding question that we cannot yet answer.

Conclusion

As Dorothy Guilford's lifelong struggle to be an active participant in American democracy demonstrates, our democracy has for much of its history strayed from the country's founding notion that all are created equal and have inalienable rights. The story of voting rights in this nation is one of high ideals coexisting with great inequality and widespread exclusion. We have noted that America's democracy has, over the course of time, become more and more inclusive. But, as we have also noted, greater inclusion has generally only occurred after prolonged struggle by those on the outside. Moreover, those on the inside have often vigorously and sometimes violently resisted those efforts. And even after rights have been given, the gains have often been reversed. To be very explicit, the White majority has often deliberately chosen to resist the expansion of the franchise to the minority population. Thus, the history of voting rights is very much one of ebb and flow—gains followed by backlash and retrogression.

The battle over voting rights persists today. Some of the current controversies continue to focus on access to the vote (e.g., voter identification laws and felon disenfranchisement laws), but since the passage of the Voting Rights Act (and its subsequent weakening when preclearance was ended in the *Shelby* decision), much of the struggle has been (and continues to be) over the quality of the vote. Racial and ethnic minorities want their votes to count as much as those of Whites, a wish that has often been flouted by race-neutral but highly effective tools like at-large elections, racial gerrymandering, and the purging of voter rolls.

The resistance of so many Americans for such a long time to a fully inclusionary electoral system is in some ways understandable. Access to the vote is access to power. And rare is the group that willingly gives up power. Moreover, there are legitimate debates about minority influence in a majoritarian democracy. We want the majority to be heard, but we also want to protect minorities from harm and exclusion. Since there are no best practices for democracy, it may be difficult to know how much influence racial and ethnic minorities should have.

Nevertheless, America clearly needs to do better in ensuring that all citizens have the same ability to vote and to influence government policies. The fact that minorities vote less often than Whites; the fact that when the votes are counted, minority votes end up on the losing side of the vote more than White votes; and the fact that some 90 percent of all elected officials are White all indicates that we have a long way to go before achieving an equal and open democracy.

As the nation looks forward, we should continue to look for ways to reduce barriers as well as to identify reforms that will incorporate a broader set of Americans in the democratic decision-making process. The simplest and most effective of these would be mandatory voting (sometimes called universal voting), which requires all eligible citizens to participate and fines those who do not show up at the polls. But barring such a drastic and unlikely move, voting-rights advocates are likely to continue to push for an expansion to automatic registration (or opt-out registration), greater access to mail-in ballots, expanded early voting, and more polls and longer poll hours. Somewhat outside the conventional box are alternative electoral systems like proportional representation (where seats are distributed according to each party's share of the overall vote), cumulative voting (where voters who get multiple votes for multiple offices can choose instead to gain some influence by using all of those votes on one office), and ranked choice voting (where voters not only indicate their first choice but also rank other candidates in order so that voters who favor third party candidates with little chance of winning do not have to waste their votes). These less conventional measures are garnering a lot of attention, and all have been tried in at least a few locations nationwide. For immigrants' rights activists and those interested in broader participation, anything that makes the naturalization process easier and faster would be a welcome change. Finally, one of our favorite reforms is to shift the timing of local elections so that they are held on the same day as statewide or national contests (see Chapter 7, "Political Participation" for a full description). This move has the potential to double turnout in localities that currently hold off-cycle elections—roughly 70 percent of the nation. It would also likely significantly increase the share of voters coming from communities of color and could, in turn, lead to local government policies that are more in line with minority interests. In short, it could radically alter local democracy to make it more inclusive.

Literacy Test Answers

1. Trial by jury only
2. False (every 10 years)
3. Habeas Corpus (immediate presentation of charges); lawyer; speedy trial.
4. January 3
5. January 20
6. Proposed change, as in a constitution
7. Life (with good behavior)
8. Nine
9. Yes
10. Affirm
11. 35
12. In God We Trust
13. False
14. U.S. Constitution
15. The governor
16. Six
17. Two
18. Executive
19. Congress
20. Population (as determined by census) less untaxed Indians
21. Cruel and unusual

KEY TERMS

Cracking
Efficiency gap

Felon disenfranchisement
Mandatory voting (universal voting)
Packing
Preclearance provisions
Redistricting
Senate malapportionment
Voter identification laws

DISCUSSION QUESTIONS

1. How much influence should a minority group have in a majoritarian democracy?
2. What kind of tools has the White majority used to limit the access of racial and ethnic minorities to the vote?
3. What kind of tools has the White majority used to dilute the quality of the racial and ethnic minority vote?
4. What is the best way to draw district lines? Which goal or goals should guide the drawing of district lines? Explain your answer.
5. Are felon disenfranchisement laws justified or discriminatory?
6. Are voter identification laws justified or discriminatory?
7. How might legislators make access to American democracy broader and more equitable?

ANNOTATED SUGGESTED READINGS

See Frank Parker. 1990. *Black Votes Count: Political Empowerment in Mississippi after 1965*. Chapel Hill: University of North Carolina Press, for an excellent account of the struggle for voting rights in the South.

See Henry Flores. 2015. *Latinos and the Voting Rights Act: The Search for Racial Purpose.* Washington, D.C.: Lexington Books, for a detailed discussion of Latinos and the Voting Right Act using Texas as a case study.

See Jessica L. Trounstine and Melody Ellis Valdini. 2008. "The Context Matters: The Effect of Single Member vs At-Large Districts on City Council Diversity," *American Journal of Political Science* 52: 554–569, for an insightful analysis of the effect of at-large elections on minority representation.

See Charles Cameron, David Epstein, and Sharyn Halloran. 1996. "Do Majority-Minority Districts Maximize Substantive Black Representation in Congress?" *American Political Science Review* 90: 794–812, providing a deeper understanding of how redistricting can shape both descriptive and substantive representation.

For two different perspectives on the debate about *Shelby* and the merits of the Voting Rights Act, see: Abigail Thernstrom. 2013. "A Vindication of the Voting Rights Act," *Wall Street Journal*, June 26; and The New York Times Editorial Board. 2013. "An Assault on the Voting Rights Act," *New York Times*, June 25.

See Jeff Manza. 2006. *Locked out. Felon Disenfranchisement and American Democracy*. Oxford: Oxford University Press, for a comprehensive analysis of how felon disenfranchisement impacts American democracy.

See John Kuk, Zoltan Hajnal, and Nazita Lajevardi. 2020. "A Disproportionate Burden: Strict Voter Identification Laws and Minority Turnout," *Politics, Groups, and Identities* 10(1): 126–134, for a discussion of the impact of voter identification laws on racial and ethnic minority turnout.

CHAPTER REFERENCES

Abbott, Carolyn and Asya Magazinnik. 2020. "At-Large Elections and Minority Representation in Local Government," *American Journal of Political Science* 64(3): 717–733.

Ahlquist, John S., Kenneth R. Mayer, and Simon Jackman. 2014. "Alien Abduction and Voter Impersonation in the 2012 U.S. General Election: Evidence from a Survey List Experiment," *Election Law Journal: Rules, Politics, and Policy* 13: 460–475.

Atkeson, Lonna Rae, Lisa Ann Bryant, That Hall, Kayle Saunders, and Michael Alvarez. 2010. "A New Barrier to Participation: Heterogeneous Application of Voter Identification Policies," *Electoral Studies* 29: 66–73.

Barreto, Matt A., Stephen Nuño, Gabriel R. Sanchez, and Hannah L. Walker. 2018. "The Racial Implications of Voter Identification Laws in America," *American Politics Research* 47: 238–249.

Bialik, Kristin. "How Americans View Some of the Voting Policies Approved at the Ballot Box," Pew Research Center, January 15. www.pewresearch.org/fact-tank/2018/11/15/how-americans-view-some-of-the-voting-policies-approved-at-the-ballot-box.

Biggers, Daniel R. and Michael J. Hanmer. 2017. "Understanding the Adoption of Voter Identification Laws in the American States," *American Politics Research* 45: 560–588.

Brischetto, Robert R. 1987. "Latinos in the 1984 Election Exit Polls: Some Findings and Some Methodological Lessons," In *Ignored Voices: Public Opinion Polls and the Latino Community* (ed.) Rudolfo O. de la Garza. Austin: Center for Mexican American Studies, University of Texas.

Cameron, Charles, David Epstein, and Sharyn Halloran. 1996. "Do Majority-Minority Districts Maximize Substantive Black Representation in Congress?" *American Political Science Review* 90: 794–812.

Chen, Keith, Kareem Haggag, Devin G. Pope, and Ryne Rohla. 2019. "Racial Disparities in Voting Wait Times: Evidence from Smartphone Data," NBER Working Papers.

Collingwood, Loren and Sean Long. 2019. "Can States Promote Minority Representation? Assessing the Effects of the California Voting Rights Act," *Urban Affairs Review* 57(3): 731–762.

Davidson, Chandler. 1999. *Minority Vote Dilution.* Cambridge, MA: Howard University Press.

Domonoske, Camila. "U.S. Appeals Court Strikes Down North Carolina's Voter ID Law," *NPR.* www.npr.org/sections/thetwo-way/2016/07/29/487935700/u-s-appeals-court-strikes-down-north-carolinas-voter-id-law.

Fraga, Bernard. 2018. *The Turnout Gap: Race, Ethnicity, and Political Inequality in a Diversifying America.* New York: Cambridge University Press.

Fresh, Adriane. 2018. "The Effect of the Voting Rights Act on Enfranchisement: Evidence from North Carolina," *Journal of Politics* 80: 713–718.

Griffin, John D. 2006. "Senate Apportionment as a Source of Political Inequality," *Legislative Studies Quarterly* 31: 405–432.

Gunter, Booth. 2014. "Alabama Woman, at 94, Reflects on Poll Taxes, Literacy Tests and New Efforts to Limit Voting," Southern Poverty Law Center. www.splcenter.org/news/2014/11/02/alabama-woman-94-reflects-poll-taxes-literacy-tests-and-new-efforts-limit-voting-0.

Hajnal, Zoltan. 2020. *Dangerously Divided: How Race and Class Shape Winning and Losing in American Politics*. Cambridge: Cambridge University Press.

Hopkins, Daniel J. 2011. "Translating into Votes: The Electoral Impacts of Spanish-Language Ballots," *American Journal of Political Science* 55: 814–830.

Jackman, Robert W. 1987. "Political Institutions and Voter Turnout in Industrial Democracies," *American Political Science Review* 81: 405–424.

Kousser, Morgan. 1974. *The Shaping of Southern Politics: Suffrage Restriction and the Establishment of the One-Party South, 1880–1910*. New Haven, CT: Yale University Press.

Kousser, Morgan. 1992. "The Voting Rights Act and the Two Reconstructions," In *Controversies in Minority Voting: The Voting Rights Act in Perspective* (eds.) Bernard Grofman and Chandler Davidson. Washington, D.C.: Brookings Institution, 135–176.

Kuk, John, Zoltan Hajnal, and Nazita Lajevardi. 2020. "A Disproportionate Burden: Strict Voter Identification Laws and Minority Turnout," *Politics, Groups, and Identities* 10(1): 126–134.

Leadership Conference Education Fund. 2019. "Democracy Diverted: Polling Place Closures and the Right to Vote." http://civilrightsdocs.info/pdf/reports/Democracy-Diverted.pdf.

Levitt, Justin. 2007. "The Truth about Voter Fraud," The Brennan Center for Justice. www.brennancenter.org/our-work/research-reports/truth-about-voter-fraud.

Lublin, David. 1997. "The Election of African Americans and Latinos to the U.S. House of Representatives, 1972–1994," *American Politics Quarterly* 25: 269–286.

Lublin, David. 2018. "Eight White-Majority Districts Elected Black Members of Congress This Year. That's a Breakthrough," *Washington Post*, November 19.

Malhotra, Neil and Connor Raso. 2007. "Racial Representation and U.S. Senate Apportionment," *Social Science Quarterly* 88: 1038–1048.

Marschall, Melissa J. and Amanda Rutherford. 2016. "Voting Rights for Whom? Examining the Effects of the Voting Rights Act on Latino Political Incorporation," *American Journal of Political Science* 60: 590–606.

McAdam, Doug. 1988. *Freedom Summer*. Oxford: Oxford University Press.

Montejano, David. 1987. *Anglos and Mexicans in the Making of Texas, 1836–1986*. Austin, TX: University of Texas Press.

Parker, Frank R. 1990. *Black Votes Count: Political Empowerment in Mississippi after 1965*. Chapel Hill: University of North Carolina Press.

Ramirez, Mark D. and David A. M. Peterson. 2020. *Ignored Racism: White Animus toward Latinos*. Cambridge: Cambridge University Press.

Rupar, Aaron. 2018. "Trump's Latest Make-Believe about Voter Fraud: Dems Change Shirts and Vote Twice." *Vox*, November 14. www.vox.com/2018/11/14/18095592/trump-voter-fraud-disguises-cars-daily-caller-interview.

Sentencing Project. 2021. "Voting Rights in the Era of Mass Incarceration: A Primer." www.sentencingproject.org/publications/felony-disenfranchisement-a-primer.

Thernstrom, Abigail. 1987. *Whose Votes Count? Affirmative Action and Minority Voting Rights*. Cambridge, MA: Harvard University Press.

Trounstine, Jessica L. and Melody E. Valdini. 2008. "The Context Matters: The Effects of Single-Member Versus At-Large Districts on City Council Diversity," *American Journal of Political Science* 52: 554–569.

Valentino, N. A. and F. G. Neuner. 2017. "Why the Sky Didn't Fall: Mobilizing Anger in Reaction to Voter ID Laws," *Political Psychology* 38(2): 331–350.

Washington, Ebonya. 2012. "Do Majority Black Districts Limit Blacks' Representation? The Case of the 1990 Redistricting," *Journal of Law and Economics* 55: 251–274.

14 Race and the Shaping of American Social Policies

It was not until early March 2020 that most Americans confronted the nearly unprecedented challenges associated with the coronavirus pandemic. By July of that year, reported deaths in America attributed to COVID-19 had skyrocketed to over 150,000. For Tashina Nunez, a nurse in Yakima County, Washington, these statistics were not just a shocking abstraction. During this time, she noticed that many of the patients she treated were familiar to her. They were either acquaintances or recognizable people from her community—and, most importantly, they were, like her, also members of the Yakama Nation.[1] Although the county is named for the local indigenous population, members of the Yakama Nation only make up about 7 percent of the county residents. However, in Ms. Nunez's estimation, a much higher fraction of the COVID-19 patients she saw were Native American. Still, because the hospital did not record information on race or ethnicity she could only rely on her informal observations. "Not being counted is not new to us," she reported in a story covered in the *New York Times* (Conger, Gebeloff, and Oppel 2021). In the absence of reliable data, public health officials in general, and Yakama Nation leaders in particular, were unable to direct the necessary resources to the communities most in need. "You don't know how bad it is until it is too late," said Ms. Nunez.

The situation regarding the disproportionate Native American incidence of COVID-19, and the difficulty of documenting this pattern, is not peculiar to Yakima County, Washington. The Centers for Disease Control and Prevention (CDC) has reported that according to information drawn from twenty-three of the fifty states, Native Americans (including Alaskan Natives) have infection rates that are 3.5 times as high as non-Hispanic Whites. Additionally, the Navajo Nation—as at May 2021, the largest federally recognized tribe in the United States, and the Indigenous group with the largest reservation covering parts of Utah, Arizona, and New Mexico—has more per capita cases and deaths from the coronavirus than any of the fifty states. However, "because reporting to the CDC is voluntary, federal data paint an incomplete picture of the prevalence of COVID-19 infection [among Native Americans]" (Hlavinka 2020).

The Indigenous population is not the only minority community to experience disproportionate fatalities from the coronavirus pandemic. According to official

---

[1] Although the county is named for the Native American tribe, the spelling is slightly different.

Photo 14.1 Nate Phillips, a member of the Omaha Nation Native American Indian tribe bows his head in prayer during the closing ceremony on November 30, 2020, for the "In America: How Could This Happen . . .," an outdoor public art installation of white flags as a reminder of the lives lost to COVID-19 in the United States. Volunteers led by artist Suzanne Firstenberg planted the flags in a field for each life lost. Native Americans were particularly hard hit during COVID-19. *Source*: Photo Roberto Schmidt © Roberto Schmidt/Contributor/AFP/Getty Images.

statistics, Hispanics, Blacks, as well as Native Hawaiians and Pacific Islanders were also more likely than non-Hispanic Whites to contract the virus and were more likely to die as a result. As at November 2021, the CDC reported that almost all groups are more likely to die from the virus compared with non-Hispanic Whites. In a country where Whites represent almost two-thirds of the population, non-Hispanic Whites have the most COVID-19 fatalities, but holding population size constant, the data shows that *the rate* at which non-Whites die from contracting the virus is much higher relative to Whites. Specifically, the CDC reports that Native Americans and Alaskan Natives are 2.2 times more likely than non-Hispanic Whites to die from COVID-19.[2] The comparable figure for the Hispanic population is 2.1 times higher than Whites. And African Americans are 1.9 times more likely than non-Hispanic Whites to die from the coronavirus. Asian Americans die as a result of contracting the virus at about the same rate as non-Hispanic Whites according to these data.

---

[2] These data are based on age-adjusted COVID-19 death rates standardized to the 2019 US standard COVID-NET catchment population, see at: www.cdc.gov/coronavirus/2019-ncov/covid-data/ investigations-discovery/hospitalization-death-by-race-ethnicity.html, last accessed December 15, 2021.

The disproportionately high rates of hospitalizations and fatalities among different racial and ethnic groups in the United States during the COVID-19 pandemic stand as a stark reminder of the longstanding impact of the nation's social policies on certain populations. This can be traced back to a variety of factors, including discrimination in the healthcare industry and the fact that these groups already suffer disproportionately from disadvantaged social conditions (e.g., poverty, crowded or inadequate housing, the inability to work from home, etc.) and pre-existing medical conditions (e.g., high blood pressure, diabetes, obesity, etc.) that make them more susceptible to the virus. Why are disadvantaged minority groups more likely to suffer from adverse social circumstances and have pre-existing medical conditions? In many cases, these outcomes are the inevitable result of decades of federal, state, and local social policies.

We have referred to social and public policies in the discussion of racial inequities throughout this book, but in this chapter we will directly address some of the politics surrounding these programs and investigate how these debates are implicated by considerations of race and ethnicity. As we will see, and as illustrated in the discussion above, even social issues that appear to be race-neutral at first glance—such as the devastating impact of the COVID-19 pandemic—can have vastly disparate racial impacts.

Social and Public Policy in the United States

Social policy refers to public policies in the domains of healthcare, education, housing, labor, human services, and social welfare (e.g., assistance to individuals and families in need). In Chapter 5, we discussed how various social programs implemented in the nation's past, particularly those, such as the Freedmen's Bureau, which was enacted during and after Reconstruction, have revealed a pattern of social bias that has had a generational impact on populations. Criminal justice practices also fall into this category, as we saw in Chapter 12. Social policies in each of these domains are generally conceived as efforts to address inequalities across various groups defined by class, race, gender, or age, and to bring conditions on the ground up to standards regarded as acceptable in society. For example, the stated goal of housing policy has been to provide adequate and affordable housing to American families. In a July 2021 press briefing from President Biden he noted that, "We need to deal with the shortage of affordable housing in America. Over 10 million renters in this country pay more than half their income for the rent on their apartment, and the lack of affordable housing prevents people from moving to communities where there are more opportunities" (Biden 2021). As we have seen in earlier chapters, these lofty goals are not always (or even often) met. Similarly, in the case of education, most would agree that children should have access to adequate schooling to acquire, at a minimum, the rudimentary literacy and citizenship skills needed to function in modern society. Unfortunately, the United States still has a long way to go before we reach these goals for all members of society. And when these goals are not met, there can be long-lasting consequences that persist across generations.

Development of Anti-Poverty Policies

As we have discussed in several chapters of this book, the United States stands apart from other advanced democracies of the world in many respects. Mass incarceration is a uniquely American phenomenon. So, too, is the inviolable and constitutionally protected right to own guns and the inordinate levels of gun ownership and gun violence in America. So, too, are the levels of extreme income inequality unseen in any other advanced economy. The United States is also anomalous and divergent in its social policies. The conventional wisdom is that the United States, despite its enormous wealth and status as the leading economic power in the world, is a "welfare laggard," unusually slow and ungenerous in providing basic social benefits like universal healthcare coverage, unemployment benefits, paid leave, and income support.

As a share of gross domestic product, the United States allocated 18 percent on social programs in 2019. France, Italy, Germany, and the United Kingdom, by contrast, allocated 31, 28, 25, and 21 percent, respectively. The contrast is even starker in terms of welfare programs in the form of income support to the working-age population. Here, the United States spent only 1.5 percent of its GDP, compared with 5.3, 4, 3.4, and 3.9 percent for France, Italy, Germany, and the UK, respectively.[3] In other areas of social policy, the United States remains the only advanced industrialized nation without paid family medical leave, to allow Americans to care for a new child or a family member with serious medical illness. And in healthcare, while the United States spends more than twice the average of advanced industrialized countries, it remains one of the few Organization for Economic Cooperation and Development (OECD) nations without universal healthcare coverage, even with the passage of the Affordable Care Act in 2010.

A chief reason for, and constant theme underlying, America's conspicuous under-investment in a social safety net for the have-nots is the enduring role of race and racial politics. Race-based considerations have helped to shape the country's social policies in a number of ways. In some cases, these policies have reduced racial hierarchies, but in other instances they have reinforced these disparities. Public opinion and the media have played a strong role in this process, especially in the development of anti-poverty programs.

American Views on and Media Coverage of Poverty

Relative to most wealthy democracies, the United States spends comparatively little on social welfare policies (Alesina, Glaeser, and Sacerdote 2001). In particular, the United States spends less money on efforts to reduce poverty than most other industrialized nations (Prasad 2016). One common explanation for the distinctiveness of the United States when it comes to social welfare spending is that Americans

---

[3] Source: OECD at: www.oecd.org/els/soc/OECD2020-Social-Expenditure-SOCX-Update.pdf.

Photo 14.2 A homeless camp on Bloomington, Indiana's west side in disarray after residents were evicted in October, 2022.
Source: Photo Jeremy Hogan © SOPA Images/Contributor/LightRocket/Getty Images.

are less supportive of such policies than are the citizens of other countries. According to this argument, Americans view the poor as lazy and undeserving whereas they envy the rich and, perhaps unrealistically, hope to someday join their ranks. In *Class Attitudes in America: Sympathy for the Poor, Resentment of the Rich, and Political Implications* Spencer Piston (2018) challenges this familiar narrative.

Piston examined nationally representative survey data from the 2008 American National Election Study (ANES) and found that respondents frequently provided spontaneous mentions of either the rich (19 percent) or poor (15 percent) when describing the parties and presidential candidates. The overwhelming majority (92 percent) of comments about the poor were positive and the vast majority (87 percent) of comments about the rich were negative. Also, using survey data of his own design from 2013–2014, Piston reports that a majority or large plurality of respondents support over a dozen downward redistributive policies. However, of the three exceptions to this rule—welfare, aid to Blacks, and the estate tax—two implicitly or explicitly involve race. Results from the 2020 ANES provide similar results. Most (59 percent) Americans support raising the minimum wage and increasing federal spending on the poor (51 percent), but less than one-third (29 percent) support increased spending on welfare programs. In short, Americans mostly support redistributive social policies except when those policies are associated with Blacks.

Do Americans overestimate the number of Blacks on welfare and, if so, does this influence their attitudes about this policy? These questions are addressed in some detail in Martin Gilens' 1999 book, *Why Americans Hate Welfare*. He reported that Americans—although he focuses only on White attitudes—do in fact overestimate the number of Blacks who are poor and who are on welfare. Moreover, Gilens described how White Americans' perceptions of welfare are linked up with attitudes about race. Specifically, the author examined nationally representative survey data and found that the main reason Whites oppose welfare policy is because of their belief that African Americans are lazy and therefore undeserving of welfare benefits. The author demonstrated this finding in several ways. First, Gilens showed that Whites who endorse the negative stereotype that Blacks are lazy were most likely to oppose increased welfare spending, even after accounting for partisanship, ideology, and negative attitudes about poor people in general. Additionally, using an experimental design, the author randomly assigned study participants to learn about a single mother on welfare described as either Black or White. Respondents with negative views of this welfare recipient were much more likely to oppose welfare spending when the mother was described as Black.

Race and Social Policy Throughout U.S. History

Racial division and racial hierarchy have been featured prominently in each of the four eras of significant social policy reforms in United States history: the Progressive era of the late nineteenth and early twentieth centuries; the New Deal era of the 1930s; the Great Society era of the 1960s; the neoliberal turn in the 1990s. In the Progressive era, the provision of welfare and social protections from disability, misfortune, and ruthlessness of private enterprises was largely left to local communities and churches. Municipalities often kept "poorhouses" for those who were too old or otherwise unable to work. These poorhouses generally offered abject living conditions and anyone living in them was subject to shame and stigma. In this era, African Americans were largely excluded from any public welfare by virtue of where they lived: the vast majority of Blacks still lived in the South, where they were subject to Jim Crow segregation and almost wholly denied any citizenship rights, including social rights such as support for the poor.

Public charity through poorhouses were eventually supplemented with benefits for veterans of the Civil War and pensions for mothers. The mothers' pensions, however, were at the initiative of state legislatures, and the aid was principally targeted to benefit White women (Neubeck and Cazenave 2001; Ward 2005). As one important study describes this period, by the end of the Progressive era, there were three distinct political and racial economies of welfare relief describing the South (where a disproportionate number of the poor were African American), the North (where the majority were immigrant-based White ethnics), and the southwest (where large numbers were Mexican Americans). Relief was most steady and flush in the North, where Eastern and Southern European immigrant groups channeled their demands to support the needy through organized political machines. And relief was significantly more meager elsewhere. In the South, tenant farming and Jim Crow laws and norms meant that most Blacks had to rely on the private paternalism of White plantation owners and community leaders. In the southwest, the precarity of seasonal migrant labor and racism against Mexicans and Mexican Americans resulted in perhaps the worst conditions at the time. Despite the fact that, according to the laws of the day, they were legally "White," Mexicans and Mexican Americans in the southwest were generally cast as "lazy" and "undeserving" and denied any social rights of citizenship and, with the onset of the Great Depression, trainloads were involuntarily deported to Mexico (Fox 2012).

This initial era of social benefits for "mothers and soldiers" was ultimately replaced by a more serious and sustained federal effort starting with the New Deal policies of the 1930s. In 1935, specifically, Congress and President Franklin Delano Roosevelt enacted the Social Security Act, which included the Aid to Dependent Children program, a program that would become known over the years as "welfare." On paper, the programs of this era represented a breakthrough in the social rights of African Americans. Like many sweeping laws in U.S. history, however, the Social Security Act of 1935 was a feat of negotiation and compromise. In this case, the coalition needed to secure its passage included Southern Democrats, who were opposed to the idea of a federal aid program that might potentially upend the existing Jim Crow social order of the South.

The resultant of the negotiation and compromise was a bill that included, among other things, several provisions that would further exacerbate rather than ease racial inequalities, as discussed previously in Chapter 5. One was that the implementation of the Aid to Dependent Children program (later Aid to Families with Dependent Children) would be left to the states and the program (like "mother's pensions" programs before it) was written in racially and morally coded ways to benefit the "deserving poor." Another was that Southern White congressmen insisted on excluding certain jobs from old-age insurance coverage—most notably, agricultural laborers and domestic servants, a labor force that was predominantly Black at the time. These occupations were also denied the right to organize into unions and the exclusionary policies were not limited to the Social Security Act. The GI Bill, which leap-frogged millions of Americans into middle-class jobs and homeownership, was implemented locally, which effectively meant that almost all Blacks in the South were excluded. One study, for instance, found that of 3,229 home, business, and farm loans backed by the GI Bill in Mississippi in 1947, only two such loans went to Black veterans. The net effect of such policies and provisions was a jump start of broad and generous benefits to Whites that left out many Black Americans. One prominent scholar thus describes this period as an era "when affirmative action was white" (Katznelson 2005, 2013; Lieberman 1998; Williams 2003).

A third era of major social reform came about in the mid-1960s, as the United States envisioned ushering in a "Great Society." Beyond the monumental twin laws, the Civil Rights Act of 1964 and the Voting Rights Act of 1965, President Lyndon Johnson declared the urgency of a "war on poverty" to stamp out structural barriers to equality. From community action programs to efforts to address hunger and housing, these programs initially had measurable impacts on racial inequality. From 1959 to 1969, poverty rates among African Americans declined from an alarming 55 percent to a still high 32 percent; Black high-school graduation rates increased from 39 percent to 56 percent; the income ratio between Whites and Blacks dropped from 1.93 to 1.63 (Massey 2011). These were hard-fought gains that were direct federal responses to decades of de jure and de facto segregation in the South and decades of protest demands for both political, social, and economic equality in the South and beyond in the United States. The progress and commitment to close the gap on racial inequality, however, ultimately floundered and fell flat for reasons that scholars and politicians continue to debate today. Northern liberals grew reluctant to embrace social and economic rights as the Civil Rights Movement moved outside the South; the nation's attention became divided and its resources strained as a result of America's entanglement in an unpopular war in Vietnam; movement activism from Blacks evolved into more aggressive demands for swifter, sweeping changes and erupted in urban uprisings in America's cities. These are among the reasons cited for the failed campaign to achieve a Great Society.

The politics of race played a crucial role through these three eras in which the United States government made serious and sustained efforts to alleviate poverty and address injustice. That continued to be the case in the most recent era of welfare reform in the mid-1990s. This period saw the convergence of neoliberalism and paternalism under the aegis of a Democratic president, Bill Clinton. The rise of neoliberalism in the 1980s and 1990s generated pressures to privatize the provision of public goods and more generally to apply economic logics to all spheres of life, pressures that were reinforced by conservative scholars who argued that public assistance programs were a cause of poverty and not a solution to it and that working was a social obligation of citizenship (Mead 1984). The "new paternalism" in social policy saw a redefined role of government policy to direct and supervise those in need, effectively "telling the poor what to do" and how they should pull themselves out of poverty (Mead 1988). Neoliberalism and paternalism together produced reforms like the Personal Responsibility and Work Opportunity Reconciliation Act (PRWORA) of 1996, which replaced the previous Aid to Families with Dependent Children program for income support with a new program named Temporary Aid to Needy Families (TANF). The language of "personal responsibility" and "temporary aid" reflected the political mood of the times, which was more focused on addressing "welfare dependency" than attacking poverty.

AFDC and the Depiction of the Poor in America

Although many Americans have negative views of welfare recipients and mistakenly believe that Blacks make up most beneficiaries, this has not always been the case. The public's linkage of Blacks with poverty and welfare began in the 1960s. Prior to this time, Black poverty was mostly ignored and poverty at the national level was viewed as a "White problem" (Katznelson 2005). Gilens argued that three factors led to changes in these perceptions. The first was the widespread migration of African Americans from the rural South into different northern cities in the 1940s and 1950s. Because of this migration, many northern cities, which had previously been overwhelmingly White, saw a dramatic increase in their African American population. The second change that was necessary for setting the stage for the racialization of poverty was the changing racial composition of the recipients of the most prominent "welfare" policy, Aid to Families with Dependent Children (AFDC). As noted in Chapter 5, most Blacks were initially prevented from accessing AFDC benefits when the program was launched in the 1930s. Over time however, as Blacks gained more political clout, these restrictions were loosened, and the Black percentage of AFDC recipients increased from about 13 percent in 1936 to a high of 46 percent in 1973. Lastly, the urban uprisings of the 1960s (e.g., Watts, Detroit, Newark, etc.) brought renewed media attention to the plight of poor Blacks.

According to Gilens, the changing demographics of the urban North and of AFDC recipients, along with the civil disturbances of the mid-1960s all contributed to the racialization of poverty. But how do we know if he is correct? Gilens tested his theory by examining press coverage on the issue of poverty over a forty-two-year period. In particular, he examined press coverage in three weekly news magazines: *Time, Newsweek*, and *U.S. News and World Report* between 1952 and 1992. Overall, he examined 1,256 stories. He also tracked the poverty rate over the same time period to assess whether changes in poverty coverage were being driven by changes in the poverty rate.

Two important trends emerge from this analysis. First, the number of news stories devoted to poverty in *Time, Newsweek*, and *U.S. News and World Report* increased dramatically after about 1964. The numbers remained high into the mid-1970s and then began to decline, until they rose again in the early 1980s. What is perhaps most noteworthy about this last increase is that it coincides with a general decline in the poverty rate. In short, the press devoted more attention to poverty just as the percentage of Americans in poverty was declining. The second trend involves *how* the poor are depicted by the press. During the forty-year period of his study, Gilens also examined whether stories on poverty were accompanied by photographs of Whites or African Americans. Overall, he identified 6,117 images in these stories, and of these images race could be determined in about 72 percent (4,388). Gilens found that during this forty-year period, Blacks represented over half (53 percent) of all poor people shown in these magazines, even though Blacks actually represented only 29 percent of the poor during this period. Interestingly, the percentage of Blacks depicted in news images about the poor is not constant throughout this forty-year period. In fact, the depiction of the Black poor increased dramatically in 1964, going from about 27 percent (which was roughly their true percentage in the population), to 53 percent in 1965–1966, and reaching as high as 75 percent of all photographs depicting the poor in 1972. Gilens reported that, since the late 1960s, Blacks have represented about 57 percent of all poor people depicted in news magazines—about twice their true proportion among Americans living in poverty.

Gilens found that the press did not simply link poverty to Blacks after the mid-1960s, but they also adopted a more critical tone. That is, after the mid-1960s, neutral descriptions of anti-poverty programs such as AFDC disproportionately showed pictures of White Americans, but stories about welfare abuse or inefficiency disproportionately showed pictures of Black Americans. Gilens also engaged in comparable analyses of network television news. He found the same pattern of results—although the effects were somewhat greater on network television—with the news overreporting images of Blacks when covering stories about poverty, especially when such stories were negative.

TANF and Continuing Racialized Public Opinion

In 1996, the AFDC program was abolished and replaced with Temporary Aid to Needy Families (TANF), a far more restrictive anti-poverty program which also provided more discretion to the states in terms of how benefits were structured. For example, unlike AFDC, the new TANF program imposed time limits on how long a family could receive aid and attached conditions to this support, such as work requirements. On paper, the policies and programs were race-neutral, but racial considerations motivated these reforms and racial consequences defined their outcomes. The lead-up to enacting PRWORA in 1996 were several decades of political rhetoric on "welfare cheats" and "welfare queens," prevailing stereotypes of Blacks and Latinos as "lazy," and media coverage that associated "Black" with "poor" in the minds of Americans (Fox 2004; Gilens 1999). The new TANF policy was ostensibly designed to address the shortcomings of the AFDC program, most notably the concern that it discouraged recipients from working. Considering these reforms, the media bias and public misperceptions regarding Blacks and anti-poverty programs should have been diminished if not eliminated. However, more recent work finds little support for this proposition. Following the work of Gilens (1999), Dyck and Hussey (2008) analyzed photos in the same news magazines from 1999 to 2004. They found that during this time Blacks made up about 25 percent of the poor but were represented in pictures of the poor in *Time*, *Newsweek*, and *U.S. News and World Report* about 43 percent of the time. Similarly, analyzing survey data from 1992 to 2004, they found that negative racial stereotypes about Blacks contributed about as much to opposition to welfare after TANF replaced AFDC, as before this transition. Our own analysis of the 2020 American National Election Study survey data reveals similar results. Even after accounting for demographic factors like education and income, as well as political factors such as ideology and partisanship, the belief that Blacks are less hardworking than Whites is significantly associated with White opposition to welfare spending in 2020. Negative views about African Americans do not, however, affect support for other anti-poverty programs such as raising the minimum wage.[4]

---

[4] Authors' analysis of the 2020 American National Election Study.

Views on Race in the Implementation of Anti-Poverty Programs

Although racial considerations may influence how anti-poverty programs are covered in the press and how the public thinks about these programs, does it also affect how these policies are implemented? The consensus in the scholarly literature is that race does influence the design and execution of anti-poverty programs. This is particularly true in the case of both AFDC and, later, TANF. For instance, even before the successful welfare reform efforts of the late 1990s, states were more likely to seek waivers—allowing them to modify the traditional AFDC program—imposing time limits and work requirements in areas where the welfare caseloads were disproportionately made up of African Americans (Fording 2003). Research focusing on the period *after* welfare reform found similar results. One such study by Soss and his colleagues (2001) found that the one factor most consistently linked to state restrictions on welfare benefits, including family caps, work requirements, and time limits, was the size of the minority population. Another, more recent, study finds that in states where Whites are more inclined to embrace negative stereotypes about Blacks a lower percentage of TANF expenditures are allocated to basic cash assistance (Fusaro 2020). In both cases, researchers argue that specifically *anti-Black attitudes* are responsible for the more punitive allocation of welfare benefits. These results are also reflected in the 2020 American National Election Study survey data. As indicated previously, one of the most powerful determinants of White opposition to welfare spending is the belief that Blacks are lazier than Whites. Indeed, the strength of the statistical association between negative racial stereotypes about Blacks' work ethic and opposition to welfare spending is similar to that of partisanship and exceeded only by political ideology. In contrast, similar analyses relying instead on the belief that Hispanics or Asian Americans are lazier than Whites has only a weak or statistically insignificant impact on White attitudes about welfare spending.

HOW IT HAPPENED: AFFIRMATIVE ACTION

On June 4 1965, Lyndon Baines Johnson made an unusual trip for a President of the United States at that time. President Johnson traveled 2 miles across town from the White House to Howard, a historically Black university. He was at Howard ostensibly to deliver a commencement address but sought with his words to signal a radical new federal commitment to equality in America. Johnson celebrated the new freedoms secured for Black Americans by the recently enacted Voting Rights Act of 1965, but then added that:

Freedom is not enough ... You do not wipe away the scars of centuries by saying: Now you are free to go where you want, and do as you desire, and choose the leaders you please. You do not take a person who, for years, has been hobbled by chains and liberate him, bring him up to the starting line of a race and then say, "you are free to compete with all the others,"

Photo 14.3 On June 28, 1978, following the Supreme Court's decision in the *Allan Bakke* case, Black leaders Vernon Jordan of the Urban League, Robert Hooks of the NAACP, and the Reverend Jesse Jackson of People United to Save Humanity (PUSH) hold a joint news conference. Hooks called the decision "a clear-cut victory for voluntary affirmative action." *Source*: © Bettmann/Contributor/Bettmann/Getty Images.

and still justly believe that you have been completely fair. Thus it is not enough just to open the gates of opportunity. All our citizens must have the ability to walk through those gates.[5]

President Johnson's speech at Howard is often seen as an early time-stamp on the origins of one of the most controversial policy initiatives in the last half century, affirmative action. Johnson followed up his Howard speech with Executive Order 11246 that same year, which required federal government contractors to "take *affirmative action* to ensure that applicants are employed, and that employees are treated during employment, without regard to their race, color, religion, sex, or national origin [emphasis added]." It was not until 1969, however, that the Nixon Administration's Labor Department issued its ambitious "Philadelphia Plan" to require specific "goals and timetables" to counter a long history of racial discrimination in that city's construction industry. In the following years, the Nixon Administration broadened their efforts to other federal agencies. At the same time, many elite universities began to revamp their admissions policies with the goal of admitting more minority students. By 1972, Congress amended the Civil Rights Act of 1964 to include provisions against discrimination on the basis of race, religion, and nationality in educational institutions.

---

[5] The full text of the speech is available at: www.presidency.ucsb.edu/documents/commencement-address-howard-university-fulfill-these-rights.

These early efforts to put Johnson's words to deeds survived mounting legal challenges. In 1978, however, the arc of affirmative action took a sharp turn with the *Regents of the University of California* v. *Bakke* case. The Supreme Court, in a divided 5–4 decision, deemed unconstitutional any admissions policies that set quotas for specific racial minorities. Justice Lewis Powell, who broke the deadlock between liberal and conservative judges, penned a more narrowly tailored legal justification for allowing affirmative action programs to continue. This justification defined a "compelling state interest" where such programs in university settings produced the specific educational benefit of a diverse student body or workplace. This "diversity" rationale supplanted any rationale rooted in rectifying historical or ongoing discrimination and served as the basis for adjudicating several decades of further legal challenges to affirmative action, including recent high-profile challenges to the college admissions policies at the University of Michigan (*Gratz* v. *Bollinger*, *Grutter* v. *Bollinger*) and the University of Texas (*Fisher* v. *University of Texas at Austin*).

Throughout the history of affirmative action, public support for such programs has been deeply contested. In California (in 1996) and Michigan (in 2006), ballot initiatives passed banned the use of race, national origin, sex, or religion in public institutions, effectively prohibiting any affirmative action programs. In public opinion polls, views are highly dependent on how the program is defined. The American National Election Studies, for instance, has long asked a single question: "are you for or against preferential hiring and promotion of blacks?" Asked this way, roughly three out of every four Americans oppose such policies.[6] A 2003 survey by the Pew Research Center similarly asks about programs to "to improve the position of blacks and other minorities ... if it means giving them preferential treatment," and 72 percent of Americans are opposed. However, in the same 2003 Pew survey, when Americans were instead simply asked if they supported "affirmative action programs designed to increase the number of black and minority students on college campuses," 60 percent agreed. Also in the same survey, 63 percent supported programs "designed to help blacks, women, and other minorities get better jobs and education."[7]

In addition, public opinion on affirmative action is also deeply divided by race. Whites are far more likely to oppose affirmative action than are Blacks, with Latinos and Asian Americans generally closer to Blacks than Whites. In the 2003 Pew survey above, only 54 percent of Whites supported programs to increase the number of underrepresented minorities in colleges while 77 percent of Latinos and 87 percent of Blacks favored such programs. In the 2012 National Asian American Surveys, 82 percent of Asian Americans supported "programs designed to help blacks, women, and other minorities get better jobs and education."

[6] See at: https://cpsblog.isr.umich.edu/?p=338, last accessed September 12, 2022.
[7] See at: www.pewresearch.org/politics/2003/05/14/conflicted-views-of-affirmative-action, last accessed September 12, 2022.

In short, on the whole Americans support the goals of affirmative action policies. But that support is divided by race, and it is further divided by the means to achieve those goals if the means entail taking race or gender into account when making hiring or college admissions decisions.

This polarization in public opinion reminds us that while President Johnson's speech at Howard University more than a half century ago held the promise of unifying a divided nation, the politics and rhetoric around affirmative action today threaten to further trouble a country already plagued by white nationalism, xenophobia, polarization, and anti-government insurrection. As we write this text, the U.S. Supreme Court is poised to hear a lawsuit against Harvard University (*Students For Fair Admissions, Inc.* v. *President and Fellows of Harvard College 2022*). Most observers expect the Court to use this case to further restrict, if not ban altogether, affirmative action programs as unconstitutional. The legal activist behind the lawsuit is notable for recruiting Asian Americans to enlist as plaintiffs in a transparent strategy to pit one racial minority group against others. A parallel fight on affirmative action is being played out in the halls of many urban "magnets," elite public high schools where admissions to the schools are based on entrance exams and where the student bodies are overwhelmingly Asian American while Blacks and Latinos remain vastly underrepresented.

The district court hearing on the Harvard case portrayed an admissions process that evokes our discussion in Chapter 5 on how inequality is baked into institutions. The judge's "finding of facts" shows that Harvard gives many other forms of preferential consideration to applicants: when they are children of alumni, athletes, children of the university's faculty and staff, and children whose parents or relatives donated large sums of money to the university. These are factors that in most instances disproportionately advantage White applicants. If Asian American students are disadvantaged, it is largely through Harvard's use of subjective "personality ratings" and through these other forms of preferential treatment, and not through affirmative action programs.[8] Admissions to the most elite, selective universities in America is thus not a zero-sum game where gains to Blacks, Latinos, and other underrepresented minorities necessarily require losses to Asian American applicants.

It is clear that if the Supreme Court rules affirmative action programs unconstitutional, it will be even harder for Blacks, Latinos, and other underrepresented minorities to gain a toehold in elite institutions of higher education. In 1996, voters in California passed Proposition 209, effectively banning affirmative action programs in public education, jobs, and contracting. Proposition 209 resulted in a drop in the enrolment of underrepresented minorities on every University of California campus, especially UCLA, Berkeley, and UC San Diego where the percentage of underrepresented minorities enrolled declined from 16 percent the year before Proposition 209 was implemented to 10 percent the year after. This shift in

---

[8] See Judge Burroughs' "Findings of Facts and Conclusion of Law" at: www.harvard.edu/admissionscase/wp-content/uploads/sites/6/2021/06/2019-10-30_dkt_672_findings_of_fact_and_conclusions_of_law.pdf.

enrolments, furthermore, had and continues to have long-term consequences on lost potential wages for these applicants.[9]

We have focused the previous theme box largely on affirmative action in higher education, but the lost wages for Blacks, Latinos, Native Americans, and Pacific Islanders due to bans on affirmative action in states like California and Michigan are an important reminder that policies have consequences beyond higher education. In the workplace and in public contracting, audit studies and other social science research continue to find rampant employment discrimination as we saw in Chapters 4 and 5. Affirmative action, for as long or as short as it survives legal challenges, is an area of social policy today where moral principles meet political millstones. It is also a policy that directly and durably opens Lyndon Johnson's "gates of opportunity" for underrepresented minorities who would otherwise not be able to walk through those gates.

Here are a few questions to ponder as you consider your own views on affirmative action: Is President Johnson's view that "freedom is not enough" still true today? Do your views on affirmative action vary depending on whether its targeted beneficiaries underrepresented racial minorities or other groups? Do they depend on which racial minorities are targeted? Do they vary depending on whether the programs concern jobs rather than schools? Are background characteristics like gender and race the only ways in which "preferential treatment" factors in employment and education decisions?

Development of Education Policy

The federal government exerts considerable influence on social policies in this country. However, one area where this influence is more limited is with education policy. This is because most of the funding for public schools (K-12) originates at the local or state level, and not the federal level. Still, despite the limited role that the national government plays in funding local schools, it can still exert control in various other ways, most notably through the federal court system. Arguably, the most notable example of the federal court's influence on education policy at the state and local level is with the case of *Brown* v. *Board of Education of Topeka, Kansas*.

The Federal Court Rules on School Segregation

As discussed in Chapter 5, the 1896 U.S. Supreme Court decision in *Plessy* v. *Ferguson* declared that racially segregated public facilities were constitutionally permissible. This decision, establishing the principle of "separate but equal,"

---

[9]   See Zachary Bleemer, "Affirmative Action, Mismatch, and Economic Mobility after California's Proposition 209," Berkeley Center for Studies in Higher Education Research and Occasional Paper Series, August 2020, at: https://cshe.berkeley.edu/sites/default/files/publications/rops.cshe.10.2020.bleemer .prop209.8.20.2020_2.pdf.

allowed for the maintenance and proliferation of segregated schools throughout the South. Although the civil rights organization, the National Association for the Advancement of Colored People (NAACP) Legal Defense and Educational Fund (LDEF), sought to challenge this practice in the federal courts throughout the 1930s and 1940s, these efforts were only partially successful until the *Brown* decision. The case commonly referred to as *Brown* v. *Board of Education* involved a series of challenges to the system of school segregation that were unsuccessful at the U.S. District Court level. The NAACP Legal Defense and Educational Fund sought an appeal to the district court decision by bringing their case to the U.S. Supreme Court in 1952. The argument of the civil rights organization was that the principle of separate but equal violated the equal protection clause of the Fourteenth Amendment to the Constitution. Segregation in public schools and other public accommodations was therefore unconstitutional. The Supreme Court rendered their decision on May 17, 1954. They agreed, unanimously, that the principle of separate but equal was incompatible with the equal protection clause. As a result, segregation mandated by law was declared to be unconstitutional.

Despite the momentous decision in *Brown* v. *Board of Education*, segregation did not go away overnight. For one thing the Supreme Court, in a follow-up decision involving the implementation of desegregation (often referred to as *Brown II*), called for these efforts to proceed with "all deliberate speed." This phrase was widely interpreted as contradictory—deliberate implies slow and cautious, whereas speed suggests quickness—and vague. In practice, the vagueness allowed for political forces in the South that opposed desegregation to organize in opposition. This opposition was manifest in what came to be known as the program of "massive resistance," originating with the efforts of U.S. Senator Harry F. Byrd (D-Virginia) and followed shortly thereafter by the "Southern Manifesto." This manifesto, which called for open defiance of the Supreme Court decision in the *Brown* case, was signed by nineteen U.S. senators and eighty-two U.S. House members—all of whom hailed from the eleven states that had previously joined the Confederacy during the Civil War.

Largely because of the open defiance of the Supreme Court decision in the *Brown* case, an estimated 99 percent of southern Blacks were still attending segregated schools as late as 1964, ten years after the Court declared segregation unconstitutional (Orfield 2001). And, although not legally mandated in most regions outside the South, in the mid-1960s most Black students attended segregated schools throughout the nation (Reardon and Owens 2014). In the 1968 Supreme Court case, *Green* v. *County School Board of New Kent County*, the court finally took a more forceful stance on the issue of desegregation. Additionally, with the 1971 *Swann* v. *Charlotte Mecklenburg* case, the Supreme Court ordered districts to use busing—where White or Black children would be bussed to schools outside their neighborhood—to achieve racially integrated schools. Lastly, in 1973, the Supreme Court ruled in *Keyes* v. *School District #1, Denver Colorado*, that districts that had never practiced legal (de jure) segregation could still be required to use busing even if their districts were segregated in practice (de facto). This case ensured that busing and other desegregation enforcement efforts would not just be confined to the South but would also include Northern school districts. With these decisions, the Court essentially held that school districts throughout the country must develop concrete plans to bring about integration. Shortly thereafter, hundreds of local school districts were operating under court-ordered desegregation plans and many other districts were motivated to act because of the threat of such mandates. As a result, Black–White school segregation levels declined significantly from the late 1960s through the mid-1970s (Reardon and Owens 2014).

The Supreme Court's commitment to desegregation would prove to be fleeting. The policy of busing to achieve racially integrated schools was controversial and deeply unpopular among Whites.[10] Prominent politicians such as President Richard Nixon, California Governor (and future president) Ronald Reagan, and Delaware Senator (and future president) Joe Biden publicly opposed the policy. In a 1974 case, *Milliken* v. *Bradley*, the Supreme Court effectively undermined its previous decisions and held that busing could not be used in the metro-Detroit area so that Black students from the city could attend the same schools as wealthy, and mostly White, students in the surrounding suburbs. In short, busing could be used only within a school district but not across school district lines. Given the persistence of de facto housing segregation, with Black and White families typically living in different school districts, this decision would eventually lead to the end of busing as a tool to achieve integrated schools.

School Segregation since the 1980s

Since the early 1980s, school segregation levels between Blacks and Whites, as well as between Hispanics and Whites, and Asians and Whites, have remained mostly stagnant (Reardon and Owens 2014). Local, state, and federal policies have generally led to this outcome as described earlier. What are the consequences of our collective deemphasis on school desegregation? In other words, do racially integrated schools make a difference? The preponderance of evidence suggests that they do. For example, the achievement gap—the disparity between the performance of White and non-White students on standardized tests—is significantly lower in racially integrated schools. In one of the more comprehensive studies on this question, Reardon (2016) examined over 100 million test scores for grades 3 through 8 in over 300 metropolitan areas from 2009 to 2012. He focused on the effects of school segregation on both White–Black and White–Hispanic achievement gaps. Reardon found that segregation, and particularly the greater likelihood that Black and Hispanic students compared with White students attended schools with classmates who are poor, was significantly associated with larger achievement gaps. According to Reardon (2016: 47), "racial segregation—specifically racial differences

---

[10] See at: www.washingtonpost.com/national/effective-but-never-popular-court-ordered-busing-is-a-relic-few-would-revive/2019/07/07/dce439c8-9d40-11e9-b27f-ed2942f73d70_story.html.

in exposure to poverty—accounts for roughly one-fifth of the average racial achievement gap."

Reardon's study suggests that educational outcomes are heavily reliant on the availability of resources, and that these disparities are often tied to race. In short, the quality of education for ethnic and racial minorities is at least partially dependent on the amount of money available for their school districts. Jackson, Johnson, and Persico (2016) reach a similar conclusion. They note first that local schools are typically funded partially by local property taxes such that wealthier communities have more resources to direct toward their schools. However, because Hispanic and Black families are less likely to own homes, and the homes they do own are devalued at least in part because of institutional discrimination, their communities tend to operate with a lower tax rate with which to fund the local schools.[11] And school funding levels matter for quality-of-life indicators measured years after students have graduated. For example, Jackson and his colleagues (2016) examined over 15,000 students born between 1955 and 1985 to see if per-student spending was associated with educational attainment and adult earnings. They found that per-pupil spending made little difference for affluent children. In the case of low-income students, however, they found that as little as 10 percent increased spending in each year from first grade to the last year of high school was associated with about half-a-year of additional post-secondary education, 10 percent higher earnings, and a 6 percent reduction in poverty. Moreover, "a 25 percent increase in per-pupil spending throughout one's school years could eliminate the average attainment gaps between children from low-income and non-poor families" (Johnson and Nazaryan 2019).

Resource Disparities for Blacks in Higher Education

Racial inequities in educational policy are not confined to primary and secondary (K-12) schools. These issues also emerge in funding for colleges and universities. Colleges and universities (post-secondary schools) in America have also been segregated, and minority serving institutions (MSIs) have historically been underfunded by the government. The first set of institutions of higher learning dedicated to educating non-White populations were Historically Black Colleges and Universities (HBCUs). Prior to the Civil War and during the subsequent Jim Crow period, most post-secondary schools in the United States prevented Blacks and other minorities from enrolling. As a result, HBCUs were established in order to provide African Americans an outlet for higher education. Although the first of the approximately 100 HBCUs, Cheyney University in Pennsylvania, was founded in 1837, most of these institutions originated in the South following the conclusion of the Civil War.

Many of the persistent resource disparities between HBCUs and Predominantly White Institutions (PWIs) can be traced back to the funding mechanism for the

---

[11] See at: www.cnn.com/2021/04/20/economy/redfin-housing-boom-race-discrimination/index.html.

nation's land-grant universities. Many of the country's major public universities were created as a result of the 1862 Morrill Act, aided and abetted by the systematic seizure of Native American land. This congressional legislation authorized the development of a single land-grant university, with an emphasis on agriculture, engineering, and science, in each state. The federal government would provide funding for these institutions provided that this funding stream was matched, dollar-for-dollar, by nonfederal sources—in practice, meaning the respective state governments. Consistent with the prevailing norms and legal practices of their day, African Americans were barred from all land-grant universities in the South. As a result, Congress passed a second Morrill Act in 1890 to provide funding for institutions dedicated to educating Black college students. However, with the 1890 Morrill Act states were *not* required to provide a 100 percent funding match for HBCUs, as had been stipulated with exclusively White (at least in the Southern states) land-grant institutions. As a result, states were disincentivized to provide funding for HBCUs.

Photo 14.4 On March 22, 1947, students of historically Black college Morgan State held a mass meeting to protest against cuts in the student budget made by the state governor.
Source: Photo Afro American Newspapers © Afro Newspaper/Gado/Contributor/Archive Photos/Getty Images.

Even though land-grant universities and HBCUs are no longer formally segregated, the legacy of inequality that led to their creation remains with us today.
Katherine Mangan (2021) illustrates this point in an article published in the
Chronicle of Higher Education. The article begins by noting the vast disparities in
infrastructure and resources at Tennessee State University (an HBCU) compared
with the University of Tennessee (a PWI). Much of the campus at the former is in
disrepair whereas the latter enjoys all the modern amenities associated with elite
post-secondary education. This is partially the inevitable result of the unequal
funding mechanisms for the two universities. But Mangan also points to a more
recent source of this inequality—often-times HBCUs did not even receive the
unequal state funding that they were due. She reports that in spring 2021 a legislative committee in Tennessee concluded that "the state has always provided the
predominantly white land-grant institution, the University of Tennessee at
Knoxville, with a full match of the dollars it received from the federal government.
Sometimes, it provided more than that. But budget documents ... indicated that,
from 1957 to 2007, the state has spent no matching dollars on TSU, its historically
Black land-grant university." The committee estimated that Tennessee State
University (TSU) had been shortchanged by as much as half a billion dollars during
this fifty-year period.[12] The case of TSU is not unique. According to the same
Chronicle of Higher Education article, between 2010 and 2012 61 percent of Black
land grant universities received less than a full match of their federal grants from
their respective states. This translates to a loss of about $57 million dollars of
funding during this period.

Resource Disparities for Native Americans in Higher Education

Tribal Colleges and Universities (TCUs) also encounter funding inequities. The first
TCU began in Arizona in 1968 as the Navajo Community College (now known as
Diné College). Today there are approximately three dozen such institutions
throughout the country serving approximately 40,000 Native and non-Native students. Many of these institutions are located on or near Native American reservations in the southwest. The TCUs were developed in order to address the
underrepresentation of Native students on college campuses and to provide an
education that would preserve and revitalize indigenous cultures. Federal funding
for TCUs began with the Tribally Controlled College or University Assistance Act
of 1978. By 1994, with the Equity in Educational Land Grant Status Act, these
institutions were officially granted land grant status. However, the funding mechanism for TCUs differs from other land grant institutions. First and foremost, state
governments are under no obligation to provide matching funds for TCUs. As a
result, few states provide such funding (Nelson and Frye 2016).

---

[12] Although some of this blatant disparity was resolved after 2007, the state of Tennessee has continued to
shortchange TSU (Mangan 2021: 17). Additionally, Black students at the University of Tennessee (6
percent) remain underrepresented relative to their share of the population in this state (17 percent).

TCUs face some additional institutional funding barriers. Because American Indian reservations, where many TCUs are located, operate under a federal trust they are unable to levy taxes to generate revenues as do many non-TCU community colleges. Moreover, as the number of students attending TCUs has increased, federal funding—which represents almost three-quarters of total revenue for such institutions—has failed to keep pace.[13] This is particularly important because students attending these institutions tend to come from low-income, heavily rural backgrounds, making it unlikely that additional funds could be acquired through increases in tuition. Lastly, TCUs receive no federal funds to support the education of non-Native students, even though they represent about 15 percent of enrolled students (Nietzel 2021). This consequently exacerbates the resource constraints facing these chronically underfunded institutions. According to Nelson and Frye at the American Council of Education, "[through] Indian treaty rights dating back as far as the late 1700s, the United States government legally and morally committed to honoring a unique set of rights, benefits, and conditions for Native people. Among those rights is the benefit of education. Given the trust responsibility and treaty obligations of the federal government to provide life-long education, which arguably included meeting fiscal and operational needs of TCUs, the chronic funding gap is especially troubling" (Nelson and Frye 2016).

Racialization of Healthcare Policy: The Case of Obamacare

In addition to social welfare policy and education policy, racial considerations are also implicated in the development of—and the public's reaction to—healthcare policy. A full exploration of this phenomenon is beyond the scope of this chapter, but a brief illustration can be found in the politics surrounding the Patient Protection and Affordable Care Act passed by Congress in 2010 and signed into law by President Obama on March 23, 2010. This legislation, more commonly referred to as "Obamacare," was arguably the signature policy accomplishment of the Obama administration. Among other things, the legislation made health insurance much more widely available and accessible to the American public by relying on a variety of mechanisms, including expanding Medicaid coverage (the federal government's health insurance policy for low-income individuals).[14]

The politics surrounding the passage of Obamacare were undeniably partisan. Only one Republican supported the legislation in the House of Representatives and not a single Republican voted in favor of the bill in the Senate. Many voters and political observers also thought the debate was influenced by racial attitudes given the close association the legislation had with Barack Obama, the first president of

---

[13] This remains true even after the passage of the Fostering Undergraduate Talent by Unlocking Resources for Education (FUTURE) Act in 2019 and the passage of the American Rescue Plan in 2021, both of which provided greater funding for TCUs.

[14] See at: www.kff.org/health-reform/fact-sheet/summary-of-the-affordable-care-act.

Photo 14.5 As the minority leader of the House of Representatives on January 16, 2017, Nancy Pelosi speaks beside House Democrats at an event to protect the Affordable Care Act in Los Angeles after the Republican-led U.S. Senate launched their effort to repeal the Affordable Care Act.
Source: © Mark Ralston/Staff/AFP/Getty Images.

African descent. The charge that racial concerns influenced opposition to the policy was sufficiently widespread that President Obama was questioned about it by reporters: "What I'm saying is this debate that's taking place [over healthcare reform] is not about race, it's about people being worried about how our government should operate" (Obama appearing on *Meet the Press* in September 2009, quoted in Tesler 2012). Despite the president's denial, there is considerable evidence that race did influence public opinion on Obamacare.

Political scientist Michael Tesler provides the best evidence on this matter (Tesler 2012). He examined multiple surveys beginning with the 1988 American National Election Study (ANES), conducted during the presidential campaign in the fall of that year, the 2008–2009 ANES Panel Study, which interviewed the same set of White respondents over multiple waves beginning in January 2008 and concluding in September 2009, and yet another panel survey, the Cooperative Campaign Analysis Project (CCAP), initially fielded in December 2007 and concluding in November 2009. The point in examining public opinion on healthcare reform during this twenty-year period was to determine whether measures of racial prejudice were more closely associated with White opposition to this policy after it became closely linked to President Obama. Tesler found that, with one exception

(1994), prejudice was more strongly associated with opposition to healthcare reform in September 2009—as the legislative battle for Obamacare was heating up in Congress—than for any other year going back to 1988.

Tesler also conducted some experiments which came to the same conclusion. In the 2009 CCAP Panel Study, Tesler briefly described to respondents key elements in the healthcare reform legislation then being discussed in Congress. However, he alternatively labeled the legislation as proposed by "some people," as part of President Clinton's 1993 health reform efforts, or as part of President Obama's current healthcare reform initiative. White survey respondents were randomly assigned to only one of these three conditions. Tesler hypothesized that respondents scoring high on measures of racial intolerance would be less supportive of healthcare reform when the policy was linked to President Obama rather than President Clinton. This hypothesis was confirmed, suggesting that at least some of the opposition to Obama's landmark legislation could be attributed to anti-Black racial prejudice rather than principled opposition to healthcare reform.

Conclusion

The overarching theme of this chapter is that social problems, and the policies designed to address them, can have racially disparate impacts and be influenced by racial considerations even when the problems are not overtly about race. We opened this chapter by describing the disparate racial impact of the COVID-19 pandemic. In short, almost all racial and ethnic minority groups in this country have suffered greater fatalities from the coronavirus than non-Hispanic Whites. This outcome is not a function of biological differences across the different racial and ethnic groups in this country. Instead, the unequal devastation wrought by the COVID-19 pandemic can be attributed to widespread and longstanding racial inequities in society. For these same reasons, and as we briefly documented in Chapter 1, racial and ethnic minority groups typically make less money, are more likely to be mired in poverty, are more likely to be unemployed, less likely to graduate from college, are less likely to own their own homes, and have lower life expectancies than do non-Hispanic Whites.

Over time, numerous social policies have sought to eliminate these disparities. Perhaps the most celebrated examples emerged during the 1960s and 1970s, in response to the Civil Rights Movement, and similar movements that it inspired such as the Chicano Movement (seeking political and social empowerment on behalf of Mexican Americans), and the Red Power Movement (efforts by Native Americans to achieve self-determination) of that era. As a result of the pressure brought to bear by these movements and their more contemporary descendants, anti-poverty programs were expanded to include people of color, more aggressive enforcement mechanisms were added to court-ordered desegregation efforts, greater funding and legal status were provided to Minority Serving Institutions of higher learning, and health insurance was extended to low-income and minority populations. Politics, however, is a story about give and take. As a result, this chapter documents how the nation's ongoing contestation surrounding issues of race are also implicated in social welfare policy, education policy, and healthcare policy. In practice, this means that ostensibly shared goals such as reducing poverty, increasing access to quality education, and improving health outcomes are often short-circuited due to intolerance and a desire to maintain the racial status quo—with Whites frequently at or near the top of the hierarchy. We therefore conclude that in order to fully address the challenges facing all Americans, we must inevitably address the deep and persistent inequities facing Americans of color.

KEY TERMS

Aid to Families with Dependent Children (AFDC)
Affirmative action
Historically Black Colleges and Universities (HBCUs)
"Obamacare"
Social Security Act 1935
Tribal Colleges and Universities (TCUs)

DISCUSSION QUESTIONS

1. How do poverty rates vary across different racial and ethnic groups?
2. Why do fatalities from COVID-19 differ by race and ethnicity?
3. Why do many Americans associate poverty and welfare with racial minorities?
4. Are school children more segregated today than in the 1950s?
5. What should be done about unequal funding levels for minority serving institutions compared to predominantly White institutions?

ANNOTATED SUGGESTED READINGS

See Sanford F. Schram, Joe Soss, and Richard C. Fording. 2003. *Race and the Politics of Welfare Reform*. Ann Arbor: University of Michigan Press, for a great overview of the research on race and welfare reform.

See Sean F. Reardon and Ann Owens. 2014. "60 Years after *Brown*: Trends and Consequences of School Segregation," *Annual Review of Sociology* 40: 199–218, to learn more about trends in school desegregation.

See Michael Telser. 2016. *Post-Racial or Most-Racial? Race and Politics in the Obama Era*. Chicago: University of Chicago Press, for an excellent analysis of race during the Obama years.

See Stephanie Fryberg and E. Martinez. 2014. *The Truly Diverse Faculty: New Dialogues in American Higher Education*. New York: Palgrave Macmillan, if you would like to know more about the challenges of minority faculty in higher education.

See Adam Harris. 2021. *The State Must Provide: Why America's Colleges Have Always Been Unequal—and How to Set Them Right*. New York: HarperCollins, for more on funding inequalities in colleges and universities.

CHAPTER REFERENCES

Alesina, Albert, Edward Glaeser, and Bruce Sacerdote. 2001. "Why Doesn't the U.S. Have a European-Style Welfare State?" *Brookings Papers on Economic Activity* 2: 1–70.

Biden Jr., Joseph R. 2021. "Remarks by President Biden on the Benefits of the Build Back Better Agenda for Working Families," *Whitehouse.gov*, July 7. www.whitehouse.gov/briefing-room/speeches-remarks/2021/07/07/remarks-by-president-biden-on-the-benefits-of-the-build-back-better-agenda-for-working-families.

Conger, Kate, Robert Gebeloff, and Richard A. Oppel Jr. 2021. "Native Americans Feel Devasted by the Virus Yet Overlooked in the Data," *New York Times*, January 3. www.nytimes.com/2020/07/30/us/native-americans-coronavirus-data.html.

Dyck, Joshua J. and Laura S. Hussey. 2008. "The End of Welfare as We Know It? Durable Attitudes in a Changing Information Environment," *Public Opinion Quarterly* 72(4): 589–618.

Fording, Richard C. 2003. "'Laboratories of Democracy' or Symbolic Politics? The Racial Origins of Welfare Reform," In *Race and the Politics of Welfare Reform* (eds.) Sanford F. Schram, Joe Soss, and Richard C. Fording. Ann Arbor: University of Michigan Press, 72–100.

Fox, Cybelle. 2004. "The Changing Color of Welfare? How Whites' Attitudes towards Latinos Influence Support for Welfare," *American Journal of Sociology* 110(3): 580–625.

Fox, Cybelle. 2012. *Three Worlds of Relief: Race, Immigration, and the American Welfare State from the Progressive Era to the New Deal*. Princeton: Princeton University Press.

Fusaro, Vincent A. 2020. "State Politics, Race, and 'Welfare' as a Funding Stream: Cash Assistance Spending under Temporary Assistance for Needy Families," *Policy Studies Journal* 49(3): 811–834.

Gilens, Martin. 1999. *Why Americans Hate Welfare: Race, Media, and the Politics of Antipoverty Policy*. Chicago: University of Chicago Press.

Hlavinka, Elizabeth. 2020. "CDC Confirms Soaring COVID-19 Rate among Native Americans: 'Excessive Absence of Data' for American Indians and Alaskan Natives Speaks to Public Health Disparity," *Medpage Today*, August 19. www.medpagetoday.com/infectiousdisease/covid19/88167.

Jackson, C. Kirabo, Rucker C. Johnson, and Claudia Persico. 2016. "The Effects of School Spending on Educational and Economic Outcomes: Evidence from School Finance Reforms," *Quarterly Journal of Economics* 131(1): 157–218.

Johnson, Rucker C. and Alexander Nazaryan. 2019. *Children of the Dream: Why School Integration Works*. New York: Basic Books/Russell Sage Foundation.

Katznelson, Ira. 2005. *When Affirmative Action Was White: An Untold History of Racial Inequality in Twentieth-Century America*. New York: W. W. Norton.

Katznelson, Ira. 2013. *Fear Itself: The New Deal and the Origins of Our Time*. New York: Liveright Publishing.

Lieberman, Robert. 1998. *Shifting the Color Line*. Cambridge, MA: Harvard University Pres.

Mangan, Katherine. 2021. "The Betrayal of Historically Black Colleges: For Decades States Have Been Funding Their White Campuses While Starving Their Black Ones. In Tennessee That Could Finally Change," *The Chronicle of Higher Education*, September 24. www.chronicle.com/article/the-betrayal-of-historically-black-colleges.

Massey, Douglas. 2011. "The Past and Future of American Civil Rights," *Daedalus* Spring: 37–54.

Mead, Lawrence. 1984. *Beyond Entitlement: The Social Obligations of Citizenship*. New York: Free Press.

Mead, Lawrence. 1988. "Telling the Poor What to Do," *National Affairs* 132: 97–112.

Nelson, Christine A. and Joanna R. Frye. 2016. "Tribal College and University Funding: Tribal Funding at the Intersection of Federal, State, and Local Funding," American Council of Education, Center for Policy Research and Strategy: Issue Brief, May. www.acenet.edu/Documents/Tribal-College-and-University-Funding.pdf.

Neubeck, Kenneth and Noel Cazenave. 2001. *Welfare Racism: Playing the Race Card Against America's Poor.* New York: Routledge.

Nietzel, Michael T. 2021. "America's Tribal Colleges and Universities Hope for Transformation Under Biden Administration," *Forbes.com,* May 14. www.forbes.com/sites/michaeltnietzel/2021/05/14/americas-tribal-colleges-and-universities-hope-for-transformation-under-biden-administration/?sh=7927f6136cec.

Orfield, Gary. 2001. "Schools More Separate: Consequences of a Decade of Resegregation," Report Civil Rights Project, Harvard University.

Piston, Spencer. 2018. *Class Attitudes in America: Sympathy for the Poor, Resentment for the Rich, and Political Implications.* Cambridge: Cambridge University Press.

Prasad, Monica. 2016. "American Exceptionalism and the Welfare State: The Revisionist Literature," *Annual Review of Political Science* 19: 187–203.

Reardon, Sean F. 2016. "School Segregation and Racial Achievement Gaps," *RSF: Russell Sage Foundation Journal of the Social Sciences* 2(5): 34–57.

Reardon, Sean F. and Ann Owens. 2014. "60 Years after 'Brown': Trends and Consequences of School Segregation," *Annual Review of Sociology* 40: 199–218.

Soss, Joe, Sanford F. Schram, Thomas Vartanian, and Erin O'Brien. 2001. "Setting the Terms of Relief: Explaining State Policy Choices in the Devolution Revolution," *American Journal of Political Science* 45(2): 378–395.

Tesler, Michael. 2012. "The Spillover of Racialization into Health Care: How President Obama Polarized Public Opinion by Racial Attitudes and Race," *American Journal of Political Science* 56(3): 690–704.

Ward, Deborah. 2005. *The White Welfare State: The Racialization of U.S. Welfare Policy.* Ann Arbor: University of Michigan Press.

Williams, Linda Faye. 2003. *The Constraint of Race: Legacies of White Skin Privilege in America.* University Park, PA: Pennsylvania State University Press.

15 Diversity and Democracy from the Bottom up: The Past, the Present, and the Future

We wrote this textbook to introduce students to racial and ethnic politics in the United States. Like most textbooks, we have curated a mountain of facts and findings, organized to inform and stimulate your critical thinking. In our case, the facts and figures concern the challenges and opportunities of democratic politics in a racially diverse society—that is, issues about which Americans have deeply felt, often polarizing opinions. Our approach to writing this text has been heavily influenced by the moment we are in. As we described in the opening section of Chapter 1, we are in a moment of convergence of at least three exceedingly rare happenings, each on its own a potential turning point in American politics. A global pandemic that has upended everyone's lives, killed millions the world over, inflicted chaos on the economy, and further divided the country. A polarizing election that spawned an insurrection on the U.S. Capitol and threatens to push America down the slippery slope of democratic backsliding toward autocracy or even civil war. A mass movement of millions of Americans pouring into the streets to protest racialized police brutality and structural racism, including the rallying cry, "Defund the Police."

Racial conflict and racial inequality are central characters in each of these narratives, just as they have been at other times in American history, both mundane and momentous. In writing this text we have been motivated to apply our knowledge and expertise as political scientists to shed some explanatory light on racial identity, inequality, and injustice in American life. The topics and themes have been organized around defining questions that the #BlackLivesMatter movement has challenged all Americans to answer: do our politics and political institutions address and ameliorate society's inequalities and injustices or do they instead reinforce and reproduce those very existing inequalities and injustices? Do all American lives matter equally in the design of our institutions and the decisions of our representatives, or do our institutions and representatives privilege some Americans at the expense of others?

To us, the answers to these questions are disquieting. The chapters of this book demonstrate that racial boundaries and racial inequality remain pervasive in American society. To be clear, the facts and findings show clear progress on some dimensions. In 2008, an American named Barack Husein Obama, who wrote a book two years earlier titled *The Audacity of Hope: Thoughts on Reclaiming the*

Photo 15.1 Supporters of Barack Obama celebrate the election results on November 4, 2008, at Grant Park, Chicago, Illinois, in anticipation of Obama's victory address—and a win that was expected to reshape American politics.

Source: © Stan Honda/Staff/AFP/Getty Images.

American Dream (2006), had the audacity to run for the highest political office in the land. When he succeeded in that aspiration, many Americans of all backgrounds and political stripes felt so uplifted that they dared to think that racial bias was behind us at last. Columnist Matt Bai penned this headline in the *New York Times*: "Is Obama the End of Black Politics?" The Black conservative author Shelby Steele wondered aloud, "Does victory mean that America is now officially beyond racism?" And the Civil Rights Movement icon Congressman John Lewis declared, "Barack Obama is what comes at the end of that bridge in Selma."

Electing Obama to the presidency represented for many Americans proof that the nation had finally vanquished its long history of racism. The nation seemed poised, as if by magical thinking, to move to a radically different kind of post-racial, post-ethnic, post-Black politics in America. That hope has proven to be short-lived. Just eight years later, the pendulum of racial progress swayed seemingly inexorably back to a new period of racial reprisal. Donald Trump launched a successful presidential campaign with the promise to "Make America Great Again." While Obama fueled his rise to power with hope for a post-racial future, albeit by exploiting familiar racial stereotypes for electoral advantage (see Chapter 8), Trump fed his base of disaffected and dispossessed voters a red-meat diet of nativist, nationalist, populist rhetoric. Along the way, at both the federal as well as state levels and in both legislative and judicial institutions, the nation readied to turn the clock back on many of the most visible markers of racial progress—dismantling the Voting Rights Act, ending affirmative action, even whitewashing the nation's racial history in classroom texts.

As educators, one of the most dismaying signs of how far we are from achieving our promise as a nation is that Americans remain intensely and stubbornly divided on matters of basic fact about whether racial bias persists and what the root causes of racial inequality are. Without agreement on where we are and how we got here, how does a nation confront the challenge of what we should do about it and where we, as a nation, can go? Consider the clashing perspectives of U.S. Supreme Court justices on the subject of racial equality in education. In *Parents Involved* v. *Seattle School District* (2007) the Court ruled against Seattle's plan to address racial inequality by intentionally integrating schools. Chief Justice John Roberts famously wrote in the majority's opinion, "the way to stop discriminating on the basis of race is to stop discriminating on the basis of race." Then, in *Schuette* v. *Coalition to Defend Affirmative Action* (2014), the Court affirmed the constitutionality of Michigan's ballot initiative to ban affirmative action in public education and employment. Justice Sonia Sotomayor filed a dissenting opinion with the following retort to Justice Roberts, "The way to stop discriminating on the basis of race is to speak openly and candidly on the subject of race, and to apply the Constitution with eyes open to the unfortunate effects of centuries of racial discrimination."

Where We Are Today

As we write this concluding chapter, it is early in 2022. Whatever some of us may have believed or hoped for after Election Tuesday in November 2008, it is clear to us as political scientists that the United States is resoundingly not a color-blind society and that we are decidedly not beyond racism. To continue to insist that race no longer matters in 2022 has the ring of an ideological commitment that is blind to the persistence of racial bias. In this book, we have followed Justice Sotomayor's exhortation to openly and candidly consider race in American politics, and that open and candid examination shows that racial inequality and discrimination remain deeply ingrained in American political life. To complete our examination, we pivot from following the evidence and research to a more open-ended exploration of where we might go—whether change is possible and how it might happen. In a democracy as diverse, divided, and fragile as ours, it is not enough to be armed with facts and findings alone, especially when those facts and findings reveal such a sobering and bleak picture. Politics today looks futile to many in part because many Americans have lost hope in their government. Democratic legitimacy is the faith that members of a polity have in a system of government, and in the United States today, that legitimacy is at a low point.

Take, for example, trust in government, an important indicator of democratic legitimacy. Since 1958, the American National Election Study (ANES) has asked a random selection of adult Americans the question, "How much of the time do you think you can trust the government luther in Washington to do what is right—just about always, most of the time or only some of the time?" In 1958 and 1964, 73 percent and 76 percent, respectively, of Americans said they trusted their government "just about always" or "most of the time." Even as recently as 2002, just after the 9/11 terrorist attacks on America a majority of Americans (56 percent) trusted the government at these levels. Those numbers have been in a tailspin since 2002, hitting 22 percent by 2012 and by the latest 2020 ANES, only 15 percent of Americans trusted the federal government at least "most of the time."

Similar signs of lost political legitimacy are found in the General Social Survey (GSS) series on institutional confidence. The GSS has, since 1973, asked a random selection of Americans the following question: "I am going to name some institutions in this country. As far as the people running these institutions are concerned, would you say you have a great deal of confidence, only some confidence, or hardly any confidence in them." Since around 1990, there has been a slow but steady decrease in confidence in most of the major institutions of government. In the last decade confidence in the "people's branch of government," Congress, hovers around 10 percent. Confidence in the news media and the criminal justice system fares only slightly better at around 20–30 percent while confidence in the presidency and the Supreme Court track each other closely at between 30 and 40 percent. Following the momentous decision to overturn *Roe* v. *Wade* in summer 2022, the Gallup organization reported that confidence in the Supreme Court has fallen to a historic low (Jones 2022). The only government institution enjoying confidence among a majority of Americans in our democratic system of government is confidence in the military, which is robustly stable at around 75 percent.

Yet other surveys suggest that a sizeable number of Americans today are open to alternatives to our current system of democracy. A 2018 study from the Voter Study Group, for example, finds that only a slim majority (54 percent) consistently express pro-democratic sentiments in a series of questions about political regimes. At the same time, nearly one in four like the idea of "a strong leader who doesn't have to bother with Congress or elections" and 18 percent say that "army rule" would be "fairly" or "very good."[1] This decline in democratic legitimacy coupled with the sobering facts and findings in this textbook offer little solace or hope for the future. To paraphrase from Martin Luther King's 1963 "I Have a Dream" speech in Washington, D.C., where out of this mountain of despair can we find a stone of hope?

---

[1] Lee Drutman, Larry Diamond, and Joe Goldman. "Follow the Leader." A Research Report from the Democracy Fund Voter Study Group. March 2018, at: www.voterstudygroup.org/publication/follow-the-leader. A more recent survey conducted by Morning Consult similarly found that 26 percent of the U.S. population could be categorized, by their measures, as "highly right-wing authoritarian," see at: https://morningconsult.com/2021/06/28/global-right-wing-authoritarian-test.

A Stone of Hope

The stone of hope is found in the fact that democracy does not work solely through our established institutions of representative government. Institutions like a free press, organized interest groups, competitive and regular elections are designed to foster a pluralist competition of ideas and uphold the will of the people in a democracy. But for an increasing number of Americans, such institutions are failing us. Or failing some of us, along racial and ethnic lines. When that happens, Americans have a right and a duty to speak truth to the power of people in a democracy. In fact, they have a long tradition of doing so. As a nation forged out of revolution, resistance and rebellion are woven into the fabric of our republic. The threads of that fabric connect the Black Lives Matter movement of today to the Civil Rights Movement of the 1950s and 1960s all the way back to Henry David Thoreau's refusal, in the 1840s, to pay taxes to protest against slavery and America's declaration of war against Mexico.

Consider, too, the long history of resistance and rebellion against slavery. The Black freedom movement in the western hemisphere has many chapters, perhaps the first among them taking place outside the United States, with the Haitian Revolution in 1791. While the slave revolt led by Toussaint L'Ouverture was set in Haiti, it captured the imagination of the anti-slavery movement throughout North America, effectively ended France's efforts to build slave colonies in North America, and stopped the expansion of slavery into the Louisiana Territories. Then, following the Haitian Revolution came Nat Turner's slave revolt in 1831 in Southampton, Virginia and another revolt of slaves in Harper's Ferry, Virginia in 1859 led by the abolitionist John Brown. Harper's Ferry is widely seen as a prelude and harbinger to the Civil War.

While these early American slave rebellions failed in their ultimate goal of dismantling the institution of slavery, there is a clear throughline from these early demands to the more sustained anti-slavery movement in the nineteenth century that Frederick Douglass, Martin Delany, Harriet Tubman and others built. And a throughline to African Americans' collective resistance to Jim Crow laws and extra-legal racial violence in the late nineteenth and early twentieth centuries led by Ida B. Wells-Barnett, W. E. B. Du Bois, Monroe Trotter, and even Booker T. Washington. Each of these chapters of organized resistance was, of course, also met with concerted campaigns by White segregationists to thwart demands for freedom and equality. Thus, there is also a history of racial violence and oppression, from lynchings and race riots to "Black codes" that determined where, when, and for how much Blacks could work. Yet in spite of these campaigns of racial violence and oppression, Black Americans organized and built and bolstered homegrown institutions, from advocacy groups like the NAACP and National Urban League, to a thriving Black press, Black colleges and universities, Black churches, and other Black organizations.

These snapshots of the African American freedom struggle here are admittedly surgically selective and short. However, they underscore two important points

Photo 15.2 Historical 1863 engraving of Nat Turner and his confederates in conference.
Source: New York Public Library Digital Collections.

about mobilizing for social change. The first is that no matter how foreboding our current state of affairs, we should remember that the structures and institutions that produce and reproduce racial injustice are not invincible or invulnerable to mass mobilization and protest. Even a structure and institution as deeply embedded into the founding of the nation as slavery—upon which the early success of the American political economy depended, was met with resistance and was ultimately dismantled. Resistance and rebellion from the bottom up is thus the stone of hope that allows a David to fell a Goliath.

Stones of hope, importantly, do not materialize out of thin air. Our politicians in power were never first to the frontlines of organized efforts to dismantle slavery. And that is the second key point. Many key legislative acts of triumph against injustice and transformative change, like the passage of the Thirteenth, Fourteenth, and Fifteenth Amendments or the Civil Rights Act of 1964 and the Voting Rights Act of 1965 have precursors which began outside of legislative and electoral politics. Part of the robustness of democracy as a system of government is that top-down change (laws and policies initiated and enacted by our political representatives) is often dependent on bottom-up demands for change. Some of the central tenets of democracy, like accountability, responsiveness, legitimacy, consent, and participation depend on the co-constructed relationship between elites who make laws and policies and the masses who make demands of the elites and are served by them.

Because *democracy* is fundamentally about the exercise of power (*kratos*) by the people (*demos*), we would be remiss to write a text about racial and ethnic politics in a diverse democracy like the United States without including our perspective on how people make politics when their politicians and political institutions fail them. Furthermore, the potential to achieve common purpose and collective interests through nonelectoral means and institutions of governance outside of the status quo is especially critical when that common purpose and those collective interests center on racial equality and justice. That is, as we have seen time and again in this text, electoral politics and the status quo institutions of governance have a proven track record of either working to deepen existing inequalities or at least failing to stem the root causes of injustice. This happens not inevitably, but with alarming regularity. Whether it is the extent to which the interests of racial and ethnic minorities are electorally "captured" as Paul Frymer describes it (see Chapter 9), or the way that a "War on Drugs" preyed on racial anxieties to erect a "new Jim Crow" as Michelle Alexander describes it (see Chapters 5 and 12), a key aspect of racial and ethnic politics has always entailed thinking beyond voting, elections, legislative politics, interest group mobilization, and judicial activism.

How Movements Happen

We conclude this book, then, by examining what social scientists have to say about protest movements and democratic politics from the bottom up. To begin, protest movements are a kind of collective behavior and there are many varieties of collective behavior, from mobs, fads, panics, cults, and revivals to urban rebellions, civil wars, and revolutions. Collective behavior is the behavior of groups, typically coordinated and aiming to reach some common purpose. It is important to keep in mind that not all such behavior is political.

Crowds gather for lots of reasons. A majestic oak is felled by lightning on the hillside of a college campus, and a crowd gathers. On a different day, an a cappella group congregates on that same hillside to sing and people come together. On April 20 yet another group meets up there to smoke pot together. And on a fourth occasion, students assemble with banners and bullhorns to holler about the administration's inaction on sexual violence on campus. We can probably all agree that a crowd gathering around a fallen tree is not *political* even if it is collective action in some sense, and that protesting sexual violence on campus is political. The a cappella performance might be political if, say, they chose to sing an arrangement of Violetta Parra's "Gracias a la Vida" or Nina Simone's "Mississippi Goddam." Similarly, the 420 get-together might be political if a petition in support of a federal law to legalize marijuana is being passed around and signed.

There are many occasions that bring a group of people together for some common purpose, but what makes the collective behavior *political* are factors like the content, context, and motivation underlying the group action. In the most consequential form, when the collective behavior is sustained over time, purposive in its objectives, oriented around change, and organized outside conventional means of participation, it is not just a political moment on a campus quad, but a broader social movement for change. The study of social movements is a huge topic that could take a semester-long class to absorb, so we simply summarize here what that literature has to say about moments and movements around racial justice. To start, social movements are typically organized and sustained efforts to promote change or to oppose change, where the efforts require in part non-institutionalized collective action and where that change cannot be achieved through regular means.

Purposive versus Spontaneous Action

The difference between spontaneous collective acts and purposive, movement-oriented collective behavior is not merely an abstract debate over definitions, but a recurring hot debate where race is concerned. Take a seemingly routine and peaceful traffic stop in the Watts neighborhood of Los Angeles on a hot summer day in August 1965. California Highway Patrol officer Lee Minikus (who is White) pulls over Marquette Frye (who is Black) for reckless driving; Frye fails a sobriety test. Stoked by a gathering crowd of onlookers and police reinforcement called to the scene, the "routine" stop goes awry and triggers a physical scuffle and multiple arrests. The ensuing six days of intense civil unrest and violence results in thirty-four deaths and Governor Pat Brown mobilizing some 14,000 National Guard troops to quell the uprising. Many interpreted the "Watts riot" in a broader context: set against a backdrop of widespread allegations of institutional racism in the Los Angeles Police Department under Chief William Parker; the 1964 ballot initiative (Proposition 14), passed with overwhelming White support, that legalized housing discrimination in California; linked to the outbreak of urban uprisings in the 1960s in cities like New York, Newark, Philadelphia, Detroit, and Chicago; and connected to the critical juncture in the Civil Rights Movement when the activism shifted from a focus on racial segregation in the Jim Crow South of the 1950s and early 1960s to a focus on economic and social justice beyond the South of the mid-1960s. Yet others saw Watts entirely differently. LAPD Chief Parker compared rioting African Americans to the Viet Cong; Governor Brown described the riot participants as "guerillas fighting with gangsters"; and the renowned political scientist Edward Banfield saw Watts and other uprisings as rioting "mainly for fun and profit."

DIGGING DEEPER: RIOT OR REBELLION?

The controversy over what kind of collective action counts as political protest also bleeds over to what terms are used to describe such events. For instance, there is a long-standing debate over whether moments of civil disorder like Watts in 1965 and South Central Los Angeles in 1992 should be described by the term "riot" and "disturbance" or "rebellion" and "uprising," among others. The term "riot" implies an event that is ruled by irrational mob behavior, senseless violence and wanton illegal action. The term "rebellion," by contrast, implies clearer purpose, motivation, even organization. This is not just a bit of trivia about the lexicon of the 1960s and 1990s, but a debate that continues to animate how we view current clashes over racial justice.

Photo 15.3 On March 15, 1966, police officers search young men following a short-lived racial flareup in Watts—the second in the strife-torn area in eight months. Two persons were killed, more than twenty-five injured, and at least thirty-one arrested during the afternoon of shootings, looting, burnings and beatings.
Source: © Bettmann/Contributor/Getty Images.

An op-ed written by Barry Latzer in the *Wall Street Journal* in response to the #BlackLivesMatter marches, for instance, is titled, "Don't Call Rioters 'Protesters'." In the body of the essay, Latzer says of the demonstrators, "Mr. Floyd's tragic death is, for them, a pretext for hooliganism" (Latzer 2020). The power of language and what terms imply about collective behavior was also a live controversy in the initial news coverage and subsequent debate over the January 6, 2021 attack on the U.S. Capitol. Press coverage on the day of the attack varied in the use of "protest," "mob," "riot," "insurrection," and "terrorist attack" (McBride 2021). President-elect Biden denounced the "siege," issuing a statement that "This is not dissent. It's disorder. It's chaos. It's bordering on sedition." Meanwhile, out-going President Trump released a statement telling his supporters who were attacking the Capitol, "We love you, you're very special." And since that fateful day, there have been continuing efforts to contest the description of the event, with some Republicans in Congress describing it as "a peaceful protest" and "a normal tourist visit" while the Republican National Committee voted to sanction Republican Representatives Liz Cheney and Adam Kinzinger for participating in a congressional investigation of what the RNC described as "legitimate political discourse" (Dawsey and Sonmez 2022).[2]

The terms we use to describe events often vary not just by the political content that is implied by or imbued to the event, but also by the race of the participants in the event. Consider an event that is far removed from protest politics, like surviving a natural disaster in the face of a failed timely government response to help local residents. In late August 2005, Hurricane Katrina, a raging Category 5 storm, rampaged across Florida and into the Gulf states, taking deadly aim at New Orleans. In its wake, Katrina left over 1,800 dead, flooded 80 percent of the city of New Orleans, and displaced over a million people. The initial federal, state, and local government response was disconcertingly slow and blundering. In that context, two photos and their captions caught the eye of Americans. The Associated Press ran a photo depicting a young African American man wading through flooded waters with a case of soda under his arms and described his activity as "looting a grocery store." By contrast, AFP/Getty ran another photo showing a white couple in the same flooded waters with the woman holding two bags of food and the caption described their deeds as "finding bread and soda from a local grocery store" (Ralli 2005).

Photo 15.4 Immigrants rights protest.
Source: © David S. Holloway/Contributor/Getty Images News.

---

[2] The full text of the RNC's resolution is worth reading in its entirety and can be accessed at: https://int.nyt.com/data/documenttools/rnc-censure-resolution/58226d40412e4f18/full.pdf.

What Prompts Collective Action?

For political scientists, whether collective behavior is seen as protest or riot hinges on whether it is seen as rational and purposive. That question invites a puzzle about why people get involved politically and collectively in the first place. At least since the publication of Anthony Downs' *An Economic Theory of Democracy* in 1957, political science texts on elections generally begin with the "paradox of voting." The paradox goes as follows. Assume that people are rational about the pursuit of their own personal interests. If I am choosing between two jobs, all else being equal, I am likely to pick the one that pays more or that better suits my career in the long term. Similarly, if I am choosing between two candidates for political office, all else being equal, I am likely to vote for the one whose political views or personal background is most similar to my own. The paradox that this seemingly innocuous assumption leads to is that it is hard to explain why anyone who is rational would vote. That anyone chooses to vote is a paradox because the expected costs in time, information, and other tangible resources are real while the expected benefits to anyone thinking about voting approximates zero. Expected benefits are practically non-existent because the chances that any one person's vote will determine the outcome of an election is effectively zero. In short, if my vote does not "matter," then why take the time and energy to vote? Keep in mind, over 155 million Americans voted in 2020 and the margin of victory in the popular vote for Joe Biden over Donald Trump exceeded 7 million votes. Over the decades, political scientists, economists, and sociologists have developed many different explanations that make voting less of a paradox. For example, people are rarely so narrowly rational that they would only participate if their vote was pivotal. Or to take another explanation, people are motivated by more than merely the expected material benefits to them personally from participating; people act as well based on their "expressive preferences" (getting value from the act of voting itself, or from seeing oneself as an active citizen) and "social preferences" (getting value from benefiting others, advancing national interest, pursuing the public good, for instance).

The Paradox of Participation

The same paradox of voting can also be a useful starting point for understanding whether and how protests materialize. Nearly half a million Californians marched through downtown Los Angeles in March 2006 to protest a proposed bill (H.R. 4437) that would have labeled unauthorized immigrants as felons and criminalized anyone helping them to enter or stay in the United States. The expected benefit of political protest—the likelihood that the participation of any one marcher among the half million would lead to the defeat of H.R. 4437 or compel Congress to pursue a broader, more humane agenda of immigration policy reform—is effectively zero. Furthermore, the costs of participating in protests is almost always higher than the costs of voting, sometimes infinitely higher. The 2006 immigration protests, for example, included thousands of undocumented Americans among the marchers and protesters who were risking their very viability as Americans given the police presence that typically accompanies large protest marches. Yet people, under the right circumstances, reliably and repeatedly show up to voice their collective grievances.

Requiring that protests meet a standard of rationality, then, is unreasonable. Whether under authoritarian or totalitarian rule, or under slavery in pre-Civil War United States, people will rise up and rebel at times even knowing that their resistance will meet with dire, even deadly consequences to them personally. Because individuals in a group that is collectively rising up appear to throw the calculus of benefits and costs to the wind, some of the earliest social science theories on collective behavior described the "crowd" as an organic form all its own and non-rational in character. Gustav Le Bon, back in the nineteenth century (1895), wrote that "crowds, doubtless, are always unconscious, but this very unconsciousness is perhaps one of the secrets of their strength." To anyone reading Le Bon today, the picture of protest participants getting caught up in a mad moment, beyond their consciousness and free will, paints a disparaging, patronizing picture of people fighting for freedom and justice. Theories of the "crowd" also fell out of favor because they were just bad as a theory, meaning that they were poor at explaining different kinds of variation in collective behavior, such as when and why movements arise, grow in strength, succeed in their aims, or peter out.

The Political Process Theory of Social Movements

Filling that gap, more contemporary accounts emphasize three key elements of what is called the political process theory of social movements, focusing on resources, frames, and opportunities. Resource mobilization theorists like McCarthy and Zald (1977) argue that the variation in protest movements can be explained by structural factors, like the availability of resources and the role of organizations. The kindling of an event like the brutally public killing of Michael Brown or George Floyd may result in burning down a city, but it will not crystallize into a social movement without resources. Resources here are broad. Money, of course, but also human capital like movement activists with prior experience, leadership and organizational skills; creativity and strategic thinking to devise situational tactics; organizational strength, such as "movement organizations" dedicated to coordinate protests and communicate demands for change. Movement organizations also create the conditions for agency, which McCarthy and Zald call "issue entrepreneurship," where leaders like Cesar Chavez and Dolores Huerta can reshape the debate over the labor rights and civil rights of farmworkers in the 1960s and 1970s, or like Alicia Garza, Patrisse Cullors, and Opal Tometi can transform a hashtag into a national movement for racial reckoning.

Next, protest movements also move people to action and transform spectators into activists when they win the war of ideas. Labor is exploited everywhere, yet only under the right conditions will workers organize around their collective bargaining rights. People are poor everywhere, yet only under the right conditions will the dispossessed demand their fair share. Mobilizing protest movements thus also requires awakening the mind to the possibility of change and agency. As Doug McAdam puts it, "before collective [action] ... can get under way, people must collectively define their situations as unjust and subject to change through group action" (1981: 51). A classic example of this kind of agentic awakening is Fannie Lou Hamer's declaration before the Democratic National Convention in 1964 that "All my life I've been sick and tired. Now I'm sick and tired of being sick and tired." This consciousness raising is facilitated by "framing." In psychology and behavioral economics, frames are cognitive representations that simplify, interpret, and bias one's understanding of a complex reality or choice. We saw in Chapter 8 how the media uses framing to depict an issue or policy dispute by characterizing it in one way as opposed to another plausible way they might have covered it. In the social movements literature, framing refers to mobilization processes by which collective acts "assign meaning to and interpret relevant events and conditions in ways that are intended to mobilize potential adherents and constituents, to garner bystander support, and to demobilize antagonists" (Snow and Benford, 1988: 198).

Snow and Benford identify three kinds of functions that collective action frames can serve: they can be diagnostic, prognostic, or motivational (spur individuals to action). Diagnostic frames identify the problem and name the source of the problem, often focusing on defining grievances, such as with the evocation of phrases like "I Can't Breathe," "March for our lives," or "Women's rights are human rights." Prognostic frames propose the goals to alleviate the problem, including specific strategies and targets to achieve those goals, such as "Defund the police" and "#StopAAPIHate." Motivational frames can focus on identity such as the shared identity of movement activists, such as with coinages like "We are the 99 percent," "#MeToo," and "Indivisible." Motivational frames can also highlight agency and group empowerment, as with the rallying cry of the 2006 immigration protests, "Sí se puede" and the 2008 Obama campaign's version of the same, "Yes, we can."

Mobilizing resources and motivating frames are two of three key ingredients to building demands for change like racial equality and justice from the bottom up. The third key ingredient in the political process model sees in every situation and society a political opportunity structure that is either more open or closed to the possibility of change. One prominent scholar defines political opportunity structures as "consistent ... signals to social or political actors which either encourage or discourage them to use their internal resources to form social movements" (Tarrow 1996: 54). It is a nebulous concept, but one that makes the important point that context matters. McAdam (1996) identifies several dimensions that make political opportunities for change likelier: the openness or closed nature of a political system; the stability or instability of current elite coalitions; the presence or absence of elite allies; the state's capacity and penchant for repressing dissent. Accounts of the emergence of the Civil Rights Movement in the 1940s and 1950s, for example, point to "windows of opportunity" that opened because America was engaged in an ideological Cold War abroad, because cracks were forming in the New Deal political alignment that forged a coalition between Northern Democrats (who favored racial integration) and Southern Democrats (who favored racial segregation), and so on.

More generally, societies facing war, economic crises, demographic transformation, political realignments, or shifts in geopolitical relations are more vulnerable to change than those that are more stable. The United States, for instance, is currently confronting four of these five factors: economic adversity, demographic change, political realignment, and upheaval in geopolitical relations. The current moment is thus rife with the possibility of wide-ranging change, but whether that change will pull us further down into democratic backsliding or lift us up ever closer to our democratic ideals remains to be seen. Importantly, our present context serves as a reminder that windows of opportunity for mobilization are also sometimes opened by *moments of threat*. The noted social movement theorist Charles Tilly, for instance, writes that "a given amount of threat tends to generate more collective action than the same amount of opportunity" (1978: 134–135). Perceptions of individual and collective threat are especially useful to understand the continuing social movement for immigrants' rights in the United States. An early manifestation of that threat emerged in the mid-1990s, when states like California passed anti-immigrant laws like Proposition 187, which would have prohibited undocumented immigrants from accessing public services like healthcare and education. Pantoja, Ramirez and Segura (2001) show that the anti-Latino rhetoric had the unintended effect of mobilizing Latinos in California to naturalize as citizens, turn out to vote in higher numbers, and become discernibly more Democratic in their voting patterns. A similar mobilizing effect has been demonstrated as a key factor in the 2006 immigration protests, where roughly 5 million Americans were roused to march against the proposed bill H.R. 4437, that would have further changed undocumented status from a civil violation to a federal felony, including for those who assisted undocumented immigrants (Zepeda-Millán 2016). More recent examples of contexts of threat against Latinos have come both locally and nationally, from Sheriff Joe Arpaio in Maricopa County, Arizona to President Trump in the White House, and will likely continue into the future.

The political process view on whether and when people organize into a movement for change, in sum, emphasizes the central roles of means (resources), motivation (frames), and mobilizing contexts (political opportunities). These preconditions usually help us to understand the onset of protest movements—from the killing of Emmett Till to a Civil Rights Movement, from the killing of Trayvon Martin to a #BlackLivesMatter movement—but social movements evolve, typically in an arc from onset to an ending. The initial stage of a protest movement often starts with the heightened awareness of a problem and the definition of common interests and of collective agency. This initial stage is also often rooted in local groups, indigenous leaders, and a prior history of activism (Morris,1986). Movements then often build strength when the potential grievants raise their awareness of an issue, begin to organize, frame their cause, and bring audiences and allies into the movement. Movements institutionalize when they build formal organizations around their movement, with paid staff, strategic long-term planning, and in their organizational form, make institutionalized demands on a system.

How Social Movements End

Finally, we have to remember that no social movements endure forever. Sometimes a movement ends because its goal of social change is achieved. Sometimes it declines because the issues, passions, and resources that drive a movement from outside the political system are co-opted within the system. Movements also sometimes fall into decline because the initial outrage and commitment cannot be sustained, and the energy behind it flags. And then movements—especially those that fundamentally challenge an existing social order—can fall into decline because the movement and its leaders are harshly repressed out of existence. The 2021 Hollywood film, *Judas and the Black Messiah*, for instance, retells the story of the FBI's counterintelligence program and its surveillance and then assassination of Black Panther leader Fred Hampton. The arc of a protest movement summons perhaps one of the toughest questions to ask about politics from the bottom up: how successful are bottom-up movements for change? Do they succeed more often than fail? Is the backlash and countermobilization worse than the force for change? How do the short-term gains or losses weigh against potential long-term consequences?

DIGGING DEEPER: BOOKER T OR W. E. B? MARTIN OR MALCOLM?

One of the tougher questions about social movements and politics from the bottom up is whether change is better achieved by working within the system or outside the system. For the African American freedom movement, this question has, historically, pitted the likes of Booker T. Washington against W. E. B. Du Bois at the turn of the last century and then Martin Luther King, Jr. against Malcolm X during the Civil Rights Movement. Washington saw protest as a largely useless weapon in the fight against Jim Crow, and he advocated for a more gradualist (and to some, accommodationist) approach to advance Black progress. Du Bois, in contrast, argued emphatically for a more activist approach, arguing that "[P]rotest is for two purposes. For its effects upon your political enemies, and secondly, for its effect upon yourself."

Martin Luther King Jr. and Malcolm X were less divided on working within the system or outside it, but more divided on how far and hard to go from the outside. Dr. King advocated for the moral virtue and strategic value of nonviolent action, while Malcolm X (and others like Stokley Carmichael, H. Rap Brown and Huey Newton) saw virtue and value in advocating for freedom, justice, and equality for Blacks even if this meant armed defense against violent racist attacks not only because it was justifiable, but also for the end of reclaiming one's self-respect and dignity. King saw nonviolent resistance as "the most potent weapon available to oppressed people in their struggle for freedom and human dignity. It has a way of disarming the opponent. It exposes his moral defenses." Malcolm X, by contrast, saw no purpose in accepting the terms of engagement set by Dr. King or an oppressive White society, exhorting that "I'm one of the 22 million black victims

Photo 15.5 American Civil Rights leader Dr. Martin Luther King Jr. (1929–1968) speaks at a rally held at the Robert Taylor Homes in Chicago, Illinois, 1960s.
Source: Photo Robert Abbott Sengstacke © Robert Abbott Sengstacke/Contributor/Archive Photos/Getty Images.

of the Democrats. One of the 22 million black victims of the Republicans, and one of Americanism. I speak as a victim of America's so-called democracy. You and I have never seen democracy—all we've seen is hypocrisy ... We don't see any American dream. We've experienced only the American nightmare."[3]

Fighting the Power

We close this chapter on political change from the bottom up with a topic that many political science textbooks might begin with: the concept of power. Harold Laswell famously defined politics in 1936 as the story of "who gets what, when, and how." He is less well known for another definition: "Political science, as an empirical discipline, is the study of the shaping and sharing of power (Laswell and Kaplan, 1950: 21)." That political science is at heart of the study of power is an idea that has survived through the generations. How do political scientists think power works? And how do you get it, if you do not already have it? For the most part, political

---

[3] See at: https://americanradioworks.publicradio.org/features/blackspeech/mx.html.

scientists see power in three "faces," each one nested within the other like layers of a matryoshka doll: visible power, hidden power, and invisible power. All three share a common definition, according to Steven Lukes: "A exercises power over B when A affects B in a manner contrary to B's interests" (2005: 30).

The Three Faces of Power

Visible power is coercive power. In Robert Dahl's oft-cited definition, "A has power over B to the extent that he [sic] can get B to do something that B would not otherwise do (1957: 202)." A police officer flashes their lights to pull over a young African American man who is just trying to get home after a long day. To the extent that the driver pulls over, keeps his hands on the steering wheel, and shows his license, registration, and proof of insurance when asked to do so—even if there is no apparent reasonable cause for the stop—the officer's power is visible. And by implication, so too is the power of law enforcement and the power of the state. To take a more directly political example, the fact that no serious legislative action has been taken on gun safety and gun control—prior to the limited gun safety measures signed into law by President Biden following the mass shooting in Uvalde, Texas in spring 2022— despite an epidemic of gun violence, mass killings, and overwhelming public support for stricter gun laws, is a visible manifestation that power on this issue still lies with the gun lobby. And for an example of visible power from the bottom up, the impact of over 5 million Americans marching against H.R. 4437 in 2016 (the bill mentioned earlier in this chapter) was that the U.S. Senate companion bill never even made it past its assigned committee. This is the "I know it when I see it" dimension of power. Visible power has winners and losers; political scientists study visible power by defining arenas of conflict (e.g., competing candidates in elections, policy debates in Congress) and explaining outcomes in terms of the mobilization of resources like money, votes, access, framing ideologies, and so on.

Of course, power is not always observable. An important source of hidden power is the power to agenda-set (Bachrach and Baratz 1962). Following Dahl's formulation, A has power over B if A can decide what issues A and B can and cannot discuss and decide on. When issues that might be debated, contested, and addressed are left off the policy agenda, the status quo governs and any potential problems, grievances, or conflicts are by definition concealed as well. Whoever wields monopoly over an agenda wields monopoly over its outcomes. For decades from the 1970s until the rise of #BlackLivesMatter, a seemingly cardinal rule for politicians was to be "tough on crime" or risk losing the next election, leading to campaigns like the "War on Drugs," "Three Strikes Laws," and "Stop and Frisk." Largely absent from any policy debates in this period were serious efforts to reform policing, redirect regularized increases in policing budgets to social needs, or revive the movement to focus on rehabilitation (and not punishment) in "correctional" facilities. Or, to take another example, a recent study by Omar Wasow (2020) demonstrates that civil rights activism played an instrumental role in "agenda-seeding," by shaping media coverage on the protests and changing public opinion about desegregation, which then moved legislative elites to push for sweeping civil rights legislation. That is the power of agenda-setting. As E. E. Schattschneider put it some six decades ago, "Some issues get organized into politics while others are organized out" (1960: 71).

Finally, there is invisible power, or the power to shape our interests, beliefs, and awareness of our interests and beliefs. A has power over B if A can shape what B thinks and how B thinks, or more specifically, how B subjectively understands their material conditions and how those conditions link to (or are unrelated to) governance and policy. In terms of actions and choices, invisible power is at work if B willingly does A's bidding of their own free will, even if doing so would make B materially worse off. Consider the decades of increasingly punitive criminal justice policies mentioned in our example of agenda-setting power. In those decades, voters continued to reelect politicians without questioning why a "War on Drugs" was necessary, whether a 100-to-1 crack versus powder cocaine sentencing disparity was just, and why "peace" officers seemed to so regularly inflict violence with lethal force on young Black men after pretextual stops. Recent phenomena like politicians who engage in "gaslighting" and media actors who pollute our information with "fake news" are further reminders of how the tools of invisible power can be exploited to shape our politics.

At the same time, many of the most transformative demands for change in recent years have been waged at this level, to rewrite the script on racial justice. The current debates over racial reparations and rethinking policing are now on the policy agenda (the second face of power) and in some local governments even on proposed legislation (the first face of power), but they began with a radical act of rethinking. Whereas most Americans assumed the history of slavery and its durable effects of racial inequality was a "Black problem," Ta-Nehisi Coates (2014) impelled anyone who read his essay, "The Case for Reparations," to understand it as a moral debt that continues to cripple us as a nation. And whereas most Americans assumed an untidy but necessary relationship between the reality of crime and the need for law enforcement (and focused on addressing its "bad apples"), #BlackLivesMatter impelled many to understand that racialized police violence occurs within an ecology of structural barriers to due process and equality of opportunity which cannot be dealt with by ratcheting up or ratcheting down levels of policing in our communities.

The "three faces of power" orthodoxy tells us a lot about the *structure* of power and how to strategize against it. When the political opportunities to win the legislation you want are foreclosed, perhaps it is time to organize around agenda-setting. And when the opportunities to agenda-set are also foreclosed, the long game requires coming up with new ideas and fresh frames that question what we assume to know about an issue. The three faces of power framework, however, is also just one way to think about the work of power. That is, as a structural account, it conceives of power as power over; what A can get B to do, decide about, or even think.

"Power to" and "Power with"

There are at least two other key senses of power to keep in mind. These are especially relevant to agency, or how we as individuals become activated to contest inequality and injustice and to rethink democratic organizing. One is power to, the ability of a person or group to do something, to achieve an end. Martin Luther King, Jr., for example, defined power as "the ability to achieve purpose" and as "the strength required to bring about social, political, and economic change."[4] *Power to* is, by definition, about agency, choice and empowerment. When *power to* is harnessed by those who are subordinated or otherwise short-changed in the sense of *power over*, it connotes resistance and opposition to domination.

The other is power with, captured by Hannah Arendt's idea that power is "the human ability not just to act but to act in concert (1969: 44)." *Power with* is the force that obtains from collectively pursuing shared ends. When it is accompanied by the further goal of contesting inequality and injustice, *power with* reflects solidarity and group consciousness. Rallying cries in protest movements capture this solidaristic aspect, such as "Sí se puede" of the United Farm Workers movement in California and its updated variant in the 2008 U.S. presidential elections, "Yes, we can!" or "Amandla … awethu!" the call and response in the anti-apartheid movement, translating from Xhosa to English as "power … it is ours!" As Hannah Arendt saw it, *power with* is a fundamentally democratic capacity and potential: "Power is always … a power potential and not an unchangeable, measurable, and reliable entity like force or strength … power springs up between men [sic] when they act together and vanishes the moment they disperse (1958: 200)."

Conclusion: The Story of Us

Social science theories about collective behavior, social movements, and power can often feel abstract and remind students why "academic" is used by many as a pejorative term. What can a young adult seeking to make a difference do with concepts like "resource mobilization," "frame alignment," "power to," and "power with?" Especially when confronted with something as seemingly forbidding as structural racism? We opened this chapter by candidly acknowledging that, for a topic like racial and ethnic politics, a concluding chapter should aim to be not only pedagogically instructive and thought-provoking, but also *useful*.

In this final section, then, we turn to some gems of insight from Marshall Ganz. Ganz is widely seen as a legendary organizer and thought leader on building movements for social change, a reputation backed up by a career dedicated to activism. Some notable moments in this career include: dropping out of Harvard College in 1964 to join Freedom Summer participants in Mississippi at the height of the Civil Rights Movement; working alongside Cesar Chavez in the rise of the United Farm Workers movement from the mid-1960s to 1981; returning to Harvard to pivot from being an activist in social movements to a thinker on organizing; applying his theories on organizing as a strategist for "Camp MoveOn" (to train MoveOn.org's local leaders) and "Camp Organizing for America" (instrumental to Barack Obama's 2008 "ground game"). Ganz offers two hopeful and helpful

---

[4] From Martin Luther King Jr.'s "Where Do We Go From Here?" speech, delivered August 16, 1967. Available at: https://kinginstitute.stanford.edu/where-do-we-go-here.

insights to transform interested bystanders into change agents. The first is that stories are vital to translating our values into action (Polletta 2006). We may all witness things happening to us and to our communities, and what we witness may spur outrage and a sense of injustice, but we need to interpret and understand things to be moved to act. The second insight is that values are most effectively translated into action when three kinds of narratives come together: stories of self, stories of us, and stories of now. The "public narrative" moves us to act by weaving together all three threads. As Rabbi Hillel put it in some two millennia ago, "If I am not for myself, who will be for me? If I am for myself alone, who am I? If not now, when?"

The backdrop to the subject matter of this book has been the epoch-making confluence of three striking trends: a growing demographic diversity that is transforming the racial and ethnic composition of America; a growing inequality that is dividing the fate and fortune of Americans by race (and with race, by class, geography, generation, and other markers); a growing political polarization that is menacing our ability to govern ourselves as a democracy. These trends, while striking, should also not be surprising. There will always be "huddled masses yearning to breathe free" who will see the United States as a land of opportunity, so demographic change is part of our national destiny. The wealthy in all societies will always seek to get wealthier if we let them get away with it. And no group that has enjoyed the bounty and privileges of being the dominant group in a society can be expected to willingly cede that bounty and those privileges, whether they are White or wealthy or both. So, the current rise of Trumpism and White nationalism is an expected evolution in the story of democracy in the United States. How that story continues to unfold will depend ultimately on all of us. Which brings us back in time to Frederick Douglass: August 3, 1857, delivering a speech at Canandaigua, New York, on the topic of "West India's Emancipation." Addressing the critical role of West Indian slaves in their own freedom struggle, Douglass penned the following stirring words, "The whole history of the progress of human liberty shows that all concessions yet made to her august claims have been born of earnest struggle ... If there is no struggle there is no progress. ... Power concedes nothing without a demand. It never did and it never will."

KEY TERMS

Agency
Collective behavior
Diagnostic frame
Framing
Hidden power
Invisible power
Motivational frame
Political opportunity structure
Political process theory
Power over
Power to
Power with

Prognostic frame
Resource mobilization
Social movement
Visible power

DISCUSSION QUESTIONS

1. What difference do you see between terms like "riot" and "rebellion" or "insurrection" and "protest"?
2. Think about a recent incident of "civil disorder" on your campus or in your community involving a large group. What words were used in the local press or on social media to describe it? What effect did those terms have, if any?
3. Is change better achieved by working within our system of electoral, representative democracy, or by working outside it? Is change outside the system better achieved by making peaceful, direct demands or by adopting more radical, even violent means?
4. Do the ends of social change always justify the means of getting there? Is it worth engaging in radical protest even if you are more likely to lose on the substantive change you want to see?
5. The current political context in the United States seems poised for historic change. How do you see our future and why? Will we go further down the road to authoritarianism? Build a durable democratic movement for racial equality? Something else?

ANNOTATED SUGGESTED READINGS

See John Gaventa. 1980. *Power and Powerlessness: Quiescence and Rebellion in an Appalachian Valley*. Oxford: Clarendon Press, for a classic look at the age-old question: why do the poor and dispossessed so often accept their fate, rather than rising up in rebellion?

See Elizabeth McKenna and Hahrie Han. 2015. *Groundbreakers: How Obama's 2.2 Million Volunteers Transformed Campaigning in America*. Oxford: Oxford University Press, showing how Obama's unexpected success in 2008 was not just about big money and data analytics, but also translating the principles and practices of community organizing to electoral politics.

See Keeanga-Yamahtta Taylor. 2016. *From #BlackLivesMatter to Black Liberation*. New York: Haymarket, which connects the current fight against structural racism and racial violence to the history of Black freedom movements and presents a blueprint for future activism.

CHAPTER REFERENCES

Arendt, Hannah. 1969. *On Violence*. New York: Harcourt.

Bachrach, Peter, and Morton S. Baratz. 1962. "The Two Faces of Power," *American Political Science Review* 56: 947–952.

Coates, Ta-Nehisi. 2014. "The Case for Reparations," *The Atlantic*. June. www.theatlantic.com/magazine/archive/2014/06/the-case-for-reparations/361631.

Dahl, Robert A. 1957. "The Concept of Power," *Behavioral Science* 2: 203–204.

Dawsey, Josh and Felicia Sonmez. 2022. "'Legitimate Political Discourse': Three Words about Jan. 6 Spark Rift among Republicans," *The Washington Post*, February 8. www.washingtonpost.com/politics/2022/02/08/gop-legitimate-political-discourse.

Downs, Anthony. 1957. *An Economic Theory of Democracy*. New York: Harper & Row.

Ganz, Marshall. 2009. *Why David Sometimes Wins: Leadership, Organization, and Strategy in the California Farm Worker Movement*. Oxford: Oxford University Press.

Jones, Jeffrey M. 2022. "Confidence in U.S. Supreme Court Sinks to Historic Low," Gallup News, June 23. https://news.gallup.com/poll/394103/confidence-supreme-court-sinks-historic-low.aspx.

Laswell, Harold and Abraham Kaplan. 1950. Power and Society: *A Framework for Political Inquiry*. New Haven, CT: Yale University Press.

Latzer, Barry. 2020. "Don't Call Rioters 'Protesters'," *Wall Street Journal*, June 4. www.wsj.com/articles/dont-call-rioters-protesters-11591293310.

Le Bon, Gustav. [1895] 2016. *The Crowd: A Study of the Popular Mind*. Sunnyvale, CA: Loki Publishing.

Lukes, Steven. [1974] 2005. *Power: A Radical View*, 2nd ed. New York: Palgrave.

McAdam, Douglas. 1981. *Political Process and the Development of Black Insurgency*. Chicago: University of Chicago Press.

McAdam, Douglas. 1996. "Conceptual Origins, Current Problems, Future Directions," In *Comparative Perspectives on Social Movements* (eds.) Doug McAdam, John McCarthy, and Meyer Zald. Cambridge: Cambridge University Press.

McBride, Kelly. 2021. "From 'Protest' to 'Riot' to 'Insurrection'—How NPR's Language Evolved," *National Public Radio*, January 14. www.npr.org/sections/publiceditor/2021/01/14/956777105/from-protest-to-riot-to-insurrection-how-nprs-language-evolved.

McCarthy, John D. and Meyer Zald. 1977. "Resource Mobilization and Social Movements: A Partial Theory," *American Journal of Sociology* 82(6): 1212–1241.

Morris, Aldon D. 1986. *The Origins of the Civil Rights Movement: Black Communities Organizing for Change*. New York: The Free Press.

Obama, Barack. 2006. *The Audacity of Hope: Thoughts on Reclaiming the American Dream*. New York: Crown Publishing.

Pantoja, Adrian, Ricardo Ramirez, and Gary Segura. 2001. "Citizens by Choice, Voters by Necessity: Patterns in Political Mobilization by Naturalized Latinos," *Political Research Quarterly* 54(4): 729–750.

Polletta, Francesca. 2006. *It Was Like a Fever: Storytelling in Protest and Politics*. Chicago: University of Chicago Press.

Ralli, Tania. 2005. "Who's a Looter? In Storm's Aftermath, Pictures Kick up a Different Kind of Tempest," *New York Times*, September 5. www.nytimes.com/2005/09/05/business/whos-a-looter-in-storms-aftermath-pictures-kick-up-a-different.html.

Schattschneider, Elmer Eric. 1960. *The Semi-Sovereign People*. Oxford: Oxford University Press.

Snow, David A. and Robert D. Benford. 1988. "Ideology, Frame Resonance, and Participant Mobilization," *International Social Movement Research* 1: 197–218.

Tarrow, Sidney. 1996. "States and Opportunities: The Political Structuring of Social Movements," In *Comparative Perspectives on Social Movements* (eds.) Doug McAdam, John McCarthy, and Meyer Zald. New York: Cambridge University Press.

Taylor, Keeanga-Yamahtta. [2016] 2021. *From #BlackLivesMatter to Black Liberation*, Updated ed. New York: Haymarket.

Tilly, Charles. 1978. *From Mobilization to Revolution*. Boston, MA: Addison-Wesley.

Wasow, Omar. 2020. "Agenda Seeding: How 1960s Black Protests Moved Elites, Public Opinion, and Voting," *American Political Science Review* 114: 638–659.

Zepeda-Millán, Chris. 2016. "Weapons of the (Not So) Weak: Immigrant Mass Mobilization in the US South," *Critical Sociology* 42(2): 269–287.

Index

Note: Page numbers in bold refer to Tables; those in italic refer to Figures, an italic *n*. refers to a note on that page